Canada: An Appraisal of Its Needs and Resources

Canada: An Appraisal of Its Needs and Resources

GEORGE W. WILSON
SCOTT GORDON
STANISLAW JUDEK

Avec un commentaire par

A. BRETON

TWENTIETH CENTURY FUND *New York*

UNIVERSITY OF TORONTO PRESS

FOREWORD

Canada is a country with vast natural resources and with an advanced industrial economy that yields its people one of the highest per capita incomes in the world. Canada, too, is an important unit in the North Atlantic Treaty Organization and in the larger, unstructured comity of nations on both sides of the North Atlantic—a grouping held to include eighteeen countries in Western Europe, along with the United States of America.

Covering the two latter areas, the Twentieth Century Fund has made large-scale surveys of *America's Needs and Resources*, published in 1947 and 1955, and of *Europe's Needs and Resources*, published in 1961, both under the direction of J. Frederic Dewhurst. More recently, the Fund has undertaken the compilation of an updated and essentially statistical survey of the nations of the whole North Atlantic region. This is still in preparation, with publication expected in 1965. The present study supplies the information about Canada needed for this North Atlantic compilation. Building on the base of the massive Gordon report of a few years ago, as well as other resources, this study includes central statistics that are co-ordinated with similar key figures being assembled by the Twentieth Century Fund for the countries of Western Europe and for the United States.

This study, however, goes much further than a mere assembly of some core figures. This is a book about Canada, written by a team of Canadian economists, and addressed primarily to the interested Canadian public. It is not a repository of source material meant only for scholars, but is designed to give the concerned citizen, the businessman, the student, the teacher, and the public official a broad and authoritative look at the economic potentials of the country. One of its virtues, we believe, is the rather refreshing willingness of its authors to discuss issues and offer viewpoints.

George W. Wilson, a professor in the School of Business at Indiana University, organized and directed the study and did much of the writing in his native Ottawa. The study is, however, a joint product of Professor Wilson, Professor H. Scott Gordon of Carleton University, Ottawa, and Professor Stanislaw Judek of the University of Ottawa.

Professor Gordon took primary responsibility for the Introduction and made a notable contribution to the rest of the volume through his penetrating suggestions and criticisms. Professor Judek was responsible for the two important chapters on population and manpower. The Epilogue was jointly prepared by Gordon and Wilson. The rest of the book was written by Professor Wilson. Throughout there was close co-operation among the three authors, so that, despite special responsibility for particular chapters, the book is in fact a joint effort.

In order to increase both the usefulness and interest of the study, arrangements were made to translate into French this Foreword, the Preface, the Introduction, and the Epilogue. The book was rounded out with a Commentary in French on themes in the study that might have special interest for the French-speaking community in Canada. The Twentieth Century Fund is grateful for the contributions of Professor Léopold Lamontagne of Laval University, who made the translations; and of Professor Albert Breton of the University of Montreal and of the Social Research Group, who wrote the very discerning Commentary.

Acknowledgment, also, is due to Miss Sherry Goldman, whose able assistance, especially during the summer of 1963, permitted a finished manuscript sooner than expected.

The Twentieth Century Fund is particularly pleased to be associated with the University of Toronto Press in a joint publishing venture. The editing, design, and manufacture of the book were handled by the University of Toronto Press with skill and intelligence. The Fund appreciates especially the warm personal interest and valuable suggestions of Mr. Marsh Jeanneret, Director of the Press; Miss Eleanor Harman, Assistant Director; and Miss Francess Halpenny, Editor. The Fund wishes to express its thanks to them, to the authors, the translator, and the commentator, and to voice the hope that this study may be found useful to Canada and Canadians and a matter of interest in the United States and elsewhere in the world.

AUGUST HECKSCHER
Director, The Twentieth Century Fund

41 East 70th Street, New York
June 1965

AVANT-PROPOS

Le Canada est un pays très riche en ressources naturelles ; son développement industriel assure à ses habitants un revenu individuel qui est un des plus élevés du globe. En outre, le Canada occupe une place importante dans l'Organisation du Traité de l'Atlantique Nord et dans l'ensemble plus vaste que constituent, des deux côtés de l'Atlantique Nord, des nations librement associées comprenant dix-huit pays de l'Europe Occidentale et les États-Unis.

Dans le cadre des deux organisations que nous venons de mentionner, le Fonds du Vingtième Siècle a publié, sous la direction de J. Frederic Dewhurst, deux études d'ensemble : *America's Needs and Resources* (1947 et 1955) et *Europe's Needs and Resources* (1961). Plus récemment, le Fonds a entrepris de réunir les éléments d'une vaste enquête avec statistiques à l'appui, sur la situation actuelle des pays de l'Atlantique Nord. Cette synthèse en préparation doit paraître en 1965. La présente étude a pour but de fournir les renseignements qui concernent le Canada. Sans pour autant négliger d'autres sources, elle est souvent fondée sur l'abondante documentation qu'offre le rapport Gordon, paru il y a quelques années ; elle donne les statistiques principales auxquelles sont confrontées les statistiques correspondantes sur l'Europe Occidentale et les États-Unis — ces dernières étant rassemblées par le soin du Fonds.

Néanmoins, les auteurs offrent ici plus qu'une étude statistique. Ce livre sur le Canada, rédigé par une équipe d'économistes canadiens, s'adresse d'abord à tous les Canadiens conscients des problèmes qui se posent pour leur pays. C'est plus qu'un catalogue de faits bruts que seuls des spécialistes pourraient consulter ; on y trouvera un tableau complet et bien documenté des possibilités économiques du pays, qui intéressera tout Canadien désireux de se tenir au courant, aussi bien l'homme d'affaire que l'étudiant, le professeur, et le fonctionnaire. Ses grands mérites et sa nouveauté résident sans doute le fait que les auteurs ont cherché à examiner certaines questions et à présenter leurs idées.

M. George W. Wilson, professeur à la Faculté de Commerce de l'Université d'Indiana, a dirigé l'enquête, coordonné les recherches, et rédigé une grande partie de l'ouvrage à Ottawa, sa ville natale. Cependant, ce livre est le fruit d'un travail collectif qui n'a été possible que grâce à la collaboration de MM. les professeurs H. S. Gordon de l'Université Carleton (Ottawa) en Stanislaw Judek de l'Université d'Ottawa.

M. le professeur Gordon s'est chargé de l'introduction, mais nombreuses sont les pages oú l'on retrouvera un écho de ses remarques et de ses critiques pleines de perspicacité. C'est à M. le professeur Judek que l'on doit les deux importants chapitres sur la population et les ressources humaines. MM. Gordon et Wilson ont écrit ensemble l'Epilogue. Quant au reste du livre, il a été rédigé par M. Wilson. Néanmoins, il est bien entendu que ce livre a été réalisé en équipe, en dépit de la responsabilité plus ou moins grande qui incombe à chacun des co-auteurs dans la rédaction de tel ou tel chapitre.

Afin de donner une plus large diffusion à un livre dont l'intérêt et l'utilité sont manifestes, il a été décidé que l'Avant-propos, la Préface, l'Introduction, et l'Epilogue seraient traduits en français. On trouvera aussi à la fin quelques pages qui reprennent en français les points susceptibles d'intéresser particulièrement les Canadiens de langue française. Le Fonds du Vingtième Siècle exprime ses remerciements à M. le professeur Léopold Lamontagne, de l'Université Laval, responsable de la traduction, et à M. le professeur Albert Breton, de l'Université de Montréal et du Groupe de Recherche Sociale, qui a rédigé en français le Commentaire, fort pénétrant.

Il faut aussi mentionner ici Miss Sherry Goldman, dont l'aide efficace, en particulier au cours de l'été de 1963, a permis d'achever la rédaction de ce livre plus tôt qu'on ne l'avait prévu.

Le Fonds du Vintième Siècle se réjouit d'être associé aux Presses de l'Université de Toronto. Comme co-éditeurs, les Presses de l'Université de Toronto se sont chargées, avec goût et compétence, de la mise au point du texte et de la préparation matérielle de l'ouvrage. Il nous est particulièrement agréable de remercier M. Marsh Jeanneret, directeur des Presses, Mlle Eleanor Harman, sous-directrice, et Mlle Francess Halpenny, rédactrice, pour leurs précieuses remarques et l'intérêt qu'ils n'ont cessé de porter à l'ouvrage. Exprimons à nouveau notre gratitude envers ceux qui, à des titres divers, nous ont aidés dans notre entreprise.

Nous espérons que la présente étude rendra service au Canada et aux Canadiens et qu'elle recevra un accueil favorable aux États-Unis et dans le reste du monde.

AUGUST HECKSCHER
Directeur du Fonds du Vingtième Siècle

41 East 70th Street, New York
juin 1965

PREFACE

The purpose of this volume is to provide a non-technical treatment of the economic realities of Canada at mid-century and of its future prospects. Our aim is to reach the intelligent layman (be he aspiring politician, journalist, or simply an observer who likes to have the facts) as well as beginning students of economics, in Canada, at home, and abroad, and to assemble in one short volume the relevant empirical evidence with a reasoned but non-technical discussion of what the evidence suggests. Although this is primarily a work on economics, we could not avoid discussion of many political, historical, social, and even psychological matters since these impinge upon economics as both cause and consequence in important respects. The book, in short, contains a large dose of statistical material and much economic and some non-economic analysis and judgment.

There are already several excellent studies of the Canadian economy such as the many volumes of the Royal Commission on Canada's Economic Prospects, and Caves and Holton's *The Canadian Economy*. However, the RCCEP is now some ten years old and much of the empirical material ends before the economic slowdown of the mid 1950's. The Caves and Holton book, although less dated, is oriented more to the professional economist than to the audience we seek to reach. Nor does *Historical Statistics* parallel the present work, although it duplicates some of the data presented here.

Originally conceived as a supplement to the Twentieth Century Fund's *Needs and Resources* series, time and space limitations prevented development of the abundance of useful detail which characterizes these volumes. We have therefore gone further in the direction of analysis and evaluation than the other Fund studies. Nevertheless, it is hoped that the material presented and discussed in the present volume will facilitate the study, already under way, of the North Atlantic economy. In all the important categories, the statistical evidence is directly additive and the concepts used are comparable to those in the Fund's larger studies of Western Europe and the United States. Most of the book was written in 1963, but the material has been updated wherever necessary or feasible.

Our aim throughout has been to blend judgment, analysis, and data into a relatively short form that covers the essential economic, social, political, and historical trends in a fashion comprehensible to non-technical readers. The Introduction traces the evolution of the Canadian polity from Confederation to the present; Part I sketches the past economic trends in important dimensions mainly since the late 1930's; Part II examines the resource base and makes estimates of the quality and quantity of the four factors of production distinguished by economists, namely, land, labour, capital and entrepreneurship, each of which is discussed conceptually and empirically in a separate chapter; Part III makes estimates of Canadian economic potential in 1970 and 1975; the Epilogue provides a short outline of Canada's unfinished business.

Canada's economic potential is among the world's brightest. As we argue throughout most of the present volume, the relative qualities and quantities of human, natural, and man-made resources are scarcely surpassed anywhere. This strong resource base has created extremely favourable conditions for a prosperous and rapidly growing economy. The economic future of Canada, as she approaches the centennial of her birth, is therefore bright with promise. But the fulfilment of this promise requires more responsible economic policies and actions, both public and private, than have prevailed over most of the past decade. Furthermore, there are a series of non-economic difficulties that have clouded the national landscape, especially as far as national cohesion and independence are concerned. Substantial US ownership of Canadian industry, the "quiet revolution" in Quebec, the national flag, and so on have all been the subjects of lengthy and sometimes emotional discussion and debate from one end of Canada to the other. What could be the subject of a healthy soul-searching and national stock-taking is, however, all too frequently, distorted by a lack of general understanding of the issues involved. It is our belief that in few areas is there more misunderstanding of Canada's mid-twentieth-century position than in the realm of economics, and that the economic problems and policies in Canada are largely responsible for many of the other difficulties besetting the Canadian scene. Until the economic problems are approached and answered more realistically by those making important decisions in both the public and private sectors, there seems little prospect of a satisfactory resolution of the divisive forces in the political and social spheres which in turn jeopardize achievement of Canada's economic potential.

Whether this volume can successfully meet the purposes indicated above is for the reader to decide. We are content to let the book speak or whisper for itself.

GEORGE W. WILSON
SCOTT GORDON
STANISLAW JUDEK

PREFACE

Nous avons voulu présenter la réalité et l'avenir économiques du Canada en évitant de faire de ce livre un ouvrage technique. Notre ambition a été d'intéresser aussi bien le profane — soit-il aspirant à la politique, journaliste, ou simplement un observateur en quête de faits — désireux de s'instruire que l'étudiant qui aborde les sciences économiques, au Canada, aux Etats-Unis, et ailleurs, et de rassembler en un court volume les faits significatifs accompagnés d'une discussion qui fait appel au bon sens plus qu'aux connaissances techniques. Bien qu'il s'agisse surtout d'économie, il nous a été impossible de laisser de côté les données politiques, historiques, sociales, et même psychologiques, qui ont nécessairement une incidence sur l'économie dans la mesure où elles la conditionnent ou sont conditionnées par elles. On trouvera donc d'assez abondantes statistiques et de nombreuses analyses, où, bien entendu, l'économie a la plus belle part.

Il existe déjà d'excellents ouvrages sur l'économie canadienne, entre autres les nombreux volumes publiés par la Commission royale sur l'avenir économique du Canada, et le livre de Caves et Holton, *The Canadian Economy*. Cependant, le premier de ces ouvrages date d'une dizaine d'années et ne traite pas de la dépression économique qui a marqué la dernière décennie ; le second, s'il est moins ancien, s'adresse davantage à un public de spécialistes qu'aux lecteurs que nous voulons toucher. Ajoutons que le volume intitulé *Historical Statistics* ne fait pas double emploi avec le présent ouvrage bien que certains renseignements que nous donnons y figurent.

Le temps et l'espace ont manqué pour faire de ce livre ce qu'il devait être à l'origine — un supplément à la collection *Needs and Resources*, publiée par le Fonds du Vingtième Siècle — et pour le présenter avec l'abondance de détails qui caractérise les volumes de cette collection. Aussi la place faite à l'analyse et à la réflexion est-elle plus grande que dans les autres études du Fonds du Vingtième Siècle. Quoi qu'il en soit, nous osons espérer que les matériaux ici rassemblés et analysés rendront plus aisée l'étude, déjà commencée, de l'économie des pays de l'Atlantique Nord. Dans l'ensemble, les données statistiques viennent compléter celles des ouvrages plus volumineux que le Fonds du Vingtième Siècle a consacrés à l'Europe Occidentale et aux États-Unis ; l'optique est d'ailleurs essentiellement la même. L'ouvrage a pour la grande partie été écrit en 1963, mais le sujet a été mis à jour là où on l'a cru nécessaire ou possible.

Comme nous l'avons déjà dit, nous avons voulu rassembler en un nombre de pages relativement réduit, des faits et des réflexions que nous proposons à l'attention des non-spécialistes. L'Introduction retrace l'histoire politique du Canada depuis la naissance de la Confédération jusqu'à nos jours. La première partie montre rapidement ce qu'a été l'économie canadienne, surtout depuis le début de la deuxième guerre mondiale ; dans la deuxième partie, on passe en revue les principales ressources du pays et l'on évalue les quatre facteurs de production que distinguent généralement les économistes : la terre, le travail, le capital, et l'entreprise. Chacun d'eux fait l'objet d'un chapitre. La troisième partie présente une estimation des possibilités économiques du Canada en 1970 et en 1975. Quant à l'épilogue, il fait le tour des problèmes restés en suspens.

L'avenir économique du Canada est un des plus prometteurs qui soit. Comme nous le montrons tout au long de notre livre, on y trouve réunies en abondance et dans des conditions presque uniques au monde, la main-d'œuvre, les richesses naturelles et les réalisations matérielles nécessaires au développement d'un grand pays. Ces moyens laissent espérer un essor économique rapide et brillant. C'est donc un avenir plein de promesses qui semble s'offrir au Canada, un siècle après sa naissance. Mais pour que ces promesses ne soient pas déçues, la nécessités s'impose à tous les échelons d'une politique économique mieux pensée. De plus, l'horizon a été assombri par des difficultés étrangères à l'économie — difficultés qui remettent en cause la cohésion et l'indépendance nationales. La mainmise des États-Unis sur une bonne partie de l'industrie du pays, le « quiet revolution » du Québec, la querelle autour du drapeau national, ont suscité de vives dissensions et passionné l'opinion publique d'un bout à l'autre du Canada. Ce qui aurait pu donner lieu à un fructueux examen de conscience et à un inventaire national n'a souvent produit aucun résultat valable, parce qu'on a méconnu les données du problème. Nous sommes persuadés que c'est dans le domaine économique que les problémes ont été le plus mal compris. De là proviennent, croyons-nous, la plupart des difficultés que connaît le Canada actuel. Tant que ces problèmes n'auront pas été abordés et résolus avec plus de réalisme par ceux chargés de la tâche importante de prendre des decisions tant dans le domaine public que privé, on ne voit guère comment pourraient être réglées de façon satisfaisante les dissensions politiques et sociales qui, à leur tour, sont un obstacle à l'épanouissement de l'économie du pays.

Au lecteur de dire si cet ouvrage atteint le but que les auteurs se sont proposé. A notre livre de se défendre lui-même.

GEORGE W. WILSON
SCOTT GORDON
STANISLAW JUDEK

CONTENTS

xx *Contents*

Introduction

A NATION STILL IN THE MAKING

There was once a railway line in New Brunswick that went by the impressive name of the "European and North American Railway." It ran between St. John and Shediac, a distance of 120 miles, and despite the strenuous efforts of its owners, got no further. In choosing this grandiose name, however, the promoters of this line were only reflecting the cavalier disregard for geography and the romantic dreams of wealth and continental conquest that characterized so much of the economic and political thinking of North America in the mid-nineteenth century. A continent, virtually empty, lay waiting to be won, beckoning with a promise and a challenge unique in history—an opportunity to build a new empire in a new world. The tide of this continental enthusiasm was at the flood in the United States in the years before the Civil War, and the great waves flowed up into British North America, as they have always done, and engendered there similar dreams of empire. Upon the crest of one such wave, the provinces of British North America bound themselves together in 1867 into a new Confederation, with its own hopes of dominion *a mari usque ad mare*.

But reality is always more austere and contingent than hope, and nowhere could the divergence between them have been as great as in the new nation of Canada. As P. B. Waite, the historian of Confederation, has reminded us:

The reality of 1867 was frightening. It showed how naïve the dreams of the colonists were: Newfoundland, its population clinging precariously to a living wrested from the Labrador current and a hard land; Prince Edward Island, complacent, defiant, parochial; Nova Scotia, afloat on seven oceans, proud of herself and jealous of Canada; New Brunswick, half-American in politics and attitude; Quebec, determined to get every jot and tittle of privilege with or without Ottawa; Ontario, sleek, bigoted, and stentorian; a thousand miles from Toronto, at Red River, 9,000 mixed settlers and the Hudson's Bay Company trying to keep the northwest from the Americans; in distant British Columbia, a dying gold rush with two small and hostile towns holding the mortgage. This was the reverse of the glory arguments that resounded in the speeches of 1864. One was the stubborn and almost intractable reality: the other was a political dream of wonderful audacity. There were many noble statements of this dream, by Howe, by McGee, by Brown; even Cartier on coming home in 1867 said, "Henceforth we shall rank among the nations." But no one knew, not Cartier, not even Macdonald, what really was involved in the creation, administration, and maintenance of a transcontinental state. An empire of this size had been created before; it could be done—that was the great example the Americans provided. But it had been done by a rich and powerful nation of twenty millions. The contemplation of the same thing by a struggling group of still discordant provinces, with a population of four millions, was surprising; perhaps it was absurd. The railway that might have given such a union a semblance of reality did not yet exist. Union of the colonies was achieved in 1867; but it was hardly more than a beginning. The railways at Rivière du Loup and Truro that stared into the empty miles between marked a cause not yet won, a nationality not yet realized. These still lay in the difficult years ahead.[1]

The difficult years, at least as they might have been foreseen in 1867, are over; the railways have been built, the northern half of the continent has been secured to Canadian sovereignty, the Canadian nationality that seemed so tenuous and uncertain in 1867 has been realized. Even the most rhapsodic of the Fathers would have cause to be proud of what has grown from this beginning. If Canada does not "rank among the nations" in the sense of being a great military power, it ranks among the first of those who have provided freedom and opportunity for their citizens: a high and rising standard of living, a political democracy free from any threat of subversion, a society open to and participant in the best that the modern worlds of science and culture have to offer. The land has proved to be rich in resources even beyond anything that might have been imagined in 1867; the system of parliamentary government, transplanted from the Old World, has proved capable of independent and sturdy growth in the New. And yet withal . . . , the struggle for Canadian nationhood is not irrefragibly won, even after a century of Confederation; perhaps even another century will not suffice to establish it beyond doubt. There is a continuing uncertainty and irresolution about Canadian nationhood, for there are more subtle and abiding strains upon it than the problems of providing the physical infrastructure of communications and the political mechanisms of public administration

[1]P. B. Waite, *The Life and Times of Confederation, 1864–1867* (Toronto, 1962), pp. 328–9.

for a large and diverse country. These strains spring from two sources—the internal cleavage between French and English, and the external proximity of the United States—and both of these are as powerful today as they were in 1867.

Paradoxically, these two major weaknesses of Canadian nationhood are also the factors that were primarily responsible for bringing about the union of the British colonies into a second continental nation in North America. Despite the grandeur of the dream of continental empire which gave to Confederation its romantic appeal, it would probably not have taken place had it not offered a practical solution to the more immediate political problems created by French-English conflict in the united provinces of Canada and the expansionist pressure from the United States. Undoubtedly the politicians of Canada had many reasons for advancing a grand scheme of British North American union at Charlottetown in 1864, but none was as compelling as the fact that such a scheme would make it possible for French-speaking Canada East and English-speaking Canada West to disengage from one another in amity instead of continuing headlong down the clear path that led to acrimonious divorce. Nor is it probable that Confederation would have come about in absence of the fear of American imperialist designs upon the British provinces. In the face of the American doctrine of "manifest destiny" and the steady thrust of American hegemony into the open territory of the west, and the more immediate tensions produced by the posturings, threats, and military adventures of the Fenians,[2] the lonely British provinces felt their helplessness with acuity and were responsive to the assurances which a larger political union seemed to offer.[3]

This sense of external threat from the United States has been slow to pass away in Canada, even in its crude military form. As late as 1895, substantial defensive preparations against American invasion were made, and even between the First World War and the Second, the only defence plans the Canadian military bothered to compile were for defence against

[2]The Fenian Brotherhood was an organization of Irishmen and Irish-Americans dedicated to freeing Ireland from British rule. They organized military expeditions against Canada after the Civil War, as a means of attacking Britain indirectly.

[3]"The new creation must be tied together with railroads. It must get as large a territorial future as possible. And the American wolf must be kept as far from the British North American door as possible: in fact but for the loud howling of the American wolf in 1864 and the following years, it is probable that the different provinces would not have come together. This fear of the great, heaving neighbour was reflected in a hundred ways, not least by the disproportionate attention given to the subject of defence: British North American union was to be union for defence against the United States." A. R. M. Lower, "Theories of Canadian Federalism—Yesterday and Today," in A. R. M. Lower, F. R. Scott, *et al.*, *Evolving Canadian Federalism* (Durham, NC, 1958), pp. 9–10.

attack from the United States.[4] Such military fears have now at last departed, but only to be replaced by deeper and more subtle ones—fears of cultural and economic penetration of Canada by the United States.

To understand Canada at all one must understand her historic attitude towards the United States, and the vital role that this has always played in Canadian internal affairs. As Professor Underhill has put it: "The oldest and most tenacious tradition in our communal memory centres around our determination not to became Americans. This is also the one tradition in which English Canadians and French Canadians have been whole-heartedly united."[5] The foundation of the French-Canadian attitude in this respect is obvious. Struggling as they have been since the victory of Wolfe over Montcalm in 1759 to maintain their language and cultural identity in a hostile English-speaking environment, French Canadians know full well how easily they would be dissolved in the great American melting pot whose acid of assimilation has always been much more powerful than that of Canada. It has always seemed to the French Canadians better to husband and protect the French soul in North America under the British flag, however limited and confined it must therefore be, than to be melted down into an American button, and lose identity for ever. The English Canadians have derived their separatism from a different, yet equally powerful, source. Ontario, the centre of English-speaking Canada, was settled, after the American Revolution and the War of 1812, by people who left their homes in the new independent United States in order to fulfil their strong determination to live and bring up their families as British subjects. From the very beginning, therefore, the heart of English Canada was composed of people who had rejected the American revolution and American aspirations to an independent, democratic, and republican nationhood. There they grew and multiplied, husbanding their anti-Americanism within the folds of a disdainful Anglo-Saxon hauteur, which was undiluted by the steady immigration of ethnic compatriots from Britain, and proceeded to supply the generations of ruling élites that have dominated the political, business, and cultural life of English-speaking Canada down to the present day.[6]

And yet . . . firm and fundamental as this decision to remain a separate nation from the United States seems to have been, it is a decision that

[4]Canadian-American Committee, *The Perspective of Canadian-American Relations* (Washington, DC, and Montreal, May 1962), p. 2.

[5]F. H. Underhill, *In Search of Canadian Liberalism* (Toronto, 1960), p. 222.

[6]A discussion of the economic élite in Canada appears below in chap. 8. This and the other Canadian élites have been examined intensively in *The Vertical Mosaic* (Toronto, 1965), by Professor John Porter of Carleton University.

can never be made final and irrevocable for Canada. The forces of geography, culture, history, and international affairs keep putting this question back on the agenda of Canadian politics again and again. It has repeatedly to be raised, and repeatedly answered. But there is something more here than has so far been said: the fact is that Canadians do not find this continual re-emergence of the question of union with the United States altogether vexatious. They are not unhappy that the great political alternative of union with the wealthiest and most powerful nation in the world is still open to them. In her relations with the United States, Canada is like the young maiden in the old song who always answered "No, John! No, John! No, John, No!" but also gave the same reply to the query whether she was determined to be single all her life.

In the hundred years that have passed since Confederation, a nation has been built, but a sense of positive nationhood has not been clearly established. The constant negative of rejection has so dominated the political life of Canada's two primary ethnic groups that positive elements have had little opportunity to flourish. Nor were positive elements of nationhood forthcoming from the European motherlands of Britain and France. If the conquest of 1759 did not break the tie of French Canada to Continental France, the French Revolution certainly did, and the Roman Catholic church, which stepped into this breach and provided French Canada with a sense of being and continuity, did so in ways that removed her from the mainstream of Canadian life, and prevented her full participation in the great developments of the nineteenth century. The ties of English Canada with Great Britain, though never broken, provided little more. English Canada drew from Britain many of the superficialities of nationalism but little of the solid political and cultural substance on which a new Canadian nationhood could be built. As for mother England herself, she had long since been anxious that these overgrown colonial infants in North America should cease their insistent clutching at the maternal breast, and heaved a sigh of deliverance when Confederation, which she herself had laboured hard (and disingenuously!) to bring about, promised relief.

It is *rejection* that is the dominant inner theme of Canadian national life: rejection *by* Canada of the challenges and opportunities of American union, and rejection *of* Canada by the motherlands of Great Britain and France. Perhaps it is this internal historical neurosis of rejection, combined with the fact of living alongside the wealthiest nation in the world—comparisons with which are as inevitable as they are inevitably unfavourable—that is responsible for one of the strongest characteristics of Canadian national life, a lack of confidence in her worth and in her position in the world of nations. No Canadian production, in literature and the arts especially, but even in the sciences and social sciences, is generally considered to be of merit, unless it has received the *imprimatur* of foreign approval. No Canadian of creative power is considered highly until he has been tested upon a foreign stage.

If a psychological interpretation of this Canadian syndrome is appropriate in this connection, it may not be altogether out of place to recount a story about Sigmund Freud. His biographer, Ernest Jones, tells of Freud's receipt of a communication from the Austrian income tax authorities expressing wonder at the smallness of Professor Freud's income "since everyone knows that his reputation extends far beyond the frontier of Austria." To this Freud replied: "Professor Freud is very honoured at receiving a communication from the Government. It is the first time the Government has taken any notice of him and he acknowledges it. There is one point in which he cannot agree with the communication: that his reputation extends far beyond the frontier of Austria. It begins at the frontier."[7] It is a remark that many Canadians would fully understand.

Just as the fear of American expansionism played a vital part in creating the Canadian Confederation, so in the years after Confederation, the policy of the national government was dominated by the same force. The three legs of post-Confederation policy—railways, immigration, and tariffs—met in a common pivotal point: so to develop the country as to render her safe from the "manifest destiny" of the expanding United States. Of these three, one was magnificently successful, one disturbingly ambiguous, and the third has contributed greatly to the opposite of its original object.

The first task of the new nation was obviously railways—a railway not only to bridge the gap between Quebec and the Maritimes and so knit the partners of Confederation together, but a railway to thrust into the empty miles around the shore of Lake Superior to Red River and then beyond over the seemingly endless expanse of the prairies, through the forbidding barrier of mountains to the sea where, after all this emptiness, another little knot of British North Americans waited to be joined. It was not merely a task. It was a race—a race against the Americans who already had purchased Alaska almost the very day that Confederation became a fact, and thus outflanked British Columbia on the north, and who would surely draw the Hudson's Bay Company

[7]Ernest Jones, *The Life and Work of Sigmund Freud*, edited and abridged by Lionel Trilling and Stephen Marcus (London, 1963), p. 362.

territories into the orbit of their power if Canada was slow to establish its own claims to sovereignty. And so the great Canadian Pacific Railway was built, with courage, daring, and speed, and with a financial recklessness that was heedless of cost in the race to win half a continent as the prize. The building of the CPR was an audacious undertaking for a new nation with such a small population, but, as Professor Underhill has remarked, it was "an exploit to which we look back now as the most magnificent expression in our history of our national faith in ourselves."[8]

The second leg of the post-Confederation tripod of national policy was immigration, and here too there was a consciousness of contest with the United States. Not only did Canadians wish the country to grow, and welcomed additional numbers to this end, but they also realized that as long as the land was empty, Canadian sovereignty over it was weak. It was not until the prairie was well settled in the first decade of the present century that this sense of national weakness began to pass away. But there has always been a considerable degree of ambivalence in Canada towards this element of national policy. Opposition to immigration has sprung from the usual sources, such as fear of labour competition and unemployment, and the customary ethnic, cultural, and linguistic bigotries, but in Canada it has, in addition, fed upon the fact that Canada has not been a melting-pot country and has not been able to anticipate the quick disappearance of ethnic loyalties that has been so distinct a feature of American development. In the United States a strong sense of unique nationality has been a very powerful assimilative force in itself and thus has served as both cause and consequence of the growth of nationhood. The immigrants who came to the United States in the nineteenth century were, for the most part, eager to lose their Old World identities and become Americans as quickly as possible. By contrast there has been in Canada, until very recently, little sense of "Canadianism" with which immigrants could identify in a similar fashion, and even today, it does not exert an assimilative force upon "New Canadians" (as the immigrants since the Second World War have been officially called) that compares in power with the romantic magnetism of American nationality achieved from the very beginning of that country's existence as an independent state. Perhaps national identity and assimilative power is one of the auxiliary characteristics of an independence won by revolutionary struggle, and is denied to the country that achieves hers by a route as timorous, irresolute, and peaceful as Canada followed. The extraordinary dominance in Canadian life of the English

[8]*In Search of Canadian Liberalism*, p. 99.

élites is also important in this connection. To have a name with a non-British ring has been more of a disability in Canada than in the United States, and there has always been a consciousness among Canadians of non-British stock that there were some very special doors in the country that were closed to them, and this has limited the ardour of their participation in the development of a Canadian nationality. The consciousness of this in French Canada has been particularly acute and has led to a distinct opposition to immigration. The "revenge of the cradle" to which the extreme nationalists in French Canada looked for many years to wipe away the dominance the English had imposed by military and political power, was threatened by immigration, which drew few New Canadians into the French-speaking orbit. But even the more moderate French Canadians, who entertained no such tight-lipped hopes of *la revanche*, could hardly look upon massive immigration as anything but a threat to the position of the French language and culture in the Canadian nation. To the extent that immigration produced other self-sustaining linguistic and cultural communities, and in the years of western expansion this seemed far from unlikely, additional strains would surely be placed upon the growth of Canadian nationality. Even today it is not clear that the country's ability to assimilate immigrants is large. Fear of the strains that might be produced has limited the liberality of Canadian immigration policy from Confederation down to the present day.

Unlike the United States, Canada has been not only a country of great immigration but of great emigration as well. The wealth and dynamism of the United States has proved insufficient to draw Canada into the American orbit, but many Canadians, both English- and French-speaking, have been so drawn. Emigration from Canada, the great bulk of which has been to the United States, has been so heavy in the years since 1867 that, over the whole of the period since then, the *net* contribution to Canadian population by migration into and out of Canada has been close to zero. This steady movement of Canadians to the United States and the rough historical correlation of periods of high immigration with ones of high emigration has led to the repeated advocacy of the "displacement theory" of immigration. This theory (which is discussed more fully in Chapter 2 below) advances the proposition that high immigration is the *cause* of high emigration—through the displacement of native Canadians from their economic opportunities by an influx of foreigners. Numerous variants on the displacement theory have been advanced in Canada from time to time and all reflect the nagging worry that migration has proven to be, for Canada, a two-edged sword that cuts as much against as for her desire to populate the land.

The third leg of the tripod, the policy of protective tariffs, had primitive beginnings in the province of Canada even before Confederation, but, from 1867 on, the plea for a "national policy" to protect domestic enterprise from foreign competition in order to develop the nation's economy came increasingly to be heard. It was twelve years before the National Policy was implemented, but when it was it marked a major turning point in Canadian history, evidenced by the fact that while it was a fiercely political issue when first introduced by the Conservatives under Sir John A. Macdonald in 1879, it was not reversed or even diluted by the Liberals when they took power under Laurier in 1896.

The object of the National Policy, as the phrase itself indicated, was the same as the policies of railway construction and immigration—to encourage the growth of the national economy, for its own sake of course, but also because of the contribution this would make to Canada's ability to withstand the pressures of American expansionism. One of the most frequently reiterated defences of the policy of tariff protection that has been advanced in Canada since 1879 is that the tariff, by encouraging the more heavily labour-using manufacturing industries, enables the country to provide employment for a larger population, which is in itself a contribution to national viability in the fashion indicated above.[9] However, most modern students of this question are inclined to argue that an effect of the tariff is to lower economic efficiency and per capita income in Canada, which casts doubt on the validity of the population argument since it is undoubtedly the case that low incomes in Canada are a potent factor in stimulating emigration to the United States. There can be no assurance therefore that the protective tariff has contributed to national viability by leading to a larger population. In some of the popular discussion indeed the connection is implicitly inverted, in that the net effect of immigration and emigration is argued to have had an adverse effect upon the educational composition of the population. Canada is seen as a "demographic railway station" in which the new arrivals are in large part non-English-speaking Europeans with low educational standards, while the departees are fully acculturated North Americans of high educational and technical attainments. What is somewhat indelicately referred to as a "haemorrhage of Canadian brains" to the United States reflects the view that the quality of the Canadian

[9]See, e.g., W. A. Mackintosh, *The Economic Background of Dominion-Provincial Relations*, Royal Commission on Dominion-Provincial Relations (Ottawa, 1939); and C. L. Barber, "The Canadian Tariff," *Canadian Journal of Economics and Political Science* (hereafter abbreviated to *CJEPS*), Nov. 1955, pp. 513–30.

population is lowered by the flow in and out of migrants—the "good-byes" in this railway station are spoken in more educated accents than the "hellos." This argument has yet to be fully documented, and when one considers the large number of highly trained immigrants to Canada, and the number of Canadians who return after receiving a (usually highly subsidized) education in the United States and overseas, it is not obvious without much further investigation on which side of the population quality equation the net weight of Canadian migration lies. Nevertheless it seems to be quite apparent, in the context of the discussion here, that the effect of the tariff has been adverse. There is no reason to believe that a lower standard of living, which is the economic effect of the tariff, leads to a larger immigration of highly trained foreigners or induces a larger number of Canadian graduate students to return from abroad.

The other major intellectual support of the National Policy was, of course, the infant industry argument. Macdonald quoted J. S. Mill's fateful paragraph in support of this argument in the House of Commons in the debates over the National Policy and it has been a major mainstay of Canadian protectionist thought ever since. The industrial consequences of the National Policy, however, have been far from those envisaged by its early supporters. "We must guard and cherish the acorn for the sake of the future oak," opined the *Canadian Monthly* in 1874 when the debate over protection was rising towards its climax. And, accordingly, the acorn of Canadian manufacturing industry was guarded and cherished by the National Policy, as lovingly as any maiden aunt tends her potted plants—but what developed was not the tall, majestic, straight, and mighty oak so common in literary reference, but the lowly scrub oak, dwarfed and weak, and unsuited to its environment.

The passage of the National Policy in 1879 was immediately followed by an influx of industrial capital into Canada from the United States.[10] The Canadian market being closed to American exports of manufactured goods, capital was exported instead. With the adoption of Imperial Preferences in the 1930's a further impetus was given in this direction since firms with plants in Canada could thereby obtain preferential entry to all Commonwealth markets. The secondary manufacturing industry of Canada today is in large part a creation of the protective tariff and its consequent stimulus to foreign direct investment. However, the manu-

[10]H. Marshall, F. A. Southard, Jr., and K. W. Taylor, *Canadian-American Industry: A Study in International Investment* (New Haven, Toronto, 1936), chap. 1. Note especially Tables 1 and 2, p. 15.

facturing industry thus created, which is subsidized by the Canadian consumer, through the tariff, to the extent of one billion dollars annually,[11] is in large part an inefficient industry, mainly because its structure is inappropriate to the Canadian economy. The consequence of this artificially stimulated inflow of foreign capital has been that many of the American manufacturing firms that were in competition with one another in their own home market entered into similar competition with one another in Canada by establishing Canadian subsidiaries. Canada has thereby acquired an industrial structure in secondary manufacturing that may be well suited to the United States economy, but is quite unsuitable for Canada. In the case of many of these manufactures, the basic conditions of Canadian productivity are good enough to enable Canada to compete successfully in unprotected home and open world markets, but such successful competition would seem to be quite impossible for the present satellite industry without considerable structural rationalizaion and fundamental change in production and marketing policies.[12] As a policy designed to increase the economic strength of Canada and to help secure her from the steady threat of American expansionism the policy of protective tariffs inaugurated in 1879 has been the most conspicuous (but least generally recognized) misdirection of national endeavour in Canada's history.

The questions of foreign investment and the control of Canadian industry by foreigners have now become major objects of Canadian political concern, and have quite displaced all the older fears of American military and direct political conquest. The public discussion of this matter in Canada in recent years has been highly charged with emotion, as has been all discussion, throughout Canadian history, of matters regarded as touching on the vital question of independence from the United States. It is difficult to believe, however, that the emotion of Canadian nationalism has ever obscured the facts and principles of an issue more than it has obscured those that are relevant to this question of foreign investment and business control. Canadians have been told in recent

[11]J. H. Young, *Canadian Commercial Policy* (Ottawa, 1957), chap. 6.

[12]Many Canadian economists have advocated, as a solution to this problem, the promotion of Canadian-American industrial integration through the mutual lowering of tariff barriers. This point has been strongly argued by Harry G. Johnson in his sapient and penetrating essays on Canadian economic and political problems recently collected and republished under the title *The Canadian Quandary: Economic Problems and Policies* (Toronto, 1963). See especially in this connection the essays in Part 2.

years not only that the size of Canada's foreign borrowings has been excessive, but that it reflects serious weaknesses in the Canadian character: a desire to "live beyond one's means," a short-sighted willingness to sell the Canadian birthright for a mess of American pottage, a crass materialism incompatible with the demands of national sacrifice. Foreign borrowing and foreign control of Canadian industry are frequently treated as if there were a one-to-one relation between them. The dominating influence of American firms in Canadian industry is taken, without even an effort at sophistication, to mean that Canadian political independence is in grave jeopardly. It is sometimes even alleged that Canada has been deliberately brought into a colonial status by American economic imperialism and that she has been marked down for ever to be a mere raw materials supplier, "hewer of wood and drawer of water" to American industry. As we argue below in Chapter 4, none of these assertions have the consequences or other attributes so frequently ascribed to them. Looked at in objective terms it is plain enough that American investment in Canada is simply part of a long-run historical trend towards the progressive integration of the North American economy,[13] a trend which has been accelerated in recent years by the worldwide movement towards regional economic intergration.[14] The concern of Canadians has deep historical and psychological roots, however, for it is part of the old Canadian syndrome of fear of American expansionism.[15] It focuses today on American ownership of Canadian industry in much the same way as it focused, a century ago, on the American pretension of a "manifest destiny" to unify the continent. To interpret the present Canadian concern over the American ownership in different

[13]H. G. J. Aitken, *American Capital and Canadian Resources* (Cambridge, Mass., 1961).

[14]Johnson, *Canadian Quandary.*

[15]It is revealing in this connection to note the extent to which a focus on "foreign" influence becomes in Canada, a focus on *American* influence. Two examples: (1) When the First National City Bank of New York took over the Dutch-held controlling interest in the Mercantile Bank of Canada in 1963, strong opposition was expressed by the Canadian Government. The Minister of Finance, Mr. Walter Gordon, is reported to have been "so emphatic in his opposition that Rockefeller (Chairman of the New York Bank) was shocked into asking, 'Does this mean that you trusted the Dutch but you don't trust us?' Gordon made it plain that this was just what he did mean...." Peter C. Newman, "Backstage in One More American Takeover," *MacLean's*, 14 Dec. 1963, p. 17. (2) The governmental regulation of television in Canada prescribes that 55 per cent of programming must be "Canadian content." For the purpose of this regulation, the term "Canadian" includes programs from the Commonwealth and, in French, from "French-language countries" including multilingual countries such as Belgium and Switzerland. It is evident that the real intent of the regulation is that no more than 45 per cent of Canadian program time should be American.

terms from those that lie deep at the heart of Canadian origins and nationhood would be a mistake. But it would also be a mistake to dismiss its importance in the contemporary political landscape of Canada because most of the arguments that have been forthcoming in public debate are tendentious, neurotic, and muddle-headed. It is almost certain that continuing efforts will be made in the next few years to attack the problem of foreign ownership by means of national policy in one way or another. The real question before Canada in this respect is whether such efforts can be turned into moderate and even constructive channels —and that may prove to be even more of a challenge to Canadian political life than the facts of foreign ownership themselves.

The fear that an independent Canadian nationhood is somehow incompatible with the growing economic integration of the Canadian and American economies[16] and, more particularly, with American control of large sections of Canadian industry, may or may not be justified by consideration of those long-term forces of historical evolution, if such things may be said to exist, that shape the fate of nations. As a basis for concrete national policy, however, such fears would seem to be too vague and irrational for a modern advanced nation of the twentieth century, and the specific Canadian policies of the past five years or so that have drawn their inspiration from this source do little to ease the disquiet of a rational observer.[17] The most important effect of the recent upsurge of nationalistic concern has been to divert Canadian attention from the important and immediate problems with which the economy has been beset. To understand the "condition of Canada" in the early 1960's it is necessary to identify these problems[18] and to examine briefly the lines of economic policy that have been pursued by the federal government in the face of them.

The basic economic problem that has faced Canada in recent years has been persistent unemployment. At no time since mid 1957 has the

[16]This was particularly evident in federal government policy during the regime of the Conservative government under John Diefenbaker between 1957 and 1962. Witness, for example, (1) the announced intention of the government in 1958 to bring about a substantial diversion of Canadian trade from the United States to the United Kingdom; and (2) the strong opposition of the Canadian government to Britain's effort to join the European Common Market in 1962 which, it was feared, would place Canada in greater dependence on the United States by weakening Commonwealth trade ties.

[17]The most astounding case, of course, is Finance Minister Walter Gordon's Budget of 1963. Despite its weaknesses, which were so palpable that its proposals were virtually all withdrawn, the experience has done little to induce in Canada a more sober spirit of questioning concerning the policies of economic nationalism.

[18]A more detailed study of them is contained in chaps. 1 and 4 below.

economy operated at close to a full-employment level despite improvements in recent years. The loss of national income due to unemployment
has probably averaged at least $2 billion a year or more since the onset
of this stagnation. On the external side, Canada has had large current
account deficits in her balance of international payments.[19] The over-all
balance of payments position, however, has been in surplus during most
of this period due to large autonomous inflows of foreign capital. The
conspicuous exception to this general statement was, of course, the period
of foreign exchange crisis which lasted from the spring of 1962 until the
end of that year. This crisis was not due to any general weakening of
Canada's external position however, but resulted from a speculative
attack on the Canadian dollar stimulated largely by official efforts to
manipulate the floating exchange rate downwards. Both before the crisis,
and since, the Canadian dollar has been a "hard" currency, the dominant
pressures upon it in the foreign exchange market being in an upward
direction.

Recent Canadian economic policy has, however, not been congruent
with these conditions of the domestic economy and the balance of payments. During the exchange crisis of 1962, of course, such congruence
was impossible since no set of policies could have attacked the domestic
unemployment and the severe weakness of the Canadian dollar at the
same time, and the authorities chose, rightly, to devote their immediate
attention to the exchange problem. The lengthy period from mid-1957
to the development of the exchange crisis was, however, one in which
simple policies of economic expansion could have been pursued since
the over-all position of the balance of payments was strong. That such
policies were not followed is due primarily to a misreading of the domestic economic environment and a misinterpretation of the Canadian
balance of payments position on the part of the authorities. Attention
was mistakenly focused on the danger of (a non-existent) inflation in
the domestic economy, and the balance of payments, though in over-all
surplus, was on account of its large deficit on current account, taken
to be in need of support. The result was that policies of economic
restraint were pursued. Such policies, designed to restrain the total level
of spending despite substantial excess capacity, were quite inappropriate

---

[19]This has led to considerable debate concerning the connection between domes-
tic unemployment and the balance of payments. See, for example, Bank of Canada,
Annual Report, 1961; C. L. Barber, "Canada's Unemployment Problem," *CJEPS*,
Feb. 1962, pp. 88–102; R. G. Penner, "The Inflow of Long-term Capital and the
Canadian Business Cycle, 1950–1960," *ibid.*, Nov. 1962, pp. 527–41; R. Dehem,
"The Economics of Stunted Growth," *ibid.*, pp. 502–10; Johnson, *Canadian
Quandry*.

and promoted the continuation of economic stagnation and high levels of unemployment.

The policies that have been developed since the ending of the exchange crisis of 1962 are especially worthy of attention since they may fore-shadow an important general trend in the character and orientation of Canadian economic policy. As in the period before the crisis, conditions have existed for the implementation of straightforward expansionary policies, but what appears to have developed is the adoption of policies that, while directed at combating unemployment domestically, are aimed at the Canadian balance of payments position as if it were a weak one.[20] Such policies are not immediately compatible with one another, but they are not impossible to devise and operate as long as one is prepared to insulate the domestic and external aspects of the country's economy from their normal interaction with one another. The principal thing that must be said about such a policy approach is that it goes against the spirit of the rules for orderly international trade and exchange that have been evolved, since the war, under the guidance of international organizations such as the General Agreement on Tariffs and Trade, and foreshadows a return to the particularist and manipulative economic policies of the pre-war period.

Since the chief weapons that are relied upon by the government of a modern economy to meet general problems such as unemployment, inflation, and balance of payments disequilibruim are the general techniques of fiscal and monetary policy, a word or two of a more specific nature about the use of these techniques by the Canadian government in recent years is in order.

Fiscal Policy. The last occasion on which the federal government budget was specifically employed for such purposes of economic management was in 1959. The economic upswing then in progress was interpreted by the Minister of Finance to be powerful enough to generate inflationary pressure and the Budget of that year raised personal and corporate income tax rates as a stabilizing measure. As it turned out, the 1959 expansion was not strong enough even to approach full employment and the chief impact of the Budget was to contribute to the premature downturn of the economy early in 1960. Income tax rates were not lowered, however, when unemployment deepened and continued, and they remain today [early 1965] at the high levels to which they were

[20]The most striking example is the policy of stimulating employment in the automobile industry by offering export subsidies to Canadian manufacturers in the form of tariff remissions on imported parts. See Harry G. Johnson, "The New Tariff Policy for the Automotive Industries," *Business Quarterly*, spring 1964.

raised in 1959. In succeeding budgets the Minister of Finance spoke favourably of the theory of counter-cyclical budgeting but no measures, either on the expenditure side or the revenue side, were actually introduced to put the theory into practice. The budgetary deficits that have been experienced by the federal government since the onset of deep unemployment in 1957 have been "passive" deficits, resulting from the low levels of national income, rather than from any active efforts to combat the sluggishness of the economy by means of a Keynesian type of fiscal policy.

The unemployment policies of the federal government in this period have consisted of introducing a series of specific measures of a sort which were believed to exert a direct and specific impact on unemployment. This approach to the problem is clearly shown in the budget speeches from the special "Baby Budget" of December 1960 (which was introduced specifically because, as the Minister acknowledged, the economic climate had significantly changed in the preceding months) down to be the most recent Budget of 1963. The December 1960 Budget, for example, introduced the principle of limited accelerated depreciation for capital expenditures in areas of substantial and sustained unemployment or for the creation of capital assets to serve production activities not before carried on in Canada; the Budget of June, 1961 repealed the excise tax on automobiles to encourage their sales and added further to the accelerated depreciation policy; the Budget of April 1962 proposed that corporate profit tax rates should be reduced on the profits earned on additional sales over a base period (this was aimed at encouraging exports); the Budget of 1963, *inter alia*, offered a bonus to employers of additional workers aged 45 years and over (conditional upon the employer providing retraining), provided tax exemptions for three years to new manufacturing and processing enterprises locating in "areas of slower growth," and again extended the applicability of accelerated depreciation. Other fiscal measures have been introduced outside the formal budget speeches, of course, but they have shared the specific and selective characteristics of the measures listed in this paragraph.

Monetary policy in Canada, for most of the period from 1957 to 1962, was dominated by fears of inflation. Such fears were the *raison d'être* of the Conversion Loan of 1958 by which $6.5 billion of the federal government debt was refinanced into longer-term issues at much higher rates of interest. In undertaking this massive refinancing the monetary authorities were, unfortunately, not only misguided as to the state of the economy but clumsy in their management of the operation. The result was exceptionally sharp upward movements of interest rates, as an immediate effect of the loan itself, and as a result of disorderly bond market conditions which materialized after its "successful" conclusion. The net impact on the economy was highly deflationary. Liquidity was greatly reduced both by the lengthening of the term of the debt and the increased risk premium that had been attached to government bonds by the disorderly market. To the already low ratio of the Canadian money supply to national income was added the further deflationary impact of a distinct shift upwards in the community's demand for money.[21] The disorder of the government bond market also had an important effect upon fiscal policy, by creating a belief in official circles, even among those of Keynesian persuasions, that active deficit budgeting should not be pursued as an anti-deflationary policy, because the deficit would be difficult to finance and because such a policy would further shake the confidence of an already nervous financial community.

The great majority of Canadian non-governmental economists have been deeply dissatisfied with the economic policy performance of the past several years and troubled at the continuing stagnation of the economy. When one surveys the official statements and policy decisions of recent years, it is difficult to avoid the conclusion that there has been a serious failure of policy advice at senior official levels in the civil service. A deep cleavage has developed between the opinions of academic economists and the senior economists of the federal government and a similar cleavage, not so deep but still important, between economists within the federal public service who are engaged in research and those who provide policy advice. One of the major tasks facing the newly created Economic Council of Canada is to repair these cleavages and to improve the quality of the economic interpretation and advice that goes forward to the cabinet.

The foregoing illustrations of inadequate policy and the growing cleavage between government and academic economists have more disquieting overtones than appear on the surface. During the Second World War and afterwards, at least till 1956, Canadian economic policy and administrative efficiency were not only highly regarded abroad but apparently quite successful domestically (see Chapter 1 for details) and consistent with the recommendations of contemporary economic analysis. Furthermore, there appeared to be widespread public acceptance of deliberate monetary and fiscal measures to arrest undesirable movements of the economy in either an inflationary or deflationary direction. Many economists and others in the United States and overseas looked wistfully

[21]Cf. C. L. Barber, "The Canadian Economy in Trouble." A brief to the Royal Commission on Banking and Finance, 1962.

at the apparent sophistication of Canadian economic policy and the willingness of Canadian authorities to accept sound economic advice. Canada likewise adopted a liberal and far-sighted position in many important international matters and in particular championed a closer approximation to free trade, even when the short-run domestic impact might be adverse. All this seemed to change rather abruptly about 1956 or 1957. The poor performance of the economy during the latter part of the 'fifties, combined with serious mistakes of policy and an international short-sightedness that was less apparent earlier, have led to serious doubts about the real foundations of Canada's earlier success. Perhaps it was, after all, due much more to a fortunate conjunction of circumstances than to the wisdom of Canadian policy. Perhaps no real consensus had existed concerning economic policy after all, and the apparent acceptance of counter-cyclical management might simply have been a passive acquiescence founded upon growing affluence and prosperity. We have recorded some of the mistakes of economic policy here, not only for their own inherent interest, but especially to portray the growing sense of uneasiness that has replaced the, perhaps excessive, self-confidence of the post-war years. Self-doubt and healthy self-criticism are desirable and useful when supported by a basic confidence in a nation's ability to resolve its problems. But when soured by disillusionment, self-criticism turns to attempts to assign blame either externally (e.g., the United States) or to particular groups internally. The recent burst of anti-American sentiment and the exacerbation of latent internal ethnic hostilities would appear to be related to the growing sense of frustration and disillusionment in both the economic and political spheres of Canadian life.[22]

It should not now be regarded as purely an accident of circumstances that the recent years of poor performance in the Canadian economy have witnessed the rapid growth of internal political problems that are now sufficiently great to be a serious threat to Canadian nationhood. Problems of federal-provincial relations and, in particular, problems of the relationship between Quebec and Ottawa, which is the political focus for French-English tensions, now share the stage with the problem of foreign ownership of industry as the major concern of Canadian politics. There can be little doubt that the disappointment of expectations, which is a result of the economic stagnation, is in large part responsible for the rapidity with which federal-provincial and French-English problems

[22]For a detailed discussion of this mood in the political realm see Peter C. Newman, *Renegade in Power: The Diefenbaker Years* (Toronto, 1963).

have moved to the forefront of public attention in recent years. The Great Depression of the 1930's had a similar impact—it generated surprisingly little creative analysis in Canada for the economics of unemployment, but an intense concern with and profound examination of the economics, finance, constitutional law, and politics of Canadian federalism. There are pervasive continuing strains on Canadian nationhood, which make themselves strongly felt when economic conditions are a source of disappointment, though it would be a mistake to believe that these strains would be completely resolved by a continuously progressing economy. Bad economic conditions exacerbate these strains, but they do not create them; good economic conditions ameliorate, but do not resolve, them.

An important element in these tensions has been the regional disparities within Canada, in incomes, educational systems, economic interests, and political attitudes, not to speak of differences of language and religion. These disparities at the purely economic level have been great, and the trends of economic development suggest that they will persist and, indeed, increase. What MacGregor Dawson called the "galling difference in the economic position of the provinces"[23] have been all the more productive of strains upon nationhood because they are widely held, in the poorer provinces, to be the result of Confederation itself and of the policies that have been pursued by the national governments. In the Maritime provinces, for example, the tariff, by which the manufacturing areas of the central provinces are subsidized at the expense of other sections of the country, is frequently blamed for the continuing economic backwardness of the region.[24] The same contention can be heard on the prairies where economic conditions are poor. In Quebec, where personal incomes have long been some 25 per cent lower than those of Ontario,[25] this is read as evidence of the fact that French-speaking Canadians do not enjoy a full partnership in Confederation.

The task of holding the disparate elements of the nation together has had to be a prime objective of the federal government ever since Confederation, and the methods by which this has been accomplished have often been rather crude. As Professor Underhill has described the difficult post-Confederation years: "the political technique was successfully being standardized by John A. Macdonald, the technique of keeping

[23]R. M. Dawson, *The Government of Canada* (4th ed., Toronto, 1963), p. 85.
[24]See, for example, W. J. Woodfine, "Canada's Atlantic Provinces: A Study in Regional Economic Retardation," in M. H. Watkins and D. F. Forster, eds., *Economics: Canada* (Toronto, 1963), pp. 312–19.
[25]André Raynauld, "The Economic Problems of Quebec," *ibid.*, pp. 325–30. See also below, pp. 138–9.

things going by a process of purely opportunistic bargaining and manipulation among the sectional units of the new Dominion, of holding the members of the Federation together through bribes first to one section and then to another."[26] Goldwin Smith, the great historian and gadfly of Canadian politics, visiting British Columbia by way of the newly completed Canadian Pacific Railway, asked a local citizen what were his politics and received the cynical reply, "Government appropriations."[27] This way of accomplishing the task of union was not confined to the early years of nationhood. It is surprising, when one surveys the matter, the extent to which Canadian confederation has been held together by "Government appropriations"—railways and other public works, federal grants, conditional and otherwise, freight rates and other forms of thinly disguised regional subsidization, "equalization payments," and a host of others. But the astonishing thing is how effective a cement this political self-bribery has been, at least for the first century of Confederation. Perhaps the genius of Canadian politics lies in the extent to which each section of the country has been able to persuade itself that the process of political blackmail that has been going on since Confederation has on the whole been favourable to itself. One should also note, and especially at the present time, the part in this process that has occasionally been played by the threat of secession. When cynically advanced, this threat has been, perhaps, a symptom of political health in Canada, like the lover who threatens suicide in order to accomplish the seduction of his inamorata (and himself!)—but at times, it has become, as perhaps it is today in French Canada, a threat of self-destruction that is neurotic and uncalculating and may, on that account, actually be carried out.

The old techniques evolved by Sir John A. Macdonald have not lost their effectiveness in dealing with immediate sectional strains, as the most recent Federal-Provincial Conference has shown,[28] but there are other sources of growing tension that it would not be wise to neglect. These spring from the changing economic and social roles of the federal and provincial governments since the Second World War, and from growing French-Canadian disaffection.

The Fathers of Confederation deliberately sought to establish a nation with a strong central government. They were impressed with the instability of the American Union, then seared by Civil War, and Macdonald himself thought of federation as only an intermediate step that would lead to full legislative union as the immediate political necessities that

---

[26]*In Search of Canadian Liberalism*, p. 173.
[27]*Ibid.*, p. 34.   [28]Held in Ottawa, Nov. 1963.

dictated a federal form of union passed away. The British North America Act specifically gave the great powers—financial, economic and other—as well as the residual power—to the central government, and it was only the perverse decisions of the Judicial Committee of the Privy Council in subsequent constitutional cases that frustrated this intent. The fiscal system established at Confederation was deliberately restrictive so far as provincial sources of revenue were concerned, in part because it was regarded as necessary to forestall any development of provincial taxation that would act as tariffs and other impediments to interprovincial trade, but also because it was not envisaged that the financial needs of the provinces would be large, since their responsibilities were then clearly of minor importance.[29]

From the very beginning however, provincial financial resources were inadequate to their responsibilities. Grants from the federal treasury were necessary, and the size of these transfers has grown steadily despite the fact that the legal scope of provincial taxing power has been greatly widened since Confederation. The heavy pressures on provincial finance resulting from the depression of the 1930's translated themselves into the transfer of more responsibility to the federal government, and the Second World War again greatly enlarged the federal sphere relative to the provincial. For a time it even appeared as if Macdonald's expectation would come true in substance if not in formal organization, since it was the federal government that was universally looked to for leadership and authority in all important matters. The high water mark in this development was probably the Report of the Royal Commission on National Development in the Arts, Letters and Sciences in 1951. This Commission under the chairmanship of the Right Honourable Vincent Massey dealt with matters that were strictly of provincial concern by constitution without engendering sectional complaint, and it recommended solutions in terms of an enlargement of federal responsibilities without exciting much opposition.

All this has changed in the past decade. The great growth in the functions of government that has been going on since the war has virtually all been in areas of provincial responsibility—education, health, social services and social welfare, roads, etc.—and although the federal government has taken an active role in all these fields, the significance of the provincial level has grown very much. Unlike the United States, Canada does not have a focus of great and unquestionable federal significance in the defence and foreign policy functions of government and

[29]See J. H. Perry, "What Price Provincial Autonomy?" *CJEPS*, Nov. 1955, p. 433.

so there has been nothing to prevent the growth of provincial importance from reducing that of the central government. The most significant development, however, is that it is now the provincial governments that display imperialistic propensities, thrusting themselves into areas traditionally and constitutionally belonging to the central government. The Ontario "trade crusade," by which that provincial government seeks to expand Canadian exports and reduce imports; the industrial promotion policies of many provinces, but especially Quebec; the suggestion by Premier Lesage of Quebec at the Federal-Provincial Conference of 1963 that the provinces should be consulted concerning such matters as monetary policy and tariff policy—are symptoms of this trend. But the great significance of these developments lies in the fact that they reflect the failure of the federal government to act effectively in its own constitutional spheres in recent years. The detailing of the deficiencies of federal economic policies earlier in this chapter has been for the purpose of illustrating this most important recent development—the widespread disappointment with the central government under successively *both* major political parties—as an effective instrument for the performance of certain essential governmental functions.

The rise of French-Canadian disaffection in recent years has added other elements of tension which, with those noted above, could make for a serious threat to Canadian nationhood. In addition to questioning the *effectiveness* of the existing constitutional structure, French Canada has begun to question its *legitimacy,* and that, if the political sociologists are to be credited, is a particularly dangerous combination of complaints.[30] The recent revival of the "contract theory" of Confederation, which has no legal or historical foundations worth mentioning, bespeaks a desire to argue that the present political system in Canada is illegitimate because the "contract" between French and English has been voided. The argument that French must be accorded equal status with English throughout the country springs from the real disabilities of French-speaking Canadians, but it often finds expression in terms that question the legitimacy of any political power in Canada that is not bilingual. The terrorist activities of the *Front Liberation Québecois* and the daubing of "Québec Libre" on monuments and buildings may be the work of isolated neurotics, but it still constitutes a significant rejection of the established political processes. Even more significant perhaps, as a reflection of the questionable legitimacy of the political system, is the lack of agreement between French and English concerning the symbols

---

[30]See S. M. Lipset, *Political Man* (New York, 1963), chap. 3.

of legitimacy—flag, anthem, days of national reverence, etc. The legitimacy of the term "nation" itself to refer to Canada as a whole, has even been decried by French Canadians and the rejection has been accepted, but not without concern and bewilderment, in Ottawa.

These are the rising internal strains on Canadian nationhood. Their relation to the old external threat from the United States is no longer that internal weakness will invite American conquest, but that a failure to solve the problems of nationhood would induce many sections of Canada, perhaps all, to seek that union with the Republic that was first rejected almost two hundred years ago. The economics, politics, culture and geography of Canada herself, and her proximity to the United States, make it unlikely that the strains on Canadian nationhood can ever be fully resolved, but it is important to note, again, how much more threatening these strains become in periods of economic stagnation. Whatever their sources, these strains can be greatly eased, and even turned into constructive channels, by an economy that is growing and progressing, offering expanding opportunities to its citizens and enabling them to be proud of themselves as belonging to a country that is held high among the free and progressive nations of the world. In the life and fortunes of a nation, economics is not everything, but it is a very great deal.

Introduction

UNE NATION EN VOIE DE FORMATION

Il y eut jadis au Nouveau-Brunswick, une compagnie de chemin de fer qui portait le nom bien retentissant de : l' « European and North American Railway ». Sa seule ligne ferroviaire reliait St.-John et Shédiac, soit un parcours de 120 milles. Malgré tous les efforts énergiques que déployèrent les propriétaires de cette sociéte, la ligne en question ne fut jamais prolongée. Mais en choisissant ce nom grandiloquent, les fondateurs de cette compagnie de chemin de fer ne faisaient que témoigner d'une certaine désinvolture à l'égard de la géographie, ainsi que des rêves romantiques de richesse et de conquête continentale qui ont tant caractérisé la pensée économique et politique de l'Amérique du Nord au milieu du 19e siècle.

Un continent vierge attendait d'être ; il offrait à l'esprit d'entreprise de vastes ressources à exploiter et une occasion, unique dans l'histoire, de bâtir un nouvel empire dans un monde nouveau. Le flux de cet enthousiasme pour la conquête du continent a battu son plein aux Etats-Unis au cours des années qui ont précéde la Guerre civile. Et les grandes vagues ont déferlé comme elles l'ont toujours fait, jusqu'en Amérique du Nord britannique, où d'autres homme ont aussi rêvé de bâtir un empire. A la faveur d'une de ces vagues, les provinces de l'Amérique du Nord britannique se sont unies en 1867 pour former une nouvelle confédération qui, à son tour, a nourri l'espoir de fonder un « dominion » *a mari usque ad mare.*

La réalité, toutefois, est toujours plus austère et plus contingente que l'espoir, et nulle part l'écart entre les deux aurait pu être aussi grand que dans la nouvelle nation canadienne. Ainsi que P. B. Waite, l'historien de la Confédération, nous l'a rappelé:

La réalité de 1867 était terrifiante. Elle montrait combien étaient naïfs les rêves des colonisateurs qui devaient compter avec les pays suivants : Terre-Neuve, dont la population arrivait tout juste à vivre en pêchant dans le courant du Labrador et en cultivant une terre aride ; l'Ile-du-Prince-Edouard, satisfaite d'elle-même, intraitable, et ayant un esprit de clocher ; la Nouvelle-Ecosse, dont les navires voguaient sur sept océans, fière d'elle-même, jalouse du Canada ; le Nouveau-Brunswick, à demi-américain sur le plan politique et dans ses façons de faire ; le Québec, décidé à obtenir chaque parcelle de droit et de prérogative, avec ou ans le consentement d'Ottawa ; l'Ontario, prospère, aux préjugés tenaces et à la voix retentissante ; à un millier de milles de Toronto, près de la rivière Rouge, un groupe peu homogène de 9,000 colons, et la Compagnie de la Baie d'Hudson, essayant de tenir les Américains à l'écart du nord-ouest ; dans la lointaine Colombie-Britannique, la ruée de l'or qui se meurt et dont l'hypothèque est recueillie par deux villes, petites et hostiles. Tout cela est bien le contraire des arguments grandioses dont retentissaient les discours prononcés en 1864. D'une part, la réalité tenace et rebelle aux efforts de l'homme, d'autre part, un rêve politique d'une audace merveilleuse. Ce rêve fut évoqué bien des fois et en termes nobles par Howe, par McGee, par Brown ; même Cartier, à son retour en 1867, disait : « Désormais, nous compterons parmi les nations » . Mais personne, ni Cartier, ni même Macdonald, ne savait vers quoi on allait en créant un Etat continental qu'il faudrait faire vivre et administrer. Un empire de cette importance avait été crée auparavant; on porrait en faire un autre, en s'inspirant du grand exemple que les Américains avaient donné. Mais cet empire avait été fondé par une nation riche et puissante de vingt millions d'habitants. Qu'un groupe de provinces encore en lutte et aux opinions opposées, disposant d'une population de quatre millions d'habitants, envisagent de faire de même, c'était surprenant et c'était peut-être même absurde. Le chemin de fer, qui aurait pu rendre quelque peu réalisable la fondation d'une telle union, n'existait pas encore. L'union des Colonies fut réalisée en 1867 ; mais c'était à peine un commencement. A Rivière-du-Loup et à Truro les tronçons de voies ferrées, encore séparés par des centaines de milles, montraient bien que la cause restait à gagner et qu'une nouvelle nation restait à créer. Et ce devait être l'œuvre d'années difficiles, encore à venir.[1]

Ces années difficiles, du moins telles qu'on les avait envisagées en 1867, sont maintenant derrière nous ; les chemins de fer ont été construits ; la moitié nord du continent a été soumise à la souveraineté canadienne, la nationalité canadienne qui semblait peu réalisable en 1867 est aujourd'hui un fait accompli. Même les Pères les plus enthousiastes de la Confédération auraient lieu d'être fiers de ce qui a été réalisé depuis le début. Si le Canada « ne compte pas parmi les nations » en ce sens qu'il n'est pas une grande puissance militaire, il se range toutefois

[1]P. B. Waite, *The Life and Times of Confederation, 1864–1867* (Toronto, 1962), pp. 328–9.

parmi les premiers peuples qui aient donné la liberté et des possibilités
de progrès à leurs citoyens : un niveau de vie de plus en plus élevé, une
démocratie politique à l'abri de toute menace de subversion, une société
qui participe activement à tout ce qu'il y a de meilleur dans les nouveaux domaines de la science et de la culture. La terre s'est révélée
riche en ressources, même bien plus riche qu'on n'aurait pu l'imaginer
en 1867 ; le système parlementaire, apporté du Vieux Monde, a montré
que, dans le Nouveau, il pouvait se développer et se fortifier en toute
indépendance. Et pourtant avec tout cela . . . , la lutte du Canada pour
devenir une nation homogène n'est pas encore gagnée de façon définitive,
même après un siècle de Confédération. Et peut-être un siècle de plus ne
suffira-t-il pas pour que ce résultat soit finalement acquis. En attendant,
l'incertitude et le doute continuent à prévaloir à l'égard de la nation
canadienne. Il faut dire qu'elle est soumise à des épreuves plus subtiles et
plus tenaces que celles qui résultent de l'équipement d'un pays vaste et
divers en moyens de transport et de communication et la création des
mécanismes politiques nécessaires à son administration. Ces épreuves
émanent de deux sources : à l'intérieur la scission entre les Français et
les Anglais, et, à l'extérieur, la proximité des Etats-Unis. Et ces deux
facteurs sont aussi puissants aujourd'hui qu'ils l'étaient en 1867.

Ces deux plus grandes faiblesses de la nation canadienne sont aussi,
de façon paradoxale, les éléments qui sont en premier lieu responsables
de l'union des colonies britanniques pour former la seconde nation continentale en Amérique du Nord. Malgré la majesté du rêve d'un empire
continental, qui a donné à la Confédération son attrait romantique, la
Confédération n'aurait sans doute jamais été réalisée si elle n'avait pas
offert une solution pratique aux problèmes politiques les plus immédiats
que posait le conflit franco-anglais dans les provinces unies du Canada,
et la pression expansionniste des Etats-Unis. De toute évidence, les
hommes politiques du Canada avaient de nombreuses raisons pour proposer le grand projet de l'union de l'Amérique du Nord britannique à
Charlottetown en 1864, mais aucune de ces raisons ne compta autant
que celle qui voulait que ce projet donnât au Canada francophone de
l'est et au Canada anglophone de l'ouest la possibilité de mettre fin, dans
un esprit de concorde, à leur rivalité, au lieu de poursuivre leur route
sur cette pente glissante qui menait tout droit à la rupture acrimonieuse.
Il n'est guère probable non plus que la Confédération eût pris naissance
sans la crainte qu'inspiraient les desseins des impérialistes américains sur
les provinces britanniques. En présence de la doctrine américaine « manifest destiny » et de la pousée persistante de l'hégémonie américaine vers

les territoires de l'ouest ouverts à la colonisation, et aussi aux diverses tensions causées par les provocations, les menaces, les aventures militaires des Féniens[2], les « provinces britanniques » , se sentant isolées, eurent le vif sentiment de leur faiblesse. Elles ont ainsi accueilli les assurances que semblait offrir une plus grande union politique[3].

Cette crainte d'une menace venant des Etats-Unis ne s'est atténuée que très lentement au Canada, même sous sa forme la plus brutale, à savoir celle d'une action militaire. Jusqu'en 1895, on se livrait encore à d'importants préparatifs de défense contre toute invasion américaine, et même entre la première Grande Guerre et la seconde, les seuls plans de défense dont se souciaient les militaires canadiens, reposaient sur l'hypothèse d'une attaque venant des États-Unis[4]. De telles craintes sur le plan militaire ont enfin disparu, pour ne faire place toutefois qu'à d'autres craintes, plus profondes et plus subtiles, relatives à la pénétration culturelle et économique du Canada par les États-Unis.

Pour bien comprendre le Canada, il faut connaître son attitude historique vis-à-vis des Etats-Unis, et le rôle vital que cette attitude a toujours joué dans les affaires intérieures canadiennes. Ainsi que s'exprimait le professeur Underhill : « La tradition la plus ancienne et la plus tenace dans notre mémoire à tous est celle qui a pour centre notre décision de ne pas devenir Américains. C'est également la seule tradition qui unisse sans réserve les Canadiens anglais et les Canadiens français »[5]. A cet égard, le fondement de l'attitude des Canadiens français est évident. Ayant lutté depuis la victoire de Wolfe sur Montcalm, en 1759, pour maintenir leur langue et leur identité culturelle dans un milieu hostile d'anglophones, les Canadiens français n'ignorent pas qu'ils auraient vite fait de disparaître dans le grand creuset américain dont le

[2]La « Fraternité des Féniens » était une organisation d'Irlandais qui avaient juré de libérer l'Irlande de la domination britannique. Ces Féniens organisèrent des expéditions militaires contre le Canada après la Guerre civile, en vue d'attaquer, de façon indirecte, la Grande-Bretagne.

[3]« Cette nouvelle union doit être pourvue de liens grâce à l'établissement d'un réseau ferroviaire. Elle doit obtenir un avenir territorial aussi vaste que possible. Et le loup américain doit être tenu aussi loin que possible de la porte de l'Amérique du Nord britannique: en effet, sans les bruyants hurlements du loup américain en 1864 et au cours des années suivantes, il est peu probable que les diverses provinces se fussent unies. Cette crainte du grand voisin entreprenant s'est exprimée de cent façons. L'importance démesurée qu'on attachait aux problèmes de défense n'en était pas la moindre : l'union britannique nord-américaine devait être une alliance défensive contre les Etats-Unis. » A. R. M. Lower, « Theories of Canadian Federalism—Yesterday and Today » , A. R. M. Lower, F. R. Scott, etc., *Evolving Canadian Federalism* (Durham, NC, 1958), pp. 9–10.

[4]Comité Américano-Canadien, *The Perspective of Canadian-American Relations*, mai, 1962, p. 2.

[5]P. H. Underhill, *In Search of Canadian Liberalism* (Toronto, 1960), p. 222.

ferment d'assimilation a toujours été beaucoup plus puissant que celui du Canada. Il a toujours semblé aux Canadiens français qu'il est préferable de garder et de protéger l'âme française en Amérique du Nord à l'abri du drapeau britannique, si limité et restreint soit-il, que de se laisser dissoudre et n'être plus qu'un « bouton américain » , et de perdre ainsi pour de bon toute identité. Le séparatisme chez les Canadiens anglais provient d'une source toute différente, et pourtant aussi puissante. Ontario, le centre du Canada anglophone, fut colonisé, après la Révolution américaine et la Guerre de 1812, par des gens qui abandonnèrent leur foyer dans les nouveaux États-Unis indépendants, afin de donner suite à leur inébranlable décision de vivre et d'élever leur famille dans la tradition britannique. Ainsi, dès le début, le cœur du Canada anglais comprenait des gens qui avaient rejeté la Révolution américaine et l'aspiration des Américains à former une nation indépendante démocratique et républicaine. C'est donc au Canada qu'ils ont grandi et se sont multipliés, entretenant leur anti-américanisme à l'abri de l'attitude hautaine et dédaigneuse des Anglo-Saxons, que l'immigration constante de compatriotes de même race venus de Grande-Bretagne ne risquait pas d'affaiblir, et ce sont eux qui ont fourni, pendant des générations, les élites dirigeantes nécessaires à la vie politique, économique, et culturelle du Canada anglophone jusqu'à nos jours[6].

Et pourtant . . . si ferme et fondamentale qu'ait été cette décision de rester une nation séparée des Etats-Unis, il s'agit d'une option que l'on ne pourra jamais rendre définitive et irrévocable pour le Canada. Les forces géographiques, culturelles, et historiques ainsi que les affaires internationales ne cessent de remettre cette question, de façon répétée, à l'ordre du jour de la politique canadienne. On doit continuellement la soulever et on doit continuellement y répondre. Mais il y a autre chose dont on n'a pas encore fait mention : les Canadiens ne trouvent pas qu'il soit, à tout prendre, fâcheux de revenir constamment sur ce sujet. L'idée d'avoir encore le choix d'une grande union politique avec la nation la plus riche et la plus puissante du monde n'est pas pour leur déplaire. Dans ses rapports avec les Etats-Unis, le Canada rappelle la jeune fille de la chanson de jadis qui répondait toujours : « Non, Jean! Non, Jean! Non, Jean! Non! » , mais qui toutefois donnait la même réponse à la question de savoir si elle était décidée à rester célibataire toute sa vie durant.

Au cours du siècle qui s'est écoulé depuis la Confédération, une nation

---

[6]Une étude sur l'élite économique du Canada paraît ci-après au chapitre 8. Cette élite et les autres élites canadiennes sont étudiées dans *The Vertical Mosaic* (Toronto, 1965) par le professeur John Porter de Carleton University.

est née, mais le sentiment d'une véritable nationalité n'a pas été établi de façon claire. L'attitude négative a tant dominé, de façon continue, la vie politique des deux principaux groupes ethniques du Canada que les éléments positifs ont eu peu d'occasions de s'affirmer. D'ailleurs les mères-patries européennes, l'Angleterre et la France, n'aidaient pas non plus à la formation d'un sentiment national. Ce n'est pas la conquête de 1759 qui a rompu les liens qui rattachaient le Canada français à la France, c'est la Révolution française. Et l'Eglise catholique romaine qui combla le vide ainsi créé et donna au Canada français une raison d'être et une continuité, le fit de telle façon que ce pays se trouva à l'écart du courant principal de la vie canadienne et ne put participer pleinement aux grands progrès réalisés au cours du dix-neuvième siècle. Les liens du Canada anglais avec la Grande-Bretagne, bien qu'ils n'aient jamais été rompus, n'ont guère été plus utiles. Le Canada anglais a importé de Grande-Bretagne de nombreux éléments superficiels du nationalisme, mais bien peu de la substantifique moelle politique et culturelle avec laquelle il eût été possible de bâtir une nouvelle nation canadienne. D'ailleurs l'Angleterre, la mère-patrie, désirait vivement depuis longtemps que ses enfants coloniaux de l'Amérique du Nord, devenus adultes, cessent de se cramponner à son tablier. Elle poussa un soupir de soulagement lorsque la Confédération, pour la naissance de laquelle elle avait elle-même beaucoup œuvré (et non sans arrière-pensée), la déchargea de sa responsabilité.

C'est le *rejet* qui est le thème intime dominant de la vie nationale canadienne ; rejet *par* le Canada des occasions uniques offertes par l'union avec les Etats-Unis et rejet *du* Canada par les mères-patries, la Grande-Bretagne et la France. Peut-être est-ce cette névrose historique interne du rejet, qui s'ajoute au fait de vivre à côté de la nation la plus riche du monde — avec laquelle les comparaisons sont aussi inévitables qu'elles sont inévitablement peu favorables — qui est responsable d'une des caractéristiques les plus fortes de la vie nationale canadienne, à savoir un manque de confiance quant à sa propre valeur et quant à sa place dans le concert des nations. Aucune production canadienne, dans les domaines littéraires et artistiques en particulier, ni même dans ceux des sciences et des sciences sociales n'est généralement reconnue, si elle n'a pas reçu l'*imprimatur* de l'approbation étrangère. On n'apprécie vivement aucun Canadien doué de puissance créatrice tant qu'il n'a pas fait ses preuves dans un pays étranger.

Si l'on peut se permettre une interprétation psychologique de ce syndrome canadien, il ne serait pas tout à fait déplacé de raconter une anecdote au sujet de Sigmund Freud. Son biographe, Ernest Jones, nous

raconte que Freud reçut un jour une communication émanant du Service
des impôts autrichiens, qui exprimait de l'étonnement que le revenu du
professeur Freud fût si minime « étant donné que tout le monde sait que
sa réputation s'étend bien au delà des frontières de l'Autriche » . Freud
y répondit : « Le professeur Freud est très honoré de recevoir une communication du gouvernement. C'est la première fois que le Gouvernement a fait attention à lui et il lui en sait gré. Il y a un seul point sur
lequel il n'est pas d'accord, à savoir que sa réputation s'étend bien au
delà des frontières de l'Autriche. En fait, elle ne commence qu'une fois
la frontière franchie » [7] . C'est une observation que de nombreux
Canadiens comprendront facilement.

De même que la crainte de l'expansionnisme américain a joué un rôle
vital dans la création de la Confédération canadienne, de même au cours
des années qui ont suivi la Confédération la politique du gouvernement
national a été dominée par le même facteur. Respectivement relatifs aux
chemins de fer, à l'immigration et aux tarifs douaniers, les trois grands
programmes de la politique canadienne après la Confédération sont au
service de la même cause : mettre en valeur le pays et le protéger de
l'expansionnisme « manifest destiny » des Etats-Unis en plein développement. De ces trois programmes, l'un a brillamment réussi, un autre
présentait une équivoque inquiétante, et le troisième a grandement contribué à atteindre, mais dans le sens opposé, l'objectif fixé à l'origine.
    La première tâche de la nouvelle nation fut évidemment la construc-
tion des chemins de fer. Il s'agissait non seulement de rapprocher Québec
des Provinces Maritimes, afin d'unir les partenaires de la Confédération,
mais aussi de pénétrer dans les régions désertes autour des rives du Lac
Supérieur jusqu'à la rivière Rouge, et ensuite par delà les immenses
étendues des prairies, de traverser les imposantes chaînes de montagnes
pour aboutir à la mer, au bord de laquelle un autre petit noyau de Nord-
Américains britanniques attendait d'être uni à la Confédération. Ce ne
fut pas seulement une tâche. Ce fut une course — une course contre les
Américains qui déjà, le jour même, pour ainsi dire, où la Confédération
avait été proclamée, avait acheté l'Alaska, tournant ainsi par le nord
la Colombie-Britannique ; les Américains auraient certainement attiré les
territoires de la Compagnie de la Baie d'Hudson dans l'orbite de leur
autorité si le Canada avait tardé à faire valoir ses droits dans ces régions.
Et c'est ainsi que le grand réseau du Pacifique Canadien fut construit,
avec courage, audace, et rapidité, et aussi, sur le plan financier, avec une

[7]Ernest Jones, *The Life and Work of Sigmund Freud,* ouvrage édité et résumé
par Lionel Trilling et Stephen Marcus (Londres, 1963), p. 362.

témérité peu soucieuse du coût, puisqu'il fallait gagner une course dont la récompense n'était pas moins de la moitié du continent. La construction de ce chemin de fer transcontinental était une entreprise audacieuse pour une nouvelle nation dont la population était peu nombreuse. Mais, comme M. Underhill l'a fait remarquer, c'était « un exploit que nous considérons maintenant comme la plus belle expression, au cours de notre histoire, de notre foi en notre destinée nationale »[8].

Le deuxième pilier de la politique nationale après la Confédération fut l'immigration. Là aussi, il y avait un sentiment de concurrence avec les Etats-Unis. Non seulement les Canadiens désiraient voir le pays se développer et accueillirent à cette fin de nouveaux immigrants, mais aussi ils se rendaient compte que là où le territoire restait inoccupé, la souveraineté canadienne était précaire. Ce ne fut que lorsque la prairie eut été bien colonisée au cours de la première décennie de notre siècle que ce sentiment de faiblesse nationale commença à disparaître. Mais il y a toujours eu au Canada deux sentiments nettement opposés en ce qui concerne la politique nationale de l'immigration. L'opposition à l'immigration provient des causes habituelles, telles que la peur qu'une main-d'œuvre abondante n'entraîne le chômage, ainsi que l'étroitesse d'esprit concernant, comme d'habitude, les questions raciales, culturelles, et linguistiques. Mais au Canada, cette opposition provient, en outre, du fait que ce pays n'a pas été un creuset de races, et n'a pas pu préparer la disparition rapide des loyautés ethniques, ce qui, par contre, a été une caractéristique marquée de l'évolution américaine. Aux Etats-Unis, un vigoureux sentiment national exclusif a été une très puissante force d'assimilation ; le développement de la nation américaine lui doit beaucoup et l'a renforcé à son tour. Les immigrants qui venaient aux Etats-Unis durant le dix-neuvième siècle étaient pour la plupart vivement désireux d'oublier leurs origines européennes pour devenir américains aussitôt que possible. En revanche, il n'y a eu au Canada, jusqu'à récemment, qu'un faible sentiment du « Canadianisme » auquel les immigrants puissent s'identifier de pareille façon. Même aujourd'hui, ce sentiment national n'exerce pas sur les « Nouveaux Canadiens » (c'est ainsi qu'on dénomme officiellement les immigrants depuis la deuxième Guerre mondiale) une force d'assimilation comparable au magnétisme romantique par lequel les Etats-Unis ont attiré les immigrants dès qu'ils sont devenus indépendants. Peut-être le sentiment national et la force l'assimilation sont les caractéristiques subsidiaires d'une indépendance arrachée par la violence et la révolution. Ces caractéristiques ne sont pas celles d'un pays

[8]*In Search of Canadian Liberalism*, p. 99.

qui a atteint son indépendance par des moyens aussi timorés, hésitants et pacifiques que ceux que le Canada a employés.

L'extraordinaire prédominance des élites anglaises dans la vie canadienne est également importante sous ce rapport. Le fait de porter un nom dont la consonance n'est pas britannique a présenté de plus graves inconvénients au Canada qu'aux Etats-Unis. Il y a toujours eu le sentiment parmi les Canadiens d'origine non britannique que certaines portes leur étaient fermées, ce qui a refroidi l'ardeur qu'ils auraient pu mettre à s'intégrer à leur nouveau pays. Ce sentiment a été particulièrement vif au Canada français, et y a provoqué une opposition très nette à l'immigration. La « revanche des berceaux » sur laquelle comptaient les extrémistes nationaux au Canada français durant de nombreuses années pour annuler la prédominance que les Anglais avaient imposée par des moyens militaires et politiques, a été menacée par l'immigration qui attirait peu de Nouveaux Canadiens du côté des francophones. Mais même les Canadiens français modérés, qui entretenaient le secret espoir de « la revanche » , ne pouvaient s'empêcher de voir dans l'immigration massive une menace pour la langue et la culture françaises au sein de la nation canadienne. Dans la mesure où l'immigration donnait naissance à d'autres communautés linguistiques et culturelles indépendantes — cette éventualité paraissait assez probable durant les années de l'expansion occidentale — de nouvelles tensions viendraient certainement mettre à l'épreuve le développement du sentiment national canadien. Même aujourd'hui, il n'est pas évident que le pays soit en mesure d'assimiler beaucoup d'immigrants. La crainte que l'immigration ne provoque des tensions a empêché le Canada, depuis la Confédération jusqu'à nos jours, d'être plus libéral en matière d'immigration.

A la différence des Etats-Unis, le Canada a été un pays non seulement de grande immigration mais aussi de grande émigration. Si la richesse et le dynamisme des Etats-Unis n'ont pas réussi à attirer le Canada dans l'orbite américaine, par contre de nombreux Canadiens, tant anglophones que francophones, en ont subi l'attraction. L'émigration du Canada — la plus grande partie se destinant aux Etats-Unis — a été si importante à partir de 1867 que, pour toute la période qui s'est écoulée depuis, elle annule presque l'apport que représente l'immigration. Cette émigration constante de Canadiens vers les Etats-Unis et la corrélation approximative, sur le plan historique, des époques de grande immigration avec celles de grande émigration ont confirmé, à plusieurs reprises, la « théorie du déplacement » en ce qui concerne l'immigration. Cette théorie (dont il est question plus longuement au chapitre 2 ci-après) prétend que la grande immigration est la cause de la grande émigration, l'arrivée d'étrangers privant les Canadiens d'origine de certains débouchés économiques et les incitant à aller chercher fortune ailleurs. De nombreuses variantes ont été faites au Canada de temps à autre sur la théorie du déplacement, et toutes semblent aboutir à la conclusion que les migrations se sont révélées pour le Canada une épée à double tranchant qui entrave, autant qu'elle le favorise, le peuplement divisé de son territoire.

Le troisième axe de la politique nationale, c'est-à-dire la politique des barrières douanières, fut amorcé dans la province du Canada même avant la Confédération, mais, à partir de 1867, on réclamait de plus en plus vivement une « politique nationale » en vue de protéger les entreprises nationales de la concurrence étrangère, et d'encourager ainsi l'économie nationale. Il a fallu douze ans pour instituer la politique nationale, mais le résultat, une fois obtenu, a marqué un tournant important de l'histoire canadienne. En effet, bien que les mêmes questions proposées aient fait l'objet de vives discussions lorsqu'elles furent présentées en 1879 par les Conservateurs sous Sir John A. Macdonald, elles ne furent ni supprimées ni même édulcorées par les Libéraux lorsqu'ils prirent le pouvoir sous Laurier en 1896.

Le but de la politique nationale, comme l'indique justement l'expression, était le même que celui de la politique de la construction des chemins de fer et de celle de l'immigration ; il s'agissait d'encourager le développement de l'économie nationale, dans son propre intérêt évidemment, mais aussi parce que cette évolution contribuerait à renforcer les possibilités qu'a le Canada de résister aux pressions de l'expansionnisme américain. Parmi les arguments le plus souvent présentés au Canada, depuis 1879, en faveur des barrières douanières il en est un selon lequel le protectionnisme, en encourageant les industries qui ont besoin d'une très forte main-d'œuvre, permet au pays de fournir du travail à une population plus importante, ce qui est en soi une contribution à la viabilité nationale, selon les principes indiqués ci-dessus[9]. Cependant, la plupart des spécialistes contemporains de cette question estiment qu'une consequence des barrières douanières est d'abaisser l'efficacité économique et le revenu individuel au Canada. Cette thèse met donc en doute la valeur de l'argument relatif à la population, étant donné qu'il est indéniable que le niveau relativement bas des revenus au Canada con-

---

[9]Voir, par exemple, W. A. Mackintosh, *The Economic Background of Dominion-Provincial Relations*, Royal Commission on Dominion-Provincial Relations (Ottawa, 1939); et C. L. Barber « The Canadian Tariff » , *Canadian Journal of Economics and Political Science* (ci-après *CJEPS*), Nov. 1955, pp. 513–30.

tribue vivement à encourager l'émigration vers les Etats-Unis. On ne peut donc pas soutenir que les barrières douanières ont contribué à la viabilité nationale en augmentant la population. En effet, quand des débats publics ont lieu sur cette question, la rapport de ces deux facteurs est interverti de façon implicite. Ainsi on prétend que les conséquences de l'immigration et de l'émigration ont eu des répercussions défavorables sur le niveau de l'instruction de l'ensemble de la population. On dit même que le Canada est une « gare ferroviaire démographique » où la plupart de ceux qui arrivent sont des Européens non anglophones dont le niveau d'instruction est bas, alors que ceux qui partent sont des Américains du Nord parfaitement assimilés et possédant une bonne formation générale et technique. Ce qu'on appelle parfois, de façon peu delicate, « l'hémorragie des cerveaux canadiens » vers les Etats-Unis confirme le point de vue selon lequel la qualité de la population canadienne baisse à la suite de l'arrivée des immigrants et du départ des émigrants. Dans cette station de chemin de fer, ceux qui partent parlent mieux que ceux qui arrivent. Cet argument ne repose pas encore sur des preuves suffisantes. Lorsqu'on pense au grand nombre d'immigrants très qualifiés qui se rendent au Canada, et aussi au nombre de Canadiens qui retournent au pays après avoir fait des études (habituellement subventionnées) aux Etats-Unis et outre-mer, il n'est pas évident, tant qu'on n'aura pas entrepris une enquête précise à ce sujet, que c'est l'immigration ou l'émigration qui favorise le mieux la qualité de la population canadienne.

Toutefois, il semble tout à fait clair, en ce qui concerne le problème qui est débattu ici, que les conséquences des tarifs douaniers ont été défavorables. Il n'y a pas de raison pour croire qu'un niveau de vie plus bas — conséquences économiques des barrières douanières — attire un plus grand nombre d'étrangers hautement qualifiés au Canada ou invite à y revenir un plus grand nombre d'étudiants diplômés canadiens, qui ont poursuivi leurs études à l'étranger.

L'autre argument intellectuel important en faveur de la politique nationale concernait, évidemment, l'industrie naissante. Au cours des débats qui se déroulèrent à la Chambre des communes sur la politique nationale, Macdonald cita le paragraphe fatidique de J. S. Mill à l'appui de cet argument. Depuis lors, les protectionnistes canadiens y sont restés fidèles. Les conséquences industrielles de la politique nationale ont, toutefois, été bien différentes de celles qu'avaient envisagées ses premiers partisans. « Nous devons garder religieusement le gland dans l'intérêt du chêne qui va croître », proclamait le *Canadian Monthly* en 1874 alors que les débats sur le protectionnisme battaient leur plein. Et, en effet, le gland de l'industrie canadienne fut gardé religieusement par la politique nationale, avec autant de soin qu'une vieille fille s'occupe de ses pots de fleurs! Mais ce qui a poussé, ce n'était pas le grand chêne, majestueux et puissant, dont on parle souvent en littérature ; ce n'était qu'un petit chêne, rabougri et affaibli, qui ne convenait pas à son milieu.

L'adoption de la politique nationale en 1879 a été immédiatement suivie d'une entrée au Canada de capitaux industriels venant des Etats-Unis[10]. Ne pouvant exporter leurs produits manufacturés sur le marché canadien, les Américains y placèrent leurs capitaux. La loi relative aux « Préférences impériales » dans les années 30 de notre siècle, a été un nouvel encouragement dans cette même direction. En effet, les firmes qui avaient des usines au Canada pouvaient ainsi bénéficier des tarifs préférentiels pour tous les marchés de la Communauté britannique. Les industries de transformation que l'on trouve aujourd'hui au Canada sont, dans une grande mesure, le résultat du protectionnisme, et de l'impulsion qu'il a donnée, par voie de conséquence, aux investissements étrangers directs. Pourtant, les industries ainsi créées, qui, du fait des tarifs douaniers, sont subventionnées par le consommateur canadien jusqu'à concurrence d'un milliard de dollars par an[11], sont dans une grande mesure d'un rendement douteux, la raison principale étant que leurs structures ne sont pas adaptées à l'économie canadienne. La conséquence de cette arrivée de capitaux étrangers, provoquée par des moyens artificiels, a été que de nombreuses firmes américaines de fabrication qui étaient entre elles en concurrence sur leur propre marché aux Etats-Unis, ont transporté cette concurrence, telle quelle au Canada, en établissant des succursales canadiennes. Le Canada a ainsi obtenu pour les industries secondaires de transformation des structures qui peuvent très bien convenir aux Etats-Unis, mais qui ne s'adaptent pas tout à fait chez nous. En ce qui concerne une grande partie de ces industries, les conditions de base de la productivité canadienne sont assez bonnes pour permettre au Canada de prendre pied avec succès sur les marchés intérieurs qui ne sont pas protégés et sur les marchés ouverts du monde. Mais il ne semble pas que l'industrie satellite actuelle puisse réussir dans ce genre de concurrence sans une rationnalisation considérable des structures et un changement fondamental dans la politique de la production et dans celle de la commercialisation[12]. En tant que politique destinée à accroître

[10]H. Marshall, F. A. Southard, et K. W. Taylor, *Canadian-American Industry: A Study in International Investment* (New Haven & Toronto, 1936), chap 1. Voir particulièrement tableaux 1 et 2, p. 15.
[11]J. H. Young, *Canadian Commercial Policy* (Ottawa, 1957), chap. 6.
[12]De nombreux économistes canadiens ont préconisé, comme solution à ce problème, l'encouragement de l'intégration industrielle américano-canadienne en

le développement économique du Canada et à l'aider à se protéger contre la menace constante de l'expansionnisme américain, la politique des barrières douanières inaugurée en 1879 représente le gaspillage le plus frappant (encore qu'il ne soit pas généralement reconnu) qu'on ait fait de l'énergie nationale dans toute l'histoire du Canada.

Les questions des investissements étrangers et la mainmise étrangère sur l'industrie canadienne préoccupent maintenant sérieusement la politique canadienne. Ces problèmes ont chassé toutes les vieilles craintes qu'on avait au sujet de la conquête américaine, soit militaire, soit politique par voie directe. La discussion publique de ce problème au Canada, au cours des années récentes, a soulevé une vive émotion comme c'est le cas chaque fois qu'on a discuté le maintien de notre indépendance vis-à-vis des Etats-Unis. Il est difficile, toutefois, de croire que l'émotion du nationalisme canadien a jamais obscurci les faits et les principes d'un problème plus qu'elle n'a obscurci ceux qui se rapportent à cette question des investissements étrangers et de la mainmise sur les entreprises. On a fait savoir aux Canadiens qu'ils empruntent trop à l'étranger et que, de plus, ces emprunts reflètent de graves faiblesses dans le caractère canadien: un désir « de vivre au-dessus de ses moyens » , et l'imprévoyance qui fait qu'on est prêt à vendre le droit d'aînesse des Canadiens pour un plat de lentilles américain — matérialisme grossier et incompatible avec les exigences du patriotisme. Les emprunts étrangers et la mainmise étrangère sur l'industrie canadienne sont fréquemment considérés comme si les échanges avec les Etats-Unis se faisaient sur un pied d'égalité. On admet, sans même faire un effort pour maintenir cette affirmation, que l'indépendance politique canadienne court un grave danger à cause de l'influence prédominante des firmes américaines dans l'industrie canadienne. On insinue même parfois que le Canada a été, de façon délibérée, poussé vers un statut colonial par l'impérialisme économique américaine, et que ce pays a été marqué à tout jamais pour n'être qu'un fournisseur de matières premières, une sorte de scieur de bois et de porteur d'eau de l'industrie américaine. Ainsi que nous le soutiendrons au chapitre 4 ci-après, aucune de ces affirmations ne correspond vraiment à la réalité. Si l'on étudie ce problème de façon tout à fait objective, il est assez évident que les investissements américains au

baissant dans chaque pays les barrières douanières. Ce point de vue a été vivement soutenu par Harry G. Johnson dans ses essais pleins de sagesse et de pénétration sur les problèmes de l'économie et de la politique canadiennes; ces textes ont été récemment groupés et republiés sous le titre *The Canadian Quandary: Economic Problems and Policies* (Toronto, 1963). Voir en particulier à ce sujet les essais dans la deuxième partie.

Canada ne font partie que d'une tendance historique de longue haleine ayant pour but l'intégration progressive de l'économie de l'Amérique du Nord[13] — tendance qui a été accélérée au cours des récentes années par le mouvement d'ampleur mondiale qui tend à l'intégration économique régionale[14]. L'intérêt parfois inquiétant que manifest les Canadiens pour ce problème a pourtant de profondes racines historiques et psychologiques, car il fait partie de la vieille crainte qu'éprouvent périodiquement les Canadiens au sujet de l'expansionnisme américain[15]. Cette crainte se concentre aujourd'hui sur les droits de propriété que les Américains exercent sur l'industrie canadienne, de la même façon qu'elle avait pour objet, il y a un siècle, les prétentions américaines d'un « manifest destiny » en vue d'unifier le continent. Ce serait une erreur d'attribuer l'inquiétude qu'éprouvent les Canadiens actuellement au sujet de l'emprise américaine à d'autres causes que celles qui sont profondément ancrées dans les origines du pays et dans la nation canadienne. Mais ce serait également une erreur de minimiser son importance dans le milieu politique du Canada contemporain parce que la plupart des arguments qu'on a avancés dans les débats publics sont tendancieux, névrosé, et confus. Il est presque certain que des efforts continus seront faits au cours des prochaines années pour s'attaquer au problème de la mainmise étrangère, en adoptant une politique nationale qui reste à déterminer. Le vrai problème auquel doit faire face le Canada à ce sujet est de savoir si de tels efforts peuvent prendre une forme modérée et même constructive. Et il se pourrait que ce problème mette la vie politique canadienne

[13]H. G. J. Aitken, *American Capital and Canadian Resources* (Cambridge, Mass., 1961).

[14]Johnson, *Canadian Quandary.*

[15]Sous ce rapport, la mesure dans laquelle une convergence sur l'influence « étrangère » devient, au Canada, une convergence sur l'influence *américaine* est assez révélatrice. Citons deux exemples : (1) Lorsque la « First National City Bank » de New York prit possession de la part d'actions prédominante (en remplaçant les Hollandais) à la « Mercantile Bank of Canada » en 1963, le gouvernement canadien s'y opposa vivement. Le ministre des Finances, M. Walter Gordon fut, dit-on, « si catégorique que Rockefeller (président de la Banque de New York), indigné, lui demanda: « Cela veut-il dire que vous mettiez votre confiance dans les Hollandais, mais que vous n'avez pas confiance en nous ? » Gordon répondit clairement que c'était exactement ce qu'il voulait dire. . . .» Peter C. Newman, « Backstage in One More American Takeover » , *MacLean's*, 14 décembre 1963, p. 17. (2) Les règlements du gouvernement relatifs à la télévision au Canada stipulent que 55 pour cent des programmes doivent être « canadiens » . En ce qui concerne ce règlement, le mot « canadien » comprend des programmes émanant de la communauté britannique; et les programmes en français proviennent des pays francophones, y compris les pays multilingues tels que la Belgique et la Suisse. Il est évident que ce règlement vise à limiter à 45 pour cent au maximum la part américaine des programmes canadiens.

à une plus rude épreuve que celle de la mainmise étrangère sur l'industrie du pays.

La crainte selon laquelle une nation canadienne indépendante serait plus ou moins incompatible avec l'intégration économique croissante des économies canadienne et américaine[16], et en particulier avec la mainmise américaine sur de vastes secteurs de l'industrie canadienne, peut être confirmée ou infirmée par l'examen de ces facteurs à long terme de l'évolution historique qui, à supposer qu'ils existent, façonnent le destin des Etats. Des appréhensions de ce genre, cependant, paraissent trop vagues et trop peu rationnelles pour qu'un Etat moderne et évolué du vingtième siècle puisse fonder sur elles une politique concrète, et les mesures que le Canada a prises au cours des cinq dernières années en s'inspirant de pareilles inquiétudes ne sont guère de nature à calmer les appréhensions d'un observateur épris de rationnel.[17] L'effet le plus important de la poussée récente de nationalisme a été de détourner l'attention du Canada des problèmes graves et immédiats auxquels l'économie doit faire face de tous côtés. Si l'on veut comprendre la « situation du Canada » au début de cette décennie, il est indispensable de diagnostiquer ces problèmes[18] et d'examiner brièvement les grandes lignes de la politique économique mise en œuvre par le gouvernement fédéral pour les résoudre.

Le problème économique fondamental auquel le Canada a eu à faire face au cours de ces dernières années est celui du chômage chronique. A aucun moment depuis l'été de 1957, l'économie ne s'est approchée de son niveau de plein emploi, malgré quelqu'amélioration pendant les dernières années, et, depuis le début de ce marasme, on peut estimer à une moyenne probable de deux milliards par an au moins les pertes qui en résultent pour le revenu national. En ce qui concerne le commerce extérieur, le Canada a enregistré des déficits de comptes courants dans

[16]Cette crainte fut particulièrement évidente dans la politique pratiquée par le Gouvernement fédéral pendant le ministère conservateur de John Diefenbaker de 1957 à 1962, ainsi qu'en témoignent (1) l'annonce par le gouvernement en 1958 de son intention de faire dévier en direction du Royaume-Uni partie importante du commerce canadien avec les Etats-Unis; (2) l'opposition résolue du Gouvernement canadien à l'effort entrepris en 1962 par l'Angleterre pour entrer dans le Marché Commun: on craignait qu'en provoquant un relâchement des liens commerciaux à l'intérieur du Commonwealth cette entrée dans le Marché Commun ne mît le Canada dans une plus grande dépendance vis-à-vis des Etats-Unis.

[17]L'exemple le plus ahurissant est ici fourni par le budget proposé en 1963 par M. Walter Gordon, ministre des Finances. En dépit des faiblesses de ce budget, qui étaient si évidentes que toutes les propositions qu'il contenait furent pratiquement retirées, cette expérience n'a guère conduit le Canada à faire son autocritique en matière de nationalisme économique.

[18]On trouvera aux chapitres 1 et 4 une étude plus détaillée de ces problèmes.

la balance de ses paiements internationaux[19]. Cependant, la balance générale des comptes à l'extérieur a été excédentaire pendant la plus grande partie de la période considérée en raison d'entrées autonomes d'importantes quantités de capitaux. La seule exception évidente à ce qui vient d'être énoncé est constituée, bien entendu, par la crise du dollar canadien, entre le printemps et la fin de 1962. Cette crise ne fut pas provoquée par un affaiblissement quelconque de la position du commerce extérieur canadien, mais par une attaque de caractère spéculatif lancée contre le dollar canadien, attaque largement encouragée par les efforts du gouvernement qui désirait manipuler les fluctuations du change dans le sens de la baisse. Avant cette crise comme après, le dollar canadien a été et reste une monnaie forte, les pressions auxquelles il est soumis sur le marché international des changes tendant à le faire monter.

Mais la politique économique du Canada au cours des dernières années n'a pas été en conformité avec ces deux facteurs, dont l'un relève de l'économie intérieure et l'autre de la balance des paiements. Assurément, pendant la crise du dollar canadien de 1962, cette conformité était impossible à réaliser, puisque aucun ensemble de mesures n'aurait pu agir simultanément sur le chômage intérieur et sur la baisse sensible du dollar sur le marché des changes ; et les autorités décidèrent alors, avec raison, de s'occuper en premier lieu du problème du change. Cependant, la longue période qui va de l'été 1957 à apparition de la crise du dollar aurait pu permettre la mise en œuvre de mesures simples d'expansion économique : en effet, la position de la balance générale des paiements était alors forte. Si de telles mesures n'ont pas été adoptées, c'est surtout parce que les autorités n'ont pas su diagnostiquer l'état de l'économie intérieure et la position du Canada en matière de balance des paiements. Elles portèrent à tort leur attention sur le risque d'une inflation dont rien ne prouvait l'existence dans l'économie intérieure, et crurent, sur la base de l'important déficit constaté en matière de comptes courants, que la balance des comptes à l'extérieur, bien qu'excédentaire, avait besoin d'être soutenue. On eut donc recours à une politique d'austérité, entièrement impropre à améliorer la situation ; elle eut pour effet de prolonger le marasme et de maintenir le chômage à un niveau élevé.

Les mesures adoptées depuis la fin de la crise du dollar canadien de

[19]Ce fait a provoqué d'amples discussions sur la relation entre le chômage intérieur et la balance des paiements. Voir, par exemple: Banque du Canada, *Rapport annuel*, 1961; C. L. Barber; « Canada's Unemployment Problem » , *CJEPS*, fév. 1962, pp. 88–102; R. G. Penner, « The Inflow of Long-Term Capital and The Canadian Business Cycle 1950–1960 » , *ibid.*, nov. 1962, pp. 527–41; R. Dehem, « The Economics of Stunted Growth » , *ibid.*, pp. 502–10; Johnson ; *Canadian Quandary.*

1962 retiennent tout particulièrement l'attention, car elles permettent peut-être d'apercevoir une importante tendance générale de la politique économique du Canada. Comme pendant la période qui précéda la crise, les conditions se trouvaient réunies pour la mise en œuvre de mesures expansionnistes simples ; mais on préféra appliquer des mesures qui, tout en visant à combattre le chômage à l'intérieur, sont conçues comme si la balance des comptes du Canada à l'extérieur était faible.[20] Certes, ces deux fins ne sont pas automatiquement conciliables ; mais il n'est pas impossible de les associer dans un même plan et de les poursuivre simultanément, si l'on est prêt à isoler l'un de l'autre l'aspect intérieur et l'aspect extérieur de l'économie du pays, de façon qu'ils ne retentissent pas l'un sur l'autre comme ils tendent normalement à le faire. Ce qu'il faut relever de plus important cependant, au sujet de cette façon de concevoir une politique économique, est qu'elle enfreint l'esprit des règles visant à mettre de l'ordre dans le commerce international et les changes qui ont été établies depuis la guerre sous la direction d'organismes internationaux, comme le GATT, et qu'on semble ainsi s'orienter vers un retour à l'autarcie.

Puisque les principales armes dont un gouvernement dispose aujourd'hui en matière économique pour faire face à des problèmes tels que le chômage, l'inflation et le déséquilibre de la balance des comptes à l'extérieur relèvent de la technique utilisée en matière fiscale et monétaire, il n'est peut-être pas inutile de dire un mot de la politique suivie dans ces deux domaines par les gouvernements canadiens des dernières années.

Politique fiscale. C'est en 1959 que pour la dernière fois le budget du gouvernement fédéral fut spécifiquement utilisé à des fins de gestion économique. Le ministère des Finances estima que l'expansion économique qui se manifestait alors était suffisamment forte pour risquer de provoquer une pousée inflationniste, et le budget de l'année éleva le taux de l'impôt sur le revenu des personnes et des sociétés afin de tenter de stabiliser la situation. En réalité, l'expansion de 1959 était trop faible pour conduire l'économie à son niveau de plein emploi, et l'effet principal de ce budget fut de contribuer au ralentissement de l'économie au début de 1960. Les taux d'impôt sur le revenu ne furent pas pour autant abaissés quand le chômage s'installa et s'aggrava, et ils restent aujourd'hui au niveau élevé où ils furent fixés en 1959. Dans les budgets qu'il présenta au cours des années suivantes, le ministre des Finances fit l'éloge

---

[20]L'exemple le plus frappant que l'on puisse donner ici est la mesure visant à stimuler l'embauche dans l'industrie automobile en offrant aux industriels canadiens des subventions à l'exportation sous forme d'exonérations tarifaires sur l'importation de pièces détachées. Voir Harry G. Johnson : « The New Tariff Policy for the Automotive Industries » , *Business Quarterly*, printemps 1964.

de la théorie des budgets anti-cycliques, mais aucune mesure, ni du côté des dépenses, ni du côté des recettes, ne fut introduite afin de mettre cette théorie en pratique. Les déficits budgétaires enregistrés par le gouvernement fédéral depuis la recrudescence du chômage en 1957 ont été des déficits « passifs », provoqués par le bas niveau du revenu national, mais non par des mesures visant à combattre activement la paresse de l'économie au moyen d'une poltique fiscale de type keynésien.

La politique du gouvernement fédéral pour lutter contre le chômage pendant cette période a consisté à adopter une série de mesures dont on croyait qu'elles agiraient directement sur le chômage. Cette façon d'aborder la question apparaît clairement dans les discours de présentation du budget, depuis le « baby budget » spécial de décembre 1960 (introduit parce que, comme le reconnut le Ministre, le climat économique avait changé au cours des derniers mois) jusqu'au dernier budget en date, celui de 1963. Le budget de décembre 1960 par exemple, introduisit, à l'intérieur de certaines limites, le principe de l'amortissement accéléré des investissements réalisés dans les secteurs de chômage grave ou prolongé, ainsi que des investissements destinés à introduire de nouveaux types de production au Canada ; le budget de juin 1961 supprima l'impôt indirect sur les automobiles afin d'en stimuler la vente, et accentua la politique d'amortissement accéléré ; le budget d'avril 1962 proposa que les taux d'impôts sur les bénéfices des sociétés fussent réduits sur les bénéfices réalisés lors de ventes supplémentaires pendant une période donnée (de façon à encourager les exportations) ; le budget de 1963, entre autres choses, offrit une prime aux employeurs d'ouvriers surnuméraires âgés de 45 ans et plus (à condition que l'employeur garantisse un ré-apprentissage), exempta d'impôts pour trois ans toute entreprise nouvelle de fabrication ou de transformation qui s'installerait dans « les zones de moindre croissance », et augmenta à nouveau le champ d'application du principe de l'amortissement accéléré. Bien entendu, d'autres mesures fiscales ont été introduites en dehors des discours de présentation du budget annuel, mais elles présentent les mêmes caractéristiques spécifiques et sélectives que celles qui viennent d'être énumérées.

Politique monétaire. Pendant la plus grande partie de la période 1957–62, elle a été dominée par la crainte de l'inflation. Cette peur fut la raison fondamentale de l'émission de l'Emprunt de conversion de 1958, grâce auquel 6.5 milliards de la dette du gouvernement fédéral furent refinancés dans des émissions à long terme à des taux d'intérêts beaucoup plus élevés. Lorsqu'elles entreprirent ce refinancement massif, les autorités non seulement se trompèrent sur la situation de l'économie mais firent preuve de maladresse dans la conduite de l'opération. Elle eut pour effet de provoquer des hausses exceptionnellement brutales et fortes des taux d'intérêt, qui résultèrent directement de l'émission de l'emprunt lui-même, ainsi que de la réunion sur le marché des valeurs, de facteurs de désordre que l'on vit apparaître clairement après l'« heureuse » conclusion de l'opération. L'effet global sur l'économie fut nettement déflationniste. La liquidité fut sensiblement réduite à la fois par l'allongement du terme de la dette et par le risque accru que présentèrent les obligations de l'Etat du fait des fluctuations du marché. Au rapport déjà faible entre le stock de monnaie en circulation et le revenu national s'ajouta l'effet déflationniste supplémentaire d'une demande d'argent nettement plus grande de la part de la population[21]. Le désordre qui régnait sur le marché des valeurs d'Etat eut aussi une incidence importante sur la politique fiscale, en accreditant dans les milieux officiels, et même dans ceux d'obédience keynésienne, l'idée que le recours aux budgets déficitaires devait être abandonné en tant que mesure anti-déflationniste, étant donné que le déficit serait difficile à financer et qu'une mesure de ce genre entamerait encore la confiance des milieux financiers déjà très inquiets.

Dans leur grande majorité, les économistes canadiens qui ne sont pas au service du gouvernement ont été fort peu satisfaits de ce qui s'est fait au cours des dernières années en matière économique, et se sont alarmés de voir la stagnation se prolonger. Lorsqu'on analyse les déclarations officielles et les décisions de ces dernières années, il est difficile de ne pas en conclure que les hauts fonctionnaires ont été conseillés de façon fort peu satisfaisante sur les mesures à prendre. Un fossé profond s'est creusé entre l'opinion des économistes universitaires et des économistes qui occupent des postes importants dans le gouvernement fédéral ; on découvre également un autre fossé, moins profond mais non dépourvu d'importance, au sein du gouvernement fédéral entre les économistes qui se livrent à la recherche et ceux qui conseillent le gouvernement. L'une des tâches les plus importantes auxquelles doit faire face le Conseil d'orientation économique du Canada, qui vient d'être créé, est de faire disparaître ces fossés et d'augmenter la qualité des analyses et des conseils en matière économique qui sont fournis au Cabinet.

Les exemples qui viennent d'être donnés de l'insuffisance de la politique suivie et l'élargissement du fossé qui sépare les économistes du gouvernement et les économistes universitaires sont plus inquiétants qu'il

[21]Voir C. L. Barber, « The Canadian Economy in Trouble » , a brief to the Royal Commission on Banking and Finance, 1962.

ne paraît. Pendant et après la guerre, à tout le moins jusqu'en 1956, la politique économique du Canada et l'efficacité de son administration furent non seulement très estimées à l'étranger mais permirent de remporter de grands succès à l'intérieur (voir, sur cette question, le chapitre 1) ; de plus, elles concordaient avec les recommandations de l'analyse économique contemporaine. En outre, il semble que le public ait alors très largement accepté l'idée que des mesures monétaires et fiscales soigneusement mises au point étaient parfois nécessaires pour mettre un terme à des mouvements indésirables de l'économie dans une direction inflationniste ou déflationniste. Bien des gens, et notamment des économistes, aux Etats-Unis et en Europe, admiraient avec une pointe d'envie ce qui paraissait être le raffinement de la politique économique du Canada, et l'empressement des autorités canadiennes à accepter de bons conseils en la matière. Parallèlement, le Canada adoptait sur de nombreux grands problèmes internationaux une attitude libérale et clairvoyante, et en particulier se faisait l'avocat d'une politique économique plus voisine du libre-échange, même quand l'effet à court terme d'une telle politique risquait d'être nuisible à l'économie intérieure. Mais vers 1956–57 on eut l'impression d'un changement brutal dans ces divers domaines. Le médiocre rendement de l'économie vers la fin de la période 1950–57, s'ajoutant à l'effet de graves erreurs politiques et d'une politique internationale dont l'imprévoyance à long terme devint alors plus visible, conduisit certains observateurs à mettre gravement en doute les raisons réelles de la réussite du Canada pendant la période précédente. Peut-être, après tout, cette réussite était-elle due à un heureux concours de circonstances beaucoup plus qu'à la sagesse des dirigeants politiques. Peut-être, en somme, n'y avait-il jamais eu unanimité réelle en matière de politique économique, et ce que l'on prenait pour l'adoption des principes d'une gestion anti-cyclique n'était-il en fait qu'une acceptation passive de ces mécanismes, engendrée par une richesse et une prospérité croissantes. Certaines des erreurs commises en matière de politique économique ont été notées ici, non seulement pour l'intérêt intrinsèque qu'elles présentent, mais surtout parce qu'elles rendent sensible l'atmosphère de malaise croissant qui a remplacé l'euphorie, peut-être excessive des années de l'après-guerre. L'esprit de critique vis-à-vis de soi-même est utile et désirable lorsqu'il s'appuie sur une confiance fondamentale dans l'aptitude du pays à résoudre ses problèmes. Mais, lorsqu'il est éveillé par des déceptions, il tend à rechercher des coupables à l'extérieur (les Etats-Unis par exemple) ou à l'intérieur (dans des groupes particuliers). La poussée récente d'anti-américainisme et l'aggravation d'une hostilité latente dans le pays, notamment entre les groupes ethniques, semblent bien être liées au sentiment croissant d'impuissance né des déceptions accumulées en matière aussi bien politique qu'économique.[22]

On aurait donc tort de considérer comme un simple effet du hasard le fait que, pendant la période de médiocre rendement de l'économie canadienne de ces dernières années, des problèmes de politique intérieure aient rapidement augmenté en gravité, au point de menacer sérieusement aujourd'hui la nation canadienne elle-même. Le problème des relations entre le fédéral et le provincial, en particulier celui que posent les rapports entre Québec et Ottawa, et qui constitue le point de fixation des heurts entre Canadiens français et Canadiens anglais, occupent sur la scène politique autant de place que le problème posé par l'emprise du capital étranger sur l'industrie, et sont devenus les thèmes centraux de la vie politique canadienne. On ne saurait sérieusement mettre en doute le fait que l'accumulation des déceptions provoquées par la stagnation économique est pour une grande part à l'origine de la rapidité avec laquelle, pendant ces dernières années, le problème des rapports entre le fédéral et le provincial et entre les deux ethnies s'est emparé du devant de la scène politique. La dépression des années 30 avait eu un effet analogue : elle avait engendré, au Canada, étonnamment peu d'analyses économiques fécondes en matière de chômage, mais elle avait conduit beaucoup d'esprits à mettre au premier rang de leurs préoccupations une analyse serrée de l'économie, des finances, de la loi constitutionnelle, et de la politique du fédéralisme canadien. Il existe dans la nation canadienne des tensions profondes et continues, qui se font sentir avec force lorsque la situation économique se révèle décevante. Cependant, on aurait tort de croire qu'une économie progressant régulièrement ferait complètement disparaître ces tensions. Une mauvaise situation économique les exaspère mais ne les crée pas ; une bonne situation économique les atténue sans les faire disparaître.

L'un des facteurs importants de ces tensions est traditionnellement constitué par les disparités régionales à l'intérieur du Canada en matière de régime fiscal, d'enseignement, d'intérêts économiques, et de conceptions politiques, sans parler bien entendu des différences de langue et de religion. Sur le plan purement économique, ces disparités sont très sensibles ; les tendances observées dans le développement économique donnent à penser que, loin de disparaître, elles iront en s'accentuant. Ce que MacGregor Dawson appelle « l'irritante différence dans la situation

---

[22]On trouvera une analyse détaillée de l'aspect politique de cet état d'esprit dans Peter C. Newman : *Renegade in Power: The Diefenbaker Years* (Toronto, 1963).

économique des diverses provinces »[23] a engendré à l'intérieur du pays
des tensions d'autant plus grandes que les provinces pauvres ont tendance
à en attribuer la responsabilité à la loi sur la Confédération même, ainsi
qu'à la politique suivie par les divers gouvernements fédéraux. Dans les
Provinces maritimes, par exemple, la politique tarifaire du Canada, grâce
à laquelle les régions industrielles des provinces centrales sont subventionnées aux dépens du reste du pays, est fréquemment considérée
comme responsable de la prolongation du sous-développement de cette
région[24]. Le même grief est également formulé dans les Prairies, dont la
situation économique est médiocre. Dans le Québec, où le revenu individuel est depuis longtemps inférieur de 25 pour cent à ce qu'il est dans
l'Ontario[25], ce fait est considéré comme prouvant que les Canadiens
francophones ne sont pas traités en partenaires égaux.

Depuis les débuts de la Confédération, la tâche consistant à maintenir
ensemble les éléments disparates de la nation a toujours été au premier
rang des préoccupations du gouvernement fédéral, et les méthodes utilisées pour y parvenir ont souvent été assez grossières. Comme l'a écrit
M. Underhill à propos des années difficiles qui ont suivi la Confédération : « la technique politique utilisée fut brillamment mise au point par
John A. Macdonald : elle consistait à faire en sorte que les choses
continuent sur leur lancée à coups de marchandages et de manœuvres
de caractère purement opportuniste entre les diverses parties du nouveau
Dominion, et à maintenir ensemble les membres de la Fédération à l'aide
d'avantages et de pots de vin accordés successivement à celui-ci, puis à
celui-là »[26]. Un jour qu'il visitait la Colombie-Britannique grâce au
chemin de fer du Pacifique Canadien qui venait d'être achevé, le grand
historien et le critique acerbe de la politique canadienne, Goldwin Smith,
s'entendit répondre avec cynisme par un citoyen de l'endroit qu'il inter-
rogeait sur ses opinions politiques : « Le bon gouvernement, c'est celui
qui subventionne » ![27] Cette façon de réaliser l'union ne se limita pas aux
toutes premières années de la Confédération. L'analyste qui examine
cette question est surpris de voir à quel point l'unité de la Confédération
canadienne a été assurée au moyen des « ressources du budget » : chemins de fer et autres travaux publics, subventions fédérales sous condi-

[23]R. M. Dawson ; *The Government of Canada* (4e édition, Toronto, 1963),
p. 85.
[24]Voir, par exemple, W. J. Woodfine ; « Canada's Atlantic Provinces: A Study
in Regional Economic Retardation » , dans M. H. Watkins et D. F. Forster, éd.,
Economics: Canada (Toronto, 1963), pp. 312–19.
[25]André Raynaud, « The Economic Problems of Québec » , *ibid.*, pp. 325–30.
Voir Aussi ci-dessous pp. 138–9.
[26]*The Search of Canadian Liberalism*, p. 173.
[27]*Ibid.*, p. 34.

tions ou sans conditions, tarifs pour le transport des marchandises et autres subventions régionales plus ou moins camouflées, « paiements destinés à égaliser les différents niveaux de revenu » , etc., etc. Mais ce qui surprend plus encore est de voir à quel point ce recours systématique aux pots de vin a assuré la solidité intérieure de la Confédération, au moins pendant son premier siècle. Il se pourrait que le génie politique canadien consiste dans l'aptitude révélée par chaque partie du pays à se persuader que le chantage politique en usage depuis le début de la Confédération lui a, dans l'ensemble, été personnellement utile. Il y a lieu à ce sujet, et particulièrement aujourd'hui, de signaler le rôle joué à l'occasion dans ce domaine par la menace de faire sécession. Brandie avec cynisme, cette menace a pu être de temps en temps un signe de santé politique ; ainsi un amoureux menace parfois de se suicider pour séduire sa bien-aimée, et se « séduire lui-même » par la même occasion. Mais, parfois, et c'est peut-être aujourd'hui le cas au Canada français, il s'agit d'une menace de caractère irresponsable et névrosique qui précisément, pour cette raison, risque un pour d'être mise à exécution.

Les vieilles techniques mises au point par Sir John A. Macdonald n'ont pas perdu leur efficacité quand il s'agit de régler dans l'immédiat des tensions entre membres de la Confédération : la dernière en date des Conférénces fédérales-provinciales le montre[28]. Mais il existe d'autres sources de tension croissante que l'on aurait tort de négliger : il s'agit de l'évolution des rôles respectifs des gouvernements fédéral et provinciaux en matière économique et sociale depuis la seconde Guerre mondiale, et de désaffection croissante que manifestent les Canadiens français.

Les Pères de la Confédération se donnèrent consciemment pour but de fonder une nation dotée d'un gouvernement central fort. Ils étaient impressionnés par l'instabilité des Etats-Unis, alors déchirés par la Guerre de Sécession, et Macdonald lui-même concevait la Fédération comme une simple étape conduisant vers une union législative totale, à mesure que disparaîtraient les nécessités politiques qui conseillaient pour l'instant la forme fédérale. La loi sur l'Amérique du Nord britannique donna au gouvernement central les pouvoirs principaux : financier, économique, etc., ainsi que le pouvoir résiduel ; et seules les décisions prises dans le sens opposé par la commission judiciaire du Conseil privé, à l'occasion de litiges constitutionnels ultérieurs, empêchèrent ce dessein d'être réalisé. Le système fiscal établi lorsque la fédération fut fondée était nettement restrictif en ce qui concernait les sources de revenu des provinces, en partie parce que l'on considérait comme indispensable de prévenir tout

[28]Tenue à Ottawa en novembre 1963.

accroissement de la fiscalité provinciale équivalant à un tarif et entravant le commerce interprovincial, mais aussi parce qu'on n'envisageait pas que les besoins financiers des provinces pussent devenir considérables, leurs domaines propres étant alors clairement d'une importance secondaire[29].

D'emblée, cependant, les ressources financières des provinces furent insuffisantes par rapport à leurs responsabilités. Des subventions du Trésor fédéral se révélèrent indispensables et le volume de ces transferts a régulièrement augmenté, bien que le domaine légal du pouvoir fiscal des provinces ait été très élargi depuis la Confédération. Les pressions auxquelles la crise des années 30 soumit les finances des provinces aboutirent au transfert au gouvernement fédéral d'une part plus large de responsabilité, et la Seconde Guerre mondiale augmenta encore le domaine du fédéral par rapport à celui des provinces. On put même croire un instant que le pronostic de Macdonald allait être confirmé en substance sinon dans l'ordre des structures juridiques, puisque tout le monde attendait du gouvernement fédéral l'initiative et l'autorité dans tous les grands domaines. Cette tendance atteignit sans doute son point culminant lorsque fut déposé en 1951 le Rapport de la Commission royale sur le développement national des Arts, des Lettres et des Sciences. Présidée par le Très Honorable Vincent Massey, cette commission s'occupa de questions qui, selon la Constitution, étaient rigoureusement de la compétence des provinces, et ce sans provoquer chez elles de protestations ; en outre, elle recommanda, sans soulever beaucoup d'opposition, des solutions qui supposaient l'élargissement du domaine du fédéral.

Tout cela a changé pendant les dix dernières années. L'accroissement, régulier depuis la guerre, du rôle joué par les gouvernements s'est manifesté presque uniquement au Canada dans des domaines relevant des provinces (enseignement, santé, services sociaux et assistance sociale, routes, etc.) ; et, bien que le gouvernement fédéral ait joué un rôle actif dans ces divers domaines, l'importance de l'échelon provincial a beaucoup augmenté. Comme, à la différence des Etats-Unis, le Canada n'a pas, dans les responsabilités du gouvernement en matière de défense nationale et de politique étrangère, un nœud commun et central de préoccupations légitimant de façon indiscutable l'existence d'une organisation fédérale, rien n'a pu empêcher le pouvoir provincial de se développer aux dépens du fédéral. Le fait récent le plus significatif sur ce point est que ce sont à présent les gouvernements provinciaux qui manifestent des tendances impérialistes en s'immisçant dans des zones relevant tra-

[29]Voir J. H. Perry, « What Price Provincial Autonomy? » *CJEPS*, nov. 1955, p. 433.

ditionnellement et constitutionnellement du gouvernement central. La « Croisade pour le Commerce » de l'Ontario, par laquelle le gouvernement de cette province cherche à augmenter les exportations et à réduire les importations canadiennes ; la politique de développement industriel poursuivie par plusieurs provinces, et notamment le Québec ; la suggestion, formulée par le premier ministre du Québec, M. Lesage, à la Conférence fédérale-provinciale de 1963, et selon laquelle les provinces devraient être consultées en matière de politique monétaire et douanière : tout cela confirme cette tendance. Mais la signification la plus importante de ces faits est qu'ils reflètent l'inaptitude du gouvernement fédéral, pendant ces dernières années, à agir efficacement dans les domaines qui relèvent constitutionnellement de lui. L'inventaire détaillé, donné au début de ce chapitre des insuffisances observables en matière de politique économique visait à éclairer l'importance de ce fait récent : la déception qu'inspire un peu partout le gouvernement central (sous la conduite successive des *deux* principaux partis) en tant qu'organe chargé de remplir certaines fonctions gouvernementales essentielles.

La poussée de désaffection constatée au cours de ces dernières années chez les Canadiens français a suscité d'autres éléments de tension qui, en s'ajoutant à ceux qui viennent d'être relevés, risquent de constituer pour la nation canadienne une menace sérieuse. Non content de mettre en doute l'*efficacité* de l'organisation constitutionnelle actuelle, le Canada français a commencé à mettre en question la *légitimité* de celle-ci, et, s'il faut en croire les spécialistes de sociologie politique, il y a là une convergence de griefs particulièrement dangereuse[30]. La réapparition récente de la « théorie du contrat » confédéral, qui ne repose sur rien de solide historiquement ou juridiquement, témoigne d'un désir de démontrer que l'organisation politique actuelle du Canada est illégitime puisque les termes du prétendu « contrat » entre Français et Anglais n'ont pas été remplis. L'argument selon lequel les Canadiens français doivent se voir accorder un statut égal à celui des Canadiens anglais tire sa source des désavantages de fait que rencontrent les Canadiens français, mais il s'exprime souvent en des termes qui contestent la légitimité au Canada d'un pouvoir politique qui ne serait pas bilingue. Les activités terroristes du Front de Libération du Québec et la multiplication des inscriptions « Québec Libre » sur les monuments et les immeubles peuvent être l'œuvre d'individus isolés et névrosés ; mais elles constituent néanmoins un rejet significatif des méthodes politiques traditionnelles. Plus significative encore, en ce qu'elle reflète une mise en question de la légitimité de l'organsation politique, est l'absence d'accord entre Français

[30]Voir S. M. Lipset, *Political Man* (New York, 1963), chap. 3.

et Anglais sur les symboles de cette légitimité : drapeau, hymne national, jours de fête nationale, etc. Même la légitimité du mot « nation » à propos du Canada a été contestée par certains Canadiens français, et le rejet de ce mot a été accepté à Ottawa, non sans susciter de l'inquiétude et de la perplexité.

Telles sont les tensions internes que l'on voit croître à l'intérieur de la nation canadienne. Le lien qui les relie à l'ancienne menace extérieure en provenance des Etats-Unis n'est plus constitué par le fait que la faiblesse à l'intérieur risque d'entraîner ceux-ci à conquérir le Canada, mais par la crainte de voir l'inaptitude à résoudre les problèmes nationaux conduire plus d'une partie du Canada, toutes les parties peut-être, à rechercher l'union avec les Etats-Unis qui fut écartée il y a plus de deux cents ans. Les conditions économiques, politiques, culturelles, et géographiques du Canada, et la proximité des Etats-Unis, rendent peu vraisemblable la disparition complète de ces tensions ; mais il importe de noter une fois de plus que celles-ci deviennent infiniment plus lourdes de menaces en période de stagnation économique. Quelles que soient leurs sources, ces tensions peuvent être réduites, et même transformées en stimulants, par une économie en progrès, qui offrirait aux citoyens la perspective d'une expansion régulière, et qui leur permettrait de s'enorgueillir d'appartenir à une nation tenue en haute estime parmi les pays libres et progressifs. Dans la vie et le destin d'une nation, l'économie n'est pas tout, mais elle compte pour beaucoup.

PART ONE

The Recent Past

The Canadian economy has a curious and almost unique combination of characteristics. On the one hand it is a "mature" economy in the sense of a high level of economic achievement as measured in terms of output per capita and other indicators,[1] while on the other hand it has many features generally attributed to underdeveloped economies, such as a substantial dependence upon the export of a few "staples," large imports of industrial and manufactured goods, and a vast frontier region (the "North") where development has scarcely begun. It is in many respects an affluent society where economic potentialities are even yet dimly perceived. While some other societies may be little less (or somewhat more) affluent than Canada, few of them still possess such vast empty spaces and such a high land-man ratio. Geographically, Canada is the world's second largest country, but its population is less than 20 million. The space for economic development well beyond the present levels clearly exists. But, of course, there is much more to growth than mere resource availability and numbers of people: the quality and quantity of both people and resources, plus all the institutional arrangements which influence the pattern of output, the intensity of and rewards for productive effort, and the skill with which economic affairs, both public and private, are managed, are at least of equivalent importance. Nevertheless, Canada's economic possibilities on the surface, would appear to be substantial. However, not only has the Canadian economy, with all its potential, failed to resolve satisfactorily the problem of cyclical and seasonable unemployment, but there has been a noticeable slowing down of the growth rate in the latter part of the 1950's and early 1960's as indicated in the Introduction. Furthermore, the growing dependence

[1]See data in Table I:1. As of 1962, Canada's output per head was second only to that of the United States.

TABLE 1.1

Indicators of Development in Selected Industrial Countries, 1962

Country	GDP US dollars (1)	Exports US dollars (2)	Steel consumption kilograms per capita (3)	Energy consumption kilograms (4)
United States	2690	114	488	8263
Canada	1850	317	345	6015
Sweden	1770	386	530	3755
United Kingdom	1370	199	332	4948
West Germany	1390	241	488	3884
France	1370	157	318	2591
Australia	1630	219	334	4070
Japan	690	52	242	1388
USSR	1000*	32	334	3046

NOTES AND SOURCES: Col (1). Average of two estimates appearing in UN, *Yearbook of National Accounts Statistics 1963* (New York, 1964), Tables 3A and 3B, pp. 322-331. One estimate converts to US dollars at official exchange rates while the other adjusts these rates to reflect relative change in prices vis-à-vis the US since 1938. Data rounded to nearest 10.

Cols (2), (3), and (4). UN, *Statistical Yearbook 1963* (New York, 1964).

*Estimated from data in S. H. Cohn, *The Gross National Product in the Soviet Union: Comparative Growth Rates* (US Dept. of Commerce, Washington, 1963), pp. 8-10.

upon the United States, the non-power status in the world power struggle, the political separatism recently manifest in Quebec, and the rising concern over political, cultural, and economic independence all attest to the enormity of the tasks, both economic and non-economic, facing Canada in the latter half of the twentieth century.

The purpose of Part I of this study is to examine the main economic tendencies especially since the late 1930's. This will fill in many of the details alluded to in the introduction and provide a broad base for projecting the several economic aggregates to 1970 and 1975 in Part III. Chapter 1 provides a general overview of the period of major concern. Chapter 2 deals more fully with the important trends and developments in demographic factors. Chapters 3 and 4 examine respectively the regional structure of the Canadian economy and the extent and kind of external economic influences.

1

DIMENSIONS OF GROWTH

A BRIEF STATISTICAL SURVEY

Between 1937 and 1962 the Canadian economy not only exhibited substantial over-all growth but also structural change. From an average gross national expenditure[1] of only $5.4 billion per year (1937–39) the economy grew to output levels over $36 billion for the years 1960–62 (see Table 1.1). Much of this, of course, reflects higher prices, but in real terms (i.e., discounting price changes) the aggregate growth is still impressive, rising from an annual average (1937–39) of about $9 billion (in 1949 dollars) to something in excess of $25 billion for the years 1960–62. As both cause and consequence of the over-all expansion in output, population increased steadily from 11.3 million in 1939 to over 18 million in 1962, the civilian labour force increasing from almost 4.7 million to over 6.6 million in that period (see Table 1.3). Per capita GNE in constant (1949) dollars rose from about $800 in the closing years of the 1930's to over $1,400 between 1959 and 1961 and reached $1,514 in 1962. The growth rate over the period of our survey was thus a respectable 2.8 per cent compounded annually. The story of the Canadian economy from 1937–39 to the present is, in general, one of growth —but a growth that has been far from steady. Although Canada has apparently become somewhat less sensitive to US recessions since the

[1]Official Canadian statistics refer to the expenditure on all final goods and services produced by a nation's economy during a time period, usually a year or calendar quarter, as gross national expenditure (GNE) which is necessarily equal in total to gross national product (GNP), a concept more widely used in other countries. The two will be used interchangeably here when only their magnitudes are under consideration.

TABLE 1.1

Components of Gross National Expenditure 1926-63
(in millions of constant 1949 dollars unless stated otherwise)

| | Personal expenditure on consumer goods and services | Business gross fixed capital formation | | | | |
		total	new residential construction	new-non residential construction	new machinery & equipment	adjusting entry
1926	5010	1206	399	402	426	−19
1929	6490	1948	426	779	734	9
1933	5272	462	168	150	154	−11
1937	6420	1112	336	317	470	−11
1938	6337	1050	310	293	456	− 9
1939	6510	1053	361	286	427	−21
1940	7034	1343	363	349	638	7
1941	7471	1682	427	456	802	− 3
1942	7692	1567	356	524	682	5
1943	7902	1234	343	513	389	−11
1944	8444	1235	401	355	496	−17
1945	9267	1420	472	352	618	+22
1946	10,323	1846	512	569	777	12
1947	10,657	2496	610	700	1186	
1948	10,451	2758	638	850	1270	
1949	10,923	3032	794	920	1318	
1950	11,642	3167	833	988	1346	
1951	11,817	3301	727	1074	1500	
1952	12,633	3588	737	1235	1616	
1953	13,338	3926	905	1306	1715	
1954	13,650	3723	946	1272	1505	
1955	14,662	3962	1040	1365	1557	
1956	15,603	4891	1110	1816	1967	
1957	16,083	5115	998	2112	1995	10
1958	16,585	4761	1219	1884	1650	8
1959	17,392	4575	1157	1683	1735	
1960	17,908	4345	937	1637	1770	1
1961	18,480	4270	941	1698	1626	5
1962	19,157	4365	989	1654	1717	5
1963*	19,980	4640	1034	1731	1866	—

SOURCE: Dominion Bureau of Statistics, *National Accounts Income and Expenditure, 1926-1956*, Table I; *ibid., 1961*, Table 5; *ibid., 1962*, Tables 5, 56, and 57.
*DBS, *Canadian Statistical Review*, May. 1965.   Data in 1949 dollars estimated for 1963.

Government expenditure on goods and services				Change in inventories			
total	current	gross fixed capital formation	adjusting entry	total	non-farm business inventories	farm inventories and grain held commercially	adjusting entry
792				253	260	− 33	26
1027				109	256	−201	54
842				−242	−134	−119	11
1056				66	210	−194	50
1127				274	−36	377	−67
1156				699	191	595	−87
1794				658	159	588	89
2531				68	216	−199	51
5189				336	−302	796	−158
5714				−309	52	−439	78
6499				−204	5	−252	43
4542				−462	211	−831	158
2294				536	562	−82	56
1850				446	520	−74	
1902				87	70	17	
2127	1620	507		49	150	−101	
2242	1680	562		561	389	163	
2806	2140	666		849	493	356	
3516	2670	846		489	81	408	
3517	2748	769		590	320	270	
3415	2676	739		−216	−39	−177	
3563	2767	796		419	134	285	
3794	2869	925		955	648	307	
3833	2867	968	2	210	246	−89	53
4093	3044	1056	7	−286	−158	−141	13
4155	3055	1109	−9	308	334	−91	65
4188	3059	1141	−12	314	219	89	6
4283	3222	1169	−8	−130	220	−497	147
4528	3255	1285	−12	500	290	288	−18
4713	—	—	—	—	—	—	—

TABLE 1.1 (*continued*)

	Exports of goods and services	Imports of goods and services	Residual error of estimate	Adjusting entry	Gross National Expenditure (GNE)	GNE index (on 1949)	Percentage change in GNE from previous year
1926	2437	2296	231	−59	7576	46.4	
1929	2603	3092	−40	16	9061	55.4	.3
1933	1903	1824	−140	86	6359	38.9	−6.5
1937	2903	2600	−117	−20	8820	54.0	9.9
1938	2623	2436	−55	−49	8871	54.3	.6
1939	2885	2599	−47	−121	9536	58.3	7.5
1940	3281	2888	157	154	10,911	66.8	14.4
1941	4298	3310	−111	−143	12,486	76.4	14.4
1942	3852	3549	−142	−129	14,816	90.7	18.7
1943	5340	4246	−181	−97	15,357	94.0	3.7
1944	5168	5020	−199	4	15,927	97.5	3.7
1945	5059	3986	−258	−30	15,552	95.2	−2.4
1946	4115	3717	−40	−106	15,251	93.3	−1.9
1947	4141	4176	32		15,446	94.5	1.3
1948	4193	3749	93		15,735	96.3	1.9
1949	4021	3853	44		16,343	100.0	3.9
1950	3999	4206	66		17,471	106.9	6.9
1951	4380	4685	79		18,547	113.5	5.8
1952	4850	4882	−167		20,027	122.5	8.0
1953	4809	5269	−117		20,794	127.2	3.8
1954	4616	5013	11		20,180	123.5	−2.9
1955	4969	5742	87		21,920	134.1	8.6
1956	5340	6662	−110		23,811	145.7	8.6
1957	5389	6571	−22	80	24,117	147.6	1.3
1958	5368	6150	−74	100	24,397	149.3	1.2
1959	5574	6776	22	−8	25,242	154.4	3.4
1960	5806	6743	69	−82	25,802	157.9	2.2
1961	6240	6823	106	−58	26,468	162.0	2.2
1962	6517	6911	153	−198	28,111	172.0	6.2
1963	7077	7105	—	—	29,404	—	5.1

| GNE in constant 1957 dollars | | GNE in current dollars | | GNE per head | |
total	percentage change from previous year	total	percentage change from previous year	current dollars	in constant 1949 dollars
		5152		545	802
		6134	1.5	612	903
		3510	−8.3	330	598
		5257	13.0	476	799
		5278	.4	473	795
		5638	6.8	500	846
		6743	19.6	592	959
		8328	23.5	724	1085
		10,327	24.0	886	1271
		11,088	7.4	940	1302
		11,850	6.9	992	1333
		11,835	−.1	980	1288
		11,850	.1	964	1241
		13,165	11.1	1049	1231
		15,120	14.8	1179	1227
		16,343	8.1	1215	1215
		18,006	10.2	1313	1274
		21,170	17.6	1511	1324
		23,995	13.3	1660	1385
		25,020	4.3	1685	1401
		24,871	−.6	1627	1320
29,018		27,131	9.1	1728	1396
31,508	8.6	30,585	12.7	1902	1481
31,909	1.3	31,909	4.3	1921	1452
32,284	1.2	32,894	3.1	1926	1428
33,398	3.5	34,915	6.1	1940	1444
34,144	2.2	36,254	3.8	2029	1444
35,023	2.6	37,421	3.2	2052	1451
37,158	6.1	40,339	7.9	2172	1514
39,145	5.3	43,180	7.0	2285	1536

TABLE 1.2

National Income, Disposition of Personal Income, and GDP
1926-63
(millions of current dollars)

	National income	Personal income	Personal taxes	Disposable Personal income
1926	4129	4014	53	3961
1929	4708	4608	68	4540
1933	2368	2790	69	2721
1937	3887	4007	112	3895
1938	4001	4068	115	3953
1939	4236	4290	112	4178
1940	5063	4914	139	4775
1941	6305	5851	296	5555
1942	8098	7393	495	6898
1943	8802	8042	698	7334
1944	9583	8865	838	8027
1945	9665	9120	809	8311
1946	9551	9719	796	8923
1947	10,361	10,375	791	9584
1948	12,003	11,901	822	11,079
1949	12,905	12,638	789	11,849
1950	14,161	13,428	740	12,688
1951	16,588	15,824	1030	14,794
1952	18,654	17,395	1323	16,072
1953	19,294	18,336	1432	16,904
1954	19,032	18,421	1437	16,984
1955	20,737	19,738	1499	18,239
1956	23,166	21,885	1732	20,153
1957	24,011	23,191	1917	21,274
1958	25,011	24,675	1795	22,880
1959	26,482	26,036	2088	23,948
1960	27,424	27,411	2360	25,051
1961	28,316	28,506	2511	25,995
1962	30,415	30,817	2720	28,097
1963	32,622	32,795	2911	29,882

SOURCES: DBS, *National Accounts, Income and Expenditure, 1926-1956*, Tables 2, 3, and 4.   *Ibid.*, 1962, Tables 2, 3, and 4. *Canadian Statistical Review*, March and May 1965.

Personal savings	Personal consumption expenditures	Personal taxes and savings as per cent of personal income	Personal savings as per cent of disposable income	Gross domestic product
419	3542	11.8	10.6	4904
81	4621	3.2	1.8	5686
263	2984	11.9	9.7	3122
11	3884	3.1	0.3	4707
56	3897	4.2	1.4	4846
194	3984	7.1	4.6	5122
287	4488	8.7	6.0	6074
452	5103	12.8	8.1	7424
1398	5500	25.6	20.3	9344
1536	5808	27.8	20.9	10,041
1753	6274	29.2	21.8	10,781
1342	6969	23.6	16.1	10,804
892	8031	17.4	10.0	10,791
494	9090	13.4	5.2	11,857
994	10,085	15.3	9.0	13,699
926	10,923	13.6	7.8	14,885
662	12,026	10.4	5.2	16,458
1334	13,460	15.0	9.0	19,126
1291	14,781	15.0	8.0	21,344
1312	15,592	14.9	7.8	22,206
809	16,175	12.2	4.8	22,213
850	17,389	11.9	4.7	24,326
1320	18,833	13.9	6.5	27,189
1202	20,072	13.4	5.7	28,455
1635	21,245	13.9	7.1	29,354
1357	22,591	13.2	5.7	31,175
1539	23,512	14.2	6.1	32,363
1509	24,486	13.6	5.8	33,416
2358	25,739	16.5	8.4	35,931
2466	27,416	16.4	8.3	37,772

TABLE 1.3
Population and the Civilian Labour Force
1926–63

| | Popu- lation | Civilian non- institutional population, 14 years of age and over | Persons with jobs | | | Persons without jobs and seeking work | Total civilian labour force |
			Non- agricul- tural	Agricul- tural	Total		
1926	9451	6326	2299	1251	3550	108	3658
1929	10,029	6820	2541	1307	3848	116	3964
1933	10,633	7366	2192	1257	3449	826	4275
1937	11,045	7870	2776	1339	4115	411	4526
1938	11,152	7997	2707	1359	4066	522	4588
1939	11,267	8122	2741	1379	4120	529	4649
1940	11,381	8140	2840	1344	4184	423	4607
1941	11,507	8056	3047	1224	4271	195	4466
1942	11,654	8085	3295	1139	4434	135	4569
1943	11,795	7871	3373	1118	4491	76	4567
1944	11,946	7920	3349	1136	4485	63	4548
1945	12,072	8048	3303	1144	4447	73	4520
1946	12,292	8779	3500	1186	4686	143	4829
1947	12,551	9007	3722	1122	4844	98	4942
1948	12,823	9141	3790	1096	4886	102	4988
1949	13,447	9490	3931	1083	5014	144	5158
1950	13,712	9615	3979	1018	4997	166	5163
1951	14,009	9726	4171	940	5111	106	5217
1952	14,459	9945	4295	891	5186	129	5315
1953	14,845	10,144	4388	858	5246	137	5383
1954	15,287	10,300	4321	873	5194	232	5426
1955	15,698	10,597	4546	819	5364	245	5610
1956	16,081	10,805	4809	776	5585	197	5782
1957	16,610	11,108	4981	744	5725	278	6003
1958	17,080	11,357	4983	712	5695	432	6127
1959	17,483	11,562	5163	692	5855	373	6228
1960	17,870	11,789	5280	675	5955	448	6403
1961	18,238	12,010	5375	674	6049	469	6518
1962	18,570	12,224(est)	5564	653	6217	391	6608
1963	18,896	12,400	5688	659	6347	401	6748

SOURCES: DBS, *National Accounts, Income and Expenditure, 1926–1956*, and *ibid.*, *1962*, Appendix, Tables I and II. Data for 1963 from DBS, *Canadian Statistical Review*, Nov. 1964.

Second World War,[2] the performance of the economy, especially between 1956 and 1961, was distinctly sluggish. Indeed, real GNE per capita reached a record peak in 1956 and fell below this level until 1962. On the other hand the wartime experience was one of unprecedented growth which quickly mopped up the excess capacity associated with the Great Depression and raised output per head to record highs. The record, in short, has been marked by sharp bursts of expansion followed by slow growth or actual decline on a per capita basis.

TRENDS IN THE NATIONAL ACCOUNTS COMPONENTS
There are various manifestations of change in the structure of the economy, as is to be expected in any economy whose aggregate real output nearly tripled in two decades. The composition of gross national expenditure has altered in three important respects. (1) Personal consumption expenditures declined from between 72 and 73 per cent of total GNE (annual averages 1927–29 and 1937–39) to an average of 65 per cent for the years 1960–62. This is largely accounted for by the rise in government purchases of goods and services from roughly 10 to 19 per cent, a rise financed mainly by taxes as is reflected in the declining ratio of disposable personal income to GNE. (2) Business gross fixed investment increased from slightly over 11 per cent in 1937–39 to almost 18 per cent by 1960–62, although this latter figure represents a steady decrease

TABLE 1.4

Trends in the Composition of GNE
selected periods 1927–61
(percentages)

	1927–29	1937–39	1947–49	1959–61
Personal consumption expenditures	72.4	72.8	67.4	65.0
Durable goods	6.3	5.9	6.5	7.4
Non-durable goods	39.6	40.1	39.8	32.6
Services	26.5	26.8	21.1	25.0
Government expenditures on goods and services	9.8	12.2	12.2	18.8
Business gross fixed capital formation	16.9	11.2	17.3	18.6
Exports of goods and services	28.3	27.2	26.2	19.6
Imports of goods and services	−30.4	−24.7	−24.9	−22.9

SOURCES: DBS, *National Accounts Income and Expenditures 1926–1954*, and *ibid.*, 1961 and 1962, Tables 2 and 47.

[2]See Irving Brecher and S. S. Reisman, *Canadian–United States Economic Relations*, a study prepared for the *Royal Commission on Canada's Economic Prospects* (hereafter abbreviated *RCCEP*) (Ottawa, 1957), Part I, for a discussion of the sensitivity issue and relevant bibliography. See also G. Rosenbluth "Changes in Canadian Sensitivity to United States Business Fluctuations," *CJEPS*, Nov. 1957.

TABLE 1.5

Various Components of Aggregate Demand as Percentages of GNE
1926-62

	National income	Personal disposable income	Personal consumption	Gross Investment by business
1926	80.1	76.9	68.8	13.6
1929	76.8	74.0	75.3	18.9
1933	67.5	77.5	85.0	6.7
1937	73.9	74.1	73.9	12.0
1938	75.8	74.9	73.8	11.2
1939	75.2	74.1	70.7	10.5
1940	75.1	70.8	66.6	11.9
1941	75.7	66.7	61.3	13.2
1942	78.4	66.8	53.3	10.3
1943	79.4	66.2	52.4	8.0
1944	80.9	67.7	52.9	7.6
1945	81.7	70.2	58.9	8.7
1946	80.6	75.3	67.8	11.7
1947	78.7	72.8	69.0	15.8
1948	79.4	73.3	66.7	17.3
1949	79.0	72.5	66.8	18.6
1950	78.6	70.5	66.8	18.6
1951	78.4	69.9	63.6	18.7
1952	77.7	67.0	61.6	18.5
1953	77.1	67.6	62.3	20.0
1954	76.5	68.3	65.0	19.2
1955	76.4	67.2	64.1	19.2
1956	75.7	65.9	61.6	22.1
1957	75.2	66.7	62.9	23.0
1958	76.0	69.6	64.6	21.2
1959	75.8	68.6	64.7	19.7
1960	75.6	69.1	64.9	18.5
1961	75.7	69.5	65.4	17.7
1962	75.8	69.5	63.7	17.2

SOURCE: DBS, *National Accounts Income and Expenditure, 1926-1956* and *ibid., 1961* and *1962*, Tables 2 and 3.

Gross investment by government	Government non-capital	Total government expenditure on goods and services	Exports	Imports
		9.5	32.0	29.5
		10.4	26.6	31.7
		13.2	23.5	23.6
		11.8	30.3	26.8
		12.6	25.7	23.8
		12.1	25.7	23.6
		16.6	26.8	24.2
		19.6	29.6	23.7
		35.6	22.9	22.3
		37.7	31.1	26.3
		42.0	30.1	30.1
		30.9	30.4	24.6
		15.2	27.1	24.3
		11.7	27.6	27.5
		11.9	26.8	24.0
3.1	9.9	13.0	24.6	23.6
3.3	9.8	13.0	23.2	25.1
3.7	11.8	15.5	24.0	26.5
4.3	13.5	17.8	23.2	22.5
3.9	13.8	17.7	21.6	23.4
3.8	14.1	17.9	20.7	22.4
3.8	13.9	17.7	21.2	23.7
4.1	13.5	17.6	20.8	25.2
4.3	13.6	17.9	20.0	24.5
4.2	14.6	18.8	19.3	22.6
4.4	14.2	18.6	19.1	23.3
4.3	14.3	18.6	19.3	22.5
4.1	15.1	19.3	20.4	22.8
4.4	14.7	19.1	20.4	22.4

TABLE 1.6

Components of GNE
1926-62
(millions of current dollars)

| | Expenditures on consumer goods and services | | | | Business gross fixed capital formation* | |
	Total	Durables	Non durables	Services	Total	New residential construction
1926		279	1840	1423	702	201
1929		417	2557	1647	1161	230
1933		173	1637	1174	234	72
1937		331	2165	1388	633	164
1938		305	2136	1456	592	148
1939		312	2186	1486	592	174
1940		390	2474	1624	803	186
1941		421	2908	1774	1085	240
1942		337	3240	1923	1064	214
1943		297	3541	1970	887	220
1944		323	3772	2179	900	267
1945		375	4193	2401	1031	318
1946		596	4829	2606	1388	368
1947		841	5390	2859	2085	494
1948		934	6070	3081	2619	609
1949		1146	6288	3489	3032	794
1950		1451	6711	3864	3348	883
1951		1480	7610	4360	3959	895
1952		1780	8051	4950	4451	933
1953		2001	8199	5392	4998	1166
1954		1970	8373	5832	4779	1227
1955		2245	9065	6079	5210	1378
1956		2431	9736	6666	6774	1526
1957		2430	10,402	7240	7335	1409
1958		2499	10,878	7868	6975	1763
1959		2678	11,373	8540	6894	1734
1960		2669	11,785	9058	6692	1443
1961		2697	12,257	9532	6635	1458
1962		2913	12,877	9959	6954	1577

SOURCES: *National Accounts Income and Expenditure, 1926-1956*, and *ibid.*, 1962, Tables 2, and 47.

*Includes capital expenditures by private and government business enterprises, private non-commercial institutions, and outlays on new residential construction by individuals and business investors.

†Includes defence expenditures.

‡The book value of inventories is deflated to remove the effect of price changes

Business gross fixed capital formation*		Government expenditure on goods and services†			Value of physical charge in inventories‡		
New non-residential construction	New machinery and equipment	Total	Current expenditure§	Gross fixed capital formation**	Total	Non-farm business inventories	Farm inventories and grain in commercial channels
240	261	488			135	154	−19
490	441	640			52	146	−94
78	84	462			−91	−68	−23
188	281	619			9	113	−104
170	274	666			57	−21	78
164	254	683			282	101	181
208	409	1116			255	87	168
287	558	1635			88	130	−42
354	496	3674			135	−202	337
364	303	4177			−180	28	−208
256	377	4978			−145	−10	−135
253	460	3656			−311	148	−459
435	585	1796			333	360	−27
597	994	1541			403	437	−34
816	1194	1797			113	85	28
920	1318	2127	1620	507	49	150	−101
1042	1423	2344	1756	588	550	399	151
1270	1794	3271	2491	780	914	564	350
1566	1952	4279	3239	1040	512	90	422
1719	2113	4432	3454	978	583	351	232
1671	1881	4461	3519	942	−130	−40	−90
1848	1984	4792	3758	1034	311	133	178
2589	2659	5386	4126	1260	1084	808	276
3103	2823	5722	4340	1382	231	305	−74
2811	2401	6180	4791	1389	−322	−197	−125
2589	2571	6490	4967	1523	357	421	−64
2577	2672	6755	5185	1570	361	275	86
2683	2491	7205	5668	1537	−144	276	−420
2668	2709	7721	5937	1784	565	375	190

and the derived "physical" change is then valued at average prices of the current period to obtain the value of physical change.

§Also includes net purchases of government commodity agencies and the defence production revolving fund. Excludes shipments of previously produced military equipment to NATO countries but includes replacement of new equipment.

**Includes outlay on new durable assets such as building and highway construction by governments, other than government business enterprises.

from the peak of 1957. (3) Exports of goods and services declined from some 27 or 28 per cent of GNE in 1927–29 to about 20 per cent by 1960–62; imports fell from 30 to 23 per cent over the same period. (See Tables 1.4, 1.5, and 1.6 for details.)

National income[3] has increased somewhat more slowly than GNE and in 1962 was not quite 76 per cent of GNE compared with slightly over 80 per cent in 1926. The ratio has, however, varied substantially over time from a high in 1945 of almost 82 per cent to a low of less than 68 per cent in 1933. In general the range of variation of this ratio has been mainly between 75 and 80 per cent compared with a slightly higher range of 80–85 per cent in the United States. The composition of national income has exhibited some tendency to change although there are less pronounced shifts here than on the expenditure side. The most noteworthy feature is the fairly substantial, although not steady, rise in the proportion accruing as wages, salaries, and supplementary labour income. Table 1.7 indicates a rise from slightly under 60 per cent in 1927–29 to almost 67 per cent in 1960–61. If military pay and allowances are included, the 1960–61 proportion becomes almost 70 per cent. The bulk of this increasing share is related to the opposite shift in net farm income—an indication of the declining relative importance of agriculture. No other shift of significance is apparent, although the steady downward drift of net income of non-farm unincorporated business since 1927–29 and rise in investment income since 1947–49 may be noted.

TRENDS IN INCOME INEQUALITY

Aggregative changes in total production and income and even variations in these magnitudes on a per capita basis are inadequate by themselves

[3]The difference between GNE and national income is composed of the following items: indirect taxes less subsidies, capital consumption allowances and miscellaneous valuation adjustments, and the residual error of estimate.

During the twelve years, 1950 through 1961, Canadian national income averaged 76.6 per cent of GNE as compared to 83.4 per cent in the United States for the same period. This differential seems to be attributable about equally to two factors. First, indirect taxes as a proportion of GNE generally run about 3 to 4 per cent higher in Canada than in the United States. This reflects the greater reliance of the US on income taxes, particularly at the federal level, and Canada's more intensive use of indirect taxes, particularly sales taxes. In 1960, for example, all levels of Canadian governments obtained 46.1 per cent of their total tax revenues from indirect taxes and only 53.9 per cent from direct taxes. In that year in the United States, on the other hand, all government levels combined obtained 58.2 per cent of all tax revenues from direct taxes and 41.8 per cent indirect taxes.

The second factor that accounts in part for the differential between GNP and national income in the two countries is the relatively higher capital consumption allowances (i.e. depreciation) in Canada. As a proportion of GNE capital consumption allowances in Canada are usually about 3 to 4 per cent greater than in the United States. This reflects the higher capital-output ratio that exists in Canada and which is discussed in more detail in chapter 7.

TABLE 1.7

Trends in National Income and its Components
Selected Periods 1927–61
(percentages)

	1927–29	1937–39	1947–49	1957–59	1960–61
Wages, salaries, and supplementary labour income	59.1	63.1	61.8	66.2	66.8
Military pay and allowances	0.2	0.4	0.8	1.9	1.9
Corporation profits before taxes	8 .7	10.6	16.2	12.9	12.3
Dividends paid to non-residents	—	—	2.3	1.9	1.9
Rent, interest, and miscellaneous investment income	7.6	6.9	5.5	8.5	9.1
Accrued net income of farm operators from farm production	11.8	8.2	10.7	4.4	4.1
Net income of non-farm unincorporated business	12.6	11.4	10.9	8.4	8.0
National income (millions of current dollars)	$4600	$4041	$11,756	$25,168	$28,782

SOURCE: DBS, *National Accounts, Income and Expenditure*, various years.
NOTE: Percentages do not add to 100 because of omission of the inventory valuation adjustment.

to convey any more than a superficial impression of how well off, even in a strictly economic sense, a nation may be. Averages and totals hide much of significance in terms of the proportion of output and income received by various groups. The most general form of analysis of income distribution involves the so-called Lorenz curve which shows the proportion of total income received by any given percentage of income recipients (individuals or families) when the latter are ranked according to income from the lowest to the highest. Since most democratic societies have as one of their major goals a more equitable distribution of income, it is important for us to examine some of the evidence on Canada's success or failure in achieving this goal.

Unfortunately in Canada the data on income distribution are rather meagre; only in recent years has much serious effort gone into this type of analysis.[4] It is possible, however, to make a rather limited comparison between 1931 and 1951, 1954, 1957, or 1959 of the distribution of

[4]Since 1954 the Dominion Bureau of Statstics (DBS) has published three reports on the size distribution of non-farm incomes, one for each of the years 1951, 1954, and 1957. A survey of some earlier work in this area in Canada as well as the 1951 study is given by Simon A. Goldberg and Jenny R. Podoluk, "Income Size Distribution Statistics in Canada—A Survey and Some Analysis," in International Association for Research in Income and Wealth, *Income and Wealth Series* VI (London, 1957), chap. 6.

wage and salary income among individuals and families taken separately. Even with this limited comparison there are problems, such as the unrepresentativeness of the year 1931 compared with 1951, 1954, or 1957. Most of the caveats regarding the data are given in the sources to be cited and we will indicate in what follows only the major conclusions to be derived.

Tables 1.8 and 1.9 and Figures 1.1 and 1.2 in current dollars summarize the relevant data. (Conversion to constant dollars would not alter the results.) Although the estimates are rather crude, it is clear that a rather substantial shift towards greater equality of wages and salaries did in fact occur between 1931 and 1951, whether computed on the basis of individuals or families. The distributions for individuals in 1951,

TABLE 1.8

Distribution of Wages and Salaries by Individuals and Families Earning Them
1930–31 and 1951
(percentages)

	Quintile				
	lowest	second	third	fourth	highest
Individuals					
1930–31	2.1	10.3	15.7	23.5	48.5
1951	3.9	12.4	18.8	25.0	39.9
Families					
1930–31	5.3	11.3	17.3	23.5	42.6
1951	8.0	13.9	17.9	22.6	37.5

SOURCE: Simon A. Goldberg and Jenny R. Podoluk, "Income Size Distribution Statistics in Canada—A Survey and Some Analysis", *Income and Wealth Series VI*, (London, 1957), Table II, p. 159.

1954, and 1957 virtually coincide (see Table 1.9), and we have thus drawn only a single Lorenz curve for these three years in Figure 1.2. Despite some problems of comparability, the sharp increase in equality is clear from Figures 1.1 and 1.2. For wage- and salary-earning families, Figure 1.1 and Table 1.8 show that the share of the lowest quintile rose from about 5.3 to 8 per cent while the share of the top 20 per cent declined from 42.6 to 37.5 per cent between 1931 and 1951. A similar pattern appears for individual wage- and salary-earners. Two other features reinforce this trend to equality. In the first place, the data are before taxes. It is well known that with a progressive income tax structure and substantial transfer payments, both of which developed more extensively after 1931, and especially after 1945, the degree of equality of disposable personal income is greater than that of pre-tax wage and salary income. Again, other income sources from property (interest, dividends, and net rental income of persons) have declined as a proportion of personal income from about 15 per cent in 1931 to 9 per cent in 1951. Since property income is more unequally distributed than labour income, the inclusion of this component of personal income in both periods would tend to reduce the degree of inequality in 1951 relative to 1930–31. A similar comment holds for net income of non-farm unincorporated businesses since the share of this component of personal income was 13 per cent in 1930–31 and only 10 per cent in 1951. Conversely, since farm income tends to be somewhat more equally distributed, the rise in its share of personal income from 5 to 13 per

TABLE 1.9

Distribution of Non-Farm Family and Unattached Individuals: Income by Size
1951, 1954, 1957

	1951		1954		1957	
Income group	Per cent of income	Per cent of families	Per cent of income	Per cent of families	Per cent of income	Per cent of families
Under $500	0.6	7.4	0.4	5.6	0.1	3.3
$ 500–$ 999	2.0	8.5	1.6	7.5	1.2	7.7
1000– 1499	3.4	8.6	2.6	7.8	1.9	7.0
1500– 1999	5.1	9.3	3.3	6.9	2.8	6.7
2000– 2499	8.0	10.9	5.4	8.9	3.9	7.4
2500– 2999	11.3	13.0	7.3	9.7	4.9	7.6
3000– 3999	20.3	18.6	19.1	19.9	13.9	17.0
4000– 4999	13.3	9.6	16.3	13.5	14.8	14.0
5000– 9999	25.7	12.4	31.0	17.5	41.0	25.6
Over $10,000	10.3	1.8	13.0	2.7	15.6	3.7
Average income	$3185		$3654		$4269	
Median income	2703		3174		3624	

SOURCE: DBS, "Distribution of Non-Farm Incomes in Canada by Size", *Reference Papers* 52, 66, and occasional report for 1957.

cent between the two dates tends to suggest a further increase in the equality of the over-all income distribution.[5] In short, the increase in equality of wage and salary income is probably less than the increase in equality of after-tax personal income from all sources.

Finally it should be mentioned that average wage and salary incomes, as well as average personal incomes, increased substantially from $964 in 1931 to $2,136 in 1951 for individual wage- and salary-earners. Even

[5]These comments are based upon *ibid.*, pp. 165–8.

in constant 1951 dollars, the increase was substantial—over 31 per cent. For family wage- and salary-earners an increase in real terms of some 34 per cent was registered.[6] Thus, not only did average real wages and salaries rise but the dispersion about the average narrowed. This is the common experience of all affluent societies with a system of progressive taxation and substantial welfare expenditures.

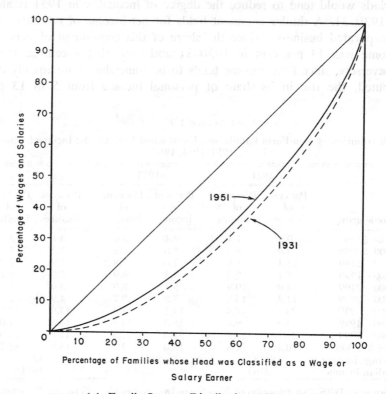

FIGURE 1.1. Family Income Distribution, 1931 and 1951

SOURCE: Computed from S. A. Goldberg and J. R. Podoluk, "Income Size Distribution Statistics in Canada," International Association for Research in Income and Wealth, *Income and Wealth Series VI*, Table IV, p. 162, for 1931.

On the other hand, trends in over-all income distribution since 1951 do not reveal any significant major change at all. Data for 1951, 1954, 1957, and 1959 tend to fall along the same Lorenz curve as shown in Figure 1.2; these data include income from all sources. Of course, the time period involved is very short and the major changes in welfare have

[6]*Ibid.*, pp. 160-1 and 163.

already been accomplished so that further tendencies toward greater equality would naturally prove more difficult although the general policy objective remains. This situation seems to be generally true of the United States as well.[7]

But one serious omission in the above discussion of trends in equality has been regional disparities. This will be discussed further in Chapter 3.

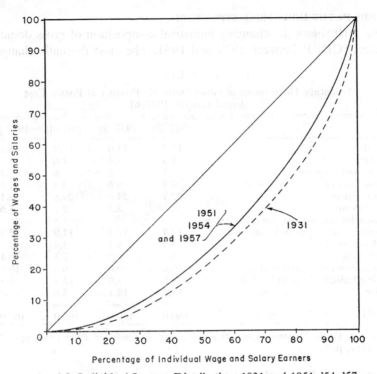

Percentage of Individual Wage and Salary Earners

FIGURE 1.2. Individual Income Distribution, 1931 and 1951, '54, '57

SOURCE: Calculated from S. A. Goldberg and J. R. Podoluk, "Income Size Distribution Statistics in Canada," International Association for Research in Income and Wealth, *Income and Wealth Series VI*, Table 1, p. 159 and p. 160, for 1931 data. Data for 1951 and 1957 from DBS, *Distribution of Non-Farm Incomes by Size*, catalogue nos. 13-503 and 2104-506.

However, it is worth mentioning at this point that the degree of inequality tends to be greater within the poorer regions of Canada than within the wealthier, a generalization that appears to apply among nations as well. In short, the discussion in this section, focused on the all-Canadian

[7]See US Department of Commerce, *Survey of Current Business* (July 1962), Table 18, p. 16.

aggregates and averages, hides a rather substantial diversity within particular regions. Desirable as the over-all trend appears to be, there is
little room for complacency so long as inequality remains significantly
higher in various regions of the economy. The problem of what is loosely
referred to as "residual poverty" remains a serious one in Canada. We
shall examine this more fully in Chapter 3 and in Part III as well.

TRENDS IN THE INDUSTRIAL STRUCTURE

Table 1.10 shows the changing industrial composition of gross domestic
product (GDP)[8] between 1927 and 1961. The most dramatic change is

TABLE 1.10

Percentage Distribution of Gross Domestic Product at Factor Cost
selected periods, 1927–61

	1927–29	1937–39	1943–45	1959–61
Agriculture	15.3	11.0	10.9	5.1
Forestry	1.3	1.4	1.6	1.2
Fishing and trapping	.7	.5	.6	.3
Mining, quarrying, and oil wells	3.4	6.6	3.2	4.4
Manufacturing	22.7	24.6	29.5	26.1
Construction	4.5	3.2	2.7	5.6
Transportation, storage, communication, electric power, gas and water utilities	12.9	12.5	11.9	12.4
Wholesale trade	3.7	4.1	3.4	4.7
Retail trade	8.8	9.0	7.5	9.4
Finance, insurance, and real estate	10.0	10.0	6.8	10.5
Public administration and defence	3.5	5.0	13.3	7.3
Service	13.2	12.1	8.6	13.0
Total	100.0	100.0	100.0	100.0

SOURCE: DBS, *National Accounts Income and Expenditure 1926–1956*, pp. 28–9;
ibid., 1961, p. 17.

the steady decline in the relative contribution of agriculture from over
15 per cent to about 5 per cent. Aside from this, the relative contributions of the other sectors are not significantly different over the years,
for the percentage decline in agriculture has been rather evenly picked up

[8]Gross domestic product refers to total production within the geographic boundaries of Canada. It is an aggregative measure comparable to gross national
product except that the latter refers to production by Canadian residents regardless
of whether their productive activity takes place within Canadian territory or not.
GDP is usually measured "at factor cost" which means that "indirect taxes less
subsidies" are to be excluded. Thus the relationship between GNP at market
prices and GNP at factor cost is as follows (omitting the residual error of
estimate): GNP minus (indirect taxes less subsidies) minus income received
from non-residents plus income paid to non-residents equals GDP at factor cost.

in construction, manufacturing, and public administration and defence. On the other hand, a comparison of the later war years, 1943–45, with the earlier periods shows a sharp rise in manufacturing and, of course, public administration and defence, with declines in services, trade, construction and mining, quarrying and oil wells. This indicates the extent of the wartime distortions and dislocations or rather a subsequent failure to maintain a high level of efficiency, since the later period, 1959–61, shows every tendency of reverting to the pre-war pattern (see within at pp. 58–61).

Selected data on the distribution of the labour force for census years are shown in Table 6.6 and generally mirror the altered composition of gross domestic product. The share of the labour force attached to agriculture has declined steadily and sharply especially since 1941. This has been partly matched by the opposite movement in the service sector. Trade and electricity (including gas and water) have increased their share of the labour force, but manufacturing, though still accounting for a larger proportion of the labour force than in 1931, has declined since 1951. Generally, almost two-thirds of the labour force was attached to the trade, service, and manufacturing sectors in 1961 compared with less than half in 1931.

The proportion of output and employment in manufacturing, trade, finance, and services can be taken as an indicator of economic development. Canada, with between 60 and 70 per cent of its output and employment in these categories, must be considered a highly developed economy, as is borne out by its high level of real per capita output.

TRENDS IN THE OCCUPATIONAL STRUCTURE

Occupations are notoriously difficult to classify at any point of time[9] and in most censuses coverage is not complete. Furthermore, comparisons over time suffer from the problem of new occupations, changing skill requirements of existing occupations, and reorganization of functions in many lines of business. Under the best of circumstances, therefore, occupational trends present substantial conceptual and statistical difficulties. In Canada, there are two additional sources of difficulty. One is that

[9]As has noted, job terminology ". . . is the resultant of such elements as academic, vocational, apprenticeship or specialized training, material worked in, conditions of work, physical demands, etc. The resulting classification, therefore, depends upon the elements or combination of elements to which chief consideration is given. In addition, the final product may be designed so as to reflect a socio-economic, a quasi-industrial, level of skill, etc., aspect." DBS, *Ninth Census of Canada, 1951, Classification of Occupations*, pp. 5–6.

many occupations bear industrial titles, a carry-over of earlier classification techniques which creates some confusion.[10] Another revolves around the fact that census data for earlier periods were collected on the basis of "gainfully employed" rather than "labour force," a concept which includes both those employed and unemployed.[11] Despite these difficulties, however, it is believed that the rather broad occupational groups shown in Figure 1.3 are sufficiently comparable over time to warrant their use as trend indicators.[12]

The figures show a substantial and fairly steady increase in the white-collar occupations since 1901 and an even more substantial decrease in primary labour. On the other hand blue-collar workers have remained a fairly stable proportion of the total. At the present time, white-collar, transportation and communication, and service workers account for almost 60 per cent of the labour force, compared with 40 per cent in 1931 and less than 30 per cent at the turn of the century. These facts are consistent with the evidence of the previous two sections and are further analysed in chapter 6. It is, however, worth commenting on the implications of this occupational pattern with respect to skill, training, and educational requirements. If occupations are arranged on the basis of the amount of skill and training each requires, the following trends in growth rates over the decade of the 1950s may be observed:[13]

Professional workers	+71 per cent
Skilled workers	+38 per cent
White-collar workers	+34 per cent
Semi-skilled and unskilled workers	+19 per cent
All other occupations	−27 per cent

Despite all the statistical hazards involved in measuring and classifying occupations the trends shown above provide unmistakable evidence that the fastest growing occupations are those requiring higher degrees of training and education. At the same time there has been an absolute decrease in "all other occupations," which refers mainly to the primary industries, and the rate of growth of the semi-skilled and unskilled occu-

[10]For example one occupation is classified as "manufacturing and mechanical" but not all people in this group are engaged in the manufacturing industry. That is, the occupational group includes such subgroups as machine operators, spinners and weavers, various types of mechanics, millwrights, welders, and so on not all of which are unique to manufacturing industry.

[11]The concept of "gainfully employed" used prior to the 1951 census excludes those seeking work for the first time, but in general is believed reasonably comparable to the labour force concept.

[12]Further details and analysis are given in chap. 6.

[13]Data from an address by W. R. Dymond to the Women's Personnel Group of Montreal, Feb. 13, 1961, entitled "The Changing Pattern of Manpower Utilization in the Canadian Economy 1950–1960," mimeo, p. 18.

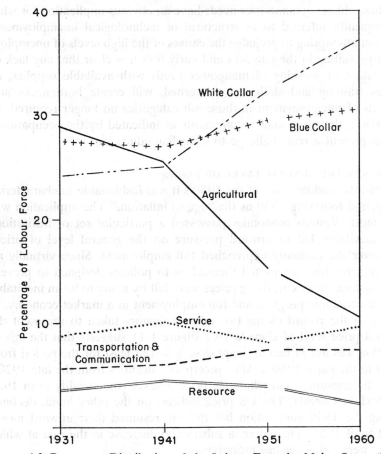

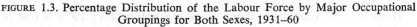

FIGURE 1.3. Percentage Distribution of the Labour Force by Major Occupational Groupings for Both Sexes, 1931–60

SOURCE: "Technological Changes and Their Impact on Employment and Occupations," Report prepared by Economics and Research Branch, Department of Labour, Ottawa, 1961, Chart 3.

pations is well below that of the professional, skilled, and white-collar groups. In short economic growth not only entails a changing industrial structure but also, as both cause and effect, ever increasing demands for higher skills and improved quality of labour. A progressing industrial economy becomes, as Harbison points out, "increasingly dependent upon the brains and much less dependent upon the brawn of its working forces."[14] Canada is no exception.

[14]S. E. Hill and F. Harbison, *Manpower and Innovation in American Industry* (Princeton, 1959), p. 3.

These changing manpower needs have an obvious implication for what is frequently referred to as structural or technological unemployment. Without attempting to prejudge the causes of the high levels of unemployment prevailing in the late 50's and early 60's it is clear that any lack of integration or meshing of manpower needs with available supplies, as far as training and skills are concerned, will create bottlenecks and pockets of unemployment in those job categories no longer required. In this sense, the rising skill requirements as indicated by the occupational trends present a real challenge to Canadian education.

TRENDS IN THE GENERAL LEVEL OF PRICES

Around the middle years of the 1950's it was fashionable to characterize the period following 1939 as the "age of inflation." The implication was that most Western economies possessed a particular set of institutions that inevitably led to upward pressure on the general level of prices whenever the economy approached full employment. Since virtually all governments had committed themselves to policies designed to prevent serious unemployment, rising prices were felt by many to be an inevitable cost of economic progress and full employment in a market economy. A glance at the record of the two price indicators taken to represent the general price level of Canada (see Figure 1.4) suggests that the age of inflation was not in fact an inapt description at least for the period from 1939 to the early 1950's. After precipitous declines from the late 1920's both the consumer and wholesale price indexes rose steadily from 1939 to 1951 in Canada. The US price indices, on the other hand, declined during the 1949 contraction but quickly resumed their upward movement until 1951. Thereafter, a substantial decrease in the rate at which prices were rising became more typical.

However, the Canadian record of price stability after 1951 is one of the best in the western world. From 1952 through 1961 and 1962 inclusive, the consumer price index increased at a rate of only 1.3 per cent per year compared with rates of increase ranging upwards from 2.1 per cent in Italy to 4.1 in France between 1953 and 1961. In Western Europe only Belgium and Switzerland had comparable degrees of price stability.[15] The US price increase was 1.4 per cent, very close to the Canadian.

Details on the movements of both the consumer and wholesale price indexes in Canada from 1926 to 1962 are given in Table 1.11. Over the whole period the consumer price index increased at an average annual

[15]Budget Papers, in *Votes and Proceedings of the House of Commons of Canada*, Tuesday, 11 June, 1963, p. 30.

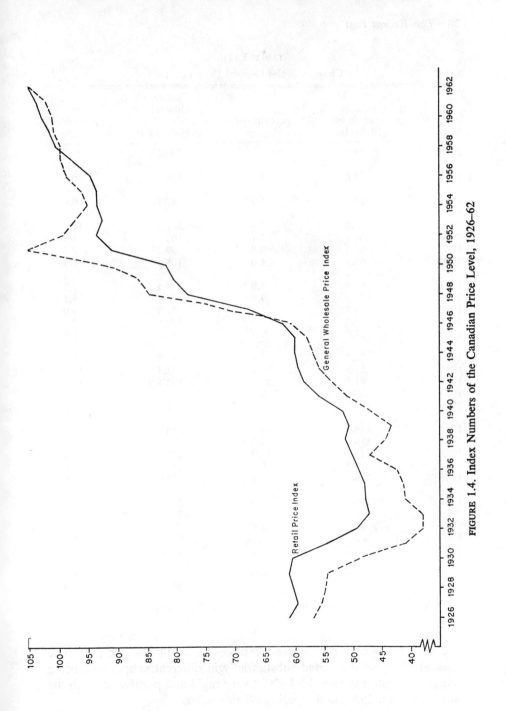

FIGURE 1.4. Index Numbers of the Canadian Price Level, 1926–62

TABLE 1.11

Changes in the General Price Level

	Retail consumer price index 1949 = 100	percentage change	General wholesale price index 1935-39 = 100	percentage change
1926	75.9		130.3	
1929	75.8	1.1	124.6	−0.8
1933	58.8	−4.7	87.4	0.6
1937	63.0	3.1	107.7	11.3
1938	63.7	1.1	102.0	−5.3
1939	63.2	−0.8	99.2	−2.7
1940	65.7	4.0	108.0	8.9
1941	69.6	5.9	116.4	7.8
1942	72.9	4.8	123.0	5.7
1943	74.2	1.8	127.9	4.0
1944	74.6	0.5	130.6	2.1
1945	75.0	0.5	132.1	1.1
1946	77.5	3.3	138.9	5.1
1947	84.8	9.4	163.3	17.6
1948	97.0	14.4	193.4	18.4
1949	100.0	3.1	198.3	2.5
1950	102.9	2.9	211.2	6.5
1951	113.7	10.5	240.2	13.7
1952	116.5	2.5	226.0	−5.9
1953	115.5	−0.9	220.7	−2.3
1954	116.2	0.6	217.0	−1.2
1955	116.4	0.2	218.9	0.9
1956	118.1	1.5	225.6	3.1
1957	121.9	3.2	227.4	0.8
1958	125.1	2.6	227.8	0.2
1959	126.5	1.1	230.6	1.2
1960	128.0	1.2	230.9	0.1
1961	129.2	0.9	233.3	1.0
1962	130.7	1.3	240.0	2.9

SOURCES: DBS, *Canadian Statistical Review, 1959 Supplement; Canadian Statistical Review*, vol. 38, no. 4.

rate of 2.1 per cent and wholesale prices at about 2.4 per cent. The rates of change have varied substantially in different subperiods, being generally negative during the 1930's, very rapid and positive through the war years until 1951, and tapering off thereafter.

The main forces underlying this pattern are not difficult to discern. The collapse of aggregate demand during the 1930's and its rapid rise during the war and immediate post-war period, the shortages, and, most recently, especially since the mid 1950's, the slow-down in the over-all rate of economic growth are causally related to the general pattern of prices. Of course, during particular periods other forces have been at work either to depress or accelerate the rate of change of prices. For example, price controls during the war and monetary policies during much of the 1950's served to moderate the pace of price increases. Working in the opposite direction have been price trends in other countries. We have already noted the generally higher rate of inflation in most of Canada's major trading partners. This has an important effect upon Canadian prices because of the high levels of imports and exports relative to GNE. Price increases abroad for such imported items as consumer durables, capital equipment, component parts, and so on are, as Firestone has observed,[16] quickly reflected in higher Canadian prices. More rapidly rising prices in other countries also encourage exports from Canada; this likewise serves to put an upward pressure on the price of the domestic counterparts of these goods.

In general, however, despite specific pressures which have varied from time to time, the main determinant of price behaviour in Canada has been the level of total spending relative to industrial capacity. Since the period as a whole from the late 1930's has generally been characterized by expansion of aggregate demand, even if at differential rates, steady upward pressure upon the price level has been exerted. The general drift has therefore been upward as Figure 1.4 shows. It is not clear, however, in view of the relative price stability characteristic of the 1950's, whether the age of inflation has come to an end. But it is evident that the slow pace of economic progress and the rise of chronic unemployment[17] since 1956 have redirected attention, however belatedly in Canada, towards matters that at the moment are more urgent.

THE MECHANISM OF ECONOMIC CHANGE

The foregoing sections have indicated the dominant trends in Canada's economic development over the past thirty or so years. These trends are familiar in the growth process of most Western countries with high levels

[16]O. J. Firestone, *Canada's Economic Development, 1867–1953* (London, 1956), p. 179.
[17]See below at page 58 and chap. 6.

of living. The decline in agriculture and rise of manufacturing and tertiary industries and their concomitant impact upon occupational structure are prevalent in the United States and Western Europe, as is the decreased reliance upon external markets, the falling share of personal consumption expenditures as a proportion of GNE, the increased equality of income distribution, and the upward drift of prices. There are, however, certain peculiarities in the Canadian situation that require a more detailed examination of the broad aggregates noted above. Later sections of the present chapter and the other chapters in Part I will analyse these aggregates.

Already at this point, however, where we are mainly trying to sketch the pattern of change since the 1930's and provide a broad indication of the magnitudes with which we are dealing, it is worthwhile commenting further on the significance of the relative decline in exports and the rise in business fixed investment and government expenditures.

It is generally believed that short-run changes in Canadian GNE depend upon the *commodity* export markets.[18] Three studies suggest a high correlation between commodity exports in any one year and national income in the following year.[19] The postulated casual mechanism runs somewhat as follows (omitting many qualifications): the level of exports and their prospects significantly affects business investment decisions and the latter is the chief determinant of short-run GNE changes. The one-year lag occurs because of the delayed response of actual business investment behind changing conditions in Canada's export markets. It has long been held that the prime mover of Canadian GNE has been exports, not investment, since the latter is deemed to depend mainly upon the former, with the other components of GNE largely passive followers.[20] However,

---

[18]The above data include commodity exports plus services. As a proportion of GNE, commodity exports accounted for 17.3 per cent in 1937–39 and 16.2 per cent in 1959–61.

[19]Gilbert Jackson and associates, *Exports and National Income* (New York, 1945); E. Munzer, "Exports and National Income in Canada," *CJEPS*, Feb. 1945; and H. E. English, "The Role of International Trade in Canadian Economic Development since the 1920's," PhD thesis, University of California, Berkeley, 1957.

[20]For example, A. F. W. Plumptre, *Central Banking in the British Dominions* (Toronto, 1940), speaking of the situation in the British dominions generally, asserted (pp. 367–8): "Despite the spread of secondary industries and the countries' growing self-sufficiency, changes in export incomes are still the independent variables of first importance. Periods of prosperity are based upon rising prices of export staples, rising volumes of exports, and—if the country is still pretty young —upon the import of capital."
Similarly, W. A. Mackintosh in *The Economic Background of Dominion-Provincial Relations*, a study prepared for the Royal Commission on Dominion-Provincial Relations (Ottawa, 1939), stated in his final chapter (p. 102): "In the

the rising share of business investment and government GNE purchases combined with the slight decline in the share of commodity exports should tend to make the economy somewhat less dependent upon external conditions and, in fact, suggest the reduced role of exports in determining short-run movements in GNE. Furthermore, the expansion of the domestic market naturally makes much private investment less dependent upon export markets. If we take annual capital expenditures in manufacturing, a sector that generally has not loomed large in Canada's exports, it is noteworthy that these virtually tripled from the post-war years to the 1957 peak. The same is true of capital expenditures in housing, wholesale and retail trade, and other domestically oriented industries.[21] It would seem therefore to be a general tendency for the degree of sensitivity of the Canadian economy to external conditions to diminish as the domestic market expands.

However, over longer time periods there is no pronounced, or even discernible, trend in the over-all degree of reliance of the Canadian economy upon commodity exports. This is true despite the fact that commodity exports have on the average constituted a slightly smaller proportion of national income in the period after the Second World War than they did in earlier years. Thus from 1926 to 1938 commodity exports were equal, on the average, to 24.2 per cent of national income, while in the years 1946 to 1962 commodity exports composed, on the average, only 22 per cent of national income. As is indicated below, however, the decrease in the proportion of national income composed of commodity exports has been offset by the even more strategic role of commodity exports since 1945.

Munzer, in his study of the relationship between commodity exports and national income lagged by one year for the period between 1923

---

past, the rate of [Canadian] economic growth has been dependent on the expansion of exports and the related volume of investment."

More recently Richard E. Caves and Richard H. Holton have argued that "the same income determination mechanism has been at work in each of Canada's major growth phases in the twentieth century..." (*The Canadian Economy: Prospect and Retrospect* (Cambridge, Mass., 1959), p. 112 and hence that Canadian dependence upon commodity exports remains undiminished. Somewhat more cautiously, Anderson pointing to the interdependence between exports and business investment (rather than a simple one-way causality), the rise of autonomous government expenditures, and, in particular, the relative decline of exports noted above, concludes that "exports would appear to have lost part of their significance in determining Canadian incomes and G.N.E. and G.N.P." (R. V. Anderson, *The Future of Canada's Export Trade*, a study prepared for RCCEP (Ottawa, 1957), p. 8.)

[21]DBS, *Private and Public Investment in Canada, 1946–1957* (Ottawa, 1959), Table 3.

and 1938, found a correlation between the two of 0.989 when current dollars were used and 0.987 when constant dollars were used.[22] This strong relationship appears to hold in the post-war period. A similar correlation for the years 1946 to 1962 reveals a correlation of 0.981 when current dollars are used.[23] Munzer obtained a regression coefficient of 3.7978 in connection with commodity exports and national income lagged by one year in current dollars. The regression coefficient for the same relationship in the 1946–62 period is 5.8448.[24] In other words, in the 1923–38 period an increase (decrease) of one dollar in commodity exports was on the average associated with an increase (decrease) of $3.7978 in national income during the subsequent year, and in the 1946–62 period a similar increase (decrease) of one dollar in exports corresponded on the average to a change in the same direction in national income of $5.8448. Thus, while commodity exports have tended to comprise a smaller share of national income in the post-war period, the significance of a marginal dollar of commodity exports has been greater in the post-war than in the pre-war period.[25]

The high correlation between commodity exports and national income in the subsequent year is consistent with what is often loosely referred to as the "staple theory,"[26] since Canada's exports consist mainly of raw materials and semi-finished goods (i.e., "staples"). Succinctly stated ". . . the staple theory declares that rapid capital formation and rising per capita incomes depend jointly on strong foreign demand for resource-based, mass producible commodities and upon technogolical developments making such production feasible."[27] Much of Canada's develop-

[22]Munzer, "Exports and National Income in Canada," p. 36.

[23]As would be expected, the relation between exports and GNE lagged by one year is about the same as in the case of national income. Indeed, in the 1946–62 period the correlation between exports and GNE lagged by one year was also exactly 0.981 when figured in current dollars.

[24]The regression equation for national income during 1945–62 period is: $Y = -3623.7901 + 5.8448x$, and that for GNE during the same period is: $Y' = -6208.444 + 7.9876x$.

[25]One would, of course, expect a high correlation between exports and national income since the former are a significant part of the latter. However, the high correlation figures obtained become more meaningful when it is realized that non-commodity exports during the same periods showed a much less significant relationship to national income, and, further, that the relationship in question is between commodity exports and the following year's national income.

[26]The staple theory is associated with the name of Professor Harold A. Innis whose pioneering works on Canadian economic history first gave prominence to this notion. See for example *The Fur Trade in Canada: An Introduction to Canadian Economic History* (Toronto, 1930) and *The Cod Fisheries: The History of an International Economy* (Toronto, 1940), as well as many others.

[27]Caves and Holton, *Canadian Economy*, p. 117.

ment from 1800 on runs in terms of rapidly rising foreign demand for particular natural resources followed by a sharp decline and subsequent emergence of a demand for new staples. From furs, fish, and timber to wheat, minerals, and fuels, the economy continues to exhibit a heavy reliance upon commodity exports, and staple exports in particular, at any given point of time.

The composition of exports is examined more fully in Chapter 4, but it should be emphasized here that although aggregate exports as a proportion of GNE have declined, the predominance of staples has remained relatively constant. Evidence of this is the constancy of the share of "fully or chiefly manufactured goods" at close to 40 per cent of total exports from 1900 to the present.[28] Raw materials and partially manufactured goods thus continue to comprise about 60 per cent of total commodity exports.

However, a substantial shift between these two components in favour of the latter has occurred. Furthermore, not only has the "partially manufactured" category of exports increased at the expense of "raw materials" but there is a far greater variety of so-called "staples" among the exports than before the 1930's. For example, in 1928 the top four commodity exports constituted about 53 per cent of total domestic exports including gold, whereas in 1955 the share of the top four was less than 40 per cent.[29] Thus, although in a general aggregative sense the role of staples continues to be a significant determinant of Canadian economic tendencies, the increased variety of such staples reduces the sensitivity to changes in external demand for particular commodities. Furthermore, as already suggested, with the growing domestic market, manifest by rising real GNE per head and greater population, the process of import substitution is slowly advancing and serves to reduce even more the degree of reliance upon and sensitivity to external conditions. It might be noted, however, that the possible increase in stability resulting from these trends may be offset in part by the tendency for larger proportions of Canadian exports to move to the United States. The proportion of Canadian exports going to the US has persistently increased from less than 40 per cent in the 1930's to close to 60 per cent in recent years.[30]

[28]The data in this case are highly tenuous, as DBS points out, and must be used with some caution. However, they support the general impression and are consistent with the relatively modest increase since the 1920's in the share of the GDP attributed to manufacturing.

[29]Anderson, *Future of Canada's Export Trade*, Table 1, p. 8. Figures for 1962 suggest a further decline.

[30]See chap. 4, p. 164.

The general overview of the economic trends for the whole economy thus suggests a continuing, though possibly reduced, heavy dependence upon exports of goods that are largely unmanufactured. The staple theory, while retaining substantial apparent validity since 1945 in aggregative terms, needs to be interpreted carefully. The Canadian economy is far more diversified than in the past, which in itself would suggest that no single or highly simplified explanation of economic tendencies could adequately account for other than the broadest aggregates and even then would be subject to a wide margin of error. It is, however, noteworthy that the strategic role of commodity exports has apparently increased, as the correlation analysis above indicates.

Nevertheless, it seems probable that Canada's export prospects will depend much more upon the conscious and deliberate cultivating by Canadians of foreign markets rather than upon the spontaneous and autonomous rise in foreign demand, to which the Canadian economy merely reacts, as it has done in the past. Especially will this be the case if exports are to become even more highly diversified, particularly in terms of manufactured goods, and hence less sensitive to fluctuations in particular primary product markets. It is not difficult to see why Canada should exert special efforts to export a wider variety of goods outside of the raw material category. As the Economic Council of Canada put it: "While raw materials will continue to occupy a very important position in Canadian export trade, the most rapidly expanding categories of world trade are in the fields of processed and manufactured goods. Similarly, the most rapidly expanding Canadian imports under conditions of sustained domestic growth would fall into these same catergories.[31]

Even more to the point is the apparent need for vigorous efforts to sell more Canadian products in markets outside the United States or at least a wider range of products within the United States. The problem of Canadian–US economic relationships is the subject of much of chapter 4.

ECONOMIC DEVELOPMENT SINCE 1939

Four sharply distinguished periods are evident since the late 1930's: (1) the forced-draught production stimulated by the demands of the Second World War; (2) the peace-time transition from 1946–1949; (3) rapid growth, which began before the hostilities in Korea superimposed a further stimulus; and (4) sluggish growth from 1956 through 1961. The

[31]Economic Council of Canada, *Economic Goals for Canada to 1970* (Ottawa, December, 1964), p. 97.

sections below will analyse these episodes in more detail and comment upon the experience since 1961.

1. THE SECOND WORLD WAR

On the eve of the Second World War, the Canadian economy, like most other countries, had substantial excess capacity. Unemployment exceeded 11 per cent of the labour force, an improvement over the depression low of over 19 per cent in 1933 but still evidence of considerable slack. The unemployment situation was, however, even worse than this figure indicates, since it fails to include the increase of 160,000 agricultural workers between 1931 and 1939. This shift into agricultural employment did not, of course, represent additional job opportunities: rather it reflected the lack of jobs in industry, a sort of push into underemployment made easier by the special conditions of agriculture. The extent of under-employment may be gauged by the fact that in the period 1940–44 the volume of agricultural output was more than 31 per cent above the 1935–39 average despite an 18 per cent decline (some 200,000 persons) in the farm work force (see Table 1.3).

Excess capacity existed not only in terms of manpower, but in the realm of capital as well. Crude estimates of industrial fixed capital suggest a slight increase between 1939 and 1945 from $24.1 to $24.9 billion[32] despite a rise in real GNE of more than 63 per cent. Other examples of the extent of slack in the Canadian economy on the eve of the Second World War may be given for particular industries. The primary iron and steel industry's ratio of production to capacity was less than 40 per cent in the mid 1930's. Even on the eve of war it was below 70 per cent, compared with some 80 per cent in 1940–42 when its capacity was much expanded. Steel ingot production almost doubled between 1939 and 1942. In rail transport an estimated 32 billion ton-miles were generated in 1939 compared to 66 billion in 1944[33] with little increase in mileage or equipment. Even in agriculture it is believed that in addition to a decline in the farm labour force, "the stock of farm capital almost certainly decreased"[34] during the war years despite a sharp rise in agricultural output.

In short, all major segments of the Canadian economy had substan-

---

[32]See William C. Hood and Anthony Scott, *Output, Labour and Capital in the Canadian Economy*, a report prepared for the RCCEP (Ottawa, 1957), p., 451.

[33]The ton-mile figures are from a paper by George A. Wagdin, submitted by the Canadian Good Roads Association and Presented at the IV World Meeting of the International Road Federation in Madrid, Oct. 14–20, 1962.

[34]J. M. Smith, *Canadian Economic Growth and Development from 1939 to 1955*, a report prepared for the RCCEP (Ottawa, 1957), p. 15.

tially greater productive capacity than was being utilized during 1938 and 1939. In fact, few other countries in the world, aside from the United States, were hit so hard by the depression as Canada. This, of course, is consistent with the fact that any economy heavily reliant upon the export of a few staples in hypersensitive to fluctuations in world markets. As Table 1.12 suggests, in almost every category for which comparable data exist, Canada and the US experienced more severe fluctuations than the other nations listed. This partly reflects the fact that the European economy as a whole did not experience the boom of the 1920's to the same extent as North America and, of course, there were special difficulties in Germany. Nevertheless, the sharp rise in unemployment and the drop in real national income for both Canada and the US far exceeded anything experienced in Europe.

TABLE 1.12

Cyclical Experience in Selected Countries
1929 to 1932 or 1933
(percentage changes 1929 to through 1932 or 1933)

Country	Unemployment as proportion of labour force	Real national income	Index of Value of merchandise exports	Index of Value of merchandise imports
United Kingdom	+112	−1.9	−64	−58
Germany	+234	−24.5	−57	−65
France	n/a	−11.7	−61	−49
Sweden	+121	−8.2	−64	−55
United States	+678	−36.7	−69	−70
Canada	+566	−28.1	−58	−69

SOURCE: Ingvar Svennilson, *Growth and Stagnation in the European Economy*, United Nations (Geneva, 1954), pp. 31 and 331.

In Canada and the US too, recovery from the deep 1932-33 trough was exceptionally slow and excess capacity persisted through the balance of the decade.

However, the outbreak of war quickly changed the situation. Even the anticipation of hostilities induced a rapid inventory build-up in early 1939 which, coupled with the declaration of war, raised the GNE for 1939 by nearly 7 per cent over 1938. But the real spurt occurred later. Indeed, the rate of growth of real GNE per capita exceeded 9.2 per cent compounded annually between 1939 and 1944. This is an unprecedentedly high growth rate under any circumstances and may be contrasted with the 2.8 per cent rate between 1937–39 and 1959–61. The dominant stimulus underlying this surprising performance was, of course, the rapid expansion of government spending. Total federal government expenditures rose swiftly from slightly less than one half billion dollars in 1939 to over five billion in 1944 with defence expenditures accounting for the bulk of the increase[35] (see Table 1.13). Provincial and municipal government spending changed very little between 1939 and 1944. As would be expected, large deficits were encountered by the federal government since taxes could not be raised by the full extent required to finance the needed spending programs. As a result, since one sector's deficits constitute surpluses for other sectors, private savings rose sharply throughout the war period. Personal savings which were running at a rate of less than $200 million per year in 1939, or 4.6 per cent of disposable income, rose progressively to over $1,750 million in 1944, almost 22 per cent of disposable personal income. At the same time business gross saving increased sharply from less than $700 million in 1939 to over $1,300 by 1944. Despite this rise in savings, however, personal consumption expenditures increased although lagging well behind personal disposable income. As in the United States, civilian levels of living, indicated by real per capita consumption outlays, increased at the same time that defence needs were successfully met. In constant 1949 dollars, personal consumption expenditures per head rose from $578 in 1939 to $707 in 1944 and $768 in 1945. The North American economies had both guns and butter during the war, unlike their European counterparts. The reason for this was, of course, the enormous excess capacity existing on the eve of the Second World War and the lack of physical destruction on the North American continent.

But there is another feature of federal government finance during the war period that requires mention at this point, namely, the alteration of dominion-provincial relations occasioned by the crisis. This constituted a structural change in the political environment that continues to enliven present-day relations between the federal and provincial governments and raises all the thorny problems of what in the United States is referred to as "states rights."

Dominion-Provincial Fiscal Relations. At Confederation in 1867 the bulk of legislative power was vested in the federal government partly in the belief that inadequate federal power in the United States was responsible for the Civil War. In the realm of fiscal affairs the federal government in Ottawa was given exclusive control over indirect taxes, then the major revenue-producer, while sharing concurrent jurisdiction with the provinces in the realm of direct taxation. However, over time two

[35]Defence spending increased from $70 *million* in 1939 ($36 million in 1938) to $4.3 *billion* in 1944.

TABLE 1.13

Federal Spending
1939–45
(millions of current dollars)

	Wages, salaries, and supplementary labour income	Military pay and allowances	UNRRA, mutual aid, and military relief	Wartime military expenditures abroad (excluding military pay and allowances)	Other purchases of goods and services	Total federal expenditures on goods and services
1939	90	32	—	4	91	213
1940	112	193	—	13	362	680
1941	119	386	—	58	624	1187
1942	172	641	1002	145	1275	3235
1943	203	910	518	603	1484	3718
1944	209	1068	960	1261	972	4470
1945	220	1117	858	630	272	3097

SOURCE: DBS, *National Accounts Income and Expenditure 1926–1956*, Tables 43, 36, 37, and 53.

developments seriously affected the relative position of Ottawa vis-à-vis the provincial governments in fiscal matters. One was the increasing importance of direct taxation compared to indirect, which enhanced the provinces' ability to raise funds since they shared jurisdiction in this field. The other was a series of legal interpretations that progressively broadened the powers of the provinces and weakened the central authority. These factors largely account for the steady decline in the proportion of federal government expenditures to total expenditures by all levels of government from over 52 per cent in 1870 to less than 25 per cent in 1930.[36] But the economic and social problems of the 1930's raised the revenue needs of both the provincial and federal governments and led to the search for additional revenues especially in the areas of concurrent jurisdiction. Increasing inability to handle the problems of the depression at the provincial level as the crisis deepened and the curtailment of federal powers resulted in an intensive inquiry into dominion-provincial relations by the famous Rowell-Sirois Commission. In fiscal affairs it was evident not only that the duties of the national and provincial governments needed to be carefully defined and probably revised but also that the jurisdiction over taxation of various types had to be clearly divided to prevent serious inequities to taxpayers in different provinces. The Commission advocated that the federal government

[36]See Firestone, *Canada's Economic Development, 1867–1953*, Table 38, p. 127.

TABLE 1.13 (*continued*)

Transfer payments	Subsidies	Transfers to provinces	Total federal expenditure	Total federal revenues	Budgetary Surplus or Deficit
190	−17	79	465	459	−5
198	53	70	1001	860	−140
218	69	54	1528	1498	−30
270	87	150	3742	2016	−1726
315	205	148	4386	2441	−1945
408	261	155	5294	2582	−2712
761	257	157	4272	2438	−1834

should have complete jurisdiction over relief payments to the unemployed, should assume all provincial debts, and have in return the sole power to tax personal and corporate incomes as well as estates. The provinces were to receive adjustment grants to enable them to maintain certain social services and other functions which were to remain provincial or municipal responsibilities both as to character and amount. Although the recommendations were rejected and the 1941 Dominion-Provincial Conference collapsed, the war emergency induced a temporary settlement of the dispute over financial jurisdiction which partly followed the Report's general recommendations. Thus in 1942 the first of a series of temporary "tax rental" agreements was entered into.

There have been five such agreements running for five years each and subject to renegotiation. The most recent one expires in 1967. But the unanimity of the first agreement, induced by the military emergency, which saw all provinces vacate the fields of personal and corporate income taxes as well as succession duties in return for payments which contained some elements of fiscal need subsidy to the poorer provinces, was broken after expiry in 1947 despite strenuous attempts by the national government to establish such a uniform system on a permanent basis.

It is not germane to our purpose here to set forth all the details of the subsequent agreements since we are mainly interested in the broad trends.[37] Suffice it to say that uniformity of treatment has not been maintained and that separate agreements on tax rentals have been made with each province. Quebec has generally refused to accept any agreement and Ontario, even when agreeing to rent, has retained one or another of the direct taxes. The subsidy elements in the payments to the agreeing provinces have been retained and even enhanced (e.g., the Atlantic Provinces Adjustment Grants, tax equalization payments, and revenue stabilization payments). But in general the situation in fiscal affairs remains to be resolved satisfactorily. Indeed the 1962 agreement provides for federal government withdrawal from the direct taxation field and provincial re-entry. The federal government is to reduce its personal income tax progressively by 16 per cent in 1962 to 20 per cent in 1966 and the federal corporate tax is reduced by 9 per cent (10 per cent where the province pays the subsidy to higher education as in Quebec) with estate taxes abated by 50 per cent as in the earlier agreements. The provinces are not restricted to the extent of federal withdrawal, although for the most part they have increased taxes in the vacated fields by roughly comparable amounts. The federal government continues to collect the personal income taxes for the provinces, except Quebec, and the corporate income taxes, except for Quebec and Ontario.

This, of course, represents a partial reversion to the state of affairs existing prior to the 1942 agreements. It is probably fair to suggest that "there can be no solution but only worse disorder . . . until all the 11 governments realize that they are governing the same nation, collecting from the same body of taxpayers and depending on the health of the same economy."[38] At the very least the problem of concurrent jurisdiction remains in a highly unsettled state and, like much else in Canada, has reverted,[39] in part at least, to the pre-war situation.

Employment, Prices, and Production in the Second World War. By June 1, 1941, unemployment had fallen to about 4.4 per cent of the civilian labour force. At the same time, the armed services increased from a mere 9,000 men in 1939 to almost 300,000, and there was an increase in non-agricultural employment of more than 300,000.

[37]Most of the details are generally available in the *Canada Year Book*. The Wartime Tax Agreements of 1942 are outlined in the 1946 edition, pp. 900–1; the 1947 and 1952 Tax Rental Agreements are summarized in the 1954 *Year Book*, pp. 1087–90; the 1957 Federal-Provincial Tax-Sharing Arrangements Act is described in the 1961 edition, pp. 1067–70 while the 1962 agreement is outlined in the 1962 edition, pp. 1015–16.
[38]Bruce Hutchison, *Ottawa Journal*, July 18, 1963, p. 7.
[39]See below at p. 46.

In industry, the rapid expansion of demand in the face of excess capacity led to sharp increases in production with little change in price. Steel production rose 120 per cent between 1939 and the wartime peak of 1942–44, aluminum output increased about 5 times, while producton of zinc, lead, and nickel recorded increases of 55, 32, and 27 per cent respectively.[40] The index of industrial production almost doubled between 1939 and 1944. Other evidence of wartime, as well as post-war, growth is presented in Table 1.14 with US comparisons where data permits. In virtually every case the growth rate of comparable Canadian output in the 1939–46 period exceeded that of the US. This reflects in part the relatively small base from which the Canadian economy grew in some lines but it also illustrates the dynamism of the accelerated wartime efforts.

But the data of Table 1.13 understate the degree of wartime expansion since in almost every case output in 1946 was below the peak war year (generally 1943 or 1944). Nevertheless, with the exception of consumer durables, some metals, and mining in general, every product shown in Table 1.13 grew from 1939 to 1946 at rates mainly in excess of 5 or 6 per cent compounded annually.

As suggested above, prices were marked by relatively modest increases during the wartime years of 1940–45. Although Canada actually entered the Second World War in September of 1939, its entry had relatively little impact on prices that year; in fact, the consumer price index fell by 0.8 per cent during 1939.[41] From the end of 1939 until 1945 the consumer price index rose by only 18.7 per cent, or an average of about 2.9 per cent a year. This increase compares with a 29.5 per cent increase in the United States' consumer price index during the same period—an average of 4.4 per cent a year.

Canada's rather considerable success in avoiding excess inflation during the war years, despite the inevitable shortages of many goods and rising incomes, is attributable to several factors. One of the most important of these has already been mentioned namely, the existence of substantial excess capacity at the beginning of the period which permitted a rapid increase in production in response to growing wartime demands without pressing against capacity. Increased government demands for goods and services were offset partially by higher wartime taxes, which kept disposable personal income from rising as rapidly as national income, and partially by the sale of government war bonds, which helped

[40]Firestone, *Canada's Economic Development, 1867–1953*, p. 214.
[41]Data on price behaviour are shown in Table 1.11.

TABLE 1.14

Annual Growth Rates of Selected Industries
1939–62

Industry and unit		1939	1946	Highest year of 1956–58 to 1962	1962
				Canadian output	
Industrial production	(DBS index	53.3	83.8	155.44	186
Industrial production total	1949 = 100)	90.3	74.3	228.55	286
Mining total		48.7	85.2	145.13	165
Manufacturing total					
Selected industries					
Metals					
Copper, production of refined	(million				
copper	pounds)	463.2	408.0	660.0§	765
Nickel, production	"	225.6	192.0	375.6||	474
Lead, production of refined lead	"	381.6	331.2	395.2‡	304
Zinc, production of refined zinc	"	351.6	370.8	511.2‡	560
Iron ore, producers' shipments	('000 tons)	123.6	1,549.2	22,348.8‡	27,128
Non-metallic minerals					
Asbestos, producers' shipments	('000 tons)	364.8	558.0	1,046.4§	1,214
Gypsum, producers' shipments	"	1,416.0	1,812.0	4,896.0||	5,317
Cement production	"	996.0	1,872.0	6,312.0§	6,842
Textiles					
Cotton, broad woven cotton					
fabric	('000 yards)	260,364	240,384	305,664‡	310,6?
Woolen and worsted fabrics	"	17,244	28,980	23,076‡	15,1?
Broad woven rayon fabric	"	51,288	78,168	86,912‡	94,1?
Forest products					
Newsprint, total shipments	('000 tons)	2,860.8	4,136.4	6,448.8‡	6,680
Exports of wood pulp	"	705.6	1,418.4	2,373.6‡	3,045
Lumber, production	(million feet				
of sawn lumber	board measure)	3,976.8	5,083.2	7,740.0‡	8,770
Electric power	(million kilowatt hours)	26,424	39,264	92,914||	115,7?
Crude petroleum,					
producers' shipments	('000 barrels)	7,824	7,584	181,848§	—
Rubber, production					
of synthetic	(million pounds)	—	114.24	302.52||	377.?
Total motor vehicles, produced	('000's)	155.4	171.48	471.36‡	508.
Mechanical refrigerators, produced	"	51.48	56.76	293.4 ‡	271.?
Washing machines, produced	"	103.92	115.2	305.88§	298.
Radio receivers, produced	"	370.8	568.8	721.2	689.
Television receivers, produced	"	—	—	597.63	420.
Air traffic, passenger	(millions of pass. miles)	21.6	206.4	2,152.8||	3,57?
Air traffic, freight,					
express, mail	(millions of ton miles)	—	1,896.0	20,232.0||	57,21?
Railroad traffic, freight	"	31,464.0	55,308.0	78,780.0‡	65,80?
Railroad traffic, pass.	(millions of pass. miles)	1,752.0	4,644.0	2,928.0§	1,95?

*Production   †Crude runs to stills.   ‡1956   §1957 ||19?
SOURCES: DBS, *Canadian Statistical Review, 1959 Supplement* (Ottawa, 196?
US Department of Commerce, Office of Business Economics, *Business Statistics, 19?*
biennial edition (Washington, DC, 1961). US Department of Commerce, *Survey ?
Current Business*, April, 1963.

	Average annual percentage change						
	Canada				United States		
1939–46	1946 to highest year 1956–58	Highest year of 1956–58 to 1962	1939–62	1939–46	1946 to highest year 1956–58	Highest year of 1956–58 to 1962	1939–62
6.7	5.8	3.7	5.6	6.5	4.9§	3.4	5.1
—	8.6	5.8	5.1	2.2	3.9‡	0.3	3.1
8.7	5.5	5.8	5.5	6.7	4.8§	3.5	5.1
—	4.1	2.8	2.2		4.7§	2.1	2.1
—	6.3	4.8	3.3				
—	1.8	0.5		1.3	1.4‖		0.2
0.8	5.5	1.5	2.0	5.3	2.6§		2.5
43.5	30.6	3.3	26.4	3.6	3.7§	—	1.1
6.3	5.9	3.0	5.4				
3.6	10.5	1.4	5.9	8.4	—	14.6	4.9
9.4	12.8	2.0	10.0	4.3	6.8‡	1.0	4.5
—	2.4	0.3	0.8	2.3	1.1§	—	0.5
7.7	—	—	—	7.2	—	—	—
6.2	1.1	1.3	2.7	3.6	—	—	0.7
5.4	4.5	0.6	3.8	—	8.2§	3.9	3.6
10.5	2.9	4.2	6.7	7.6*	7.6‡	3.9*	6.6*
3.6	4.3	2.1	3.5	4.5	1.2‡	—	1.2
5.8	7.4	5.6	6.6	7.6	8.6‖	9.3	8.0
—	8.3	—	—	4.9†	5.3†‡	0.9	4.0
—	8.5	5.7	—	132.1	3.8§	7.1	33.7
1.4	10.6	1.3	5.3	—	8.0§	2.5	3.6
1.4	17.9		7.5	—	—	—	—
1.5	8.5	—	4.7	5.1	8.2‡	—	4.2
6.3	2.2	—	2.7	5.8	—	4.4	2.5
38.0	21.6	7.1	24.9	36.4	12.6‖	12.6	19.0
—	21.8	26.7	—	30.0	14.5‖	14.4	19.7
8.4	6.1	—	2.6	8.2	0.5‡	—	—
14.9	—	—	0.5	16.2	—	—	—

somewhat in reducing the demand for consumer goods and services. All these measures however, would doubtless have been inadequate to hold down the price level in the absence of direct government action to control prices. In Canada this direct action took the form of rationing, production directives, maximum price controls, subsidies, etc. The first three methods of control were common in most countries during the war, but subsidies to keep prices down were somewhat less so. Subsidies of certain commodities that were scarce in Canada were underwritten by the Wartime Prices and Trade Board to keep their prices below what the market would otherwise have established.

The wholesale price index followed a somewhat similar pattern as shown in Table 1.11. After registering declines during both 1938 and 1939, the index had increased rapidly by about 33 per cent at the end of 1945. Although almost double the rate of increase in the consumer price index, this was still a smaller increase than recorded in the US where the wholesale price index rose by more than 37 per cent. Furthermore, the rate of increase appears greater owing to the sharp declines in the immediate pre-war years. Taking the increase from 1937 suggests a rise of only about 23 per cent in the wholesale price index. By either standard, however, the record of Canada in terms of price stability was little less remarkable than the record of production.

Effects of the War. The Canadian economy emerged after the war in a far stronger position than at the beginning. Not only had industrial research begun on a large scale but many entirely new industries had been established (e.g., synthetic rubber, roller bearings, diesel engines, antibiotics, high octane gasoline, aircraft manufacturing, and ship-building[42]). Further processing of some manufactured goods hitherto imported likewise gave the Canadian economy a taste of new manufacturing capabilities that it was hoped would prove to be irreversible. In many industries (e.g., steel) basic capacity was permanently enlarged.

Our concern here is mainly with the post-war experience which we shall treat in considerably greater detail. However, the wartime performance of the Canadian economy had a substantial impact and provided the experience, structural adaptation, and optimism which hopefully were to prevent a complete reversion in the post-war period to the situation of the thirties. It is perhaps not too much to say that the wartime industrial pressures induced or forced a degree of economic maturity and confidence that would not otherwise have occurred and provided a base

[42]The latter two had existed before the war but on such a small scale compared with wartime production levels that they became, in essence, "new" industries.

from which, after a period of readjustment, a kind of economic take-off might well prove to be not only rapid but perhaps viable. Indeed, at war's end a substantial alteration of the economic structure had already taken place, as was natural in all belligerent countries. But for Canada, in particular, the new industries, the proof of industrial and technological capabilities, the wide diversification of output, even within agriculture[43] but more pronounced in other sectors, and the substantial rise in exports of a greater variety of products, seemed to augur well for the future. The lesson that government expenditures could be extremely stimulating, even with high rates of taxation, likewise created greater acceptance of so-called functional finance[44] and the tax rental schemes provided the means for carrying out a national counter-cyclical fiscal policy. Furthermore, the problem of inflation had been kept within manageable bounds. If these positive aspects of the war upon the Canadian economy could be maintained and the trends continued, Canada's economic future could be one of sustained and relatively slump-free dynamism.

But two aspects of Canada's position at the end of the war raised nagging doubts. The first, and the one receiving the bulk of public attention and concern, was the problem of conversion to a peace-time economy. The possibility of a major contraction haunted the minds of policy-makers. We shall deal with the reconversion process in the next section. The second aspect, more subtle and long-run, did not receive nearly the appropriate degree of attention: the great growth of the economy, especially in secondary manufacturing but in other sectors as well, had taken place under extremely sheltered circumstances with supplies from Europe and the US either cut off or sharply curtailed. In addition the federal government provided special assistance such as accelerated depreciation and the fruits of its research and development programs. This happy conjunction of rising demand, reduced competition, and various forms of governmental assistance could scarcely prevent even the least motivated entrepreneur from responding positively. As the Gordon Commission's *Final Report* put it "in this protected hot-house atmosphere, where costs were of relatively minor importance, secondary manufacturing grew like a beanstalk."[45] The vital question for the further

[43]For details of the shifting patterns of agricultural output during the war period, especially prior to 1944, see V. C. Fowke, "Canadian Agriculture in the Postwar World," in R. H. Coats, ed., *Features of Present-Day Canada*, Annals of the American Academy of Political and Social Science, vol. 253 (Philadelphia, 1947), esp. pp. 46 and 47.
[44]Recent indications are that this may no longer be true as far as the general public is concerned.
[45]RCCEP, *Final Report* (Ottawa, 1957), p. 87.

rapid progress of the Canadian economy was whether industries so stimulated could maintain their output when the heady hot-house climate
cooled under the winds of European recovery and the conversion of the
US economy to a peace-time basis. In short, was the wartime experience
of the economy a passing phase or had it set the stage for a further drive
toward economic viability and maturity? Could Canadian manufacturing
industry perform successfully in competitive world markets thereby reducing the validity of the staple theory and ushering in a new and more
independent pattern of economic growth and development? The reversion, if that is an appropriate term, of the industrial composition of gross
domestic product from the wartime structure to pre-war patterns has
already been noted. This may be interpreted either as re-establishment
of "normalcy" following the wartime distortions or as a failure to retain
the impetus given to manufacturing—a failure caused by increased competition from Western Europe, the United States, and Japan which
forced or induced the Canadian economy to resume its historic emphasis
upon resource-oriented production.

On balance, we are inclined to the view that this is an unfortunate
reversion occasioned by serious mistakes of public policy especially after
1956 combined with a lack of aggression by private firms in seeking or
retaining foreign markets in a wide variety of manufactured products.
To be sure, Canada's large comparative advantage in natural resources
would doubtless have manifest itself in any event but not to the same
extent had these factors been absent. "Reversion" is in our opinion a
more valid interpretation of post-war experience in Canada—a reversion
moreover that was largely avoidable and unfortunate for the sustenance
of a high level of output, employment and efficiency.

We have already noted several other aspects of "reversion." The public
acceptance of deliberate governmental deficits as a stimulus to economic
activity seems to have diminished sharply, if indeed the public had ever
come to regard such deficits as any more than a necessary evil in time
of war. Reversion from the 1942 tax rental agreements has been a
feature of post-war dominion-provincial arrangements, the federal government in the latest agreement vacating some proportion of the major
revenue sources. The relative price stability of the late 1950's is reminis-
cent of the 1920's and the slow rate of growth over the decade of the
fifties as a whole has a certain parallel with the thirties, although at a
far higher level and for totally different reasons. On the other hand there
are several obviously permanent structural changes such as the decline
of agriculture, the rise in demand for improved labour skills, and the
increased variety of domestic output which the war merely accelerated.

2. THE TRANSITION FROM WAR TO PEACE

In current and constant value terms, GNE reached its wartime peak during 1944. With the end of the war in Europe (May 1945) and in the Far East (August 1945), federal government spending was sharply curtailed from a high of almost 38 per cent of GNE in 1944 to 26 per cent in 1945. Thereafter the decline proceeded rapidly and steadily until in 1948 the share of the federal government, in a not-much-changed total GNE, was less than 5 per cent. Contrary to the general fears of policy-makers at the time, this sharp reduction in government spending did not precipitate a cumulative contraction of the whole economy. Partly this was a result of certain stimuli given to the economy as outlined in the White Paper on Employment and Income (April 1945), but for the most part the decline in government spending was offset by a sharp increase in private expenditures. In constant dollar terms, personal consumption expenditures increased from about $9.3 billion in 1945 to almost $11 billion in 1949. Business capital formation increased even more dramatically from $1.4 billion in 1945 to over $3 billion in 1949 (see Table 1.1). The reasons for such increases are in retrospect obvious: pent-up demands following the war, accumulation of substantial savings in both businesses and households, policy measures to prevent contraction of the economy, and the continuing needs of Western Europe for the products of North America. Holdings of liquid assets in the form of government securities, savings by business and households, inactive savings deposits, currency, and active deposits held by the general public increased from about $6½ billion in 1940 to around $17 billion in 1945.[46] At the same time and closely related to these large accumulations the ratio of consumption to disposable income increased from a wartime low of 78.2 per cent to a more normal figure of around 92 per cent (see Table 1.2). Interestingly enough, although national income declined slightly in 1946, personal income was over 6 per cent higher than in 1945 due mainly to the rise in transfer payments from $546 million to $1,106 million, most of which represented payments to veterans, and a modest reduction in personal income taxes. Business investment (in constant 1949 dollars) increased from $1.2 billion, or 7 per cent of GNE in 1944, to $3.0 billion, or 18 per cent, by 1949. As a result of these offsets to the decline of government expenditures total GNE fell very slightly from the wartime (1944) peak of $15.9 billion in 1949 dollars to a low in 1946 of $15.3 billion. In current dollar figures, GNE was in fact identical at $11.9 billion in both 1944 and 1946. Indeed, using

[46]Bank of Canada, *Annual Report of the Governor to Minister of Finance for the Year 1949* (Ottawa, Feb. 1950), p. 4.

current dollars the drop in GNE was a mere $15 million and occurred between 1944 and 1945. However, in real terms GNE did not surpass its wartime peak until 1949 although the extent of the decline was, as we have just seen, not large.

In the labour market, the transition likewise proceeded smoothly. Although some 620,000 servicemen were released between June 1, 1945, and June 1, 1946, as well as a roughly equal number of employees working in munitions plants or employed on other wartime contracts, the rate of unemployment never exceeded 5.6 per cent on a monthly basis. For the years 1945 and 1946 as a whole the unemployment rate was only 1.6 and 3.0 per cent respectively and fell to around 2 per cent in 1947 and 1948. Generally, the reduction of employment in war industries and the armed services was largely offset by the rapid expansion of output in non-military lines as the relaxation of wartime controls, combined with the release of pent-up demand by households and business, pushed production in the latter industries to new record highs.

As far as particular segments of the economy are concerned some of the evidence, especially as regards output of consumer durables, is shown in Table 1.14. Table 1.15 summarizes some of the output data in terms of GDP at factor cost by industry. In manufacturing, transportation, and public administration and defence, output contracted sharply from the wartime peak until 1946 and in the latter case even until 1948. But by 1948 a good deal of the slack so created had been absorbed by increases in construction, electric power, and wholesale and retail trade; in each of these broad sectors, output levels by 1948 were well above the wartime peak. By 1949 or 1950 virtually all sectors of the economy had achieved or passed the peak; agriculture, durable goods, manufacturing and, of course, public administration and defence were notable exceptions. Generally, however, the economy as a whole maintained the greater part of the wartime gains in total output and employment.

In a very real sense, therefore, the transition to a peacetime economy proceeded with an ease that even the most optimistic forecaster in 1944–45 could not have foreseen. But there were various trouble spots. In the first place the decontrol of prices showed the extent to which inflation had successfully been suppressed in the latter period of the war. The subsequent price rise was doubtless inevitable given the elimination of excess capacity during the war and the low level of capital formation (including new housing). Faced with mounting demands from households and businesses in directions where slack no longer existed, upward pressure on the price level could scarcely have been avoided once the controls were removed. By 1949 the consumer price index had risen by

TABLE 1.15

Quantity Indexes of Gross Domestic Product at Factor Cost by Industry of Origin
1939-62
(1949 = 100)

Year	Manu-facturing	Con-struction	Electric power and gas utilities	Trans-portation	Whole-sale trade	Retail trade	Public adminis-tration and defence
1939	48.7	43.4	49.7	51.0	53.4	53.3	61.6
1943	104.0	65.6	77.2	103.3	82.9	62.0	311.2
1944	106.1	53.5	78.2	105.3	86.8	66.1	342,1
1946	85.2	68.4	79.4	93.2	89.7	89.2	124.7
1948	97.3	89.2	94.8	102.4	97.4	95.3	92.3
1950	106.2	106.7	113.2	102.1	103.2	108.9	106.6
1951	115.0	110.6	129.4	111.4	111.2	106.5	119.0
1952	118.5	123.2	140.7	116.6	117.2	113.3	136.3
1953	126.4	130.1	147.9	117.1	122.3	120.8	144.2
1954	122.9	129.8	161.4	110.6	118.8	121.6	151.3
1955	134.7	139.8	183.3	127.9	129.4	133.4	156.3
1956	145.1	165.7	204.9	143.3	144.7	143.9	158.9
1957	142.9	174.7	220.3	141.0	144.9	144.4	163.7
1958	140.7	178.4	239.1	135.2	147.6	147.3	171.3
1959	149.8	170.7	268.7	150.8	161.9	153.5	175.0
1960	149.3	163.0	298.0	151.8	161.8	153.9	177.8
1961	153.0	168.4	317.7	159.7	162.7	155.9	183.9
1962	164.9	171.0	337.7	166.4	174.9	162.6	187.9

SOURCE: DBS, *Indexes of Real Domestic Product by Industry of Origin, 1935-1961*
(Ottawa, 1963).

a third over the 1945 level while the wholesale price index had increased
by a substantial 50 per cent (see Table 1.11). Superimposed on this
came further sharp price increases associated with the Korean hostilities
to be discussed in the following section.

Secondly, an exchange crisis occurred in 1947 which, although immediately related to specific phenomena unlikely to recur (i.e., the extensive
loans and advances to overseas countries for reconstruction), nevertheless provided unmistakable evidence that the changing circumstances of
Canada's major trading partners was to be a source of continuing difficulty. Briefly the crisis involved a sharp reduction in reserves of foreign
exchange from a level of over $1.5 billion in terms of US dollars at the
end of 1945 to barely $0.5 billion at the end of 1947. The bulk of the
decline (over $0.7 billion) occurred in 1947. The immediate cause of
this very substantial loss in the reserves, despite a current account surplus
in both 1946 and 1947, was the financing *via* Canadian loans and
advances of much of the net exports to overseas countries. Some $0.6

TABLE 1.16

Exports, Imports, and Balance of Payments
on Current Account
1926–62
(millions of current dollars)

	Exports				Imports		
	Mer-chandise	Services	Gold production available for export	Total	Mer-chandise	Services	Total
1926	1272	348	30	1650	− 973	− 549	1522
1929	1178	417	37	1632	−1272	− 673	1945
1933	532	212	82	826	− 368	− 460	828
1937	1041	405	145	1591	− 776	− 663	1409
1938	844	351	161	1356	− 649	− 608	1257
1939	906	361	184	1451	− 713	− 615	1328
1940	1202	403	203	1808	−1006	− 623	1629
1941	1732	531	204	2467	−1264	− 712	1976
1942	2515	30	184	2361	−1406	− 901	2307
1943	3050	247	142	3444	−1579	−1338	2917
1944	3590	81	110	3561	−1398	−2171	3569
1945	3474	27	96	3597	−1442	−1468	2910
1946	2393	721	96	3201	−1822	−1055	2877
1947	2723	818	99	3640	−2535	−1086	3621
1948	3030	901	119	4050	−2598	−1035	3633
1949	2989	893	139	4021	−2696	−1157	3853
1950	3139	881	163	4183	−3129	−1384	4513
1951	3950	989	150	5089	−4097	−1516	5613
1952	4339	1084	150	5573	−3850	−1550	5400
1953	4152	857	144	5400	−4210	−1633	5843
1954	3929	1063	155	5147	−3916	−1658	5574
1955	4332	1277	155	5764	−4543	−1900	6443
1956	4837	1378	150	6365	−5565	−2150	7715
1957	4894	1335	147	6391	−5488	−2325	7813
1958	4887	1290	160	6340	−5066	−2357	7423
1959	5150	1385	148	6683	−5572	−2559	8131
1960	5392	1774	162	7008	−5540	−2632	8172
1961	5889	1580	162	7631	−5716	−2826	8542
1962	6364	1695	165	8224	−6209	−2824	9033

SOURCE: DBS, *National Accounts Income and Expenditure, 1926–56*, and *ibid.*, *1961* and *1962*, Table 55.

NOTE: Data refer to estimates consistent with the National Income and Expenditure Accounts and exclude from "Services" both mutual aid to NATO countries and inheritances and immigrants' funds.

Balance of Payments on Current Account		
Balance on commodity account	Balance on other current items	Net balance on current account
299	− 172	127
− 94	− 217	− 311
164	− 166	− 2
265	− 85	180
195	− 95	100
193	− 67	126
196	− 47	149
468	23	491
1109	− 8	1101
1471	− 265	1206
2192	−1174	1018
2032	− 486	1546
571	− 208	363
188	− 139	49
432	19	451
293	− 116	177
10	− 344	− 334
− 147	− 370	− 517
489	− 325	164
− 58	− 385	− 443
13	− 445	− 432
− 211	− 487	− 698
− 728	− 638	−1366
− 579	− 864	−1455
− 199	− 952	−1131
− 422	−1082	−1504
− 148	−1095	−1243
+ 173	−1155	− 982
+ 155	−1003	− 848

billion of Canada's sales overseas were financed in this way; this meant that no immediate cash return was received. At the same time Canada paid cash for her imports from other countries, but total sales to these did not exceed purchases by more than a meagre amount. "Consequently [in 1947] we had a cash deficiency on our current transactions with other countries of some $530 millions, and a drain on our foreign exchange reserves of an equivalent amount. This, together with payment of $74 millions on our subscription to the International Monetary Fund, redemptions of Canadian bonds held abroad, and other net capital payments abroad, account for the over-all reduction of $743 millions in our gold and foreign exchange reserves. . . ."[47]

In order to rebuild the reserves, import restrictions and restrictions on pleasure travel involving the use of US dollars were imposed in late 1947. These actions combined with more buoyant exports relative to imports in subsequent years served to raise reserves to over $1.1 billion by the end of 1949. The crisis, in short, was over, and by 1949, despite a recession in the United States, the Canadian economy again moved forward and embarked upon a vigorous period of expansion through the first half of the 1950's.[48]

3. CONTINUED RAPID GROWTH, 1949–56

The year 1949 was notable in many respects. Not only did it represent the first year in which GNE (in constant 1949 dollars) exceeded the 1944 wartime peak, but the year as a whole exhibited the first significant post-war increase in real output, a somewhat modest rise of about 3 per cent, excluding Newfoundland, but significantly above the increases since 1945. Furthermore, the downturn in the US, mild though it was, had little effect upon Canada. Seasonally adjusted GNE in constant (1957) dollars fell by less than 1 per cent between the peak attained during the fourth quarter of 1948 and the first quarter of 1949. Thereafter, real GNE rose in every quarter resulting in the annual increase of 3 per cent over 1948.

From the first quarter of 1949 to the fourth quarter of 1953 real GNE (in constant 1957 dollars) grew steadily (with two exceptions: third and fourth quarters of 1951) from $20,980 million to $27,656 million or by over 30 per cent.

[47]Bank of Canada, *Annual Report, 1947* (Ottawa, Feb. 1948), p. 21.
[48]A more complete discussion of the exchange crisis is given in DBS, *The Canadian Balance of International Payments in the Post-War Years, 1946–1952* (Ottawa, 1953), chap. II.

By the end of 1956 GNE had reached a level some 46 per cent above 1949 despite a slight contraction in 1954. The growth rate, compounded annually, exceeded 2.8 per cent on a per capita basis, well below the wartime spurt but a respectable performance compared with other countries. Indeed the year 1956 represents the high water mark of the 1950's in terms of real output per head. Thereafter, this index of economic growth, crude as it is, declined and in fact for the balance of the 1950's and 1961 remained below the 1956 peak. It is important therefore that we examine in more detail the forces which early in the fifties propelled the economy forward at a very rapid rate and then appeared to lose steam until late in 1961.

A glance at the major components of GNE suggests that the dynamic elements in the period 1949–56 were government spending and business gross fixed capital formation which increased (in real terms) by some 80 and 60 per cent respectively. The most dynamic component of government spending was, naturally enough, for purposes of defence following the Korean war. Defence spending, however, reached a peak in 1953 and has maintained almost that level ever since. The most volatile component of business fixed investment was construction. Residential construction expenditures increased almost 40 per cent between 1949–1956 while non-residential outlays more than doubled. In national accounting terms these two components, added together, rose from $1.7 billion (in constant 1949 dollars) to over $2.9 billion—an increase of roughly 70 per cent. The quantity index of construction in terms of gross domestic product at factor cost rose by some 66 per cent between these two dates. Thus underlying the rapid expansion was the defence build-up in the early years plus the sustained upswing of a construction boom. Although non-residential construction increased further in 1957, housing declined and the rate of growth of the two combined tapered off. Absolute declines occurred after 1958 so that by 1961 total construction outlays amounted to $2.6 billion (in 1949 dollars) or less than in 1956, 1957, or 1958.

At the same time various shifts were taking place within the private consuming sector. Although personal consumption expenditures increased from $10.9 billion in 1949 to some $15.6 billion (in 1949 dollars) in 1956, this no more than paralleled the rise in personal disposable income. In fact, consumption spending declined as a proportion of GNE from 66.8 per cent in 1949 to 61.6 per cent. The changing composition of consumer spending is shown in Table 1.17 for selected years. All categories of consumer spending were higher in 1956 than in 1949, although there were differences in the rates of increase. In the durable,

TABLE 1.17

Consumption Expenditures, 1949–62
(millions of constant 1949 dollars; percentages)

Category	Percentage average 1927-29	1949	1950	1951	1952	Percentage average 1950-52	1953	1954	1955	1956	1957	1958	1959	1960	1961	Percentage average 1959-61	1962
Food	26.5	2887	3072	3089	3251	26.2	3452	3598	3785	4023	4178	4272	4485	4661	4694	25.7	4756
Tobacco and alcoholic beverages	5.3	883	907	879	960	7.4	1029	1049	1109	1198	1265	1319	1372	1394	1417	7.8	1474
Clothing and personal furnishings	14.2	1947	1520	1493	1615	12.4	1672	1662	1744	1855	1901	1948	2020	2076	2093	11.5	2149
Shelter	13.8	1200	1272	1350	1406	11.8	1473	1536	1645	1710	1824	1928	2059	2140	2212	11.9	2292
Household operation	14.0	1416	1501	1473	1604	12.6	1699	1795	1966	2169	2208	2274	2391	2426	2533	13.7	2642
Transportation	9.1	1109	1303	1207	1369	10.8	1519	1541	1817	1928	1927	2029	2149	2205	2265	12.3	2445
Personal and medical care and death expenses	6.6	691	734	750	775	6.3	818	842	883	968	1001	1079	1149	1225	1306	6.8	1374
Miscellaneous	10.5	1240	1333	1576	1653	12.5	1676	1627	1713	1752	1762	1713	1730	1733	1886	9.9	1938
Total*	100.0	10,923	11,642	11,817	12,633	100.0	13,338	13,650	14,662	15,603	16,083	16,585	17,392	17,908	18,480	100.0	19,157
Durable goods	8.7	1146	1432	1297	1526	11.7	1737	1724	2066	2209	2121	2151	2262	2258	2329	12.7	2521
Non-durable goods	54.7	6288	6574	6667	7016	55.6	7348	7535	8187	8705	9059	9268	9659	9958	10,278	55.6	10,667
Services	36.6	3487	3636	3853	4091	32.7	4253	4391	4409	4689	4884	5127	5416	5623	5801	31.3	5021

SOURCE: DBS, *National Accounts Income and Expenditure, 1926-1956*, Table 48, p. 91; *ibid, 1961*, Table 58, p. 59; *ibid., 1962*, Table 58, p. 65.
*Includes adjusting entry for 1957-1962.

non-durable, and services categories, the steady rise in the latter two components compared to the rather wavering rise in durables is apparent; however, the increase in durable good purchases between 1949 and 1956 was much higher—at about 93 per cent—than in the other two categories; non-durables rose by close to 40 per cent and services by 34 per cent. As a result durables accounted for almost 14 per cent of total consumption spending in 1956 compared with slightly more than 10 per cent in 1949. After 1956, however, the growth of durables tapered off.

It is evident that private consumption spending provided less of a stimulus to the increase in GNE in this period than in the immediate post-war years, and this fact, coupled with the investment boom, resulted in the emergence of excess capacity in many consumer goods industries by 1956 or 1957.

Exports, however, rose by less than GNE between 1949 and 1956, but their role was in reality more strategic than this relative decline might suggest. The export boom was mainly in the resource industries, as the belief in scarcity of strategic raw materials came to be widely held especially in the US. The rise in exports induced a substantial investment in those sectors of the economy heavily reliant upon world markets and partly underwrote the construction boom as new areas were opened up. The proportion of gross domestic investment in the "mining, quarrying, and oil wells" category increased sharply in the period 1953–56 in response to the upsurge in world demand for raw materials,[49] and more than offset the tapering-off of defence spending. Output of the mining sector (defined in terms of GDP at factor cost) more than doubled between 1949 and 1956.[50] Much of this investment was later to prove excessive relative to other sectors and future demands.

In short, strong autonomous forces pushed the economy ahead rapidly until 1956. These were (1) the upswing of the residential housing cycle and non-residential construction, (2) the sharp rise in world demand for natural resources which Canada had in abundance, and (3) the great jump in defence spending which had stabilized at or close to the 1953 peak.

Since the behaviour of exports had a strategic importance beyond the extent of their aggregate increase, it is worthwhile to examine these in somewhat greater detail although the changing magnitude and composition of Canadian exports is dealt with more fully in Chapter 4.

World demand for natural resources rose rapidly in the late 1940's

[49]See Caves and Holton, *Canadian Economy*, p. 103, Table 4.
[50]DBS, *Indexes of Real Domestic Product by Industry of Origin 1935–61* (Ottawa, 1963), Table 1, p. 67.

and early 1950's. World production of certain basic commodities is, of course, a reflection of this demand, and the trend in world production of those items important in Canada's exports provides some insight into the stimulus given the Canadian economy during the period in question by both exports themselves and by investment in facilities for increasing their production. Aluminum, lead, newsprint, nickel, wood pulp, copper, and iron ore were among the most important Canadian exports influenced by this increase in world demand for natural resources. World production of the first four of these commodities rose each year from 1949 to 1957, and during the same period wood pulp showed a decline in production only in 1952, iron ore only in 1954, and copper ore only in 1957. However, world demand for all of these commodities seems to have weakened, at least temporarily, around 1956–57, since production was marked by a decline in either 1957 or 1958. In the meantime, however, the dollar value of Canadian exports of these seven commodities almost doubled between 1949 and 1955 and, as a proportion of total domestic exports (including gold), it rose from some 29 per cent in 1949 to over 38 per cent in 1955.

But the slackening of world demand occasioned declines in Canadian production. Output of newsprint, wood pulp, iron ore, and lead ore fell in both 1957 and 1958, aluminum production dropped in 1957 and the output of copper and nickel declined in 1958. Production of all these commodities, except aluminum and copper, generally remained below the 1956 or 1957 peak until 1960. As a result the share of the seven commodities in the exports of 1960 was slightly below the 1955 proportion.[51]

Prices in the early part of the 1949–56 period increased sharply as a result of the Korean conflict. The consumer price index jumped from 102.9 in 1950 to 113.7 in 1951 and further to 116.5 in 1952. It remained relatively stable until 1956 when it showed a slight further increase of 1.7 points (see Table 1.11). The wholesale price index also increased sharply in 1951 (from 211.2 in 1950 to 240.1), but its course thereafter was one of steady decline until 1955, when it rose from 218.9 to become 225.6 in 1956. The general pattern is thus one of a significant increase following Korea, with its attendant scare-buying by households and rising aggregate demand generally, followed thereafter, at least until 1955, by relative price stability or actual declines.

These are some of the salient features of the period 1949–56. It may generally be regarded as one of rapid expansion despite the 1953–54

[51]See Table 4.2 for details of the export consist.

contraction.[52] But the weaknesses of the boom are fairly obvious. In the first place there appears to have been an excessive concentration of investment in the resource area, as became apparent when world demand slackened. Total gross business investment in all sectors reached a record high of 23 per cent of GNE in 1957, a rate that could not be sustained without a large rise in aggregate demand. The brief reappearance of inflationary pressures between June 1950 and December 1951, however, induced the monetary authorities to become mildly restrictive. Although the degree of restraint has varied during the 1950's, monetary policy was broadly one of attempting to curb actual or anticipated inflationary pressures. At the same time as monetary policy became restrictive the federal government budget changed from a deficit of $100 million (computed on a nation accounts basis) in 1954 to surpluses of $176 million in 1955 and a substantial surplus of $544 in 1956.

The combination therefore of tight money and budgetary restraint tended to curb aggregate demand at the very time when forces previously maintaining it were beginning to weaken. That this was a major policy blunder can scarcely be denied. As the Porter Commission concludes after a careful examination of post-war Canadian monetary fiscal and debt management policies: "the record shows that the major errors of the post-war period have arisen in large part because of a reluctance to use the general policy instruments appropriately or because hasty and haphazard expedients have been resorted to when well thought-out and carefully co-ordinated programs would have accomplished the task more satisfactorily."[53] Thus in 1956, the mistakes of policy were no longer hidden or offset by the other factors inducing economic expansion. The consequence of the conjunction of these depressive forces was naturally to slow down the growth rate. It is no accident therefore that GNE per head reached a level in 1956 which was not to be matched until 1962.[54]

[52]Details on the cyclical behaviour of the Canadian economy in the postwar world may be found in a report by William C. Hood, "The Demand for Labour" which appears as Appendix 1 of the *Proceedings of the Special Committee of the Senate on Manpower and Employment*, No. 2, Dec. 8, 1960 (Ottawa, 1960).

[53]*Report of the Royal Commission on Banking and Finance* (Ottawa, 1964), p. 536.

[54]There is, of course, much more to policy problems than indicated here, but the general consensus among economists is that both the fiscal and especially the monetary policies pursued by Canadian authorities during most of the 1950's, but particularly from 1957 on, were mistaken in the sense that at best they did little to offset undesirable trends and at worst probably aggravated them. For details of policy see R. Craig Ivor, *Canadian Monetary, Banking and Fiscal Development* (Toronto, 1958), chaps. IX and X. General comments on such policies may be found in T. N. Brewis and others, *Canadian Economic Policy* (Toronto, 1961), chaps. 7, 9, 10 and 13; Johnson, *Canadian Quandary*; H. G. Johnson, "Economic

4. THE SLOW-DOWN 1957–61

The forces generating the post-war boom and the expansion of the first half of the 1950's could not be sustained during the latter part of the decade. Year-to-year increases in real GNE were generally less than 2 per cent (except for 1958–59 when the increase was 3.5 per cent using 1957 dollars). This was not adequate to sustain the level of output per head achieved in 1956, since the population was increasing faster than 2 per cent (see Table 1.1). Rates of unemployment in the range of 6 per cent and higher came to typify what we have designated as the slowdown.

TABLE 1.18.

Changes in GNE and Components
1957-61
(percentages based on constant 1957 dollars)

GNE		+9.8
Personal consumption expenditures		+14.9
Business gross fixed capital formation		−16.5
New residential construction	−5.7	
New non-residential construction	−19.7	
New machinery and equipment	−18.5	
By industry		
Agriculture	32.7	
Forestry	4.2	
Mining, quarrying and oil wells	−25.9	
Manufacturing	−26.6	
Construction	−13.9	
Transportation and storage	−38.1	
Communications	8.0	
Electric power, gas and water utilities	−25.2	
Trade	−17.0	
Finance, insurance, and real estate	14.6	
Service	45.4	
Exports of goods and services		+15.8
Imports of goods and services		+3.8
Government purchases of goods and services		+14.4

SOURCE: DBS, *National Accounts Income and Expenditure, Fourth Quarter and Preliminary Annual 1962*, Table 18; *ibid., 1961*, Table 5; *ibid., 1962*, Table 25.

Real GNE (in constant 1957 dollars) increased from $31.9 billion in 1957 to only $35.0 in 1961, yielding an average rate of increase of only about 2.3 per cent compounded annually which compares with a 5.3 per cent annual rate of growth between 1950 and 1956. As shown in Table 1.18 three components of aggregate demand, namely, consumer

Nationalism in Canadian Policy," *Lloyds Bank Review*, Oct. 1964; and Paul Wonnacott, *The Canadian Dollar, 1948–1958* (Toronto, 1961).

spending, exports of goods and services, and government purchases of goods and services, all increased by 14 to 16 per cent between 1957 and 1961; this increase is somewhat in excess of the 10 per cent rise in real GNE but well below the increase in the earlier period. The striking factor is the sharp decline in business gross fixed capital formation. It is clear, as indicated by the almost 17 per cent drop in business investment, that this is the key component in any assessment of the declining level of income per head and must be examined in more detail.

As Table 1.18 indicates, the bulk of the decline was concentrated in new non-residential construction and in new machinery and equipment, both of which fell by 18 to 20 per cent between 1957 and 1961. In other words, the behaviour of business investment, normally the most volatile component of GNE, accounts for the slow pace of progress during this period. The incidence of the decline in investment by industry sheds further light upon its causes. As Table 1.18 shows, the largest decreases occurred in mining, quarrying and oil wells, manufacturing, transportation and storage and electric power, gas and water utilities. All other industrial categories registered slight declines or even rather large increases, especially in several of the tertiary industries. The decline in manufacturing investment was particularly large in both absolute and percentage terms. Aside from this, declines took place mainly in resource-oriented industries. In fact, however, some of the reduction in manufacturing investment was also directly related to exports. The OECD has estimated that, whereas in 1957 "resource and related development" accounted for over 35 per cent of business investment in Canada, by 1960 the share had fallen to less than 27 per cent of a greatly reduced total.[55] By 1961 business investment had declined even further.

Thus despite the almost 16 per cent rise in exports of goods and services, there was no further stimulus to investment in the area of export-oriented and related industries. Likewise for domestic industries, the inducement to invest diminished sharply.

The roots of the slowdown are thus to be found partly in the excesses and imbalances generated in the earlier period which were aggravated by three specific factors: (1) The world demand for primary commodities which underlay much of the previous dynamism tapered off abruptly in 1957 and 1958 partly because of a recession in the US and a somewhat changed attitude to stock-piling. (2) The emergence of European and Japanese competition, especially in manufactured goods, not only caused difficulties for Canadian manufactured exports but reduced the incentive to invest in this sector domestically. (3) After 1955 monetary and fiscal

[55]Computed from OECD, *Canada* (Paris, November 1962), Table 2, p. 9.

policy on balance tended to restrict or at least not vigorously encourage aggregate demand.[56] In other words, while a decline in the GNE growth rate would naturally be expected in or around 1956 or 1957 for reasons already noted (see pp. 0000), the continuation of sluggish growth in Canada until 1961 must be attributed to the persistence of these three factors in the face of the rapid expansion of capacity earlier.

It is difficult to overestimate the importance of external conditions. As already suggested in the previous section, a large part of the residential construction, as well as social and business capital investment in the 1950-56 period, was made in response to the rising world demand for primary products. When this tapered off at the same time as the manufacturing industries in Canada faced intensified competition from a revived Europe and Japan, the investment basis for the previous boom fell sharply. The persistent sluggishness of the US economy, with which the Canadian economy is so closely related, provided a further depressing influence.[57] Nor did government or household spending pick up the slack in investment and exports. Thus output per head declined. The period of slack was undoubtedly protracted by a series of events leading to increased uncertainty as far as private capital formation was concerned. On the economic scene, Britain's policy with respect to the Common Market was a source of doubt and not a little worry, although this occurred later in the period. The potential loss of sales to the UK should she join the Common Market hung over the heads of policy-makers. On the political front, the Diefenbaker administration added to uncertainty by frequent assertions to the effect that 15 per cent of Canada's trade should be diverted from the US. Widespread publicity about the extent of Canadian assets under foreign (chiefly US) control tended to create a somewhat less appealing climate for capital flows. The effects of the changed political climate and the rising nationalistic spirit in Canada (which took a strongly negative, anti-American bent) are difficult to assess fully, but uncertainty about the specific techniques to effect a substantial "trade diversion" and greater Canadian participation in branch

[56]It is true that rather large federal government deficits occurred from 1958 through 1962 but for the most part the magnitudes if not the deficits themselves were essentially due to the failure of the economy to grow more rapidly and hence may be termed "passive deficits." At the same time a generally restrictive monetary policy typified the situation through the first half of 1961.

[57]The US difficulties especially in the realm of the balance of international payments still persists. Policies designed to arrest the US gold and dollar outflow have a serious potential impact on Canada in view of Canada's substantial reliance on foreign (mainly US) financing. See the following section for some details and further discussion in chap. 4.

plans of US firms did little to create a favourable atmosphere for invest-ment. Nor did the nationalization of electric power facilities in British Columbia and Quebec do much to stimulate private investment, although these actions should not be overstressed. In sum, domestic and inter-national uncertainties and other depressive, or at least not vigorously expansive, forces kept the Canadian economy hesitant and slow from 1957 to early 1961.

5. A NEW RESURGENCE

The 1957–61 period, then, was a disappointing one for Canada from the standpoint of growth and development in many respects. The increase in real output was only about 2 per cent a year, a rate insufficient to main-tain per capita real income at the level reached in 1956. Public and pri-vate capital expenditures in 1958, 1959 and 1960 were below the 1957 level both in absolute terms and as a per cent of GNE. Unemployment was at a high level throughout the period, and the performance of the Canadian economy was generally below what it had been in the 1949– 1956 period as already noted.

In 1961 the Canadian economy began a recovery that carried forward into 1965. It is not possible to answer the question of whether 1961–65 heralds a new and sustainable take-off point for the economy or whether a repetition of the experience of the 1950's is in sight. We are, however, inclined to the former view. While it is premature to argue that business cycles are a thing of the past, as some analysts are suggesting, it is obviously possible to do a better job of forecasting and remedying con-tractions in the level of economic activity than before.

The upturn which began after the first quarter of 1961 has yielded gains in real output on an annual basis through 1964 averaging over 5½ per cent. Nor does the pace appear to be faltering, in view of the increase in real output in 1964 of 6½ per cent over 1963. Although the expansion is continuing at the present writing (June, 1965), national accounts data are only available through the fourth quarter of 1964. Using this date, the increase in real GNE since the first quarter of 1961 has been almost 25 per cent. Related to this aggregate growth has been a fairly steady decline in the proportion of the labour force that is unemployed to less than 4.5 per cent during the last quarter of 1964[58]— the best showing in over seven years. Furthermore, the expansion has not been marked by sharply rising prices. Both the wholesale and con-sumer price indexes have increased at rates close to those experienced

[58]The rate during March, 1965, was down to 3.9 per cent.

during the 1953–63 decade which itself was notable for price stability. Nor has inventory accumulation been excessive. Thus, Canada is experiencing the longest sustained and most balanced expansion since Korea and one of the longest booms in peace-time history.

As would be expected, the leading sectors have been exports and business investment. From the first quarter of 1961 through the fourth quarter of 1964, these major components of GNE have risen by about 32 and 29 per cent, respectively—far more than any other component. Consumption expenditures rose by almost 21 per cent and government expenditures by only 9 per cent. The dynamic elements have thus been a rather spectacular revival of foreign demand for Canadian products and an investment boom. To be sure, there were specific factors initiating, supporting, and sustaining the growth in foreign demand. The wheat sales to China and the Soviet Union, devaluation of the Canadian dollar in mid-1962, and a resurgence of economic growth in the United States and the United Kingdom all contributed greatly to the increase in demand for Canadian exports. At the same time, devaluation prevented the sharp increase in imports that normally accompanies an economic boom in Canada. Indeed imports rose by barely 20 per cent between the first quarter of 1961 and the first quarter of 1964, well below the percentage increase in exports. The sharp decline in Canada's over-all deficit on current account during 1964 to less than third of the 1959 deficit is directly attributable to these factors. The exchange crisis of 1962, in short, did not seriously impair the continuation of economic growth.[59]

[59]The crisis itself was triggered by a sharp increase in the outflow of short-term capital which was not counterbalanced by the usual net inflow of long-term capital. As a result there was a serious reduction in official exchange holdings of $374 million during the first quarter of 1962 and a further reduction of $634 million during the second quarter which was in sharp contrast with the experience of previous years. As a result Canadian authorities devalued and pegged the Canadian dollar. Following the election in June of 1962 international financial assistance was received and emergency measures like those of late 1947 were instituted. That the crisis reflected short-term temporary influences is evident by the quick recovery. As Slater concludes the crisis was almost completely a crisis of confidence "complicated by the election campaign and the enormous difficulty of mobilizing Canada's international monetary arrangements effectively at the time." (David W. Slater, *Canada's Balance of International Payments—When is A Deficit a Problem?* (Montreal, Nov. 1964), p. 23.) Furthermore this lack of confidence was exacerbated by Canadian monetary and fiscal policy. It is difficult to avoid the conclusion that the vacillation of policy at this time and the acrimony of the election campaign were the main causes of what would otherwise have been a very mild, manageable and temporary decrease in official exchange holdings. As Slater puts it the crisis "in no way reflected Canada's real position in external trade or finance." (*Ibid.*, p. 24–5.)

The vital question is whether the present momentum can be sustained or whether the favourable conjunction of circumstances is a once-for-all stimulus that will soon be dissipated. The foundations of the boom arise primarily from a more realistic valuation of the Canadian dollar vis-à-vis other currencies, the agricultural difficulties of China and the Soviet Union, the resurgence of the UK and, more important, the US. Since the Canadian government has returned to a fixed exchange rate below the level prevailing in mid-1962, it seems unlikely that this will be changed again in the near future. The wheat sales to China and the Soviet Union, as well as other East European countries, which began in 1961, may be expected to continue since there is little prospect of an immediate improvement in the Soviet or Chinese agricultural situation. Finally, the tax cut in the United States during the first quarter of 1964 has served to sustain and accelerate the rise in the tempo of US economic activity already begun. Britain may experience some slowing down in the rate of expansion shown during 1962 and 1963, but, for the US and UK together, growth may be expected to proceed and thus provide a continuing stimulus to the Canadian economy. In short, with the momentum already begun and the broad base of the expansion in Canada, the situation appears to be closely analogous to the early 1950's, without the excesses of that period. The present expansion may therefore be expected to continue well into 1965 and, assuming that domestic policy will be rather more enlightened than it was during the mid and late 1950's, there is every reason to believe that the Canadian economy will achieve as high a growth rate through 1970 and 1975 as during any other non-war period, or perhaps even higher. Details of our projections and the assumptions underlying them are contained in Part Three. As this juncture is it sufficient to note that a new take-off has apparently begun which will hopefully be sustained.

2

POPULATION PATTERNS

Canada's population has always exhibited relatively rapid growth over long periods of time. At the middle of the nineteenth century, the colonies of British North America had a population of 2.5 million; at its end, the people of Canada numbered 5.3 million. Thus, within a half-century, Canada more than doubled her population—an annual average compound rate of growth of 1.58 per cent. This rate was, however, exceeded by the 2.04 per cent growth rate between 1901 and 1961. At the latter year Canada's population amounted to 18.2 million. The estimated population of Canada in January 1965 was 19.4 million.

Such growth rates have generally been among the highest of the developed countries in the Western world. But like the trends in total production, population growth has been uneven. Indeed, there is a kind of rough relationship between the state of the economy and population trends. Prosperous conditions in Canada tend to raise marriage and birth rates and at the same time attract more immigrants and discourage emigration. As a result both natural rates of population growth and net immigration are stimulated during periods of sustained economic growth and prosperity; conversely during periods of relative economic stagnation or depression. This relationship between economic and demographic factors is, however, far from precise. Indeed, it is no simple task to isolate cause and effect since an increase in population may be at the same time a stimulus to growth *via* an increase in demand and a source of growth through a rise in the labour force. In addition, if we examine birth, death, and marriage rates, the relationship of each to economic factors is beset with lags of varying length and distorted by numerous non-economic factors as well. A decline in the birth rate may be associated with high levels of economic activity as well as low. For example, birth rates declined steadily during the prosperous late 1920's and continued the downward trend through the depressed 1930's until the revival after 1937. Death rates have declined steadily and are obviously more closely related to improvements in health standards which themselves are related to economic factors in a very loose fashion at best. Marriage rates *over short periods* do not correlate closely with economic conditions nor does average family size. Immigration is affected by domestic policy and economic and political conditions in other countries and is subject to important lags of varying duration. Thus, during the Second World War, despite economic prosperity, both immigration and emigration were extremely low and during the depression of the thirties, for example, net immigration was negative.

Nevertheless, it is generally true that sustained rates of economic and population growth are associated in Canada. In the sections to follow, this will be illustrated. However, it must not be presumed that the interrelationship is simple or necessarily stable. Population growth is in fact subject to a large number of non-economic factors; hence whatever impact economic conditions have on births, deaths, and net migration operates through channels that are mostly indirect and more or less remote.

POPULATION GROWTH BY DECADES, 1901–61

The over-all trend in population growth and the variations by decade are set forth in Table 2.1 for the present century. The Canadian population almost doubled during the first thirty years of this century as compared with the sixty-year period required for doubling the world's population. From 1931 to 1961, Canada's population increased from 10.4 million to 18.2 million, or about 76.0 per cent.[1]

In the first decade of this century, the intercensal growth of population amounted to 1,836,000, an increase of 34.2 per cent. This rate has not been exceeded by any other decennial period up to 1961. This early rapid growth was due mainly to the development of the West which was accompanied by unusually heavy immigration. The number of new settlers in Canada between 1901 and 1911 amounted to 1.8 million. At the same time, however, the number of emigrants was slightly in excess of one million. Nevertheless, migration accounted for almost two-fifths of the increase of population during this decade.

---

[1]A small part of this increase was due to the Newfoundland's entry into the Confederation in 1949. Newfoundland at that time had a population of 345,000.

TABLE 2.1

Growth of Population in Canada,
1901–61
(000's)

| | Population at beginning of period, June 1 | Natural increase* | | Immigration | Emigration |
		Number	Per cent		
1901–11	5371	1120	61.0	1759	1043
1911–21	7207	1350	85.4	1612	1381
1921–31	8788	1360	85.6	1203	974
1931–41	10,377	1222	108.1	150	242
1941–51†	11,507	1972	92.1	548	379
1951‡–56	14,009	1473	71.1	783	184
1956–61	16,081	1675	77.6	760	278
1961	18,238				

SOURCE: 1901–51 data based on Wm. C. Hood and Anthony Scott, *Output, Labour and Capital in the Canadian Economy*, Table 4.1, p. 156.
1951–61 data DBS Census Division, Population Section.
NOTES: *Natural increase equals births minus deaths.
　　　†Not including Newfoundland in both years. Including Newfoundland in 1951 but not in 1941, the increase amounted to 2,502,000 or 21.8 per cent.
　　　‡Including Newfoundland.

Population growth slowed down in the next decade, 1911–21, not only in percentage, but in absolute, terms as well. Immigration, though still very high prior to 1914, fell off substantially during the First World War (in which Canadian casualties amounted to about 60,000). Emigration reached an all-time record level of 1.4 million in this decade. Consequently, despite heavy immigration of 1.6 million and an estimated natural increase of about 1.4 million, the population of Canada in 1921 had increased by only 22.0 per cent over the 1911 figure, about one third less than during the previous decade.

The 1920's saw another increase of 1.6 million, or 18.1 per cent. The total increase in population between 1921 and 1931 exceeded the natural increase by only 230,000, for, although immigration still remained at a relatively high level of 1.2 million, almost one million Canadian residents left the country in that decade.

The 1930's, characterized by the Great Depression, experienced the lowest growth in population since Confederation. The increase of barely over one million people between 1931 and 1941 represented a mere 11 per cent gain over the 1931 figure. Depressed economic conditions contributed to a further reduction of the birth rate to slightly over 20 per

TABLE 2.1 (*continued*)

Net immigration			Intercensal growth		
Number	Per cent	Population at end of period, June 1	Number	Per cent change	Average annual rate of growth
716	39.0	7207	1836	34.2	3.0
231	14.6	8788	1581	21.9	2.0
229	14.4	10,377	1589	18.1	1.7
−92	−8.1	11,507	1130	10.9	1.0
169	7.9	13,648	2141	18.6	1.7
599	28.9	16,081	2072	14.8	2.8
482	22.4	18,238	2157	13.4	2.6

1,000 population as compared with the rate of 27.4 in the 1921–25 period and 24.1 in the years 1926–30. Immigration fell off to 150,000, the lowest inter-censal total during this century, while emigration amounted to about one-quarter million.

The upward trend in population growth was, however, resumed in the next decade, 1941–51. Excluding Newfoundland, population increased over this decade by over two million or 18.6 per cent. Including the latter province, population grew by 22.0 per cent to just over 14.0 million. An even faster rate of population growth occurred during the second part of the decade because of increases in both the volume of immigration and the rate of natural increase during the early post-war years. During the first half of the period, immigration amounted to only 84,000,[2] while between June 1, 1946, and June 1, 1951, about 460,000 immigrants entered Canada. These immigrants included a substantial number of Canadian soldiers' war-brides and also "displaced persons" from war-devastated Europe. About 380,000 residents of Canada left the country during this decade. Natural increase was also high, particularly during the second half of the decade as the number of marriages increased following the termination of hostilities. About 61 per cent of the natural increase of almost 2 million took place in the second half of the decade.[3]

[2]DBS, *1961 Census of Canada, General Review*, Bulletin 7.1–1, p. 1–4.
[3]*Ibid.*, p. 1–4. These figures are exclusive of the natural increase in Newfoundland.

During the most recent decennial period, 1951–61, Canada's population increased more rapidly. Indeed, the total growth of over 30 per cent constituted the most rapid intercensal rate of growth since the first decade of the twentieth century. In the first half of the 1950's population rose by 14.8 per cent or at 2.8 per cent average annual rate of growth, while in the second half the rate of increase fell to 2.6 per cent per year.

During the years 1949–56, Canada experienced a rapid rate of economic expansion, as noted in Chapter 1. The concurrent gains in population from both natural increase and net immigration were very large. The number of marriages remained high, despite a relatively low number of native-born young people reaching marriageable age in the early 1950's —a result of the diminished birth rates of the 1930's. It is very likely that the inflow of young immigrants, within the age range of 20–35 years, helped to maintain high rates of marriages and births. During the first half of the last decade about 780,000 immigrants entered this country and with a diminished flow of young Canadians emigrating, net immigration contributed about 29 per cent of the increase in population between 1951–56. This percentage was somewhat lower (22.4) during the second part of the decade, partly because of higher emigration occasioned by the economic slowdown. But, over the whole period, 1951–61, the contribution of net immigration was larger than in any other decennial period except the first decade of this century. A high proportion of post-war immigrants appears to have remained in the country partly because of the United States immigration quota regulations restricting the entry of non-Canadians to that country.

The relatively small differences between the over-all rates of increase in 1951–56 and the following five years conceal, however, a slowdown in the rate of population growth especially in the years after 1960. The lower rate of economic growth between 1957 and 1961 appears to have adversely affected the birth rate, reduced the annual inflow of immigrants, and increased emigration. Net immigration has, temporarily at least, ceased to contribute substantially to Canada's population growth.

NATURAL GROWTH

NATURAL INCREASE

The rate of natural increase is the difference between the crude birth rate and the crude death rate per year. In general, in societies where mortality has been brought under control by improved medical care and public health services, it is changes in the birth rate rather than in the death rate that are primarily responsible for fluctuations in the rate of natural increase. For the last few decades the Canadian rate of natural increase has exceeded that of other countries whose economic structure and development are roughly comparable. In general, the long-term rate of natural increase in Canada's population has remained relatively stable because the decline in the death rate, particularly in recent decades, has been matched by some decline in the birth rate since its peak in the years immediately following the Second World War.

BIRTHS

The standard measure of births is the crude birth rate, that is, the number of live births per 1,000 of population per year. However, since crude birth rates are based on *total* population, they do not reflect the fertility or proportion of women in the reproductive age group. Indeed the crude birth rate is also affected by the average age at marriage, the proportion of women who are married to total number of women, and the general economic conditions of a country. Nevertheless, it is a useful and widely used measure of one aspect of demographic change. We have therefore brought together data on the crude birth rate, as well as crude death and marriage rates, in Table 2.2 and will comment briefly on the broad trends indicated.

The Canadian birth rate by this measure, using five-year averages, exhibits rather prolonged cyclical movements. It declined steadily from

TABLE 2.2

Crude Birth, Death, Marriage and Natural Increase Rates,*
by Five-Year Periods
†1921-60

Period‡	Crude birth rate	Crude death rate	Crude marriage rate	Natural increase rate
1921-25	27.4	11.2	7.3	16.2
1926-30	24.1	11.1	7.3	13.0
1931-35	21.6	9.8	6.5	11.7
1936-40	20.7	9.9	8.7	10.8
1941-45	23.7	9.8	9.7	13.9
1946-50	27.6	9.3	9.8	18.3
1951-55	28.0	8.5	8.7	19.5
1956-60	27.5	8.0	7.8	19.5

SOURCE: 1921-30 data, *Canada Year Book, 1956*, p. 201. 1931-60 data, *1961 Census of Canada, General Review*, Bulletin 7.1-1, Table II, p. 1-5.
*Per 1,000 population.
†Not including Yukon and Northwest Territories.
‡1921-30 data exclude Newfoundland.

27.4 per 1,000 of population in 1921–25 to a depression low of about 21. Thereafter it rose steadily until the end of the post-war "baby boom" in 1955, reaching a high of 28. Since then the crude birth rate has declined once more. Indeed for 1961 and 1962, the rate was down to 26.1 and 25.3 respectively.

There is a rough relationship, as indicated in Table 2.2, between the crude marriage (i.e., number of marriages per 1,000) and birth rates. The birth rate in one period generally changes in the same direction as the marriage rate in the previous period. In the post-war period as a whole, however, there was a decline in the crude marriage rate but the birth rate remained at high levels. The "baby boom" in fact came despite a smaller number of women within the age group of 20–29 years, itself a consequence of the low birth rate in the 1930's. It has been suggested that "Increases in the proportions of marriages, a decline in the average age at marriage, a reduction in the number of women remaining child-less, and a slight increase in the average size of completed families . . ."[4] were the major factors contributing to higher fertility and birth rates. In addition, the sustained period of prosperity until 1957 and various social welfare measures also created favourable conditions for higher birth rates. Fertility rates for women aged 15–24 years have increased almost 80 per cent since the mid 1930's, while the rate for women in the 25–29 age group has risen about 40 per cent.[5] Thus, the fertility rates among the most reproductive groups of Canadian women have significantly contributed to the baby boom.

DEATHS

General mortality, or crude death rate per 1,000 population, indicates mortality without regard to causes of death or changes in the age and sex composition of the population. This measure of mortality is, however, independent of the changes in the size of the population. The crude death rate is being used here because it generally reflects the more significant changes in mortality and can be used for comparisons with other countries where more refined measures such as the standardized death rate or the age-proportional death rate, are not readily available. The differences in the crude death rates between widely separated periods reflect not only better health but also the changed age and sex composition of the population.

The crude death rate in Canada, as in other similarly developed

[4]Dennis H. Wrong, "Trends in Class Fertility in Western Nations," *CJEPS*, May 1958, p. 226.
[5]See DBS, *Canada Year Book 1962*, p. 191, and *ibid., 1946*, p. 148.

countries, has been declining steadily during the last century but most of the improvement in mortality took place in the twentieth century. Table 2.2 shows that the five-year average crude death rate has declined from 11.2 per 1,000 population in 1921–25 to 8.0 in the 1956–60 period. This reduced mortality may be regarded as a rough measure of improved health and sanitation.

This improvement in the mortality rate has not been evenly distributed between males and females of the Canadian population. The crude death rate in 1960 stood at 9.1 per 1,000 male population and 6.6 for females as compared with the over-all rate of 7.8 in the same year. In fact, the difference between the mortality rates for males and females has been widening steadily in terms of the standardized rates.[6] In 1930 the standardized death rate for males was 13.5 and for females 12.4. The corresponding rates for 1940 were 11.8 and 10.2 respectively, while in 1950 the male rate was 10.1 and for females 8.1. By 1960, the standardized mortality rate for the male population stood at 9.3 and only 6.6 for females.[7]

Although infant mortality is about one-third of what it was in 1930, it is still very high as indicated in Table 2.3. Mortality then reaches its minimum during childhood, adolescence, and early adulthood. In general, the mortality rates for people under the age of 45 during the period 1930 to 1960 have been roughly halved. Death rates have, however, been falling only slightly for all male age groups of 45 and over but more significantly for all females of the same age range.

LIFE EXPECTANCY

The life span is a direct result of the prevailing mortality patterns. The average age at death reflects the length of life of those dying during the current year and roughly reflects health conditions existing at the time. The life expectancy at birth indicates what the life span would be for babies born today if the current mortality rate were to prevail throughout their lives.

The Canadian average age at death for males in 1960 was 59.5 and for females 62.7 years. The corresponding figures for 1930 were 42.2 and 43.5.[8] There is a slightly widening gap in average age at death as between sexes in favour of females. These figures are not, however, adjusted to the age structure of the population.

[6]This rate is adjusted so as to eliminate the effect of a changing sex composition of the population. In this case the adjustment was made as if the sex composition of the population remained throughout the same as it was in 1956.

[7]DBS, *Vital Statistics, 1960.*

[8]*Ibid.*

TABLE 2.3

Some International Comparisons of Population Growth
1941-61

Growth of population	Canada	US	France	Federal Republic Germany
(000's)				
1941	11,810	133,894	38,800	
1951	14,009	154,955	42,056	48,369
percentage increase	18.6	15.7	8.4	
growth rate per annum (41-51)	1.72	1.46	.81	
1961	18,238	183,650	45,960	54,214
percentage increase	30.2	18.5	9.3	12.1
growth rate per annum (51-61)	2.69	1.72	0.91	1.16
CRUDE RATES				
1941				
Birth	22.2	18.9	13.1	
Death	10.0	10.5	17.0	
Natural increase	12.2	8.4	−3.9	
1950-54				
Birth	27.8	24.5	19.5	16.1
Death	8.7	9.5	12.8	10.7
Natural increase	19.1	15.0	6.7	5.4
1960				
Birth	26.9	23.6	18.0	17.7
Death	7.8	9.5	11.4	11.4
Natural increase	19.1	14.1	6.6	6.3
INFANT MORTALITY RATES				
1941	59.7	45.3	73.5	
1950-54	37.0	28.1	46.2	49.3
1960	27.3	25.6	27.4	33.8

SOURCE: UN, *Demographic Year Books*.

The life expectancy at birth has steadily been increasing. In 1931, it was 60.0 years for males and 62.1 years for females, while in 1956 the corresponding figures were 67.6 and 72.9 years respectively.[9] This increase in life expectancy is due in part to decreased infant mortality, reduction in maternal mortality, and improved control over contagious and infectious diseases.

[9]*Ibid.*

TABLE 2.3 (*continued*)

Italy	Netherlands	Sweden	UK	Australia	New Zealand
44,202	8965	6389	48,216	7110	1629
46,996	10,264	7073	50,574	8422	1947
6.3	14.5	10.7	4.9	18.4	19.5
.60	1.37	1.02	.049	1.70	1.79
49,549	11,637	7520	52,925	10,508	2420
5.4	13.4	6.3	4.6	24.8	24.3
.53	1.28	.60	.46	2.24	2.19
20.9	20.3	15.6	14.4	18.9	22.8
13.9	10.0	11.3	13.7	10.6	9.8
7.0	10.3	4.3	.7	8.3	13.0
18.4	22.1	15.5	15.9	23.0	25.8
9.9	7.5	9.7	11.7	9.4	9.3
8.5	14.6	5.8	4.2	13.6	16.5
18.5	20.8	13.7	17.5	22.4	26.5
9.7	7.6	10.0	11.5	8.6	8.8
8.8	13.2	3.7	6.0	13.8	17.7
115.2	43.6	37.0	59.7	39.7	29.8
61.0	23.2	20.0	29.0	23.8	26.6
43.8	16.5	16.6	22.5	20.2	22.6

SOME INTERNATIONAL COMPARISONS

Table 2.3 compares the growth of Canadian population for the years 1941–61 with other Western countries. It shows clearly that Canada has been among the leading countries during the last two decades in terms of population growth. During this period only two other Commonwealth countries, Australia and New Zealand, showed comparable decennial percentage increases and average annual rates of population growth. This fact is to be explained by heavy post-war immigration to the two countries indicated. It is of interest to note, however, that the high rates of population growth of the United States and the Netherlands are principally due to high natural increase rather than net migration.

The table provides some vital statistics for selected countries and years during the last two decades. As may be seen in this table, the Canadian crude birth rate in 1960 was the highest among those listed and it was generally higher than those of the developed countries of Western Europe. On the other hand, the crude death rate in 1960, as well as during the two decades, 1941 to 1960, was among the lowest in the same group of countries. Consequently, the Canadian natural increase rate was one of the highest among these countries.

This favourable over-all Canadian crude death rate, however, hides the fact that the infant mortality rate, although greatly reduced as indicated earlier, is still higher than the rate prevailing in the United States, Czechoslovakia, Finland, Netherlands, Sweden, Switzerland, United Kingdom, Australia, and New Zealand. This suggests that as an increasing proportion of children are born in hospitals,[10] and as obstetrical and post-natal care improve, the Canadian infant mortality rate will be further reduced in the years to come. This in turn implies that, as long as the crude birth rate does not continue to decline, the high rates of natural population growth could rise even further in Canada since significant scope for reduction in infant mortality still exists.

AGE AND SEX DISTRIBUTION

The age composition of the population is significant because of its effects upon the demands made upon the economy and upon the supply of labour. In this way, population and economic growth are closely interrelated. The age distribution is also important for other types of analysis since the age factor influences marriage, birth and death rates as well as the needs for education, health, and other facilities.

Table 2.4 shows the age and sex distribution of the population of Canada at census dates from 1901 to 1961. The number of males has consistently exceeded the number of females at every census since 1901, particularly in 1911 when there were 113 men to every 100 women, because of a significant addition to the population during the preceding

[10]In 1960 about 95 per cent of live births in Canada were in hospitals, a significant improvement over the 79 per cent figure as late as 1951. However, there is substantial regional variation: the figure was only 85 per cent in Quebec, compared with about 99 per cent in most other provinces. (*Canada Year Book 1962*, Ottawa, 1962.)

decade by largely male immigration. Since then the proportion of men to women has steadily declined and in 1961 there were only 102 men for each 100 women. There is, however, significant variation as between rural and ruban areas. As of June 1961, there were 118 males to 100 females for the rural farm population sector as compared with 109 for rural non-farm and 98 for urban population.[11] These figures are representative of all provinces and territories and are a reflection of the female employment opportunities in urban centres. In addition, the excess of men does not occur at all age levels. As of June 1961, most of the excess was found within the age groups of 0–19 years, 25–34, and 45–59, but in other age groups there was a small surplus of women.

The pre-school age group, 0–4 years, accounted for 12.3 per cent of the total Canadian population in 1961 as compared with 9.1 per cent in 1941. The elementary school age group, 5–14 years old, constituted 21.6 per cent of the population in 1961 as compared with 18.7 per cent in 1941 and 18.1 per cent in 1951. A high post-war birth rate together with a low death rate among children added to the population under 15 years of age and raised the proportion of this group to the total population.

At the other end of the age scale, people 65 years and over accounted for 7.6 per cent of the population in 1961 as compared with 6.7 per cent in 1941 and 7.8 per cent in 1951. Thus as a result of the disproportionate increase in the young and the elderly people, there has been a rise in so-called "ratio of dependency" of the Canadian population. The dependents (age groups of 0–14 years and 65 and over) have increased their percentage share of total population from 34.5 in 1941 to 38.2 in 1951 and to 41.5 in 1961. The number of older people will tend to increase, but on the other hand the number of younger people (0–14), because of the post-war baby boom, will also steadily increase, and this factor should provide an important element on the demand side for sustained economic growth.

The main family formation age group, 20–29 years, has declined relatively from 17.4 per cent in 1941 to 15.9 in 1951, and to 13.1 in the last census year. This decline, of course, reflects the low birth rates of the 1930's and early 1940's. Thus, for example, in 1961 there were 127,000 marriages as compared with 133,000 in 1957. However, due to the baby boom, larger numbers of young people will reach marriageable age in the next few years.

The same trend is to be observed with respect to the labour force recruiting age group, 15–24 years, which has also declined from 18.7 per

[11]DBS, *1961 Census of Canada, Population, Sex Ratios*, Bulletin 1.2–1.

TABLE 2.4
Age and Sex Distribution of Population of Canada
1901-61

Age group	1901			1911		
	Male %	Female %	Total %	Male %	Female %	Total %
0-4	11.8	12.2	12.0	11.7	12.9	12.3
5-9	11.3	11.6	11.5	10.3	11.5	10.9
10-14	10.7	10.9	10.8	9.3	10.2	9.7
15-19	10.2	10.4	10.3	9.2	9.7	9.4
20-24	9.3	9.6	9.5	10.1	9.5	9.8
25-29	7.9	7.9	7.9	9.7	8.5	9.1
30-34	6.8	6.7	6.7	8.1	7.2	7.7
35-39	6.3	6.1	6.2	6.7	6.2	6.5
40-44	5.5	5.3	5.4	5.6	5.2	5.4
45-49	4.6	4.3	4.4	4.7	4.5	4.6
50-54	3.9	3.7	3.8	4.0	3.9	4.0
55-59	3.0	3.0	3.0	3.0	3.0	3.0
60-64	2.6	2.6	2.6	2.5	2.5	2.5
65-69	2.0	2.0	2.0	1.8	1.9	1.8
70-74	1.4	1.4	1.4	1.2	1.4	1.3
75 and over	1.6	1.6	1.6	1.4	1.6	1.5
not stated	1.1	0.7	0.9	0.7	0.3	0.5
Total number	2751.7	2619.6	5371.3	3822.0	3384.6	7206.6
Male and female as percentage of total	51.2	48.8		53.0	47.0	

Age group	1941			1951*		
	Male %	Female %	Total %	Male %	Female %	Total %
0-4	9.0	9.2	9.1	12.4	12.2	12.3
5-9	9.0	9.2	9.1	10.1	9.9	10.0
10-14	9.4	9.7	9.6	8.1	8.0	8.1
15-19	9.6	9.9	9.7	7.5	7.6	7.6
20-24	8.8	9.2	9.0	7.6	8.0	7.8
25-29	8.3	8.5	8.4	7.8	8.4	8.1
30-34	7.3	7.4	7.3	7.2	7.7	7.4
35-39	6.7	6.5	6.6	7.1	7.2	7.1
40-44	5.9	5.8	5.9	6.3	6.1	6.2
45-49	5.6	5.4	5.5	5.5	5.2	5.3
50-54	5.4	4.9	5.1	4.8	4.7	4.7
55-59	4.7	4.2	4.5	4.1	4.0	4.1
60-64	3.7	3.4	3.5	3.7	3.5	3.6
65-69	2.7	2.6	2.7	3.2	3.0	3.1
70-74	1.9	1.9	1.9	2.3	2.3	2.3
75 and over not stated	2.0	2.2	2.1	2.3	2.5	2.4
Total number	5900.5	5606.2	11506.7	7088.9	6920.6	14,009.5
Male and female as percentage of total	51.3	48.7		50.6	49.4	

SOURCE: *Census of Canada.*
*Newfoundland included since 1951.

	1921			1931	
Male %	Female %	Total %	Male %	Female %	Total %
11.8	12.3	12.0	10.1	10.6	10.4
11.7	12.2	11.9	10.7	11.2	10.9
10.2	10.6	10.4	10.1	10.6	10.3
8.9	9.4	9.2	9.8	10.3	10.0
7.7	8.4	8.1	8.6	8.9	8.8
7.7	8.0	7.8	7.6	7.5	7.6
7.6	7.3	7.4	6.8	6.8	6.8
7.6	6.8	7.2	6.7	6.6	6.6
6.3	5.6	6.0	6.5	6.0	6.2
5.2	4.7	5.0	6.0	5.3	5.6
4.3	3.9	4.1	5.0	4.4	4.7
3.3	3.1	3.2	3.7	3.4	3.5
2.8	2.7	2.7	2.8	2.8	2.8
2.0	1.9	2.0	2.2	2.2	2.2
1.3	1.3	1.3	1.6	1.7	1.7
1.4	1.6	1.5	1.6	1.7	1.7
0.2	0.2	0.2	0.2	0.0	0.2
4529.6	4258.3	8787.9	5374.5	5002.2	10376.7
51.5	48.5		51.8	48.2	

1961					
Male		Female		Total	
Number (000's)	%	Number (000's)	%	Number (000's)	%
1154.1	12.5	1102.3	12.2	2256.4	12.3
1063.9	11.5	1015.7	11.3	2079.5	11.4
948.2	10.3	907.8	10.1	1856.0	10.2
729.0	7.9	703.5	7.8	1432.6	7.9
587.1	6.4	596.5	6.6	1183.6	6.5
613.9	6.7	595.4	6.6	1209.3	6.6
644.4	7.0	627.4	7.0	1271.8	7.0
631.1	6.8	639.8	7.1	1270.9	7.0
560.0	6.0	559.0	6.2	1119.0	6.1
515.5	5.6	499.8	5.5	1015.3	5.6
442.9	4.8	420.3	4.7	863.2	4.7
362.1	3.9	343.7	3.8	705.8	3.9
292.6	3.2	291.1	3.2	583.6	3.2
239.7	2.6	247.4	2.7	487.1	2.6
196.1	1.4	206.1	1.6	402.2	1.5
238.3	3.4	263.5	3.6	501.9	3.5
9218.9	100.0	9019.3	100.0	18,238.2	100.0
	50.6		49.4		

cent in 1941 to 15.4 per cent in 1951 and again to 14.4 in 1961. However, the age group of 15–19 years old is increasing and Canada is already experiencing a difficult problem in providing jobs for the rising number of new entrants into the labour force, especially in the face of the economic slowdown of the late 1950's.

The portion of the population 15–64 years old represents the age group from which the potential labour force is normally drawn. This decreased from 65.5 per cent in 1941 to 61.9 per cent in 1951 and to 58.5 in 1961 as a consequence of the low birth rates of the 'thirties. This is the age group which must provide for the economic needs of the whole population. It is certain that, without the large post-war immigration, the proportion of this labour force potential would have been much lower.

Such are the salient facts with respect to the proximate determinants of *natural* rates of population growth. But as indicated earlier, immigration has played a major though varying role in determining demographic patterns in Canada as well as representing an important cultural influence. This is the subject of the following section.

THE POST-WAR IMPACT OF IMMIGRATION

It has recently been argued that post-war immigration ". . . helped to raise the level of national production, to increase capital investment, and to expand the volume of international trade."[12] The other main economic arguments for immigration, which have to do with potential advantages of a larger population, include spreading the burden of social capital, increasing the supply of labour and its mobility, and providing larger domestic markets. The bulk of the post-war immigration was concentrated in the tax-paying category and this should help to reduce the individuals' tax burden as the high overhead costs incurred in maintaining the Canadian standard of living are spread over a wider base. This immigration has been to a considerable extent family immigration, and thus those joining the labour force were accompanied by an almost equal number of wives, children, and other dependents. The post-war immigration, roughly, provided ten consumers of goods and services for about every six who entered the labour market. Moreover, these immigrants were comparatively young as a group and thus contributed to the high Canadian marriage and birth rates that prevailed until recently. Many

[12]J. W. Pickersgill, "Million and a Quarter Immigrants to Canada in Past Decade," *Monetary Times*, Annual National Review, 1957, p. 73.

immigrants brought with them capital assets and settlers' effects. Some established themselves in small businesses and industries introducing new and improved production processes.

But immigration has more than quantitative and economic significance. The Canadian culture and way of life, however defined, have been greatly enriched by the diverse traditions, points of view, habits, and tastes, of the immigrants, who largely came from Europe, without however changing Canada's bilingual character. There are, for example, over 150 newspapers and periodicals in Canada that are printed in languages other than English or French. There are also many cultural and educational organizations of various ethnic groups.

There has, however, long been a view of immigration known as the "displacement theory." This notion, accepted until recently, implied that employment opportunities in Canada could at best grow at a slightly higher rate than the natural rate of population increase. Consequently, according to this view, the operating principles of immigration policy, not being adjusted to the absorptive capacity of the Canadian economy, permitted too large a flow of immigrants. This created unemployment and drove out of Canada a corresponding number of emigrants, who went mainly to the US which has served as a safety valve for any "excess" population. The people from the Maritimes tended to settle in New England, while the French Canadians settled south of Quebec and emigrants from Ontario concentrated in New York State and Michigan. Emigrants from Western Canada moved into Minnesota, North Dakota, Washington, and Oregon. There are also large numbers of Canadian emigrants in California and Florida.

However, the Royal Commission on Canada's Economic Prospects rejected the displacement theory on the grounds that immigration into and emigration from Canada are not causally related to each other and that in any case some Canadian residents would always be leaving this country, which increases the need for immigrants here. The Commission concluded that it should not be assumed that ". . . the Canadian economy has a fixed and ascertainable absorptive capacity at any one time and that if the flow of immigrants exceeds that amount, other Canadian residents will be forced out in consequence."[13] Other studies have indicated that the pattern of Canadian settlement in the United States does not accord with the displacement theory,[14] that the long process of the settlement and economic development of the North American continent

[13]RCCEP, *Final Report* (Ottawa, 1957), p. 116.
[14]Richard E. Caves and Richard H. Holton, *The Canadian Economy: Prospect and Retrospect* (Cambridge, Mass., 1959), p. 53.

must be considered as a whole, and that population movements therefore into and within the areas of this continent are integral aspects of the distribution process, geographically and occupationally, of the population as a whole.[15]

POST-WAR IMMIGRATION POLICY[16]

The regulation of immigration policy has been left to the federal government. Prior to the Second World War, immigration policy set up a screening process which permitted the government to tighten or relax the requirements, according to particular circumstances in Canada. It also imposed a test of individual suitability in physical and mental health, character, literacy, means of support, and so on, as do immigration regulations in most other countries. However, it specifically limited immigration from Asiatic and African countries and gave preference to immigrants from other countries, especially those of Northwestern Europe and the United States, and for certain occupational groups. These general features have been retained through the present.

The general principles of post-war immigration policy were announced by the then prime minister, Mackenzie King, in a debate of the House of Commons on May 1, 1947. He stressed the need for a larger population through immigration but argued that the government should seek to ensure careful selection and permanent settlement of such numbers of immigrants as can advantageously be absorbed in the national economy. He indicated the importance of relating the flow of immigrants to absorptive capacity that varies from year to year in response to economic conditions. As to the sources of immigration, he stated that no alien has any basic right to enter Canada and that "the people of Canada do not wish, as a result of mass immigration, to make any fundamental alteration in the character of our population. Large-scale immigration from the Orient would change the fundamental composition of the Canadian population" and "would, moreover, be certain to give rise to social and economic problems of a character that might lead to serious difficulties in the field of international relations." In short, there would be no "open door" policy as far as Canada was concerned. Indeed, even certain Commonwealth countries with whom Canada has special relationships are limited

[15]Brinley Thomas, *Migration and Economic Growth* (Cambridge, 1954), pp. 134–8.

[16]Details of Canadian immigration policy, practice and results have been neatly summarized in DBS, *Canada Year Book 1957–58*, pp. 154–76, and *ibid.*, *1959*, pp. 175–8 for both the pre- and post-war periods. A more thorough survey and analysis can be found in D. C. Corbett, *Canada's Immigration Policy: A Critique* (Toronto, 1957).

to a small handful of immigrants each year, despite the general absence of a quota system. For example, immigrants from India, Pakistan, and Ceylon cannot exceed 300, 100, and 50 persons respectively per year. At the other extreme is the regulation that permits entry conditioned only upon the possession of sufficient means to tide the immigrant over until employment is found as far as British (defined to exclude Asiatic or African Commonwealth nations or dependencies except the Union of South Africa), French, or US subjects are concerned. In general there exists a hierarchy of admissibility which has the effect of determining the pattern of actual immigration on the basis of nationality with white Anglo-Saxons or French citizens ranking first and Asiatics and Africans ranking last with people from the Middle East somewhere between. The absence of a detailed quota system by nationality, in short, does not preclude a *de facto* selection procedure having the same effect.

The selective principle also applies with respect to the occupational background of potential immigrants. Also admissable are wives, single children under 21 years, fathers of 65 and mothers of 60 of legal residents in Canada, who are in a position to receive and look after such dependents.

Over the years, the Immigration Act has been changed to modify specific references to the underlying pattern of racial preference. But the general policy remains one of relative degrees of preference according to the hierarchy indicated above. The way in which such a preference scheme manifests itself can be subtle and not obviously based on racial or national origins. For example, active recruiting of immigrants is concentrated in the United States and Northwestern Europe, the United Kingdom in particular, whereas consular officials in, say, India seldom recruit and frequently discourage potential immigrants in a variety of ways. Furthermore, there are relatively more offices in Europe than in Asia or Africa.[17]

But in saying all this, we do not wish to suggest that immigration policy is necessarily unrealistic. The Canadian people are no less, or no more, subject to prejudice than others and any large-scale migration to Canada of people whose cultural and racial characteristics are substantially different from the Canadian would, in fact, create difficulties of assimilation or integration. However much this attitude may be lamented, it would be foolish to deny its existence. What may be criticized is a failure to take some lead in breaking down the barriers of prejudice and thereby, in effect, acquiescing in them. It is not too much to say that the ranking of nations in terms of acceptability to Canadians in general,

[17]See Corbett, *Canada's Immigration Policy*, p. 58.

whether explicitly or implicitly, merely supports the kind of prejudice that has long been felt unworthy. It is not unrealistic in the sense indicated above, but at the same time it is clearly nothing to be proud of. To be sure, Canadian policy regarding refugees may have been *relatively* generous. For example, the Department of Citizenship and Immigration states that between 1945 and 1964, Canada admitted over 300,000 refugees while during the Hungarian crisis Canada accepted about 38,000, "more proportionately to population than any other country in the world. Canada was also the first overseas country to accept handicapped tubercular refugees from Europe."[18]

But even if these actions may be construed as generous, they are really exceptions to the general rule and have been carried out under the glaring spotlight of world opinion and the periodic waves of intense compassion for unfortunate victims of aggression and persecution. If the humanitarian spirit underlying such actions could become the rule rather than the exception, Canadians could be proud of their immigration policy. Indeed, if Canada would adopt and enforce a policy along the lines that the desired attitude to immigration is not where a person comes from but what are his personal qualities and needs, this would reduce the racist implications of present policy. This can, of course, easily be thwarted in administration since much depends upon the estimation of

[18]Immigration Branch, Department of Citizenship and Immigration, "Canadian Immigration Policy," Ottawa, September, 1964, p. 2, (mimeo). A less charitable assessment has been given as follows: "The degree of generosity which Canada has shown in her international relations is reflected in the admission of refugees. In 1949, the peak year of overseas resettlement of refugees by the International Refugee Organization, the United States accepted almost five times as many refugees as Canada; Australia more than three times as many; and Israel twice as many. In 1950, Canada took even fewer refugees than the previous year; however, in 1951 our total increased significantly to thirty thousand, one-third of the American total. From 1952 onward, refugee resettlement administration has been under the United Nations High Commissioner for Refugees, replacing the IRO. From 1952 to the middle of 1954, Canada's reception of refugees was second only to the United States, and amounted to eleven thousand, nearly half the American total. All told, we have accepted about one hundred thousand refugees. However, they have been carefully selected, and most of them would have satisfied our standards if they had been applying as immigrants. The IRO did not keep a record of the numbers of so-called "difficult cases" which the receiving countries accepted. The "difficult cases" were people who for various reasons including ill health and age would not normally be acceptable by immigration countries. On the other hand, records were kept of the number of refugees requiring permanent care in institutions whom the receiving countries accepted. Of the nearly ten thousand such cases resettled, Canada accepted so few that she was not even listed among the countries which received two hundred cases or more, in a report issued by the Office of the United Nations High Commissioner for Refugees." Corbett, *Canada's Immigration Policy*, pp. 198–9.

the particular immigration officer.[19] But a clear intent to move in this direction can prevent the more blatant forms of ethnic discrimination.

The legal procedure applied to immigrants seeking Canadian citizenship is as follows: They must file with the clerk of court in the judicial district in which they live, a declaration of intention to become a Canadian citizen. They must be able to speak either English or French and indicate an understanding of the responsibilities and privileges of Canadian citizenship. There are no prescribed examinations for this purpose. Before they can obtain from the court the Certificate of Citizenship, they must reside in Canada for five years. Language classes are organized for the immigrants and government authorities and voluntary agencies assist them in establishing themselves in Canadian society.

In general, in the post-war period, the emphasis has been on "integration" rather than "assimilation." The latter aimed at the complete absorption of the immigrants, culturally and socially, in order to create a more homogeneous society. Integration, on the other hand, ". . . recognizes and respects the cultural contributions that may be made by people of diverse ethnic backgrounds who, nevertheless, are devoted to the welfare of the same country."[20]

Although Canadian immigration policy may be considered as generally restrictive and highly selective, the government does assist and encourage "desirable" immigrants. Since 1951, the Canadian government has advanced loans, under the Assisted Passage Loan Scheme, to certain immigrants to help cover the cost of their transportation to Canada. Immigrants receiving such assistance are required to agree to work for a Canadian employer and remain in the same type of employment until the amount advanced has been repaid. Between February 1, 1951 and the end of 1962, the sum advanced under this scheme amounted to $22.0 million, of which $19.7 million has been repaid. The number of immigrants admitted to Canada, under this scheme, was 130,537 or 7.6 per cent of the total immigrants admitted during this period. Many Canadian firms have extended similar assistance to immigrants, particularly to those possessing the skills that they needed.

In view of these policies, we would expect to see some relationship between the numbers of immigrants and economic conditions in Canada. Furthermore, application of the general policies determines the ethnic composition of the migrants independently of their numbers. Some of the details are examined in the following sections.

[19]*Ibid.*, pp. 77–89.
[20]DBS, *Canada Year Book 1959*, p. 177.

POST-WAR IMMIGRATION
It has been suggested that "The inflow of immigrants into Canada tends
to vary with the business cycle as a consequence, in part, of the fact that
over the course of the cycle, immigration regulations tend to be applied
with varying restrictiveness."[21] However, economic conditions, while in-
fluential, are not immediately effective because of a time-lag of six to
eighteen months involved in the immigration process connected with
selection, medical examination, documentation, etc., and the time required for an immigrant to decide to act following news of improved
economic opportunities. Consequently, immigration may be relatively low
in years of economic expansion and high in years of recession. A planned
immigration policy, adjusted to varying economic and employment conditions, is thus difficult to apply. It has been suggested therefore that
". . . the economic advantages of continued immigration are substantial
enough to justify an attempt to maintain a stable immigration policy even
through periods of mild recession in Canada."[22]

TABLE 2.5.

Immigrant Arrivals
1946-64
(000's)

Year	Arrivals	Year	Arrivals
1946	71.7	1955	109.9
1947	64.1	1956	164.9
1948	125.4	1957	282.2
1949	95.2	1958	124.9
1950	73.9	1959	106.9
1951	194.4	1960	104.1
1952	164.5	1961	71.7
1953	168.9	1962	74.6
1954	154.2	1963	93.1
		1964	102.6*

SOURCE: DBS, *Canada Year Book 1962*, to 1962.   The 1963
and 1964 figures are from DBS, *Canadian Statistical Review*,
Oct. 1964, p. 1.
*Yearly rate for first 6 months.

As Table 2.5 shows, there has been, in fact, wide variation over these
post-war years in the number of immigrants. Arrivals for the whole
period, 1946–62, amounted to over 2 million. Many of the persons who

[21]Mable F. Timlin, "Economic Theory and Immigration Policy," *CJEPS*, Aug.
1950, p. 378.
[22]RCCEP, *Final Report*, p. 120.

arrived in 1946 and 1947 were the wives and children of Canadian servicemen. By 1948, as more shipping facilities became available, the number of immigrants doubled. The latter included a high proportion of "displaced persons" from Eastern Europe as well as many Germans and Italians, who had been removed from the "enemy alien" category. As the immediate post-war period of rapid economic expansion ended, there was a decline in immigrant arrivals in 1949 and 1950. The Korean War in 1950 provided a new economic stimulus and during the next three years immigration remained high. As a result of the mild recession of 1953–54, the government decided to restrict the number of immigrants but, because of the inevitable time lag, the effects of this policy showed themselves only in 1955, when immigration fell to 110,000. By this time, however, the Canadian economy again was moving upwards and some shortages of labour became evident. Partly for this reason, immigration increased in 1956. The Hungarian uprising and the Suez crisis of 1956 account for the record level of post-war immigration in 1957. This high immigration occurring at a time when economic conditions in Canada began to deteriorate, aggravated the unemployment situation, which rose to levels around 7 per cent in 1958. With a somewhat lower rate of economic growth in Canada between 1957 and 1961 and improved economic and political conditions in Western Europe, there was a steady decline in immigrant arrivals until 1961; only in 1962, 1963, and 1964 was the downward trend halted.

The Royal Commission on Canada's Economic Prospects indicated that a substantial net inflow of immigrants would be needed until 1963 and 1964 and perhaps until 1970 to make up the possible shortage of native-born entrants into the labour force.[23] However, Canada may well experience some difficulty in obtaining the desired number of suitable immigrants from Western Europe because of improved economic and social conditions there. No large immigration from Eastern Europe can be expected in the foreseeable future. Besides, the current idea among some potential immigrants that the rate of expansion in this country may be slower in future and that high unemployment may persist will make Canada a less attractive place to come to. But, if the economy can continue the momentum of the years 1962 to 1964, Canada's net attractiveness will not be much further diminished, as the more recent figures suggest (see Table 2.5).

Migrants to Canada come almost entirely from Western Europe including the United Kingdom (see Table 2.6). During the period 1946–

[23]*Ibid.*, p. 116.

TABLE 2.6
Immigrants by Country of Former Residence
1946-62

Country of last permanent residence	Number (000's)		Percentage of total
United Kingdom		608.1	28.3
Republic of Ireland		21.4	1.0
Continental Europe		1,207.3	56.1
Austria	46.1		2.1
Belgium	33.0		1.5
Denmark	30.2		1.4
France	51.5		2.4
Germany	246.6		11.5
Greece	47.6		2.2
Hungary	50.3		2.3
Italy	287.6		13.4
Netherlands	150.7		7.0
Poland	93.8		4.4
Other European countries	169.9		7.9
United States		168.3	7.8
Other countries		146.4	6.8
Total		2,151.5	100.0

SOURCE: Department of Citizenship and Immigration, Statistics Section.

62, 29.3 per cent of the immigration flow came from the United Kingdom and Ireland; 56.1 per cent from Continental Europe; 7.8 per cent from the United States, and only 6.8 per cent from all other countries combined. Among the European countries, Italy, Germany, the Netherlands, and Poland were the main sources of immigrants to Canada. Immigrants from the United Kingdom were relatively numerous in the immediate post-war years and again in 1956 and 1957, after the Suez crisis. Immigrants from Italy steadily increased their share of the total number of immigrants to Canada and in more recent years even surpassed the number of British immigrants. The proportion from Continental Europe, after reaching a peak in 1959, gradually decreased, reflecting the improved economic conditions in Western Europe in the recent past. The relative share of immigrants from the United States has been increasing in the last few years.

The percentage distribution of the post-war immigrants by ethnic origin differs only slightly from that by country of last residence. The difference is due to wartime and post-war population movements in Europe, and in particular, to the movement of "displaced persons." Of the 2.2 million post-war immigrants, 25.8 per cent were of British origin;

13.9 per cent Italian; 12.2 per cent German (Austrians were included with Germans prior to 1953), and 7.3 per cent Dutch.

Sex and Age Distribution of Post-War Immigration. Table 2.7 indicates in terms of annual averages for five-year periods the numerical sex distribution and percentage age distribution of the post-war immigrants.

TABLE 2.7

Annual Average of Age and Sex Distribution of Immigrants
1946-62

Age Group	Males	Females
0-14	21.7	22.3
15-19	7.5	7.4
20-24	17.7	18.7
25-29	18.3	16.4
30-39	20.5	17.8
40-49	9.1	8.4
50-59		
60-64	5.2	8.7
65 and over		
Number of immigrants		
annual average	66,441	60,118

SOURCE: Department of Citizenship and Immigration, Statistics Section.

During the period 1946–50, female immigrants slightly exceeded male. This was mainly due to the arrival, in the early post-war years, of the war-time brides of Canadian soldiers. Between 1951 and 1960, males constituted more than half of the total immigrants, while in 1961 and 1962 there were again more female immigrants than males. Over the whole period, 1946–62, however, male immigrants accounted for about 53 per cent of all the immigrants to Canada.

The pre-school and elementary school age groups (0–14 years old) accounted for 21.7 and 22.3 per cent of total male and female immigration respectively during the 1946–62 period, as compared with corresponding figures of 34.3 and 33.6 per cent for the Canadian population in June, 1961. Thus immigration imposed a relatively weaker immediate demand upon school facilities and family allowances than the Canadian average. At the other end of the scale, immigrants 65 years and over during 1956–60 and 1961–62, accounted respectively for 1.0 and 2.6 per cent of the male and 2.2 and 3.8 per cent of the female immigrants. These percentages were lower than the corresponding 7.4 per cent for males and 7.9 per cent for females for the Canadian population at the 1961 census. Thus, the "ratio of dependency" or dependency burden (including age groups of 0–14 years and 65 years and over) of immigrants, was lower than that of the Canadian population as a whole in 1961.

The main family formation age group, 20–29 years old, of male and female immigrants during the years 1946–62, accounted for 36.0 and 35.1 per cent respectively. These percentages were much higher than the corresponding percentages of 13.1 and 13.2 for the Canadian population in 1961. Thus, immigration partially made up the indicated deficiency in this age group of the Canadian population and contributed to the high marriage and birth rates in Canada during the post-war period. Among the immigrants the labour force recruiting age group, 15–24 years, was also higher than that of the Canadian population in 1961.

During the periods 1956–60 and 1961–62, the 15–64 year old age group, representing the potential labour force, accounted respectively for 76.4 and 72.5 per cent of all male immigrants and 75.0 and 76.6 per cent of all females. These percentages were higher than the corresponding percentages of about 58 per cent for the male and female Canadian population in 1961. It is evident that the post-war immigrants have added significantly to the Canadian labour force and, since they received their training and education elsewhere, they were immediately available as productive manpower. Newcomers have, in short, partly corrected the imbalance in the age pyramid of the Canadian population caused by the low birth rate of the 1930's. At the same time, there is no guarantee that the already acquired skills are those needed by modern technology. In this sense immigration may simply aggravate the excess supply of particular kinds of labour and necessitate more retraining.

EMIGRATION

Emigration of Canadian-born and other Canadian residents offsets the gains from immigration. Unfortunately, there are no official statistics in Canada on emigrants. However, the annual reports of the Immigration and Naturalization Service of the US Department of Justice provide fairly accurate figures on the movement of Canadian residents to the United States, which is the major recipient of Canadian emigrants. These figures, however, include only those persons who have expressed their intention of establishing permanent residence in the United States.

Table 2.8 illustrates the annual flow of total and Canadian-born emigrants to the United States between 1946–62. Between July 1, 1945 and July 1, 1962, 585,000 Canadian residents entered the United States, of which number three-quarters were Canadian-born persons. Such figures, however, give an exaggerated impression of Canadian population losses

TABLE 2.8

Emigration from Canada to the United States
1946-62
(Year end June 30)
(000's)

	Number			Number	
Year	Total from Canada	Canadian-born	Year	Total from Canada	Canadian-born
1946	20.4	17.6	1955	32.4	23.1
1947	23.5	21.0	1956	42.4	29.5
1948	24.8	21.8	1957	46.4	33.2
1949	24.5	20.8	1958	45.1	30.1
1950	21.9	18.0	1959	34.6	23.1
1951	25.9	20.8	1960	46.7	30.3
1952	33.4	28.1	1961	47.5	31.3
1953	36.3	29.0	1962	44.3	30.4
1954	34.9	27.1			

SOURCE: Immigration and Naturalization Service, US Department of Justice.

because of an important omission in the statistics. During the decade 1951–61, US immigration statistics showed the registered entry of about 280,000 Canadian-born persons. But, during the same decade, Canada had a net loss of only about 54,000 Canadian-born persons, apart from deaths. It has been estimated that between 1951 and 1961 approximately 175,000 Canadian-born persons returned to Canada after residence abroad and were resident in Canada at the 1961 census. Thus, *net* emigration of Canadian-born persons during 1951–61 was much less than the gross emigration figures would indicate. The same conclusion can be drawn from the fact that in 1950 the number of Canadian-born living in the US was 990,000 as compared with 950,000 in 1960. While the number of Canadian-born in the US decreased, the number of American-born living in Canada remained all but static (i.e., 282,000 in 1951 and 284,000 in 1961).

Female Canadian-born emigrants to the United States constituted a somewhat higher proportion of the total than male emigrants. About one-third of the total Canadian-born emigrants between 1951–62 were young persons below 20 years of age. The age group 20–29 accounted for 30.4 per cent, and 30.5 per cent were within the 30–59 year group, while people of 60 years and over accounted for only 1.7 per cent. It would appear then that, in general, younger people are leaving Canada.

Of some concern is the skill composition of Canadian emigrants to the US. Data concerning "professionals," which include engineers, lawyers, doctors, teachers, and so on, suggest that net emigration of this group to the US has been rising from 1,676 to 3,663 per year between 1950 and 1959. A very large increase took place during 1957 when net professional emigration exceeded 4,400.[24] Since the demand for professionals presently exceeds the available supply in Canada, this is a loss out of all proportion to the numbers involved. It occurs chiefly because the US suffers from similar skill shortages and regularly makes more attractive job offers than typically prevail in Canada for many professional positions. The ease of entry to the US for those born in Canada, the cultural similarity, and proximity also serve to make emigration less painful.

Thus, not only are younger Canadian-born persons emigrating to the US but there is a relatively heavy incidence of the more highly skilled, a fact that has always been of great concern in Canada, but which, with developing technology and rising social needs not readily met by the labour force as presently trained, may well become one of the most significant demographic problems facing the nation in the future.[25]

ETHNIC DISTRIBUTION OF CANADIAN POPULATION

For purposes of the census, the ethnic origin and mother tongue of the original immigrant ancestor in the male line, as declared by each individual, is traced. Of course, the individuals so classified may have already been assimilated into one of the two basic stocks of the Canadian people, the French and Anglo-Saxon group. Evidence showing the diverse racial origin of the Canadian population is given in Table 2.9.

The proportion of the population that is French has not changed greatly owing to the high birth rate among French Canadians which enabled them to increase as fast as the population of the country as a whole. Immigration from France has been too small to change the relative share of French Canadians in Canada's population. French Canadians are located mainly in and closely adjacent to the Province of Quebec, New Brunswick, and in small settlements in southern Manitoba and elsewhere. The proportion of British origin on the other hand has declined, particularly during the last decade, while the proportion of other origins has correspondingly increased. Canada's third largest composite group is mainly represented by Germans, Ukrainians, Dutch, Scandinavians, Italians, and Poles.

[24]Data from *Proceedings of the Special Committee of the Senate on Manpower and Employment*, Fourth Session, 1960–61, no. 2, Dec. 8, 1960, p. 56.
[25]This is discussed more fully in chapter 6.

TABLE 2.9

Ethnic Origin of the Canadian Population
1931-61

Origin	1931 %	1941 %	1951 %	1961 Number	1961 %
British	51.9	49.7	47.9	7,996,669	43.8
English	26.4	25.8	25.9	—	—
Irish	11.9	11.0	10.3	—	—
Scottish	13.0	12.2	11.0	—	—
Other	0.6	0.7	0.7	—	—
Other European	45.8	48.0	49.1	9,657,195	53.0
French	28.1	30.3	30.8	5,540,346	30.3
Austrian	0.5	0.3	0.2	106,535	0.6
Belgian	0.3	0.2	0.2	—	—
Czech & Slovak	0.3	0.4	0.5	73,060	0.4
Danish*	0.3	0.3	0.3	386,534	2.1
Finnish	0.4	0.4	0.3	59,436	0.3
German	4.6	4.0	4.4	1,049,599	5.8
Greek	0.1	0.1	0.1	—	—
Hungarian	0.4	0.5	0.4	126,220	0.7
Icelandic	0.2	0.2	0.2	—	—
Italian	0.9	1.0	1.1	450,351	2.5
Jewish	1.5	1.5	1.3	173,344	1.0
Lithunian	0.1	0.1	0.1	—	—
Netherlands	1.4	1.8	1.9	429,679	2.4
Norwegian	0.9	0.9	0.9	—	—
Polish	1.4	1.4	1.6	323,517	1.8
Roumanian	0.3	0.2	0.2	—	—
Russian	0.8	0.7	0.7	119,168	0.6
Swedish	0.8	0.7	0.7	—	—
Ukranian	2.2	2.7	2.8	473,337	2.6
Yugoslavic	0.2	0.2	0.2	—	—
Other†	0.1	0.1	0.2	346,068	1.9
Asiatic	0.8	0.6	0.5	121,753	0.7
Chinese	0.5	0.3	0.2	58,197	0.3
Japanese	0.2	0.2	0.2	29,157	0.2
Other	0.1	0.1	0.1	34,399	0.2
Other Origins	1.5	1.7	2.5	462,630	2.5
Native Indian and Eskimo	1.2	1.1	1.2	220,121	1.2
Negro	0.2	0.2	0.1	—	—
Other and not stated	0.1	0.4	1.2	—	—
Totals	10,376,786	11,506,655	14,009,429	18,238,247	100.0

SOURCE: Numerical data 1931-51, *Canada Year Book, 1961*, p. 191. Numerical data 1961, *1961 Census of Canada*, Bulletin 1.3-2, Table 81, pp. 81-1 to 81-8.

*In 1961 Danish includes all Scandinavian, i.e., Danish, Icelandic, Norwegian and Swedish.

†1961 data includes Belgian, Greek, Lithuanian, Roumanian, and Yugoslavic origins.

Post-war immigration, unlike previous immigrations, was not entirely an economic immigration but consisted of a high proportion of political exiles and refugees, who cannot return to their own countries for political reasons. The new immigrants also differ from their predecessors in that ". . . they represent more of a cross-section of their original society, with the disproportion rather on the side of the more highly educated and qualified."[26] This partly offsets the loss of Canadian-born professionals to the US.

CANADIAN FAMILIES

The total number of families in the population at any given time is affected by the rate of net family formation, i.e., the excess of new families formed by marriages and by the immigration of married people over the number of families dissolved by a natural cause, divorce, or by the emigration of married persons. The 1961 census defines a family as a husband and wife (with or without children) or a parent with an unmarried child (or children) living together in the same dwelling. Unmarried sons and daughters under 24 years of age and living with their parents are classified as children, as are wards and guardianship children under 21 years of age.

Canadian families grew steadily over the last three decades examined, adding each year to the total as the number of new families exceeded the number of families dissolved. This net increase in the number of families has had repercussions on the Canadian economy in terms of its effects on housing construction and demand for furniture, appliances, etc. Similarly, the high rate of net family formation also influenced the birth rate.

Table 2.10 shows the rate of growth of family formation, average size of family, and average numbers of children per family in Canada during the 1931–61 period.

The number of families in Canada rose from about 2.1 million in 1931 to over 2.5 million in 1941, at an annual average rate of 1.6 per cent (compound), which was higher than the average annual rate of population growth during the same decade. In the next decade, 1941–51, families grew at the rate of 2.7 per cent as compared with 1.7 per cent of population growth. The Second World War induced many people to marry earlier and a large number of Canadian soldiers brought their war-brides to Canada after the end of the war. It is estimated that in

[26]Sheila Patterson, "This New Canada: A Study of a Changing People," *Queen's Quarterly*, vol. XLII, no. 1 (1955–56), pp. 84–5.

TABLE 2.10

Families, Persons in Families, Average Size of Family,
and Average Number of Children per Family
1931-61

Year	Number of families	Intercensal percentage increase	Average annual rate of growth	Number of persons in families	Average no. of persons per family	Average no. of children per family
1931	2,149,048	—	—	8,971,311	4.2	—
1941	2,525,299	17.5	1.6	9,937,986	3.9	1.9
1951*	3,287,384	30.2	2.7	12,216,103	3.7	1.7
1961	4,147,444	26.2	2.4	16,095,721	3.9	1.9

SOURCE: *Censuses of Canada.*
*Excludes Newfoundland, Yukon, and Northwest Territories before 1951.

1946 and 1947 some 40,000 war-brides entered Canada. The prosperous economic conditions in the period following the war made earlier marriages possible and, in addition, the opportunities for married women to continue working after marriage also encouraged many young people to marry. Another factor has been family immigration, already referred to, which contributed to the net addition of families in Canada.

During the last decade, 1951–61, the annual average rate of family formation of 2.4 per cent was slightly lower than the 2.7 per cent of the population growth. Marriage rates in Canada had been very high until 1957, and the result was that a higher proportion of the adult population was married than before. In 1961, two-thirds of the population 15 years of age and over was married as against 64.0 per cent in 1951, and 57.0 per cent in 1941. More people are now marrying earlier. Of the young people who were 20–24 years of age in 1961, 30.4 per cent of the males and 59.2 per cent of the females were married as against 25.0 per cent of the males and 51 per cent of the females in 1951. The corresponding percentages in 1941 were 16.0 and 39.0 respectively.

Families in Canada, excluding the Yukon and Northwest Territories, rose to an estimated 4,239,000 as of June 1, 1962, an increase of 92,000 or 2.4 per cent compared with the 1961 census. The average number of persons per family on June 1, 1962, was 3.9, unchanged from 1961, and slightly higher than in 1951.

The average number of children per family in Canada was 1.9 in 1961 as compared with 1.7 in 1951 and 1.9 in 1941. Young married people are having somewhat larger families, although large families have become less common than twenty years ago. There is an apparent tendency towards more families of three or four children rather than one or two, as shown in Table 2.11.

The 445,800 post-war immigrant families comprised 1,607,500 per-

TABLE 2.11

Percentage of Families with Average Number of Children, 1941–61

Average number of children	1941	1951	1961
No children at home	31.2	32.3	29.3
1–2 children at home	41.1	43.3	40.8
3–4 children at home	17.0	16.7	20.9
5 or more children at home	10.7	7.7	9.0

sons or an average of 3.6 per family with an average number of children of 1.6.[27] Both these averages were somewhat lower than the corresponding over-all national averages.

URBANIZATION

Concurrently with the growth of Canadian population there have been shifts from farms and rural non-farm areas to urban centres, particularly to metropolitan areas. At the same time within major urban and metropolitan areas there has been a significant movement out from their centres to the suburbs. The Canadian population has become not only more urban, but also more suburban.

These population movements reflect the structural changes in the Canadian economy and the shifting location of industries and enterprises. As noted in Chapter 1 the steady decline in importance of employment in agriculture during the whole of the twentieth century and the rise of trade and services in particular has given an increasingly urban orientation to productive activity. At the same time high birth rates in rural areas, mechanization, and other technological improvements in agriculture have accentuated the growth of surplus population in these areas. This rural-to-urban movement was, of course, accelerated during the Second World War by the growth of armament industries. But the increasing concentration of industrial jobs in larger cities and metropolitan areas continued during the post-war period. However, the rates of urbanization have been rather uneven among different sized cities and consequently the financial burden of providing schools, hospitals, and other social facilities has been unequally distributed.

Changes in the definition of "urban" and "rural" population in the censuses make it difficult to trace precisely the historical shifts in the geographical distribution of the Canadian population. Until the 1951 census, the urban population was defined as the population residing in

[27]DBS, *1961 Census of Canada, Households and Families, Post-War Immigrant Families*, Bulletin 2.1–8.

incorporated cities, towns and villages, while the remainder were considered as rural. Since 1951, however, the population residing in cities, towns, and villages of 1,000 population or over, whether incorporated or unincorporated, as well as the population of census metropolitan areas including suburbs, was defined as urban and that outside such localities as rural. The 1956 census also included in the urban category the suburban population of major urban centres, while the 1961 census added "urbanized" or built-up residential areas surrounding all cities and towns with 10,000 or more persons. Beginning with the 1931 census, the rural-farm segment of the rural population was separated from the total rural population.

Despite these statistical and conceptual difficulties, the broad trends in the rural-urban distribution of the Canadian population can be established. Table 2.12 shows the rural-urban population of Canada by census

TABLE 2.12

Rural and Urban Distribution and Intercensal Rates of Growth of
Population*
1901-61

| | | Population | | | | | | | Increase in urban population as a per-cent of total population increase |
| | | Rural | | Urban | | Intercensal percentage | | | |
Year	Total '000	Number '000	Per cent	Number '000	Per cent	Total	Rural	Urban	
1901	5371.3	3381.1	62.9	1990.2	37.1				
1911	7206.6	4059.3	56.3	3147.3	43.7	34.2	20.1	58.1	63.0
1921	8787.9	4530.5	51.6	4257.4	48.4	21.9	11.6	35.3	70.2
1931	10,376.8	4802.8	46.3	5574.0	53.7	18.1	6.0	30.9	82.9
1941	11,506.6	4958.3	43.1	6548.3	56.9	10.9	3.2	17.5	86.2
1951*	14,009.4	5191.8	37.1	8817.6	62.9	21.7	4.7	34.7	90.7
1956	16,080.8	5365.9	33.4	10,714.9	66.6	14.8	3.4	21.5	91.6
1961†	18,238.2	5266.3	28.9	12,971.9	71.1	13.4	−1.9	2.11	104.6

SOURCE: Data 1901-1941, *Census of Canada 1956, Analytical Report,* Bulletin: 3-2, Table II, p. 2-4; data 1951-1961, *1961 Census of Canada, General Review,* Bulletin 7.1-2, Table IV, p. 2-7.

*Includes Yukon and Northwest Territories.

†Adjusted broadly to the 1956 definition, i.e., urban defined as all incorporated and un-incorporated cities, towns and villages of 1,000 and over, as well as all fringe parts of metropolitan and other major urban areas. Newfoundland is not included prior to 1951.

periods, 1901–61, according to the 1956 census definition. The dramatic shift from rural to urban areas is immediately apparent. In 1901, 63 per cent of the population of Canada resided in rural areas; by 1961 about 71 per cent lived in urban areas, including the "fringe" parts around the larger cities. In the US, at the time of the 1960 census, about 70.0 per cent of the population was also urban and 30.0 per cent rural. Between 1901 and 1931 the intercensal percentage increase in the Canadian urban population was much more rapid than in the rural population. In 1921 the proportion of urban and rural populations was about equal. During the 1930's, there was some reverse population movement from urban to rural areas and consequently the proportion of urban and rural in 1941 changed only slightly as compared with that in 1931. However, during the Second World War and the post-war years, the intercensal rate of urban population growth once again accelerated. In all intercensal periods since 1901 urban areas have accounted for from two-thirds to over 90 per cent of the increase in Canada's total population.

A further indication of the shift from rural to urban living that has taken place since the beginning of the twentieth century can be gained from the statistics relating to incorporated cities, towns, and villages of 1,000 population and over. In 1901, the incorporated localities numbered 325 and accounted for 1,867,000 persons or about one-third of the total Canadian population, while in 1961 there were 892 incorporated areas (excluding 30 in Newfoundland), which comprised a population of 10,467,000 or almost 60 per cent of Canada's population (exclusive of Newfoundland).[28]

RELATIVE GROWTH OF URBAN CENTRES BY SIZE
Since the beginning of the present century, there has been a tendency towards increasing concentration of urban population in larger cities and decreasing relative importance of the smaller urban centres. The proportion of the total urban population living in incorporated urban centres of 100,000 population and over increased from about one quarter in 1901 to almost two-fifths in 1961 (excluding Newfoundland), while, during the same period, the percentage of the population living in the smallest size group, 1,000–4,999, decreased from 29 to 13. Similarly, a percentage decline occurred in urban centres between 5,000–9,999, from 15 to 9 per cent. The proportion of the population residing in incorporated cities of 10,000 to 29,999 on the other hand increased from about 12 per cent in 1901 to 19 per cent in 1961, and in the 30,000–99,999 class the increase was from 18 to 21 per cent between these two dates.[29]

However, the growth of the larger urban centres and metropolitan areas has been even more spectacular, when the growth of suburbs and "fringe" areas is included. Between 1951 and 1961, the growth in the

[28]DBS, *1961 Census of Canada, General Review, Rural and Urban Population,* Bulletin 7.1–2, pp. 2–11.
[29]*Ibid.,* Table VI, p. 2–13.

largest size group, 100,000 population and over, was almost 60 per cent as compared with less than 50 per cent for the over-all urban population increase during the same decade. The size group, 10,000–29,999, also grew faster (53 per cent), while other size groups showed a much lower rate of growth than the over-all urban population growth rate. In 1961, the population living in urban centres of 100,000 and over accounted for about two-thirds of Canada's urban population of almost 13 million.

An important feature of urban population growth has been a steady shifting of population for the last several decades into metropolitan areas. This phenomenon has been associated with the increasing industrialization of the country and improved transportation. The number of metropolitan areas in Canada has increased from 12 in 1941 to 15 in 1951 and 17 in 1961.[30] These seventeen metropolitan areas comprised 8,164,000 people or about 45 per cent of Canada's population on June 1, 1961. Between 1951 and 1961, the metropolitan areas increased in population by 2,527,000 which accounted for 60 per cent of the total population increase in Canada between 1951 and 1961.

This growth of the metropolitan area took place largely through the growth of the suburbs. As of June 1, 1961, 55.0 per cent of the total metropolitan area population resided within the central city and 45.0 per cent within the suburbs. The growth of suburbs is indicated by the fact that in 1951 only a little less than one-third and in 1941 only one-quarter of the population in metropolitan areas resided in the suburbs.[31] This movement of population from the city "proper" to suburbs has been so extensive that some metropolitan areas are beginning to merge into still larger metropolitan areas.

The movement of urban population to the suburbs is explained, in part, by "suburbanization" of jobs within metropolitan area limits. For example, in 1939 about 82 per cent of the manufacturing jobs in the two major industrial areas (Toronto–Hamilton, Montreal) were located in their centres as compared with 71 per cent in 1956.[32] This change has taken place mainly in the post-war years. Another factor influencing the growth of the suburbs is the middle class search for more space, privacy, and modern housing. This movement has stimulated the building boom in the suburbs, but, at the same time, it has created other problems such as the need for building expressways and subways, extending the supply

[30]Metropolitan census areas are Calgary, Edmonton, Halifax, Hamilton, Kitchener, London, Montreal, Ottawa, Quebec, Saint John, St. John's, Sudbury, Toronto, Vancouver, Victoria, Windsor, and Winnipeg.
[31]DBS, *1961 Census of Canada, General Review, Rural and Urban Population,* p. 2–13.
[32]David W. Slater, "Decentralization of Urban Peoples and Manufacturing Activity in Canada," *CJEPS,* Feb. 1961, p. 76.

of gas, electricity, water, etc., developing shopping centres, new schools, hospitals, churches, and other facilities and services. In some cases, this move to the suburbs has created slums out of the former residential districts in the centres of the cities. On the other hand, there is some evidence of a growing preference for the central districts because the suburban growth was less rapid in 1956–61 than in the previous five years, and that of the central districts somewhat greater. Another indication of this has been the large-scale construction of apartment buildings in the centres of the cities. However, it would be premature at this stage to suggest that "reurbanization" is in full swing. What has apparently occurred in Canada as well as the US is a change in the role of the central city from a place of job location and residence for workers to a cultural, service, and financial centre within which reside many people beyond the working age or exempt from the type of activity formerly associated with the core area. The transition of the function of the central city area will be accompanied by some residential movement back, perhaps stimulated by such things as high-rise apartments and redevelopment of cultural facilities. But this reurbanization will be of a different character than formerly and, on balance, it is doubtful whether there will be any significant net increase in the number of people living in these areas.

FARM AND NON-FARM RURAL POPULATIONS, 1931–61

The "farm" population refers to the population living on farms in rural areas and, hence, its size is dependent both on the definition of the "farm" and "rural" segments of the population. In the following analysis, the 1956 definition of "farm" is used,[33] which is also applicable to farm population in other census years. It was necessary to break down the whole period of 1931–61 into two subperiods, 1931–51 and 1951–61, because of different definitions of the rural population. Table 2.13 shows the distribution of the rural population of Canada between farm and non-farm for the 1936–61 period.

Throughout the whole period under consideration there has been an increase in the rural non-farm population mainly because of a rise in population of areas surrounding the unincorporated rural communities. However, the most striking feature is the accelerating decline of the farm population in Canada, which has been associated with the significant

---

[33]In the 1951 and 1956 censuses, a farm was defined as a holding on which agricultural operations were carried out and which was (*a*) 3 acres or more in size, or (*b*) to 3 acres in size with agricultural production during the previous year valued at $250 or more.

TABLE 2.13

Farm and Non-farm Rural Population
1931-61*
(000's)

Population	1931	1941	1951	1931-41	1941-51
		1931-51†		Intercensal percentage change	
Rural	4,907.8	5,236.2	5,375.3	6.7	2.7
Farm	3,237.7	3,112.8	2,815.7	−3.9	−9.5
Non-farm	1,670.1	2,123.4	2,559.6	27.1	20.5

Population	1951	1956	1961	1951-56	1956-61
		1951-61‡		Intercensal percentage change	
Rural	5,191.8	5,365.9	5,266.3	3.4	−1.9
Farm	2,769.3	2,631.6	2,237.6	−5.0	−15.0
Non-farm	2,422.5	2,734.3	3,028.7	12.9	10.8

SOURCE: 1931-51, *1951 Census of Canada*, vol. X, Table VIII, p. 45. 1951-61, *1961 Census of Canada*, Bulletin 1.1-7, Table 13, pp. 13-1 to 13-8.

*Newfoundland, Yukon, and Northwest Territories excluded in 1931-51, but included in 1951-61.

†According to 1951 census definition of rural with the exception that in incorporated places of 1,000 and over were included in the rural population since they could not be separated out in the 1931 and 1941 census figures.

‡1956 census definition of rural.

decrease in the farm labour force. During the 1931–41 period, Canada's farm population decreased by 3.9 per cent, with the Maritime provinces, Ontario, and Saskatchewan experiencing declines in farm population significantly greater than the country as a whole. During the next decade, 1941–51, the rate of decline of the farm population of Canada amounted to 9.5 per cent. All regions, except British Columbia, showed a decline in farm population, particularly the Prairie and Maritime provinces. It is estimated that during this period the farm population of Canada decreased by 300,000 as compared with 125,000 during the previous decade. The rate of decline of the farm population of about 20 per cent in the 1951–61 period was double that of the previous decade, with the decrease particularly pronounced in the second half the the last decade.

CONCLUSION

The foregoing outline of Canada's changing population reveals a general pattern typical of most Western countries during the twentieth century although significant differences in the rates of change are apparent in some aspects. Over-all, Canada's population has increased in every year since Confederation in 1867 but at widely varying rates. The general growth rate has been high by Western standards due mainly to a large gap between crude birth and death rates. But during periods of sustained prosperity, the over-all growth of population has been considerably enhanced by net migration and conversely somewhat offset during periods of war or prolonged depression.

The steady decline in death rates, the much higher though more volatile birth rates, and the rapid urbanization, especially since the 1930's, are familiar patterns in other developed countries as well.

But despite substantial population as well as economic growth, Canada remains a relatively underpopulated nation with sharply defined regional differences in climate, soil, resource conditions, ethnic and demographic concentrations and rates and patterns of economic growth. The nature and implications of these important differences need to be spelled out more fully for an understanding of the internal problems that regularly threaten the apparently fragile political and economic viability of Canada as a whole. The first two chapters of this study have concentrated upon national trends and aggregates. We must now turn to regional and international development and their influence on Canada as a whole. Chapters 3 and 4 will examine respectively these internal and external problems that loom so large on the Canadian scene.

3

REGIONAL DIFFERENCES

To this point we have treated the Canadian economy as a single integrated unit. However, the vast geographical size of Canada inevitably means that the country contains distinct economic regions, if only because of the concentration of diverse natural resources in particular localities. But the Canadian economy is beset with a degree of regional diversity extending well beyond that implicit in disparate resources. The existence of US markets close to the Canadian border that are generally larger than any Canadian market a similar distance away creates a southward pull on the thinly settled band that represents the greater part of the Canadian economy. This pull attracts the outlying regions east and west of Central Canada more to the US than toward the rest of Canada. To create a viable economy stretching east-west implies therefore strenuous efforts not only to overcome the great distances involved but also to curb the powerful orthogonal pull towards the south which constantly threatens the very existence of east-west trade within Canada.

Despite the fact that each region of Canada has closer economic similarities to the adjoining region in the United States than to other Canadian regions,[1] which would have the natural effect of rendering the US and Canada highly competitive, the overwhelming size of the American market serves as an economic magnet which has led to close north-south regional economic ties based on the working out of comparative

[1]The Atlantic provinces are more a part of New England than the rest of Canada in a variety of contexts: Ontario and Quebec have less, though somewhat comparable, similarities and connections with the states adjoining the Great Lakes; the Prairie provinces are a continuation of the great plains states, and British Columbia is more naturally tied to and is an extension of the Pacific Northwest in the US.

advantages. North America has in fact experienced a high degree of economic integration which, it is believed, makes the job of maintaining a viable and independent Canadian economy all the more difficult.[2] Indeed, the border between Canada and the US cuts across the main channels of trade. In the absence of this political boundary it is doubtful whether much interregional trade north of the border would have taken place. From an economic point of view the US-Canadian border is clearly illogical. But of course this is true of most political boundaries and logic, especially of the economic variety, seldom prevails. Hence, by the processes and exigencies of history, mainly colonial developments including the US Revolutionary War, the British and French colonies to the north were drawn together and created a precarious political and economic unity and independence designed to stem the encroachments of the economic dynamism of the colossus to the south. Few other large nations have been so conceived and few face the tremendous magnetism which constantly threatens, almost unconsciously, the high degree of independence sought by most Canadians. By the same token, however, this benign threat provides one of the new forces tending to draw most Canadians together whether they live in Vancouver, Saskatoon, Chicoutimi, or Digby.

THE REGIONS OF CANADA

Five major political regions are normally distinguished in Canada.[3] These are: (1) the Atlantic provinces, which includes the provinces of Prince Edward Island, Nova Scotia, New Brunswick and, since 1949, Newfoundland,[4] (2) Central Canada, made up of Quebec and Ontario, (3) the Prairie provinces of Manitoba, Saskatchewan, and Alberta, (4) British Columbia, and (5) the North which consists of the federal re-

[2]There is some equivocation regarding this point although it is a widely held belief in Canada. If the extent of North American economic integration has raised GNP per capita in Canada to levels not otherwise attainable, as is clearly the case, this creates greater economic space for manoeuvre and in this sense enhances Canada's ability to make needed adjustments in her own interests. In some areas, however, the very close economic ties between the two countries increases the economic penalty of particular policies that Canadians may feel to be desirable. For example, Canadians favour exports even from US subsidiaries in Canada to countries that may be unfriendly to the US while the subsidiary is reluctant or forbidden to make such sales. The mounting concern over the size and kinds of capital flows from the US to Canada creates a unique vulnerability should these flows be curtailed. These, and many others discussed in later chapters, pose problems of policy in Canada that may conflict with accelerated growth.

[3]These differ from the physical regions discussed in chap. 5. Recently sixty-eight regions in Canada have been distinguished which will prove suitable for more detailed economic analysis. See P. Camu, E. P. Weeks, and Z. W. Sametz, *Economic Geography of Canada* (Toronto, 1964), esp. part III.

[4]Without Newfoundland, the three provinces are referred to as the Maritimes.

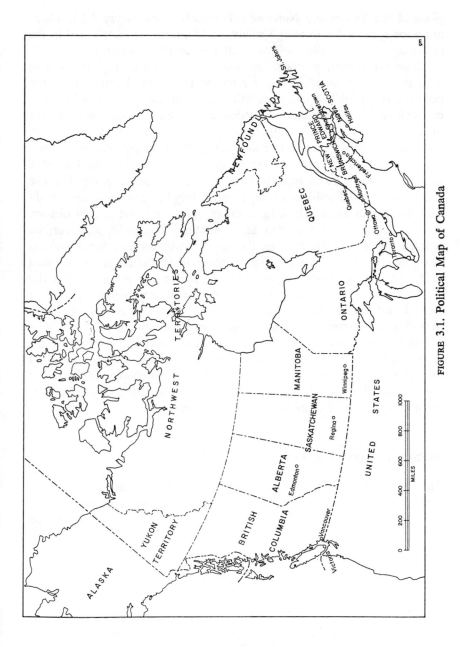

FIGURE 3.1. Political Map of Canada

gions of the Yukon and Northwest Territories (see Figure 3.1). There are good reasons for treating Quebec and Ontario separately and in the following discussion they will be dealt with in this manner.

There are serious problems involved in defining a "region" and, in fact, the appropriateness of any regional boundary depends upon the purpose. It is usually found in practice that political boundaries are most convenient if only because the statistical evidence and discretionary power of authorities is normally limited to such units. There may, indeed, be considerable overlapping in terms of what comprises an economic region when segregated by political boundaries. This is somewhat less of a problem in the various regions listed above in Canada partly because each region so defined is very large but mainly because there are significant differences among them in terms of natural resources, past history, culture, and economic growth and structure. It should, however, be pointed out that, while data availability necessitates a regional division along provincial (or groups of provinces) lines, for all provinces west of the Maritimes the important economic region encompasses primarily the southern sections. The northern parts of these provinces are better viewed as distinct regions in themselves in terms of climate and resources as well as the extent and nature of economic activity conducted therein. A more detailed and more appropriate regional division is shown on the map in Chapter 5. However, estimates of production and so on are not available for this degree of refinement. The present chapter will examine regionalism along provincial lines as already described and will indicate the major aspects of economic differentiation.

PRESENT ECONOMIC STRUCTURE

The land area, population, and population density for each region, province, and territory is shown in Table 3.1. The most striking aspect of the data, as perhaps of Canada itself, is the extremely low man/land ratio. Compared with other geographically large countries (the US, the USSR, China, India, and Brazil; see Table 3.2) the over-all Canadian density of slightly over 5 people per square mile varies between a fourth and one-seventeenth of these more populous nations. The phenomenon of space and vast distances is no journalistic myth and indeed is the opposite of the pressure of population on the land which so typifies the poorer countries of the world. Even the most densely populated province, Prince Edward Island with 48 people per square mile, has a degree of elbow room to make most countries in the world envious. Probably

TABLE 3.1

Population Density by Region, Province, or Territory 1961

Region, province, or territory	Area Square miles	Percentage	Population Thousands	Percentage	Number of people per square mile of land
Atlantic provinces	208,148	5.5	1898	10.4	9.8
Newfoundland	156,184	4.1	458	2.5	3.2
Prince Edward Island	2184	0.1	105	0.6	48.1
Nova Scotia	21,425	0.6	737	4.0	36.1
New Brunswick	28,354	0.7	598	3.3	21.5
Quebec	594,860	15.4	5259	28.8	10.0
Ontario	412,582	10.7	6236	34.2	18.1
Prairie provinces	757,985	19.6	3179	17.4	4.7
Manitoba	251,000	6.5	922	5.1	4.4
Saskatchewan	251,700	6.5	925	5.1	4.2
Alberta	255,285	6.6	1332	7.3	5.4
British Columbia	366,255	9.5	1629	8.9	4.5
Yukon and Northwest Territories	1,511,979	33.9	38	0.3	0.03
Canada	3,851,809	100.0	18,238	100.0	5.1

SOURCE: DBS, *Canada Year Book, 1960*, p. 2; and DBS, *1961 Census of Canada, Series 1.1, Population*, (Ottawa, 1963).

TABLE 3.2

Population Densities of Selected Countries
1960

	Area (000 sq. m.)	Population (000's)	Number of people per square mile
Brazil	3287	65,743	20
Canada	3851	18,238	5
China	3692	646,530	175
India	1262	433,060	343
United States	3615	180,670	50
Union of Soviet Socialist Republics	8650	214,400	25

SOURCE: *Canada Year Book, 1962*, Table 8, pp. 155.

not more than a third of Canada's vast area is "developed" in any meaningful sense of that term. The occupied farm land is less than 8 per cent of the total area while the forest land now accessible is only 19 per cent of the forested area.[5]

[5]*Canada Year Book 1961*, p. 15, and DBS, *Canadian Forestry Statistics, Revised 1959*, Table 1, p. 7.

Since all regions have such enormously high ratios of land per head there is little point in analysing the implications of these differences among them. A frequent exercise in international comparisons is to correlate national income per head with some variant of land/man ratios. But for the Canadian regions no such relationship appears to exist. Nor is there any reason to expect such a pattern, since all regions are well below what is loosely referred to by many economists as "optimum population density." For example, the two most economically prosperous regions, Ontario and British Columbia, have widely varying population densities, roughly 18 and 5 per square mile respectively, while the relatively depressed provinces of Prince Edward Island and Newfoundland have population densities of about 48 and 3. Thus, the relative degree of economic development among the regions in Canada cannot be rationalized on grounds of population pressure or lack thereof.

Of course, for Canada as a whole, the extremely low ratio is mainly due to the presence of the Yukon and Northwest Territories, a vast region which accounts for almost one and a half million square miles—more than a third of the total area of Canada—but which contained as of 1961 a mere 38,000 people. The North has in fact become a symbol of one of the world's last remaining new frontiers and has a position in Canadian affairs bordering on mystique.[6] Its development, however, is exceptionally difficult. For present purposes perhaps a better index of the over-all population density would be a figure around 8.6 people per square mile obtained by deducting the land area and population of the North, instead of the mere 5.1 including these empty spaces. But even this figure of less than 10 persons per square mile is extremely low relative to most other major countries of large geographical size as shown in Table 3.2.

It should be recalled, however, that about 70 per cent of the Canadian population lives in urban or village areas containing over 1,000 people while almost 45 per cent lives in cities with populations over 100,000. Indeed the bulk of Canada's population (almost three-quarters) is concentrated in a narrow band stretching almost 4,000 miles from east to

[6]This should not be taken to imply that there is much widespread popular support for or emotional attachment to what is loosely referred to as "the North." For most Canadians there is but a dim awareness of this vast region: few have visited it and fewer still have any intimate knowledge of its prospects or problems. Indeed, it is often used as a kind of psychological prop to bolster what many politicians see as sagging morale by providing the opportunity to talk in grandoise terms of its enormous potential. The vision of the North as holding the golden key to Canada's future, as a kind of economic insurance policy should external affairs cause difficulties, as a direction in which Canada "could move if only she chose" and so on, is frequently cultivated but generally fails to evoke much widespread response.

west and lying within 200 miles of the United States border. Even within this band population is unevenly distributed; it is estimated that 90 per cent of Canada's population live on a mere 10 per cent of the land area. These facts mean that not only is "crowding" greater than is implied in the average population density of less than 10 people per square mile, but also that there are enormous distances between major urban centres, except for the highly industrialized region of south-eastern Ontario. But regardless of how one chooses to examine Canadian population density, the fact of space, about 4 million square miles of it, and easy access to uninhabited regions even from within the largest cities (except perhaps Toronto and Montreal) provides an almost unique feeling of freedom in the sense of absence of overcrowding, easy escape from urban life and, perhaps most important of all, a feeling of great future possibilities.[7] The bald facts of Table 3.1 are therefore presented not to explain or rationalize regional income disparities but to give a more distinct impression of the emptiness of virtually all parts of Canada.

Of more interest than these broad averages are differences in regional economic structure and incomes. The usual indicator of these differences would, of course, be national income or gross national product on a per capita basis, a figure normally used (and often misused) when comparing nations. However, national accounts data are not generally available on a regional or provincial basis. Thus we must examine other evidence to obtain some indication of economic disparities and differences. Table 3.3 indicates an almost two-to-one disparity between the highest per capita regional income figures in Ontario and the lowest in the Atlantic region. The data must be used with some caution, however, since they contain rather rough estimates of income in kind, especially farm income, which has different significance among the regions. Nor are they adjusted for different levels of taxation.[8] Furthermore, the disparities narrow significantly using an income per family measure mainly because of larger

[7]While there may be substantial future possibilities, the fact of space and the great distances involved impose a serious transportation cost burden on the economy as a whole. It has even been suggested that "space ... is our greatest single negative asset; we do our work in an oasis set in a desert of distance;" and that "it is obvious to all that Canada is too big." F. Kenneth Hare in *Proceedings of the Resources for Tomorrow Conference* (Ottawa, 1962), vol. 3, p. 27.

[8]Although personal income has many weaknesses, as already noted, an experimental study of provincial gross domestic product made several years ago by DBS indicated that the regional rankings and to a lesser extent the magnitude of the differences among regions were roughly the same whether using personal income or gross provincial product. No data on the latter have been published and the experimental study has not been put on a continuing basis. There is no choice then but to use personal income in the present context. However the consistency of these estimates with the results of the unpublished study of GDP by province, encourages one in the use of what would otherwise be a less desirable measure.

TABLE 3.3

Personal Income per Head by Regions: Annual Averages of Major Components
1959-61

| | Personal Income per head | Percentage of total | | |
		Earned income	Interest and dividends	Government transfer payments
Atlantic provinces	1062	74.5	7.7	16.6
Quebec	1311	79.5	9.9	11.9
Ontario	1807	79.4	11.6	9.5
Prairie provinces	1488	79.5	8.8	12.3
British Columbia	1786	79.1	10.4	12.3
Yukon and NWT	1261	93.3	2.2	5.3
Canada	1529	78.9	9.7	11.3

SOURCE: Calculated from DBS, *National Accounts Income and Expenditure 1961.*
(Ottawa, 1962).   Data are in current dollars.   Totals may not add to 100 because of
rounding.

TABLE 3.4

Composition of Families by Province
1961

	Average number of persons per family	Average number of children per family
Newfoundland	4.7	2.7
Prince Edward Island	4.2	2.2
Nova Scotia	4.0	2.0
New Brunswick	4.3	2.3
Quebec	4.2	2.2
Ontario	3.6	1.6
Manitoba	3.7	1.7
Saskatchewan	3.8	1.8
Alberta	3.8	1.8
British Columbia	3.6	1.6
Yukon and NWT	4.3	2.3

SOURCE: *Census of Canada.*

average family size in the Atlantic and Quebec regions (see Table 3.4).
On this basis the disparity between the lowest and highest (once again
the Atlantic region and Ontario respectively) declines from almost
two-to-one to about three-to-two.

There are several ways in which such average measures may be interpreted. On the one hand they may be viewed as indicators of general
welfare; on the other as measures of economic potential. Either view-

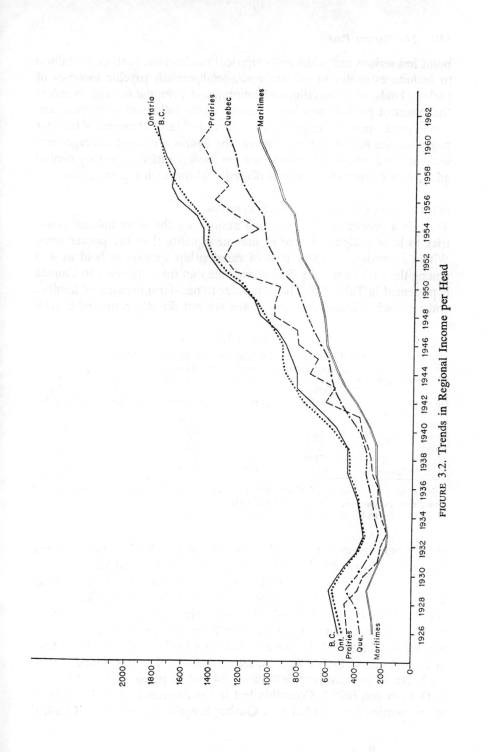

FIGURE 3.2. Trends in Regional Income per Head

point has serious analytical and empirical weaknesses, such as the failure to include estimates of private and social capital, psychic incomes of various kinds, and the failure of estimates of *personal* income to reflect the extent of publicly provided facilities or the full range of current economic production and opportunity since rather large elements of transfer payments are included. Furthermore, the figures are rough averages and without some additional information on income distribution they cannot adequately convey the extent of diversity within each region.

DISTRIBUTION OF INCOME WITHIN REGIONS

There is a general tendency among nations for the more affluent countries to have a higher degree of income equality than the poorer ones. Within countries, a similar type of relationship appears to hold as well among the various regions. Some evidence that this is the case in Canada is presented in Table 3.5. The data refer to non-farm incomes of families and unattached individuals and hence are not directly comparable with

TABLE 3.5

Non-Farm Income Distribution by Regions, 1959*
(percentage of total regional income)

Quartile	Atlantic provinces	Quebec	Ontario	Prairie provinces	British Columbia
Lowest	6.5	7.7	7.2	5.1	6.9
Second	16.8	18.5	19.0	16.6	17.8
Third	25.7	25.8	26.8	27.5	28.2
Highest	51.0	48.0	47.0	50.8	47.1
Average Incomes	$3262	$4438	$4680	$3993	$4494

SOURCE: DBS, *Survey of Consumer Finances, 1960*, and DBS, *Distribution of Non-Farm Incomes in Canada by Size, 1959.*
*Data refer to families and unattached individuals.

the personal incomes per head shown in Table 3.3. However, they are the only data available for computing even crude regional income distributions. Table 3.5 suggests that the proportion of income, so defined, accruing to the upper 25 per cent of families and unattached individuals is lower in Ontario and British Columbia, the two most affluent regions by all measures, than elsewhere. Similarly, the proportion of income received by the lowest 25 per cent is higher in these two provinces than in the Atlantic or Prairie regions, although lower than in Quebec. Again, the lower 50 per cent receive between 24 and 27 per cent of total income in Ontario and British Columbia but in the Atlantic and Prairie regions the proportion is somewhat less. Quebec is again an exception, if ranked according to the estimates of Table 3.3. However, Quebec is ranked third in terms of the income concept used in Table 3.5 and hence is not an exception in terms of these estimates. Indeed, these figures suggest a very close correspondence between average non-farm regional incomes and inequality. Ontario, British Columbia, and Quebec, in that order, have non-farm incomes per family and unattached individuals' incomes averaging over $4,500, the Prairies close to $4,000, and the Atlantic provinces less than $3,300. At the same time the degree of inequality appears to be greatest in the latter two regions. In general, the evidence, crude as it is, bears out the general pattern of income distribution observed among nations at different levels of average incomes. Not only then is average income lower in the Atlantic region than in other regions, but a greater proportion of the population receives incomes below the average. Thus, in a welfare sense, the Atlantic region is relatively worse off than the figures showing average incomes suggest. It is little wonder that Canada's Atlantic provinces are considered to be a special problem area.

COMPONENTS OF PERSONAL INCOME

If one is mainly interested in viewing incomes per head in terms of basic economic factors, rather than in a more subjective welfare sense, a closer look at the components of personal income is essential. This is shown in Table 3.3. The concept of "earned income" refers to non-property income accruing from current contributions to productive effort and includes, (1) wages, salaries, and supplementary labour income, (2) net income received by farm operators from farm production, and (3) net income of non-farm unincorporated business.[9] It is used here to represent relative regional productivity and appears to be a better indicator of production originating within any region than personal income since there are greater statistical problems in allocating interest and dividends: in fact, these do not necessarily emerge from economic activity within the region in which they are received. Transfer payments are, by definition, not received in return for current contributions to productive effort and hence should be excluded from any productivity measure.

An examination of Table 3.3 shows an even greater regional disparity among earned incomes than among personal income per head. Earned income constitutes only about 75 per cent of personal income for the Atlantic provinces but almost 80 per cent for each of the other regions (excluding the North). The relatively high proportion of government

[9]See DBS, *National Accounts Income and Expenditure, 1926–1956* (Ottawa, 1958), sec. C, and pp. 173–5.

transfer payments to the Atlantic provinces suggests that in terms of economic resources and productivity personal income seriously under-states the regional differentials.

Despite all the conceptual and statistical hazards in the foregoing data, the pattern of regional inequality seems sufficiently large and persistent to warrant an attempt to account for it in economic terms. That is to say, if it is fair to interpret the differences in earned or even personal incomes as rough indicators of over-all economic levels, then an examina-tion of the industrial structure, population, labour force, wage patterns, and degree of urbanization should highlight the major factors accounting for the regional disparities.

TABLE 3.6

Regional Industrial Structure
1959/60

| Region | Per cent of Canadian total (1960) | | Per cent of employment and manufacturing output accounted for by leading four manufacturing industrial groups (1959) | |
	Net value of commodity production (1)	Value of manu-facturing (2)	Employment (3)	Value added (4)
Atlantic provinces	5.6	3.9	73.1	73.2
Quebec	25.8	30.1	42.3	43.6
Ontario	41.4	50.5	51.2	52.6
Prairie provinces	17.3	7.4	61.9	58.5
British Columbia	9.7	8.1	73.3	71.1

SOURCES: Columns (1) and (2), *Canada Year Book*, p. 1073. Columns (3) and (4), DBS, *General Review of the Manufacturing Industries of Canada 1959* (Ottawa, 1962), Part II, Table 1, pp. 120-2.

Note.   The industrial groups included here are more broadly defined than those in Table 3.7. Total manufacturing by industrial groups used here includes 19 sub-divisions whereas the data used in Table 3.7. includes 40 sub-divisions.

REGIONAL INDUSTRIAL STRUCTURE

The data summarized in Table 3.6 indicate the overwhelming predomi-nance of the central provinces in commodity production.[10] Over two-thirds of the net value of all commodity production originates in Ontario

[10]Commodity production rather than gross domestic product is used in the present section because a geographical distribution of the latter is not available. As DBS points out "a major advantage of the net value of commodity production series is that it can be broken down by province. Also, in compiling the gross domestic product series it is difficult to allocate corporate profits according to the provinces in which they are generated by productive activity, but it should be borne in mind that the commodity production estimates by provinces exclude the non-commodity-producing industries." *Canada Year Book 1962*, p. 1069.

and Quebec. Even more concentrated in these two provinces is manu-facturing—over 80 per cent of net value added in manufacturing in Canada is accounted for by the central provinces. The smallest propor-tion of both commodity production and manufacturing activity emanates from the Atlantic provinces. In addition, Table 3.6 indicates a greater variety of manufacturing production in the central provinces, since the leading four industry groups account for a substantially smaller propor-tion of total output and employment than in the other regions. The finer industrial breakdown used in Table 3.7 reveals not only a smaller degree of concentration, in terms of proportion of value added by the leading four industries to total value added for each region, in Ontario and Quebec, but likewise a higher degree of processing and less concentra-tion in resource-oriented activities.[11]

Details of the composition of commodity output are shown in Table 3.8. Not only do Quebec and Ontario account for a disproportionate share of commodity output in the aggregate but more than 81 per cent of their production is concentrated in secondary industry (defined as manufacturing and construction). The other regions have a much higher proportion of commodity production in what is classified as the primary industries. The data shown here may even understate the degree of con-centration. Howland has reclassified some of the activities designated as manufacturing above, such as fish-processing, saw milling and pulp and paper production, and included these in the category of "resource indus-tries" while reserving "secondary manufacturing" for those industries "which undertake a higher degree of processing, which produce more end products than industrial materials and which normally produce for the Canadian domestic market."[12] When this adjustment is made, not only does the proportion of total Canadian manufacturing, so defined, rise in Ontario and Quebec, but these are the only two provinces in which the resource industries, including primary processing as well as the pri-mary stages of agriculture, fishing, mining, and forestry, comprise less than half the value of commodity production.[13]

But, however defined, it is clear that by far the greatest proportion of Canadian manufacturing activity takes place in Ontario and to a lesser extent in Quebec. Since manufacturing, as defined in Table 3.8 accounted

[11]It should be noted that the value added by iron and steel mills in the Atlantic region was about $33 million in 1960. This has been left out of Table 3.7 since this activity is confined to Nova Scotia only and not generally typical of the Atlantic region.

[12]R. D. Howland, *Some Regional Aspects of Canada's Economic Development,* a study prepared for RCCEP (Ottawa, 1957), p. 166.

[13]For details, see *ibid.,* Table 3, p. 19.

TABLE 3.7

Leading Manufacturing Industries by Region
1960

Region and industry	Value added $ millions	Value added percentage
Atlantic provinces:		
1. Pulp and paper mills	98.9	
2. Fish products	30.7	
3. Sawmills	16.0	
4. Dairying	11.7	
Total	157.3	39
Quebec:		
1. Smelting and refining	172.8	
2. Pulp and paper mills	305.9	
3. Aircraft and parts	109.4	
4. Communications equipment	87.7	
Total	675.8	21
Ontario:		
1. Motor vehicles	330.0	
2. Iron and steel	285.5	
3. Smelting and refining	248.4	
4. Pulp and paper mills	232.6	
Total	1096.5	21
Prairie provinces:		
Manitoba: 1. Slaughtering and meat packing	26.1	
2. Railway rolling stock	16.8	
3. Fabricated structural metal	15.8	
4. Petroleum refining	13.3	
Total	72.0	24
Saskatchewan: 1. Petroleum refining	18.5	
2. Slaughtering and meat packing	10.4	
3. Flour mills	10.0	
4. Breweries	7.8	
Total	46.7	39
Alberta: 1. Slaughtering and meat packing	32.5	
2. Petroleum refining	30.8	
3. Industrial chemicals manufacturing	21.2	
4. Pulp and paper mills	14.7	
Total	99.2	28
British Columbia:		
1. Sawmills	168.4	
2. Pulp and paper mills	148.6	
3. Veneer and plywood mills	34.8	
4. Printing and publishing	26.8	
Total	378.6	46

SOURCE: DBS, *Canada Year Book 1962* pp. 653–62.

TABLE 3.8

Relative Importance of Commodity-Producing Industry
Groups by Regions
1960
(percentages)

	Atlantic provinces	Quebec	Ontario	Prairie provinces	British Col.	Yukon, NWT	Canada
Primary							
industry groups	35.0	18.9	18.0	51.6	31.1	96.4	26.4
Agriculture	7.6	5.7	6.7	30.6	4.7	—	10.4
Forestry	7.4	3.5	1.7	0.9	14.7	2.8	3.6
Fisheries	5.2	0.1	0.1	0.2	1.5	2.0	0.5
Trapping	—	—	—	0.2	0.1	2.7	0.1
Mining	9.6	5.0	5.7	16.3	5.2	80.2	7.7
Electric power	5.2	4.6	3.8	3.4	4.9	8.7	4.1
Secondary							
industry groups	65.0	81.1	82.0	48.4	68.9	3.6	73.6
Manufactures	37.9	64.0	66.6	23.4	45.9	3.6	54.7
Construction	27.1	17.1	15.4	25.0	23.0	—	18.9
Totals	100.0	100.0	100.0	100.0	100.0	100.0	100.0

SOURCE: *Canada Year Book, 1962*, pp. 1068-73.

for about 55 per cent of total commodity production in 1960, the importance of this degree of concentration in the central provinces is considerably enhanced.

The largest single industry in the Prairie region is, of course, agriculture which accounts for some 30 per cent of net value of commodity output. As indicated in Table 3.9, the agricultural output of the Prairies is over 50 per cent of the Canadian total while Ontario produces over a quarter, although agriculture is relatively less important in Ontario's total net output. Indeed, agriculture comprises less than 8 per cent of each region's commodity output except in the Prairies. Table 3.9 likewise illustrates the great relative importance of Ontario as a commodity producer even outside of secondary industry and agriculture. In 1960 Ontario was third largest in the forestry category, second in mining, and first in electric power. Quebec, which ranks second in secondary industry, likewise accounts for a significant proportion of all other commodity production except fisheries in which the Atlantic provinces predominate. Tables 3.8 and 3.9 therefore highlight the extreme concentration of production in the central provinces in virtually all categories.

On a per capita basis some of the foregoing comparisons emerge even more vividly. Table 3.10 shows that in forestry and fisheries the two outlying regions predominate by rather substantial margins. Agriculture output per head in the Prairie region is many times that of any other region, while Ontario and Quebec stand out sharply in manufacturing

TABLE 3.9

Value of Commodity Production by Region
1960

Region	Agriculture		Forestry		Fisheries	
	Million Dollars	Per cent of Canadian total	Million dollars	Per cent of Canadian total	Million dollars	Per cent of Canadian total
Atlantic provinces	81.1*	4.1	79.2	11.5	56.0	55.7
Quebec	280.8	14.0	171.2	24.9	4.5	4.5
Ontario	532.7	26.6	132.2	19.2	5.0	5.0
Prairie provinces	1018.8	50.9	30.9	4.5	6.5	6.5
British Columbia	87.7	4.4	273.2	39.7	28.0	27.9
Yukon and NWT	....		1.0	0.2	0.7	0.7
Totals	2001.1	100	687.7	100	100.5	100

SOURCE: *Canada Year Book 1962*, p. 1073.   Details may not add to totals because of rounding.
*Excludes Newfoundland.   †Included with British Columbia.

output per head although the margin is less than total manufacturing output as indicated in Table 3.7.

The foregoing evidence of industrial structure reveals the very heavy concentration in the central provinces of those activities deemed to represent a high degree of industrial maturity. The outlying regions are, on the other hand, highly dependent upon primary processing, mostly of

TABLE 3.10

Commodity Production per Head
by Industry and Region
1960
(dollars)

Region	Agriculture	Forestry	Fisheries	Mining	Electrical power	Manufacturing	Construction	Total
Atlantic provinces	43.4	42.4	30.0	55.3	29.2	217.6	155.4	573.3
Quebec	54.6	33.3	0.9	47.8	44.5	616.8	165.1	963.0
Ontario	87.2	21.6	0.8	74.0	49.4	867.9	201.1	1302.0
Prairie provinces	327.3	9.9	2.1	174.3	36.9	250.4	269.0	1069.9
British Columbia	54.7	170.5	17.5	60.8	57.4	533.0	267.7	1161.6

SOURCE: DBS, *Canada Year Book, 1962*, M.1072-3 for net value of commodity production. Population data for 1960 from DBS, *National Accounts Income and Expenditure, 1961*.

TABLE 3.9 (*continued*)

Mining		Electric power		Manufacturing		Construction	
Million dollars	Per cent of Canadian total	Million dollars	Per cent of Canadian total	Million dollars	Per cent of Canadian total	Million dollars	Per cent of Canadian total
103.3	7.0	54.6	6.9	406.2	3.9	290.2	8.0
246.1	16.7	229.0	28.8	3172.8	30.1	849.2	23.4
452.0	30.7	302.1	38.0	5303.8	50.5	1229.3	33.8
542.5	36.9	114.9	14.4	779.4	7.4	837.1	23.0
97.4	6.6	92.0	11.6	853.8	8.1	428.9	11.8
29.1	2.0	3.2	0.4	1.3	—	†	—
1470.4	100	795.8	100	10577.3	100	3634.6	100

resources located within their boundaries. Closely associated with the latter is a disproportionate share of marginal and subsistence activities especially in agriculture and fishing. Small-scale operations requiring relatively less capital thus tend to predominate in the regions outside Ontario and, to a lesser extent, Quebec. What this implies is that the industrial structure of the central provinces is concentrated in the more productive and more capital-intensive activities relative to the rest of Canada. Where economies of scale are important, especially in manufacturing, these activities tend to concentrate in the larger market areas of Ontario and Quebec, which thereupon become the sources of supply to the rest of Canada for Canadian manufactured products. This in turn attracts a greater population which expands the market in Ontario and Quebec and thus justifies an even greater concentration of facilities. Given these features of the regional industrial structure, it is scarcely surprising that output per head in Ontario is the highest in Canada. But there are other factors as well, related to the foregoing as both cause and consequence, which contribute to regional inequality.

REGIONAL DISTRIBUTION OF THE LABOUR FORCE
Aside from the relatively heavy concentration of the more highly productive industries in Ontario, it is also noteworthy that the proportion of the people in the labouring age category (over 14) is higher as is also the participation ratio. The participation ratio is the proportion between the size of the labour force and the number of people in the labouring age category. Ontario, in other words, has fewer dependent people per member of the labour force than any other province. This fact, when

TABLE 3.11

Age Distribution of Canada's Population, by Province
1961
(percentages)

Province or territory	Total number (000's)	Age group					
		0-4	5-9	10-14	15-19	20-24	25-29
Newfoundland	457.9	14.8	14.1	13.0	9.6	6.6	5.8
Prince Edward Island	104.6	12.6	11.7	11.7	8.5	6.1	5.4
Nova Scotia	737.0	12.4	11.5	10.9	8.7	6.7	6.0
New Brunswick	597.9	13.1	12.7	12.2	8.9	6.3	5.6
Quebec	5259.2	12.8	11.9	10.8	8.9	7.0	6.9
Ontario	6236.1	11.9	10.8	9.5	7.0	6.2	6.8
Manitoba	921.7	11.7	11.0	9.9	7.7	6.4	6.2
Saskatchewan	925.2	12.3	11.6	10.2	7.9	6.2	6.0
Alberta	1331.9	13.5	11.9	9.8	7.4	6.7	7.2
British Columbia	1629.1	11.5	10.5	9.3	6.9	5.8	6.3
Yukon	14.6	16.0	12.0	8.1	5.2	7.6	9.8
Northwest Territories	23.0	16.9	12.7	10.5	7.4	9.7	9.4

SOURCE: *Census of Canada.*

combined with the fact of higher average earnings per worker (to be examined in the next section), makes Ontario's earned income per head the highest in Canada.

In general, the ratio of the labour force to total population shown in the last columns of Table 3.12 correlates with the ranking of regional income per head except that the positions of the Prairie provinces and British Columbia are reversed. The Atlantic provinces by all the measures of Table 3.12 rank lowest, which implies that a larger number of people are supported by a given number of productive workers than elsewhere in Canada.

It is also noteworthy that both the male and female participation rates are highest in Ontario and lowest in the Atlantic provinces. This reflects in large part the greater range of economic opportunity in Ontario than in the Atlantic region. To a lesser extent this is true of the other regions as well. Indeed the entire pattern of regional population and labour force characteristics is bound up with economic differentials as both cause and effect. The age structure of the poorest region is partly due to emigration of those in the productive age category to more wealthy regions in Canada or the US; this in turn serves to keep per capita incomes low in the Atlantic region and high in the already more wealthy regions.

AVERAGE EARNINGS DIFFERENTIALS

In addition to the above, part of the difference in regional income per head is related to earnings differentials even in "comparable industries."

TABLE 3.11 (*continued*)

30-34	35-39	40-44	45-49	50-54	55-59	60-64	65-69	70-74	70 and over
5.6	5.4	5.3	4.7	3.8	2.9	2.5	2.1	1.6	2.2
5.1	5.5	5.4	5.4	4.7	3.8	3.7	3.4	2.8	4.1
5.9	6.1	6.0	5.6	4.7	3.7	3.2	2.9	2.3	3.3
5.7	6.0	5.6	5.1	4.4	3.5	3.0	2.7	2.2	3.0
7.1	6.8	5.8	5.2	4.5	3.6	2.8	2.2	1.7	2.0
7.4	7.5	6.4	5.8	5.0	4.1	3.5	2.9	2.3	2.9
6.5	6.8	6.3	5.9	5.0	4.1	3.5	3.1	2.7	3.3
6.3	6.4	6.2	5.7	4.8	4.0	3.3	3.0	2.7	3.5
7.3	6.9	6.1	5.3	4.4	3.6	2.9	2.4	2.1	2.5
6.9	7.1	6.6	6.2	5.1	4.1	3.5	3.1	3.0	4.1
10.4	8.2	6.2	4.8	3.7	2.7	2.0	1.2	0.9	1.2
8.0	6.5	5.0	4.1	3.3	2.4	1.6	1.1	0.7	0.7

The problem of ascertaining comparable industries is, however, very great and the figures that we have drawn together in Table 3.13 involve rather broad categories which cast some doubt regarding comparability. For example, there are many different kinds of forestry activities, and it is not clear that the average weekly earnings discrepancy shown in Table 3.13 between the over \$90 in Ontario and British Columbia and the \$58 in New Brunswick represents a true earnings differential for comparable activity or a variation due to different activity. The same is true of every category listed. However, it is reasonable to suppose that some part of the differentials shown, which correlate well with the levels of regional income per head, is due to an earnings differential even where industries and activities are comparable. The generally higher weekly wages shown for Ontario and British Columbia contrast with the low levels in the Atlantic provinces in most industries. Although it has not been possible to isolate the extent to which the varying industrial "profiles" contribute to these differentials, other information confirms that much of it is due to differences in earnings. For example, hourly wage rates in Toronto, Hamilton and Vancouver for a large number of specific occupations are consistently above those in Halifax and Saint John with the levels obtaining in Winnipeg, Regina, Edmonton, and Calgary in between.[14] Living costs doubtless parallel these differences, so that in real terms they may be less pronounced than the 50 cents to

[14]For details see *Canada Year Book 1962*, Table 20, p. 729. Figures refer to October, 1961.

TABLE 3.12

Population and Labour Force Relationships by Region
1962
(percentages)

Region	Proportion of population 14 years of age and over			Labour force participation rate			Ratio of labour force to total population		
	Total	Male	Female	Total	Male	Female	Total	Male	Female
Atlantic provinces	63.9	31.8	32.1	48.8	74.3	23.5	31.2	23.6	7.5
Quebec	65.0	32.1	32.9	52.5	78.7	26.9	34.1	25.2	8.9
Ontario	67.2	33.1	34.1	56.1	81.6	31.4	37.7	27.0	10.7
Prairie provinces	64.3	32.6	31.7	56.1	80.9	30.7	36.1	26.4	9.7
British Columbia	68.1	34.5	33.6	52.9	77.1	28.0	36.0	26.4	9.6
Canada	65.7	32.7	33.0	54.0	79.5	28.9	35.5	26.0	9.5

Source: DBS, *The Labour Force*, May, 1962, p. 7.

$1.00 per hour discrepancy which frequently prevails between the lowest and highest rates for the same occupations. Nor are the figures pertaining to large cities necessarily representative of regional or provincial averages, although a similar set of differences exists with respect to male farm help, except that the Prairie region ranks above Ontario.[15]

Despite all of the data deficiencies, statistical as well as conceptual, and lack of comparability, the general pattern that emerges is one of earnings differentials that roughly coincide with regional disparities. Again this is a cause and effect relationship. With greater economic opportunity and higher productivity, earnings in the same occupational lines tend to be higher than where economic conditions are more circumscribed and less efficient.

URBAN-RURAL PATTERNS BY REGION

The proportion of the population of the poorer regions—the Atlantic provinces and the Prairies—residing in urban areas is about 50 and 58 per cent respectively whereas for the other regions the proportion is over 70 per cent (see Table 3.14). Since average incomes in urban areas exceed those in rural areas, the urban-rural ratio is yet another factor relating, as both cause and consequence, to regional average income differentials. According to recent evidence average family income in towns with a population of 30,000 and more (here called "metropolitan" centres) was $5313 for 1957 for all of Canada compared with a non-farm average family income in non-metropolitan centres of only $3728.[16] Since these figures exclude farm income they do not adequately portray urban-rural differences. However, a somewhat comparable discrepancy to that shown above also appears to exist between farm and non-farm remuneration, although the data are not strictly comparable. Thus, in a very rough sense the average income differences between centres above and below a population of 30,000 may be taken as broadly representative of the urban-rural pattern. If so, Table 3.15 also suggests

[15]For example, pay with board for male farm help as of May 15, 1961, was as follows:

	Daily	Monthly
Maritimes	$5.10	$107
Quebec	6.00	110
Ontario	6.40	119
Prairie provinces	6.40–7.00	135–145
British Columbia	7.80	144

See *Canada Year Book, 1962*, Table 23, p. 734. A similar pattern exists with respect to pay without board.

[16]See DBS, *Distribution of Non-Farm Incomes in Canada by Size, 1957* (Ottawa, 1959), Table 4, p. 22.

TABLE 3.13

Average Weekly Wages by Industry and Province
(1961 annual averages)
(dollars)

Industry	Newfoundland	Nova Scotia	New Brunswick	Quebec
Forestry	78.8		57.7	62.8
Mining	89.9	70.4		92.7
Manufacturing	72.3	66.5	66.6	75.6
Food and beverages	43.2	49.7	51.5	71.3
Sawmills	—	—	47.6	57.2
Pulp and paper mills	113.7	—	95.7	102.3
Transportation equipment	—	71.8	75.2	91.6
Building and general engineering	83.2	70.7	64.1	86.2
Steam railways	—	78.1	83.9	87.7
Trade	51.7	54.3	54.3	66.2
Industrial composite	71.4	64.0	63.6	75.3

SOURCE: DBS, *Review of Employment and Payrolls, 1961* (Ottawa, 1962), Tables 8 and 9.

NOTE: The Northwest Territories (excluding Baffin Island) are included in Alberta, Baffin Island in Quebec, and the Yukon in British Columbia. Prince Edward Island has been omitted because not enough data were available for comparison.

TABLE 3.14

Urban-Rural Population Differentials by Region
1961
(percentages)

Region	Rural	Urban
Atlantic provinces	50.3	49.7
Quebec	25.7	74.3
Ontario	22.7	77.3
Prairie provinces	42.4	57.6
British Columbia	27.5	72.5
Yukon and NWT	63.0	37.0
Canada	30.3	69.7

SOURCE: *Canada Year Book, 1962*, p. 1197.

that the gap between urban and rural average incomes is greater in the poorer regions. This is consistent with the previous evidence showing a higher degree of inequality of income distribution in the Atlantic and Prairie provinces.

Part of the urban-rural differential is explained by the heavier concentration of large-scale productive activities within urban areas. As Table 3.16 shows, not only are there more and larger manufacturing establishments in urban centres but in terms of value of shipments these account

TABLE 3.13 (*continued*)

Ontario	Manitoba	Saskatchewan	Alberta	British Columbia
91.8				99.4
97.0	98.9	106.6	110.2	98.9
84.9	72.6	78.2	82.7	88.6
74.2	76.1	74.7	79.3	77.3
64.8	—	—	—	83.3
102.6	—	—	—	107.8
96.7	79.4	—	79.9	94.3
94.3	84.4	82.9	92.6	103.5
86.2	87.6	83.8	90.0	88.6
69.1	66.4	64.2	66.6	72.6
81.1	73.5	74.2	80.5	85.0

for a greater proportion of total provincial manufacturing shipments in Ontario and Quebec than elsewhere. The proportion is likewise high in the Prairie provinces and low in British Columbia. The latter is doubtless attributable to the heavier incidence of non-urban-oriented manufacturing in British Columbia especially in saw mills and pulp and paper mills. The high ratio for the Prairies may emerge as a result of the relative importance of urban industry such as slaughtering, meat packing, and petroleum refining which tend to locate near larger markets.

TABLE 3.15

Metropolitan–Non-Metropolitan Income Differences by Region
1957*

Region	Average provincial income	(a) Average income metropolitan area	(b) Average income non-metropolitan area	Ratio b : a
Atlantic provinces	$3085	4183	2502	.60
Quebec	4144	4584	3219	.70
Ontario	4340	4752	3746	.79
Prairie provinces	3601	4438	2605	.59
British Columbia	4401	4472	4268	.95

Source: DBS, *Distribution of Non-Farm Incomes in Canada by Size, 1957* (Ottawa 1959), Table 5, p. 23.

*Metropolitan centres have populations of 30,000 and over: non-metropolitan centres have less than 30,000, Data refer to average incomes of families and unattached individuals.

TABLE 3.16

Concentration of Manufacturing in Urban Centres
1959

	Urban centres with shipments over $1,000,000 each	Establishments in urban centres with shipments over $1,000,000	Shipments of urban centres having $1,000,000 or over as a proportion of total regional shipments
			%
Atlantic provinces	46	965	68.4
Quebec	179	7927	93.3
Ontario	181	8873	82.2
Prairie provinces	42	2504	78.4
British Columbia	27	1967	47.5
Canada	475	22,236	81.9

SOURCE: *Canada Year Book, 1962*, p. 663.

CONCLUSION

The explanation of the existing differences in earned income per head in the regions of Canada runs in terms of a set of interrelated factors tending to concentrate the high-productivity industries in areas with large urban agglomerations; this in turn leads to a greater proportion of the population (both male and female) being involved in productive activity (i.e., a lower over-all dependency burden). Furthermore, the skill composition of the labour force is generally higher in the wealthier provinces. Table 3.17 indicates that the proportion of the labour force in the managerial, professional, and technical occupations is greatest in British Columbia, Ontario, Quebec, and Alberta, and lowest in Prince Edward Island and Saskatchewan. Although adequate data are not available, it is doubtless the case that, again as cause and consequence, the ratio of capital to labour tends to be higher in the more wealthy provinces. But not only are the goods-producing secondary industries concentrated in Ontario, Quebec, and British Columbia but also the banking, commerce, and finance activities as well. This aspect of industrial structure is likewise related to the concentration of population, labour force, and manufacturing in a self-reinforcing pattern of cumulative causation.

A convenient way of summarizing some of the reasons for the large discrepancies in earned incomes per head would be to attempt to assess their relative importance. A recent study[17] has performed such an exercise for the largest differential between Ontario and the Atlantic prov-

[17]Howland, *Regional Aspects of Canada's Economic Development*, p. 158.

TABLE 3.17

Proportion of Total Labour Force in
Managerial, Professional, and
Technical Occupations by Province
1961

Province	Number (000s)			Per cent of total to labour force over 15 years of age
	Male	Female	Total	
Newfoundland	11.7	6.5	18.2	16.2
Prince Edward Island	2.9	1.9	4.8	14.1
Nova Scotia	25.2	14.2	39.4	16.7
New Brunswick	19.3	11.1	30.4	17.0
Quebec	224.2	93.6	317.8	18.0
Ontario	331.5	115.4	446.9	18.7
Manitoba	39.1	15.8	54.9	16.0
Saskatchewan	35.0	16.3	51.3	15.7
Alberta	64.4	23.9	88.3	18.0
British Columbia	83.2	30.4	113.6	19.7
Yukon and NWT	0.7	0.3	1.0	16.1

SOURCE: DBS *1961 Census of Canada*, Series 3.1, *Labour Force*, (Ottawa 1963).

inces and, while it is evident that the basic factors are interrelated, it is at least suggestive to attempt to isolate them so long as it is acknowledged that no unique causality is implied.

Howland has attempted to deduce the degree of responsibility of the various factors already outlined in explaining the 1951 disparity of $545 between earned income per head in the Atlantic region and Ontario. His results are summarized in Table 3.18. Briefly stated, the evidence, after evenly dividing interaction effects, suggests that almost half of the difference is caused by the different wage rates. That is, for comparable industries, the rate of remuneration is higher in every case in Ontario than in the Atlantic region. The second most significant factor is the population and labour force characteristics, for, as already stressed, not only is the age structure of the Atlantic provinces more heavily concentrated outside of the 14–65 year age group than in Ontario but the participation rate, especially of females, is much lower than in Ontario. Table 3.18 ascribes almost 30 per cent of the differential to the population structure and participation rate.

This exercise is, of course, no more than a mechanistic way of attempting to pinpoint the major reasons for observed differentials and in no sense can be deemed to have adequately isolated the basic causal factors. Not only does it exclude such measurable variables as urban-

TABLE 3.18

Relative Contribution to the Disparity in Income per Head of
Various Factors between Ontario and the Atlantic Region
1951

		Dollars	Per cent
Total disparity	545		100
Proportion accredited to			
1. Relative size of labour force	158		29
(a) Due to different age distribution of population		103	19
(b) Due to different participation rates		55	10
2. Number of weeks worked per year by paid workers	55		10
3. Occupational or industrial pattern	65		12
4. Rates of earnings	267		49

SOURCE: Howland, *Regional Aspects of Canada's Economic Development*, Table 50, p. 158.

rural differentials and capital-labour ratios but the intangible effects of government policy, entrepreneurial and labour skills and incentives, climate, resource availability, past history, social attitudes, and so on are also neglected. The evidence that, for example, the age distribution of the Atlantic provinces accounts for much of the discrepancy with respect to Ontario says nothing about the reasons for such an age distribution. In fact, it is the existence of the higher earnings in Ontario that induces much of the emigration from the Atlantic region. While therefore the population structure may partly "explain" the earned income differences, it is equally true that the income differential partly explains the population structure.

The above exercise is, however, heuristic and a simple way of bringing together much of the preceding discussion. But of greater importance than the static picture drawn above are the long-term trends in incomes per head and, underlying these, the changes in industrial structure and population. The dynamics of regional growth will be examined next.

TRENDS IN REGIONAL DEVELOPMENT

POPULATION GROWTH, 1906–61

As would be expected, the additions to Canada's population by natural increase and immigration have not been evenly distributed among the provinces. Moreover, a considerable interprovincial movement of population has been taking place during the last forty years, particularly from

the Atlantic provinces and, until very recently, from the Prairie provinces
into the central provinces and British Columbia. This net migration
naturally accelerated the growth of population in the latter provinces,
and depressed it in others below what it might have been as a result of
natural increase.

The record of population growth by provinces and regions since 1901
given in Table 3.19 indicates the rapid expansion that took place in the
Prairie provinces up to 1921. The total population of these provinces
increased from 420 thousand in 1901 to almost 2 million in 1921, an
increase of nearly 370 per cent as compared with 62 per cent for the
nation as a whole during the same period. This spectacular population
growth in the Prairie region was, of course, associated with the settlement of the western provinces and the growth of the wheat economy.
During the twenties this population expansion slowed down. In the
thirties it became almost stationary: the Prairie provinces gained only
2.9 per cent—Saskatchewan actually lost about 26,000 people—as compared with a 10.8 per cent increase for the country as a whole; the
natural increase of 318,000 in the Prairies during this decade was offset
by nearly a quarter million net emigration. During the 1940's also, net
emigration from the Prairies greatly reduced the actual increase in the
population. In particular, Saskatchewan showed a net emigration of over
200,000 people and suffered a reduction in population between 1941
and 1951 of approximately 65,000. During the last intercensal period,
1951–61, the Prairie provinces as a whole increased their population by
about a quarter and showed positive net immigration although Saskatchewan once more had net emigration of 78,000. As a result of these
migratory trends the Prairie provinces reduced their share in Canada's
population from 21.6 per cent in 1921 to 17.5 per cent in 1961. These
facts, of course, reflect the declining importance of agriculture as a
source of employment, while the large net movement of people, especially from Saskatchewan during the depression, is a consequence of the
peculiar instability of a one-commodity economic region. More recently
the development of oil and natural gas in Alberta has stimulated large
net immigration and its population grew by some 42 per cent between
1951 and 1961, the largest proportional increase in Canada outside of
the North.

The relation between economic and demographic conditions is also
illustrated in the Atlantic provinces. This region experienced only a slight
gain in population between 1901–21, from about 1.1 million in 1901 to
barely 1.3 million in 1921—an increase of roughly 13 per cent. Indeed,
Prince Edward Island actually lost about 15,000 people over this period.

TABLE 3.19

Growth of Population in Provinces
1901-61
(000's)

Census year	Factors in the growth of population	Nfld.	PEI	Nova Scotia	New Brunswick	Quebec
1901	Population	221.0	103.3	459.6	331.1	1648.9
	Per cent of Canada	4.0	1.9	8.2	5.9	29.5
1911	Population	242.6	93.7	492.3	351.9	2005.8
	Actual increase	21.6	−9.6	32.7	20.8	356.9
	Per cent increase	9.8	−9.2	7.1	6.3	21.6
1921	Population	263.0	88.6	523.8	387.9	2360.5
	Actual increase	20.4	−5.1	31.5	36.0	354.7
	Per cent increase	8.4	−5.5	6.4	10.2	17.7
1931	Population	281.5	88.0	512.9	408.2	2874.7
	Actual increase	18.5	−0.6	−10.9	20.3	514.2
	Per cent increase	7.0	−0.7	−2.1	5.2	21.8
	Natural increase	32.0	8.2	51.3	56.5	499.1
	Per cent of actual increase	173.0			278.3	97.1
	Net migration	−13.5	−8.8	−62.2	−36.2	15.1
	Per cent of actual increase	−73.0			−178.3	2.9
1941	Population	303.3	95.0	578.0	457.4	3331.9
	Actual increase	21.8	7.0	65.1	49.2	457.2
	Per cent increase	7.7	8.0	12.7	12.0	15.9
	Natural increase	35.0	9.7	56.7	59.0	456.9
	Per cent of actual increase	160.6	138.6	87.1	119.9	99.9
	Net migration	−13.2	−2.7	8.4	−9.8	0.3
	Per cent of actual increase	−60.6	−38.6	12.9	−19.9	0.1
1951	Population	361.4	98.4	642.6	515.7	4055.7
	Actual increase	58.1	3.4	64.6	58.3	723.8
	Per cent increase	19.2	3.6	11.2	12.7	21.7
	Natural increase	73.9	15.8	103.8	99.9	727.0
	Per cent of actual increase	127.2	464.7	160.7	171.4	100.4
	Net migration	−15.8	−12.4	−39.2	−41.6	−3.2
	Per cent of actual increase	−27.2	−364.7	−60.7	−71.4	−0.4
1961	Population	457.9	104.6	737.0	597.9	5259.2
	Per cent of Canada	2.5	0.6	4.0	3.3	28.8
	Actual increase	96.5	6.2	94.4	82.2	1203.5
	Per cent increase	26.7	6.3	14.7	15.9	29.7
	Natural increase	110.0	17.6	127.4	119.2	991.9
	Per cent of actual increase	114.0	283.9	135.0	145.0	82.4
	Net migration	−13.5	−11.4	−33.0	−37.0	211.6
	Per cent of actual increase	−14.0	−183.9	−35.0	−45.0	17.6

SOURCE: *Census of Canada*

Ontario	Man.	Sask.	Alberta	BC	Yukon & NWT	Canada
2182.9	255.2	91.3	73.0	178.7	47.3	5592.3
39.0	4.6	1.6	1.3	3.2	0.8	100.0
2527.4	461.4	492.4	374.3	392.5	15.0	7449.3
344.5	206.2	401.1	301.3	213.8	−32.3	1857.0
15.8	80.8	439.5	412.6	119.7	−68.3	33.2
2933.7	610.1	757.5	588.5	524.6	12.3	9051.0
406.3	148.7	265.1	214.2	132.1	−2.7	1601.7
16.1	32.2	53.8	57.2	33.7	−18.1	21.5
3431.7	700.1	921.8	731.6	694.3	13.5	10,658.3
498.0	90.0	164.3	143.1	169.7	1.2	1607.3
17.0	14.8	21.7	24.3	32.3	9.8	17.8
346.3	100.6	153.8	104.6	49.1	−0.3	1401.1
69.5	111.8	93.6	73.1	28.9	−25.0	87.2
151.7	−10.6	10.5	38.5	120.6	1.5	206.2
30.5	−11.8	6.4	26.9	71.1	125.0	12.8
3787.7	729.7	896.0	796.2	817.9	16.9	11,810.0
356.0	29.6	−25.8	64.6	123.6	3.4	1151.7
10.4	4.2	−2.8	8.8	17.8	25.1	10.8
279.4	78.3	133.0	106.7	40.4	0.4	1255.5
78.5	264.5	—	165.2	32.7	11.8	109.0
76.6	−48.7	−158.8	−42.1	83.2	3.0	−103.8
21.5	164.5	—	−65.2	67.3	88.2	−9.0
4597.6	776.5	831.7	939.5	1165.2	25.1	14,009.4
809.9	46.8	−64.3	143.3	347.3	8.2	2199.4
21.4	6.4	−7.2	18.0	42.5	48.2	18.6
504.7	109.1	137.2	149.8	116.0	2.4	2039.8
62.3	233.1		104.5	33.4	29.3	92.7
305.2	−62.3	−201.5	−6.5	231.3	5.8	159.6
37.7	−133.1		−4.5	66.6	70.7	7.3
236.1	921.7	925.2	1331.9	1629.1	37.6	18,238.2
34.2	5.1	5.1	7.3	8.9	0.2	100.0
638.5	145.2	93.5	392.4	463.9	12.5	4228.8
35.6	18.7	11.2	41.8	39.8	49.8	30.2
937.0	148.3	171.5	260.7	220.3	8.8	3112.8
57.2	102.1	183.4	66.4	47.5	70.4	73.6
701.5	−3.1	−78.0	131.7	243.6	3.7	1116.0
42.8	−2.1	−83.4	33.6	52.5	29.6	26.4

During the last four decades these provinces have consistently recorded net emigration, which amounted to 342,000 as compared with a natural increase of 976,000 over the same period. Consequently, except during the 1930's, the Atlantic provinces showed lower intercensal percentage increases in population than Canada as a whole and their proportion of total population in Canada declined from 14 per cent in 1921 to 10 per cent in 1951.

The rate of population increase in the Province of Quebec by decades over the last sixty years has been generally comparable to that of the country as a whole. Quebec's share of the total population decreased only slightly from 29.5 per cent (1.7 million) in 1901 to 28.8 per cent (5.3 million) in 1961. With the exception of the last decade, 1951–61, the growth of population in Quebec was principally due to the natural increase rather than additions contributed by net migration during the years 1921–61. It is of interest to note that the decennial rate of population increase in the Province of Quebec over the first fifty years of this century was consistently greater than in Ontario, but by 1961 Ontario had taken the lead mainly because a larger proportion of post-war immigrants tended to locate there.

The population of Ontario recorded consistent growth throughout the period under consideration. In the first two decades of this century, Ontario's intercensal percentage population increase was below the national rate, while during last two decades it was above it. The 1901 population of 2.2 million in Ontario accounted for 39.0 per cent of Canada's population as compared with 6.2 million or about 34 per cent in 1961. Ontario, like British Columbia, experienced additions to her population by net migration during all the decennial periods over the years 1921–61. These additions ranged from one-fifth to two-fifths of the actual intercensal increases in population and reflect the relatively greater economic dynamism and opportunity.

British Columbia, together with the Yukon and Northwest Territories, had a population of 226,000 in 1901 or only 4 per cent of the total Canadian population. However, throughout the whole period 1901–61, the population of British Columbia showed consistently higher intercensal rates of growth than those of the country as a whole. By 1961, the population of British Columbia amounted to 1.6 million and that of Yukon and Northwest Territories to 38,000; together they now account for about 9 per cent of Canada's population. Net immigration has been a significant factor in this spectacular population growth of British Columbia, accounting for over 70 per cent of the increase in population in the 1920's. Corresponding percentages for the 1930's and the 1940's were

67.3 and 66.6 respectively. During the last decennial period this percentage declined somewhat to 52.5. But despite this reduction, British Columbia is the only province in which net immigration consistently exceeded natural increase during the period 1921–61.

Crude birth and death rates, along with number of marriages per 1,000 of population, are shown by province in Table 3.20. The birth rates in most provinces followed a similar trend, but there were some provincial differences in the pattern in more recent years. Prior to the Second World War, the Province of Quebec usually recorded the highest birth rate in Canada, although during the years 1936–40 New Brunswick and Newfoundland experienced slightly higher rates. All provinces recorded high birth rates immediately following the war. However, five-year average birth rates in Ontario and the Prairie provinces were higher during 1951–55 than those for 1946–50, while those for Quebec and the Maritimes (Newfoundland being an exception) were lower. In fact, in the post-war period, Quebec's rate steadily declined from the average 30.4 per thousand in 1946–50 to 28.6 in the second part of the 'fifties. The same trend prevailed in the Atlantic provinces, while Ontario, British Columbia, and Alberta, the more rapidly developing parts of Canada, actually increased their five-year average birth rates during the 1945–60 period, although, as indicated above, the annual rates have been declining in the latter years of the 1950's and early years of the 1960's.

Crude death rates in every province have exhibited a steady decrease with the most spectacular decreases occurring in Newfoundland and PEI. Also noteworthy is a narrowing of the provincial disparities between 1931–35 and 1956–60 which mirrors in part the geographical diffusion of improved health facilities.

The figures of net migration by themselves do not reveal the complex process of interprovincial movement of population and its consequences without an examination of the age and sex characteristics of migrants. A study of net migration during the years 1951–56 indicated that the provinces (the Maritimes) that experienced net losses on account of migration lost mainly younger people. The loss among the women in the most mobile age group of 20–34 years was greater than that among men, while the provinces which gained from migration absorbed more young men than women. In the Maritimes, for instance, about 65 per cent of the net loss through migration in the 20–34 age group, were women, while in British Columbia approximately 62 per cent of the net gain in the same age group due to migration were men. "The preponderance of men in the stream of migration into the rapidly expanding provinces

TABLE 3.20

Crude Birth, Death, Marriage, and Natural Increase Rates*,
by Five-Year Periods, by Provinces
1931-60

	1931-35				1936-40			
Province	Birth	Death	Marriage	Natural in-crease	Birth	Death	Marriage	Natural in-crease
Newfoundland	23.4	12.7	6.0	10.6	25.8	12.4	7.5	13.4
Prince Edward Island	21.8	11.1	5.5	10.7	21.9	11.5	6.6	10.4
Nova Scotia	21.9	11.6	6.7	10.3	21.7	11.0	8.6	10.7
New Brunswick	24.9	11.3	6.5	13.6	25.1	11.4	8.6	13.7
Quebec	26.6	11.0	5.8	15.6	24.6	10.4	8.5	14.2
Ontario	18.5	10.2	6.9	8.3	17.5	10.3	8.9	7.2
Manitoba	19.4	7.7	7.1	11.7	18.8	8.5	9.6	10.3
Saskatchewan	21.9	6.5	6.1	15.4	20.4	7.0	7.2	13.4
Alberta	22.1	7.3	7.4	14.8	20.8	7.7	9.2	13.1
British Columbia	14.0	8.9	6.0	5.1	15.6	9.9	9.1	5.7

	1941-45				1946-50			
Province	Birth	Death	Marriage	Natural in-crease	Birth	Death	Marriage	Natural in-crease
Newfoundland	29.7	11.8	9.5	17.9	36.2	9.3	7.9	26.9
Prince Edward Island	23.7	10.5	7.5	13.2	30.5	9.8	7.2	20.7
Nova Scotia	25.2	10.5	10.5	14.7	28.9	9.7	8.9	19.2
New Brunswick	28.2	10.9	9.6	17.3	34.0	9.8	9.8	24.2
Quebec	28.4	9.9	9.6	18.5	30.4	8.9	9.2	21.5
Ontario	19.9	10.2	9.7	9.7	24.6	9.9	10.3	14.7
Manitoba	21.8	9.1	10.0	12.7	25.9	9 0	10.2	16.9
Saskatchewan	21.7	7.6	7.7	14.1	26.3	7.8	8.9	18.5
Alberta	23.7	8.0	10.0	15.7	28.4	8.0	10.6	20.4
British Columbia	19.8	10.5	10.7	9.3	24.0	10.2	10.7	13.8

	1951-55				1956-60			
Province	Birth	Death	Marriage	Natural in-crease	Birth	Death	Marriage	Natural in-crease
Newfoundland	34.1	7.6	7.4	26.5	34.6	7.2	7.0	27.4
Prince Edward Island	27.2	9.2	6.2	18.0	26.6	9.5	6.4	17.1
Nova Scotia	27.5	8.8	8.0	18.7	26.9	8.5	7.4	18.4
New Brunswick	31.0	8.6	8.1	22.4	29.0	8.1	7.6	20.9
Quebec	30.0	8.0	8.3	22.0	28.6	7.3	7.5	21.3
Ontario	26.1	9.1	9.2	17.0	26.4	8.5	8.0	17.8
Manitoba	26.4	8.4	8.8	18.0	25.6	8.3	7.5	17.2
Saskatchewan	27.5	7.7	8.0	19.8	26.9	7.5	7.1	19.3
Alberta	30.7	7.4	9.6	23.3	30.6	6.9	8.5	23.7
British Columbia	25.1	9.8	8.9	15.3	25.7	9.2	7.9	16.4

SOURCE: *1961 Census of Canada, General Review*, Bulletin 7.1-1, Table II, pp. 1-5 to 1-6.
*Per 1000 population.

may be accounted for in part by the substantial share of [foreign] immigrants those provinces have received."[18]

Foreign immigration also accentuated the regional disparities in overall population growth. As of June 1961, foreign immigrants numbered 1.5 million since the Second World War. More than half of them located in Ontario, approximately a sixth in Quebec, another sixth in the Prairie provinces, and over a tenth in British Columbia. The Atlantic provinces absorbed only 2.2 per cent. As Table 3.21 indicates, more than nine out

TABLE 3.21

Distribution of Post-War Immigrants by Province and Period of Immigration
1946-61

	1946-50		1951-55		1956-61*		1946-61*	
Province	Number 000	Per cent	Number 000	Per cent	Number 000	Per cent	Number 000	Per cent
Newfoundland	1.3	0.4	1.2	0.2	1.7	0.3	4.2	0.3
PEI	0.4	0.1	0.5	0.1	0.6	0.1	1.5	0.1
Nova Scotia	4.4	1.4	5.3	0.9	6.5	1.0	16.2	1.1
New Brunswick	3.2	1.1	2.9	0.5	4.4	0.7	10.5	0.7
Quebec	38.5	12.7	87.9	15.5	121.4	19.1	247.8	16.4
Ontario	169.1	55.6	323.5	57.1	340.7	53.6	833.3	55.3
Manitoba	15.9	5.2	21.1	3.7	25.4	4.0	62.4	4.1
Saskatchewan	8.1	2.7	9.5	1.7	11.4	1.8	29.0	1.9
Alberta	25.4	8.4	48.3	8.5	48.0	7.5	121.6	8.1
BC	37.3	12.3	65.9	11.6	74.3	11.7	177.5	11.8
Yukon & NWT	0.4	0.1	1.1	0.2	1.6	0.2	3.1	0.2
Canada	304.0	100.0	567.2	100.0	635.9	100.0	1507.1	100.0

SOURCE: *1961 Census of Canada, Citizenship and Immigration*, Bulletin 1.2-8, Table 58, pp. 58-1 to 58-6.
*Includes the first five months only of 1961.

of every ten post-war immigrants resided at the time of the 1961 census in Ontario, Quebec, British Columbia, and Alberta. It is of interest to note that Quebec, which traditionally does not favour immigration, steadily increased its relative share of the post-war immigration. Approximately one-fifth of the immigrant arrivals during the 1946–62 period indicated the Province of Quebec as their intended destination,[19] but only 16.4 per cent of the total were actually located in that province

[18]A. H. Le Neveu and Y. Kasahara, "Demographic Trends in Canada, 1941–56, and Some of Their Implications," *CJEPS*, Feb. 1958, p. 14.
[19]Department of Citizenship and Immigration, Statistics Section, *Immigration 1962*, Table 15, p. 28.

at the time of the 1961 census. The same is true of the Atlantic provinces, which, like Quebec, probably lost some of their post-war immigrants to other parts of Canada.

The foreign-born population of Canada rose from 2 million to 2.8 million, or from 14.7 per cent to 15.6 per cent of the total population, between the 1951 and 1961 censuses. Regionally, the Prairies showed a decrease of 3.8 per cent in the ratio of the foreign-born population residing there, despite the large addition to their population by immigration. British Columbia also experienced a ratio decrease of 3.1 per cent, while Ontario's ratio went up by 3.2 per cent and Quebec's ratio by 1.8 per cent. The Atlantic provinces showed very insignificant gains. Table 3.22 indicates the proportion of foreign-born to total populations in the provinces as of June, 1961. As would be expected, Ontario and the four western provinces including the Yukon have the largest proportions.

TABLE 3.22

Ratio of Foreign-Born to Total Population,
by Province
June 1961

Province	Ratio (percent)
Newfoundland	1.4
Prince Edward Island	2.9
Nova Scotia	4.6
New Brunswick	3.9
Quebec	7.4
Ontario	21.7
Manitoba	18.4
Saskatchewan	16.1
Alberta	21.7
British Columbia	26.0
Yukon	18.6
Northwest Territories	8.5

But aside from the regional disparity, there is also a heavy urban concentration of post-war immigration (see Table 3.23). Especially noteworthy is the very heavy concentration of immigrants in urban areas of 100,000 and over; less than one-sixth of the immigrants have settled in rural areas. The largest numerical concentration of immigrant families was in Toronto, Montreal, Vancouver, Hamilton, Winnipeg, Edmonton, and Calgary. In the Toronto metropolitan area, slightly more than one out of four families was a post-war immigrant family; in Hamilton, one out of every five; in Calgary and Edmonton, one out of every six; in Montreal, one out of every seven. In other major urban areas the post-

TABLE 3.23
Urban and Rural Distribution of Post-War Immigrants*
1946-61

Locality and population	Immigrants		Percent	Percentage distribution of Canada's population
	Number 000			
Rural		204.2	13.5	30.4
Rural farm	68.3		4.5	11.4
Rural non-farm	135.9		9.0	19.0
Urban		1302.8	86.5	69.6
100,000 and over	1027.1		68.2	43.4
30,000 to 99,999	126.2		8.4	9.3
10,000 to 29,999	56.1		3.7	5.8
2500 to 9999	63.4		4.2	6.8
1000 to 2499	30.0		2.0	4.3
Total		1507.1	100.0	100.0

SOURCE: *1961 Census of Canada, Citizenship and Immigration*, Bulletin 1.2-8, Table 58, p. 58-1.
*Includes the first five months only of 1961.

war immigrant families concentrated in St. Catharines, Oshawa, Fort William–Port Arthur, Niagara Falls, Sault Ste Marie, and Sarnia. In these cities in 1961 one out of every five or six families was a post-war immigrant family.[20] There is, of course, a close relationship between the urban and regional concentration of immigrant families since more of the larger urban centres are in Ontario.

The urban orientation of post-war immigration however merely accentuates a trend discernible since the turn of the century (see Table 3.24). The 1901 census indicated that over half of the population lived in rural areas in Ontario and British Columbia, while in the Maritimes and the Prairies the rural population was over 70 per cent. Indeed, Saskatchewan was almost 94 per cent rural in 1901. Since then each province and region has exhibited a steady and virtually uninterrupted decline in the proportion of population living in rural areas so that by 1961 urban populations accounted for over three quarters of the population of Ontario, Quebec, and British Columbia and over half in the other regions.

The broad demographic trends by region including interregional migration, location of foreign-born immigrants, and urban-rural patterns are interrelated with economic factors to which we now turn.

[20]DBS, *1961 Census of Canada, Households and Families, Post-War Immigrant Families*, Bulletin 2.1–8.

TABLE 3.24

Provincial Percentage Distribution of Population by Rural and Urban*
1901-61

Province	1901		1911		1921		1931	
	Rural	Urban	Rural	Urban	Rural	Urban	Rural	Urban
Newfoundland	—	—	—	—	—	—	—	—
Prince Edward Island	85.5	14.5	84.0	16.0	81.2	18.8	80.5	19.5
Nova Scotia	71.2	28.8	62.0	38.0	56.3	43.7	54.5	45.5
New Brunswick	73.7	26.3	70.1	29.9	65.4	34.6	65.3	34.7
Quebec	61.8	38.2	54.1	45.9	48.0	52.0	40.3	59.7
Ontario	56.4	43.6	47.2	52.8	39.3	60.7	34.7	65.3
Manitoba	75.1	24.9	58.3	41.7	55.9	44.1	51.1	48.9
Saskatchewan	93.9	6.1	83.9	16.1	83.2	16.8	79.7	20.3
Alberta	83.8	16.2	70.6	29.4	69.9	30.1	68.9	61.1
British Columbia	53.6	46.4	49.1	50.9	43.9	56.1	32.7	67.3

SOURCE: Data 1901-41, *Census of Canada, 1956, Analytical Report*, Bulletin 3-2, Table 1, pp. 2-26 to 2-27; data 1951-61, *1961 Census of Canada, General Review*, Bulletin 7.1-2, Table IV, p. 2-7.

*Adjusted broadly to the 1956 definition, i.e. urban defined as all incorporated and unincorporated cities, towns and villages of 1000 and over, as well as all fringe parts of metropolitan and other major urban areas.

REGIONAL TRENDS IN INCOME

One of the mose striking aspects of regional growth patterns is their comparative stability in terms of personal income per head. Tables 3.25 and 3.26 provide the relevant data. If we compare general trends (see Figure 3.2) all regions have for the most part followed the same path between 1926 and 1962. A rising trend in the late 1920's followed by the contraction to 1932, then a slow rise until about 1940, and a fairly persistent upward movement ever since, typify all the regions. Although the prairie provinces show a far higher degree of cyclical variation than the other regions, as would be expected in view of the heavy reliance upon agriculture in general and wheat in particular, there is likewise a comparable pattern of cyclical variation among the regions. Table 3.26, showing regional incomes per head as a percentage of the Canadian average, confirms the relative stability especially if the comparison is made using 1927–29 and 1959–61. Only the Maritimes increased its relative position and this was matched by an almost equivalent drop in the average for British Columbia. The other regions show little change between the two dates. The evidence, using personal income per head, therefore seems to suggest, as Howland puts it, that "there is considerable uniformity in regional reactions to national and international

TABLE 3.24 (*continued*)

1941		1951		1956		1961	
Rural	Urban	Rural	Urban	Rural	Urban	Rural	Urban
—	—	57.3	42.7	55.4	44.6	48.1	51.9
77.9	22.1	74.9	25.1	69.3	30.7	67.6	32.4
50.0	50.0	44.7	55.3	42.6	57.4	43.4	56.6
61.7	38.3	57.4	42.6	54.2	45.8	50.9	49.1
38.3	61.7	33.0	67.0	30.0	70.0	25.1	74.9
30.8	69.2	26.6	73.4	24.1	75.9	20.8	79.2
50.7	49.3	43.4	56.6	39.9	60.1	35.0	65.0
78.5	21.5	69.6	30.4	63.4	36.6	57.0	43.0
66.6	33.4	52.0	48.0	43.4	56.6	36.1	63.9
32.2	67.8	29.2	70.8	26.6	73.4	23.3	76.7

phenomena. . . ."[21] On the other hand, the persistence of the relative differentials cannot be regarded with any complacency since, as already suggested, the wide absolute and growing disparity in levels of living and the concentration of secondary manufacturing in the central provinces, which is both cause and consequence of such difference, create persistent difficulties in regard to interprovincial as well as federal-provincial relations.

However, personal income per head is not an adequate index of comparative well-being, as indicated earlier, due to lack of adjustment for taxation, varying levels of provincial transfer payments, and a probable under-estimate of farm income in kind. Yet as a trend indicator, other evidence suggests that the pattern revealed is roughly correct. Crude calculations of gross provincial product for the Atlantic provinces related to gross national product per head for all Canada from 1930 through 1958 suggest a very slight decline over the period as a whole. Considerable variation exists however, but mostly within a relatively narrow range of 60–65 per cent for Nova Scotia, 53–58 per cent for New Brunswick, and 41–44 per cent for Newfoundland for the years 1949–58. Prince Edward Island has exhibited a far higher degree of variation in its ratio of provincial gross product to GNE between 43 and 54 per cent. There is stronger indication of a relative deterioration especially since 1946 for the region as a whole.[22]

[21]Howland, *Regional Aspects of Canada's Economic Development*, p. 66.
[22]Data from A. C. Parks, *The Economy of the Atlantic Provinces, 1940–1958*, Atlantic Provinces Economic Council (Halifax and Fredericton, 1960), pp. 9–11.

TABLE 3.25

Provincial and Regional Personal Income per Head
1926-62

Province and Region	1926	1929	1932	1935	1937	1938
Maritime provinces	277	312	197	216	262	258
Quebec	360	470	269	280	329	325
Ontario	486	562	360	392	456	456
Prairie provinces	457	385	214	235	280	293
British Columbia*	515	586	372	395	465	470
Yukon and NWT*						
Canada	425	459	287	309	363	365

Province and Region	1948	1949	1950	1951	1952	1953
Maritime provinces	641	664	693	749	805	826
Quebec	779	789	836	928	995	1047
Ontario	1069	1120	1182	1325	1410	1459
Prairie provinces	979	975	947	1262	1328	1287
British Columbia*	1090	1120	1204	1346	1434	1478
Yukon and NWT*				840	920	960
Canada	928	940	979	1130	1203	1235

*For the years 1926-50 inclusive Yukon and Northwest Territores are included with British Columbia.

SOURCE: DBS, *National Accounts Income and Expenditure, 1926-1956*, and *ibid.*, *1962.*

TABLE 3.26

Regional Income per Head as a Percentage of Canadian Average
selected periods 1927-61

	Annual averages				
	1927-29	1937-39	1943-45	1947-49	1959-61
Maritimes*	65.6	70.8	72.5	71.9	70.2
Quebec	87.7	89.2	81.4	84.3	85.7
Ontario	117.6	124.6	121.3	116.9	118.2
Prairies	97.8	80.5	90.6	103.1	97.3
British Columbia†	123.0	127.0	115.2	117.4	117.7
Canada ($)	$454	$370	$726	$898	$1529

SOURCE: Computed from DBS, *National Accounts Income and Expenditure, 1926-1956*, and *ibid.*, *1961*, Tables 28, 29 and Appendix Table 1.
*Excludes Newfoundland.
†Includes Yukon and NWT.

TABLE 3.25 (*continued*)

1939	1940	1941	1942	1943	1944	1945	1946	1947
265	303	353	427	489	529	569	626	632
336	371	441	516	571	593	610	645	702
472	544	658	763	844	886	914	913	962
322	361	387	626	566	730	678	813	823
475	526	612	727	822	825	861	898	951
381	432	508	634	682	742	755	791	827

1954	1955	1956	1957	1958	1959	1960	1961	1962
846	861	927	962	1002	1049	1104	1128	1171
1059	1073	1149	1204	1238	1265	1308	1361	1417
1446	1504	1594	1668	1714	1770	1800	1851	1938
1106	1272	1397	1311	1420	1457	1530	1476	1691
1476	1538	1667	1705	1696	1758	1783	1817	1896
1000	1069	1387	1355	1182	1206	1333	1243	1205
1205	1257	1361	1396	1445	1489	1534	1563	1658

Yet if we examine the components of personal income and the mechanism whereby the degree of stability with respect to the Canadian average has been maintained over the period 1926–61, the economic base of the Maritime provinces in particular seems to have deteriorated relatively to the rest of Canada. A comparison of the increase of the three components of personal income per head, shown in Table 3.27, suggests that between 1926 and 1960, government transfer payments to the Maritimes increased some 22 times and as a proportion of the Canadian average rose from 78 per cent in 1926 to almost 104 per cent in 1960. Transfer payments as a percentage of total personal income per head have risen in the Maritime provinces from less than 3 per cent in 1926 to over 16 per cent by 1960. Earned income has fallen from about 90 per cent in 1926 to less than 76 per cent by 1960. In no other region did earned income in 1960 constitute less than 78 per cent of total personal income, even though transfer payments have risen sharply in the Prairie provinces and Quebec and despite the fact that transfer payments per head in British Columbia and the Prairies exceed those of the Maritimes. It seems generally true therefore that "living standards, lower in the Atlantic provinces than they are in the rest of Canada, would have been lower still if it had not been for certain policies of the Federal

TABLE 3.27

Personal Income per Head by Components
1926 and 1960
(current dollars)

	Earned income		Interest, dividends and net rental income		Government transfer payments	
	1926	1960	1926	1960	1926	1960
Maritime provinces	245.49	818.89	25.05	90.20	6.11	178.29
Quebec	307.72	1043.56	49.17	130.29	3.46	152.47
Ontario	407.39	1427.75	69.53	211.59	9.48	172.48
Prairie provinces	403.77	1210.15	45.45	136.25	8.22	195.69
British Columbia	465.34	1413.23	44.55	185.39	19.80	219.73
Canada	365.25	1211.08	52.27	158.70	7.83	171.56

SOURCE: DBS, *National Accounts Income and Expenditure 1926-1956*, and *ibid.*, *1961*, section C.

Government."[23] Furthermore, the data on transfer payments exclude various other forms of regional assistance such as the reduced freight rates to and from the Maritimes, the Crows Nest Pass rates on export grain from the Prairies, and the tariff which provides protection to secondary manufacturing. In addition, the Maritimes has only maintained its investment position during the 1950's through the incidence of heavy government investment.[24] Even with such investment, however, total new capital expenditures per head in the Atlantic provinces for 1949–56 inclusive were less than 60 per cent of the Canadian average.[25] On the basis of earned income, as previously defined, Canada's eastern region has in fact fallen further behind. Since earned income and new investment are better measures of economic capability than personal income, the evidence suggests that the stability of the shares of personal income may be non-sustainable in the future without major structural changes.

But in addition to the role of governmental transfer payments in sustaining personal incomes in the Atlantic provinces, the pattern of population growth is likewise important. Not only has the decennial rate of population growth been well below the Canadian average, as already

[23]RCCEP, *Final Report*, p. 404.
[24]Howland, *Regional Aspects of Canada's Economic Development*, p. 5.
[25]The data on average annual capital expenditures per head for 1949–56 in constant 1949 dollars are as follows:

Canada	$297	Ontario	328
Atlantic provinces	174	Prairie provinces	360
Quebec	242	British Columbia	391

Data from *ibid.*, Table 31, pp. 95–97.

noted, but every province in the Atlantic region has recorded net emigration since 1931. As is usually the case, the greater proportion of those who emigrate are in the labour force age group (14–65) and especially in the 20–34-year-old age group; hence emigration tends to worsen the dependency burden. It is not therefore surprising to find that the Maritime labour force rose more slowly than population between 1931 and 1955 and that between 1946–55 the labour force actually declined slightly.[26] The adverse economic impact is even greater than the data regarding the dependency burden would suggest,[27] for those who emigrate are generally the more aggressive members of the labour force and not infrequently the more highly educated especially considering the rising demand for skilled manpower since the Second World War. As Howland puts it, "there has been a relatively greater acquisition of new skills in the regions which have experienced the greater diversity and momentum of industrial activity."[28] Even as early as 1951, the proportion of the labour force with only 0–4 years of school in the Atlantic provinces was over 13 per cent (over 10 per cent if Newfoundland is excluded) compared with less than 5 per cent in Ontario and British Columbia. On the other hand, the proportion of the labour force having more than 13 years of schooling was only 6 per cent in the Atlantic provinces (6.5 per cent excluding Newfoundland) but over 12 per cent in Ontario and British Columbia.[29] The impact upon personal earned income per head tends therefore to be adverse although in the present instance the emigration has tended to reduce total population more rapidly than earned incomes. Thus, slow rates of population growth and a sharp rise of transfer payments represent the main forces accounting for the failure of the relative gap between personal income per head in the Atlantic provinces and other regions to widen significantly. However the absolute gap has increased substantially. On the average for the years 1926–29, the level of Maritimes personal income per head was roughly $154 below the Canadian average and $329 below Ontario.[30] By 1959–61, the discrepancies had risen to $429 and $707 respectively. Despite the relatively slow population growth[31] and increase in transfer payments, the Maritimes and Newfoundland have fallen behind in terms of

[26]See *ibid.*, p. 77, Tables 21 and 22.
[27]For details see Tables 3.9 and 3.11.
[28]*Ibid.*, pp. 78–9.
[29]*Ibid.*, Table 24, p. 79.
[30]During this early period, Ontario's personal income per head averaged $522 which was below that of British Columbia with an annual average of $548.
[31]Or perhaps because of it since the net emigration in the productive age bracket tends to affect adversely the dependency burden and over-all productivity.

absolute differences which may be a more critical index of well-being than the relationship to the Canadian average. As it is, a slight downward trend is apparent using estimates of gross provincial product related to gross national product, although the data are not sufficiently accurate nor the trend sufficiently pronounced to read anything of great significance into them.

For the other regions, excluding the North (i.e., Yukon and Northwest Territories), the persistence of the differentials, which in any event narrow considerably when the Atlantic region is omitted, is more symptomatic of general economic dynamism rather than the adjustment process apparently at work in the Atlantic region. It is true that Saskatchewan and Manitoba experienced not only net emigration in the decades of the '30's, '40's and '50's (see Table 3.28), but Saskatchewan's population actually declined in the '30's and '40's while Manitoba's

TABLE 3.28

Net Inter-Provincial Migration, by Province
1941-51 and 1951-61

Province	1941-51	1951-61
Newfoundland	n.a.	−6277
Prince Edward Island	−11,451	−8844
Nova Scotia	−35,414	−41,119
New Brunswick	−40,040	−24,462
Quebec	4569	−34,122
Ontario	181,070	110,387
Manitoba	−69,152	−49,383
Saskatchewan	−203,564	−102,000
Alberta	−33,759	23,523
British Columbia	203,744	133,400
Yukon and NWT	4997	−1103

SOURCE: DBS, Census (Demography) Division.

rate of population growth was among the lowest for any province during the same period. But these population tendencies reflect mainly the incidence of the great depression and the peculiar sensitivity of the wheat economy. Indeed, personal income per head in Saskatchewan was the lowest of any province for several of the depression years. In general, however, the postwar experience of the other regions has been one of basic economic dynamism, at least until the over-all slowdown. New discoveries in the prairies (oil, uranium, natural gas), new industries, heavy investment especially in British Columbia and the prairie provinces, rather than rising transfer payments (although these too have increased) and emigration, are the main forces sustaining a high and growing level of personal per capita incomes in these regions.

REGIONAL TRENDS IN THE LABOUR FORCE

The evidence of Tables 3.29–3.33 concerning the labour force by region and province, broadly confirms the foregoing economic and demographic trends. Briefly the picture is as follows. Since the turn of the century the proportion of Canada's total labour force accounted for by the Atlantic provinces has declined while that of the prairie provinces and British Columbia has increased sharply. Ontario has decreased its share slightly and Quebec's share is roughly what it was in 1901. Despite problems of comparability of the data over time, it is also apparent that labour force participation rates in the Atlantic provinces are now below the 1901 level after rising somewhat until 1941. For all other provinces, except Alberta and British Columbia, participation rates are above the 1901 levels. The very high rates in these two provinces in the earlier years were attributable to the disproportionate number of men in the total population and are related to the opening up of these provinces; hence the decline in the participation rates does not represent the same kind of phenomenon that it does in the Atlantic region. For all provinces female participation rates have rather steadily increased since 1901 and are now over double the earlier figure. But though much higher than previously shown, female participation rates in the Atlantic provinces are substantially below those of the other provinces, a situation not generally true in 1901. Male participation rates have declined more rapidly in the Atlantic region than in most other sections of Canada.

A comparison of the industrial distribution of the labour force in 1931 with 1961 indicates a sharp decline for all regions in the agriculture, forestry, and fishing categories with the largest increase in the trade and service groups. For all regions, except the Prairies, the proportionate decline in agriculture was almost completely absorbed by increases in trade and service. In the Prairie region, employment in transportation and communication also contributed significantly to the relative increase in employment outside of agriculture.

In terms of occupational distribution a comparison between 1931 and 1961 roughly parallels the changes in industrial distribution by region. White-collar workers almost doubled as a proportion of the total for every region while manual occupations exhibited comparative stability over the thirty-year period. Primary employment was, of course, sharply down.

In very broad terms it is apparent that the changes in industrial and

TABLE 3.29

Growth of Labour Force* in Regions
1901-61
(000's)

Census Year		Atlantic provinces			Quebec		
		M	F	T	M	F	T
1901	Labour force	265.0	35.8	300.8	435.0	77.3	512.3
	Per cent distribution	88.1	11.9		84.9	15.1	
	Per cent of Canada	17.1	15.1	16.9	28.2	32.5	28.7
1911	Labour force	280.3	44.8	325.1	552.1	101.1	653.2
	Per cent change	5.8	25.1	8.1	26.9	30.8	27.5
1921	Labour force	296.0	52.5	348.5	642.2	138.6	780.8
	Per cent change	5.6	17.2	7.2	16.3	37.1	19.5
1931	Labour force	298.5	54.2	352.7	820.1	202.1	1022.2
	Per cent change	0.8	3.2	1.2	27.7	45.8	30.9
1941	Labour force (a)	344.6	69.7	414.3	977.3	260.5	1237.8
	(b)	299.4	69.6	369.0	928.5	260.2	1188.7
	Per cent change (a)	15.4	28.6	17.5	19.2	28.8	21.1
	(b)	0.3	28.4	4.6	13.2	28.7	16.3
1951	Labour force*	416.6	99.9	516.5	1121.7	341.5	1463.2
	Per cent change	20.9	43.3	24.7	14.7	31.2	18.2
1961	Labour force	397.6	135.2	532.8	1275.4	477.7	1753.1
	Per cent distribution	74.6	25.4		73.8	27.2	
	Per cent change	−4.6	35.3	3.2	13.7	39.8	19.8
	Per cent of Canada	8.7	7.7	8.4	27.8	27.1	27.6

SOURCE: Census data.
a. Including persons on Active Service.
b. Not including persons on Active Service.
*Including Newfoundland.

occupational structure during the twentieth century have not differed significantly among the various regions. The categories are overly aggregative for a complete analysis but do imply that these factors have a high degree of regional comparability in terms of direction of change. The large discrepancies are related more to demographic factors and especially trends in participation rates which, as already noted, tend to keep the Atlantic provinces at a relative disadvantage as far as incomes per head are concerned. Furthermore, the incidence of unemployment,[32] especially in recent years, has been heaviest in the Atlantic region as

[32]For details see chap. 6.

TABLE 3.29 (*continued*)

Ontario			Prairie provinces			British Columbia		
M	F	T	M	F	T	M	F	T
645.6	108.6	754.2	122.7	11.6	134.3	76.6	4.7	81.3
85.6	14.4		91.4	8.6		94.2	5.8	
41.8	45.6	42.3	7.9	4.8	7.5	5.0	2.0	4.6
836.1	154.9	991.0	500.8	47.4	548.2	189.5	16.6	206.1
29.5	42.6	31.4	308.1	308.6	480.2	147.4	253.2	153.5
922.2	194.9	1117.1	620.9	77.5	698.4	194.1	25.5	219.6
10.3	25.8	12.7	24.0	63.5	27.4	2.4	53.6	6.6
1096.2	249.4	1345.6	779.5	115.7	895.2	262.4	43.8	306.2
18.9	28.0	20.5	25.5	49.2	28.2	35.2	71.8	39.4
1257.5	315.4	1572.9	809.3	133.1	942.4	287.9	55.3	343.2
1140.1	315.0	1455.1	736.4	132.9	869.3	258.7	55.1	313.8
14.7	26.5	16.9	3.8	15.0	5.3	9.7	26.3	12.1
4.0	26.3	8.1	−5.5	14.9	−2.9	−1.4	25.8	2.5
1412.0	444.8	1856.8	762.1	179.8	941.9	338.6	97.9	436.5
12.3	41.0	18.0	−5.8	35.1	−0.1	17.6	77.0	27.2
1663.0	691.3	2854.3	835.7	300.6	1136.3	410.1	155.7	565.8
70.6	29.4		73.5	26.5		72.5	27.5	
17.8	55.4	26.8	9.6	67.2	12.1	21.1	59.0	29.6
36.3	39.3	37.1	18.2	17.1	17.9	9.0	8.8	8.9

indicated in Table 3.33 and thus aggravates the structural problems that have persisted over long periods of time.

CONCLUSION

If relative poverty or affluence is its own cause or at least subject to a significant degree of self-perpetuation, as the interrelationships among the more proximate determinants suggests, then our description is scarcely surprising. Nor does the persistently higher level of unemployment, particularly noteworthy in the Atlantic region, facilitate narrowing of the differentials. Yet their perpetuation can scarcely be viewed with equanimity.

TABLE 3.30

Labour Force Participation Rates by Sex, by Province
1901-61*

Census Year	Newfoundland			Prince Edward Island		
	Male	Female	Total	Male	Female	Total
1901†				87.3	10.0	48.5
1911				86.1	12.1	48.9
1921				86.6	13.1	50.3
1931				86.6	14.6	52.0
1941a				85.6	15.7	52.2
b				73.3	15.6	45.7
1951	76.1	15.6	46.7	78.8	18.2	49.1
1961	63.4	18.3	41.6	73.0	24.5	49.3

Census Year	Ontario			Manitoba		
	Male	Female	Total	Male	Female	Total
1901†	83.6	14.1	48.9	84.5	12.1	52.9
1911	88.1	17.5	54.1	88.2	16.6	57.3
1921	87.0	18.7	53.2	86.6	17.1	54.3
1931	84.7	20.1	53.1	85.1	19.4	54.4
1941a	84.7	21.9	53.7	83.5	18.9	52.6
b	75.8	21.8	49.7	74.9	18.9	48.1
1951	82.5	26.1	54.3	79.5	23.8	52.0
1961	79.0	32.6	55.7	75.5	31.4	53.7

SOURCE: Census data.

*10 years of age and over in 1901 and 1911; 14 years in 1921-51 and 15 years and over in 1961.   Members of the armed forces excluded in 1951 and 1961.

†Low rates are due to Indians being included in the population but not in the labour force.

a Including persons on Active Service.

b Not including persons on Active Service.

Chronic disparities among regions of a nation lead to certain inevitable frictions and difficulties. As far as Canada is concerned, the entire basis of Confederation is from time to time jeopardized. During the 1930's, the Prairie provinces threatened to secede, blaming central Canada for siphoning off undue amounts of the incomes generated in the West. More recently, Quebec has come to question whether Confederation has been a failure, from its point of view, and has begun to speculate about the gains and losses of secession. Newfoundland has likewise expressed doubts about the wisdom of joining Canada in 1949. It is noteworthy, however, that these sentiments become more vocal and prevalent when economic conditions are seriously depressed or even when they are merely relatively static. Under these circumstances, one

TABLE 3.30 (*continued*)

Nova Scotia			New Brunswick			Quebec		
Male	Female	Total	Male	Female	Total	Male	Female	Total
85.6	12.0	49.4	87.5	12.7	50.7	83.3	14.7	48.9
86.6	14.8	51.5	87.8	14.4	51.0	85.3	16.1	51.2
86.0	16.4	51.8	85.9	15.8	51.6	84.9	18.3	51.6
83.1	16.1	50.7	84.1	16.6	51.2	85.1	21.3	53.4
82.3	18.2	51.1	82.6	17.7	51.1	83.4	22.3	52.9
71.4	18.1	45.5	72.2	17.7	45.7	79.2	22.3	50.8
74.9	19.4	47.4	78.2	20.0	49.0	82.5	24.5	53.1
65.8	24.4	45.3	67.3	24.8	46.1	75.9	27.8	51.6

Saskatchewan			Alberta			British Columbia		
Male	Female	Total	Male	Female	Total	Male	Female	Total
66.7	5.8	40.3	—	—	—	82.8	10.8	51.6
92.8	10.9	62.7	90.8	12.6	62.3	91.2	16.9	67.3
89.9	12.2	56.5	88.1	12.9	56.0	87.3	15.8	57.3
87.2	13.8	54.9	87.9	15.1	56.3	86.1	19.0	57.2
84.6	14.5	52.5	85.3	15.3	53.6	81.7	18.3	52.4
77.8	14.4	48.8	77.7	15.3	49.4	73.4	18.2	47.9
80.3	18.3	51.0	80.4	20.0	52.0	75.4	23.0	49.9
77.2	26.4	52.9	78.4	30.8	55.6	72.1	28.3	50.5

region's gain tends to be another's loss and the degree of discontent is thereby felt more strongly. There is little question that a rapid and highly diffused rate of economic growth would quiet much of the discontent in the less affluent regions even though relative discrepancies were widening. Losing out relatively is less painful when all areas are making absolute gains (as has indeed been happening since 1960–61).

But more specifically, the problem of dominion-provincial relations, especially in the area of fiscal arrangements, is chronically aggravated by the extent of regional economic differences. It is no accident that Quebec and Ontario have regularly balked at tax rental arrangements, part of whose purpose is to provide a higher degree of regional equality. Not only fiscal agreements but also the various subsidies to transportation, the welfare schemes, government investment policy, and so on are designed to alleviate regional inequality. Especially in the short run, these may slow down the over-all growth rate but appear essential if political unity is to prevail. They may be regarded as the economic price

TABLE 3.31

Percentage Distribution of the Labour Force
by Sex and Major Industry Groups for Regions
1931 and 1961

1931	Atlantic provinces			Quebec		
	M	F	T	M	F	T
All industries	100.0	100.0	100.0	100.0	100.0	100.0
Agriculture	35.2	4.4	30.5	27.0	2.3	22.1
Forestry	2.0	(1)	1.7	2.1	(1)	1.7
Fishing	5.8	0.2	5.0	0.8	(1)	0.6
Mining	6.1	(1)	5.1	1.0	(1)	0.8
Manufacturing	13.1	10.9	12.8	21.7	25.1	22.4
Electricity	0.5	0.2	0.4	0.7	0.2	0.6
Construction	6.1	0.2	5.2	9.7	0.2	7.8
Transportation and communication	7.9	3.3	7.2	7.6	3.1	6.7
Trade:	7.5	13.3	8.4	9.8	9.8	9.8
Wholesale	1.3	1.3	1.3	1.5	0.8	1.3
Retail	6.2	12.0	7.1	8.3	9.0	8.5
Finance	1.1	1.8	1.2	2.4	3.6	2.6
Service:	6.6	65.3	15.6	11.0	55.1	19.8
Community						
Business	2.1	24.2	5.5	3.5	23.4	7.5
Government	2.2	2.2	2.2	3.2	1.2	2.8
Recreation	0.3	0.4	0.3	0.4	0.3	0.4
Personal	2.0	38.5	7.6	3.9	30.2	9.1
Industry not stated	8.1	0.4	6.9	6.2	0.6	5.1

1961	Atlantic Provinces			Quebec		
	M	F	T	M	F	T
All industries	100.0	100.0	100.0	100.0	100.0	100.0
Agriculture	8.4	1.5	6.6	9.0	3.3	7.5
Forestry	5.4	0.2	4.1	3.3	0.1	2.4
Fishing	5.4	0.1	4.0	0.2	(1)	0.2
Mining	3.9	0.2	3.0	2.0	0.2	1.5
Manufacturing	17.9	9.5	15.8	29.5	24.7	25.2
Electricity	1.3	0.3	1.0	1.3	0.3	1.0
Construction	11.5	0.6	8.8	10.4	0.5	7.7
Transportation and communication	10.5	3.4	8.7	8.4	3.6	7.1
Trade:	14.3	20.5	15.9	12.9	13.0	12.9
Wholesale						
Retail						
Finance	1.6	3.8	2.2	2.9	5.4	3.6
Service:	17.5	57.5	27.6	17.3	45.8	25.0
Community						
Business	5.7	30.7	12.0	6.6	26.7	12.0
Government	9.0	7.0	8.5	6.0	3.8	5.4
Recreation	0.4	0.5	0.4	0.6	0.4	0.6
Personal	2.4	19.3	6.7	4.1	14.9	7.0
Industry not stated	2.3	2.4	2.3	2.8	3.1	2.9

	Ontario			Prairie provinces			British Columbia	
M	F	T	M	F	T	M	F	T
100.0	100.0	100.0	100.0	100.0	100.0	100.0	100.0	100.0
27.1	2.8	22.6	55.8	7.4	49.6	15.9	3.4	14.1
0.9	(1)	0.7	0.2	(1)	0.2	5.9	0.2	5.1
0.5	0.1	0.4	1.0	0.2	0.9	3.6	(1)	3.1
1.7	(1)	1.4	1.8	0.1	1.6	4.8	0.2	4.1
24.9	22.4	24.5	7.8	5.8	7.5	18.7	9.4	17.3
1.1	0.4	0.9	0.4	0.2	0.4	1.2	0.5	1.1
8.2	0.2	6.8	4.4	0.3	3.9	8.9	0.2	7.7
7.9	3.5	7.1	7.2	2.8	6.6	10.3	5.7	9.6
10.4	14.1	11.1	7.7	13.3	8.4	10.4	17.2	11.4
1.6	1.3	1.5	1.8	2.0	1.8	2.1	2.3	2.1
8.8	12.8	9.6	5.9	11.3	6.6	8.3	14.9	9.3
2.4	4.3	2.8	1.6	3.5	1.8	2.2	4.1	2.5
10.7	51.6	18.2	8.6	66.0	16.0	12.4	58.6	19.0
3.2	19.6	6.3	2.7	25.0	5.5	3.2	22.7	6.0
3.5	3.2	3.4	2.3	2.3	2.3	3.4	2.5	3.3
0.6	0.4	0.5	0.4	0.3	0.4	0.6	0.7	0.6
3.4	28.4	8.0	3.2	38.4	7.8	5.2	32.7	9.1
4.2	0.6	3.5	3.5	0.4	3.1	5.7	0.5	5.0

	Ontario			Prairie provinces			British Columbia	
M	F	T	M	F	T	M	F	T
100.0	100.0	100.0	100.0	100.0	100.0	100.0	100.0	100.0
8.7	3.5	7.2	29.7	11.2	24.8	4.8	2.2	4.1
1.0	0.1	0.8	0.6	(1)	0.4	5.0	0.4	3.7
0.1	(1)	0.1	0.4	(1)	0.3	1.1	0.1	0.8
2.5	0.1	1.8	2.9	0.8	2.4	1.9	0.2	1.4
31.8	20.4	28.4	11.7	7.3	10.5	25.4	9.8	21.1
1.5	0.6	1.2	1.3	0.4	1.1	1.3	0.6	1.1
9.5	0.7	6.9	9.4	0.7	7.2	9.5	0.7	7.1
7.2	3.2	6.0	9.6	4.1	8.1	10.3	4.4	8.7
13.9	17.3	14.9	13.8	18.6	15.0	15.0	21.5	16.8
3.1	6.8	4.2	2.2	5.3	3.0	2.9	6.7	4.0
15.3	45.6	26.3	16.1	49.2	24.9	19.9	50.4	28.3
6.8	23.9	11.8	6.2	27.3	11.8	7.8	27.0	13.1
7.0	6.0	6.7	6.4	5.3	6.1	7.2	5.3	6.7
0.7	0.7	0.7	0.5	0.7	0.6	0.7	0.9	0.7
3.8	15.0	7.1	3.0	15.9	6.4	4.2	17.2	7.8
2.4	1.7	2.2	2.3	2.4	2.3	2.9	3.0	2.9

TABLE 3.32

Percentage Distribution of the Labour Force
by Sex and Major Occupation Groups for Regions
1931 and 1961*

1931	Atlantic provinces			Quebec		
	M	F	T	M	F	T
White Collar:	14.1	43.4	18.6	22.4	40.6	26.0
Proprietary and managerial	5.4	2.2	4.9	6.8	1.6	5.7
Professional	2.5	20.0	5.2	4.2	18.0	6.9
Clerical	2.6	12.7	4.2	5.2	13.9	7.0
Commercial and financial	3.6	8.5	4.3	6.2	7.1	6.4
Manual:	34.6	10.9	31.2	43.2	24.0	39.4
Manufacturing and mechanical†	7.4	7.4	7.4	12.7	18.7	13.9
Construction	4.8	(1)	4.1	7.1	(1)	5.7
Labourer‡	15.6	1.3	13.4	16.4	3.3	13.8
Transportation and communication	7.1	2.2	6.3	7.0	2.0	6.0
Service:	3.1	40.3	8.8	4.3	33.1	10.0
Personal	2.0	40.1	7.9	3.0	33.0	9.0
Protective and other	1.1	0.2	0.9	1.3	0.1	1.0
Primary:	47.9	5.4	41.4	30.1	2.3	24.6
Agricultural	35.1	5.2	30.6	26.8	2.3	22.0
Fishing, hunting and trapping	5.8	0.2	4.9	0.8	(1)	0.6
Logging	1.7	—	1.4	1.8	—	1.5
Mining and quarrying	5.3		4.5	0.7	—	0.5
Not stated	(1)	(1)	(1)	(1)	(1)	(1)

1961	Atlantic provinces			Quebec		
	M	F	T	M	F	T
White collar:	25.9	60.0	34.5	31.7	52.8	37.4
Proprietary and managerial	8.5	4.4	7.7	9.1	2.7	7.3
Professional	5.8	20.3	9.4	8.0	16.8	10.4
Clerical	5.7	22.6	10.0	7.7	25.0	12.4
Commercial and financial	5.6	12.7	7.4	6.9	8.3	7.3
Manual:	44.6	9.0	35.6	45.8	19.7	38.7
Manufacturing and mechanical†	14.6	5.8	12.4	20.3	16.3	19.2
Construction	8.3	(1)	6.2	8.2	(1)	5.9
Labourer‡	9.4	0.8	7.2	7.4	1.4	5.8
Transportation and communication	12.3	2.4	9.8	9.9	2.0	7.8
Service:	5.6	27.1	11.1	6.5	21.0	10.5
Personal	3.6	26.9	9.6	4.4	20.8	8.8
Protective and other	2.0	0.2	1.5	2.1	0.2	1.7
Primary:	21.3	1.4	16.2	13.0	3.3	10.3
Agricultural	8.6	1.3	6.7	9.2	3.3	7.6
Fishing, hunting and trapping	5.4	0.1	4.1	0.3	(1)	0.2
Logging	4.6	0.0	3.4	2.5	(1)	1.8
Mining and quarrying	2.7	0.0	2.0	1.0	(1)	0.7
Not stated	2.6	2.5	2.6	3.0	3.2	3.1

SOURCE: Census data.

*14 years of age and over in 1931 and 15 years and over in 1961. Newfoundland
included in 1961. Not including Armed Forces.

	Ontario			Prairie provinces			British Columbia	
M	F	T	M	F	T	M	F	T
22.9	48.5	27.8	16.1	46.0	19.9	21.7	51.1	25.9
7.0	1.5	6.1	5.3	1.3	4.8	7.1	2.5	6.5
4.2	15.6	6.3	2.9	20.5	5.2	4.1	18.3	6.1
5.2	21.9	8.3	3.2	17.0	5.0	4.3	19.9	6.5
6.5	9.5	7.1	4.7	7.2	4.9	6.2	10.4	6.8
42.8	18.5	38.3	22.2	6.1	20.1	43.2	11.1	38.6
15.5	14.4	15.3	5.5	3.8	5.3	11.2	6.3	10.5
6.2	(1)	5.1	3.2	—	2.9	6.6	—	5.7
13.3	1.4	11.1	8.2	0.3	7.0	16.1	0.7	13.9
7.8	2.7	6.8	5.3	2.0	4.9	9.3	4.1	8.5
4.4	30.1	9.2	3.4	40.4	8.2	6.9	34.5	10.9
3.0	30.0	8.0	2.6	40.3	7.5	5.4	34.1	9.5
1.4	0.1	1.2	0.8	0.1	0.7	1.5	0.4	1.4
29.8	2.8	24.7	68.3	7.5	51.8	28.2	3.3	24.6
27.1	2.7	22.6	55.7	7.4	49.6	16.0	3.2	14.2
0.6	0.1	0.5	1.0	0.1	0.9	3.6	0.1	3.1
0.8	—	0.6	0.2	—	0.1	4.7	—	4.0
1.3	—	1.0	1.4	—	1.2	3.9	—	3.3
0.1	0.1	(1)	(1)	(1)	(1)	(1)	(1)	(1)

	Ontario			Prairie provinces			British Columbia	
M	F	T	M	F	T	M	F	T
34.1	59.8	41.6	27.3	55.0	34.6	32.8	62.7	41.1
10.5	2.7	8.2	9.3	2.6	7.5	11.3	4.2	9.3
8.7	13.8	10.2	6.8	15.9	9.2	8.3	15.1	10.2
7.6	32.5	14.9	5.3	26.4	10.9	5.6	31.2	12.7
7.3	10.8	8.3	5.9	10.1	7.0	7.6	12.2	8.9
45.3	13.6	36.0	32.9	7.5	26.2	46.0	7.9	35.5
22.4	10.1	18.7	11.3	4.2	9.5	19.2	4.5	15.2
7.2	0.1	5.1	6.0	(1)	4.4	7.1	(1)	5.1
6.7	1.2	5.2	5.7	0.8	4.4	7.7	1.0	5.8
9.0	2.2	7.0	9.9	2.5	8.0	12.0	2.4	9.4
6.6	21.4	10.9	5.3	24.1	10.2	7.2	24.3	11.9
4.5	20.3	9.4	3.7	23.8	9.0	5.1	23.8	10.3
2.1	1.1	1.5	1.6	0.3	1.2	2.1	0.5	1.6
11.4	3.3	9.1	32.2	10.9	26.6	10.9	2.1	8.4
9.0	3.3	7.2	30.1	10.9	25.0	5.2	2.0	4.3
0.2	(1)	0.1	0.4	(1)	0.3	1.2	0.1	0.9
0.7	(1)	0.5	0.5	(1)	0.4	3.3	(1)	2.4
1.5	(1)	1.1	1.2	(1)	0.9	1.2	(1)	0.8
2.6	1.9	2.4	0.2	2.5	2.4	3.1	3.0	3.1

†Includes stationary enginemen and occupations associated with electric power production.
‡Laborers in all industries except those in primary occupations.
(1) Less than 0.1 per cent.

TABLE 3.33

Unemployment Rates* by Region
annual averages 1946–62†

	1946	1947	1948	1949	1950	1951	1952	1953	1954	1955	1956	1957	1958	1959	1960	1961	1962
Atlantic provinces‡	5.5	4.7	4.5	4.7	7.8	4.3	4.6	5.5	6.6	6.5	6.0	8.3	12.5	10.8	10.6	11.1	10.7
Quebec	4.0	2.5	2.5	3.4	4.4	2.9	3.7	3.8	5.9	6.2	5.0	6.0	8.8	7.9	9.1	9.3	7.5
Ontario	2.8	1.8	1.7	2.3	2.4	1.7	2.2	2.1	3.8	3.2	2.4	3.4	5.4	4.5	5.4	5.5	4.3
Prairie provinces§	2.2	1.4	1.5	1.9	2.1	1.6	1.9	1.9	2.5	3.1	2.2	2.7	4.1	3.3	4.2	4.6	3.9
British Columbia	3.9	2.8	3.5	3.4	4.4	3.5	3.8	4.0	5.2	3.8	2.8	5.0	8.5	6.4	8.7	8.5	6.7

*The unemployed as a percentage of the labour force.
†Averages for 1953 to 1962 are based on monthly surveys. Before 1953 the labour force survey was carried out on quarterly intervals, and averages for 1946 to 1952 are based on quarterly surveys.
‡Newfoundland included only from 1950.
§In June 1950, no interviewing was carried out in Manitoba due to flood conditions in the Red and Assiniboine valleys and all estimates for that month excluded Manitoba. A calculation has been made of what the estimates might have been if there had been no flooding and figures on this basis were included in calculating annual averages for 1950.

of attempting to create and maintain a separate national identity stretching from east to west. Indeed, it is probably not too much to say that the future political and economic viability of Canada depends to a large extent on a significant narrowing of the outstanding regional disparities. Especially *within* some of the regions, where the inequality tends to be even larger than *among* them, more pronounced trends towards equality are necessary. This refers mainly to Quebec where ethnic differences are not only substantial but tend to induce a charged emotional atmosphere.

Indeed it has been cogently argued that the nationalistic sentiment among French Canadians, accentuated by these differences, has led the Quebec government to initiate actions designed to redistribute income in favour of the French Canadian middle-class. Specifically Albert Breton concludes that "resources which could have been invested to increase the social income of the community (i.e. Quebec) have been used in the case of nationalization to buy new high-income jobs for members of the French-Canadian middle class and, in the case of the General Investment Corporation (Société Générale de Financement) to keep already existing high-income jobs for the same middle class."[33] Such actions, which Canada in general likewise employs to redistribute jobs and income to Canadians in preference to foreign and especially US investors,[34] serve to reduce the over-all growth rate in the interest of nationalism and tend to accentuate the rift among English- and French-speaking Canadians in Quebec.

Unless, then, a higher and sustained rate of over-all dynamism for the Canadian economy in general can be achieved, easy progress towards greater equality is unlikely and specific actions to redistribute income but which may not increase productive capacity are encouraged. It is in this sense that the economic slowdown of the latter 1950's, discussed in Chapter 1, has a special significance from the problem of regionalism and separatism. In addition, however, regionalism is being strengthened in Canada by the altered pattern of foreign trade—a matter to which we turn in the following chapter.

[33]Albert Breton, "The Economics of Nationalism," *Journal of Political Economy*, Aug. 1964, p. 385.
[34]See next chapter for details.

4

FOREIGN INFLUENCE

Previous chapters have indicated the extent to which external forces tend to shape Canadian economic development. So important is this relationship that it needs more extensive analysis than we have thus far been able to devote to it. The present chapter therefore will examine in some detail the changing magnitude, composition, and direction of Canada's imports and exports. However, much of the contemporary discussion of problems of dependence and independence revolves around foreign ownership and control of Canadian industrial assets and natural resources, especially by firms incorporated in the United States. Indeed this particular issue goes well beyond the economic impact of such ownership and control. It involves important but elusive questions of national identity and political, cultural, and social independence, which lie at the roots of Canadian–United States relationships.

The first section of the present chapter will examine the trends in exports and imports. The second will discuss the problem of capital flows, which carries with it the issue of foreign ownership.

EXPORTS AND IMPORTS

The over-all position of Canada in total world trade is shown in Table 4.1 for 1961. As a proportion of total world exports Canada's share rose from 4.4 per cent in 1937 to 6.5 per cent in 1952.[1] The ratio then declined to 5.7 per cent in 1955 and to about 5.1 per cent in 1960 and 1961 as exports from a revived Western Europe and Japan began to rise dramatically. On a per capita basis Canada ranks among the top

[1] R. V. Anderson, *The Future of Canada's Export Trade*, a study prepared for RCCEP (Ottawa, 1957), p. 30.

TABLE 4.1

World Trade, by Leading Countries
1961

Country	Exports fob	Imports cif	Total trade	Trade per capita
	U.S.$ '000,000	U.S.$ '000,000	U.S.$ '000,000	U.S.$
United States	20,192	16,115	37,027	200
Germany, Federal Republic	12,690	10,948	23,638	417
Britain	10,754	12,318	23,072	437
France	7222	8679	13,901	301
Canada	6107	6298	12,315	675
Japan	4236	5810	10,046	106
Italy	4188	5222	9410	189
Netherlands	4288	5087	9375	800
Belgium and Luxembourg	3924	4219	8143	858
Sweden	2738	2921	5659	750
Switzerland	2043	2707	4750	864
Australia	2325	2395	4720	449
World Totals	118,500	124,000	242,500	119

SOURCE: *Canada Year Book, 1962.*

five exporting nations, a position she has held for many decades. These data coupled with the large (though declining) proportion of exports and imports to GNE already noted in Chapter 1, indicate the continuing importance of foreign trade for the Canadian economy and, at the same time, the relatively large contribution Canada makes to total world trade.

Of greater importance than these broad aggregates and averages is the composition of exports and imports. Broadly speaking exports and imports each consist of two major components, goods and services. The former is composed of commodities (or merchandise) and may or may not include an item referred to as "gold production available for export" while the main subdivisions of the services (or "invisibles") category are travel expenditures, interest and dividends, freight and shipping, inheritances, and immigrants' funds. In Canada, merchandise or commodity exports have accounted for about three-quarters of total current receipts in the post-war period while merchandise imports generally comprise about two-thirds of total current payments. We will examine first the dimensions of commodity trade since this is the most important aspect of Canada's external economic relations in both an aggregative and strategic sense as pointed out in Chapter 1. However, a rising imbalance in the service account has become a serious problem in recent years and will be examined later.

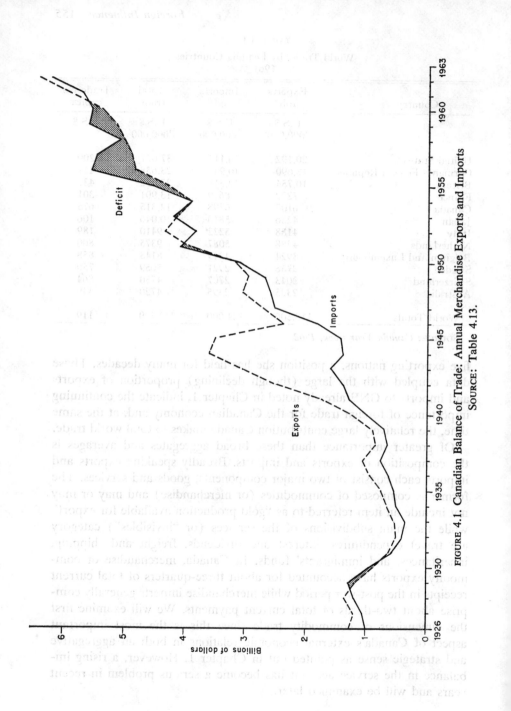

FIGURE 4.1. Canadian Balance of Trade: Annual Merchandise Exports and Imports
SOURCE: Table 4.13.

The over-all trends of merchandise exports and imports are sketched in Figure 4.1 and detailed in Table 4.13. Both merchandise exports and imports have risen erratically over time. For most periods Canada has had a surplus on merchandise transactions with the noteworthy exception of the period of the slowdown in the latter half of the 1950's. The early part of the 1960's has witnessed a re-emergence of surpluses and in 1963 Canada's favourable merchandise balance reached a level rivalling the excellent performance of the first post-war decade.[2]

Another feature of Canada's merchandise balance is its pattern as between the United States on the one hand and all other countries on the other. Deficits with the US have always typified this aspect of international trade, but generally these have been more than offset by surpluses with overseas countries and in particular the United Kingdom.[3]

COMPOSITION OF EXPORTS

The composition of domestic commodity exports in percentage terms for selected years from 1928 to 1960 is shown in Table 4.2. The most dramatic change indicated is the sharp and steady decline in the relative importance of wheat and wheat flour from over 36 per cent of total commodity exports in 1928 to less than 9 per cent in 1960. On the other hand, the lumber, wood pulp, and newsprint exports have risen from 17 per cent in 1928 to over 26 per cent in 1960 after reaching 30 per cent in 1955. The metals and minerals listed in the table have displayed an even greater change. Asbestos, aluminum, copper, lead, nickel, zinc, and iron ore accounted for a mere 6 per cent of Canada's exports of commodities in 1928 but over 20 per cent in 1960. With the exception of lead, all the metals and minerals have shown large increases over the 32-year period. The chemicals group (which also includes synthetic fertilizers and uranium) has, however, exhibited an even faster rate of relative growth especially between 1955 and 1960, much of which is accounted for by uranium whose future prospects, however, appear bleak.

The "sundry manufactures" group contains some fifteen commodity classes. We shall not outline the detailed pattern of each component here. It is sufficient to note the comparative stability of the group over time with a slight tendency to decline since 1954.

New gold available for export has shown wide relative fluctuations from between 3 to 12 per cent of the total and even became Canada's second most important actual or potential source of foreign exchange

[2]The significance of this is discussed towards the end of chap. 1.
[3]See Tables 4.14, 4.15, and 4.16.

TABLE 4.2

Canada's Domestic Exports of Selected Commodities
selected years 1928–60
(percentages of total domestic exports, including gold)

	1928	1932	1937	1954	1955	1960
Wheat and wheat flour	36.1	26.1	15.5*	11.5	9.3	8.7
Barley, oats and rye	3.5	2.5	1.0	3.2	2.2	1.3
Meats	1.4	1.1	3.5	1.3	0.9	0.8
Fish and products	2.6	3.2	2.4	3.2	2.8	2.5
Lumber	3.5	2.3	3.8	8.1	8.7	6.4
Wood pulp	3.3	3.4	3.6	6.7	6.7	6.0
Newsprint	10.2	14.8	10.7	15.8	15.0	14.0
Asbestos and products	0.8	0.5	1.3	2.1	2.2	2.2
Aluminum and products	0.7	0.7	1.6	4.6	4.8	5.0
Copper and products	1.7	2.9	4.8	3.3	3.9	4.1
Lead and products	0.8	0.6	1.5	1.0	0.8	0.5
Nickel	1.6	1.2	5.0	4.5	4.8	4.8
Zinc and products	0.6	0.7	1.3	1.4	1.6	1.2
Iron ore	0.0	0.0	0.0	1.0	2.3	2.9
Chemicals†	1.3	2.0	1.9	4.0	4.7	9.3
Sundry manufactures‡	9.6	7.0	9.8	9.5	8.0	7.8
New gold available for export	2.9	12.5	12.3	3.8	3.5	3.0
All other commodities	19.3	18.6	20.2	14.9	17.7	19.5
Total	100.0	100.0	100.0	100.0	100.0	100.0

SOURCES: DBS, *Trade of Canada;* and Bank of Canada, *Statistical Summary;* R. V. Anderson, *The Future of Canada's Export Trade,* a study prepared for RCCEP, (Ottawa, 1957), Table 1, p. 8.
*Based upon Board of Grain Commissioners' rather than customs data.
†Fertilizers, synthetic rubber, uranium and other chemicals.
‡Alcoholic beverages; rubber products; textiles and products; electrical apparatus; engines and boilers; farm machinery and implements; non-farm machinery; automobiles, trucks and parts; other vehicles, chiefly of iron; guns, rifles and other firearms; railway track material of iron; other manufactures of iron and steel; ships and vessels; aircraft and parts; cartridges, gun and rifle.

in 1937 as far as commodity exports are concerned. In the postwar period, gold has resumed its earlier relative position.

But the most noteworthy feature of Canada's exports is the preponderance of resource-based production. Although Table 4.2 includes a high degree of processing in some of the mineral and wood products categories, and hence cannot be used as an indicator of the degree of manufacturing, additional evidence is given in Table 4.3 which shows a continuing preponderance of raw materials and partially manufactured goods in the export content. We have already noted that caution must be exercised in using these classifications.[4] However, the evidence, crude as it may be, suggests a reversion to the 1926–29 pattern with over 62

[4] See also Anderson, *Future of Canada's Export Trade,* p. 13.

TABLE 4.3

Canada's Domestic Exports to All Countries by Degree of Manufacture*
selected periods 1926-59
(percentages)

	1926-29	1936-39	1946-49	1951-54	1958-59
Raw materials	46.7	32.2	27.2	30.5	34.6
Partially manufactured	14.8	25.0	24.9	30.6	28.2
Fully or chiefly manufactured	38.5	42.8	47.9	38.9	37.2
Total	100.0	100.0	100.0	100.0	100.0

SOURCE: DBS, *Review of Foreign Trade, Calendar Year 1955*, pp. 42 and 45; *Canada Year Book, 1962*, p. 980.
*Data refer to annual averages of fiscal years for 1926-29 and 1936-39 and calendar years for later periods.

per cent of the commodities in the non-fully or non-chiefly manufactured group, after the relative importance of the latter group had decreased to barely over one half in the immediate postwar period. This suggests that with European and Japanese recovery the more highly manufactured Canadian products failed to retain their promising foothold. The data also reflect the sharp rise in the new staples, namely, minerals and metals which have replaced some of the older staples, notably wheat, in terms of relative importance. But the fact remains that "the past 30 years show no evidence of a shift away from basic primary commodities in their raw or processed form."[5] Only the composition, and variety of staples has changed, not the degree of dependence upon them in an aggregative sense. However, the extent of Canadian dependence upon exported basic materials and food is not especially high compared to roughly comparable countries (in terms of economic well-being) such as Sweden, Australia, or Denmark. The implications of this may be more serious for Canada as far as maintaining a high degree of political independence is concerned, particularly when coupled with other features of Canada's export trade to be discussed below.

COMPOSITION OF IMPORTS

Table 4.1 suggests that the role of Canada as an importing nation is analogous to her role as an exporter. As in the case of exports, comparable downward trends in the ratio of imports to GNE have been registered since the late 1920's although both commodity exports and imports have more than quadrupled in value since 1928–29.

[5]*Ibid.*, p. 15.

The commodity composition of imports is shown in Table 4.4. The heavy concentration in capital goods and consumer durables which accounted for 35 to 40 per cent of total commodity imports in recent years is noteworthy compared with the figure of less than 25 per cent for the years before the Second World War. At the same time the food, drink, and tobacco component as well as the furs, hides, leather, and textile group have each declined from about 20 per cent to around 12 per cent in 1955 and 1960. Fuels and lubricants and the chemicals group have not changed significantly, although since 1937 the former has shown a downward trend, to be expected in view of the new fuel discoveries since the Second World War, while the chemicals group has risen steadily. Table 4.4 indicates that unlike the export composition the extent of fully or chiefly manufactured commodities is extremely large. Indeed, a classification by degree of manufacturing (Table 4.5) shows

TABLE 4.4

Canada's Imports of Selected Commodities
selected years 1926-60
(percentages of total commodity imports)

	1926	1929	1937	1954	1955	1960
Food, drink and tobacco:						
Fruits, nuts and vegetables	4.0	3.9	4.4	4.6	4.1	4.6
Sugar and its products	3.8	2.2	2.6	1.5	1.4	1.3
Other food, drink and tobacco	12.4	12.8	8.5	7.1	6.2	6.7
Furs, hides and skins, leather and textile products:						
Wool, manufactured	3.9	3.1	2.4	1.5	1.3	1.3
Cotton, manufactured	3.3	2.6	2.5	1.9	1.8	2.2
Other furs, hides, etc.	14.1	12.3	11.9	5.8	6.1	6.8
Capital goods and consumer durables:						
Motor vehicles and parts	5.2	6.5	6.1	6.4	7.7	9.9
Machinery other than agricultural	3.8	5.4	5.7	9.3	9.5	10.6
Electrical apparatus and supplies	1.7	2.8	1.9	51.	4.8	4.7
Other capital goods and consumer durables	8.0	9.6	9.1	18.0	18.4	11.7
Industrial materials for manufacture of durables:						
Non-ferrous metals (excluding electrical apparatus)	3.4	4.2	3.9	3.7	3.6	3.8
Primary iron and steel	5.4	5.7	6.1	2.8	3.2	2.9
Other	6.6	5.4	6.4	4.2	5.1	8.8
Chemicals: Fuels and lubricants:	3.1	3.1	4.6	5.4	5.5	6.2
Coal and products	6.7	4.9	5.2	2.1	2.6	1.7
Petroleum and products	5.2	6.0	7.3	8.4	7.9	7.2
Miscellaneous goods—mainly for consumers	9.4	9.6	9.6	11.5	10.8	9.6
Total	100.0	100.0	100.0	100.0	100.0	100.0

SOURCE: D. W. Slater, *Canada's Imports*, Appendix D, Table II; and DBS, *Trade of Canada*, various years.

TABLE 4.5

Canada's Imports from All Countries by Degree of Manufacture
selected periods 1926-59

	1926-29	1936-37	1947-49	1953-54	1958-59
Raw materials	24.3	28.4	25.6	18.9	17.2
Partially manufactured	8.9	9.5	6.9	5.0	5.3
Fully or chiefly manufactured	66.8	62.1	67.5	76.1	77.5
Total	100.0	100.0	100.0	100.0	100.0

SOURCE: DBS, *Trade of Canada*, various years.   Data refer to annual averages.

that in 1958–59 over three-quarters of Canada's commodity imports
were fully or chiefly manufactured. This compares with less than 40 per
cent for a similar group in the exports. Furthermore, there appears to
be a rising trend for the former and a general decline in the latter. However, the rise in the importance of manufactured imports, which appears
to conflict with prevalent notions of industrial development, although
not necessarily inconsistent with comparative advantage, is largely due
to the increasing importance of a few subclasses of imports having the
highest degree of manufacture. As Slater points out, however, "the typical situation is for the degree of manufacture to be smaller now than in
the late 1920's for many sub-groups of imports."[6]

The general pattern indicated by the foregoing may be summarized as
follows: the long-run trend in the relative importance of both exports
and imports has been downward although the degree of dependence
upon foreign trade is still substantial and indeed strategic. On the other
hand, the degree of reliance upon staples among the exports generally
has not altered significantly, while there has been a rising proportion of
fully manufactured goods relative to total imports. Given Canada's comparative advantage in natural resources this pattern is not perhaps surprising. Yet with the level of economic maturity or development already
achieved it would be expected that a greater degree of manufacturing
for export would have occurred and that the extent of import substitution in more completely manufactured products would have progressed
farther.

Part of the explanation of this apparent paradox lies in the changing
export and import markets. On the export side the overwhelming predominance of the United States is obvious from Table 4.6. Indeed, the

[6]D. W. Slater, *Canada's Imports*, a study prepared for RCCEP (Ottawa, 1957),
p. 20.

United States accounts for well over half the total value of Canadian commodity exports and about two-thirds of Canada's imports. The United Kingdom is Canada's second largest trading partner taking about 16 to 20 per cent of exports from Canada in recent years and providing a little over one-tenth of the imports. The US and UK combined therefore have accounted for between 75 and 80 per cent of total Canadian trade in commodities in the last several years.

TABLE 4.6

Canadian Exports by Area:
Percentages of Total Domestic Exports, excluding Gold, to All Countries
except Newfoundland
selected years 1928-62

Year	United States	United Kingdom	Continental Western Europe*	Japan	All other
1928	36.3	21.8	26.3	2.9	12.4
1932	32.8	31.1	19.8	2.5	13.8
1937	36.2	37.6	8.6	2.5	15.1
1954	59.7	16.8	8.5	2.5	12.5
1955	59.8	18.0	8.4	2.1	11.7
1960	55.8	17.4	11.3	3.4	12.1
1961	53.7	15.9	10.6	4.0	15.8
1962	58.1	14.8	9.8	3.4	13.9

SOURCE: Anderson, *The Future of Canada's Export Trade,* p. 19 and DBS, *Trade of Canada,* various years.
*Continental Western Europe refers to OEEC countries and includes all of Germany prior to 1954.

The long-term trend in distribution of exports has been toward the US and away from Western Europe. Indeed just prior to the Second World War (1937), the UK alone took 38 per cent of Canada's commodity exports compared with only 36 per cent by the US. If the rest of Western Europe is added to the UK, then the European orientation of Canada's export trade relationships was such that that area took approximately 47 per cent of the total commodity exports.[7] On the other hand, looking at imports, Canada has generally received over 60 per cent of her merchandise imports from the US.[8] The proximity to the US as well as the relative efficiency of US production, especially in important lines of manufacturing, have always tended to concentrate a high degree of Canadian import dependence on the American market.

[7]See also Anderson, *Future of Canada's Export Trade,* p. 36.
[8]See Slater, *Canada's Imports,* Table 8, p. 31 for selected data from 1926 to 1955. The proportion of Canadian imports emanating from the US varied from 61 per cent in 1935–39 to 73 per cent in 1955. The figure for 1960 was 67 per cent and for 1963 was almost 68 per cent (see Tables 4.13 and 4.14).

But as far as exports were concerned, Canada's staples were largely of a kind that tended to be competitive with US output rather than complementary to it:[9] hence, the wheat economy, for example, became tied more to Western Europe than to North America as was the case earlier in Canadian history with respect to furs, timber, and fish. So long therefore as Canada concentrated upon the exportation of commodities which the US could well supply itself, the Canadian economy had a distinct European as well as US orientation. In fact, as we shall examine later, a kind of triangular trade developed with Canada's current account surpluses from Western Europe, including the UK, serving to balance the chronic deficits with the US. But the point here is that the pre-war pattern of international transactions tended to create and maintain strong economic and commercial ties with *both* the United States and Western Europe, the UK in particular. It is important to note at this juncture that a European orientation, especially of commodities produced to the west of the Atlantic provinces, helps maintain an east-west pattern of trade within Canada itself and hence serves as a kind of counterbalance to the more natural north-south economic tendencies. So long as a large proportion of Canadian trade involved overseas countries, the economic stability and security of the economy was to that extent enhanced. The east-west orientation of economic activity within Canada has, of course, (with some exceptions) always been bolstered by deliberate policy in the form of tariffs, taxes, railroad subsidies, and so on. But the economic penalty, the real economic cost, of maintaining a separate nation north of the 49th parallel was considerably reduced and in fact rendered tolerable so long as trade had a large overseas orientation. Furthermore, and perhaps more important, the overseas countries created a diversity of markets in which to sell and reduced, to that extent, the significance of economic and political change in one country. Canada had a higher degree of economic choice and discretion when a large proportion of exports went to *both* the United States and overseas countries. This not only enhanced her economic viability but also served as a basis for financing the import surpluses from the US since export surpluses with other countries have been traditional. In addition Canadian exports of manufactured products are largely concentrated in markets outside the US, despite their relatively high cost, due to a combination of imperial preference in Commonwealth countries and the American tariff against manufactured imports. Thus, the pre-war pattern of overseas trade served to diversify not only the composition of Canadian exports but to provide a greater variety of export possibilities by destination.

[9]There were and still are some exceptions, notably newsprint and pulp.

The Second World War, however, changed Canada's trading pattern dramatically. The proportion of commodity exports alone going to the United States jumped from 36 per cent in 1937 to levels close to 60 per cent in the 1950's at the same time that exports to the UK fell from 38 per cent of the 1937 total to between 15 and 20 per cent. Exports to continental Western Europe, already down from 26 per cent in 1928 to 9 per cent in 1937, remained at levels constituting less than 10 per cent of the total. The sharp reorientation of Canadian trade thus reduced the east-west counterpoise and range of market discretion. At the same time this tended to permit the more natural economic integration of North America to go forward relatively unchecked. That this enhanced the already strong forces of regionalism in Canada has been noted earlier and with it came increasing difficulties in maintaining a viable and inter-related economy. It is against this background that recent efforts to re-direct a certain proportion of Canadian trade must be examined. Canada has always resisted to a greater or lesser extent the economic pull from the US and thus has constantly fought against the easier and more natural lure of North American economic integration.

The reasons underlying the shift in direction of exports to the US reside partly in institutional factors, such as the non-convertibility of the pound, but mainly they reflect the rise of the new staples as already shown. The new minerals and metals have become uniquely complementary to US industry as dwindling supplies of comparable US domestic resources and new needs have induced a more intensive search beyond American borders. Canada was, of course, a natural source of supply not only because of resource availability, of which more will be said in Part II, but also due to proximity and cultural, political, linguistic as well as ethnic similarity.

If we examine the destination of particular commodities, the predominance of the US in the new staples as well as some of the old ones becomes even more apparent. Table 4.7 shows the proportion of Canada's leading exports going to the US. The only significant items appearing in Table 4.2 that are omitted from Table 4.7 are wheat and wheat flour, barley, oats, and rye. As would be expected, the US, having large surpluses in these agricultural products, does not need to import further amounts. But aside from these items, which constituted 10 per cent of total Canadian commodity exports in 1960, the remaining commodities listed in Table 4.7 comprise over 45 per cent of total Canadian exports of all commodities to all destinations. It is noteworthy that, except for copper, nickel, and aluminum, over 50 per cent of each of the important Canadian export items goes to the United States. For most

TABLE 4.7

Domestic Canadian Exports to the United States,
1958
(millions of dollars)

Rank in 1958	$000,000	US Share of exports of each item %
1. Newsprint	690	86
2. Uranium ores and concentrates	263	95
3. Wood pulp	240	84
4. Planks and boards	227	78
5. Nickel, primary and semi-fab.	104	49
6. Aluminum, primary and semi-fab.	98	44
7. Farm implements and parts (except tractors)	87	93
8. Cattle, chiefly beef	84	100
9. Iron ore	78	72
10. Petroleum, crude and partly refined	73	100
11. Fish, fresh and frozen	70	99
12. Whisky	64	91
13. Asbestos, unmanufactured	48	53
14. Copper, primary and semi-fab.	43	31
15. Fertilizers, chemical	40	87
16. Zinc, primary and semi-fab.	37	67
17. Pulpwood	30	86
18. Beef and veal, fresh	20	99
19. Shingles	19	95
20. Abrasive, artificial and crude	19	83
Total, above items	2334	
Total all domestic exports to US	2832	
Percentage of above items to total	81	

SOURCE: Benard Goodman, *Industrial Materials in Canadian-American Relations* (Detroit, 1961), Table 5, p. 11.

commodities, namely newsprint, uranium, wood pulp, farm implements, cattle, petroleum, fish, whiskey, chemical fertilizers, and several others, the US market absorbs virtually all of Canada's exports.

Another way of looking at US-Canadian trade relations is to examine the leading commodities which Canada exports to and imports from the US as a proportion of total Canadian trade with the US. Table 4.8 indicates this comparison. The data suggest a high degree of complementarity between the two economies with Canada exchanging mainly raw or semi-processed natural resources for highly manufactured capital and consumer goods. To some extent this pattern arises from US commercial policy, in particular the US tariff which discriminates against the more advanced stages of manufacturing, but that a somewhat comparable though less pronounced pattern would exist in the absence of such

TABLE 4.8

Canada–United States Trade by Leading Commodities and Commodity Groups
1957

Canadian exports to United States			Canadian Imports from United States		
Rank	Millions of dollars	Percentage of total	Rank	Millions of dollars	Percentage of total
1. Newsprint	610	21	1. Machinery (non-farm) and parts	552	14
2. Wood pulp	235	8	2. Autos, trucks and parts	336	8
3. Planks and boards	205	7	3. Rolling mill products (including tubes)	275	7
4. Nickel, primary and semi-manufactured	153	5	4. Electrical equipment	209	5
5. Petroleum, crude and products	141	5	5. Tractors and parts	122	3
6. Uranium, ores and concentrates	128	4	6. Coal	113	3
7. Iron ore	110	4	7. Engines and parts	107	3
8. Aluminum, primary and semi-manufactured	101	4	8. Petroleum and products	91	2
9. Copper, primary and semi-manufactured	70	2	9. Cotton, raw and fabrics	91	2
10. Fish, fresh and frozen	62	2	10. Aircraft and parts	79	2
11. Whisky	61	2	11. Tourist purchase	74	2
12. Farm machinery and parts (ex. tractors)	58	2	12. Farm implements and parts (ex. tractors)	72	2
13. Zinc, primary and semi-manufactured	42	1	13. Fresh fruit and vegetables	69	2
14. Cattle, chiefly beef	42	1	14. Books and printed matter	60	2
15. Pulpwood	39	1	15. Synthetic plastics	47	1
16. Fertilizers	39	1	16. Cooking and heating equipment	37	1
17. Abrasives	31	1	17. Refrigerators	34	1
18. Barley	25	1	18. Iron ore	33	1
19. Machinery (non-farm) and parts	22	1	19. Tools	28	1
20. Fur skins	20	1	20. Medical, optical, dental equipment	24	1
Above total	2194	76	Above total	2453	61

SOURCE: Grant L. Reuber, *The Growth and Changing Composition of Trade between Canada and the United States*, National Planning Association and Private Planning Association of Canada, 1960, Table 7, p. 38.

NOTE: Owing to rounding, percentage figures do not add to totals shown.

a policy can scarcely be doubted. The evidence also suggests one dimension of the extent to which the North American economy has become economically integrated despite the existence of two separate nations and despite Canadian attempts to resist such a degree of US predominance. Indeed, it seems a little paradoxical that while other major regions of the world are deliberately trying to move towards closer economic and even political unification, North America has already attained a high degree of economic integration despite efforts to thwart it from the Canadian side and with no vigorous movement favouring it on the American side. It has emerged rather spontaneously and from the Canadian point of view it causes mounting concern. It may even be, as H. J. G. Aitken has recently argued, that *de facto* Canadian economic and political independence is incompatible with her continued growth.[10]

NON-MERCHANDISE TRADE

Although trade in services is less important than merchandise, nevertheless the service account is far from negligible. Table 4.9 summarizes the major components of this aspect of foreign trade for selected years between 1926 and 1962. The steady rise in the deficit, recording more than a five-fold increase since 1926, parallels the growing gap between commodity imports and exports especially since 1950. Furthermore, every item listed in Table 4.9 has contributed to the net deficit since the early 1950's. There have been some exceptions to this in the past, such as travel expenditures from 1926 to 1951 and freight and shipping after the war, but recent experience shows rising deficits on all service accounts (except travel expenditures in 1962 and 1963) as indicated in Tables 4.10, 4.11 and 4.12.

For all non-merchandise transactions, which include more than the items shown in Table 4.9, the rising deficit with the US since 1949 is especially sharp—more than 300 per cent between 1949 and 1961. The largest single contributor to this rise is the changing pattern of travel expenditures which accounted for about 46 per cent of the $457 million increase in the service deficit with the US. From a surplus of over $100 million in 1949 to a deficit of almost $90 million in 1960, the travel expenditure component progressively deteriorated, although the deficit has been eliminated over the last few years. Net payments of interest

[10]Aitken believes that the economic interrelationship between Canada and the US is the "leading contemporary example of regional economic integration. The process of integration has already gone very far and, if present trends continue, will go farther. What is emerging in North America is continental economic integration on a massive scale." *American Capital and Canadian Resources* (Cambridge, Mass., 1961), p. 7.

TABLE 4.9

Non-Merchandise Imports and Exports from and to All Countries
selected years 1926–62

	1926	1928	1932
Service exports: total ($ million)	$363	$407	$243
Travel expenditures (% of total)	41.9	43.5	46.9
Interest and dividends (%)	8.8	11.3	15.2
Freight and shipping (%)	26.5	23.6	15.6
All other current receipts (%)	22.8	21.6	22.3
Service imports: total ($ million)	$565	$611	$506
Travel expenditures (%)	17.5	16.0	9.7
Interest and dividends (%)	42.5	45.0	59.7
Freight and shipping (%)	18.6	19.0	13.0
All other current payments (%)	21.4	20.0	17.6
Surplus (+) or deficit (−) on non-merchandise transactions* ($ million)	−$202	−$204	−$263

SOURCE: DBS, *The Canadian Balance of International Payments, 1926–1948* (Ottawa, 1949), DBS, *The Canadian Balance of International Payments 1960* (Ottawa, 1962) and *Quarterly Estimates of the Canadian Balance of International Payments, Fourth Quarter, 1963* (Ottawa, 1964).

*Excluding gold production available for export, official contributions and mutual aid to NATO countries.

and dividends to the US have always typified the service component of the current balance. Especially since 1953, the deficit in this category has risen sharply and in 1960 was almost double the figure seven years earlier. Indeed, the deficit on this account continued to rise and in 1963 reached an all-time high of $614 million.

But if deficits with respect to the United States have always been a feature of the non-merchandise, as well as the commodity, balance, the same was not generally true of all other overseas countries until 1953. From 1953 to 1961 there was a steady rise in the non-merchandise deficit with other countries to almost $400 million. This has substantially reduced the net balance for all current account items and in 1959 more than offset the small surplus on merchandise trade. As in the case of the non-merchandise deficit with the US the biggest contribution has been travel expenditures which increased 14-fold between 1949 and 1963. The bulk of this deficit occurred as a result of sharply increased Canadian travel abroad especially in the UK and Western Europe.

In general, the behaviour of the non-merchandise account has paralled that of the commodity balance: rising deficits on almost all items during the 1950's which aggravated the over-all deficit (but with some improve-

TABLE 4.9 (*continued*)

1937	1950	1954	1958	1960	1962
$407	$938	$1152	$1390	$1556	$1819
40.8	29.3	26.5	25.1	26.9	30.8
18.7	9.7	12.8	12.1	11.4	11.6
27.5	30.3	27.2	28.9	28.3	27.4
13.0	30.7	33.5	33.9	33.4	30.2
$637	$1440	$1741	$2449	$2752	$2955
13.7	15.7	22.3	22.1	22.9	20.6
47.4	33.0	24.3	25.0	24.5	26.4
21.5	20.9	20.5	18.8	19.5	19.9
17.4	30.4	32.9	34.1	33.1	33.1
−$230	−$502	−$589	−$1059	−$1196	−$1136

TABLE 4.10

Travel Expenditures between Canada and Other Countries
1948-60
(millions of dollars)

	Account with United States			Account with overseas countries			Account with all countries		
Year	Receipts	Pay-ments	Net	Receipts	Pay-ments	Net	Receipts	Pay-ments	Net
1948	267	113	+154	12	21	− 9	279	134	+145
1949	267	165	+102	18	28	− 10	285	193	+ 92
1950	260	193	+ 67	15	33	− 18	275	226	+ 49
1951	258	246	+ 12	16	34	− 18	274	280	− 6
1952	257	294	− 37	18	47	− 29	275	341	− 66
1953	282	307	− 25	20	58	− 38	302	365	− 63
1954	283	320	− 37	22	69	− 47	305	389	− 84
1955	303	363	− 60	25	86	− 61	328	449	−121
1956	309	391	− 82	28	107	− 79	337	498	−161
1957	325	403	− 78	38	122	− 84	363	525	−162
1958	309	413	−104	40	129	− 89	349	542	−193
1959	351	448	− 97	40	150	−110	391	598	−207
1960	375	462	− 87	45	165	−120	420	627	−207
1961	435	459	− 24	47	183	−136	483	642	−160
1962	510	420	+ 90	50	190	−140	560	610	− 50
1963	549	392	+157	53	197	−144	602	589	+ 13

SOURCE: DBS, *Canadian Balance of International Payments 1900* (Ottawa, 1962), p. 21, and *Quarterly Estimates of the Canadian Balance of International Payments*, March 1964.

TABLE 4.11

Receipts and Payments of Interest and Dividends between Canada and Other Countries

1946–60

(millions of dollars)

Year	Account with United States					Account with United Kingdom					Account with all countries				
	Receipts		Payments		Net	Receipts		Payments		Net	Receipts		Payments		Net
	Interest	Dividends	Interest	Dividends		Interest	Dividends	Interest	Dividends		Interest	Dividends	Interest	Dividends	
1946	8	39	101	149	−203	1	6	21	33	−47	13	57	125	187	−242
1950	11	39	90	321	−361	1	5	15	39	−48	28	63	109	366	−384
1951	15	42	95	287	−325	24	6	15	42	−27	54	61	114	336	−335
1952	23	62	96	248	−259	23	6	15	41	−27	60	85	115	298	−268
1953	24	77	101	233	−233	24	4	16	41	−29	63	102	121	283	−239
1954	15	54	108	237	−276	24	11	17	45	−27	53	94	130	293	−276
1955	15	63	107	281	−310	25	16	16	59	−34	54	106	127	356	−323
1956	21	59	107	320	−347	2	12	16	57	−59	38	104	128	395	−381
1957	27	68	129	351	−385	2	8	17	61	−68	44	110	154	435	−435
1958	24	76	153	347	−400	25	7	18	58	−44	63	105	181	431	−444
1959	31	68	179	368	−448	24	11	20	70	−55	70	112	210	461	−489
1960	41	64	205	343	−443	24	10	18	63	−47	78	100	239	430	−491

SOURCE: DBS, *Canadian Balance of International Payments*, 1960 p. 22.

TABLE 4.12

Freight and Shipping Transactions between Canada and Other Countries
1953–60

(millions of dollars)

Item	1953	1954	1955	1956	1957	1958	1959	1960
RECEIPTS BY CANADA								
Ocean shipping:								
Canadian operated ships:								
Gross earnings on exports	58	61	78	76	69	65	59	75
Charter receipts	7	3	9	20	21	9	4	3
Revenues between foreign ports	17	18	28	40	38	29	29	25
Sub-totals	82	82	115	136	128	103	92	103
Expenditures of foreign ships in Canada	41	35	45	48	44	43	48	55
Gross shipping receipts	123	117	160	184	172	146	140	158
Inland freight on exports	161	159	185	204	194	190	201	207
Intransit revenues	29	29	32	33	38	37	40	38
Other receipts	5	8	21	36	41	28	39	39
Gross receipts	318	313	398	457	445	401	420	442
PAYMENTS BY CANADA								
Ocean shipping:								
Expenditures abroad by Canadian shipping companies and charter payments	60	67	95	104	113	96	107	114
Freight on imports via Canadian ports	75	66	77	105	108	113	146	157
Gross shipping payments	135	133	172	209	221	209	253	271
Inland rail freight in US on imports:								
Coal via vessel	48	39	40	53	50	34	36	35
Coal via rail	26	22	20	25	16	13	12	8
Other rail freight	121	112	121	143	142	114	121	110
Sub-totals	195	173	181	221	208	161	169	153
Miscellaneous payments	44	50	62	72	86	109	103	109
Gross payments	374	356	415	502	515	460	525	533

SOURCE: DBS, *Canadian Balance of International Payments* 1960, p. 26.

ment in the travel component in 1962 and 1963). There is one point of major difference, however: namely, the sharp rise in the deficit on non-merchandise account with the US as well as overseas countries which was only partly reduced in 1962 and 1963 as a result of devaluation and other restrictions. Whereas the favourable commodity balance with overseas countries remained fairly high and somewhat stable during the past decade, the non-merchandise balance deteriorated substantially. It is clear therefore that the triangular pattern of settlements which has historically prevailed has been seriously disrupted in large part by the deterioration in non-merchandise trade[11] combined with a failure of commodity exports to both the US and overseas countries to rise more rapidly than imports (except during 1962 and 1963).

TRENDS IN BALANCE OF PAYMENTS AND CAPITAL MOVEMENTS

The gap between exports and imports of goods and services for any period of time must, of course, equal the increase or decrease in net claims against the rest of the world. We have therefore to put together the foregoing data on exports and imports in the more familiar form of the balance of payments statement and in particular examine the source of financing or financial disposition of the import-export gap. Table 4.13 summarizes the relevant data. A quick overview of the net balance on current account from 1926 to the present suggests that large surpluses or deficits do not tend to persist for any substantial period of time although there are significant year-to-year fluctuations. This is especially apparent when related to gross national product, so that even the big deficits since 1956 seem somewhat less significant than would appear at first glance.

For a nation as reliant upon external conditions as Canada it is perhaps surprising that there have not been more severe balance of payments crises and difficulties over extended periods as world demand and supply conditions have altered sometimes drastically. As Slater puts it, imports have been "kept within [the] bounds of Canada's means of payments without such serious long-run anomalies as protracted non-cyclical unemployment, or persistent use of special import restrictions or continued deterioration in her terms of trade."[12] Although the experience since 1956 may belie this generalization, it is noteworthy that recovery from the balance of payments crisis of 1962[13] has been very

[11]A detailed analysis of non-merchandise transactions appears in John W. Popkin, *Non-Merchandise Transactions Between Canada and the United States*, Canadian American Committee (Washington, DC, and Montreal, 1962).

[12]Slater, *Canada's Imports*, p. 56.

[13]Discussed above in chap. 1, p. 62.

rapid, indicating that a fundamental weakness in Canada's foreign trade position was not the immediate source of trouble although chronic unemployment has been disturbingly persistent.[14] Before examining in detail the balance of payments data, it is worthwhile outlining the mechanism of adjustment that appears to have been operative over time.

Consistent with the staple theory, periods of rapid growth in Canada have generally been associated with expansion of export opportunities which in turn stimulate domestic investment. But as we have seen, the proportion of investment goods that are imported is relatively large. Thus, a rise in investment expenditures, typically associated with or induced by export expansion, carries with it an increase in imports.[15] At the same time, since many of the imported consumer goods are in the durable or even quasi-luxury class (or at least represent expenditures which are deferrable) they tend to be highly sensitive to changes in incomes. That is, they have a high income-elasticity of demand. Thus, when incomes rise in connection with general expansion induced by growing export opportunities, there tends to be a rather sharp increase in imports of manufactured consumer goods. The mechanism works in reverse if exports or export prospects decrease. In this way exports and imports of both capital and consumption goods tend to move rather closely together over time without serious crises or prolonged difficulties. Furthermore, when imports rise more rapidly than exports, especially during boom periods, this is usually associated with sharp increases in

[14]The problems surrounding Canada's balance of payments have been succinctly and simply presented by D. W. Slater in a useful monograph *Canada's Balance of International Payments—When is a Deficit a Problem?* Private Planning Association of Canada, Montreal, 1964. Referring to the 1962 exchange crisis, Slater concludes that it was "a short-term emergency phenomenon, related almost completely to the development and resolution of a crisis of confidence." *Ibid.*, p. 23.

[15]This sharp response of imports to changes in GNP tends to reduce the degree of cyclical fluctuation. As Professor Brewis puts it, "Fortunately for Canada, Canadian imports are highly sensitive to changes in the general level of economic activity within the country and thus exert an important cushioning effect on the economy. Declines in economic activity are likely to be accompanied by a sharp fall in imports, a large proportion of Canadian imports being capital goods. Conversely, increases in economic activity are likely to be accompanied by a sharp rise in imports. In this regard imports exert a stabilizing effect on the Canadian economy." T. N. Brewis *et al.*, *Canadian Economic Policy* (Toronto, 1961), p. 263.

At the same time, however, the high import elasticity may act as a deterrent to an expansionistic monetary and fiscal policy both because of the high import leakage effect and the adverse impact upon the balance of payments. There is, of course, no quarrel with the stabilizing impact of the behaviour of imports in response to GNP changes but to the extent that this inhibits pursuit of a vigorous anti-unemployment policy, it may mean stability at a rather high level of unemployment.

TABLE 4.13

Canada's Current Account with All Countries
1926–62
(millions of dollars)

	1926	1929	1932	1936	1939
Current receipts					
Merchandise exports (adjusted)	1272	1178	495	954	906
Mutual aid to NATO countries	—	—	—	—	—
Gold prod. available for export	30	37	70	132	184
Travel expenditures	152	198	114	142	149
Interest and dividends	32	61	37	75	57
Freight and shipping	96	92	38	80	102
Inheritances and immigrants' funds	*	*	*	*	*
All other current receipts	83	80	54	47	59
Total current receipts	1665	1646	808	1430	1457
Current payments					
Merchandise imports (adjusted)	973	1272	398	612	713
Travel expenditures	99	108	49	75	81
Interest and dividends	240	322	302	311	306
Freight and shipping	105	130	66	97	119
Inheritances and emigrants' funds	*	*	*	*	*
Official contributions	—	—	—	—	—
Mutual aid to NATO countries	—	—	—	—	—
All other current payments	121	125	89	91	112
Total current payments	1538	1957	904	1186	1331
Balance on merchandise trade	+299	− 94	+ 97	+342	+193
Balance on other transactions†	−171	−180	−190	− 98	−319
Official contributions	—	—	—	—	—
Current accounts balance	+128	−274	− 93	+244	−126

Sources: DBS, *The Canadian Balance of International Payments, 1926–1948* (Ottawa, 1949), Tables III and VII, pp. 154 and 158. DBS, *The Canadian Balance of International Payments, 1960 and International Investment Position* (Ottawa, 1962), Table II, p. 66. DBS, *Canadian Balance of International Payments, Fourth Quarter, 1962, and Preliminary Estimates for the Year 1962*, pp. 19–21; and DBS, *Quarterly Estimates of the Canadian Balance of International Payments*, March 1964.
*Included with all other current receipts or payments.
†Excluding official contributions.

long- rather than short-term capital inflows. In some cases, not insignificant in aggregate amount, the import of goods by Canada and the inflow of capital arc rigidly connected. This occurs when a foreign firm decides to make a real investment in Canada and exports to Canada the real investment goods to bring this about. In such a case the import by Canada of investment goods carries its own finance. Even when this connection between real and financial flows is not as rigid, the typical

TABLE 4.13 (*continued*)

1946	1949	1953	1957	1959	1960	1961	1962	1963
2393	2989	4152	4894	5150	5392	5889	6364	7064
—	—	246	107	63	43	35	—	—
96	139	144	147	148	162	162	165	166
221	285	302	363	391	420	482	560	602
70	83	165	154	182	173	200	211	228
311	303	318	445	420	442	486	498	550
65	68	91	124	109	102	103	124	149
209	222	319	388	392	419	403	426	444
3365	4089	5737	6622	6855	7153	7769	8348	9203
1822	2696	4210	5488	5572	5540	5716	6209	6580
135	193	365	525	598	627	642	610	589
312	390	404	589	671	653	770	781	842
219	253	374	515	525	533	568	163	635
35	59	91	157	165	181	174	163	182
97	6	25	40	72	61	56	32	61
—	—	246	107	63	43	35	—	—
382	315	465	656	693	758	790	813	835
3002	3912	6180	8077	8359	8396	8751	9196	9724
+571	+293	− 58	− 594	− 422	− 148	+ 173	+155	+484
−111	−110	−360	− 821	−1010	−1034	−1099	−971	−944
− 97	− 6	− 25	− 40	− 72	− 61	− 56	− 32	− 61
+363	+177	−443	−1455	−1504	−1243	− 982	−848	−521

situation is one where the financial decisions (to invest financially in Canada by foreigners or to borrow financially abroad by Canadians) is the primary autonomous decision and the import of real goods and services follows later on as a result. It is not usually the case that the Canadian economy first generates an import surplus and then must seek means of financing it, though this is the dominant view of the balance of payments adjustment mechanism in the popular press of Canada. Mistaken interpretation of this point has been responsible for a great deal of the public concern for the balance of payments current account deficits of recent years, since they are interpreted as being the *cause* of the sale of Canadian assets to foreigners and the consequent growth of foreign ownership of Canadian industry. The real nature of the balance

TABLE 4.14

Current Transactions Between Canada and the United States
selected years 1926–63
(millions of dollars)

	1926	1929	1932	1936	1939
Current receipts					
Merchandise exports (adjusted)	476	519	169	369	344
Gold production available for export	30	37	70	132	184
Travel expenditures	140	184	103	129	137
Interest and dividends	12	30	18	31	27
Freight and shipping	64	68	25	41	46
Inheritance and immigrants' funds	*	*	*	*	*
All other receipts	65	61	37	36	42
Total current receipts	787	899	422	738	780
Current payments					
Merchandise imports (adjusted)	652	875	246	352	472
Travel expenditures	70	81	30	54	67
Interest and dividends	130	202	205	222	220
Freight and shipping	85	103	48	53	61
Inheritance and emigrants fund	*	*	*	*	*
All other payments	73	75	61	58	76
Total current payments	1018	1336	590	739	896
Balance on merchandise trade	−176	−356	− 77	+17	−128
Balance on other transactions	− 55	− 81	− 91	−18	+ 12
Current account balance	−231	−437	−168	− 1	−116

SOURCES: DBS, *The Canadian Balance of International Payments, 1926–1948*
(Ottawa, 1949), Tables V and X, pp. 156 and 161. DBS, *The Canadian Balance of
International Payments, 1960 and International Investment Position* (Ottawa, 1962),
Table II, p. 67. DBS, *The Canadian Balance of International Payments, Fourth
Quarter 1962 and Preliminary Estimates for the Year 1962*, Table I, p. 19; and DBS
*Quarterly Estimates of the Canadian Balance of International Payments, Fourth
Quarter, 1963*, March 1964.
*Included with "all other receipts".

of payments adjustment mechanism has meant that over-all balance of
payments difficulties have not been present even when current account
deficits have been large, except in exceptional conditions such as the
immediate postwar period when the Canadian government was itself
financing a large part of Canadian exports. The performance since 1956
has raised some doubts about the continuation of the adjustment mechanism and especially its relationship to high levels of unemployment.

At this point we are interested in outlining the varying current account
surpluses and deficits by Canada's two dominant trading partners, the
US and UK. Tables 4.14, 4.15, and 4.16 show the trends in current

TABLE 4.14 (*continued*)

1946	1949	1953	1957	1959	1960	1961	1962	1963
948	1521	2458	2931	3191	3040	3213	3742	3952
96	139	144	147	148	162	162		
216	267	282	325	351	375	435		
47	40	101	95	99	102	109	1441	1522
101	126	164	222	228	220	230		
19	18	41	47	52	50	51		
140	158	253	303	311	330	310		
1567	2269	3443	4070	4380	4279	4510	5183	5474
1378	1899	3046	3878	3727	3713	3828	4217	4464
130	165	307	403	448	462	459		
250	325	334	480	547	531	642		
169	193	296	351	326	324	333	2082	2168
31	44	74	124	123	141	134		
216	244	290	413	439	469	500		
2174	2870	4347	5649	5610	5640	5896	6299	6632
−430	−378	−588	− 947	− 536	− 673	− 615	− 475	− 512
−177	−223	−316	− 632	− 694	− 688	− 771	− 641	− 646
−607	−601	−904	−1579	−1230	−1361	−1386	−1116	−1158

account relationships with these two countries and "all others." As previously noted, chronic deficits with the US have typified the past with even greater deficits incurred since the Second World War. While therefore Canada sells more to the US, both relatively and absolutely, the demand for American imports has risen even more rapidly. At the same time the redirection of trade to the US has been accompanied by a virtual stagnation, especially between 1950 and 1960, in total exports to all other overseas countries. This means that the previous pattern which saw the deficits with the US more than adequately financed by surpluses from all other countries is no longer relevant. Indeed, as the deficits with the US have risen the surpluses with other countries have declined, the net impact being extremely high over-all current deficits. Deliberate attempts to correct this situation provided strong psychological foundations for a speculative movement against the Canadian dollar which finally led to the emergency measures of mid-1962 and devaluation of the Canadian dollar. The results of devaluation have been

TABLE 4.15

Current Transactions between Canada and the United Kingdom
selected years 1926–63
(millions of dollars)

	1926	1929	1932	1936	1939
Current receipts					
Merchandise exports (adjusted)	315	224	149	342	332
Travel expenditures	8	9	7	8	7
Interest and dividends	2	2	1	2	2
Freight and shipping	15	8	5	23	34
Inheritance and immigrants' funds	*	*	*	*	*
All other receipts	12	13	14	7	27
Total current receipts	352	256	176	382	636
Current payments					
Merchandise imports (adjusted)	148	188	61	120	133
Travel expenditures	21	20	14	15	2
Interest and dividends	97	113	91	84	74
Freight and shipping	8	12	11	26	32
Inheritance and emigrants' funds	*	*	*	*	*
Official contributions	—	—	—	—	—
All other payments	20	22	13	15	52
Total current payments	294	355	190	260	293
Balance on merchandise trade	+167	+ 36	+ 88	+222	+199
Balance on other transactions†	−109	−135	−102	−100	+144
Official contributions	—	—	—	—	—
Current account balance	+ 58	− 99	−14	+122	+343

SOURCES: DBS, *The Canadian Balance of International Payments, 1926–1948*,
Tables IV and VIII, pp. 155 and 159; DBS, *The Canadian Balance of International
Payments 1960 and International Investment Position*, Table II, p. 68. DBS, *The
Canadian Balance of International Payments, Fourth Quarter 1962* and *Preliminary
Estimates for the Year 1962*, Table I, p. 19; DBS, *Quarterly of the Canadian Balance
of International Payments, Fourth Quarter 1963*, March 1964.
  *Included with "all other receipts".
  †Excluding official contributions.

promising and in 1963 the current account deficit was less than half what
it had been in 1960 and about one third of the record deficit of 1959.

Deficits on both merchandise and service account with the US have
risen since 1949. Indeed, the service component tripled between 1949
and 1960 while the merchandise component moved erratically but
remained in the $500–$600 million range during the latter part of
the decade and early 1960's. Likewise for overseas countries, the steady
dynamic element was in the non-merchandise category with surpluses
on service account dwindling until 1953 and thereafter steadily rising

TABLE 4.15 (*continued*)

1946	1949	1953	1957	1959	1960	1961	1962	1963
626	701	656	734	781	924	924	924	1017
3	11	12	18	18	20	21		
7	9	28	10	35	32	34		
107	89	79	95	80	93	100	227	262
45	38	18	40	26	26	25		
52	49	37	41	43	−50	−49		
840	897	830	938	983	1145	1153	1151	1279
138	300	463	520	618	611	593	575	525
3	17	31	47	62	70	71		
54	55	57	78	90	83	86		
32	32	42	69	85	89	93	363	360
3	10	12	20	26	25	23		
—	—	—	—	—	3	—		
110	37	92	86	89	98	100		
340	451	697	820	970	979	966	938	885
+488	+401	+193	+214	+163	+313	+331	+349	+492
+ 12	+ 45	− 60	− 96	−150	−144	−144	−136	− 98
—	—	—	—	—	− 3	—	—	—
+500	+446	+133	+118	+ 13	+166	+187	+213	+394

deficits until 1961 which reduced the total current account surpluses to amounts well below those required to finance the deficits with the US.

Details of the non-merchandise account are shown in Table 4.13. The two most important items outside of the omnibus "all other" category are travel expenditures and interest and dividends as already discussed. The latter are directly related to the large net inflow of capital during the 1950's and earlier to which we now turn.

FOREIGN INVESTMENT

Few issues have so dominated the Canadian political scene in recent years as that of foreign ownership and control of Canadian assets in one form or another. Some observers believe that such control is not only inconsistent with a high degree of political autonomy but is responsible

TABLE 4.16

Current Transactions between Canada and Countries other than the
United Kingdom and United States
selected years 1926–63
(millions of dollars)

	1926	1929	1932	1936	1939
Current receipts					
Merchandise exports (adjusted)	481	435	177	243	230
Mutual aid to NATO countries	—	—	—	—	—
Travel expenditures	4	5	4	5	5
Interest and dividends	18	29	18	42	28
Freight and shipping	17	16	8	16	22
Inheritance and immigrants' funds	*	*	*	*	*
All other current receipts	6	6	3	4	8
Total current receipts	526	491	210	310	293
Current payments					
Merchandise imports (adjusted)	173	209	91	140	135
Travel expenditures	8	7	5	6	3
Interest and dividends	5	7	6	5	8
Freight and shipping	12	15	7	18	22
Inheritance and emigrants' fund	*	*	*	*	*
Official contributions	—	—	—	—	—
Mutual aid to NATO countries	—	—	—	—	—
All other payments	28	28	15	18	20
Total current payments	226	266	124	187	188
Balance on merchandise trade	+308	+226	+86	+103	+ 95
Balance on other transactions	− 8	− 1	0	+ 20	+ 10
Official contributions	—	—	—	—	—
Current account balance	+300	+225	+86	+123	+105

SOURCES: DBS, *The Canadian Balance of International Payments, 1926–1948,*
Tables VI, IX and XI, pp. 157, 160 and 162. DBS, *The Canadian Balance of International Payments, 1960 and International Investment Position,* Tables II, III and IV,
pp. 66–68. DBS, *The Canadian Balance of International Payments, Fourth Quarter
1962,* and *Preliminary Estimates for the Year 1962* (Ottawa 1963), Table I, p. 19;
DBS, *Quarterly Estimate of the Canadian Balance of International Payments, Fourth
Quarter 1963,* Ottawa, March, 1964.
  *Included with "all other receipts".

as well for the slowdown following 1956 and for preventing a vigorous
expansion of Canadian exports to overseas countries.[16] On the other
hand, there is a general belief that the ability of Canada to grow at rates
approximating those of the early 1950's may require even greater
amounts of foreign capital regardless of the form this may take. Indeed,
foreign financing has always constituted a relatively large proportion of

[16]See for example Roger Dehem, "The Economics of Stunted Growth," *CJEPS,*
Nov. 1962, p. 509.

TABLE 4.16 (*continued*)

1946	1949	1953	1957	1959	1960	1961	1962	1963
819	767	1038	1229	1178	1428	1752	1698	2095
—	—	246	107	63	43	35		
2	7	8	20	22	25	26		
16	34	36	49	48	39	60	316	355
103	88	75	128	112	129	156		
1	12	32	37	31	26	27		
17	15	29	44	38	39	44		
958	923	1464	1614	1492	1729	2106	2014	2450
306	497	701	1090	1227	1216	1295	1417	1591
2	11	27	75	88	95	112		
8	10	13	31	34	39	42		
18	76	36	95	114	120	142		
1	5	5	13	16	15	17	542	616
97	6	25	40	72	58	56		
—	—	246	107	63	43	35		
56	34	83	157	165	191	190		
488	145	1136	1608	1779	1777	1889	1959	2207
+513	+270	+337	+139	− 49	−212	+457	+281	+504
+ 47	+ 68	+ 16	− 93	−166	−202	−184	−226	−261
− 97	− 6	− 25	− 40	− 72	− 58	− 56		
+463	+332	+328	+ 6	−287	− 48	+217	+ 55	+243

Canadian capital formation.[17] This is at present a very controversial issue and no final judgment is possible. The present section therefore will present the relevant statistical information and merely allude to the broader implications. The intent is mainly positive rather than normative at this juncture.

NET INTERNATIONAL INDEBTEDNESS

The measure of net international indebtedness is simply the excess of Canada's liabilities to non-residents over its holdings of foreign assets and includes both long- and short-term assets and liabilities except for short-term commercial indebtedness. As a general overview of the rise in net debt, Table 4.17 indicates the totals for various years from 1926 to 1960. Since 1926, gross liabilities have more than quadrupled while gross

[17]See within at pp. 192–4.

TABLE 4.17

Canadian Net Debt
selected years 1926-60
(billions of dollars)

Year	Gross liabilities	Gross assets	Net international indebtedness
1926	6.4*	1.3*	5.1*
1930	8.0*	1.5*	6.5*
1933	7.7*	1.4*	6.3*
1939	7.4*	1.9*	5.5*
1945	8.0	4.0	4.0
1949	9.3	5.5	3.8
1951	11.3	6.3	5.0
1953	12.9	6.9	6.0
1954	14.1	7.2	6.8
1955	15.3	7.4	7.9
1956	17.7	7.7	10.0
1957	19.9	8.1	11.8
1958	21.8	8.4	13.4
1959	24.3	8.8	15.5
1960	26.1	9.3	16.9

SOURCES: DBS, *The Canadian Balance of International Payments, 1960 and International Investment Position*, Table V, p. 74.
*Excludes short-term commercial indebtedness.

assets have risen about sevenfold.[18] However, in 1926 assets were only about one-fifth of liabilities so that the absolute value of the net debt has more than tripled having risen from $5.1 billion in 1926 to $16.9 in 1960. The ratio of assets to liabilities has risen to about one-third in 1960 from only a fifth in 1926. As a proportion of GNP the net external debt has dropped sharply from pre-war levels, when it generally exceeded annual GNP, to about one-third of present levels of GNP. Since GNP may be taken as one indicator of a nation's ability to handle foreign indebtedness, in the same sense that a person's income is relevant in determining reasonable levels of personal debt, it is clear that despite a large absolute increase in external net Canadian debt, Canada's ability to sustain such levels has risen even more rapidly. This may somewhat overstate the case because GNP in constant dollars only tripled between 1926 and 1960, an over-all increase which about matches that of net

[18]It is worth noting that the value of foreign assets held by Canadians on a per capita basis is among the highest in the world. Indeed the per capita value of US stock held by Canadians was about $51 in 1961 whereas the per capita value of *all* portfolio investments in Canada held by US residents was only $31 at the end of 1961. (Canadian estimates from DBS, *Canadian Statistical Review*, Aug. 1963, pp. i–iii. US figures from Table 4.20.

TABLE 4.18

Cost of Servicing Canada's External Debt
selected years 1926–61

Year	Receipts of interest and dividends	Payments of interest and dividends	Net payments	Ratio of net payments to GNP	Ratio of payments to total current receipts
	(millions of dollars)			(percentages)	
1926	32	240	208	4.0	14.4
1930	59	348	289	5.0	26.8
1933	38	264	226	6.4	31.8
1939	57	306	249	4.4	21.0
1945	80	251	171	1.4	5.6
1949	83	390	307	1.9	9.5
1951	115	450	335	1.6	8.5
1953	165	404	239	1.0	7.0
1954	147	423	276	1.1	8.1
1955	160	483	323	1.2	8.0
1956	142	523	381	1.3	8.1
1957	154	589	435	1.3	8.9
1958	168	612	444	1.4	9.5
1959	182	671	489	1.4	9.8
1960	178	669	491	1.4	9.4
1961	196	771	575	1.5	9.9

SOURCE: See Table 1.1 for GNP. Other data from DBS, *Canadian Balance of International Payments*, various years.

external debt. However, current dollar comparisons are more relevant in the present context since interest and principal payments on indebtedness are made in terms of current values. None the less, in periods of rising prices the ratio of net external debt to GNP in current dollars tends to be understated because the figures on assets and liabilities are couched in terms of book and par values. Regardless of these caveats Canada's ability to service present levels of debt has risen and in fact is substantially above that of earlier periods. A similar conclusion emerges from comparing the cost of servicing Canada's external debt as indicated in Table 4.18.

One striking feature shown in Table 4.17 is the accelerated increase in gross liabilities between 1949 and 1960. Indeed, the increase was over 250 per cent compared with a rise in gross assets of around 50 per cent. Looking only at foreign long-term capital (see Table 4.19) this is an increase in about ten years which exceeded the rate of increase from a smaller base in the sixteen-year period 1914–30. Although the rate of increase from 1949 to 1960 did not quite match the pace set between 1900 and 1914, the absolute increase was more than six times the earlier experience. In fact, of course, even the rate of increase in the recent

TABLE 4.19

Foreign Capital Invested in Canada
selected year ends 1900–59

	Owned in United Kingdom		Owned in United States		Owned elsewhere outside Canada		Total non-resident investment
Year	$ million	Per cent	$ million	Per cent	$ million	Per cent	$ million
1900	1050*	85	168	14	14	1	1232
1914	2778†	72	881	23	178	5	3837
1918	2729	60	1630	36	177	4	4536
1926	2637	44	3196	53	170	3	6003
1930	2766	36	4660	61	188	3	7614
1939	2476	36	4151	60	286	4	6913
1945	1750	25	4990	70	352	5	7092
1948	1610	22	5567	74	332	4	7509
1954	2181	17	9692	77	704	6	12,577
1955	2356	17.5	10,275	76.3	842	6.2	13,473
1956	2668	17.1	11,789	75.7	1112	7.1	15,569
1957	2917	16.7	13,264	76.0	1283	7.3	17,464
1958	3088	16.2	14,436	76.0	1481	7.8	19,005
1959	3199	15.4	15,811	75.9	1823	8.8	20,833
1960	3359	15.1	16,718	75.3	2137	9.6	22,214
1961	3385	14.3	17,966	76.2	2219	9.5	23,570

SOURCES: Irving Brecher and S. S. Reisman, *Canada-United States Relations*, Table 16, p. 88. DBS, *The Canadian Balance of International Payments 1960 and International Investment Position*, Table II, pp. 68–9. Roy A. Matthews, "Canada's Balance of Payments", *The Conference Board Record*, Vol. I, No. 4, p. 30.

*Estimated by Dr. Jacob Viner, *Canada's Balance of International Indebtedness, 1900–1913* (Cambridge, Mass., 1924).

†Estimated by Professor F. A. Knox from Excursus appearing in H. Marshall, F. L. Southard, Jr., and K. W. Taylor, *Canadian-Americacn Industry* (New Haven, 1936).

period from a much higher base is not significantly lower than the boom after 1900 and took place over a shorter time span—namely, a 250 per cent increase in between ten and eleven years compared with 300 per cent over fourteen. By any standards the rate of increase in gross liabilities, long-term capital, and net debt has been exceptionally high and accelerating during the 1950's. This is part of the phenomenon giving many Canadians cause for concern.

But of equivalent importance to the absolute and relative changes in the total levels of external indebtedness are the trends in source and type of foreign investment in Canada.

The rising predominance of the US as a supplier of capital is evident from Table 4.19. This has, however, been a much longer-run phenomenon than the redirection of Canadian exports to the US, which is mainly a product of the post-war period; as early as the late 1920's, US capital investment in Canada already exceeded that of the UK. The war and post-war problems of the UK merely hastened a trend already well established from the beginning of the century so that the proportion of long-term capital from the UK to total foreign capital invested in Canada dropped from over 60 per cent prior to 1918 to less than 15 per cent by 1961. At the same time the US share rose from about 36 per cent in 1918 to 76 per cent in 1961. The proportion owned by residents of all other nations has fluctuated narrowly between 3 and 10 per cent of the total. The US and UK, in short, account for almost all foreign capital invested in Canada, with the US especially predominant. Heavy as is the concentration of Canadian exports to and imports from the US, the degree of foreign ownership by the US is even more substantial. Thus, in terms of international trade and finance, which are crucial factors in Canadian economic development as already emphasized, the over-all significance of the United States is exceptional and has been growing at a rapid pace since the Second World War. While therefore Canada as a whole may be somewhat less reliant upon international trade than in the past, if measured by the ratio of exports and imports to GNP, the dependence upon a single mass market, the United States, has risen sharply, thus leading to a far higher level of economic integration within North America than Canada has in the past been willing to accept. As Aitken puts it: "Of fundamental importance is the relative decline of Great Britain as a source of capital and as a market, depriving Canada of its historic counterpoise to the weight of the United States. Current concern over the relations of Canada and the United States reflects the absence of this traditional balance."[19]

FORMS OF FOREIGN INVESTMENT
There are additional features to the foreign capital inflows into Canada that render the aggregates and trends possibly even more significant as far as the issue of foreign control is concerned. Broadly speaking capital inflows may take two major forms: (1) direct investment and (2) portfolio investment. The former category, as far as Canada is concerned, consists mainly in subsidiaries or branch plants of foreign companies although more formally direct investment is defined for statistical purposes by DBS as follows:

The category of direct investments shown here generally includes all concerns in Canada which are known to have 50% or more of their voting

[19]H. G. J. Aitken, J. J. Deutsch, W. A. Mackintosh, *et al.*, *The American Economic Impact on Canada* (Durham, NC, 1959), p. 9.

stock held in one country outside Canada. In addition a few instances of concerns are included where it is known that effective control is held by a parent firm with less than 50% of the stock. In effect this category includes all known cases of unincorporated branches of foreign companies in Canada and all wholly-owned subsidiaries, together with a number of concerns with a parent company outside of Canada which holds less than all of the capital stock. In addition there are a relatively small number of Canadian companies included in cases where more than one-half of their capital stock is owned in a single country outside of Canada where there is not a parent concern.[20]

Portfolio investment refers to stocks and bonds issued by firms in Canada and purchased by non-residents. Typically portfolio investment involves sales of bonds and debentures by governments or large enterprises designed to finance expansion in the development of social overhead capital. Such things as railroads, ports, harbours, water works, roads, major electrical installations, schools, and so on are generally financed in this way and the securities frequently offered for sale in the London and New York money markets. Unlike direct investment, the concentration of ownership is considerably less and hence the possibility of non-resident control is reduced. This is not only because much of portfolio investment takes the form of debt (i.e., bonds) rather than ownership (stocks) but even in the case of stock sales the holdings are generally scattered. By the same token this implies that the initiative comes from the borrower in the case of portfolio investment, while direct investments typically mean that the user of the funds not only supplies a large proportion of them but often the technical knowledge, skills, and direction as well. From the point of view of control it is evident that its extent, actual or potential, is highest in direct investment.

It is not, of course, easy in practice to make these distinctions especially in the case of mortgage, real estate, and other investments of private investment companies. The intent to control or otherwise direct the policy of the activity in which funds are invested is not so clear-cut in these and other instances as implied in the above distinction. Hence, DBS lists a third category of investment termed "miscellaneous" which combines several of the aforementioned characteristics of both direct and portfolio investment.[21]

Table 4.20 presents the data, showing the amounts of total foreign capital invested by type in Canada for selected year-ends from 1926 to 1960 along with a breakdown among US, UK, and all other countries.

---

[20]DBS, *Canada's International Investment Position, 1926–1954* (Ottawa, 1958), p. 24.

[21]Further comments on the nature of the statistical estimates to be examined below are given in *ibid.*, pp. 64–70.

Aside from the substantial increase from barely $6 billion in 1926 to over $22 billion in 1960, there are significant shifts among the relative importance of the various components. As would be expected, the demise of the international capital market due to the great depression and the Second World War has naturally reduced the extent of portfolio investment. Indeed, it is part of a general world-wide phenomenon in the postwar period that direct investments, and with them the issue of foreign control, have come to predominate as far as private capital movements are concerned.[22] It is scarcely surprising then to find a steady rise in the proportion of direct to total foreign investment in Canada from 30 per cent in 1926 to 57 per cent in 1955. The ratio stabilized at roughly 57–58 per cent from 1955 until 1960. But in fact this is relatively low compared to the composition of foreign investment in other countries. Also noteworthy is the even larger proportion of US ownership in the direct investment category. Although direct investments by the United Kingdom increased rapidly after the war, the US accounted for by far the largest part of the increase. Between 1945 and 1960, for example, total direct foreign investment increased by about $10.3 billion, of which some $8.3 billion, or 81 per cent, came from the US.

Not all the increase in foreign direct investment in Canada represents fresh capital inflows or actual capital movements. The definition of direct investment given above includes undistributed profits as well as other factors such as revaluation of assets and sundry accounting adjustments. Indeed of the total increase of $10.3 billion in foreign direct investment from 1946 to 1960 only $5.1 billion represented fresh capital inflows as reflected in the balance of payments. Undistributed earnings of foreign-controlled companies (i.e., direct investment) constituted about $4.2 billion with the balance of $1 billion made up of the other factors noted above.[23]

If we examine the trends in interest and dividend payments abroad, these facts on undistributed profits plus the declining share of portfolio investment and in particular the decline in debt relative to equity capital

[22]It is perhaps hardly necessary to remark that the capital movements to Canada have been almost entirely from private sources. Foreign aid and other aspects of bilateral governmental lending have been of no concern to Canada in the sense of a recipient country. Governmental lending by Canada is, however, another story. However the important capital movements discussed in the present chapter are private in the sense of originating in private capital markets abroad even though provincial and municipal governments in Canada have borrowed heavily abroad.

[23]See DBS, *The Canadian Balance of International Payments, 1960, and International Investment Position* (Ottawa, 1962), Table 12B, pp. 34–5.

TABLE 4.20

Foreign Long-Term Capital Invested in Canada: Direct and Portfolio
selected years 1926–60

Type of investment	1926		1945	
	Billions of dollars	Per cent	Billions of dollars	Per cent
All countries				
Direct	1.8	30	2.7	38
Portfolio	4.0	66	4.1	58
Miscellaneous	0.3	4	0.3	4
Total	6.1	100	7.1	100
United States				
Direct	1.4	44	2.3	46
Portfolio	1.7	53	2.6	51
Miscellaneous	0.1	3	0.1	3
Total	3.2	100	5.0	100
Other countries				
Direct	0.4	14	0.4	20
Portfolio	2.3	80	1.5	73
Miscellaneous	0.2	6	0.2	7
Total	2.8	100	2.1	100

SOURCES: Brecher and Reisman, *Canada–United States Economic Relations*, Table 18, p. 91; DBS, *The Canadian Balance of International Payments, 1960*, and *International Investment Position*, Table XIII, p. 81.

have a significance for future international capital transactions in Canada. The data on the "burden" of servicing the external debt, which may be defined as the ratio of interest and dividend payments abroad to GNP or to all current receipts from abroad, are given in Table 4.18. In general, since the 1920's and 1930's, both indexes of the "burden" as defined above have shown a marked decline in the post-war years. However, as would be expected in view of the substantial capital inflows during the decade of the fifties, each index has shown some tendency to rise in recent years. Furthermore, the substantial retention of undistributed profits in Canada of foreign-controlled firms and the fact that earnings for some large-scale capital projects financed by foreign direct investment have not yet begun to appear suggest that the "burden" of servicing Canada's external debt will tend to rise in the future, despite the rising trend of Canadian receipts of interest and dividends from abroad, for the latter have lagged, and will doubtless continue to lag, behind payments of interest and dividends. It is not to be expected, however, that the servicing of the external debt will constitute much of a burden on the Canadian economy, since a large part of the foreign

TABLE 4.20

1955		1958		1960	
Billions of dollars	Per cent	Billions of dollars	Per cent	Billions of dollars	Per cent
7.7	57	10.9	57	13.0	58
5.1	38	7.0	37	} 1.3	42
0.6	5	1.1	6		
13.5	100	19.0	100	22.3	100
6.5	63	9.0	63	10.6	63
3.4	33	4.9	34	5.6	33
0.4	4	.5	3	.6	4
10.3	100	14.4	100	16.8	100
1.2	38	1.8	39	2.4	44
1.7	54	2.2	48	} 3.1	56
0.3	8	.6	13		
3.2	100	4.6	100	5.5	100

investments have gone into the export field; this implies that profits of many foreign-controlled companies will fluctuate with export proceeds and hence dividend payments as a proportion of current international receipts will tend to stabilize automatically.[24] The general reduction in the proportion of debt to equity capital reduces the rigidity of Canada's payments abroad, and this too tends to stabilize the burden. Furthermore, exports being an important determinant of the level of Canadian GNP, the burden defined as in column 5 of Table 4.18 should likewise tend towards greater stability, since both numerator and denominator move in the same direction, assuming the ratio of dividends paid to earnings does not change drastically. In any event, despite the rising trend manifest in recent years there is little reason for believing that the servicing of the external debt will be a burden on the Canadian economy

[24]In the case of foreign investment in resource areas where the purpose is to obtain raw materials for the parent company, the calculation of profits for the Canadian subsidiary depends upon the pricing policy of the parent company which, in essence, is selling to itself the raw materials from Canada. At the same time the pricing policy actually followed is largely dependent upon the tax laws in the two countries. Thus, the relationship between profits and exports indicated above is apt to be much more tenuous in these situations than for other types of foreign investment.

in the future, unlike the situation in most underdeveloped countries at the present time. The impact of rapid inflows of foreign capital into already developed economies differs greatly from a similar inflow into an underdeveloped economy. Canadian concern over foreign investments is not, in short, occasioned by the increase in interest and dividend payments abroad which such investments inevitably entail. Rather the concern is over the consequences to Canada of having such a large proportion of industrial assets owned and controlled by non-residents. Such phrases as "dominance," "dependence," "satellite status," and so on have frequently been used to describe the present situation. However, definition of these phrases is most imprecise and their frequent use serves mainly to cloud the issues. Presumably what is meant is that foreign-owned or controlled firms operate differently from domestically owned or controlled firms and that this difference regularly works to the disadvantage of Canada in certain ways. Some of the more cogent arguments specifying the ways in which Canadian economic development has been influenced and possibly deterred are examined in a later section. In the meantime it is important to examine the reasons for this capital inflow and its resulting pattern.

As already noted it is mainly private from the supply side and does not involve borrowing from foreign governments or international agencies except occasionally under emergency conditions. The motivation then is the relatively higher profitability of investment or lending in Canada than elsewhere in many lines combined with a greater security of private investment and a lesser likelihood of expropriation. This in turn results from three main factors: (1) the need for many companies to secure access to important raw materials which Canada has in abundance, (2) the Canadian tariff, and (3) the higher interest rates prevailing in Canada than in the US.

The first two factors are mainly relevant to direct investment (although portfolio investment may also be involved) but give rise to different kinds. The need for raw materials induces investment in natural resource industries. The aim is then to export the raw materials to the parent company, usually owned in the US. For this type of investment the ties between parent and subsidiary are likely to be very close and the extent of non-resident control and direction substantial. In some cases, even if wholly Canadian-financed, the materials would be exported to US mills (e.g., iron ore). On the other hand investments designed to sell within the Canadian market, stimulated by the Canadian tariff against manufactured imports, are likely to require more discretion on the part of the subsidiary in meeting the needs of the domestic market. Part of the investments in Canadian secondary industry may on the other hand be motivated by export prospects to other Commonwealth countries and locate in Canada largely to take advantage of "imperial preference" tariffs that may not be available to US incorporated firms.

The spread between Canadian and US interest rates induces short-term capital inflows as well as longer-term investments of the portfolio variety.[25] Municipal and provincial governments in particular have floated rather substantial loans in the New York market in recent years. Tight money policy in Canada, especially in the late 1950's has been the major determinant of this differential with respect to the United States where monetary policy has generally tended to be somewhat less restrictive. The important point here is that much of the capital inflow was motivated by Canadian policy which induced Canadian borrowers to go to cheaper capital markets and offer attractive terms to obtain funds. It is less a case of "living beyond our means" than of creating a situation which renders it economically favourable to borrow abroad.

The general motivation for the large capital inflows remains the higher profitability (or lower cost) of obtaining needed raw materials in Canada or, due to the tariff, of entering the Canadian or Commonwealth market. In addition the interest differential induces foreign portfolio investment in both government and industry.

The predominance of the US as a source of capital inflow to Canada is determined not only by the fact that the US is the world's leading capital exporter (both public and private) but also by the proximity of Canadian resources and markets and by the cultural, political, linguistic, and ethnic similarities, which induce US private investments in Canada out of all proportion to such investment elsewhere. The US has traditionally shown a preference for direct over portfolio foreign investments and there is a particularly high ratio of direct to portfolio US investment in Canada. Direct investment involves a higher degree of control compared with portfolio investment, causing many Canadians, regardless of political affiliation, to regard the situation with some alarm. The important though nebulous question of what extent of foreign ownership is consistent with economic and political independence is not surprisingly

[25]The differential in interest rates on long-term government bonds from 1954 to 1961 rose fairly steadily from about a half of one per cent to over 1 per cent. A somewhat comparable trend exists as far as Canadian provincial and municipal bonds are concerned compared with US corporate bond yields. Although there are more fluctuations in the latter yield differentials they have generally averaged about one per cent especially since 1958. The same is true of industrial bonds. See Bank of Canada, *Annual Report of the Governor to the Minister of Finance for the Year 1960* (Ottawa, 1961), p. 96.

raised with greater frequency as the degree of North American economic integration proceeds apace.

But there are several other aspects to be examined before an accurate picture of the extent of Canadian dependence upon the US can be drawn. One of these is the proportion of new foreign investment (mainly US) to total investment in Canada. It is one thing to say that the US has the major share of foreign investment and quite another to suggest that this is a major factor in total Canadian capital formation. Again, the full impact of foreign influence cannot be assessed without a clear conception of the industries into which foreign capital has been poured, for the effects and the degree of Canadian discretion will obviously differ depending upon the extent to which foreign capital has entered domestically or export-oriented activities. The relevant evidence on these issues is presented in the following sections.

FOREIGN FINANCING OF TOTAL CANADIAN INVESTMENT

Two general approaches in determining the extent of the foreign contribution to capital formation in Canada have been employed in recent years. One involves an estimate of the amount of savings contributed by non-residents. This has been measured by adding to the current account deficit the amount of earnings retained by foreign-controlled enterprises in Canada plus the depreciation and depletion allowances of these companies and deducting retained earnings and allowances of Canadian direct investment abroad. This figure, which is taken to measure the net amount of resources of other countries made available to Canada, is then related to total (i.e., public and private) gross capital formation, including the value of the physical change in inventories, as measured by the national accounts. These figures may also be used on a net basis by subtracting depreciation (capital consumption allowances) from both. The data are beset with numerous difficulties both conceptually and empirically,[26] and can only give a rough approximation of the extent to which non-residents make a net contribution to Canadian investment. However, the evidence is suggestive and consistent with tendencies already noted. As shown in Table 4.21 this approach suggests that the use of foreign resources as a proportion of Canadian gross investment rose from about 17 per cent in the first half of the 1950's to 27 per cent in the latter half. In terms of net investment the proportions increased from 19 to 35 per cent. In the early post-war period Canada was a net

[26]For details see DBS, *Canadian International Investment Position, 1926–1954*, pp. 45–7.

TABLE 4.21

Use of Foreign and Domestic Resources in
Gross Capital Formation in Canada
1946-60
(billions of dollars)

Year	Gross capital formation	Net use of domestic resources	Net use of foreign resources
1946	2.0	2.2	− .2
1947	2.8	2.6	.2
1948	3.2	3.3	− .1
1949	3.6	3.5	.1
1950	4.5	3.8	.6
1951	5.7	4.8	.9
1952	6.0	5.6	.4
1953	6.6	5.4	1.2
1954	5.6	4.4	1.2
1955	6.6	4.9	1.7
1956	9.1	6.7	2.4
1957	8.9	6.3	2.6
1958	8.0	6.0	2.0
1959	8.7	6.2	2.6
1960	8.5	6.3	2.2

SOURCE: DBS, *The Canadian Balance of International Payments, 1960
and International Investment Position*, Statement 20, p. 49.

exporter of capital,[27] as we have already seen: hence from 1946 to 1949 the net use of foreign resources was negative.

The second measure disregards outflows of capital and is referred to as "direct foreign financing."[28] Using this concept and relating it to gross investment also reveals a substantial increase from 25 to 33 per cent of gross capital formation between the annual average for 1950–55 and 1956–60. As a proportion of *net* capital formation for the same

[27]Canada was also a net exporter of capital from 1933 to 1937 inclusive, and during much of the Second World War as well. In the former period this was mainly due to the much sharper decline in imports than exports during the great depression which illustrates the very substantial import elasticity of the Canadian economy already discussed. During and immediately after the war, the capital outflow was less a product of undesirable circumstances than deliberate policy to permit the UK in particular to purchase Canadian goods on easy credit terms.

[28]The items included in this concept are as follows: (a) direct investment in Canada, (b) retained earnings on foreign direct investment, (c) new issue of Canadian securities sold to non-residents, (d) other long-term financing, (e) change in accounts payable, (f) depreciation allowances, etc. related to non-resident investment.

periods the direct foreign financing increased from 33 to 45 per cent. These compare with the immediate post-war percentages of 19 and 24 per cent for gross and net capital formation respectively.[29]

By either method, therefore, the significance of foreign financing of the crucial determinant of growth, namely capital formation, has risen sharply in the postwar period. Very crude and tentative estimates for the late 1920's and the earlier boom period 1900–14 suggest that both the use of foreign resources and direct foreign financing, as defined above, represented over half of net Canadian capital formation, although the data are not directly comparable with the above estimates.[30] While therefore it may have been fair to say in 1955 that since the turn of the century "there has been a very considerable increase . . . in the capacity of the country to generate the savings required to finance its investment programme,"[31] more recent evidence suggests a return to the earlier conditions, since 45 per cent of net investment, using the "direct foreign financing" concept, emanated from non-residents in the 1956–60 period compared with the rough guesses of about 50 per cent during 1900–14 and the late 1920's. Of course, much of the failure to generate higher savings domestically from 1956 to 1960 was due to the persistence of levels of output and employment well below economic capacity. The slowdown in the latter half of the fifties combined with a monetary policy which tended to keep interest rates higher than in the US naturally had the effect of raising the proportion of total investment financed from foreign sources. Thus the return to earlier conditions may therefore be due simply to a peculiar set of circumstances rather than indicate a reversal of the trend in the nation's ability to finance a bigger proportion of its investment needs.

Some additional insights into the reasons for this reversion or rapid rise in the relative importance of foreign sources of finance may be had by examining the sectors of the economy into which non-resident capital has gone. Indeed, the above aggregates tend to understate the significance of foreign investment and control since they fail to point out that, as both cause and consequence of capital inflows, the sectors that have proven most attractive to foreign capital are among the fastest-growing in Canada. To this we now turn.

[29]See DBS, *Canadian Balance of International Payments, 1960*, Statement 19, p. 49.

[30]See *ibid.*, p. 49, and Brecher and Reisman, *Canada–United States Economic Relations* (Ottawa, 1957), p. 97 including n. 11.

[31]Brecher and Reisman, *Canada–United States Economic Relations*, p. 97.

NON-RESIDENT OWNERSHIP AND CONTROL BY SECTOR AND INDUSTRY

At the end of 1959 the proportion of total capital employed in manufacturing, petroleum and natural gas, and mining and smelting, that was accounted for by Canadian residents was only 44 per cent while that owned by US residents was larger at 46 per cent (see Table 4.22).[32] Other areas of investment, such as agriculture, housing, utilities, institutional services, and government are, of course, predominantly financed by Canadians due to their very nature. In other words, the above ratios include only one broad segment of the Canadian economy (mostly the commodity-producing sector less agriculture) and, as noted in the footnote above, the concept of capital is rather broad and not directly comparable with other available estimates of total capital stock. It has, however, been estimated that the net stock of social capital (government, housing, and institutions) is approximately equal to the net stock of industrial plus agricultural capital.[33] Thus, the figures showing non-resident ownership of the industries included in Table 4.22 considerably overstate the position with respect to the whole economy although comparable data are not available to specify more inclusive ratios. Nevertheless, it is rather remarkable that such a large proportion of the strategic manufacturing, mining, and smelting as well as petroleum and natural gas sectors of the economy are owned by non-residents for these are the more dynamic sectors and the ones normally taken as symbols of industrial maturity, at least in the case of manufacturing. Furthermore, in terms of control,[34] the share of non-residents rises to 63 per cent as Table 4.22 indicates. For particular industries the proportion of control is even more striking. In the rubber and automobile and parts industries the degree of non-resident control is virtually complete while in electrical

[32]The concept of capital used in these estimates is the value of investment after depreciation and depletion allowances as used by the companies in their financial statements. The estimates thus include "investments in inventories and other working capital, land, and other assets, as well as in the physical assets which would arise from expenditures on new construction and for machinery and equipment." DBS, *Canada's International Investment Position, 1926–1954*, p. 30. The data are therefore more inclusive than the investment concept used in the national accounts.

[33]Wm. C. Hood and Anthony Scott, *Output, Labour and Capital in the Canadian Economy*, a report prepared for RCCEP (Ottawa, 1957), pp. 450–1. Data refer to 1955.

[34]The difference in the ratios of ownership and control arises from the treatment of minority investments. Estimates of control include minority investments from other countries and attribute these to the country where control is held. On the other hand, foreign minority investments in Canadian-controlled companies are omitted. Thus, industry ratios of ownership and control may differ sometimes substantially.

TABLE 4.22

Ownership and Control of Selected Canadian Industries
1959

Company classification	Total Canadian and external capital (in millions of dollars) in companies controlled in:		
	Canada	United States	Elsewhere outside Canada
Manufacturing*			
Beverages	394	56	6
Rubber	5	182	16
Textiles	479	88	55
Pulp and paper	961	721	207
Agricultural machinery†	77	93‡	....
Automobiles and parts	14	391	2
Transportation equipment n.o.p.	73	71	123
Primary iron and steel	544	61	102
Electrical apparatus	102	351	73
Chemicals	250	561	262
Other	2087	2553	711
Sub-total	4986	5128	1557
Petroleum and natural gas	1373	3737	343
Mining			
Smelting and refining of non-ferrous native ores	311	611	—
Other mining	863	1002	256
Sub-total	1174	1613	256
Total of above industries	7533	10,478	2156

SOURCE: DBS, *The Canadian Balance of International Payments, 1960 and International Investment Position*, Table XV, pp. 82 and 83.

*Includes "Other enterprises".

†Includes enterprises also engaged in the manufacture of other heavy equipment which tends to overstate foreign-owned and controlled proportion of capital actually engaged in the manufacture of agricultural implements only.

‡Includes minor amounts attributable to United Kingdom and other countries; an offsetting adjustment has been made in line 11.

apparatus, chemicals, petroleum, and natural gas the proportion is about 75 per cent.

Of greater significance are the trends in degree of foreign control. Table 4.23 indicates the developments for selected year ends from 1926 to 1961 and includes data for additional sectors of the Canadian economy, such as railways and other utilities. The significant feature of this evidence is the steady increase in non-resident, especially US, control which is seemingly unaffected by depression, boom, war, or peace. In

TABLE 4.22 (*continued*)

Percentage of capital employed owned in:				Percentage of capital employed controlled in:		
Canada	United States	United Kingdom	Other countries	Canada	United States	Elsewhere outside Canada
74	23	3	—	87	12	1
14	79	7	—	2	90	8
78	13	9	—	77	14	9
49	43	7	1	51	38	11
57	43‡	....	....	45	55‡	....
11	89	—	—	3	96	1
42	27	30	1	27	27	46
75	15	9	1	77	9	14
26	65	5	4	19	67	14
39	44	14	3	23	52	25
48	41	8	3	39	48	13
49	41	8	2	43	44	13
37	57	3	3	25	69	6
44	42	7	7	34	66	—
40	53	5	2	41	47	12
41	50	5	4	39	53	8
44	46	7	3	37	52	11

manufacturing, foreign ownership rose steadily from 38 per cent in 1926 to 51 per cent in 1959 while control rose from 35 to 59 per cent. A comparable pattern exists in mining and smelting. At the same time, foreign ownership and control in railways and other utilities have steadily declined.

Much additional specific information is available along these lines, but the general point is made clear by the evidence of Tables 4.22 and 4.23 namely, that a very large and strategic part of Canada's industrial assets are owned and controlled by non-residents, much of them being directly controlled *via* the foreign parent-domestic subsidiary relationship. In addition such concentration tends to be in the larger enterprises and in industries whose growth prospects appear to be among the most dynamic in the whole economy. Indeed, the concentration is extremely

TABLE 4.23

Trends in Non-Resident Control in Various Sectors
of Canadian Industry
selected year-ends 1926–61

	1926	1930	1939
Percentage of total control by all non-residents:			
Manufacturing*	35	36	38
Mining, smelting and petroleum exploration			
and development*	38	47	42
Railways	3	3	3
Other utilities	20	29	26
Total of above industries, merchandising			
and construction	17	20	21
Percentage of control of US residents:			
Manufacturing*	30	31	32
Mining, smelting and petroleum exploration			
and development*	32	42	38
Railways	3	3	3
Other utilities	20	29	26
Total of above industries, merchandising			
and construction	15	18	19

SOURCES: Brecher and Reisman, *Canada-United States Economic Relations*, Table 25, p. 101, DBS, *The Canadian Balance of International Payments, 1960, and International Investment Position*, Table XIV, p. 81. Figures for 1960 and 1961 provided by DBS.

*Investment in exploration and development of petroleum by companies engaged principally in refining and production of petroleum products are included in manufacturing.

heavy in various key export areas as well as important sectors of domestic secondary manufacturing both of which tend to be prime movers of the Canadian economy. To a very large extent therefore it appears that Canada's economic growth is increasingly dominated by non-residents and will be strongly conditioned by decisions made by companies located in the United States and subject to US laws, customs, and attitudes.[35] It seems fair to conclude that "no other nation as highly industrialized as Canada has such a large proportion of industry controlled by non-resident concerns"[36] and, we might add, so much controlled by foreign concerns located in one country. This does not mean that the consequences for Canada are necessarily undesirable. Indeed there is little evidence to show that corporate actions in foreign-controlled companies are very much different than those under Canadian control. If the quest

[35]See Kingman Brewster, Jr., *Law and United States Business in Canada*, Canadian-American Committee (Washington, DC, and Montreal, 1960).

[36]C. D. Blythe and E. B. Carty, "Non-Resident Ownership of Canadian Industry," *CJEPS*, Nov. 1956, p. 451.

TABLE 4.23 (*continued*)

1948	1953	1954	1957	1959	1960	1961
43	51	54	56	57	59	59
40	57	59	67	67	67	64
3	2	2	2	2	2	2
24	12	11	5	5	5	5
25	28	28	32	32	33	32
39	44	45	43	44	44	44
37	55	57	60		59	56
3	2	2	2	2	2	2
24	11	10	4	4	4	4
22	24	25	27	26	26	25

for profits is the prime motivation in the conduct of privately owned economic enterprises, the nationality of the locus of control, especially between two such culturally similar nations as Canada and the US, should not make any major difference on balance. This issue is, however, very complex and in the following section some interpretative comments are offered. To this point we are simply recording the facts concerning the extent of control.

IMPLICATIONS OF THE PATTERN OF FOREIGN CONTROL

There are many actual or assumed effects of the pattern of control outlined in previous sections. For present purposes we will examine only those that appear to have direct relevance to Canada's over-all rate of economic growth and industrial structure and which have been the subject of some scholarly concern rather than popular polemics.[37] The purpose here is not to render any definitive judgment regarding the net impact of the high degree of foreign control. Indeed, considering the

[37]We will omit any discussion of the problem of Canadians in high supervisory or managerial posts in non-resident controlled enterprises or the freedom of Canadians to buy stock in such affiliates partly because whatever evidence exists suggests that "the participation of Canadians as executives or directors of the major non-resident controlled companies is widespread [which is] in striking contrast to the limited participation available to Canadians in the equity ownership of most such companies." (Brecher and Reisman, *Canada–United States Economic Rela-*

enormous variety of situations regarding both direct and portfolio investments in Canada, little can be said that is generally valid. The intangibles are simply too important to permit final judgment. We are mainly interested in outlining some of the more plausible pro's and con's, from the Canadian point of view, regarding the present situation and probable future trends. This becomes especially important in making forecasts because of the emotional nature of many aspects of foreign control which could well lead to actions on the part of the Canadian government designed to reverse or halt the trends so apparent since 1946. As the *Preliminary Report* of the Royal Commission on Canada's Economic Prospects puts it:

It is quite clear from the evidence presented before this Commission and from public discussion that many Canadians are worried about such a large measure of economic decision-making being in the hands of non-residents or in the hands of Canadian companies controlled by non-residents... If, as seems likely, the present trend continues, under which foreign investment in Canada is heavily concentrated in the resource and manufacturing industries, it seems probable that this will continue to cause concern in this country. And conceivably, if this proves to be the case, it could lead to actions of an extreme kind being taken at some future time.[38]

Indeed, in the first budget brought down under the Pearson administration in June 1963, there were several important proposals designed to lessen the degree of non-resident ownership, if not control. While the more drastic of these were subsequently removed by pressure from the Canadian financial community, this was done on the basis of administrative difficulty in carrying out the measures. There was, in fact, general sympathy with the *intent* of the legislation even from its most vigorous critics: the legislation was modified on the basis of feasibility not purpose. It will doubtless be the case that other attempts to arrest these trends will be made: hence some discussion of the economic consequences of the degree of foreign control, already detailed for the Canadian economy, is essential for an understanding of the attempts to reduce it.

---

tions, p. 135.) But the major reason for neglecting these issues is that their economic consequences do not seem to be particularly important and they tend to be far more emotional than rational in nature. For similar reasons we will omit discussion of non-resident "corporate behavior" such as the alleged failure to participate more fully in Canadian local life, to contribute to charity and so on. These are highly nebulous claims and in general probably untrue. For further details see *Policies and Practices of United States Subsidiaries in Canada*, Canadian-American Committee (Washington, DC, and Montreal, 1960).

[38]RCCEP, *Preliminary Report* (Ottawa, 1958), p. 89.

There are two general areas in which foreign investments may have an economic impact: (*a*) the over-all rate of growth, and (*b*) the structure of Canadian industry. Even these two aspects are interrelated but for expository purposes we will present some of the more cogent arguments for each taken separately.

(*a*) *Impact on the Growth Rate.* The positive impact upon the rate of growth is obvious. If the volume of savings in Canada at full employment is not adequate to sustain high levels of investment it may be supplemented by foreign sources. Given stability in the capital-output ratio, as appears to be the case in Canada and elsewhere,[39] this must necessarily raise the level of output. A rapidly rising foreign capital inflow, which carries with it not only new productive facilities or new savings but frequently entrepreneurial talent and skills as well, must likewise raise the over-all rate of economic growth. There is no quarrel with this general view, although as just stated it is vastly oversimplified. However, the form that foreign investment takes may be as important as its amount. We have already noted the prevalence of direct investment much of which takes the form of a parent-subsidiary relationship with control of the policy of the subsidiary, though operating in Canada, residing elsewhere, usually the United States. It is this aspect of the problem that warrants further discussion although the extent of control varies substantially from firm to firm.

There are some rather obvious advantages to Canada of this relationship. In the first place, the parent company may make capital available to the subsidiary in the manner and amounts needed and possibly at lower rates of interest than a non-affiliated company could obtain. But beyond this, the relationship permits readier access to more advanced technology and research than would otherwise be the case if the subsidiary were forced to do it on its own. Indeed the transmission of new technology is no easy matter in practice and the parent-subsidiary relationship vastly simplifies the problem by providing, along with the capital and techniques, the managerial and technical manpower as well. This access to advanced technology and research has even been termed "one of Canada's most important assets."[40]

The parent company, being larger and in business longer, likewise is able to provide training facilities where needed, market contacts, and possibly sources of supply which might not be so readily available to a

[39]See for example Hood and Scott, *Output, Labour and Capital*, and chap. 7 below.
[40]Brecher and Reisman, *Canada–United States Economic Relations*, p. 140.

smaller non-affiliated company. The provision of a larger market than might be possible in Canada through having the subsidiary supply the parent is often a major reason for establishing a plant or separate firm in Canada in the first place. In such cases of vertical integration, it is possible that without the corporate relationship implied in direct investments that the undertaking would not be made at all. Finally, the accumulated experience of the parent firm is not infrequently cited as providing a high degree of efficiency and viability for the Canadian subsidiary without undergoing an often painful and lengthy process of trial and error.

Looked at from a slightly different point of view many of these advantages to growth of the subsidiary may have more or less offsetting disadvantages as far as other sectors of the economy are concerned.

The easy access to research performed outside of the country may well retard development of research facilities within Canada geared to particular Canadian problems. The incentive to establish research and development departments within Canada is to that extent blunted. This has other implications involving, for example, a high proportion of skilled Canadian technicians emigrating to the US, a matter of great concern and serious loss to the whole economy.[41] Of course, in situations where cost considerations would preclude the setting up of research and development facilities in Canada, easy access to the fruits of research performed elsewhere confers a net benefit. Cost considerations rather than nationality of ownership are doubtless more frequently overriding.

Yet there is much to be gained by initiating new processes rather than simply borrowing them. Borrowing is likely to mould Canadian subsidiaries along US lines and tends to inhibit incentives to strike out in new directions more uniquely relevant to the Canadian setting. In truth, not much is known about the impact upon research of foreign control although it is of some interest to note both the relatively small expenditures on research undertaken in Canada and the rather large proportion performed by government and educational institutions compared with the US and UK.[42] But the definition of what constitutes research and the great variety of practices of Canadian affiliates in this regard makes it hazardous either to infer the significance of "research" to economic growth or to assess the over-all behaviour of US-controlled companies in Canada.

One of the more frequent complaints concerning the parent-subsidiary

[41]More will be said about this point in Part Two, chapter 6.
[42]For details see Part Two, chap. 8.

relationship is that the degree of processing permitted to the subsidiary is relatively small and that the bulk of manufacturing activity is concentrated in the parent leaving the Canadian plant in the position of supplier or raw or semi-processed resources. This, combined with the structure of the US tariff, in many cases has the effect of keeping the Canadian economy highly resource-oriented. We have already pointed to the stability over time of raw and semi-processed materials in the export consist. There is indeed a close relationship between US direct investments in Canada and US materials imports from Canada. Table 4.24 presents

TABLE 4.24

United States Imports from Canada Originating in US Direct
Investment Companies in Canada, by Selected Commodities
1955

	Total imports from Canada (millions of dollars)	Imports from US companies in Canada (millions of dollars)	Per Cent imports from US companies
Crude Oil	42	30	71
Newsprint	597	240	40
Copper	67	50	75
Sawmill Products	286	30	10
Paper Base Stocks	276	250	91
Nickel	144	135	94
Aluminum	71	70	98
Lead	20	5	25
Fertilizers	51	20	39
Zinc	46	10	22
Silver	19	5	26
Asbestos	53	25	47
Iron Ore	79	70	89
Imports of Selected Commodities, Total	1751	940	54
Total imports	2675	940	35

SOURCE: US Department of Commerce, *Survey of Current Business*, vol. XXXVI, Aug., 1956, p. 24.

some of the pertinent evidence. More than a third of total US imports from Canada in 1955 emanated from companies controlled in the US.[43] The proportion varies among commodities with US-controlled firms less important in lead, sawmill products, zinc, and newsprint than in other commodities. The very high proportion of total US imports from US-controlled companies is especially noteworthy in copper, crude oil,

[43]See S. Pizer and F. Cutler, "Growth of Foreign Investments in the United States and Abroad," *Survey of Current Business*, US Department of Commerce, Aug. 1956, pp. 22–4.

nickel, aluminum, and iron ore, all commodities of substantial importance to the Canadian economy.

This aspect of the foreign control relationship has both growth and
structural implications. On the growth side it is not clear why this should
do anything but stimulate growth through raising the level of exports.
However, it may well be that the relationship prevents the Canadian
subsidiary from aggressively seeking export markets in third countries
or even in the US itself. This is particularly important in cases where the
parent and subsidiary are not vertically integrated as in much of secondary manufacturing. Indeed Roger Dehem has recently argued that ". . . a
basic factor inhibiting the growth of secondary manufacturing in Canada
is not the smallness of the home market but the satellitic nature of most
of our important firms."[44] He goes on to assert that "the organic . . .
structure of Canadian manufacturing is such that there is a built-in
ceiling to its growth. Canadian subsidiaries have been established with a
limited horizon and with a restricted ambition. Unlike many fast-growing
European firms . . . Canadian subsidiaries are not free to conquer world
markets."[45]

On the other hand, some US-controlled companies have been located
in Canada mainly to get behind the tariff and make export sales to other
Commonwealth countries. A recent study concluded that "in the typical
case ownership as such is not a significant deterrent to the exports of
nonresident-owned firms."[46] Much ambiguity concerning the relationship
between ownership and exports therefore remains. Generalization in this
context is misleading, and *general* policies designed to raise exports by
increasing the degree of Canadian ownership are based upon assumptions having little empirical foundation and even less economic justification.

But if, in some instances, subsidiaries may not be free to entertain
orders from buyers wherever situated, it may also be that subsidiaries
are required to purchase available goods from the parent company out-

[44]Roger Dehem, "The Economics of Stunted Growth," *CJEPS*, Nov. 1962,
p. 509.

[45]*Ibid.*, pp. 509–10. There is a related feature, namely the occasional intrusion,
from the Canadian point of view, of US law especially regarding export sales to
mainland China, but since the dollar volume of *bona fide* offers to purchase has
been small we shall not comment further on it. Nor for present purposes is it
germane to discuss the US antitrust laws although both of these are problems
arising from the parent-subsidiary relationship. For a brief resumé of both these
issues see Brewster, *Law and United States Business in Canada.*

[46]A. E. Safarian, "The Exports of American-owned Enterprises in Canada,"
American Economic Review, Papers and Proceedings, May 1964, p. 456.

side of Canada rather than from other suppliers in Canada. As Brecher and Reisman put it: it is an "observable fact that imports from the parent, and from the parent's suppliers, remain high."[47]

There are many variants on the above themes but the foregoing should suffice to suggest that from the Canadian point of view many of the direct investments in Canada are not an unmixed blessing. How extensively subsidiaries behave or are required to behave is not known. Examples of varying degrees of freedom and control can be found to illustrate either viewpoint. Other illustrations can be found, for example, of substantial research expenditures conducted within Canada by subsidiaries and *vice versa*. This means that no clear-cut judgment of the net impact is possible. For example, after examining many of the above issues and others, Brecher and Reisman conclude that ". . . by comparison with the gains from foreign investment, [the] adverse effects do not appear to be of large dimension."[48] On the other hand Dehem attributes the economic slowdown in the latter 1950's to the nature of foreign investment (i.e., the satellitic relationship) in Canada. A more balanced view is given by Aitken as follows: "United States capital flows into Canada principally to accelerate development in sectors that will serve the United States market. Since the United States is already a highly industrialized economy with a very productive agricultural sector, the market demand that it exerts on Canada is predominantly a demand for industrial raw materials. The rate of economic development in Canada depends largely upon exploiting such demand."[49] Since this general pattern of *demand* would exist regardless of the form foreign investment took, it is evident that the predominance of subsidiaries and direct investments merely strengthens this pattern while the over-all rise in quantity has accelerated economic growth. But the reinforcement of the natural pattern has implications with respect to Canadian industrial structure, to which we now turn.

(*b*) *Impact on Economic Structure.* From what has already been said, it appears that the Canadian economy may have been kept more heavily reliant upon the resource industries than would otherwise have been the case and that secondary manufacturing for export may also have been retarded. Indeed it is a plausible conclusion that US influence, reinforced by commercial policy and the parent-subsidiary relationship, "is in the

[47]*Canada–United States Economic Relations*, p. 146.
[48]*Ibid.*, p. 153.
[49]Hugh G. J. Aitken, *American Capital and Canadian Resources* (Cambridge, Mass., 1961), pp. 11–12.

direction of perpetuating Canada's traditional status as a staple-producing economy."[50] But this refers mainly to the composition of exports, for if direct investments have tied Canada more closely to the US and hence hastened North American economic integration, they have also accelerated the expansion of the resource industries. This has at least bolstered, if not caused, the over-all growth rate to be higher than it would otherwise have been, at least over a reasonably short span of years. With economic growth, the Canadian economy has become more diversified as we have already seen. Despite the heavy resource orientation the share of manufacturing has not in fact declined and the variety of output has increased. Economic growth, even if resource-based, has raised incomes in Canada and, combined with the protective tariff, has thus widened the market for Canadian manufacturing. Again, many of the resource industries supply domestic manufacturing at lower cost even though the bulk of resource output is exported. From the point of view of the domestic economy it is fair to say that the closer North American integration has not prevented diversification despite its stimulus to natural resource production. The effects therefore are mainly to be seen in exports and imports. Despite many exceptions which make valid generalization difficult, the evidence suggests that the parent-subsidiary relationship, if not causal in this respect, at least reinforces present patterns of international trade as far as Canada is concerned and to this extent perpetuates a dependence upon staples and upon the US that many Canadians find disturbing. However, it needs to be constantly kept in mind that Canada has a distinct comparative advantage in natural resources and in terms of economic efficiency the present composition of exports may simply reflect these facts.

Finally, mention should made of what H. E. English refers to as the "miniature replica effect." That is, in many product lines several US firms establish subsidiaries in Canada but with the more restricted Canadian market there are too many firms to take advantage of economies of scale. There is, in short, a tendency to duplicate the US structure in a smaller market which makes each firm less efficient than it might otherwise be with a larger sales volume. This clearly influences adversely the ability of US-owned Canadian firms to compete in export markets and creates more enterprises in particular industries than the Canadian market can justify. As such "Canadian industry would appear to be a branch of US industry."[51] But, as English argues and as we have pre-

[50]*Ibid.*, p. 9.
[51]H. E. English, *Industrial Structure in Canada's International Competitive Position*, Private Planning Association of Canada (Montreal, 1964), p. 39.

viously suggested, the fact of foreign ownership by itself is subservient to Canadian and foreign tariffs in assessing its impact upon either growth of exports or industrial structure. Indeed, data are provided showing that "foreign firms export about as high a share of their products as Canadian manufacturing generally."[52] Once again we must stress the difficulty of making valid generalizations as far as foreign ownership is concerned.

Such are the major alleged effects of the extensive and growing US direct investments in Canada. For the most part they have accelerated North American economic integration and heightened the natural complementarity between the two countries. But if there is much ambiguity regarding the economic desirability of this process, there is no question that the political implications, from the Canadian point of view, are alarming. The conflict for Canada, real or imagined, has been vividly expressed as follows: "Every economic inducement, every opportunity for economic development impels Canada to accede to the continental pressures that now impinge on her. Every memory of historical tradition, every hope for the future preservation of national identity impels her to resist them."[53]

The resurgence of the US economy since late 1961 accentuates the conflict posed by Aitken at the very time when political intransigence in Canada is at a new height, despite the even more buoyant Canadian economic expansion which has thus far failed noticeably to calm the conflicts aggravated by the earlier economic slowdown.

[52]*Ibid.*, Table 14, p. 41.
[53]Aitken, *American Capital and Canadian Resources*, p. 16.

PART TWO

Resources

In 1962, as noted in Part One, the 18 million Canadian people were producing and consuming a volume of output per head second only to that of the United States. Within the next decade population is expected to increase to 23 million and each member of the increased population will be demanding even higher levels of consumption and public services than in 1962. At the same time Canadian commitments to aid the underdeveloped countries of the world may be expected to rise and contributions toward the defence of North America and Western Europe could also increase, at least absolutely, over the next ten years. Substantial as is the present level of Canadian output, it will need to expand greatly to satisfy future domestic demands and external commitments.

The question to which this Part addresses itself is whether the economy will possess adequate resources to meet the probable increase in needs. Part Two will therefore examine the supply of the four factors of production generally distinguished in economic analysis, namely, land, labour, capital, and management or entrepreneurship. We are interested in this part in the situation on the supply side as it existed in the late 1950's and early 1960's and the probable rate of increase in the future for productive assets and trends in manpower availability and skills.

It is gratuitous to remark that the possibility of meeting the increasing needs of the Canadian as well as the world economy depends upon the rate of increase in the factors of production. This is more than a mere quantitative relationship, although by definition the value of output equals the value of resources used up. Of equal, if not greater, importance is the change in the quality of the resources mentioned above. This is most evidently true in labour, capital, and management where the advances in education and skills of the human factors of production not only improve the calibre of human wants and create new wants but also make possible a far greater output per unit of resource input. Likewise, the improved quality of capital equipment has been more significant in raising over-all productivity than any increase in its quantity could have accomplished. Multiplying the number of bateaux would never have raised the efficiency of transportation to the extent of the internal combustion engine. But even in the case of land and natural resources, despite their frequent definition as "original and indestructible" and hence to that extent fixed, there can be qualitative improvements in the sense of new uses for known reserves or more efficient extraction techniques which have the effect of generating more output per unit of natural resource input. Clearly, however, this means that all resources, human and non-human, are closely interrelated especially in the qualitative dimension, for improvements in capital imply the embodiment of new skills, ideas, and so on which constitute a higher quality of the human factor as well. Likewise, the enhanced ability to tap or find natural resources, new or known, implies an improved quality of the man-hours devoted to productive effort. "Investment in human capital," as it has come to be called, is a prerequisite to improvement in the non-human factors of production as well. While therefore in this part we will treat the factors of production separately it must be remembered that this is a matter of convenience only, for all resources, human and non-human, are both interrelated and more or less substitutable in the production of any given bundle of output.

Furthermore, although we will examine the resource base apart from demand influences, this is again a matter of convenience. The incentive to enlarge the capital stock, extend the search for additional raw materials, and so on depends upon prospective effective demand as seen by business and government. In this respect supply and demand are closely interrelated with additional supply often forthcoming in response to increasing needs. At the same time the terms upon which various factors of production are available, the relative economic costs of using them, will condition both the magnitude and composition of real GNE.

There is one further point to emphasize at the outset, namely, that what constitutes an economic resource depends upon its ability to satisfy an economic want at a price that people are willing and able to pay. Before it was known how to control and use atomic energy, uranium was not much regarded as an economic resource although its presence was known in various parts of the world. But in a very brief space of time it became very important and effective demand outstripped the supply, but soon demand was less than potential supply. The same is true of certain skills with regard to human resources, the fireman on a freight train in railroad service being perhaps the most dramatic recent example of what happens when the need for such service changes in the face of improved technology (the diesel replacing the steam engine). In short, the availability of certain types of resources in given quantities does not necessarily guarantee that they are the right kind and available in adequate quantities to meet a particular constellation of demands at reasonable costs. In this context as well demand and supply are inter-related as both cause and consequence of actual output in total and composition.

These considerations mean that, even after specifying resource avail-ability, little can be said about its adequacy until the pattern of demand has been determined, for what constitutes an adequate resource base for one type of society at a particular level of economic well-being may be totally inadequate for another society especially if standards of living differ widely. The same is true of a given society at different economic levels over time. Thus a final assessment of resource adequacy must await the projections of future demand in Part Three.

5

LAND AND NATURAL RESOURCES

The possibilities of achieving ever higher levels of economic well-being are conditioned to large extent by the availability or otherwise of good land suitable for crop production and the resources needed by modern industry. This is not to suggest that such availability is the key or even a strategic factor in economic growth. Under some conditions, such as serious population pressure or lack of a highly skilled, industrious labour force, poverty of resources will accentuate the difficulties of engendering rapid economic growth. But this is less likely in the absence of these other factors. Obviously natural resources alone cannot be wholly determining since various countries such as Japan and Switzerland have achieved substantial economic success without large amounts of natural resources, including land, in the aggregate or on a per capita basis. This is especially true as compared with China, India, Indonesia, or Burma. Much else is clearly required for growth than the mere abundance of resources.

Nevertheless the natural resource base conditions the pattern of development and for those countries wishing to industrialize in the face of resource scarcity the necessity to import the required industrial materials as well as industrial capital, and not infrequently foodstuffs as well, creates special concern over the ability to finance them which, in turn, forces attention to the cultivation of export markets. This is indeed the plight of most underdeveloped countries today, especially in South Asia. Paradoxically Canada has been no less concerned over export markets despite a substantial resource endowment and a high degree of affluence. In fact, it is precisely because Canada's resource base is so substantial that it is economically sound to exploit it and be a net exporter of industrial raw materials as well as of agricultural produce. At the same time, the domestic market is such that it would not be economical to develop natural resources to the present extent solely for national use. Thus the very high level of land, mineral, and energy resources per head strongly favours heavy reliance upon their exportation in order to import more highly manufactured goods from other countries where they are produced more efficiently. Unlike most underdeveloped countries, which have little to sell to the rest of the world that cannot be obtained elsewhere at reasonable cost, Canada to this extent is extremely fortunate. That the general pattern of Canadian economic development has been strongly conditioned by the resource endowment, despite the long established and deliberate policy measures designed to alter this pattern, can scarcely be denied. It is in this sense that the resource base must be viewed as a factor contributing to the general orientation of the economy even if it cannot validly be held to determine the rate of over-all economic growth.

In the present chapter we will examine the physical features of the land along with the Canadian climate since these are important determinants of soil characteristics which in turn largely dictate what types of crops and forests will tend to predominate and the nature of the investments needed to offset whatever undesirable features of topography and climate may exist or to exploit natural advantages. Secondly we will survey the water resources of Canada including their actual or potential uses as far as the fishing industry is concerned and also from the point of view of electrical power generation and freshwater consumption by home and industry. Finally, we will examine some of the evidence concerning the extent and kind of mineral resources available which have loomed so large among the exports of the last several decades and which, in fact, have become the important "new staples" of the post-war period.

THE LAND

The physical features of Canada are shown in Figure 5.1. Broadly speaking there are four major zones, the Arctic, Sub-Arctic, Transitional and the Ecumene. The Arctic zone comprises the Queen Elizabeth Islands and the Eastern and Western Arctic regions as shown on the map. This area is a vast plain, treeless, dry and cold, with long dark winters and extremely short summers. There are few direct economic assets in the entire region: the absence of trees precludes lumbering while the year-round cold[1] does not permit agricultural activities. This is the habitat of

---

[1]The warmest month averages below 50° F while average January temperatures are between —10° and —35° F.

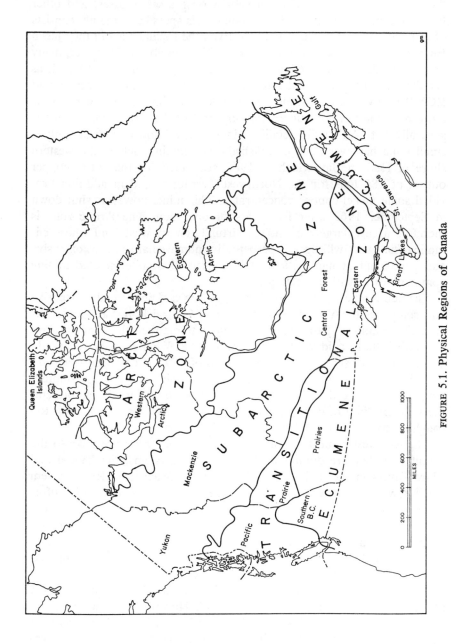

FIGURE 5.1. Physical Regions of Canada

the musk ox and caribou which subsist on grasses, mosses, and other forms of tundra vegetation. The population is sparse and mainly consists of Eskimos who hunt, trap, and fish. Even the Eskimos avoid the Queen Elizabeth Islands because of their general inaccessibility. However, many of the islands are believed to contain oil and natural gas, although as yet there are no permanent settlements except for weather stations and RCMP posts. The easternmost portion of the Eastern Arctic region is more mountainous and rugged than the rest of the Arctic zone which is generally flat. Although metallic minerals are known to exist, only a small mine has ever been established—at Rankin Inlet on the western shore of Hudson Bay which in 1961 accounted for the entire copper output of 486 tons for the Northwest Territories and in addition provided some nickel-copper concentrates. This mine, however, shut down in September 1962 after five years of operation. The Arctic zone is therefore a vast, largely unknown, virtually empty wasteland whose climatic deficiencies will keep it perpetually submarginal as far as extensive and permanent human settlement is concerned despite isolated mining communities in various sections.

The Sub-Arctic region bordering the Arctic is almost equally extensive and comprises the Yukon, Mackenzie, and Central Forest Regions. The climatic variations of this zone are more extreme than those of the Arctic, with bitterly cold winters (a low of −81° F has been recorded) and short warm summers (a record high of 103° F has been reached) lasting up to 90 days with long periods of sunshine and average summer temperatures exceeding 60° F. The southern boundary is, at present, the northern limit of commercial agriculture as the area in general is too rough or cold for any major agricultural development.

The two westernmost regions of the Sub-Arctic zone are alike to the extent that they are dominated by large river systems, the Yukon and Liard Rivers in the Yukon and the extensive Mackenzie River system which flows some 1,700 miles from Waterways, Alberta, to the Beaufort Sea with little obstruction to navigation. Both areas are rich in resources such as petroleum, gold, uranium, lead, zinc, silver, and smaller quantities of coal and asbestos and have permanent settlements of some size such as Whitehorse and Yellowknife with important villages like Inuvik, Aklavik, Pine Point, and Norman Wells. Although more populous than the Arctic zone for obvious reasons, it is still one of the least populated and least developed regions in the world. However, the two westerly regions differ in terms of topography. The Yukon is a hilly region with some high mountains whereas the Mackenzie region is flat with an elevation generally less than 1,000 feet above sea level, and is covered with muskeg, swamp, and lakes.

The Central Forest region, comprising a wide and lengthy belt around Hudson Bay is part of the northern or boreal forests of Canada, like the Yukon and Mackenzie regions. However, it consists mainly of a network of rivers, lakes and swamps and is not dominated by a single river system. It is likewise a mineral area, sparsely populated though with such important settlements as Goose Bay, Fort Chimo, Moosonee, Fort Churchill, and Lynn Lake. It comprises much of the Canadian Shield, Canada's most significant geological formation.

These two zones, the Arctic and Sub-Arctic, are what most Canadians mean by the North, although sometimes only the political areas of the Yukon and the Northwest Territories are implied. The North then is an important part of every province in Canada, save the Maritime provinces. In area, as defined in Figure 5.1, it comprises over half of the central provinces, close to half of the prairies, and a significant fringe of British Columbia. It stands as a perpetual challenge, an area whose exploitation and settlement is as difficult as it could be significant for Canada's future. A large proportion of the mineral resources of the Western World are doubtless buried in this vast region but transport costs, other necessary capital investments, and climate make this among the most difficult areas in the world to develop economically. Unless forced by economic necessity there is little prospect of any significant growth in the greater part of the Canadian North in the near future.

The Transitional zone divides the underdeveloped regions of the north from the more developed strip north of the United States border. Like the other major zones it is divided into three main segments: the Pacific, Prairie, and Eastern Transition regions. The Pacific region is mountainous and less suited for agriculture than the other two segments of the Transitional zone. However, in the Pacific Transitional zone the forests and rivers provide the basis for substantial fishing and fish processing activities, power production (the incentive for the establishment of aluminum smelting facilities at Kitimat), lumbering, and pulp and paper manufacturing.

Agriculture is possible in the Prairie portion of the Transitional zone and is extensively conducted in the Peace River district which, despite cold winters, has a growing season of 160 days, long enough for special types of grain to ripen. There is also some cattle farming and oil and gas production in this area.

In the Eastern Transition region agriculture is less predominant than in the Prairie region due to the presence of the Canadian Shield. The region is typified mainly by mining and smelting activities located at places such as Sudbury, where about two-thirds of the world's supply of nickel is produced as well as copper, gold, cobalt and other minerals.

The area from Timmins to Val d'Or is known as Canada's "gold belt," while Steep Rock is famous for iron ore, Arvida for power and aluminum production, and Elliot Lake for uranium.

The basic difference between the Transitional zone and the two Arctic zones is the ease of accessibility due to climatic differences and proximity to markets, which permit more extensive agriculture and greater ease of exploitation in the former. As a result there is greater, though still sparse, population density and a far higher degree of economic development, including a wider variety of production.

Moving south we come to the "thin band" wherein the great majority of Canadians live and an even greater proportion of economic activity takes place. But even this strip, referred to as the Ecumene of Canada, is sharply divided into four separate links which illustrate, if the brief outline of the other geographic regions has not already done so, the enormous problems involved in attempting to create or maintain a viable economic system in such an environment. The major centres in the Atlantic provinces are separated from the industrial area of central Canada by the Appalachian Highlands and a distance of between 500 and 800 miles. The populous hub of Central Canada is in turn separated from the prairies by almost 1,000 miles of lakes and the craggy Canadian Shield. Even within the Prairie provinces, population clusters about three main centres spread over 800 miles—Winnipeg, Regina, and Calgary-Edmonton—although no natural barrier provides serious obstacles to communication. Finally, Southern British Columbia is cut off from the rest of Canada by the Rocky Mountains and a distance of between 600 and 800 miles from its population centre at Vancouver to Calgary and Edmonton.

The economy of the Ecumene has already been discussed by implication in Chapter 3 of Part One in so far as virtually all economic activity for each political region emanates from the Southern belt. It therefore remains only to comment briefly upon the topography and climate. The westernmost portion is mountainous, drained by the Columbia and Fraser Rivers, typified by heavy year-round rainfall and contains one of the largest reserves of hydroelectric power in the world. It is protected from the severity of the continental winter partly by the Rockies but mainly by the moderating influence of the Pacific Ocean. The Prairie portion of the Ecumene is flat, fertile, dry, with the average annual rainfall tapering off from 20 inches in Winnipeg to around 15 inches in Alberta, forcing the latter area into irrigation for crop farming. The low precipitation and high evaporation preclude any substantial growth of trees and the relatively long, sunny summer quickly ripens crops thereby making this area the breadbasket of Canada. The grain belt is flanked on the western side by cattle raising, where the land is more rugged, and by dairying on the east, where the rain is heavier.

The Great Lakes–St. Lawrence region, as its name implies, is dominated by this enormous water system. Hydroelectric power is plentiful and cheap, especially since completion of the St. Lawrence Seaway, while access to minerals on the perimeter of the Canadian Shield and other areas within the region is relatively easy. But the area is also a fertile one for agriculture, though in fact dominated by manufacturing, and produces the bulk of Canada's output of such special crops as tobacco, fruit, maple products and so on. The climate is relatively mild and precipitation regular, a fit setting for almost three-quarters of Canada's population.

The Gulf region is dominated by the sea, a region of islands and peninsulas where in-shore and deep-sea fishing naturally prevail. The general topography is hilly which combined with a cool marine climate renders the area less suitable for agriculture except where flat areas prevail as in Prince Edward Island, the Annapolis Valley in Nova Scotia, and the Avalon Peninsula of Newfoundland. The climate is rainy (annual precipitation over 40 inches) and cooler than that along the St. Lawrence–Great Lakes system.

This, in very brief and general terms, provides some rough idea of the over-all physical and climatic setting of the Canadian economy. Table 5.1 specifies in greater detail the agricultural land area by province, and Table 5.5 the forested land. About 157,000 square miles or over 100 million acres is designated as improved and occupied agricultural land while an additional 960,000 square miles is classified as productive forested land. Thus only about one-third of the land area of Canada is at present in an improved or productive state. As already noted much of the land area is too cold for commercial agriculture and even where climatic conditions are more favourable, rough terrain, swamps, and inferior soils prohibit extensive agricultural development. The same is true as far as forestry is concerned. As Table 5.1 indicates close to half of the forested land is deemed to be non-productive. In other words, the productive portion of the land mass is severely circumscribed by climate and topography.

AGRICULTURAL LAND AND PRODUCTION

In the aggregate Canada consumes about 70 per cent of the value of domestic agricultural production. Although the proportion of domestic production exported varies a great deal among commodities (see Table

TABLE 5.1

Land Area Classified as Occupied Agricultural or Forested, by Province
square miles

	Newfoundland	Prince Edward Island	Nova Scotia	New Brunswick	Quebec
Occupied agricultural land	112	1665	4337	4658	24,860
Improved					
Crops and summerfallow	25	659	655	985	8776
Pasture	9	314	252	395	4129
Other	4	36	77	106	579
Unimproved					
Forest (woodland)	42	522	2447	2662	7622
Other	32	134	906	510	3754
Forested land	87,792	934	16,389	24,329	378,132
Net productive land‡	33,947	1955	16,906	25,804	237,510
Other land§	55,183	107	2123	1510	128,490
Totals, land area**	143,045	2184	20,402	27,835	523,800

SOURCE: *Canada Year Book 1960*, p. 29.

NOTE: Figures for occupied agricultural land were obtained from the 1956 Census; areas of forested land were compiled by the Department of Forestry from estimates supplied by the Forestry Service in each province.

*Less than one square mile.   †Included in Forested land; duplication eliminated in the item Net productive land.   ‡Includes only occupied agricultural land (less forest woodland) plus productive forested land.   §Comprises all urban land, road allowances, grass and brush land and all waste land such as open muskeg, swamp and rock.   **Net productive land plus Non-productive forested land plus Other land.

5.2), as far as food is concerned, Canada is more than self-sufficient. Indeed, Canadians are among the best fed, or overfed, people in the world. Data on per capita consumption of selected foodstuffs are given in Table 5.3. There is clearly no scarcity of agricultural produce in Canada. This abundance of food for domestic use was produced on about 63 million acres of improved crop land and roughly 10 million acres of pasture land. In other words, only three-quarters of the so-called "improved" land, defined as land that has been once subject to ploughing, is used for actual production, the rest being left to summer fallow. Trends since 1901 in land use are given in Table 5.4. The total improved land has more than tripled since 1901 but in the last two decades the increase has slowed down drastically. The large early increases in improved land are associated with the opening up and development of the West, that is the Prairie Provinces and British Columbia, since improved land in Eastern Canada had actually declined slightly from 24.1 million acres in 1901 to less than 23.5 million acres in 1961.

Some additional unoccupied land suitable for farming is still available. It has been estimated that perhaps 10 million additional acres in Ontario

TABLE 5.1 (*continued*)

Ontario	Manitoba	Saskat- chewan	Alberta	British Columbia	Yukon and N.W.T.	Canada
31,062	28,018	98,116	71,829	7092	7	271,756
13,365	16,427	60,428	34,284	1215		136,819
5423	929	1763	2000	500		15,715
856	540	1100	820	108		4226
5217	2448	3717	4517	1337	1	30,532
6201	7674	31,108	30,208	3932	5	84,464
261,747	123,305	117,738	159,064	267,638	275,800	1,712,868
191,586	84,237	135,407	184,056	214,166	75,706	1,201,370
56,500	62,900	8045	22,424	85,886	1,182,978	1,606,146
344,092	211,775	220,182	248,800	359,279	1,458,784	3,560,238

and Quebec and 7½ million more acres in Western Canada would be suitable for agriculture although their yields would be lower and substantial investments would be required to open up these regions for they lie in the northerly parts of the provinces.[2]

Of greater importance than bringing the present unoccupied land into cultivation is the more intensive cultivation of existing occupied and even improved land. Canadian agriculture is one of the most extensive in the world. The number of acres of arable land[3] per capita is 5.66 compared with 2.49 in the US and .64 in Western Europe.[4] Considerable scope therefore exists for improved use of land presently devoted to crops and pasture and for raising the ratio of improved to occupied land. In Western Canada some 4 million additional improved acres may be available from currently occupied land,[5] and an even greater amount from the very high proportion of land left to summer fallow, which accounted for nearly 30 per cent of the improved land area of the Prairie region. Part of this summer fallow is necessary to conserve moisture, but in the northern parts of the prairies there is adequate rainfall to support a form of crop rotation that would significantly raise annual yields.

[2]W. M. Drummond and William MacKenzie, *Progress and Prospects of Canadian Agriculture*, a study prepared for the RCCEP (Ottawa, 1957), chap. III.

[3]Includes land under permanent crops as well as land temporarily fallow and temporary meadows.

[4]Data from *Production Yearbook*, Food and Agriculture Organization of the United Nations (Rome, 1962), pp. 3, 4, and 13.

[5]Drummond and MacKenzie, *Progress and Prospects of Canadian Agriculture*, p. 73.

TABLE 5.2

Average Acreages, Production, Yields, and Values of Principal Field Crops
excluding Newfoundland
1955-59

Crop	Area (000 acres) (1)	Yield per acre (bu.) (2)	Production (000 bu.) (3)	Average price ($ per bu.) (4)	Total Value ($000) (5)	Per cent exported 1954-58 (6)
Wheat	22,104	20.4	452,595	1.31	590,957	66
Oats	11,222	37.8	424,690	0.63	266,108	4
Barley	9103	26.7	241,295	0.79	190,159	31
Rye	576	16.1	9393	0.92	8627	70
Flaxseed	2627	8.8	22,729	2.68	60,980	63
Peas	76	16.8	1273	2.17	2759	31
Beans	68	17.2	1170	3.79	4432	8
Soybeans	248	25.2	6256	1.98	12,379	29
Potatoes	309	131.7 (cwt)	40,685 (cwt)	1.93*	78,461	8
Field roots	36	10.9 (ton)	393 (000 tons)	21.49†	8444	14

SOURCES: Columns (1)–(5) *Canada Year Book, 1962*, pp. 414-16.   Column (6)
Rachel Berthiaume, *Exports, Imports and Domestic Disappearance of Agricultural
Products as a Percentage of Production, Canada, 1935 to 1958*, Department of Agriculture, Ottawa, May, 1960.
*price per cwt.
†price per 1000 tons.

TABLE 5.3

Net Food Supply per Capita
1960-61
(calories)

Country	Total calories	Milk	Fruits and vegetables	Cereals	Potatoes and other starches	Meat	Fats and oils
Canada	3090	440	153	660	142	566	460
United States	3100	409	179	662	92	587	501
Western Europe							
France (1959-60)	2990	281	150	1009	209	418	443
Germany	2920	301	139	784	247	368	615
Italy	2790	190	220	1312	106	130	431
Sweden	2940	476	139	681	164	356	539
Switzerland	3210	466	215	910	129	380	465
United Kingdom	3250	371	121	804	187	526	558
India	2040	104	27	1357	28	6	89
Japan	2240	41	100	1403	153	19	106
Brazil	2710	106	120	1039	361	190	161
Mexico	2550	202	127	1214	20	126	263
Libya (1959)	2100	103	242	1107	33	36	181

SOURCE: *Production Yearbook*, Food and Agriculture Organization of the United
Nations (Rome, 1962), pp. 250-52.

TABLE 5.4

Trends in Land Use
1901-61
(million acres)

Year	Occupied land	Crops	Summer fallow	Pasture	Total improved land*
1901	62.4	20.1	—	—	30.2
1911	109.0	35.7	2.4	—	48.7
1921	140.9	50.0	12.0	7.6	70.8
1931	163.1	58.3	17.0	8.0	85.7
1941	173.6	56.3	23.5	8.5	91.6
1951	174.0	62.2	22.0	10.0	96.8
1956	173.9	62.9	24.6	10.1	100.3
1961	172.6	62.4	28.2	10.3	103.4

SOURCES: DBS Reference Paper 25, Part III, *Trends in Canadian Agriculture;* and *Census of Canada, 1956* and *1961.*
*Includes "other land uses" such as buildings, farm yards, farm lanes, etc.

Other actions may be taken to raise yields. Irrigation and fertilizer application are as yet very minor items in the whole of Canadian agriculture. It has even been suggested that "almost all the grain grown in Canada comes from land on which fertilizers have never been used."[6] Recent estimates show that in terms of weight of plant nutrients applied per acre of arable land Canada uses less than one-fifth the fertilizer applied in the US and close to one-twentieth of the West European average.[7] Since yields per acre correlate closely with the amount of fertilizer applied, it is apparent that there are enormous possibilities in Canada for increasing output on presently cultivated land.[8]

Technological improvements have advanced far more rapidly than farming practice both with respect to crops and livestock.[9] The real

[6]*Ibid.*, p. 74.
[7]John O. Coppock, *North Atlantic Policy and the Agricultural Gap* (New York, 1963), p. 145.
[8]For example, in the US roughly 42 kilograms of plant nutrient are used per hectare of cropped land and yields per hectare were about 1,380 kilograms of wheat equivalent. In the Netherlands, over ten times this amount of fertilizer was used and yields per hectare averaged 4,700 kilograms of wheat equivalent. *Ibid.*, p. 146. This probably understates the possibility of raising output per hectare in Canada since present fertilizer use is so low. Diminishing returns to increased use of fertilizer appear to set in after much higher levels of fertilizer application have been reached than prevail in Canada today.
[9]For details on the extent to which present practices yield inferior results compared with present possibilities see N. R. Richards, "Production Possibilities and Technology Fertility and Soil Management—Eastern Canada," *Resources for Tomorrow* (Ottawa, 1961), vol. I, pp. 55–65.

TABLE 5.5

Forested Land Classification, by Provinces
1959
(million acres)

	Newfound-land (and Labrador)	Prince Edward Island	Nova Scotia	New Brunswick	Quebec
Forested land:					
Accessible productive:					
Softwood					
Merchantable	14,241	50	4653	4040	40,506
Young growth	2131	119	505	1853	12,937
Mixedwood					
Merchantable	79	85	3493	4684	13,949
Young growth	620	78	293	1310	11,528
Hardwood					
Merchantable	17	8	422	1244	1990
Young growth	135	7	29	611	3794
Unclassified*	—	1	273	1495	1158
Total accessible	17,223	348	9668	15,237	85,862
Potentially accessible	2300	—	—	—	55,112
Total productive	19,523	348	9668	15,237	140,974
Non-productive	34,091	—	715	334	110,954
Total forested land	53,614	348	10,383	15,571	241,928
Non-forested land	37,935	1050	2674	2244	93,342
Total land area	91,549	1398	13,057	17,815	335,270

SOURCE: DBC, *Forestry Statistics 1959* (Ottawa, 1960).
*Includes areas of recent burn, cut-over, or windfall, not yet re-stocked.

barrier to a drastic rise in yields through adoption of available techniques and equipment is the chronic tendency for the supply capabilities, even with the less efficient farm practices now in vogue, to run ahead of demand which reduces the incentive to adopt improved techniques. At the same time, government policies designed to support farm incomes slow up the process of agricultural adaptation and foreign support of domestic agricultural interest curtail the demand for Canadian agricultural output.

The point of this is simply that the potentialities of Canadian agriculture are extremely great both in the sense of extending the margin of cultivation and intensifying the use of existing areas. The stumbling block to higher output per acre in Canada is not diminishing returns but limited markets and protective policies elsewhere. No difficulty on the supply side in the sense of *ability* to raise output is to be anticipated within the time span for which forecasts in the present study are to be made.

TABLE 5.5 (*continued*)

Ontario	Manitoba	Saskat-chewan	Alberta	British Columbia	North-west Territories	Yukon Territory	Total Canada
17,592	6514	3637	8431	42,483	3136	3584	148,867
17,011	5847	792	9018	52,227	640	1280	104,360
13,517	2974	3126	7619	—	2560	2496	54,582
19,944	2665	1033	6095	—	640	640	44,846
3646	2117	5544	3095	2508	320	768	21,679
11,134	1793	1087	8184	4983	192	320	32,269
761	1927	1103	29,000	15,239	—	—	50,957
83,605	23,837	16,322	71,442	117,440	7488	9088	457,560
22,469	13,710	9923	2438	15,943	14,016	17,856	153,767
106,074	37,547	26,245	73,880	133,383	21,504	26,944	611,327
61,444	41,368	49,107	27,579	37,905	103,040	25,024	481,561
167,518	78,915	75,352	101,459	171,288	124,544	51,968	1,092,888
52,701	56,621	65,564	57,773	58,650	677,656	79,454	1,185,664
220,219	135,536	140,916	159,232	229,938	802,200	131,422	2,278,552

FORESTS

Canada has been generously endowed with forests. Almost 50 per cent of the total land area is forested and of this over half is designated as productive. It is estimated that there are some 611 million acres of productive forested land (see Table 5.5). Although at some future time it may be possible to extend the productive forest area, this does not seem feasible at the present time and in view of the extensive reserves already available is not a problem of concern. For purposes of calculating the supply we may limit our attention to the present productive area.

The total productive forest land is composed of two parts, one called "accessible" which consists of 458 million acres or about three-quarters of the total, and the other part called "potentially accessible" which consists of 154 million acres. The definition of accessible is not, however, clear-cut nor absolute and indeed varies among the provinces. Essentially it means forested land which is at present suitable for economic exploitation.[10] Rough as is the definition it is adequate for present purposes.

[10]The forest industry itself apparently construes accessible in terms of forest land that is within three miles of a main road. This, however, is a much narrower

The volume of merchantable timber on the accessible land is estimated at 589 billion cubic feet composed of 475 billion cubic feet of softwoods and 114 billion cubic feet of hardwoods. If we add the potentially accessible these totals increase by 87 billion cubic feet for softwoods and 10 billion cubic feet for hardwoods making a total of 685 billion cubic feet.[11]

The natural productivity, defined as the "annual yield . . . which could be expected from well stocked stands harvested at maturity,"[12] has been estimated at 12.9 billion cubic feet which reduces to 12.2 billion cubic feet after an adjustment for losses due to fire, insects, and disease. The allowable cut may fluctuate above or below the figure for natural productivity depending upon the inventory and the quality of management, but in general must be consistent with natural productivity if the forest stock is not to be depleted or excessively filled with overmature trees. The net allowable cut, shown by region in Table 5.6, for 1959 was about 10.2 billion cubic feet or roughly 80 per cent of the natural productivity. This indicates that "most provinces are making no allowances in their allowable cut calculations for the possible liquidation of the excessive inventory or old timber . . . [and suggests] a very low level of management."[13] Furthermore, both the allowable cut and natural productivity could be raised substantially so that the levels shown in Table 5.6 are on the conservative side.

The actual utilization in 1957 was a mere 2.9 billion cubic feet for industrial purposes[14] and 0.3 billion cubic feet for non-industrial.[15] Historically total utilization has always been below 3.5 billion cubic feet. Even when fire losses are included along with an estimate for insect and disease losses the total depletion generally remains below 4 billion cubic feet except in years when fire losses have been extremely heavy.[16] In short, the actual use of the forests has been at most about one-third of the conservatively estimated productivity.

---

construction of accessibility than is used in the above statistics. See D. V. Love, "Potentialities of the Forest Resource Base," *Resources for Tomorrow*, vol. II, p. 643, n. (b).

[11]DBS, *Canadian Forestry Statistics, revised 1959* (Ottawa, 1960), Table 3, pp. 11–12.

[12]Love, "Potentialities of the Forest Resource Base," p. 641, n. (a).

[13]*Ibid.*, p. 648.

[14]Defined to include wood for logs and bolts, pulpwood, and other primary products.

[15]Includes fuelwood and wood for charcoal.

[16]In 1956 a record high of almost 0.7 billion cubic feet of merchantable timber were lost to fires. All data in this paragraph from *Canadian Forestry Statistics*, Table 5, p. 16.

Canada typically exports a substantial proportion of its output of wood products. For example, in terms of physical units roughly half the lumber production, a fifth of the woodpulp output, and almost three-quarters of paper production were exported, mainly to the United States from 1956 to 1958. In value terms, close to 40 per cent of total gross value of production of wood, wood products, and paper was exported. When these facts are considered along with the above evidence on the great gap between actual and allowable cut, it is clear that Canada possesses a reserve of forest wealth for domestic use virtually unparalleled in any other country.[17] This does not mean that production of some species of wood, such as birch and white pine, in some areas may not be encroaching upon the available supply but in general the ratio of allowable cut to accessible reserves is less than 2 per cent (see Table 5.6). Thus even if natural growth were zero and if the allowable cut were to be matched with the actual cut, the Canadian forests would last at least for the next fifty years.

OTHER LAND USES

The amount of occupied farm land plus accessible forests comprise less than 35 per cent of the total land area of Canada. The remaining land area consists chiefly of wasteland and non-productive forests. Some estimates place the amount of wasteland at about 1,586,000 square miles and non-productive forested land at 753,000 square miles.[18] All other land uses, including residential and industrial, transportation routes, recreation areas, and so on take up a mere 21,000 square miles or less than 1 per cent of total land area. Even excluding the total land area of the Yukon and Northwest Territories, all other non-waste land uses comprise barely 1 per cent of the remaining land area in Canada. Rough estimates of these other land uses are made in Table 5.7. The figures are very crude approximations but appear consistent with estimates made for the United States. For example, urban land in the US in 1960 was approximately 0.12 acres per person while land for transportation purposes was slightly over 0.14 acres per head.[19] The slightly higher figures for Canada, if we construe urban as comprising most of what is classified

---

[17]This is not inconsistent with the growth of imports of certain specialty wood products, such as plywoods, in recent years. The above facts apply to broad aggregates and just as in the case of food, particular varieties are imported despite large exports of food and forestry products in general.

[18]Data derived from *Canada Year Book 1962*, p. 24 and memorandum supplied by Mr. G. Haase of the Department of Agriculture.

[19]H. H. Landsberg *et al.*, *Resources in America's Future* (Baltimore, 1963), Table 18-15, p. 373.

TABLE 5.6

Gross and Net Allowable Cut and Natural Productivity
(millions of cu. ft. 1956 and 1959)

Region	Gross			Losses			Net			Allowable annual cut for 1956 adjusted to 1959 inventory
	Allowable cut		Natural productivity	Insect and disease	Fire	Total	Allowable cut		Natural productivity (based on 1959 accessible Area)	
	1956	1959					1956	1959		(percentage)
ACCESSIBLE FOREST AREA										
Atlantic										
Softwood	567	835	621	45	1	46	521	789	575	2.74
Hardwood	195	290	205	9	—	9	186	281	196	3.44
Total	762	1125	826	54	1	55	707	1070	772	2.89
Central										
Softwood	1778	1606	3127	230	28	258	1517	1348	2869	1.70
Hardwood	1003	1085	1651	83	—	83	920	1002	1568	2.13
Total	2781	2691	4778	313	28	341	2440	2350	4437	1.84
Prairies and North										
Softwood	797	961	1842	28	31	59	738	902	1783	2.07
Hardwood	696	895	2014	70	31	101	595	794	1913	2.49
Total	1493	1856	3856	98	62	160	1333	1696	3696	2.25

British Columbia										
Softwood	1347	3680	1834	111	5	116	1231	3564	1718	1.22
Hardwood	41	46	46	4	—	4	37	42	42	2.52
Total	1388	3726	1880	115	5	120	1268	3606	1760	1.24
All regions										
Softwood	4489	7082	7424	414	65	479	4010	6603	6945	1.64
Hardwood	1935	2316	3916	166	31	197	1738	2119	3719	2.35
Total	6424	9398	11,340	580	96	676	5748	8722	10,664	1.81
POTENTIALLY ACCESSIBLE AREA										
All regions										
Softwood	1758	1245	1245	(All losses assumed to have			1758	1245	1245	1.44
Hardwood	439	282	282	occurred in accessible area)			439	282	282	2.91
Total	2197	1527	1527				2197	1527	1527	1.51
TOTAL PRODUCTIVE AREA										
All groups										
Softwood	6247	8327	8669	414		479	5768	7848	8190	
Hardwood	2374	2598	4198	166		197	2177	2401	4001	
Total	8621	10,925	12,867	580		676	7945	10,249	12,191	

NOTE: Data for 1959 referring to allowable cut represent increase in forest inventory due to surveys conducted after 1956

SOURCE: D. V. Love in *Resources for Tomorrow*, Vol. 2 (Ottawa, 1941), Table 7, p. 652.

in Table 5.7 as residential, commercial, and industrial, reflect the low population density in general and the abundance of land despite concentration in specific uses.

TABLE 5.7

Estimated Land Use in Canada excluding
Farm, Forest, Unproductive and Waste Lands
1963

Land use category	Acres per capita	Total (000 acres)
Residential	0.12	2160
Commercial and industrial	0.02	360
Transportation	0.20	3600
Recreational	0.20	3600
Military and defence	0.13	2340
Service	0.06	1080
Totals	0.73	13,140

SOURCE: Memorandum from Economics Division Department of Agriculture, Ottawa, June 14, 1963.

Urban Land. The increasing numbers of Canadians living in urban areas clearly requires a geographical expansion of city size that will lead to some reduction in farmland. The question is how important will this be in terms of total productive land? A crude calculation suggests that for every increase of 1,000 in urban population some 382 acres of farmland is lost.[20] This figure was derived from an examination of selected Canadian cities with a population over 100,000 between 1951 and 1956 and may not be representative of smaller urban areas nor for the future. However, if it can be assumed that average city density corresponds to the incremental density, the figure seems rather high. Indeed Crerar suggests that a generous land ratio would be a density of 108 acres per 1,000 people.[21] Other estimates of average US urban density for 1960 are between 117 and 171 acres per 1,000 people.[22] Although there are serious conceptual differences in virtually all aspects of these calculations, it would appear that the incremental Canadian farm loss due to urban growth should lie somewhere between 108 and 382 acres per

[20]A. D. Crerar, "The Loss of Farmland in the Growth of Metropolitan Regions of Canada," in *Resources for Tomorrow*, supplementary vol. (Ottawa, 1962), pp. 190–1.
[21]*Ibid.*
[22]See Landsberg *et al.*, *Resources in American's Future*, Table 18-14, p. 371, for the high estimate and Table 18-15, p. 373, for the lower estimate in 1960.

1,000, say 245. This would be in line with the US evidence and consistent with the apparent smaller degree of crowding in Canada's larger centres than in the US. Some offset to the amount of farm loss due to urban growth may arise with increased crowding, although this is not believed to be especially significant. Using the 245 acres per 1,000 increase in population of cities over 100,000, and assuming that by 1970 there will be an increase in number of people in and around such centres of about 4 million, this would imply a loss of some 980,000 acres of farmland or less than 1 per cent of improved farmland in 1961. Although in particular areas the loss of farmland may be more significant, from an over-all point of view urban growth cannot be viewed as a serious threat to the supply of productive land.

Transportation. The amount of land devoted to transportation in Canada is about 3.6 million acres used for railroad rights of way, highways, airports, and landing strips. With economic growth, increasing amounts of land will be needed for transportation. However, present intercity rights of way can accommodate substantial traffic increments and it is not to be expected that space needs for transport will rise at anywhere near the speed of expected traffic. Increased efficiency in providing transport service will likewise keep the land use in transportation from rising in proportion to traffic. But with economic development in Canada new areas will be opened up and new rights of way needed. This will tend to raise space needs faster than if the traffic growth is concentrated along existing patterns. Any estimate of future transportation land requirements thus depends upon the extent of opening up new regions. In the US, it is estimated that roughly 6 per cent more land will be needed for transportation by 1975.[23] But this is based upon a decline in railway mileage in the US while in Canada railways are extending into new areas. The "filling out" of Canada will require far more additional land for transport than in the US. Consequently an increase of around 20 per cent in Canada may not be unreasonable and has in fact been projected for 1975.[24] Thus, an additional 720,000 acres will be needed for transportation purposes by 1975. But this is a negligible amount over-all and since much of the land required will be in hitherto uninhabited areas, there will be little diversion from alternative uses, and certainly less than implied in urban growth.

Recreation. At present the amount of land used for recreational purposes is estimated at 3.6 million acres or the same amount taken up by

[23]Calculated from *ibid.*, Table 18-15, p. 373.
[24]Memorandum from Economics Division, Department of Agriculture, Ottawa, June, 1963.

transportation. But unlike the estimated growth in land transport requirements, recreational land needs are expected to expand sharply. As the
economy grows and incomes per head rise, more and more will be spent
on recreation. In the United States recreational land needs are expected
to rise by about 50 per cent between 1960 and 1975. There is little
reason to believe that Canadian needs in this area will be much less.
Thus, an additional 1.8 million acres may be needed for recreational
purposes by 1975. Again, however, the land for such use need not be
taken from other uses and there is no apparent over-all shortage of good
land for recreation even though serious crowding may occur especially
close to large urban areas.[25]

Military, Defence, and Service. Even if military needs should accelerate in the future, much of the land now used for such purposes could
be utilized more intensively. An estimate for these uses plus "service"
(i.e., reservoirs, churches, cemeteries, rural schools, etc.) suggests that
perhaps an additional 180,000 acres may be needed by 1975, a negligible amount which is not expected to encroach seriously upon other
uses.

The upshot of the foregoing is simply that Canada possesses abundant
land to accommodate easily even the highest estimates of future land
needs. The absence of crowding at present, the extensive form of agriculture, and so on imply no serious problems in land use, even though
in some categories of use there will have to be recourse to land further
removed from present population centres.

WATER

Water resources are important in three main contexts: (1) for direct
consumption or for waste disposal in homes, farms, and factories, (2)
as a source of energy, and (3) as the natural environment for the fishing industry. Each of these may be viewed separately, although under
some circumstances these various uses may come in conflict. Generally,
however, the first use implies some withdrawal of fresh water from available gross run-off, while the other uses do not reduce the over-all supply.
In this section we will examine the available supply of fresh water for
withdrawal and both fresh water and seawater in the context of the

---

[25]*Ibid.* projects an increase in land for recreation of only 240,000 acres, or well
below the transportation needs. This appears unduly low but suggests that the
estimate in the text may be on the high side. In any event, since even the high
projection would not apparently result in much diversion of land for other uses,
the Canadian situation in this respect is quite favourable.

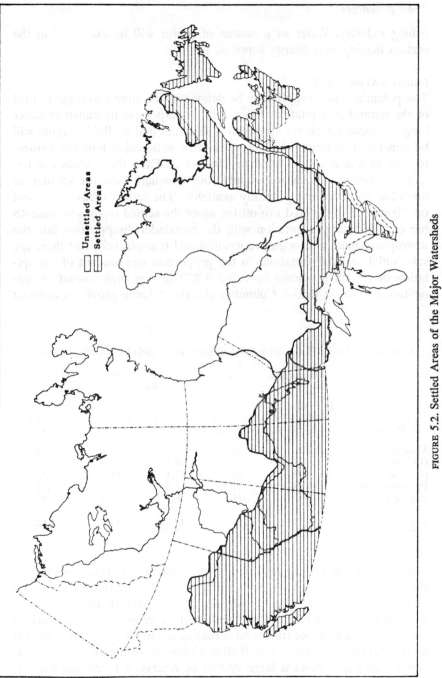

Unsettled Areas
Settled Areas

FIGURE 5.2. Settled Areas of the Major Watersheds

fishing industry. Water as a source of power will be examined in the section dealing with energy supplies.

FRESH WATER SUPPLY

The potential water supply may be defined as the annual average run-off of the natural precipitation. Since it is too expensive to transport water long distances a regional approach is essential and available supply will be construed in terms of the settled areas subdivided into the various regions of Canada as defined in Chapter 3. Even these areas are too large to represent localized supply, but adequate data for smaller or unsettled areas are not generally available. The settled areas are shown on Figure 5.2. Estimated run-off for all of the settled regions is some 48 per cent of total precipitation with the remainder disappearing into the atmosphere mainly through evaporation and transpiration. But there are substantial regional variations in the proportion and amount of precipitation of run-off as shown in Table 5.8. The very high run-off to precipitation ratios in British Columbia and the Atlantic provinces contrast

TABLE 5.8

Estimate of Annual Run-off for Settled Areas of Canada by Principal Regions
(long-term average)

Region	Precipitation (millions of acre-feet)	Run-off			
		Millions of acre-feet	Per cent of precipitation	Depth in inches	Ratio to Canadian average
Maritimes	234	145	62.0	25.6	1.95
Quebec	433	167	38.6	14.5	1.10
Ontario	240	89	37.1	11.2	.85
Prairie provinces	295	51	17.3	2.8	.21
British Columbia	402	314	78.1	24.4	1.85
Total settled area	1,604	766	47.7	13.2	1.00

sharply with the Prairie provinces and highlight the water problem of the latter region, which is only partially alleviated by the concentration of the rainfall in the May to August growing season. Drought in the Prairies is an ever-present threat and existing irrigation facilities are as yet inadequate to make the threat a remote possibility. The large run-off in the Atlantic provinces and British Columbia overstate the available supply. Indeed without a large system of reservoirs to control run-off, which is not at present available, "it is necessary to take the minimum flow as being all that in practice is available to meet the demand."[26] Thus, a reasonable estimate of normal supply that is generally available throughout the year would involve taking the minimum average monthly flow and multiplying by twelve. Table 5.9 shows the seasonal run-off pattern for settled areas by region.

The annual run-off generally available for withdrawal purposes such as public water supply, rural domestic and stock watering use, irrigation, industrial use, and even hydro power (to the extent that hydro power diverts water to the ocean or another watershed) must be compared with present use in order to place it in proper perspective. Estimates of use in 1956 and 1960 are shown in Table 5.10 and compared with the available supply as calculated above. Once again the substantial resource base of the Canadian economy is apparent with respect to water as well as the other natural resources already examined. The table indicates that even a conservative estimate of available supply is more than adequate to satisfy consumption demands. Indeed, as of 1960, the ratio of annual consumption to annual supply is below 10 per cent for every region in Canada. In the Atlantic provinces and British Columbia barely 2 per cent of available supply is used and the Canadian average is only 4.1 per cent. It should also be noted that the data refer only to what is called the "settled" area of Canada and the calculations use the lowest average monthly rainfall for the entire year. These factors suggest that the ratios of consumption to supply shown in Table 5.10 may be on the high side, especially since the available fresh water supply is augment-able through a system of reservoirs designed to control run-off. On the other hand future water use will rise sharply. What is clear, however, is the present substantial excess of supply over current consumption.

THE FISHERIES

The natural fishing resources available to Canada are remarkably extensive and abundant. The coastline on the Atlantic totals some 12,000 miles from the Bay of Fundy to Hudson Strait, including Newfoundland and other islands while the Pacific Coast is about 7,000 miles long. The waters and large shallow banks adjoining these areas provide an environment suitable for a wide variety of fish species which are available in considerable numbers. Indeed, the Grand Banks off the Newfoundland coast have long been world-famous and a major source of supply for many nations. Not only does Canada have access to substantial fishing in salt water but freshwater fishing resources are likewise plentiful. The

[26]D. Cass-Beggs, "Water as a Basic Resource," *Resources for Tomorrow*, vol. I, p. 183.

TABLE 5.9

Seasonal Pattern of Run-off for Settled Areas of Canada by Principal Regions
(long-term average)

Region	Jan.	Feb.	March	April	May
(A) *Depth in inches*					
Maritimes	1.14	.83	1.33	4.59	6.44
Quebec	.71	.61	.80	1.94	2.84
Ontario	.82	.79	.86	1.07	1.35
Prairie provinces	.16	.12	.12	.12	.27
British Columbia	.69	.61	.57	1.21	3.51
Canada	.56	.48	.56	1.28	2.22
(B) *Ratio to average month*					
Maritimes	.53	.39	.62	2.15	3.02
Quebec	.59	.51	.67	1.62	2.37
Ontario	.88	.85	.92	1.14	1.45
Prairie provinces	.68	.50	.51	.51	1.15
British Columbia	.34	.30	.28	.60	1.74
Canada	.52	.44	.52	1.18	2.05

TABLE 5.10

Water Consumption
Compared with Available Supply, by Regions
1956 and 1960

Region	Thousands of acre feet			Ratio of 1960 consumption to available supply (percentage)
	Available* supply	Consumption		
		1956	1960	
Atlantic provinces	56,307	558	674	1.2
Quebec	84,326	2615	3386	4.0
Ontario	75,500	4009	5148	6.8
Prairie provinces	25,574	1586	2159	8.4
British Columbia	87,917	1417	1728	2.0
Canada	321,024	10,185	13,095	4.1

SOURCE: D. Cass-Beggs, "Water as a Basic Resource," *Resources for Tomorrow*, Vol. I (Ottawa, 1962).

*Available supply computed as follows: number of square miles of settled area (each region) × 640 × lowest monthly rainfall in inches = number of acre feet available. Data from above source.

inland waters comprise some 260,000 square miles and provide a substantial supply of a wide variety of freshwater fish for commercial as well as recreational or sporting purposes.

Canada's annual catch is roughly 2 billion pounds of fish (including shellfish) valued at close to $200 million in 1960. Some two-thirds is

TABLE 5.9 (*continued*)

June	July	Aug.	Sept.	Oct.	Nov.	Dec.	Average month
2.29	1.43	1.03	1.02	1.60	2.29	1.57	2.13
1.97	1.10	.84	.78	.93	1.05	.80	1.20
1.05	.92	.88	.83	.87	.89	.86	.93
.39	.38	.32	.29	.26	.22	.18	.24
5.36	4.24	2.62	1.76	1.50	1.20	.89	2.01
2.05	1.53	1.06	.84	.87	.88	.68	1.08
1.08	.67	.49	.48	.75	1.07	.74	1.00
1.65	.92	.70	.65	.78	.87	.67	1.00
1.12	.99	.95	.89	.93	.96	.92	1.00
1.65	1.62	1.35	1.24	1.10	.91	.78	1.00
2.66	2.11	1.30	.87	.75	.60	.44	1.00
1.89	1.41	.98	.78	.80	.81	.63	1.00

generally exported, which makes Canada the third ranking exporter of fish and fish products. While this constitutes less than 3 per cent of the total value of Canadian commodity exports and less than one per cent of the net value of commodity production there are significant regional variations in the relative importance of the fishing industry which make it quite important to the Atlantic provinces and only slightly less so to the economy of British Columbia. For the Prairie provinces and Ontario in particular, fishing is of little consequence.

Before presenting estimates of the fish stock and current catch it should be noted that there is a certain resemblance here to the forest reserves. That is, an unexploited fish stock may become so dense that future natural growth is retarded in the same way that failure to cut mature timber may lead to an excessive density of over-mature trees. By "fishing up the accumulated stock" and removing the older fish of any particular species, the natural rate of growth tends to be stimulated. Thus, a simple comparison of current catch with estimated stock may be misleading for it is quite possible that larger future catches may be obtained without depleting the stock or even from a smaller stock, although in most cases fishing intensity is beyond the point where larger catches would tend to increase the yield without encroaching upon the stock.[27] On the other hand failure to exploit the fisheries may reduce

[27]For a fuller discussion see Department of Fisheries of Canada and the Fisheries Research Board, *The Commercial Fisheries of Canada*, a study prepared for the RCCEP (Ottawa, 1956), chap. 2.

both the quality and quantity of available species. These considerations should be kept in mind when interpreting the physical data of this section.

As in the case of fresh water resources, a regional approach to the fishing industry is essential because of its diversity. There are about 150 different commercial species of fish and marine life from which are produced over 400 differing products such as haddock, seal skins, lobsters, and cod liver oil. The enterprises engaged in fishing activity range from part-time, casual employment using small primitive, manually-operated equipment to giant enterprises employing large vessels with electronic equipment. In very general terms these differences have a regional orientation and we will outline briefly the resources and present levels of production for the Atlantic fisheries, British Columbia, and the inland freshwater lakes.

As Table 5.11 indicates, cod and lobsters are the mainstay of the Atlantic fisheries in terms of landed value. Lobsters are the prime source of income for fishermen in the Maritimes while two-thirds of the cod catch is landed in Newfoundland. On the Pacific coast salmon and herring predominate. There are other distinguishing features of these two salt fishing areas besides the type of catch which will influence the future supply from each area. In very general terms, the Atlantic fisheries tend to be more of a marginal operation yielding very low incomes per head, whereas the salmon industry on the Pacific coast is highly commercialized with more modern equipment and provides substantially higher incomes per head. For example, the average annual value landed per person employed in the primary fishing industry was barely $1,300 in the Atlantic provinces for 1958–60 but almost $2,500 in British Columbia. Although these figures possibly overstate the position since the per capita value landed in British Columbia fell to only about $1900 in 1960, it none the less indicates the magnitude of the discrepancy. Partly this discrepancy is due to the generally low productivity and lack of alternative opportunities in the entire Atlantic region which prevents easy departure from the fishing industry; this contrasts with the situation in British Columbia. The impact of the existing characteristics and past trends on future potential supply suggests that the Atlantic fisheries face generally greater difficulties in raising productivity than the Pacific.

As far as the inland fisheries are concerned the bulk of the catch comes from three large freshwater bodies, namely, the Great Lakes, Lake Winnipeg, and Great Slave Lake, although 600 smaller lakes are fished commercially. The most important species are perch, pickerel, and whitefish, which together accounted for slightly over half the total value landed in 1960 as shown in Table 5.11.

Some rough estimates of the stock of sea fish by major species are shown in Table 5.12 along with the utilization or catch for the period corresponding to the stock calculation, namely, the mid-1950's. The table suggests that on the Atlantic coast, the utilization of the cod, herring, and swordfish fisheries is capable of substantial expansion although some difficulty may be encountered in the case of haddock and even more serious problems in raising output of the important revenue producer, lobsters. On the Pacific coast halibut would appear to be in adequate supply while the all-important salmon may face some future difficulty in maintaining the 1955 utilization.[28]

As far as freshwater fishing is concerned data on stocks are not available. However, it is believed that with appropriate management practices, such as catch restrictions, regular restocking, and perhaps maintenance of hatcheries, the catch could sustain an over-all increase of about 40 per cent.[29] Although this estimate involves chiefly increases for the "coarser" species (i.e., those species other than whitefish, pike, perch, and trout) it does not consider the prospects for improvements

---

[28]The data on stocks related to annual catch must be interpreted with care. The following statement suggests why stock computations may not be the most appropriate indicator of production potential: "The actual size of a fish stock is a much less useful statistic than an estimate of its yield potential. Different fish stocks may be able to yield anywhere from about five per cent to possibly 200 per cent of their weight annually, depending mainly on the rate of growth and age at maturity of the fish. Yields of more than 100 per cent a year indicate that the stock is producing an annual surplus greater than its own bulk—something which is quite easy under tropical conditions, as every guppy fancier knows. In Canada's cool-temperature and subarctic climates potential yields are usually 50 per cent a year or less, sometimes much less. For example, commercial-size whitefish in cool Great Slave Lake increase in weight by 10–12 per cent a year, whereas in Lake Erie, with its warm water and much longer growing season, the weight increase is 30–40 per cent a year. The harvestable surplus produced by the two stocks is in much the same proportion. In general, the farther north you go, the smaller is the annual yield that can be expected from a fish stock of any given size. Stock size can be a misleading guide to potential yield in another way. A stock of salmon, cod or any other fish decreases in abundance when man begins to use it, and its adult fish must remain less numerous as long as an annual crop is removed. For long-lived fish, the original period of *fishing-up the accumulated stock* may extend over quite a few years, and it is a time of better fishing and larger catches than can ever be obtained again. It is like the harvest of trees from a virgin forest—there is a big initial yield of mature timber, after which the annual sustained yield from yearly growth will be much less. For example, some of the northern redfish stocks of the west Atlantic are today in this early phase of utilization, and are yielding catches which cannot be maintained for more than a few years. For them it is necessary to predict much smaller yields 20 years from now. By contrast, stocks that have long been fished are likely to have come to equilibrium and will continue to produce at least at the present rate." W. E. Ricker, "Productive Capacity of Canadian Fisheries—An Outline," in *Resources for Tomorrow*, vol. II, p. 775.

[29]*The Commercial Fisheries of Canada*, p. 35.

TABLE 5.11

Selected Data on Chief Commercial Fish
1960

Area and species	Quantity landed (000,000 lbs.)	Value landed ($'000,000)	Marketed value of products ($'000,000)
Atlantic coast:			
Cod	605	16.5	34.8
Flounder and sole	121	3.8	8.6
Haddock	95	3.7	9.0
Herring and sardines	246	3.7	15.9
Lobsters	52	18.0	28.8
All other	220	14.0	27.7
Total	1339	59.7	124.8
Pacific coast:			
Cod	5	0.3	0.8
Halibut	27	4.4	6.8
Herring	188	2.2	3.5
Salmon	75	18.4	36.0
All other	40	2.7	6.8
Total	335	28.0	53.9
Inland freshwater			
Perch	14	1.4	1.6
Pickerel	14	3.0	4.6
Whitefish	27	3.5	6.0
Trout	4	0.5	0.9
All other	46	3.6	5.4
Total	105	12.0	18.5

SOURCE: *Canada Year Book, 1962*, pp. 586–7.

TABLE 5.12

Estimated Stock of Sea Fish by Major Species
and Utilization
(around 1955)

Species	Stock (million lbs.)	Utilization			Rate (percentage)
		Canada	Others (million lbs.)	Total	
Atlantic:					
Cod	6800	710	400	1100	16.3
Haddock	480	112	90	202	42.1
Herring	3800	240		240	6.3
Lobster	73	48		48	65.8
Swordfish	50	4		4	8.0
Pacific:					
Herring	790	380		380	48.1
Halibut	700	24	38	62	8.9
Salmon	417	181	52	233	55.9

SOURCE: The Department of Fisheries of Canada and the Fisheries Research Board, *The Commercial Fisheries of Canada*, a study prepared for the RCCEP (Ottawa, 1956), chap. 2.

in trout fishing in the Great Lakes especially through elimination of the predatory lamprey which has virtually depleted the Great Lakes trout stock.[30] The estimated 40 per cent increase in freshwater fish take may therefore be on the conservative side.

Except for the few important instances noted, all of which may be susceptable to improvement by changes in management techniques, the Canadian fisheries in general seem capable of sustaining much larger increases in the annual catch. When it is recalled that two-thirds of the catch is exported, there is clearly no foreseeable dearth in terms of domestic consumption of fish and fish products from the supply side.

MINERALS

As we have already noted, the Canadian economy has remained heavily dependent upon natural resources. The previous sections showed that in agriculture, forestry, and fishing there still exist abundant opportunities in general so long as the demand situation is favourable. On the supply side at least there is no reason to expect problems in the production of the traditional staples from the farm, forest, and, with some exceptions, the sea. But Canada has long had a major position in world output of minerals as well. As indicated in Table 5.13, Canadian production of a large variety of important minerals ranked within the top four of all countries for which adequate data is available in recent years. Furthermore, the prosperity of the early 1950's, as noted in Chapter 1, was underwritten mainly by the new staples in the mineral class, especially metallic minerals and fuels. It is, therefore, of considerable importance to examine the resource availability of these crucial raw materials.

It is more difficult to determine the supply of these items because, unlike the situation in agriculture and forestry, they are less visible and much more difficult to survey, especially in a country like Canada with vast and relatively inaccessible areas. Nevertheless, no appraisal of Canadian resources would be complete without attempting to deal with some of the evidence, however tentative, showing mineral reserves.

Table 5.14 therefore provides some very rough estimates of reserves of various mineral resources. These must not be taken to imply absolute fixity in any sense whatsoever.[31] This is due mainly to the incomplete

[30]Since 1955 the attack on the lamprey has achieved considerable success.

[31]Indeed, since the summer of 1963 when this section was written three vivid examples of this point have occurred. One is the major ore discovery near Timmins, Ontario, made in April 1964 which indicated the presence of 25 million tons of zinc, copper, and silver ore. Another is the Athabasca oil sands estimated to contain more than 600 billion barrels of oil reserves from which almost 300

TABLE 5.13

Canada's Position in World Mineral Output
1962

Mineral	Canadian output as a per cent of world total	Canada's rank
Aluminum	11.5	2nd
Asbestos	40.0	1st
Barite	6.9	5th
Cadmium	8.4	2nd
Cobalt*	10.7	2nd
Columbium*	17.7	2nd
Copper	9.2	4th
Gold	8.4	3rd
Gypsum†	10.4	2nd
Iron ore	4.9	4th
Lead	7.6	4th
Magnesium†	5.6	3rd
Molybdenum†	1.1	4th
Natural gas‡	31.3	2nd
Nickel	59.2	1st
Selenium*	23.8	2nd
Silver	12.7	4th
Zinc	13.0	2nd

SOURCE: Bureau of Mines, US Dept. of the Interior, *Commodity Data Summaries,* Washington, Feb. 1964, and R. B. Toombs, *Canadian Minerals in National and International Perspective,* Dept. of Mines and Technical Surveys, Ottawa, 1964, p. 62.
*Excludes Sino-Soviet bloc.
†Separate data on individual countries within the Sino-Soviet bloc not available.
‡Excludes Middle East.

geological mapping. For example, the Canadian Metal Mining Association believes that about one million square miles, or over a quarter of Canada's land, are potentially available for prospecting but only about one-fifth of this has been "closely prospected or geologically mapped."[32] The Gordon commission concluded that less than one-third of the land area has been geologically mapped and "an even smaller portion sur-

---

billion barrels of synthetic crude could be recovered—an amount about equal to the world's known conventional oil reserves. New techniques for "wringing" oil out of these long known sands have just been developed. The first commercial production project was approved by the government of Alberta in the spring of 1964. Finally mention should be made of the prospects of major potash production from the lode in Saskatchewan, estimated at 5 billion tons or more, which has the potential to make Canada the world's second major potash producer in the next ten years from almost zero output in 1960. None of these significant developments have been included in Table 5.13. We prefer to let this stand as a reminder of the problems of estimating Canada's available natural resources.

[32]Cited in Bernard Goodman, *Industrial Materials in Canadian-American Relations* (Detroit, 1961), p. 89, n. 25.

TABLE 5.14

Mineral Resource Availability and Recent Levels of Production

Resource	Estimated reserves (quantity)	Production (quantity)
Minerals:		
Metallic:		
Copper	17-20 billion lbs.	878 million lbs. (1960)
Lead	16 billion lbs.	411 million lbs. (1960)
Nickel	12 billion lbs.	429 million lbs. (1960)
Zinc	33.4 billion lbs.	814 million lbs. (1960)
Uranium	474 million lbs.	25 million lbs. (1960)
Iron ore	6,066 million tons	21.5 million tons (1960)
Non-metallic:		
Asbestos	86 million tons	1.1 million tons (1960)
Sulphur from elemental gas	260 million tons (from "ultimate gas reserves") 50 million tons (from proven reserves)	0.3 million tons (1960)
Fuels:		
Natural gas	35.4 trillion cu. ft.	956 billion cu. ft. (1962)
Petroleum (crude)	4.5 billion bbls	244 million bbls (1962)
Coal	90-100 billion tons	11.0 million tons (1960)

SOURCES: Production figures from DBS, *Preliminary Report on Mineral Production, 1961* (Ottawa, 1962) for all except natural gas and crude petroleum. For these items both production data and reserves are from *Survey of Oils, 1963*, Financial Post (Toronto, 1963). All other estimates of reserves are from H. H. Landsberg *et al.*, *Resources in America's Future* (Baltimore, 1963), pp. 433, 443, 456, 464, 485, except asbestos, copper, and uranium, coal. The coal reserve estimates are from Caves and Holton, *Canadian Economy*, pp. 481 and for copper the estimate is from A. F. Gillin, *Survey of the Copper Industry in Canada 1958*, Mineral Information Bulletin No. 37, Dept. of Mines and Technical Surveys (Ottawa, 1959), and Bernard Goodman, *Industrial Materials in Canadian American Relations* (Detroit, 1961), p. 104. Asbestos reserves of ore from John Davis, *Mining and Mineral Processing in Canada*, p. 258; fibre recovery is roughly 9% of the rock milled and asbestos ore reserves are 958 million tons. Uranium reserves refer to content, *ibid.*, p. 264.

veyed on a scale adequate for mineral exploration."[33] In addition, efforts to find new reserves are directly related to considerations of profitability and hence demand. If demand is strong enough more intensive search for particular minerals will be undertaken and while this is no guarantee of fruitful results it nevertheless provides a rather close positive relationship between known reserves and expected demand—a good example of the interrelation between supply and demand.

For these reasons estimates of reserves are subject to very wide margins of error especially if divorced from anticipated needs. Furthermore,

[33]RCCEP, *Final Report* (Ottawa, 1957), p. 223.

without details of the location of these reserves estimates of their magnitudes can be distinctly misleading. Coal may be cited as an example. As suggested by Table 5.14, coal reserves are adequate for the next 9,000 years at current rates of production. Yet the location of Canadian coal reserves is generally away from the centres of manufacturing in Ontario and Quebec, which import coal from the nearer US fields. As a result, despite enormous untapped reserves, Canada is a net importer of coal. Likewise the accessibility of many of the other minerals is such that without large investments in facilities to move the resources to markets they would not be exploited. While, therefore, even if one considers the vast areas in which substantial supplies of useful resources remain buried—resources which would make the very high reserve to current output ratios even higher—enthusiasm on this score must be tempered by their general remoteness from the markets for the bulk of the resource potential. This is not a fatal weakness in Canada's resource position, and in fact nothing can hide the vastness of Canadian resource potential, for if demand is sufficiently large it becomes worthwhile to construct the needed auxiliary facilities as well as to conduct a more extensive search. But this involves a higher capital-output ratio than other countries would appear to possess, especially when the transport overhead and the investments needed to offset the rigors of the northern climate are considered. The problem of capital intensity, however, requires a more careful examination of capital needs and resources and is the subject of a later chapter.

Despite all these caveats, we have drawn together some recent estimates of the reserves of key minerals in Table 5.14 along with current rates of production. The metallic minerals shown in Table 5.14 accounted for almost 93 per cent of the total value of metallics production, excluding gold, in 1960, while the two non-metallic items shown comprised about 63 per cent of total non-metallic production and the mineral fuels over 97 per cent of total fuels. Over-all, the items shown accounted for almost three quarters of the total value of mineral production in 1960. Thus, although far from a complete listing of all minerals, those included in Table 5.14 are the most significant.

Even though there are doubtless far more extensive, though as yet unknown, reserves of these items, the evidence of Table 5.14 suggests the same picture as found in the case of agriculture, forestry, fisheries, and water—namely, that Canadian mineral resources are likewise substantial. Furthermore, alternative estimates exist for several of the metals which suggest that the figures in Table 5.14 are on the conservative side.

For example, Davis[34] estimated copper reserves of some 29 billion pounds in 1958 and Landsberg *et al.* have a comparable estimate of some 28 billion pounds.[35] These are about 50 per cent higher than the figure used in Table 5.14. Lead reserves may be about 25 per cent higher than the 16 billion pounds shown in the table[36] and this does not apparently include recent estimates of lead reserves in New Brunswick of almost 3 million tons.[37] Reserves of zinc may be as high as 46 billion pounds instead of the 33.4 billion pounds shown in the table.[38] These alternative estimates not only suggest that the figures shown may be on the low side, but also illustrate the variable and elusive nature of the estimating techniques.

However, using these conservative figures and applying 1960 production data indicates that, at these rates of production, Canada has adequate reserves ranging from a low of 18 years in the case of petroleum (excluding tar sands) to a high of 282 years in the case of iron ore, if we exclude coal for reasons already noted and the sulphur from "ultimate" gas reserves. It is evident that current production levels will not, however, be maintained. For several of the minerals listed production may be expected to decline, but for the greater part of them continued expansion is to be expected. A brief glance at past productive trends suggests a rapid rise in output.[39] Thus, the estimates of the time at which Canada may "run out" of certain materials needs to be revised downwards rather drastically in some cases. We need not be unduly pessimistic, however, in view of the incomplete surveying noted above and the positive correlation between demand and the incentive to search more extensively. As the *Final Report* of the Gordon Commission put it: "production of base metals in the 25 years ending in 1955 exceeded the reserves known to exist in 1930, yet by 1956 base metal reserves in Canada had increased substantially over the reserves of 1930. Perhaps of even more significance ... is the trend, over the years, of the ratio of known reserves to production. As this ratio is being maintained or increased in Canada, mineral resources would appear to be more than adequate to support current and expected output."[40] In addition, of

[34]John Davis, *Mining and Mineral Processing in Canada*, a study prepared for the RCCEP (Ottawa, 1957), p. 256.
[35]Landsberg *et al.*, *Resources in America's Future*, p. 456.
[36]Davis, *Mining and Mineral Processing*, p. 260.
[37]Landsberg *et al.*, *Resources in America's Future*, p. 465.
[38]Davis, *Mining and Mineral Processing*, p. 265.
[39]See chap. 9.
[40]RCCEP, *Final Report*, p. 225.

course, a large proportion of all the minerals listed is exported. In 1963, for example, over 90 per cent of the domestic production of nickel, uranium, zinc, and asbestos was exported while between 50 and 90 per cent of the output of copper, gold, lead, silver, gypsum and elemental sulphur was exported.[41] Hence, in terms of domestic needs there is no doubt that Canada is in an especially strong resource position.

ENERGY

Few other single indicators of economic growth and industrial maturity are used so frequently as that of energy consumption. Indeed the correlation between per capita energy consumption and national income per head appears extremely close.[42] There is undoubtedly much to be said for the view that the level of per capita energy consumption is a good index of relative economic well-being although the cause and effect relationship is not to be casually presumed. Yet it is not so much the total amount of energy used even on a per capita basis as the efficiency of the use and the source from which the energy is derived that may be taken to represent a high level of economic development. Energy is derived from a wide variety of sources. In North America over the past century six main energy resources have predominated: (1) human beings, (2) work animals, (3) wind power, (4) water power, (5) mineral fuels, and (6) fuel wood. Energy generated from all these sources, except (4) and (5), is scarcely symbolic of industrial maturity. As has been pointed out:

While there is an equivalence in physical terms between human effort exerted chopping wood, animal energy expended hauling a wagon, fuel wood burning in an open fireplace, wind power turning a windmill to pump water or propelling a sailing vessel, coke produced from bituminous coal used in a blast furnace to smelt iron, kerosene from petroleum providing light in an oil lamp, natural gas burned to provide carbon black for use as a coloring material, and gasoline exploding in an internal combustion engine to drive a truck, these varied forms in which energy appears and is used differ widely in their economic significance.[43]

---

[41]R. B. Toombs, *Canadian Minerals in National and International Perspective*, Department of Mines and Technical Surveys (Ottawa, 1964), p. 63. Percentages based upon physical quantities produced and exported.

[42]See for example E. S. Mason and others, *Energy Requirements and Economic Growth*, National Planning Association, Washington, 1955.

[43]J. F. Dewhurst and associates, *America's Needs and Resources: A New Survey* (New York, 1955), pp. 1101–2.

From the point of view of modern industrial society, inanimate energy sources, excluding wind power, are obviously of greatest significance since well over 90 per cent of energy demands are satisfied by "commercial" forms of energy as distinguished from such non-commercial forms as wood and other agricultural power (including animal wastes and animal muscle), usually consumed on the farms or within the area where they originate. As far as Canada is concerned, the sources of commercial energy (over 95 per cent of total inanimate energy produced[44]) are shown in Table 5.15 along with trends in their relative importance. The small proportion of energy currently emanating from coal and wood compared with 85 per cent in 1926 and 70 per cent on the eve of the Second World War is especially noteworthy and, of course, reflects the development of oil and natural gas resources especially following the war and the continued, though modest, rise in water power chiefly as a source of electricity.

TABLE 5.15

Energy Supply by Source
selected years 1926-60
(percentage of total)

Energy source	1926	1939	1949	1953	1955	1958	1960
	(1)	(2)	(3)	(4)	(5)	(6)	(7)
Coal	69	56	52	39	31	22	17
Petroleum	10	20	29	42	49	56	58
Natural gas	2	3	3	4	6	8	11
Wood	16	14	9	7	5	4	3
Water power	3	7	7	8	9	10	11
	100	100	100	100	100	100	100

SOURCE: John Davis, Canadian Energy Prospects, A study prepared for the RCCEP, (Ottawa, 1957), p. 368, for columns (1) through (5). Columns (6) and (7) calculated from H. Lee Biggs, *Developments in the Exploitation and Use of Energy in Canada*, prepared for the World Power Conference, Sixth Plenary Meeting, 1963, Melbourne, Australia.

At this point, however, we are mainly concerned with the available supply of heat- and energy-producing resources. As all the energy sources indicated in Table 5.15 except water power have already been examined in previous sections, it remains only to assess potential water power reserves.

Use of water power does not deplete a nation's resources. Although annual rainfall may fluctuate from year to year, nevertheless the reliable

[44]John Davis, *Canadian Energy Prospects*, a study prepared for the RCCEP (Ottawa, 1957), p. 21.

hydraulic energy from any continuous stream flow can be estimated with a fair degree of accuracy. Estimates of available and developed water power are given in Table 5.16 by regions. It should be emphasized that the estimates of available power represent only the minimum water power possibilities of Canada since "many unrecorded power sites exist

TABLE 5.16

Available and Developed Water Power
as at January 1, 1962
(thousands of kilowatts)

Region	Available 24-hour power at 80% efficiency at ordinary six months flow ('000 hp)	Installed turbine capacity ('000 hp)	Per cent installed capacity to available supply
(1)	(2)	(3)	(4)
Atlantic provinces	3778	845	22.4
Quebec	23,706	12,577	53.1
Ontario	7701	7960	103.4
Prairie provinces	9371	1545	16.5
British Columbia	19,400	3701	19.1
Yukon and NWT	6495	60	0.9
Canada	70,451	26,688	37.9

SOURCE: *Canada Year Book 1962*, p. 544.

on rivers and streams throughout the country."[45] As power surveys are extended, estimates of potential power reserves are revised upwards often substantially. For example, estimated water power available as at December 31, 1955, was about 51 million horsepower[46] compared with over 70 million shown in Table 5.15 as of January 1, 1962. In the course of seven years therefore estimated reserves increased about 40 per cent. Earlier estimates were 32 million horsepower in 1923 and about 40 million in 1946. The data of column (2), Table 5.16 should then be viewed as very conservative if past experience is any criterion. Of course, most of the as-yet-unrecorded available power is in the more remote sections of the country which will tend to raise the costs of such development. Yet improved transmission systems and the availability of

[45]*Canada Year Book 1962*, p. 544.
[46]See Davis, *Canadian Energy Prospects*, p. 219 where data are given in terms of kilowatts (1 kilowatt = 1.34 horsepower) and *Canada Year Book 1956*, p. 553.

water transport which will continue to attract the more power-intensive industries should offset to some extent the increased developmental costs.

Furthermore, the ratios shown in column (4) tend to overstate the situation since capacity may be installed which operates for only a few months in any typical year. Davis has suggested that the measured water power resources might well support a total installed turbine capacity some 30 per cent in excess of the ordinary six-months flow.[47]

Taking all of these considerations into account, it seems apparent that not much more than a quarter of Canada's available hydro-electric power has been utilized. In very rough terms this suggests that from water power resources now surveyed about 30 per cent of Canada's total energy consumption could be supplied by hydro power alone which compares with the close to 10 per cent figure for 1955 shown in Table 14. Since we have already concluded that Canada's oil and natural gas reserves are abundant, even though their full extent is largely unknown and hence the estimates made are on the low side, there seems to be little prospect of any dearth in the major sources of commercial energy supplies. Nor is Canada deficient in supplies of fuel required to produce nuclear energy. Indeed, it has been pointed out that "if the uranium oxide taken out in 1959 were converted into uranium and utilized within a one-year period for the generation of electric power at the design efficiency now feasible in natural uranium plants such as the Canadian 'Candu,' that annual production would be sufficient ... to generate ... 90 times the thermal power which was generated in 1960 in Canada, or 6½ times all the electric power produced in that year."[48] Even in the fast declining energy sources of wood and coal, Canada has a reserve for energy purposes that, despite locational disadvantages, could be utilized in the unlikely event that this should become necessary. Davis' judgment that "energy, in the physical sense, is not likely to be a scarce commodity,"[49] appears an understatement.

CONCLUSION

The foregoing brief survey of key Canadian natural resources indicates that the Canadian economy has a superabundance of agricultural and

[47]Davis, *Canadian Energy Prospects*, p. 219.

[48]H. Lee Briggs, *Developments in the Exploitation and Use of Energy in Canada—A National Survey*, prepared for the World Power Conference, Sixth Plenary Meeting, 1962, Melbourne, Australia, p. 26.

[49]Davis, *Canadian Energy Prospects*, p. 334.

industrial raw materials, energy, and water. If computed on a per capita basis there is little doubt that this abundance combined with the small population would place Canada at the top of the list in most resources throughout the world. Despite problems of accessibility, climate, and great distances there is every indication that on the supply side Canada has been exceptionally generously endowed with the wherewithal for agricultural and industrial advance. The bottleneck, if such exists, can therefore come from other productive factors coupled with demand pressures. No serious shortage of raw materials in Canada is envisaged at least until 1975, even on the most optimistic forecast of needs both domestic and foreign.

There can be no question that Canada's comparative advantage lies in her raw materials (including foodstuffs) and, indeed, it is her abundance in this area that is mainly responsible for the pattern of Canadian economic development along the "staple" lines examined in chapters 1 and 4.

6

THE LABOUR FORCE

Like the other factors of production, the labour force changes in quality and quantity over time. But unlike resources and capital, these changes are not solely motivated by economic considerations. Although, as we shall see, economic conditions influence the labour force in many ways, people are not "produced" for reasons of pecuniary profit. As Marshall put it long ago "free human beings are not brought up to their work on the same principles as a machine, a horse, or a slave."[1] The labour force is an important factor of production but it is more important as a consumer. Comprising as it does some 35 per cent of the Canadian population, the labour force is both a means and an end of production. It is this dual role that renders the discussion of labour a complex interplay of economic and non-economic factors.

The Canadian labour force which numbered over 6.8 million at the end of 1963 has generally increased at the same rate as the population.[2] But the aggregate growth of the labour force is not uniquely linked to demographic factors, although these obviously constrain the variability in the numbers of people commonly designated as part of the labour force. There are in addition powerful economic and social influences that have influenced the present size and especially the composition of Canada's work force. The broad trends since the turn of the century have tended to counterbalance one another and have prevented, until recently, the labour force from growing at a faster rate than over-all population. For example, on the one hand, there has been a tendency

[1]Alfred Marshall, *Principles of Economics* (London, 1890), Book VI, chap. I, sec. 1.
[2]See chap. 2.

towards later entry into the labour force because of compulsory schooling and the greater opportunities for education. At the same time there
has also been a long-term trend towards earlier retirement owing to the
higher level of economic welfare and more comprehensive retirement
provisions both private and public. These factors, if not offset, would
imply a slow labour force growth. But two main factors have tended to
offset them, namely, the entry of steadily increasing numbers of women
into the labour market and the additions made by immigrants, who have
a higher participation rate than native Canadians.

But of equal or perhaps greater importance is the changing industrial
and occupational structure of the Canadian labour force which has
already been briefly highlighted in Chapter 1. The present chapter will
outline these important developments and in particular will examine the
growing problems associated with unemployment and the influence of
rapid technological change on the pattern of employment opportunities.

THE LABOUR FORCE

The proportion of the general population which is willing and able to
work in the production of goods and services constitutes the labour
force. It includes employees, self-employed persons, as well as unpaid
family members discharging other than purely household activities. The
work force consists of employed persons, who work full-time or part-
time, and the unemployed, who have temporarily lost jobs.

In Canada, the Dominion Bureau of Statistics carries out a national
census every ten years and periodically conducts labour force sample
surveys designed to gather information on the labour force for intercensal periods. These surveys were initiated in November 1945 and until
November 1952 were carried out quarterly. Since then they have been
conducted on a monthly basis. The survey classifies people 14 years of
age and over according to age, sex, and also their economic activity.
The information is compiled from interviews carried out by enumerators
in a sample comprising approximately 35,000 households across the
country. The DBS defines the civilian labour force as being composed
of that portion of the civilian non-institutional population (members of
the armed forces and inmates of institutions are excluded) of 14 years
of age and over who, during the survey week, were employed or unemployed. Not in the labour force are those going to school, keeping
house, too old or otherwise unable to work, and voluntarily idle or

retired. The DBS definitions for the employed and unemployed[3] include a number of people who are only loosely and temporarily attached to the labour force, such as housewives and students. The survey statistics may in short indicate changes in the labour force which do not reflect actual changes either in the size of population or in the numbers of people of working age.

The total labour force, as shown in Table 6.1, has grown from 1.8 million in 1901 to 6.3 million in 1961, i.e., an increase of almost 260 per cent as compared with a 240 per cent increase in the general population of Canada during the same period. As of March, 1965, the estimated labour force stood at 7.1 million. The work force has grown somewhat more rapidly than the population, although the proportion of the population in the labour force has varied from time to time depending partly on the age structure of the population and partly upon economic conditions. There have been times when the rate of growth of the labour force was significantly higher than that of the general population. This was particularly true in the first decade of this century, when many adult male immigrants greatly boosted the Canadian labour force. In that decade the average annual rate of population growth amounted to 3.0 per cent as compared with 4.3 per cent in the labour force. During the 1920's, the rate of growth of the labour force was again somewhat higher than that of the general population. The depressed economic conditions of the 1930's experienced low intercensal average annual rates of growth both for the population and labour force. During the decade 1941–51 the rate of labour force growth was 1.2 per cent as compared with the 1.7 per cent of the population (in both cases, Newfoundland is excluded). This rather low rate of labour force growth reflected, of course, the effects of the low birth rates of the 'thirties. During the Second World War the National Selective Service directed labour in order to accomplish the greatest possible production of war materials and for that purpose facilities for training and retraining of women were

[3]The employed category includes all persons who during the survey week: (*a*) did any work for pay or profit; (*b*) did any work which contributed to the running of a farm or business operated by a related member of a household; or (*c*) had a job, but were not at work, because of bad weather, illness, industrial dispute, or vacation, or because they were taking time off for other reasons. The unemployed includes all persons who, through the survey week: (*a*) were without work and seeking work; or would have been looking for work except that they were temporarily ill, were on indefinite or prolonged lay-off, or believed no suitable work was available in the community; or (*b*) were temporarily laid off for less than 30 days. Prior to September, 1960, those on temporary lay-off were not included among the unemployed.

TABLE 6.1

Growth of Labour Force

1901–61*

(thousands)

| Census year | Labour Force | | | | Total |
| | Male | | Female | | |
	No.	%	No.	%	
1901	1544.9	86.7	237.9	13.3	1782.8
1911	2358.8	86.6	364.8	13.4	2723.6
1921	2675.3	84.5	489.1	15.5	3164.4
1931	3252.3	83.0	665.3	17.0	3917.6
1941†	3676.6	81.5	834.0	18.5	4510.6
1941‡	3363.1	80.2	832.8	19.8	4195.9
1951**	4051.0	77.7	1163.9	22.3	5214.9
1951§	3962.3	77.6	1146.8	22.4	5109.1
1961	4581.8	72.2	1760.5	27.8	6342.3

SOURCE: Census data.

*Not including Yukon and Northwest Territories. The "gainfully occupied" rather than "labour force" concept was used prior to 1951 for determining labour force status. 10 years of age and over in 1901 to 1911; 14 years of age and over in 1921 to 1951; 15 years of age and over in 1961.

†Including persons on Active Service (216,052 males and 767 females on Active Service at the date of the census were employed as wage-earners prior to enlistment).

‡Not including persons on Active Service.

**Including Newfoundland.

§Not including Newfoundland.

1931, 1951, and 1961 figures do not include armed forces.

created.[4] Wage ceilings were introduced in December 1940. With the termination of hostilities the bulk of the armed forces (some 700,000) was discharged within a year. Discharged soldiers had a prior claim to the jobs they vacated. Others pursued further education under special financial support of the federal government. Many younger women and older persons left the labour force and a shift of workers from expanded wartime industries to peacetime production took place.

During the last decade 1951–61, the labour force expanded at a rate of 2.0 per cent as compared with 2.7 per cent annual rate of the general population growth. Thus, heavy immigration with a high proportion of working age group during the fifties has not altered this long-term trend of a relatively slow growth of labour force resulting from the demographic trends of the 1930's. However, during the latter part of the last

[4]In 1944 the labour force (including members of the armed forces) reached a level of 5.3 million and the over-all participation rate reached the peak of 61.2 per cent compared with a peacetime rate of about 52 per cent, indicating the untapped labour reservoir that becomes available during emergency conditions.

TABLE 6.1 (*continued*)

	Intercensal Growth					
	Percentage change			Average annual rate		
Male	Female	Total		Male	Female	Total
52.7	53.3	52.8		4.3	4.4	4.3
13.4	34.1	16.2		1.3	3.0	1.5
21.6	36.0	23.8		2.0	3.1	2.2
13.0	25.4	15.1		1.2	2.3	1.4
3.4	25.2	7.1		0.3	2.3	0.7
10.1	40.0	15.6		1.0	3.4	1.5
7.8	37.5	13.3		0.8	3.2	1.2
13.1	51.2	21.6		1.2	4.2	2.0

decade the labour force began to increase more rapidly reflecting the high birth rates of the war and immediate postwar years. This labour force "explosion" will continue for at least the next decade and will require a sharp expansion of job opportunities if severe unemployment is to be avoided. Dramatic increases in the labour force during the summer months have already occurred in the last few years. During 1963, for example, there was an increase of almost 400,000 in the labour force between May and June, about 300,000 of whom were teenagers. The full demand for work will be felt more strongly when this group becomes older and their labour participation rates maintain a high level throughout the year. The two most important problems involved with the young entrants into the labour force are the appropriateness of the career decisions and the adequacy of the education and training which they have received.

The table also indicates that the intercensal average annual rate of growth of females in the labour force has exceeded that of males in every decade since 1901. Over the whole period 1901–61, the male labour force has tripled while the female labour force has increased seven times: as a result the share of women in the labour force has more than doubled from about 13 per cent in 1901 to almost 28 per cent in 1961.

The expansion of female employment has corresponded with the industrial development of Canada, social and cultural changes, and the increasing urbanization of the population. The development of service industries, the use of industrial machines, rationalization of industrial processes, and the growth of commercial and financial activities have all helped create greater job opportunities for women. In addition, employment of women has increased with the expansion of social security programs and government services, which require administrative and clerical types of work. At the same time women's educational and cultural opportunities have improved. Finally, two world wars have encouraged women to enter the labour market. After the war, many women continued to work or, following an absence of a few years, again re-entered the work force on a full or part time basis.

PARTICIPATION RATES

The labour force participation rate is defined as the percentage of the population of working age that is in the labour force. The definition of the working age population has changed over time from 10 years of age and over in the 1901 and 1911 census years to 14 years and over from 1921 to 1951 and 15 years and over in the 1961 census. The trends in participation rates are shown in Table 6.2. The data from 1921 to 1961, for which the measure of the working age population is most comparable, shows a high degree of stability in the over-all ratio: about 53 per cent of the population 14 years and over has regularly been classified as the labour force. But this over-all stability is the result of opposite trends in the male and female participation rates. The male rate has declined steadily since 1921 while the female rate has increased sharply. The reasons for these divergent movements become clearer when participation rates by both age and sex are examined (see Table 6.3).[5]

MALE PARTICIPATION RATES

The most significant change during the period 1946–62 has been in the participation of those aged 14–19 years. Just after the war, about three-fifths in this age group were either working or looking for work. Today, however, the need and desire to obtain more education, together with the comparative scarcity of attractive jobs for teenage boys, account for only two-fifths of them being in the labour market. It may be expected that this trend will continue because of growing demands for skilled and professional manpower, and the increased ability of many families to finance education.

[5]The record on participation rates by age as well as sex in Canada goes back only to late 1945.

TABLE 6.2

Labour Force Participation Rates by Sex*
1901-61

	Participation rates		
Census year	Male	Female	Total
1901†	83.4	13.5	49.3
1911	88.0	16.0	55.0
1921	86.7	17.2	53.4
1931	85.3	19.1	53.7
1941‡	83.9	20.2	53.0
1941§	76.7	20.2	49.3
1951	80.8	23.6	52.4
1961	75.9	29.4	52.8

SOURCE: Census data.

*Not including Yukon and Northwest Territories. Newfoundland included since 1951. 10 years of age and over in 1901-11; 14 years in 1921-51; and 15 years of age and over in 1961.

†Low rates are due to Indians being included in the population but not in the labour force.

‡Including persons on Active Service.

§Not including persons on Active Service.

At the other end of the male age spectrum, 65 years and over, the increasing number of pension plans, the rising ability of younger people to support older ones, secular shifts of the labour force, particularly out of primary industries, together with a shortage of jobs for older workers, have induced many men to withdraw completely from the labour force when reaching the retirement age. Consequently, in 1962, less than one-third of the men 65 years and over were working or looking for work as compared with about one-half at the end of the war. Part of this reduction, however, is due to enforcement of compulsory retirement. Coming at a time when the expected life span has lengthened and affecting, as it does now, people who grew up in an era when education was neither so widespread nor so important, compulsory retirement has a peculiarly harsh impact on many people, in good health, who are forced to retire at a particular age. Furthermore, since the normal retirement age is 65 while the so-called "old age pension" does not begin until 70, there is a peculiar gap that requires either a relaxing of retirement age or a lowering of the age when federal pensions begin, if some serious hardship is to be reduced.

However these two tendencies (declining participation rates of young men of 14–19 years of age and of older workers) together with a higher proportion of men 20–24 years of age seeking further education and training have caused the decline in the over-all male participation rate.

TABLE 6.3

Labour Force Participation Rates by Age and Sex
1946–62

Age groups by sex	1946*	1948*	1950†	1952	1954	1956	1958	1960	1962
Both Sexes									
14-19	49.4	45.6	44.4	42.9	41.9	41.0	38.8	37.9	35.4
20-24	67.4	68.3	69.0	69.2	68.6	68.8	69.0	69.1	68.8
25-34	59.9	60.2	59.6	59.7	59.9	60.7	61.7	62.4	63.0
35-44	}	}	59.6	60.4	59.8	60.6	61.7	63.1	63.9
45-54	55.9	56.1	58.4	59.5	59.6	61.4	62.8	64.1	64.8
55-64	}	}	51.2	50.8	50.3	51.6	53.4	54.3	55.2
65 and over	26.6		22.7	20.5	18.6	19.3	18.5	17.5	16.5
Total, all age groups	55.0	54.6	53.7	53.5	52.9	53.5	53.9	54.3	54.1
Males									
14-19	60.5	57.9	55.9	52.8	50.2	48.1	45.6	43.0	39.6
20-24	88.9	92.1	93.0	92.9	92.0	91.7	91.6	91.2	89.0
25-34	97.1	98.0	96.9	97.8	97.3	97.6	97.9	97.9	97.6
35-44	}	}	98.1	97.9	97.3	97.6	97.9	97.7	97.8
45-54	93.4	93.0	96.0	95.9	95.6	96.0	96.1	96.4	95.6
55-64	}	}	86.8	86.5	85.4	86.4	87.1	86.8	86.1
65 and over	47.5	44.0	40.4	36.7	33.2	34.1	32.2	30.2	28.4
Total, all age groups	85.1	85.1	84.0	83.4	82.2	82.2	81.7	80.8	79.3
Females									
14-19	37.7	33.3	33.0	33.1	33.6	33.9	32.1	32.6	31.0
20-24	48.0	45.4	46.4	47.1	46.6	47.1	47.4	48.1	49.7
25-34	23.2	22.8	24.0	24.1	24.4	25.1	26.2	27.3	28.3
35-44	}	}	20.5	22.5	22.1	23.8	26.2	29.4	31.0
45-54	15.3	16.2	18.9	20.6	21.1	24.4	27.5	30.4	33.3
55-64	}	}	13.2	13.4	14.0	15.9	19.0	21.2	23.8
65 and over	5.0	5.1	4.2	3.9	3.7	4.5	5.2	5.5	5.5
Total, all age groups	24.7	23.5	23.2	23.7	23.7	24.9	26.3	28.0	29.1

SOURCE: Special Surveys Division, DBS.
*Breakdown of 25-44 years and 45-64 years into 10-year age groups was not available before 1950.
†Newfoundland included only from 1950.

This changing pattern of male participation has also moderated the over-all growth of the labour force during recent years and hence kept unemployment rates below levels that would otherwise have occurred.

FEMALE PARTICIPATION RATES

Despite a slight tendency for women in the 14–19 age group to withdraw from the labour force, the over-all participation rate and that of women in all other age groups has increased as shown in Table 6.3. The highest female participation rate is found in the 20–24 age group, about 50.0 per cent, partly because it is more usual for women of this age to work and partly because of an increase in the proportion of young women who remain in the labour market after marriage.

The percentage of women in the age group 20–54 entering the labour force has been increasing steadily, particularly since the mid 1950's and there is, as yet, no evidence of a levelling off. The same tendency is noted for women in the age group 55–64, while the participation rate for women 65 years of age and over showed only a moderate increase. It should also be noted that a much smaller proportion of women of this age group was in the labour force as compared with men.[6]

An important factor in the marked advance in the female proportion of the aggregate labour force has been the increase in the number of married women, which is clearly shown in Table 6.4. By 1961, married women accounted for about a half of the total female labour force as compared with less than one-third in 1951 and only one-tenth in 1941. In the older age groups of women, there has been an increasing tendency for mothers to seek employment after their children have grown up. It also appears that among the younger women (under 24 years of age), among whom the proportion of those married has increased considerably during the postwar years, there is a growing tendency for wives to remain in the labour force in order to supplement their husbands' income.

The participation of married women in the labour force is, naturally, influenced by current employment prospects and by availability of part-time jobs. The latter have been increasing largely because of the growth of service industries and retail trade. Industrial production, however, does not lend itself readily to the use of part-time labour.

Increased life expectancy after child-bearing, coupled with earlier marriages and earlier families, more compact homes, furnished with

[6]It is probable that a somewhat higher over-all percentage of the total female population actually participates in the work force than the proportion indicated, because the mobility of women, particularly housewives, into and out of the labour market is higher than that of men.

TABLE 6.4

Distribution of the Female Labour Force, by Marital Status*
1941, 1951, and 1961

	1941†		1951		1961	
Marital status	Number	Per cent	Number	Per cent	Number	Per cent
Single	665,623	79.9	723,433	62.1	747,267	42.3
Married	85,633	10.3	348,961	30.1	879,141	49.8
Other:						
Widowed	56,964	6.8	78,672	6.8	117,592	6.6
Divorced	24,582	3.0	13,255	1.1	22,332	1.3
Total	832,840‡	100.0	1,164,321	100.0	1,766,332	100.0

SOURCE: Census data.
*Excluding Newfoundland prior to 1951 and the Yukon and Northwest Territories.
†Excluding women in Active Service.
‡Includes conjugal condition not stated.

labour-saving devices, together with the availability of processed foods, have contributed to an easier home-life and longer working-life for married women. The reduction in average hours of work enables married women to work part-time and still discharge domestic responsibilities. Changing attitudes and the social climate towards the employment of married women are also responsible for the increase in the proportion of married women working shown in each succeeding census year. These are some of the many reasons explaining the steady increase in the proportion of married women in the labour force.

US PARTICIPATION RATES
The trends in the US are shown in Table 6.5 as they may presage future tendencies in Canada and, in any event, are of interest in themselves. The over-all participation rate in the US was slightly higher than that in Canada in 1961 and has been increasing, unlike the Canadian experience. The higher US rate is principally due to greater female participation in the labour force. As of 1961 the US participation rate for men of the age 14–19 years was somewhat higher than the corresponding rate in Canada. This was not so in the case of women. The more significant difference, however, emerges in the female participation rates of women 25–64 years of age, where the US rates were substantially above those for Canada. Approximately two-fifths of US women in that age group were in the labour force as compared with less than one-third in Canada. One may reasonably expect that Canadian female participation will increase once public opinion generally accepts their employment

TABLE 6.5

Labour Force Participation Rates, by Age and Sex, in the United States
selected years 1940–61

Age and sex	1940	1946	1951	1956	1961
Total labour force	55.3	56.6	58.2	58.6	57.2
Male					
Total	82.6	82.5	83.6	82.4	78.8
14 – 19 years	44.0	53.5	53.3	50.9	44.5
20 – 24 years	95.2	81.0	89.1	89.5	90.5
25 – 44 years	96.7	94.3	96.0	96.4	96.2
45 – 64 years	90.4	92.0	90.7	91.5	90.8
65 and over	44.2	47.4	43.8	39.1	29.0
Female					
Total	27.9	31.1	33.6	35.6	36.5
14 – 19 years	23.1	32.1	31.8	31.7	29.7
20 – 24 years	49.1	46.2	46.4	46.2	47.3
25 – 44 years	32.1	34.3	37.3	38.9	39.9
45 – 64 years	21.7	27.9	34.1	40.4	45.2
65 and over	7.2	8.3	8.7	10.6	9.9

SOURCE: 1940–56, "Historical Statistics of the United States, Colonial Times to 1957", Series D 13-25. 1960 rates computed from Tables No. 281 (Labour Force, age and sex) and No. 20 (Population, age and sex). *Statistical Abstract of the United States, 1962.*

and when employment and family conditions are adjusted further to facilitate the acceptance of the working mother. Other factors working in the same direction are the continuing relative decline of primary industries in Canada, which are not suitable for female employment, further expansion of the commercial and service industries, and continued urbanization of the Canadian population (since female participation rates increase with the size of cities and the shifts of population from rural to urban communities).

INDUSTRIAL DISTRIBUTION

The industrial basis of the Canadian economy has been broadened over the past few decades and, at present, Canadian industry is moving rapidly from the primary and secondary stages to the tertiary, characterized by the rapid growth of such sectors as public utilities, trade, finance, real estate, and services, both private and public. This industrial shift is the consequence of changing patterns of demand, at home and abroad, and new technology. Naturally, the industrial composition of

TABLE 6.6

Numerical and Percentage Distribution of the Labour Force by Sex and
Major Industry Groups,
1931–61*
(thousands)

Industrial group	1931			1941		
	Male	Female	Total	Male	Female	Total
All industries	3252.3	665.3	3917.6	3363.1	832.8	4195.9
Agriculture	1099.8	24.2	1124.0	1063.0	19.1	1082.1
Forestry operations† }	96.8	0.8	97.6 {	93.2	0.5	93.6
Fishing and trapping }			{	50.7	0.4	51.1
Mining	71.5	0.4	71.9	92.4	0.6	93.0
Manufacturing	600.8	122.8	723.6	784.7	181.3	966.0
Electricity	23.6	1.8	25.4	23.6	2.0	25.6
Construction	248.2	1.6	249.8	218.7	1.5	220.2
Transportation and communications	254.5	22.7	277.2	246.8	19.8	266.6
Trade:	302.5	85.1	387.6	352.2	112.8	465.0
Wholesale	52.0	8.8	60.8	84.5	15.8	100.3
Retail	250.5	76.3	326.8	267.7	97.0	364.7
Finance and real estate	67.4	25.0	92.4	61.3	28.4	89.7
Service:	321.7	377.4	699.1	335.4	461.6	797.0
Community }	101.4	148.1	249.5 {	98.7	165.1	263.8
Business }			{	9.1	3.1	12.2
Government	94.1	15.4	109.5	109.2	28.0	137.2
Recreation	15.2	2.4	17.6	14.5	3.1	17.6
Personal	111.0	211.4	322.4	103.8	262.3	366.1
Industry not stated	165.5	3.7	169.2	41.1	4.9	46.0

SOURCE: Census data and Employment and Occupation Section, DBS. Industries
were rearranged on the basis of the 1951 classification.

*14 years of age and over for 1931 to 1951 and 15 years and over for 1961. Not
including armed forces. Not including Yukon and Northwest Territories. Newfoundland included in 1951 and 1961.

†Separate figures for Forestry and Fishing, Community and Business Services
not available for 1931.

the Canadian labour force has been remoulded accordingly. The substantial growth of industries in the field of commerce and services and
the relatively slow development of others, such as secondary manufacturing or a decline in still others (e.g., agriculture), have influenced the
direction of new entrants to the labour force into expanding industries
and the shifting of workers from declining to growing industries. On the
whole, this transformation of the labour force has resulted in the transfer
of part of the labour force from low- to high-productivity industries
which has contributed materially to the higher real income of Canadians.

The numerical and percentage distribution of the labour force by sex
and major industry group for the census years 1931–61 is shown in

(thousands)

1951			1961		
Male	Female	Total	Male	Female	Total
4051.0	1163.9	5214.9	4581.8	1760.5	6342.3
791.9	35.1	827.0	560.9	78.7	639.6
127.5	2.3	129.8	106.3	2.2	108.5
50.3	0.4	50.7	34.1	0.5	34.6
101.5	2.3	103.8	114.1	4.7	118.8
1085.9	274.8	1360.7	1178.0	308.8	1486.8
56.5	5.3	61.8	62.0	8.4	70.3
344.8	6.0	350.9	454.5	11.5	466.0
353.9	48.8	402.7	391.9	63.3	455.2
498.4	211.7	710.1	629.0	298.9	927.9
159.1	36.4	195.5	240.1	52.7	292.7
339.3	175.3	514.6	389.0	246.2	635.2
80.0	64.0	144.0	124.3	104.6	228.8
505.8	500.1	1005.9	810.6	837.1	1647.7
136.9	234.8	371.7	225.5	415.3	640.8
40.5	18.4	58.9	77.9	42.1	120.0
179.3	53.6	232.9	310.7	93.5	404.2
21.7	7.0	28.7	28.7	11.1	39.8
127.4	186.3	313.7	167.7	275.2	442.9
54.5	13.0	67.5	116.3	41.9	158.2

(*continued*)

Table 6.6. The major industry groups may be broadly classified into two principal categories: goods-producing and service-producing industries, each of which, to a considerable degree, provides employment for different kinds of workers. The goods-producing industries, including agriculture, fishing and trapping, forestry, mining, manufacturing, and construction, have declined relatively in terms of employment, while service-producing industries, including public utilities, trade, finance and real estate and services proper, have become more significant as job providers. Much of this growth of service-producing industries has reflected the increased importance of social and personal services.

Between 1931 and 1961, goods-producing industries increased their total employment by only 26 per cent and their relative share in the total labour force declined from 58 per cent to 45 per cent. On the other hand, the service-producing industries more than doubled their employment during the same period and by 1961 they had assumed a dominant

TABLE 6.6 (*continued*)

(percentages)

Industrial group	1931			1941		
	Male	Female	Total	Male	Female	Total
All industries	—	—	—	—	—	—
Agriculture	33.8	3.6	28.6	31.7	2.3	25.8
Forestry operations† }	3.0	0.1	2.5	2.9	0.1	2.3
Fishing and trapping }				1.5	—	1.2
Mining	2.2	0.1	1.8	2.7	0.1	2.2
Manufacturing	18.4	18.5	18.5	23.3	21.8	23.0
Electricity	0.7	0.3	0.6	0.7	0.2	0.6
Construction	7.6	0.2	6.4	6.5	0.2	5.2
Transportation and communications	7.8	3.4	7.1	7.3	2.4	6.4
Trade:	9.3	12.8	9.9	10.5	13.5	11.1
Wholesale	1.6	1.3	1.5	2.5	1.9	2.4
Retail	7.7	11.5	8.3	8.0	11.6	8.7
Finance and real estate	2.1	3.8	2.4	1.8	3.4	2.1
Service:	10.0	56.7	17.9	9.9	55.4	19.0
Community }	3.1	22.2	6.4	2.9	19.8	6.3
Business }				0.3	0.4	0.3
Government	3.0	2.3	2.9	3.2	3.4	3.3
Recreation	0.5	0.4	0.4	0.4	0.4	0.4
Personal	3.4	31.8	8.2	3.1	31.4	8.7
Industry not stated	5.1	0.5	4.3	1.2	0.6	1.1

relative position in the total labour force. Indeed between 1951 and 1961 almost all the increase in employment was accounted for by the service sector.

Thus the decade of the fifties marks an important milestone in the changing structure of the Canadian labour force. From being 600,000–900,000 workers ahead in 1931 and 1941, the material-goods sector was trailing the service sector in 1961 by almost 600,000. The same phenomenon occurred about a decade earlier in the United States. This suggests that technology and automation may have placed a ceiling on employment in the goods-producing industries, despite the pressures of increasing population and military hardware expenditures which might have been expected to stimulate employment in material output. That this did not happen, "underscores the fact that something new has indeed happened in our economy. . . ."[7] The new technology has therefore profoundly affected the kinds of work opportunities available in the future. The rise to predominance of the service sector in terms of employment is, as Hansen puts it, "a significant turning point in our history." Another

[7]Alvin H. Hansen, *Economic Issues of the 1960's* (New York, 1960), p. 73.

(percentages)

1951			1961		
Male	Female	Total	Male	Female	Total
—	—	—	—	—	—
19.5	3.0	15.9	12.3	4.5	10.1
3.1	0.2	2.5	2.3	0.1	1.7
1.2	—	1.0	0.7	—	0.6
2.5	0.2	2.0	2.5	0.3	1.9
26.9	23.6	26.0	25.7	17.5	23.4
1.4	0.5	1.2	1.4	0.5	1.1
8.5	0.5	6.7	9.9	0.7	7.3
8.7	4.2	7.7	8.6	3.6	7.2
12.3	18.2	13.6	13.7	17.0	14.6
3.9	3.1	3.7	5.2	3.0	4.6
8.4	15.1	9.9	8.5	14.0	10.0
2.0	5.5	2.8	2.7	5.9	3.6
12.5	43.0	19.3	17.7	47.5	26.0
3.4	20.2	7.1	4.9	23.6	10.1
1.0	1.6	1.1	1.7	2.4	1.9
4.4	4.6	4.5	6.8	5.3	6.4
0.5	0.6	0.6	0.6	0.6	0.6
3.2	16.0	6.0	3.7	15.6	7.0
1.4	1.1	1.3	2.5	2.4	2.5

significant consequence of this shift in the industrial structure of the Canadian economy has been the rapid increase in job opportunities for women. Generally speaking, in service-producing industries, automation and mechanization have, as yet, been less effectively applied than in goods-producing industries, and this largely accounts for the relative employment shift. Over three-quarters of all women employed in 1961 were working in service-producing industries; their number had increased from 516,000 in 1931 to 1,354,000 in 1961, 163 per cent. Some gains in female employment have occurred in financial business such as banks, insurance companies, real estate, in retail trade, in some sectors of transportation, such as air transport, and in communication, for example, radio and television. The most significant gains in employment, however, have taken place in the services sector proper, where the number of women employed increased from 377,000 in 1931 to 837,000 in 1961. Within this major category, female employment increased most in community services, such as schools, hospitals and social agencies, in government, and in personal services, such as laundries, dry cleaning establishments, hotels, and restaurants.

As has been true for women, so also, though to a lesser degree, the increase in jobs for men has occurred mainly in the service-producing industries. Between 1931 and 1961, the number of men employed in these industries increased by 88 per cent as contrasted with only a 16 per cent increase in male employment in goods-producing industries. The latter fact accounts for the relatively sluggish growth in total male employment, particularly during the more recent past. The greatest concentration of men in service-producing industries in 1961 was in trade, public utilities, and government service.

Looking at the main industry groups between 1931 and 1961, the basic change has been the decline in agricultural employment, particularly during the postwar period, despite the steadily growing volume of agricultural output. Relative employment in this industry decreased from 28.6 per cent of the total labour force in 1931 to 10.1 per cent in 1961. Between these two periods about half a million jobs were lost due to mechanization of agricultural production and the consolidation of farms into larger units, particularly since 1945, which led to the disappearance of the underemployment in that sector of the economy.

Despite Canada's advanced industrial status, other primary industries have generally maintained their relative position as job providers. Some decline in employment in fishing and forestry was due to technological advance and shifts in consumers' spending patterns. In mining, during the more recent past, coal and uranium have been depressed. But expansion of output, particularly in oil and natural gas, involved insignificant increases in direct employment in relation to capital investment. Resource development after the war necessitated a considerable expansion in other industries such as capital goods, manufacturing, and power, and, thus, led indirectly to greater employment outside the resource industries themselves.

Manufacturing increased its proportion of total employment from 18.5 per cent to 26.0 per cent between 1931 and 1951. Manufacturing, as a source of employment, surpassed agriculture in the early 'forties. During the Second World War, heavy industries, such as iron and steel, electrical apparatus, chemical, aluminum, aircraft-, truck-, and ship-building greatly expanded. It has been estimated that, at the peak of the war effort in 1943, about three out of five persons employed in manufacturing were producing war materials, and that in the postwar period, about two-thirds of the industrial war structure was adapted to peacetime uses.[8] Employment has continued moderately upwards during the last

[8]O. J. Firestone, *Canada's Economic Development, 1867–1953* (London, 1956), p. 215.

decade in such industries as food and beverages, tobacco products, chemicals, and telecommunication equipment. It has declined, however, in durable goods industries producing for consumers and industrial capacity. More substantial decreases have occurred in the industries manufacturing automobiles and parts, electrical apparatus, aircraft, ships, and railway rolling stock. Consequently, manufacturing's share of total employment had declined somewhat by 1961, to a figure similar to that of 1941.

Public utilities (electricity, transportation, and communication) have largely maintained their relative share of the work force though there was some decrease in employment in railways due to improved technology. A more notable change was the shift to trade from less than 10 per cent in 1931 to about 15 per cent in the labour force in 1961. A similar trend has taken place in finance and real estate business. Heavy investment in new industrial capacity, power projects and housing during the postwar years were reflected in the larger volume of construction employment. Finally, the service industries proper showed a pronounced shift from less than 18 per cent of the labour force in 1931 to 26 per cent in 1961, growth in government and community services being particularly buoyant.

For the most part, these changes in the industrial distribution of the labour force in Canada are expected to continue, that is to say, a further decrease in the proportion of the labour force employed in agriculture, a further increase in the service industries' proportion, and smaller increases in the proportion in construction and primary manufacturing, largely due to the impact of technology and automation.

OCCUPATIONAL COMPOSITION

The occupational classification of the labour force implies grouping together all individuals of a given profession or craft irrespective of the industries in which they may be working. Industrial changes, discussed in the previous section, together with technological progress and the shifts from direct-production labour to indirect-office and supervisory work have caused occupational regroupings and variations in the relative importance of different occupations in the Canadian labour force. These changing patterns of occupational composition have in general, required an upward adjustment in the level of education and training of our manpower resources. This adjustment, which has been partly accomplished by better trained entrants to the labour force, postwar immigration, and upgrading and retraining of the older workers, has not always been smooth and, in fact, has resulted in shortages in some occupations and surpluses in others. Some unemployed workers were not equipped with the skills which the economy required. Thus, as in the US, a large proportion of the unemployed are those of low education and young workers, who have not yet had the opportunity to obtain training on the job. The failure of the skill composition of the Canadian labour force to adjust as rapidly as the changing industrial requirements has aggravated the persistently high levels of unemployment since the mid 1950's. The study of past occupational trends in Canada may therefore indicate the probable directions of future occupational needs and assist in evaluating the tasks that Canada's educational and training institutions will face in the future. The occupational patterns of employment during the past three decades for men and women are summarized in Table 6.7.

WHITE-COLLAR OCCUPATIONS

Over the period 1931–61, the white-collar occupations increased at a faster rate, both absolutely and relatively, than any other major occupational group. In absolute terms the gain amounted to 1.5 million, which constituted more than three-fifths of the total increase in the labour force during this period. In relative terms, this major occupational group increased by 155 per cent, i.e., about two and one-half times the rate of increase in the total labour force. The rate of growth was particularly high during the decade 1941–51, but during the last decade, 1951–61, the growth rate was below that of the service occupations. As a result of this fast rate of growth, the white-collar share of the labour force increased from two out of every ten workers in 1931 to almost four out of every ten workers in 1961.

The employment of women in the white-collar occupations increased twice as fast as male employment. Consequently, the female share in all white-collar occupations increased from 31 per cent to 41 per cent between 1931 and 1961. In the latter year, 57 per cent of all female workers were engaged in that major occupational group as against 31 per cent in 1931.

Looking at some occupations within the white-collar category, it is evident that clerical occupations experienced the fastest growth rate. The clerical group added about 560,000 workers to its ranks and tripled its number as compared with the 1931 figure. This growth of clerical occupations is due to the expansion of record-keeping and "paper-work" required to meet the complex requirements of modern business organization. About half of the total increase in clerical occupations occurred during the 1940's. The rate of growth was lower in the following decade. It has been suggested that during the last decade only about 5 per cent of the growth in clerical employment can be attributed to the increased intensity of their employment in specific industries. Most of the growth was due to the over-all expansion of industries already employing such workers.[9] Women tend to replace men (in relative terms) in clerical work. The men now assume the supervisory and more technical jobs while women predominate in typing, stenographic, and secretarial jobs. In 1961, approximately one-third of all women employed were in clerical occupations.

Professional occupations experienced a stable growth rate over the period 1931–61. By 1961, this group was more than two and one-half times its size in 1931, having added about 400,000 persons. The professional group had the second highest rate of growth in the major white-collar occupations group. Its share of the labour force increased from 6 per cent in 1931 to 10 per cent in 1961. This growth reflects the higher standard of living of Canadians, who tend to spend relatively more on health and education, and technological changes in industry which increasingly require the services of professionally trained personnel in production, administration, and research. It also reflects the rise of government and community services. The industrial expansion based on oil, base metals, and chemical processes has created heavy demands for scientists, engineers, and technicians.

MANUAL OCCUPATIONS
This major occupational group increased at less than half the rate of the white-collar occupations over the period under consideration. It showed a gain of only 6 per cent during 1931–41 years, but increased by about 40 per cent during the next decade and 12 per cent during the most recent decade. The over-all rate of growth of 67 per cent during 1931–61 was the smallest of any major occupational group, with the exception of the declining primary industry occupations. The share of manual occupations in the labour force increased only slightly from 33.8 per cent to 34.9 per cent during the 1931–61 period. In the last decade, its share of the labour force showed a significant decline. It is interesting to note that women increased their share of employment at a faster rate than did males. Consequently, the proportion of women in the manual occupations increased from 8.5 per cent in 10.6 per cent. Within the manual group, manufacturing and mechanical occupations grew faster

[9] *Financial Post*, "Jobs and Machines," Feb. 11, 1961.

TABLE 6.7

Numerical and Percentage Distribution of the Labour Force by Sex and
Major Occupation Group
1931–1961*
(thousands)

	1931			1941		
	Male	Female	Total	Male	Female	Total
All occupations	3252.3	665.3	3917.6	3363.1	832.8	4195.9
White collar:	656.6	301.5	958.1	687.3	371.4	1058.7
Proprietary and managerial	209.1	10.7	219.8	209.2	16.3	225.5
Professional	120.3	117.8	238.1	152.2	130.1	282.2
Clerical	143.0	117.6	260.6	151.4	152.2	303.6
Commercial and financial	184.2	55.5	239.7	174.5	72.8	247.3
Manual:	1210.9	112.5	1323.4	1247.3	154.3	1401.6
Manufacturing and mechanical†	367.5	84.8	452.3	544.8	128.2	673.0
Construction	183.5	—	183.5	195.8	0.3	196.1
Labourers‡	430.1	11.7	441.8	254.1	11.7	265.8
Transportation and communication	229.8	16.0	245.8	252.6	14.1	266.7
Service:	133.2	226.4	359.6	153.6	286.2	439.8
Personal	98.3	225.7	324.0	105.9	285.3	391.2
Protective and other	34.8	0.7	35.5	47.6	0.9	48.5
Primary:	1250.3	24.5	1274.8	1265.3	19.3	1284.6
Agricultural	1103.6	24.0	1127.7	1064.8	19.0	1083.8
Fishing, hunting and trapping	47.2	0.5	47.7	51.1	0.3	51.4
Logging	42.1	—	42.1	78.8	—	78.8
Mining and quarrying	57.3	—	57.3	70.5	—	70.5
Not stated	1.4	0.3	1.7	9.7	1.7	11.4

SOURCE: Census data and Occupation and Employment Section, DBS.
*14 years and over prior to 1961, and 15 years and over in 1961. Not including armed forces. Not including Yukon and NWT. Including Newfoundland in 1951 and 1961. Occupations were rearranged on the basis of the 1951 classification.
†Includes stationary enginemen and occupations associated with electric power production.
‡Labourers in all industries except those engaged in primary occupations.
**Does not include Indians living on reserves.

than any other subgroup, doubling their numbers and adding about 585,000 workers over the thirty-year period. The growth rate of this subgroup, however, was constantly declining over each decade. Manufacturing and mechanical occupations are predominantly male. In fact, the proportion of males increased from 81 per cent to 83 per cent between 1931–61.

(thousands)

1951			1961		
Male	Female	Total	Male	Female	Total
4051.0	1163.9	5214.9	4581.8	1760.5	6342.3
1045.9	644.8	1690.7	1436.8	1010.1	2446.9
357.9	35.0	392.9	449.2	51.9	501.1
217.9	167.8	385.7	360.5	273.8	634.3
243.9	319.2	563.1	315.3	503.7	819.0
226.2	122.8	349.0	311.9	180.7	492.6
1737.6	225.9	1963.5	1977.9	235.4	2213.3
737.2	170.3	907.5	862.4	174.3	1036.7
290.5	0.9	291.4	335.1	0.8	335.9
330.3	20.9	351.2	322.9	20.9	343.8
379.6	33.7	413.3	457.5	39.3	496.8
198.9	247.2	446.1	288.6	395.3	683.9
137.0	245.2	382.2	198.0	390.5	588.4
61.9	1.9	63.8	90.7	4.9	95.6
1017.2	32.9	1050.1	753.8	76.4	830.2
797.9	32.6	830.5	573.0	75.9	648.9
52.7**	0.3**	53.0**	36.6	0.4	37.0
101.3	—	101.3	79.6	0.1	79.7
65.3	—	65.3	64.6	—	64.6
51.4	13.2	64.6	124.7	43.3	168.0

(continued)

The rate of growth of 83 per cent for the construction occupations was higher than for the manual group as a whole, although below that of manufacturing and mechanical occupations (129 per cent). The increase occurred mainly in the 1940's reflecting the war and immediate post-war construction of houses and industrial establishments.

Labourers outside primary industries experienced a substantial decrease in numbers between 1931 and 1961, i.e., about 100,000 or 22 per cent. The largest decrease occurred in the 1930's, reflecting the depressed economic conditions, and subsequent increases were due to rapid growth of the industries employing such workers. These changes, however, reduced their share in the labour force from 11.3 per cent in 1931 to 5.4 per cent in 1961.

TABLE 6.7 (*continued*)

(percentages)

	1931			1941		
	Male	Female	Total	Male	Female	Total
All occupations	100.0	100.0	100.0	100.0	100.0	100.0
White collar:	20.2	45.4	24.4	20.4	44.6	25.2
Proprietary and managerial	6.4	1.6	5.6	6.2	2.0	5.4
Professional	3.7	17.7	6.1	4.5	15.6	6.7
Clerical	4.4	17.7	6.6	4.5	18.3	7.2
Commercial and financial	5.7	8.4	6.1	5.2	8.7	5.9
Manual:	37.2	16.9	33.8	37.1	18.5	33.4
Manufacturing and mechanical†	11.3	12.7	11.5	16.2	15.4	16.0
Construction	5.6	—	4.7	5.8	—	4.7
Labourers‡	13.2	1.8	11.3	7.6	1.4	6.3
Transportation and communication	7.1	2.4	6.3	7.5	1.7	6.4
Service:	4.2	34.0	9.3	4.6	34.4	10.5
Personal	3.0	33.9	8.3	3.1	34.3	9.3
Protective and other	1.2	0.1	1.0	1.5	0.1	1.2
Primary:	38.4	3.7	32.5	37.6	2.3	30.6
Agricultural	33.9	3.6	28.8	31.7	2.3	25.8
Fishing, hunting and trapping	1.4	0.1	1.2	1.5	—	1.2
Logging	1.3	—	1.0	2.3	—	1.9
Mining and quarrying	1.8	—	1.5	2.1	—	1.7
Not stated	—	—	—	0.3	0.2	0.3

SERVICE OCCUPATIONS

This group increased by about 90 per cent over the thirty-year period, adding about 320,000 to the labour force. The largest gain occurred during the last decade and by 1961 service occupations accounted for about 11 per cent of the labour force. It is interesting to note that the number of males in service occupations increased steadily over the whole period, whereas females showed a decline in the personal service group during the 1941-51 years. Consequently, the over-all rate of increase for males was 117 per cent as compared with the 75 per cent for females in service occupations group. In 1961, females accounted for 58 per cent of the total number in service category as compared with 63 per cent in 1931.

PRIMARY INDUSTRY OCCUPATIONS

This is the only major occupational group which showed an absolute

(percentages)

	1951			1961		
	Male	Female	Total	Male	Female	Total
	100.0	100.0	100.0	100.0	100.0	100.0
	25.7	55.3	32.5	31.4	57.4	38.6
	8.7	3.0	7.5	9.8	2.9	7.9
	5.4	14.4	7.4	7.9	15.6	10.0
	6.0	27.4	10.9	6.4	28.6	12.9
	5.6	10.5	6.7	6.8	10.3	7.8
	43.0	19.4	37.6	43.2	13.3	34.9
	18.2	14.6	17.4	18.9	9.9	16.4
	7.2	0.1	5.6	7.3	—	5.3
	8.2	1.8	6.7	7.0	1.2	5.4
	9.4	2.9	7.9	10.0	2.2	7.8
	4.9	21.4	8.6	6.3	22.5	10.8
	3.4	21.1	7.3	4.3	22.2	9.3
	1.5	0.3	1.3	2.0	0.3	1.5
	25.1	2.8	20.1	16.4	4.3	13.1
	19.7	2.8	15.9	12.5	4.3	10.2
	1.3**	— **	1.0**	0.8	—	0.6
	2.5	—	1.9	1.7	—	1.3
	1.6	—	1.3	1.4	—	1.0
	1.3	1.1	1.2	2.7	2.5	2.6

decline in employment—by about 445,000 or 35 per cent over the thirty-year period. Its share of the labour force decreased from 32.5 per cent in 1931 to 13.1 per cent in 1961. The most significant decrease occurred in agricultural occupations with a net loss of 480,000 or 42 per cent since 1931. Within this group of primary industry occupations, logging experienced a high rate of growth in the 1930's but a drop in the 1950's. Mining occupations increased their number over the period as a whole, particularly in the 1930's.

In conclusion, it becomes clear that, as the Canadian economy matures, relatively more people are required to administer and co-ordinate the production of goods and in the financing, insuring, and distributing sides of business operations. The further automation and mechanization of the production process will increase white-collar occu-pations and this, of course, will require more highly skilled and educated manpower.

TABLE 6.8

Labour Force Status and Intended Occupation of Immigrants to Canada
1946–62

Labour force status and intended occupation	Annual average		1956	1957
	1946-50	1951-55		
Destined for the labour force:				
Intended occupation				
Managerial*	—	843	996	1216
Professional	1823	7082	9343	16,040
Clerical	3136	6221	9492	16,829
Transportation	1339	1527	1646	4127
Communication*	—	200	609	1127
Commercial	2261	2790	3561	6132
Financial*	—	95	262	427
Service†	3842	10,047	13,800	17,574
Agricultural	12,026	15,613	7500	10,838
Construction	2911	7592	9506	15,748
Fishing, trapping, logging	1213	1373	505	827
Mining	1029	977	1144	1866
Manufacturing and mechanical	9617	20,002	19,758	38,628
Labourers	1217	10,532	12,482	19,471
Others	974	878	435	661
Total	41,388	85,772	91,039	151,511
Immigrant workers as per cent of Grand Total	48.1	54.2	55.2	53.7
Not destined for the labour force:				
Status				
Housewives	20.904	29,565	30,547	52,533
Children	19,896	37,964	38,461	70,673
Others	3890	5085	4810	7447
Total	44,690	72,614	73,818	130,653
Grand total	86,078	158,386	164,857	282,164

SOURCE: "Immigration 1962", Table 16, p. 129. Department of Citizenship and Immigration, Statistics Section.
*Available as a separate occupational group since 1953 only.
†Includes domestic servants.

IMMIGRATION SINCE 1945

Post-war immigration has significantly altered the size and composition and increased the mobility of the Canadian labour force. The labour force status and intended occupations of the post-war immigrants who arrived in Canada between 1946 and 1962 are shown in Table 6.8.

Between 1946 and 1962 (inclusive) over two million immigrants came to Canada, of whom some 52 per cent entered the labour force immediately upon entry. The proportion of immigrants destined to the

TABLE 6.8 (*continued*)

1958	1959	1960	1961	1962	1946-62 Total	%
944	837	825	896	1093	11,020	1.0
7553	6947	7436	6696	8218	106,759	9.5
6745	5459	5860	4232	4898	100,303	9.0
902	760	913	413	369	23,461	2.1
327	239	310	161	120	3894	0.3
2066	1953	2008	1164	1050	43,191	3.9
163	154	144	77	164	1865	0.2
11,501	9740	8768	6557	5853	143,253	12.8
5071	4965	5321	2341	1923	176,154	15.7
5560	4272	4152	2345	2667	96,766	8.6
169	123	188	65	78	14,883	1.3
344	248	479	90	100	14,300	1.3
11,916	8520	9399	5731	7018	249,065	22.3
9388	8940	7482	3982	3145	123,633	11.0
429	394	293	59	52	11,578	1.0
63,078	53,511	53,573	34,809	36,748	1,120,107	100.0
50.5	50.1	51.4	48.6	49.3	52.1	
24,795	21,223	20,654	15,882	15,674	433,655	
30,444	26,133	24,626	17,315	18,137	515,087	
6534	6021	5258	3683	4027	82,656	
61,773	53,377	50,538	36,880	37,838	1,031,398	
124,851	106,928	104,111	71,689	74,586	2,151,505	

labour force has been a relatively stable one at about one-half of the total immigrant arrivals each year, whereas only one-third of the whole Canadian population was in the labour force. Over the same period, the total labour force grew by approximately 1.8 million. An official estimate places Canada's post-war immigrant workers as of the fall of 1961 at 740,000.[10] Thus, a rough estimate would indicate that about 42 per cent of entrants to the labour force were immigrants. This addition to the labour force by immigrants was even more significant since it compensated for the shortages of Canadian-born new entrants to the work force which resulted from the low birth rates of the depressed 1930's. Indeed, it has been argued that "Without large-scale immigration, labour shortages would have been even more acute than they were, and the degree of

[10]DBS, *Canadian Statistical Review*, Nov. 1962, pp. iii to viii.

economic growth actually experienced could not have been achieved."[11]
On the other hand, such immigration accentuates the extent of unemployment when the economy is less buoyant.

Immigration authorities obtain information from immigrants about their "intended" occupation, though the immigrant may follow a different occupation than the one he indicated. Nevertheless, the distribution of immigrants by broad categories of intended occupation does reveal the nature of their skills, training, and occupational background. The largest concentration of immigrant workers, as shown in Table 6.8, has been in manufacturing and mechanical occupations, followed by agricultural, service, manual labour, professional, clerical, and construction, in that order. It is of special interest to note that about one out of ten immigrant workers was in the professional occupation group. This proportion was the same as that for the whole Canadian labour force in 1961.

The relative proportion of the post-war immigrant professionals in a number of selected fields to the total number of professionals in those same fields in Canada at the time of the 1961 census is shown in Table 6.9. Immigration made the greatest proportionate contribution in the case of architects (62.1 per cent), followed by electrical engineers, mechanical engineers, draftsmen and designers, all of whom exceeded 50 per cent. Immigrant chemists and civil, mining, and chemical engineers also contributed significantly to the numbers in their respective professions in Canada.

In short, the labour force has been significantly increased by immigration in the post-war decades and, on balance, the quality probably enhanced especially in professions contributing much to the exploitation of Canada's abundant natural resources. In this sense, immigration may have performed a strategic role. This becomes more obvious in view of emigration from Canada to which we now turn.

EMIGRATION OF CANADIAN WORKERS

As already pointed out, there are no official Canadian data on emigration and the only data available are those for Canadian residents leaving for the United States. These figures, however, have to be treated with caution because they give an exaggerated impression of Canadian population and labour force losses since many Canadians return after residence abroad. The data used in this section serve only to indicate broad trends and no direct numerical comparisons with the data on immigration in the previous section is meaningful.

[11]RCCEP, *Final Report* (Ottawa, 1957), p. 79.

TABLE 6.9

Professionals Admitted to Canada by Intended Occupation,
1946–62, as a Percentage of Canadian
Labour Force, 1961

Occupation	(a) Immigrant professionals 1946–62	(b) Canadian labour force 1961	(a) as % of (b)
Accountants	4543	30,670	14.8
Architects	1825	2940	62.1
Chemists	2947	6144	48.0
Chemical engineers	971	2996	32.4
Civil engineers	5290	11,917	44.4
Electrical engineers	4700	8763	53.6
Mechanical engineers	4307	8137	52.9
Mining engineers	721	2349	30.7
Dentists	450	5469	8.2
Draftsmen and designers	10,396	20,623	50.4
Laboratory technicians and assistants	4701	53,550	8.8
Graduate nurses	16,442	61,699	26.6
Physicians and surgeons	5182	21,290	24.3
Teachers and professors	14,774	189,172	7.8

SOURCE: Statistics Section, Department of Citizenship and Immigration; and *Census of Canada, 1961*, Bulletin 3.1-3, Table 3, pp. 6–2 to 6–15.

Information on the type of Canadian emigrants destined for the US labour force and the number of those not destined for work for the period 1946–62 is summarized in Table 6.10. The number of workers leaving Canada for the United States has been increasing since 1946. The fluctuations in emigration, generally, are related to employment conditions in the United States. Out of the 585,000 residents who left Canada during the period, about half of them were destined for the US labour force. Canadian emigration to the US is heavily weighted by professionals (23.8 per cent), clerical and sales (25.2 per cent), craftsmen and foremen (17.2 per cent). Operatives and managerial occupations comprised respectively 10.5 and 7.5 per cent of the Canadian workers emigrating to the United States. Unskilled workers accounted for only a small percentage (6.2) of the Canadian workers who left the country.

The largest numbers of emigrant professionals were nurses, teachers, draftsmen and designers, accountants, engineers and physicians, in that order (see Table 6.11). The drain on Canadian professional manpower by emigration is indicated by the percentage of emigrant professionals

TABLE 6.10

Emigration from Canada to the United States by Labour Force Status and
Intended Occupation
1946–62
(Years ending June 30)

Labour force status and intended occupation	Annual average		1956	1957
	1946-50	1951-55		
Destined for US labour force				
Intended occupation				
Managerial	1286	1324	1391	1279
Professional	2712	3512	4991	5985
Clerical*	} 2811	4071 {	4365	4667
Sales*			1147	1151
Craftsmen and foremen	1450	2741	4590	4635
Operatives	1232	2047	2002	2116
Service	1110	1449	1826	1703
Farm Labour	18	69	371	323
Unskilled Labour	494	826	1417	1324
Total	11,113	16,039	22,100	23,183
Emigrant Workers as Per Cent of Grand Total	48.3	49.3	52.2	50.0
Not destined for US Labour force				
Status				
Housewives	—	—	8519	9164
Children	—	—	9150	11,068
Others	—	—	2594	2939
Total	11,905	16,526	20,263	23,171
Grand total	23,018	32,565	42,363	46,354

SOURCE: Immigration and Naturalization Service, US Department of Justice, Washington, DC.
*Breakdown between Clerical and Sales not available prior to 1952.

to the manpower in their respective fields in Canada in 1961. These data suggest that the most important losses occurred in the following professions: chemists and chemical engineers, nurses, draftsmen and designers, mechanical engineers and physicians, the very ones to which immigration contributed significantly; hence, the strategic nature of immigration in helping to maintain the skill balance of the labour force (even although many of the professional emigrants may have been recent immigrants).

UNEMPLOYMENT

Thus far we have treated the labour force as if at any moment of time all of its members were actual contributors to the nation's total output.

TABLE 6.10 (*continued*)

1958	1959	1960	1961	1962	Total 1946-62 Number	%
1347	1023	1354	1271	1193	21,907	7.5
5749	5146	5768	5562	5561	69,881	23.8
4971	3664	4781	4744	4394		
1175	966	1262	1310	1256	74,257	25.2
4713	2884	4518	4487	3833	50,615	17.2
2057	1589	2351	2434	2081	31,026	10.5
1831	1540	2025	2186	2313	26,219	8.9
214	182	210	188	198	2122	0.7
1643	1239	1851	1950	2067	18,094	6.2
23,700	18,233	24,120	24,132	22,896	294,121	100.0
52.5	52.7	51.7	50.8	51.7	50.3	
8393	6623	8160	8072	7379	—	
10,278	7576	11,381	11,727	10,358	—	
2772	2167	3007	3539	3639	—	
21,443	16,366	22,548	23,338	21,376	290,663	
45,143	34,599	46,668	47,470	44,272	584,784	

The fact is, of course, that with freedom to change jobs, even abstracting from those people absent from work due to vacation or illness for varying periods of time, the total labour force cannot be expected to be at work. There are always some people between jobs even in the best of times. Thus, when about 97–98 per cent of those defined as being in the labour force have jobs, this is considered to be "full employment," the remaining 2 or 3 per cent being construed as "frictionally" employed. When unemployment is 3 per cent or less the situation is deemed generally satisfactory and conversely for unemployment rates above the so-called frictional level.

There are other types of unemployment such as seasonal, cyclical, and structural but, except for the seasonal type, they cannot be neatly separated and measured because at any one time the unemployment total reflects the influence of all of them simultaneously.

TABLE 6.11

Canadian Professionals Admitted to the United States
by Intended Occupation, 1950–62,
as a Percentage of the Canadian Labour Force, 1961

Occupation	(a) Emigrant professionals 1950–62	(b) Canadian labour force 1961	(a) as % of (b)
Accountants	2872	30,670	9.4
Architects	359	2940	12.2
Chemists	1274	6144	20.7
Dentists	153	5469	2.8
Draftsmen and designers	3637	20,623	17.6
Chemical engineers	508	2996	17.0
Mining engineers	122	2349	5.2
Civil engineers	734	11,917	6.2
Electrical engineers	1227	8763	14.0
Mechanical engineers	1337	8137	16.4
Graduate nurses	15,516	61,699	25.1
Physicians and surgeons	2670	21,290	12.5
Teachers and professors	5805	189,172	3.1

SOURCE: Immigration and Naturalization Service, US Department of Justice; and *Census of Canada, 1961*, Bulletin 3.1-3, Table 3, pp. 6-2 to 6-15.

Thus, the evidence on unemployment in Table 6.12 cannot be used to indicate the underlying cause. But the interpretation of rates of unemployment close to or below 3 per cent as satisfactory and above 3 per cent as unsatisfactory appears to be a reasonable judgment and the data should be viewed in this context.

Looking at the post-war trends, four distinct periods may be distinguished: the first period from 1946 through 1953, which coincided with the post-war and Korean boom, had an average rate of unemployment less than 3 per cent and in fact represented one of the best peacetime records in Canadian history; the second period, 1954 through 1957, witnessed a rise above the assumed frictional level and averaged almost 4.3 which, although not recognized at the time, presaged the slowdown in economic activity; the third period, at least through 1961, revealed rates of unemployment more than double those deemed acceptable and far above those prevailing in Western Europe; the final period, 1962 to date, showed substantial improvement but as late as March 1965 the unemployment rate, at 3.9 per cent, was still well above levels deemed acceptable.[12]

[12]See chap. 1, pp. 44–63, for details.

TABLE 6.12

Unemployment by Sex
1946–61*
(thousands)

Year	Males			Females			Total		
	Labour force	Unemployed	Unemployment rate	Labour force	Unemployed	Unemployment rate	Labour force	Unemployed	Unemployment rate
1946	3746	137	3.7	1082	26	2.4	4829	163	3.4
1947	3869	92	2.4	1074	18	1.7	4942	110	2.2
1948	3923	95	2.4	1066	19	1.8	4988	114	2.3
1949	3969	122	3.1	1086	20	1.8	5055	141	2.8
1950	4050	159	3.9	1112	27	2.4	5163	186	3.6
1951	4076	103	2.5	1147	24	2.1	5223	126	2.4
1952	4144	129	3.1	1180	26	2.2	5324	155	2.9
1953	4206	143	3.4	1191	19	1.6	5397	162	3.0
1954	4263	218	5.1	1231	32	2.6	5493	250	4.6
1955	4341	213	4.9	1269	33	2.6	5610	245	4.4
1956	4436	171	3.9	1346	26	1.9	5782	197	3.4
1957	4570	244	5.3	1433	33	2.3	6003	278	4.6
1958	4634	378	8.2	1493	54	3.6	6127	432	7.1
1959	4679	326	7.0	1549	47	3.0	6228	373	6.0
1960	4750	388	8.2	1653	60	3.6	6403	448	7.0
1961	4782	404	8.4	1736	65	3.7	6518	469	7.2
1962	4820	333	6.9	1789	59	3.3	6608	391	5.9

SOURCE: Special Tables, Special Surveys Division, DBS.
*1946-51, four-month annual average; 1952, five month annual average; and 1953-62, twelve-month annual average. Newfoundland included since 1950.

Poor as has been the over-all unemployment picture in Canada since the mid 1950's, the incidence by sex and age suggests an even greater social problem because unemployment rates for men have been consistently above those for women. Since men are normally the sole breadwinners in most families, this unequal incidence as between male and female unemployment rates is more serious than even the high over-all levels would suggest, at least for males over 20 years of age. The reasons for this disparity are due to the fact that women are concentrated in the service industries and white-collar occupations which, as shown earlier, have been expanding over the whole post-war period. Again, married women are less attached to the labour force and when they lose their jobs they tend to withdraw from the labour force and hence are not counted as unemployed.

Unemployment rates have also been consistently much higher for young people than for people in older age groups. This applies both to males and females, but regardless of age group male unemployment rates have regularly exceeded the female by substantial amounts that have even widened over time (see Table 6.13).

TABLE 6.13
Unemployment Rates by Age and Sex
1951-61

| Age group | Average percentage of labour force unemployed | | | | | |
| | 1951-55 | | 1956-60 | | 1961 | |
	Male	Female	Male	Female	Male	Female
Under 20 years	7.8	4.2	13.5	6.5	16.6	9.0
20-24	5.5	2.4	9.8	3.0	11.8	4.1
25-44	3.2	1.6	5.5	2.1	7.3	2.6
45-64	3.3	⎫	5.4	⎫	7.3	⎫
		⎬ 1.2		⎬ 1.9		⎬ 2.3
65 and over	3.1	⎭	4.6	⎭	6.0	⎭
All ages	3.8	2.2	6.5	2.9	8.4	3.7

SOURCE: DBS, *Unemployment in Canada* (Ottawa, 1962), Table 4, p. 14.

The higher unemployment rates among younger workers partly reflect "job security," due to seniority provisions in many industries, and partly inadequate skills, education, and lack of experience. To the extent that the economy fails to create new job opportunities for the larger numbers of young men and women entering the labour market, there will be a tendency for the present high unemployment rates to be further increased. Seniority provisions, however, tend to encourage discriminatory hiring practices against older workers making it difficult for them to secure new employment once they lose their jobs. Thus, for example, in 1961 men who had been unemployed for seven months or more accounted, on the average, for 23 per cent of the total unemployed in the 45 and over age group, but only 15 per cent in the 25–44 age group, and 15 per cent in the age group under 25 years.[13] Since November 1, 1963, the federal government has been paying employers half of the monthly wage or $75 whichever is less, up to a full year, for unemployed persons over 45 years of age whom they employ. For the employer to qualify for this assistance under the program it is necessary that the worker be kept on the job for at least three months and given some training.

In measuring the level of unemployment, some consideration should be given to the average duration of unemployment. This tends to increase during the periods of higher levels of unemployment. In the earlier post-war years, as shown in Table 6.14 when unemployment rates were lower, about one-fifth of the unemployed had been seeking work for more than four months, but after 1957, as unemployment increased, so did the average duration and about one-third of the unemployed had been looking for work for longer than four months.

Another characteristic of the unemployed is that the unemployment rates tend to be much higher for single persons than for married people. In 1961, the average rate for single men (including widowed and divorced) was more than double the rate for married men—that is 14.1 per cent as compared with 6.4 per cent. The same was true of women, the rates being 4.9 and 2.3 respectively. On the average, about half of the unemployed in 1961 were married men, single men accounted for about two-fifths and single women for one-tenth, while married women accounted for only 4 per cent of the total.[14]

It is also a significant fact that unemployment rates tend to be much higher for people with little formal education. A special survey of educational attainments of the unemployed made in February 1960, showed that those who did not finish primary school experienced an unemployment rate of 18.7 per cent, more than double the rate of 8.0 per cent for those who completed primary but not secondary school, and seven times the rate of 2.7 per cent for those who finished secondary or more school. This relationship between unemployment and level of education was evident in all age groups, but the younger and

[13]DBS, *Unemployment in Canada* (April, 1962), Table 14, p. 27.
[14]*Ibid.*, Table 6, p. 18.

TABLE 6.14

Duration of Unemployment: Number of Months Unemployed as a Percentage of
Total Unemployed
annual averages 1946-62*

Year	Total %	Under 1 month %	1-3 months %	4-6 months %	7 months and over %
1946	100	23	50	16	11
1947	100	23	55	13	11
1948	100	21	60	12	7
1949	100	15	64	14	8
1950	100	30	40	19	12
1951	100	44	36	13	9
1952	100	43	38	13	6
1953	100	47	34	13	6
1954	100	34	38	18	10
1955	100	33	37	18	13
1956	100	39	38	15	8
1957	100	39	40	15	6
1958	100	29	37	22	13
1959	100	31	36	20	14
1960	100	31	37	20	12
1961	100	27	35	22	17
1962	100	30	36	18	16

SOURCE: Special Surveys Division, DBS.
*1946-52 averages are based on quarterly surveys; 1953-62 averages are based
on monthly surveys.

unskilled and untrained experienced higher levels of unemployment.
Thus, about one-third of the people under 25 years of age who did not
finish primary school were unemployed. This survey also indicated that,
while persons who had not finished primary school accounted for only
21 per cent of the labour force, they accounted for 44 per cent of the
total unemployed. Approximately 90 per cent of the unemployed were
persons who had not finished secondary school, and the remainder had
finished secondary school or better.[15]

Unemployment rates also vary by industry. The forestry, fishing, and
trapping industries had the highest average rate of 29.3 per cent in
1961, construction was second with 21.1 per cent; mining, quarrying
and oil wells, 9.3 per cent; manufacturing, 6.7 per cent; transportation
and other utilities, 6.6 per cent; and trade, finance, and service together,
only 4.1 per cent. The construction industry accounted for about 8 per
cent of the labour force but it was responsible for about one-quarter of
the total unemployed, while manufacturing, which accounted for about
a quarter of the total labour force, was also responsible for one-quarter

[15]*Ibid.*, Tables 7 and 8, p. 20.

of the unemployed. On the other hand, the trade, finance, and service industries as a group accounted for about a half of the labour force but only for a quarter of the unemployed. Primary industries, including agriculture, accounted for about one-eighth of the labour force and for about one-sixth of the unemployed. Finally, transportation and other utilities, which accounted for about one-tenth of the work force were responsible for almost an equal proportion of the total unemployed.[16]

SEASONAL UNEMPLOYMENT
The high annual rates of unemployment still prevailing in Canada are cause for serious concern, as we have repeatedly stressed. But Canada also suffers to a greater extent than perhaps any other advanced country from severe fluctuations in employment during the year. The failure to grapple with this problem effectively or even to recognize it as serious and worthy of attention until recently, constitutes, we believe, an inexcusable lapse on the part of both professional economists and policy-makers. It is all too easy to adopt the posture that seasonal unemployment is due solely to the Canadian climate and since this cannot be changed, the fluctuations associated therewith are likewise inevitable. The facts are, however, that such fluctuations are caused by much else besides the weather and that, even so, the consequences of such unemployment can be effectively mitigated as has been done in the Scandinavian countries.

Seasonal fluctuations in employment and unemployment are partly imposed upon the economy by the fixed rhythm of the seasons, but they are also the result of "conventional" factors, some of which originate in holiday periods such as Easter and Christmas, while others are due to business practices, consumer buying customs and habits, model changes, and fashion. These natural and conventional forces affect the conditions of production, demand, and hence employment.

Primary industries such as agriculture, logging, and fishing are directly affected by weather. Similarly, road building, inland navigation, construction, sports, the tourist industry, and most out-of-door activities have distinct seasonal swings. The seasonal pattern of activity in primary industries, in turn, affects some of the secondary industries such as transport, food processing, and others. The demand for clothing, automobiles, agricultural implements, and certain types of food and services such as hotels, restaurants, and laundries, is likewise affected by habits related to weather. The conventional aspects of seasonal variations may be illustrated by the increase in retail trade at Christmas and Easter.

[16]*Ibid.*, Tables 11 and 12, p. 24.

All of the above factors affecting employment cause workers to be laid off for a part of the year and those who do not withdraw from the labour force become unemployed. The amount of seasonal unemployment is, in part, dependent on the general level of economic activity, i.e., seasonal employment variations tend to be submerged by cyclical forces during the recovery and prosperity phases and become more pronounced during recessions. In Canada the volume of seasonal unemployment increased between 1955 and 1961 because economic conditions deteriorated. In addition, however, the number employed in the country's seasonal industries increased.

It is important to differentiate between seasonal employment and unemployment, because not all workers affected become unemployed: either they find work in some other industries or they withdraw from the labour force entirely, like housewives. It is estimated that under reasonably full employment conditions, with a labour force of about 6.5 million, about 250,000 are seasonally unemployed. For Canada as a whole, employment reaches its peak at the beginning of July or August and then it gradually declines and by February or March the seasonal upturn begins again.

Seasonal variations in employment may be measured either in terms of the absolute number of workers involved or in terms of percentages of average employment for the years covered. In 1962, the peak employment of 5.8 million in non-agricultural industries was reached in July and lowest employment of 5.3 million in February, while in agricultural industry, peak employment of 0.8 million was reached in August and 0.6 million in February. This pattern of employment is also indicated by seasonal employment indices.[17] Agriculture had in 1961–62 an amplitude of seasonal employment variation (i.e., the average difference between peak and trough employment when both are expressed in terms of seasonal indices) of 35.6 percentage points (120.8 in August 1961 minus 85.2 in February 1962), while non-agricultural industries had an amplitude of 8.1 percentage points (103.9 in July 1961 and 95.8 in February 1962). The difference between the peak and trough indices for total employment was 10.9 (105.5 in July 1961 and 94.6 in February 1962).

Table 6.15 shows the average extent to which major industry groups were subject to seasonal employment variations during the years 1954–57 and 1958–62. It also indicates the changes in amplitude in recent

[17]The seasonal employment index is the average over several years of the ratio of employment in any given month to the average level during the twelve nearest months.

TABLE 6.15

Average Amplitudes of Seasonal Employment Variations
in Selected Industries
1954-57 and 1958-62

Industries and trades	Average amplitude 1954-57	Average amplitude 1958-62	Changes in amplitude Amount	%
All industries	8.8	9.6	+ 0.8	+ 9.1
Agriculture	27.0	30.1	+ 3.1	+11.5
Forestry	54.6	58.2	+ 3.6	+ 6.6
Fishing and trapping	86.1	104.7	+18.6	+21.6
Mining and quarrying	4.8	8.5	+ 3.7	+77.1
Other primary industries	24.0	29.1	+ 5.1	+21.2
Manufacturing	3.8	6.0	+ 2.2	+57.9
Construction	36.8	39.2	+ 2.4	+ 6.5
Transportation, storage and communication	8.3	8.1	− 0.2	− 2.4
Public utilities	9.6	9.2	− 0.4	− 4.2
Trade	4.3	5.4	+ 1.1	+25.6
Finance, insurance and real estate	1.6	1.8	+ 0.2	+12.5
Service	1.9	2.5	+ 0.6	+31.6

SOURCE: Raw statistical data provided by Economics and Research Branch, Department of Labour.

years. The table reveals that with the exception of transportation, storage, and communication and public utilities, all other major industries increased in their seasonal employment amplitudes between 1954–57 and 1958–62. A change in amplitudes, due to technological changes in industry or in consumer and business habits and practices, affects the degree of utilization of human and material resources. The average amplitude of all industries, which reflects movements of the component industries, increased from 8.8 in 1954–57 to 9.6 in 1958–62, i.e., by 0.8 points or nearly 10 per cent. The major industries, whose amplitudes of seasonal employment showed the most pronounced increase, include mining and quarrying, manufacturing, service, trade, fishing and trapping, and other primary industries. The increase in seasonal amplitudes in more recent years suggests that there has been a tendency for some Canadian industries to shift their operations to summer months as compared with winter months, although part of the increase is due to the higher average unemployment rates prevailing in 1958–62.

The number of workers affected by seasonality of employment in various industries is shown in Table 6.16. These may be called seasonally "disemployed," i.e., the number of workers who, on the average

TABLE 6.16

Average Seasonal Disemployment, by Industry
1958-62

Industries	Percentage of average amplitude to average peak seasonal index	Average actual employment at peak ('000)	Seasonal disemployment
All industries	9.2	6235	573.6
Agriculture	25.8	793	204.6
Forestry	46.4	109	50.6
Fishing and trapping	68.3	276	188.5
Mining and quarrying	8.2	97	8.0
Other primary industries	26.2	214	56.0
Manufacturing	5.8	1549	89.8
Construction	33.4	498	166.3
Transportation, storage and communication	7.8	458	35.7
Public utilities	8.8	80	7.0
Trade	5.3	994	52.7
Finance, insurance and real estate	1.8	233	4.2
Service	2.5	1455	36.4

SOURCE: Economics and Research Branch, Department of Labour.

over several years, are seasonally laid off in an industry, as employment moves from peak to trough. Not all of these workers will become unemployed because some will move into other industries, and others will leave the labour force. Data on seasonal disemployment are useful, however, because they indicate the gross contribution of each industry to the seasonal unemployment problem.

The industries showing highest disemployment are the industries that employ mainly men. Manufacturing industry as a whole shows only a moderate seasonal pattern, although certain industries such as food-processing and wood-products are highly seasonal. While the employment pattern of some service industries, such as hotels and restaurants, is very seasonal, they do not contribute much to seasonal unemployment because they employ students and housewives who are loosely attached to the labour force.

The level of seasonal unemployment is indicated by Table 6.17 which shows the total number of persons unemployed per month and the corresponding percentage of the labour force during the years 1958–62.

A rough indication of the volume of unemployment in different occupations can be secured by subtracting the average number of registrations at the National Employment Service offices during the summer months from the average number registered during the winter months.

TABLE 6.17
Unemployment in Canada
1958–62 monthly
(in thousands and as percentage of labour force)

	1958		1959		1960		1961		1962	
	No.	%	No.	%	No.	%	No.	%	No.	%
January	579	9.7	578	9.5	547	8.8	693	10.8	545	8.5
February	601	10.1	571	9.4	599	9.6	719	11.3	583	9.1
March	637	10.6	554	9.1	609	9.8	705	11.1	560	8.7
April	554	9.1	467	7.6	552	8.8	622	9.7	485	7.5
May	389	6.4	355	5.7	419	6.6	457	7.0	336	5.1
June	340	5.5	249	4.0	315	4.9	370	5.6	301	4.5
July	311	4.9	240	3.7	330	5.0	354	5.2	308	4.5
August	318	5.0	258	4.0	352	5.3	323	4.8	280	4.1
September	285	4.6	225	3.6	327	5.0	308	4.7	260	3.9
October	329	5.3	251	4.0	368	5.7	318	4.9	283	4.3
November	379	6.2	317	5.1	429	6.6	349	5.4	342	5.2
December	467	7.6	406	6.5	528	8.2	413	6.4	414	6.3

SOURCE: Special Surveys Division, DBS.

This difference and the percentage of change in registrations from summer to winter are one measure of the extent of seasonal unemployment in selected occupations. Table 6.18 shows the percentage changes in registrations from summer to winter for 1961–62 in selected skilled and unskilled occupations.

The federal government in co-operation with the provincial and municipal governments as well as national labour and business organizations has attempted for a number of years to stimulate winter employment mainly through publicity and promotion campaigns. In addition, efforts are made to shift public construction and repair works to the winter months. In order to stimulate employment in the construction industry during the winter months, the Central Mortgage and Housing Corporation increases the availability of the loan funds in the autumn. In the winter of 1963–64, the dominion government introduced the incentive of a direct payment of $500 to the first purchaser or owner of a house substantially built during the four winter months, December to March inclusive. Since the 1958–59 winter, the federal government has initiated the Municipal Winter Works Incentive Programme, under which

TABLE 6.18

Variations in Registrations for Employment, by Selected Occupations
1961-62

Occupations	Summer, 1961 (July-Sept.) average number	Winter, 1961 (Jan.-March) average number	Absolute change	Percentage of absolute change to summer registrations
Skilled:				
Carpenters	8150	40,994	32,844	403.0
Loggers and bushmen	6970	32,570	25,600	367.3
Taxi, truck and tractor drivers	14,081	45,027	30,946	219.8
Auto mechanics and repairmen	2668	6424	3756	140.8
Protective service workers	9996	16,765	6769	67.7
Sales clerks	17,464	28,713	11,249	64.4
Welders and flame cutters	3510	6185	2675	76.2
Secondary textiles	7979	12,528	4549	57.0
Miners	1269	2146	877	69.1
Unskilled:				
Construction	30,585	108,831	78,246	255.8
Lumber and lumber products	7009	24,033	17,024	242.9
Food and tobacco products	6250	20,141	13,891	222.3
Pulp, paper and paper goods	1509	4060	2551	169.1
Metal working	5325	8641	3316	62.3
Textiles (primary and secondary)	2565	3583	1018	39.7

SOURCE: Economic and Research Branch, Department of Labour.

it agrees to pay half the direct payroll costs, and 60 per cent of such costs in areas where there has been a high level of unemployment,[18] of approved municipal projects, constructed in the winter months. The number of men employed under this program totalled 41,000 in 1958–59, 51,000 in 1959–60, and then rose substantially to 121,000 in the winter of 1960–61. During the last two winters it remained at the level of 145,000. The number of man-days of employment created by this program numbered 1.6 million in 1958–59, 1.9 million in 1959–60, and then rose to 5.2 million in the 1960–61 winter; and for the next two winters the man-days expanded less significantly reaching 5.8 and 6.2 million in 1961–62 and 1962–63 respectively.[19] In other words, belatedly, some positive action has begun and has thus far met with success. It goes without saying, however, that this is merely a beginning since the seasonal unemployment fluctuations remain disturbingly large and represent a continuing and serious form of economic waste.[20]

STRUCTURAL UNEMPLOYMENT

This type of unemployment arises from a permanent decline in certain industries, such as agriculture or shipbuilding, or because of technological changes in others which reduce manpower requirements. Structural unemployment affects particular localities and regions, or groups of workers, while the advantages of technological progress are available to society as a whole.

A study of the impact of technological change and automation on manpower in a number of firms in the electrical, electronics, heavy machinery, household appliances, and automobile parts industries, verified the fact that, apart from absolute changes in the volume of employment, there are also important changes in the occupational structure of the work force following technological progress. Over the decade, 1948–58, in the automobile industry, direct production labour as a percentage of total employment declined from 83 to 73, and from 78 to 68 per cent in the household appliances industry. In both industries office employment increased.[21]

One of the features of the postwar economic development in Canada has been the persistence of localized unemployment even during periods

---

[18]As of September 1963 there were forty-five National Employment Service areas designated as "high winter unemployment" areas.

[19]Economics and Research Branch, Department of Labour.

[20]For a brief discussion see Douglas Hartle, "Seasonal Unemployment in Canada, 1951–7," *CJEPS*, Feb. 1958, pp. 93–8.

[21]See "Skilled Manpower Training," Bulletins nos. 2, 3, and 8, Economics and Research Branch, Department of Labour.

of general prosperity. On the basis of registrations at the National Employment Service offices, eighteen labour market areas were identified as having a considerable labour surplus over a period 1953–59.[22] Most of these areas were located in the Atlantic provinces and the Province of Quebec. This study revealed that chronic unemployment resulted from technological changes in some industries such as car manufacturing, reflecting the impact of automation; or from changes in domestic and foreign demand for some commodities such as coal and textiles; or from the highly seasonal nature of other industries such as construction, lumbering, fishing, transportation, service, etc. These same industries are not capable of absorbing the reserve of labour in the depressed areas even during the peak of their activities in the summer months. The lack of industrial diversification in some areas and excessive dependence on primary industries as providers of employment for men accounted for most of the persistent, localized unemployment.

As of September 1963, there were thirty-five NES areas designated as "development areas" (thirteen in the Atlantic provinces, thirteen in Quebec, eight in Ontario, and one in Alberta) by the federal government.[23] Three tax incentives are available in such areas in order to attract new employment-creating industries, namely: a three-year exemption from corporation tax; accelerated capital cost allowances for machinery and equipment at the rate of 50 per cent a year instead of 20 per cent; and permission to write off the capital cost of new buildings at the rate of 20 per cent per year instead of 5 per cent. The accelerated rate of depreciation may be deferred until the firm becomes liable for income tax, so that, in some cases, the company would be excused from income taxes for more than a three-year period. The federal government has also accelerated government winter construction projects which are located in development areas. The government has established the Area Development Agency in the Department of Industry which is to work in close co-operation with industry and buiness to assist the economic development of depressed areas.

To meet effectively the technical and professional manpower requirements of the Canadian economy in the future, improved education and training of youth are essential if severe and persistent unemployment is to be avoided. The federal government, in partnership with the pro-

[22]S. Judek, "Canada's Persistent Unemployment Problem—Labour Surplus Market Areas," *Proceedings of the Special Senate Committee on Manpower and Employment*, no. 7, Feb. 2, 1961, pp. 465–601.
[23]The statistical criteria for the selection of such areas have been based on the unemployment record, far above the national level, for summer months (May to October) only to avoid undue emphasis on winter unemployment.

vinces, has thus undertaken a vast expansion of technical and vocational training facilities under the Technical and Vocational Training Assistance Act of 1960. By November 1963, about 270 new technical and vocational schools had been or are being built across the country, together with major and minor alterations of some of the existing ones at a total cost of about $530 million, of which the federal contribution amounted to about $340 million. This will mean that additional places will be provided for approximately 145,000 students. The federal government covers in most cases 50 per cent or more of the operating costs of vocational high school training, technical training at the post-high school level, training for supervisors and for upgrading other persons in co-operation with industry, as well as of unemployed, who are registered with the National Employment Service offices, and of disabled persons. These measures are becoming increasingly important as the needs for technical and professional manpower grow, as the economy adjusts to changes in technology and consumers' tastes as well as to increased foreign competition in both domestic and export markets.

CONCLUSION

The Canadian labour force has both grown in numbers and improved in quality since the turn of the century. At the same time, it has been subject to certain difficulties which themselves have changed from decade to decade. The problem of unemployment in the 1930's was associated with the general collapse of aggregate demand throughout the world which hit Canada with special severity. The general prosperity from 1940 to 1956 submerged many growing difficulties that have only come to light or been the subject of serious study in the last decade. It is not surprising that the problems of seasonal and technological (or structural) unemployment have received little attention until recently. But despite the recent resurgence there are few grounds for complacency as far as full and effective utilization of the labour force is concerned. Policies for improvements have generally been sporadic, *ad hoc*, and quite inadequate in scope. There is a serious and growing gap between the new and more highly skilled manpower requirements and the rate at which these are currently being met. A failure to mesh particular categories of labour more closely with the rapidly changing needs can only thwart the growth of productivity that is so important if Canada is to obtain new markets in an increasingly competitive international environment. The past failure to use effectively and promptly the tools of monetary and fiscal policy to offset cyclical unemployment can only make it more difficult to introduce those more direct measures designed to bring the skill composition of the labour force into closer harmony with the needs of changing technology and to offset seasonal and chronic regional unemployment. In short, Canadian policy-makers and the public in general have not yet learned the lessons of the thirties and must therefore face the new labour problems of the sixties, which are superimposed upon those related to fluctuations in aggregate demand, at a considerable disadvantage. There are, however, many hopeful signs and the beginning of a more realistic labour and employment policy has been made. But it is only a start, and it threatens to be thwarted by the growth of provincial intransigence and the new take-off which reduces the apparent urgency of direct measures to alleviate seasonal and technological unemployment. There is little doubt that if Canada is to achieve the economic potential that we postulate in Part Three unremitting attention must be paid to unemployment in all of its manfestations. An affluent society may for a time subsidize inefficiency and tolerate economic waste, but for a country like Canada so heavily reliant upon foreign trade and so vulnerable to strategic manpower losses through emigration, this is a policy that can only be self-defeating over time. The misuse and waste of manpower in Canada, while perhaps no greater than in some other countries, is not something to be contemplated with equanimity or as an inevitable accompaniment of economic and demographic change. Rather it stands as a challenge that can effectively be met only if Canada has the will and sense to do so.

7

CAPITAL

Capital, the third factor of production to be discussed, is a unique productive asset in the sense that it is man-made in response to actual or assumed economic needs; at the same time, being man-made, it is a composite of the other factors of production, a crystallization of raw materials and labour in physical form. From the point of view of economic analysis these two features plus the time dimension, which arises because capital assets yield values over some future period of time, make the explanation of the determinants of capital formation extremely complex. Our purpose here, however, is not to peer into the murky waters of capital theory, but rather it is the more mundane task of attempting to measure the amount of capital available for productive use and, from the supply side, examine the possibilities for further augmentation in the future.

It should be clear from the foregoing that the concept of capital used here is a strictly physical one. Indeed we define capital as the stock of physical assets used or usable for the production of those goods or services that are deemed to represent more immediate want satisfaction. Capital therefore includes those intermediate goods such as machinery, factories, buildings, equipment, roads, dams, housing, and so on whose employment contributes to the production of "more final" output and whose durability extends beyond a single production period.

There are clearly many alternative concepts of capital, such as, for example, any current outlay that will serve to enhance future production. Expenditures on education may be viewed as a kind of investment in man or an improvement in human capital that will increase productivity in the future. Indeed, there are a variety of expenditures which, despite formal treatment as "consumption" expenditures, have certain properties of capital such as durability, efficiency, and/or profit-enhancing capability. Such things as research and development, psychological testing of employees, and health expenditures may legitimately be placed in the category of capital broadly construed. If capital is defined as any productivity-increasing use of resources then it may well include such additional factors as religious activities, leisure, social security payments, and so on since these yield real and psychological benefits to certain people that may persist over time and enable or induce them to perform their work more effectively. There is clearly nothing wrong with construing capital more broadly. The difficulty is that this is not the way it has usually been defined and thus little in the way of empirical evidence is available for purposes of measurement. We shall then, accept the narrow and physical concept of capital both because this is and has been the most prevalent usage of the term and the one for which some factual evidence is available.[1]

However, it is one thing that statistics on capital stock exist and quite another to interpret the meaning of such data. As is well known, the value of any capital asset in the market place is the present discounted value of the expected net future receipts (or benefits). This is a rather subjective valuation process since it involves future expectations as well as an "appropriate" rate of discount and thus is subject to short-run changes independently of any change in the physical stock. Capital assets may also be valued at cost less accumulated depreciation plus the cost of improvements. However, this is scarcely more tangible or definite than the present-value formula for two main reasons: (1) the cost may refer to original or reproduction cost and these will differ if the price level and/or relative productivities have changed; and (2) estimates of depreciation are far from concrete and definite since there are many alternative techniques for calculating the reduction in value of an asset over time. Furthermore, these accounting estimates are wholly inadequate for conveying the change in productivity of capital through use during any time period. Indeed, it has been argued that "most capital goods do retain most of the efficiency of their early years until they are finally

[1]There has been growing dissatisfaction with the strictly physical conception of capital especially in discussions of education and health. A rather substantial literature has developed in recent years attempting to measure the "investment in man" and to compute rates of return on such investments. Thus, it is not strictly accurate to imply that no data exists with regard to measurement of non-physical capital. See, for example, Theodore W. Schultz, "Investment in Human Capital," *American Economic Review*, March, 1961 and references cited therein, and Edward F. Denison, *The Sources of Economic Growth in the United States*, Supplementary Paper No. 13, Committee for Economic Development (New York, 1962), chap. 7. The entire Supplement to the *Journal of Political Economy*, Oct. 1962, deals with these issues.

discarded."[2] Estimates of depreciation may therefore be seriously misleading as evidence of efficiency changes.

We raise all of these points simply to indicate that the data presented
below on the value of the capital stock must be viewed with great caution and interpreted carefully. This would be true even if the data were
based on a complete enumeration of all items of capital in the whole
economy, each of which was valued and reported in a consistent fashion.
In fact, as we show later, there are enormous statistical gaps in capital
stock estimates which, when added to the conceptual difficulties, render
the exact meaning of such figures at best somewhat ambiguous. Even in
the case of "investment," a term frequently used earlier and which is
defined as the net *change* in capital stock during a time period, there
are the same definitional problems or alternatives as mentioned above,
although the measurement of investment is on somewhat firmer ground
since, as part of the national accounting system, it fits into an integrated
conceptual framework for which statistics have been collected and refined over a fairly lengthy period of time.

THE DISTINCTION BETWEEN CONSUMPTION AND INVESTMENT

It is worth noting at this point that the distinction between an act of
consumption and an act of investment as defined above is somewhat
arbitrary. Consumption is deemed to be the "using up" of goods and
services for direct want satisfaction and results in no increase in productive capability. Indeed, if such a proportion of total output is used up
that not enough is left over to provide for depreciation of capital, productive capacity may be impaired. This view of consumption, however,
implies a fairly high level of economic achievement in the sense that
large segments of the population are free from diet deficiency diseases,
have plenty to eat, adequate clothing and shelter, and so on. When these
conditions prevail, it is clear that increases in consumption have generally
very little impact on efficiency. In this sense, consumption is truly an
activity that uses up output, decreases the stock of goods, and does not
enhance the productivity of the labour force. On the other hand, in
societies where the level of food intake is such that the majority of the
people and labour force are perpetually semi-starved, beset with anaemia
and susceptible to chronic illness and periodic epidemics, an increase in
consumption as defined above may permanently increase efficiency by
improving health, increasing the ability to work harder, and reducing
absenteeism due to frequent illness. Under such conditions, there is a
substantial blurring of the distinction between consumption and invest-

2Wm. C. Hood and Anthony Scott, *Output, Labour and Capital in the Canadian Economy*, a study prepared for the RCCEP (Ottawa, 1957); p. 253.

ment. Indeed additional "consumption" may at the same time represent investment in the broader sense of raising future output per unit of labour input.

But even where a high degree of affluence exists, there are many activities, such as education and the others noted above, that use up resources and do not leave behind a physical product but that undoubtedly have a permanent influence on efficiency. The classification of expenditures for such purposes as consumption is therefore a convention only and not the result of any compelling logic in so far as productivity is concerned. In addition, it should be mentioned that purchases of such items as automobiles, refrigerators, and other consumer durables having a life span of several years are regularly treated as "consumption" in the year of their acquisition by households.

CANADA'S CAPITAL STOCK

As indicated above the valuation of a nation's productive assets is not only a most difficult statistical process but may also be approached in a variety of ways. The results will differ depending upon the measurement technique adopted. Data limitations in Canada, however, dictate a procedure known as the "cumulation method." This involves obtaining estimates of annual investment, which are available and rather firm, and estimates of the service lives of the various assets, which are much more difficult to come by and tend to be rather shaky in any event. However, the method is fairly simple assuming the data can be obtained. Briefly stated, if the service life of capital is determined to be x years, then the annual gross investment data are cumulated for x years to arrive at the gross stock in the xth year. For each subsequent year the capital stock may be computed by adding the investment for that year and deducting the investment x years previous which by this time is believed to have used up its productive life.[3] Estimates using this technique were prepared for the Gordon Commission and are updated and summarized in Table 7.1 for the period 1945–60. It must be emphasized that the figures are based on highly restrictive assumptions concerning an average service life for a complex bundle of assets and in deriving a constant dollar series.[4] The reader is warned that the resulting evidence is little more

[3]More precisely the gross stock at the end of year $(t + 1)$ equals gross stock at the end of year t plus gross investment in year $(t + 1)$ minus gross investment in year $(t - x)$. Net stock at the end of year $(t + 1)$ equals net stock at the end of year t plus gross investment in year $(t + 1)$ minus capital consumption in year $(t + 1)$. Further details and illustration of the technique are given in *ibid.*, chap. 6, pp. 234–7.   [4]See *ibid.*, pp. 239–45.

TABLE 7.1

Capital Stock Estimates
(billions of 1949 dollars)
1945–60

Year	Gross capital stock	Net capital stock
1945	50.8	27.8
1946	52.2	28.7
1947	55.4	30.1
1948	56.9	31.8
1949	59.5	33.7
1950	62.3	35.5
1951	65.0	36.6
1952	68.2	39.6
1953	71.5	42.3
1954	74.6	44.5
1955	77.9	46.9
1956	82.6	50.4
1957	88.2	53.8
1958	91.5	56.7
1959	95.7	59.3
1960	99.2	61.5

SOURCES: Data from 1945 through 1955 from Wm. C. Hood and A. Scott, *Output, Labour and Capital in the Canadian Economy*, a study prepared for the RCCEP (Ottawa, 1957), appendix to chap. 6. Data from 1955 to 1960 derived from an unpublished OECD study.

than an informed guess and is best used as an indicator of trend since the estimate for any particular year may or may not provide a close approximation to what one is trying to measure.[5]

With these caveats in mind, the evidence of Table 7.1 indicates a fairly steady rise in both the gross and net capital stock. Gross capital stock, which includes both industrial and social[6] capital, virtually doubled between 1945 and 1960, while net capital stock, which also includes

[5]DBS has been working on capital stock estimates for several years. To date they have published only estimates for the manufacturing sector [DBS, *Daily Bulletin*, Supplement 2, December 22, 1964]. A comparison with the Hood and Scott estimates for manufacturing shows the DBS gross stock figures to be higher for the years 1946 to 1950 and lower thereafter with the discrepancy steadily widening as one moves away from 1950 in either direction. On the other hand, the DBS estimates of *net* capital stock in manufacturing are consistently below those of Hood and Scott by amounts ranging from $200–$500 million. This is further evidence of the frailty of the data.

[6]Social capital is taken to include government-owned assets such as roads, buildings, machinery, and equipment as well as private capital such as houses, and the capital assets of schools, universities, churches, and hospitals. Excluded from both industrial and social capital are consumer durables, and the value of land and other natural resources, even though these have features comparable to "capital" as defined above.

industrial and social capital, somewhat more than doubled over this same time period.

The composition of total capital stock has altered somewhat.[7] If we distinguish between machinery and equipment on the one hand and construction on the other, approximately 80 per cent of the gross capital stock in Canada in 1945 consisted of buildings, houses, roads, and other forms of construction capital or structures and only 20 per cent in the form of machinery and equipment. By 1955, the latest date for which this kind of distinction is readily available, the proportion of machinery and equipment had risen to about 25 per cent. A far sharper rise in the share of machinery and equipment has occurred if one considers only industrial capital. Indeed in 1945, machinery and equipment as a proportion of gross industrial capital accounted for barely 25 per cent whereas by 1955 it was almost 50 per cent. This rising share of machinery and equipment relative to total industrial capital has also been observed in the United States. As far as social capital is concerned, it is composed mainly of structures. In 1945, the construction component of gross social capital totalled about $25 billion (in 1949 dollars), while machinery and equipment amounted to only $1.2 billion. By 1955 this construction component amounted to about $35 billion, while machinery and equipment totalled barely $1.6 billion.

Social capital in 1945 was slightly over half (54 per cent) of the combined industrial and social gross capital stock, but by 1955 the position vis-à-vis social and industrial capital was reversed. There is an apparent trend towards a relative reduction in the share of social capital in Canada's total gross capital stock. A similar and somewhat more pronounced trend is discernible as far as net capital stock is concerned as well. This is associated with the more rapid increase in the machinery and equipment component of capital stock which is largely concentrated in the industrial sector.[8]

The importance of capital stock estimates lies primarily in the nature of the relationship between capital and output. That is, capital along with labour is generally believed to be the main determinant of potential levels of output. Indeed, the efficiency of labour appears to be closely tied to the quantity of capital available per worker, although the quality of both capital and labour is perhaps more important. Nevertheless, capital stock and changes therein (i.e., investment) is one of the critical factors in

[7]The following data are from Hood and Scott, *Output, Labour and Capital*, Appendix to chap. 6.

[8]A more detailed breakdown over the period 1945–55 is given in *ibid.*, appendix to chap. 6.

explaining levels of economic achievement. It is no accident, therefore, that many theories of economic growth concentrate upon the so-called capital-output ratio.

We have therefore computed the average gross and net capital-output ratios for Canada and compared these with the United States in Table 7.2. The evidence, crude as it is, suggests that the Canadian capital-output ratio not only has exceeded that of the US in every year since 1949, which is consistent with our previous findings regarding the greater economic costs in Canada due to climate, distance, and the smaller domestic market, but has also been rising somewhat in recent years. The increase may be attributable to the slowing down of the rate of growth of output and the increasing difficulties of extending the Canadian economy in a northerly direction. Generally, however, it appears that

TABLE 7.2

Average Capital-Output Ratios: Canada and the United States
1945-60

Year	Gross capital-output ratio		Net capital-output ratio	
	Canada	US	Canada	US
1945	3.3	3.9	2.2	2.8
1946	3.4	4.0	2.3	2.8
1947	3.6	3.7	2.5	2.6
1948	3.6	3.5	2.6	2.4
1949	3.6	3.6	2.6	2.5
1950	3.6	3.3	2.6	2.4
1951	3.5	3.0	2.5	2.1
1952	3.4	2.9	2.6	2.1
1953	3.4	2.8	2.6	2.1
1954	3.7	2.9	2.9	2.2
1955	3.6	2.8	2.8	2.1
1956	3.5	2.7	2.8	2.0
1957	3.7	2.6	3.0	2.0
1958	3.8	2.7	3.0	2.0
1959	3.8	n/a	3.1	n/a
1960	3.9	n/a	3.2	n/a

NOTES AND SOURCES:

Canadian data 1945 through 1955 for both gross and net capital stock estimates from Hood and Scott, *Output, Labour and Capital in the Canadian Economy*, appendix to chap. 6. For 1956 to 1960 data on capital stock from unpublished OECD study. The gross capital-output ratio is the gross capital stock divided by GNP, both expressed in 1949 dollars for Canada. The net capital-output ratio is the net capital stock divided by national income both in 1949 dollars.

The US capital stock estimates are from Raymond Goldsmith, *The National Wealth of the United States in the Postwar Period*, a study by the National Bureau of Economic Research (Princeton, 1962), Table A-2, p. 114. These data are in constant dollars of 1947-49. The output data refer to GNP and national income both converted to dollars of 1947-49 for the US.

Canada's average gross capital output ratio, for example, in recent years may be as high as 3.9 compared with less than 3.0 in the US. This means that every dollar's worth of real output requires $3.90 of capital on the average in Canada and about $1.00 less than this in the United States. Furthermore, since the average appears to be increasing, the extra capital required for producing an extra dollar's worth of output may be well over $4.00. Computations between various pairs of years suggest that the marginal gross capital-output ratio is between 4.3 and 4.8 and the marginal net capital-output ratio is between 2.5 and 4.0.

There is however another way to construe the capital-output ratio that does not rely on the admittedly rough calculations of total capital stock. Indeed most growth models use a measure of *marginal* or *incremental* capital-output ratio which relates the *increase* in real output to the increase in capital stock. But the increase in a nation's stock of capital assets is simply net investment (excluding inventory changes): hence the marginal or incremental capital-output ratio may be defined as net investment divided by the increase in GNE less depreciation. Selected data on the marginal capital-output ratio are shown in Table 7.3.[9] The wide variation from year to year is immediately apparent and suggests that the ratio is highly unstable and far from being a fixed "technical" coefficient. Even if we examine successive years in which unemployment was less than 4 per cent (i.e., "full" employment years) the marginal capital-output ratio still exhibits substantial though less variability. The reasons for this lack of stability even assuming the data to be accurate are given in the appendix to the present chapter.

Some observers have detected a declining tendency in Canada's incremental capital-output ratio[10] which is not consistent with the findings of Table 7.3 when the capital stock estimates are used to deduce the incremental ratio. However, the Caves and Holton estimates do not include all government capital formation.[11] Yet public investment has accounted for between 10 and 20 per cent of total investment in Canada ever since the late 1920's. Since public investment cannot validly be presumed less productive than that undertaken privately, we see no reason for its exclusion in constructing a capital-output ratio for the whole economy. When

[9]The depression and war years have been excluded because in each period whatever relationship might normally exist between a change in capital and output was seriously distorted. In the depression the economy operated at levels well below capacity while during the war forced-draft production led to output above levels that could be sustained without serious inefficiencies developing.

[10]See R. E. Caves and R. H. Holton, *The Canadian Economy: Prospect and Retrospect* (Cambridge, Mass., 1959), pp. 335–6.

[11]Their estimates apparently include government constructed housing. All other public investment has been excluded.

TABLE 7.3

Marginal Capital-Output Ratio
selected years 1927-62

Year	Marginal capital-output ratio*
1927	1.00
1928	1.13
1929	14.93
1947	1.12
1948	0.95
1949	1.88
1950	1.42
1951	0.88
1952	1.18
1953	4.27
1954	(−7.39)
1955	1.57
1956	1.43
1957	4.92
1958	4.08
1959	2.46
1960	3.51
1961	3.34
1962	1.44

*This ratio is defined as net public and private investment divided by change in net GNE. Data from DBS, *National Accounts Income and Expenditure*, various issues and DBS, *Private and Public Investment in Canada*, various issues.

public investment is included there is no trend towards a reduction in the capital coefficient. Indeed, for the period 1957–61, the ratio on average is higher than for any other years except 1929, 1938, and 1945, when GNE increased by such small amounts that the ratio is extremely large (i.e., over 13 in each year), and excluding years in which either net investment or the change in GNE was negative. If the war years are excluded the average incremental capital-output ratio for years in which labour unemployment was less than 4 per cent, works out at about 1.7. This is substantially below the estimates using capital stock data and so casts serious doubt upon their validity.

The above figures are thus extremely rough and must obviously be interpreted cautiously. Moreover, it is quite possible that the estimates are seriously misleading, particularly for marginal ratios. Nevertheless, the best available evidence, imperfect though it is, suggests not only that Canada's average capital-output ratio is relatively high but that it has been increasing in recent years, unlike US experience. Despite all the statistical weaknesses, it may well be true that Canada's investment requirements to sustain a high and growing level of output are themselves high and growing. Of course, many other factors intrude between investment and output which make the nature of the relationship much less deterministic than would otherwise be implied. Indeed the capital-output ratio is so frequently misused that a brief note on its limitations is in order.[12]

It is not, of course, possible to assess the adequacy of Canada's capital stock from recent estimates of the average capital-output ratio. As the war demonstrated, it is possible to squeeze more output from a given stock than is currently being produced from it, especially when substantial excess capacity exists, as has been the case since the end of 1956.[13] But unless replacements are regularly made for that portion of capital equipment which is constantly being used up, it will not be possible to maintain a given level of output even if for a few years the level of output is below capacity. As the capital stock decreases, so does productive capacity. There is no possibility therefore of maintaining current rates of output for, say, 20 or 30 years by using up the existing capital stock as is the case with some natural resources. Even with the degree of excess capacity that currently exists, output could not long be sustained without replacements of or additions to the stock of capital. Nor are "new discoveries" of existing capital assets possible.

If any nation seeks to raise its output levels to heights that are sustainable over time, fresh capital investment over and above replacement needs is essential. The precise amount of the new capital needed depends, of course, on what is being produced as well as the hoped-for rise in total output and it cannot be arithmetically deduced from aggregative average or marginal capital-output ratios. But the point is that capital is functionally related to output even if the relationship is not precise.

[12]See Appendix to this chapter.

[13]A crude calculation of the degree of excess capital capacity in Canada from 1957 through 1960 may be obtained by assuming a "normal" gross capital-output ratio of 3.6, which typified the late 1940's and early 1950's. If the ratio is 3.6, then real GNE in 1949 dollars "should or could have been" about $28 billion in 1960 instead of the $25.8 billion actually recorded. If we consider the extent of labour unemployment, it is not too much to suggest that perhaps $3 billion (in 1949 dollars) more real output could have been produced in 1960 if full employment of both labour and capital had been achieved. Only during 1962, 1963, and 1964 has this full employment gap narrowed to any important degree.

The crucial question then with respect to capital is not whether the present stock is large in some sense relative to output but whether it can be increased enough to maintain or raise national income per head in the face of a steady rise in total population. The maintenance or increase of the stock of capital is chiefly a function of man's future efforts and decisions to save and invest. Specifically this requires some degree of abstention from current consumption at full employment levels so that the resources so released can be devoted to capital formation. The following sections examine the levels and trends in investment and saving in Canada.

CAPITAL INVESTMENT

As already noted the creation of a new factory, machine, or other capital asset requires that resources be diverted from the production of consumption goods assuming that full employment exists. The question then is one of choice between two major competing uses of society's scarce resources. How has the Canadian economy made such choices in the past?

The "sacrifice" required to add to the stock of capital and to repair or maintain the existing stock, excluding inventory changes and the trade balance,[14] is one measure of current consumption foregone. Data showing the magnitude of expenditures for additions and repairs to the capital stock are shown in Table 7.4 for the period 1926–62. Several tendencies may be noted from this table. One is that the ratio of outlays for repairs to those for new capital formation fell from roughly half in the late 1920's to about a third in the late 1950's. Perhaps of greater interest is the different behaviour of repair and new capital expenditures. The former have increased rather steadily, especially since 1938, which parallels the steady growth in total capital stock. On the other hand, capital expenditures have exhibited a far higher degree of volatility. Since they are deferable in a way that consumer outlays for food, clothing, and shelter are not and furthermore are made on the basis of expectations, at least as far as business capital outlays are concerned, such erratic behaviour is to be expected. Private and public capital outlays are shown in Table 1.5 as a proportion of GNE. Business investment expenditures have varied from a low of less than 7 per cent of GNE in 1933 to a high of 23 per cent in 1957.

The volatility of investment expenditures may be contrasted with the relative stability of personal consumption expenditures which since 1926

[14]These are examined below.

TABLE 7.4

Capital and Repair Expenditures
1926-62
(millions of dollars)

Year	Capital expenditures	Repair expenditures	Capital and repair expenditures
1926	808	517	1325
1929	1344	619	1963
1933	319	373	692
1937	809	518	1327
1938	754	518	1272
1939	746	538	1284
1940	1028	588	1616
1941	1465	690	2155
1942	1556	760	2316
1943	1521	826	2347
1944	1343	959	2302
1945	1320	1004	2324
1946	1674	1087	2761
1947	2440	1260	3700
1948	3087	1470	4557
1949	3539	1574	5113
1950	3936	1695	5631
1951	4739	1968	6707
1952	5491	2085	7576
1953	5976	2206	8182
1954	5721	2222	7943
1955	6244	2309	8553
1956	8034	2520	10,554
1957	8717	2624	11,341
1958	8364	2614	10,978
1959	8411	2749	11,160
1960	8262	2985	11,247
1961	8172	3021	11,193
1962	8715	3161	11,876

SOURCE: DBS, *Private and Public Investment in Canada, 1946-1957* (Ottawa, 1959), Table 1, p. 11.

have constituted a fairly stable proportion of personal disposable income, if the war years are eliminated. Indeed, the year-to-year changes in personal consumption spending stand in sharp contrast to the extreme variability of business investment spending.

But in general the ratio of gross domestic investment to GNE in Canada has been relatively high. Since 1949 business plus public investment has regularly exceeded 20 per cent of GNE and in 1957 reached the very high proportion of 27 per cent. Compared with other Western countries this is a large percentage indeed. Evidence for 1955 for the nations of Western Europe and the US indicates a substantially smaller ratio of investment to GNE. There are, of course, certain statistical ambiguities in the data and, as far as the US is concerned, no estimate of public investment is included. But in general, Canada appears to devote a larger share of current output to net capital formation and replacement than most countries. Only a few of the smaller countries shown in Table 7.5 have higher ratios and the weighted average for either the EEC or EFTA countries is well below the Canadian experience. Furthermore, Canada, with domestic capital expenditures of $418 per head, stands far above the highest of Western Europe of $298 registered by Ireland and Luxembourg and is over two and one half times the West European average, omitting the changes in stocks. How Canada is able to finance such large investment outlays will be examined later.

COMPOSITION OF CAPITAL OUTLAYS

Annual investment spending by type is summarized in Table 7.6 for the years 1946–61. Investment in private housing typically accounts for around 20 per cent of total public and private investment and has risen from less than one billion dollars annually prior to 1952 to about one and a half billion dollars since 1956. The largest components of domestic investment are machinery and equipment, expenditures for which have quadrupled since 1946, and non-residential construction which has exhibited a six-fold increase between 1946 and 1961. Much of this increase reflects the low levels prevailing after the war, although these two largest components of domestic investment have continued to account for about 60–65 per cent of total investment. Indeed, the investment boom of 1957, which proved non-sustainable, was concentrated principally in these two components,[15] as was the subsequent decline.

Public investment outlays have risen sharply from not quite $290 million in 1946 to over $1.5 billion by 1961, mostly because of the rise in non-housing construction. As a proportion of total domestic investment, public capital outlays have increased slightly from about 14–15 per cent between 1947 and 1951 to roughly 18–19 per cent in the late

[15]Of the increase in 1957 over 1956 of $683 million, $678 millions of it came from private non-residential construction and machinery and equipment outlays.

TABLE 7.5

Gross Domestic Capital Formation as a
Percentage of GNP and Per Capita
Selected Countries
1955

Country	Fixed investment as to GNP			Changes in stocks	Domestic investment per capita
	Total	Non-residential	residential		
Western Europe	20.2	14.2	4.5	1.5	$151
Iceland	32.2	18.5	10.3	3.4	297
Norway	30.2	23.8	5.8	0.6	288
Finland	26.9	20.1	5.3	1.5	179
Austria	25.8	19.6	4.4	1.8	142
Germany*	25.7	16.9	5.7	3.1	218
Luxembourg	24.9	18.7	3.8	2.4	298
Netherlands	23.3	18.7	4.0	0.6	170
Switzerland	22.1	16.8	5.8	−0.5	284
Sweden	21.9	14.6	5.1	2.2	263
Italy	21.6	14.9	5.3	1.4	98
Spain	18.1	12.3	4.9	0.9	50
France	17.7	12.7	4.3	0.7	165
Denmark	17.2	14.5	2.7		160
United Kingdom	16.3	11.5	3.2	1.6	170
Belgium	15.6	11.7	3.8	0.1	168
Ireland	15.6	11.4	2.3	1.9	80
Greece	15.2	9.1	4.9	1.2	39
Portugal	14.5	11.1	3.0	0.4	30
Canada	23.0	16.3	4.6	2.1	418
United States	16.1	9.9	4.7	1.5	387

SOURCE: For all countries except Canada and the United States, data from J. F. Dewhurst and associates, *Europe's Needs and Resources* (New York, 1961), Table 14-1, p. 445. Canadian data from Tables 3, 5, and 6 of chap. 1. US data from *Annual Report of the Council of Economic Advisers, January 1962* (Washington DC, 1962). US estimates refer to private investments only.
*Includes the Saar and West Berlin.

1950's and early 1960's as office, road, and other transport and military building programs were accelerated.

So far we have looked mainly at investment construed in terms of producers' capital equipment as well as public and private housing and non-housing expenditures. There are, however, two other components of "investment" that must be mentioned in the present context. Inventories of finished or semi-processed goods held by business, whether in the form of consumer or producer goods, represent investment in the sense that they are part of the nation's production not yet used up and hence can yield services or satisfactions at some future date. They are part of the necessary expenses of running a business and take up the slack when sales differ from production. As such, inventories are clearly a form of investment.

The other component of investment is the difference between exports and imports of goods and services already examined in Chapter 4. When Canada sells more to other countries than she buys, the difference, termed "net foreign investment," represents that part of current output not used up by Canadians and constitutes an increase in Canadian claims against the rest of the world emanating from current production. As such, net foreign investment yields future foreign output or income much as domestic investment yields future national output. The opposite situation obtains when Canada buys more from the rest of the world than she sells. In the latter case net foreign investment is a negative quantity signifying that part of future Canadian GNE will be needed to satisfy the increase in foreign claims against the Canadian economy.

Figure 7.1 summarizes the behaviour of inventory change and net foreign investment over time.[16] As would be expected the inventory change is a highly volatile component of GNE although relatively small. This is due to the fact that the initial impact of any change in sales and production is felt or cushioned by the size of inventories. Generally, since the end of the war there has been net non-farm inventory accumulation although at widely differing rates ranging from the non-sustainable high of over $800 million in 1956 to a low accumulation of only $85 million in 1948. Inventory liquidation occurred in 1954 and again in 1958, both related to the downturns in GNP of those years. There is no apparent long-run trend in the inventory change component either in absolute terms or as a proportion of GNE. It is more symptomatic of short-run, cyclical adjustments than long-run tendencies.

We have already discussed the growing gap between exports and imports,[17] which represents net foreign borrowing and rising claims

[16]The data on inventories have been divided into two components (1) non-farm business inventories and (2) farm inventories and grain in commercial channels. The former "includes the change in inventories occurring in private business and government business enterprises, without any deduction for inventory reserves. Investment in grain inventories by the Canadian Wheat Board is included, but net purchases by various government commodity agencies not organized as business enterprises are excluded. . . . Government net purchases of strategic materials and the pre-financing of private inventories by the government . . . are. . . excluded." DBS, *National Accounts Income and Expenditure, 1926–1956* (Ottawa, 1962), p. 165. There are likewise important adjustments made to value inventory change in a manner consistent with national accounting requirements. For a detailed discussion of the procedure see *ibid.*, pp. 165–70.

[17]See Part One, chap. 4.

TABLE 7.6

Investment by Type
1946–61
(millions of dollars)

	Total private and public investment in Canada	Private					
		Housing		Non-residential construction		Machinery and equipment	
Year		Amount	Percentage of total	Amount	Percentage of total	Amount	Percentage of Total
1946	1674	360	21.5	435	26.0	585	34.9
1947	2440	494	20.2	597	24.5	994	40.7
1948	3087	609	19.7	816	26.4	1194	38.7
1949	3539	794	22.4	920	26.0	1318	37.2
1950	3936	883	22.4	1042	26.5	1423	36.2
1951	4739	895	18.9	1270	26.8	1794	37.9
1952	5491	933	17.0	1566	28.5	1952	35.5
1953	5976	1166	19.5	1719	28.8	2113	36.9
1954	5721	1227	21.4	1671	29.2	1881	32.9
1955	6244	1378	22.1	1848	29.6	1984	31.8
1956	8034	1526	19.0	2589	32.2	2659	33.1
1957	8717	1409	16.2	3103	35.6	2823	32.4
1958	8364	1763	21.1	2811	33.6	2401	28.7
1959	8437	1754	20.9	2589	30.8	2571	30.5
1960	8262	1443	17.5	2577	31.2	2672	32.3
1961	8109	1458	18.0	2647	32.6	2388	29.4

SOURCES: Computed from DBS, *Private and Public Investment in Canada, 1946-1957* (Ottawa, 1959); and DBS, *National Accounts Income and Expenditure, 1956-1961* (Ottawa, 1962).

against the Canadian economy by the rest of the world, chiefly the United States, and need not say more at this point.

INVESTMENT IN DIFFERENT SECTORS OF THE ECONOMY

The amount of capital expenditures going to or undertaken by the various sectors is shown in Table 7.7 for selected years. Taking the period between 1947 and 1961, total annual capital outlays more than tripled, but there were differences in the growth rates by sectors. Agriculture, fishing, and forestry barely doubled the amount of annual capital spending while public utilities, other than electric power, stepped up the pace of investment very sharply as did the various commercial and institutional services and government departments. The three largest sectors in 1947 from the point of view of new capital formation were manufacturing, utilities, and housing; together they accounted for 60 per cent of

TABLE 7.6 (*continued*)

	Public				
Housing		Other construction		Machinery and Equipment	
Amount	Percentage of total	Amount	Percentage of total	Amount	Percentage of total
39	2.3	202	12.1	45	2.7
32	1.3	274	11.2	49	2.0
26	0.8	373	12.1	69	2.2
28	0.8	424	12.0	55	1.6
40	1.0	488	12.4	60	1.5
52	1.1	654	13.8	74	1.6
38	0.7	897	16.3	105	1.9
23	0.4	848	14.2	107	1.8
11	0.2	828	14.5	103	1.8
19	0.3	924	14.8	91	1.5
21	0.3	1137	14.2	102	1.3
21	0.2	1251	14.4	110	1.3
19	0.2	1237	14.8	133	1.6
18	0.2	1368	16.3	137	1.6
13	0.2	1420	17.2	137	1.7
9	0.1	1460	18.0	147	1.8

new investment. By 1961 their share had fallen to about 52 per cent as investment by government departments and the other fast-growing sectors outpaced housing and manufacturing.

By 1961 all sectors were spending more on capital formation although some of this is due to rising prices. In general, however, the changing pattern of investment allocation reflects broadly the sectoral trends indicated in Chapter 1, namely the relative decline in agriculture, forestry, and fishing, as well as manufacturing, and the rise of services of all kinds and utilities.

THE SOURCES OF INVESTMENT FUNDS

The main sources of financing Canada's high rate of investment expenditures are shown in Table 7.8. By far the largest proportion of national savings emanates from the business sector. Business gross savings as a

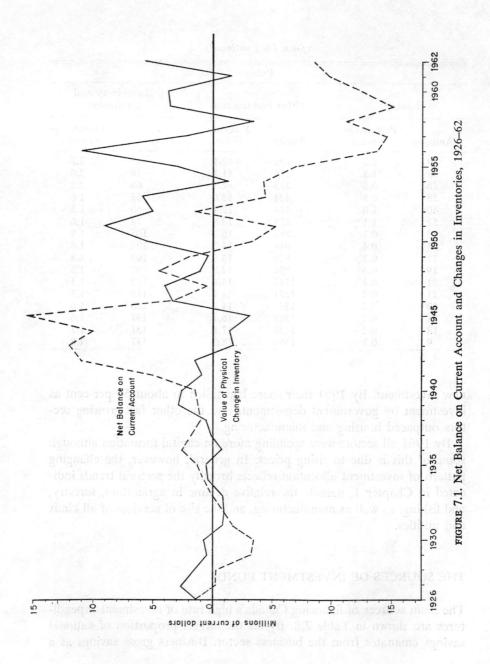

FIGURE 7.1. Net Balance on Current Account and Changes in Inventories, 1926–62

TABLE 7.7

Gross Capital Expenditure by Sector*
selected years 1947-63
(millions of dollars)

Sector	1947	1950	1954	1957	1961	1963†
Agriculture and fishing	278	482	400	434	576	659
Forestry	32	34	46	48	50	61
Mining, quarrying and oil wells	42	114	278	606	449	492
Manufacturing	528	502	822	1479	1085	1414
Utilities	410	759	1164	2308	1698	1819
Electric power	119	372	445	803	570	655
All other utilities	291	387	719	1505	1128	1164
Construction industry	52	71	97	158	136	151
Housing	526	923	1238	1430	1467	1643
Trade—wholesale and retail	119	234	368	370	307	314
Finance, insurance, and real estate	21	61	107	136	312	285
Commercial services	62	104	107	184	228	250
Institutional services	91	213	338	454	617	887
Churches	11	33	34	57	62	57
Universities	14	14	20	42	112	173
Schools	31	89	155	217	253	432
Hospitals	33	73	122	131	178	207
All other institutional services	2	4	8	8	12	18
Government departments	279	439	756	1110	1247	1366
Total	2440	3936	5721	8717	8172	9341

SOURCES: DBS, *Private and Public Investment in Canada, 1946-1957* (Ottawa, 1959), pp. 13-33. DBS, *Private and Public Investment in Canada Outlook, 1963* (Ottawa, 1963), pp. 11-15. DBS, *Private and Public Investment in Canada Outlook, 1963, Mid-Year Review* (Ottawa, 1963), pp. 5-9.

*Figures may not add to total due to rounding.
†Forecasts as of mid-1963.

proportion of total gross savings amounted to almost 90 per cent for the years 1959–61 when the substantial government deficits reduced the total recorded savings. Business saving was about four times that of the personal sector over the same period. There has been a rather important shift in the composition of national savings with the business sector accounting for a sharply growing proportion. For example, for the years 1947–49 business saving was only about 70 per cent of the total and between two and three times the size of personal savings. A fairly steady rise in the relative importance of business vis-à-vis personal savings is discernible over the postwar period.

The largest single component of business saving is depreciation which has risen steadily since 1946, except for 1958, as the industrial gross stock has grown.

TABLE 7.8

Post-War Savings by Source
1946–62
(millions of dollars)

	1946	1947	1948	1949	1950	1951	1952
Personal net saving	892	494	994	926	662	1334	1291
Business gross saving							
(a) Undistributed corporation							
profits	488	628	790	587	752	662	618
(b) Capital consumption							
allowances	998	1223	1441	1673	1913	2203	2422
(c) Adjustment on grain							
transactions	22	34	−100	−111	166	− 12	43
Inventory valuation adjustment	−254	−571	−506	−112	−374	−643	106
Government surplus (+) or							
deficit (−)	−154	753	708	373	585	985	253
Residual error of estimate	31	− 27	− 89	− 43	− 68	− 90	202
Total savings	2023	2534	3238	3293	2638	4439	4935

SOURCE: DBS, *National Accounts Income and Expenditure, 1926-1956*, and *1961*.

A comparison between gross national saving and domestic investment[18] suggests that in recent years about 82 per cent of such investment has been financed from domestic savings. Compared with the more highly developed countries in Western Europe and the United States this ratio is very low (see Table 7.9). Indeed no country listed in Table 7.8 had a ratio below 93 per cent which indicates the relatively high proportion of Canadian capital formation financed from external sources.

But this may even overstate the extent of domestic financing from Canadian sources for as shown in Chapter 4 much of Canada's industry is owned by non-residents. Thus some proportion of business saving in reality is performed by non-residents. If one is interested in the extent of self-financing of Canadian domestic investment by residents a deduction from the ratios shown in Table 7.8 is necessary. In fact, as indicated in Table 4.21, the proportion of domestic resources to gross capital formation for the same years used in Table 4.21 was only 73 per cent when foreign ownership is considered rather than the 82 per cent calculated by using the United Nations' measure (see Table 7.9) which excludes consideration of the role of non-residents.

There is, however, another way of viewing national investment that is more realistic than limiting the concept generally to business and net foreign investment. The usual treatment of government expenditures, at

[18]Domestic investment as used here is based upon the United Nations accounting system which equates the sum of domestic saving plus the current account deficit (or minus the net foreign surplus) with gross domestic capital formation.

1953	1954	1955	1956	1957	1958	1959	1960	1961	1962
1312	809	850	1320	1202	1635	1357	1539	1509	2331
729	571	962	1131	854	876	986	873	778	979
2673	2905	3266	3642	4009	3899	4204	4459	4539	4755
−24	8	64	20	—	− 1	− 5	6	26	− 11
−11	86	−189	−238	−78	− 35	−122	− 80	− 67	− 14
175	−131	106	350	100	−1007	−556	−711	−905	−770
142	− 13	−108	141	28	102	− 30	− 99	−150	−221
4996	4235	4951	6366	6115	5469	5834	5987	5750	6931

least in North America, is to construe them as entirely current and hence used up (i.e., consumed) during the fiscal period. However, government capital formation (the investment of government enterprises is already included in the business sector) is just as legitimately part of the national investment total and should be so included as we have done in an earlier section. However, in the national saving account (Table 7.8), government receipts are netted against expenditures regardless of type of outlay and shown only as government surplus (or positive savings) or government deficit (or dissavings). This amounts to treating government capital formation (e.g., roads, schools, and so on) as current consumption. Since estimates of government investment are available the amounts involved for each fiscal period may be added to the totals in the national saving and investment accounts. This involves treating part of government revenues and/or part of the deficit when this occurs, as positive savings in the same fashion as business retained income.[19] Likewise since the saving and investment account is in gross terms (i.e., includes depreciation), there is no need to become involved in the hazardous procedure of estimating depreciation on government assets.

When this is done, the proportion of total investment financed from domestic savings naturally rises. Using the same definition of investment and savings as in Table 7.9, except that the amount of public investment

[19]That is, the government surplus in total national savings would be increased by the amount of government investment, or the deficit would be decreased by the same amount, and a separate item, government investment, would be added to the national investment account.

TABLE 7.9

Sources of Finance for Gross Domestic Capital Formation in Selected Countries
Annual Averages 1955-57
(millions of dollars)

Country and area	Savings as percentage of domestic capital formation	Total savings	Domestic capital formation	Current foreign surplus
Western Europe				
Luxembourg	127	123	97	26
Belgium	113	1903	1701	222
United Kingdom	106	10,101	9571	530
France	93	7945	8500	−556
Germany	113	12,811	11,291	1520
Denmark	102	822	804	18
Netherlands	99	2169	2200	− 31
Norway	97	1058	1097	− 39
North America				
Canada	82	5808	7126	−1318
United States	102	67,200	66,100	1100

SOURCES: Western Europe from Dewhurst and Associates, *Europe's Needs and Resources* (New York, 1961) Table 14-11, p. 464. For Canada DBS, *National Accounts Income and Expenditure, 1961*. For the US *Economic Report of the President January, 1963* (Washington, DC, 1963), Table C-18, p. 193, omitting statistical discrepancy.

expenditure is added to both the totals of investment and savings, the proportion of the larger investment total financed by domestic savings (part of which represent those tax revenues applied to public investment) rises to slightly over 86 per cent. This is not a very significant increase over the 82 per cent figure shown above and is still below the proportion of any country listed in Table 7.9. Nevertheless, it represents a higher proportion of a larger total investment figure and is more realistic than the estimates that treat government investment as a form of consumption.

However, even with the revised concepts of investment and savings, the evidence suggests that any increase of Canada's stock of physical assets is dependent to a large extent upon external sources of capital inflows to augment Canadian savings, unless these savings can be increased substantially, perhaps by as much as 20–25 per cent. It is considerations such as these that render the Canadian economy so sensitive should any restrictions be placed upon the outflow of US capital by the

TABLE 7.10

Trends in National Savings
selected periods, 1927-61

	Annual averages					
	1927-29	1937-39	1947-49	1953-55	1957-59	1960-61
Total gross savings ($ millions)	1057	813	3022	4686	5808	5643
Total savings as per cent of GNE	18.0	15.0	20.3	18.4	17.5	15.6
Depreciation as per cent of GNE	11.3	11.3	9.7	11.4	12.2	11.9
Undistributed profits as per cent of GNE	4.2	3.8	4.5	2.8	2.7	2.2
Personal savings as per cent of disposable income	4.2	2.1	7.3	5.8	5.7	5.0
Government surplus (+) or deficit (−) as per cent of GNE	+0.6	−1.8	+4.2	+0.2	−1.4	−2.1

SOURCE: DBS, *National Accounts Income and Expenditure*, various issues.

American authorities.[20] The very substantial proportion of foreign-financed new investment in Canada is yet another illustration of the vulnerability of the Canadian economy and, of course, is closely linked to the pattern of Canada's international trade. Furthermore there is no discernible trend away from this particular pattern as far as foreign investment is concerned, except to the extent that more and more of it now emanates from the US.

PAST TRENDS IN DOMESTIC SAVING

Evidence on various savings ratios is presented in Table 7.10. In absolute amounts, total annual national savings during the late 1950's were over five times the levels prevailing during the late 1920's. However, since GNE in current dollars increased even more rapidly, the proportion of total output (or income) devoted to savings declined from about 18 per cent in the late 1920's to less than 16 per cent in the late 1950's. There has, furthermore, been a fairly steady decline in the savings ratio since the end of the Second World War. The main elements in this

[20]The US proposal to discourage outflows of capital made on July 18, 1963, invoked the following not atypical comment: "Can the Canadian people much longer hope to survive as a proud and prosperous community without a very basic reshaping and redirecting of the Canadian economy? ... the whole embarrassing episode should focus fresh attention on ... our humiliating inability to direct our national affairs in our own national interest." *Financial Post*, July 27, 1963, p. 1.

behaviour of saving are the decline in the proportion of personal savings to GNE, occasioned primarily by the drop in the share of disposable income to GNE from about 75 per cent in the late 1920's to about 70 per cent in the late 1950's. Government savings and undistributed profits have also decreased relative to GNE. Depreciation reserves are now slightly higher than in the late 1920's and, indeed, account for the bulk of national savings (as already noted) since the other components of total saving have decreased relatively to GNE.

On the other hand, as indicated on page 314, a more appropriate conception of national savings would include that portion of governmental receipts expended on new capital assets. When this adjustment is made, the ratio of savings to total GNE is regularly 2 to 4 percentage points higher. The apparent decline in the savings ratio shown in Table 7.10, from about 20 per cent for 1947–49 to barely 16 per cent for 1960–62, is matched by the alternative definition of savings although the savings ratio is at a higher level. In 1947–49 this ratio was slightly over 23 per cent but declined to about 21 per cent during 1960–62. Although the decline in the ratio is less pronounced when public investment is added to the usual estimates of national savings, it is none the less a fairly steady downward trend since the early 1950's.

When matched against the steady rise in the proportion of public and private investment to GNE from about 22 per cent in 1949 to over 27 per cent in 1957, despite a subsequent fall to about 22 per cent by 1960, 1961, and 1962, the financing of domestic capital formation from national savings is apparently diminishing. When the excess of imports over exports is considered, the gap between domestic savings and total national investment appears substantial, as already noted.

THE NEEDED AMOUNT OF SAVINGS AND INVESTMENT

A common form of analysis regarding the amounts of needed savings and investment involves comparisons between the ratio of domestic savings to GNE and the incremental gross capital-output ratio. We shall criticize this kind of analysis in the Appendix to the present chapter and do not propose to dwell upon it here. However, it is of some interest to note that, if the savings ratio in Canada, excluding government savings and investment, is normally 16–18 per cent and the incremental gross capital-output ratio is roughly between 4 and 5, this implies a "warranted" rate of growth of GNE of between 3 and 4 per cent while if government savings and investment are included, the warranted growth rate is a little over 4 per cent. These growth rates are close to the historical long-term trends in real aggregate GNE. The implication is that, so long as the Canadian public is satisfied with this rate of growth, there is no apparent difficulty in maintaining it, judging by the past willingness to abstain from current consumption. In short, if there were much validity to this approach, and the Appendix suggests that it involves not only monocausality but a host of additional assumptions regarding efficiency of capital use, allocation among sectors, degree of excess capacity, and so on which renders whatever degree of apparent precision in the above estimates at best crude approximations, no particularly drastic altera- tion would be required in contemporary Canadian economic habits or behaviour.

Yet as noted in Chapter 4 over 25 per cent (and possibly as much as one third) of gross capital formation in Canada is financed from abroad. Could Canadians finance all needed capital formation, if this were felt to be a desirable objective, without drastic changes or a slower growth rate?

As discussed in Chapter 4, there are various motives for foreign fin- ancing of domestic capital formation. The desire of nonresident-owned firms to secure access to certain raw materials found in Canada, the desire to sell in the Canadian or Commonwealth markets and jump the tariff barriers, the profit prospects in Canada, and the relatively high interest rates all tend to raise the proportion of capital formation financed from external sources. All of these are subject to policy changes in terms of tariffs, interest rates, restrictions on sale of securities to non-residents, differential tax treatment of foreign-owned enterprises, and so on. In- deed, some of these policies have explicitly been introduced to reduce the extent of foreign ownership.[21]

Let us assume that the aim is to reduce the foreign contribution to gross capital formation to negligible proportions. During the late 1950's estimates were that foreign financing constituted roughly 30 per cent of gross investment. This implies that domestic savings would have to be raised by about this proportion if financial inflows from abroad are to be reduced without curtailing the amount of gross investment.

The possibilities of raising gross savings by this amount need to be examined. During the 1956–61 period aggregate gross domestic savings averaged about $7 billion (including that portion of government revenues devoted to capital formation) while gross domestic investment (i.e., excluding net foreign investment) averaged over $8 billion. The gap, including the foreign deficit, amounted to an annual average of about

[21]For details see Canadian-American Committee, *Recent Canadian and U.S. Government Actions Affecting U.S. Investment in Canada*, National Planning Association (Washington, DC, 1964).

$2 billion, which was provided by foreign sources. However, the relatively low level of savings in Canada was due mainly to the sluggish growth from 1956 to 1961. If GNE had averaged $3 to $4 billion more, in current dollars, and if the savings ratio had been about 18 per cent, as consistent with past experience, instead of 16 per cent, then gross domestic savings as defined above would have worked out to be slightly in excess of gross domestic investment. It is clear that the extent of excess capacity in the Canadian economy from 1956–61 would easily have permitted $3–$4 billion more output valued at current prices and the actual savings ratio of only some 16 per cent is well below previous savings rates. The feasible conjunction of both greater output and a higher propensity to save, would more than have sufficed for the financing of actual domestic investment, ignoring the foreign balance.

But it is one thing to suggest that savings could have increased enough to cover actual investment and quite another to assume that with larger output investment would have been the same. In addition, part of the increase of savings would have emanated from nonresident-owned firms. Thus, the above exercise does not permit any firm conclusion regarding the extent of needed foreign financing even assuming a higher average GNE and an increase in the savings ratio. It does, however, suggest that with more rapid growth and a return to levels of the propensity to save consistent with past experience, the Canadian economy is capable of sustaining high and growing levels of investment with no drastic alteration in institutional patterns. If this is the case, then the extent of foreign financing is mainly a product of interest rate differentials, ease of access to Canadian vis-à-vis foreign capital markets, greater vigour and ability of foreign enterprises in identifying and exploiting economic opportunity in Canada, and the state of the foreign balance. It is not so much any inherent inability of Canadians to save enough to finance needed capital expenditures as it is the set of incentives provided in Canada to foreign capital and enterprise which induces relatively large amounts of foreign ownership and finance.

In particular, if Canadian authorities had pursued an easier monetary policy in the latter 1950's, this would have raised the growth rate and likewise the amount of domestic savings. This action would however have had two divergent effects upon the incentives of non-residents to provide finance for Canadian investment and of Canadians to borrow abroad. In the first place, with lower interest rates, the incentive of non-residents to buy Canadian securities would be reduced, if interest rates in other countries remained what they were. On the other hand rapid growth in Canada is normally associated with an investment boom which in the past has generally relied heavily on imports of parts and machinery. Since much of this goes to foreign-owned enterprises located in Canada, the financing of it comes from or is arranged by the parent company located outside of Canada. Thus foreign capital inflows are closely associated with rising Canadian growth rates.

In addition, rapid growth in Canada has generally been associated with an increase in imports greater than the rise in exports which makes net foreign investment (exports less imports) negative and thus requires additional foreign finance or reduction in holdings of foreign exchange or gold.

Even abstracting exchange rate fluctuation and changes in price levels in the domestic economy, there are divergent forces affecting foreign capital inflows. If the boom is strong enough relative at least to Canada's two major trading partners, the US and UK, lower interest rates in Canada are unlikely to offset the stimulating impact of higher profit prospects in Canada and a rising current account deficit. But if the boom continues long enough, this will tend to raise interest rates, increase the relative value of the Canadian dollar, assuming a free exchange rate—or decrease reserves if the exchange rate is pegged—and raise prices and costs in Canada. Especially will this be the case if the rate of growth of total spending in Canada impinges upon physical capacity. The increase in the exchange rate of the Canadian dollar and the rise in Canadian costs and prices will adversely affect exports and stimulate imports thereby augmenting the current account deficit unless capital imports are discouraged, to a greater degree than other imports are encouraged by lower costs in terms of the appreciated Canadian dollar. The combination then of high domestic interest rates and rising current account deficits will raise both the *incentive* of foreigners to lend to Canada and the *incentive* of Canadian borrowers to seek cheaper sources of finance, despite a rise in domestic savings, and will increase the *need* for Canada to borrow more from abroad.

But if the investment boom tapers off and if costs begin encroaching upon prices, profit prospects and the growth rate will both diminish and lead to a reversal of the above-mentioned processes which in turn will reduce both the need and incentive to borrow abroad.

The above interrelated set of adjustment processes are rendered all the more complex by the admixture of short- and long-run influences, occurrences in other countries, and policies with respect to tariffs and interest rates pursued in Canada. To unravel those factors that positively influence foreign capital inflows from those that have a negative impact and then assess quantitatively the net result is scarcely feasible. It is not, therefore, possible to determine empirically the effects of policies designed to reduce the degree of foreign capital inflows. However, this much may be said: such capital inflows are part of the mechanism of Canadian economic growth and are essential to prevent any long-term imbalance between exports and imports. But if we assume that current account imbalances are kept minimal by other means, then to eliminate foreign financing of economic activity in Canada would entail strict embargoes on foreign finance. The impact of such a policy would be to force reliance upon the domestic capital market. Since this is less developed than, say, the New York or London capital markets, in the sense that large-scale borrowing would be more difficult to arrange due to the smaller size and possibly greater fragmentation of the Canadian market, then, even if interest rates were no higher, even if Canadian savings were equal in amount to planned investment, and Canadians did not invest abroad, there would be delays and uncertainties in negotiating the necessary finance. Furthermore, if it is the case that Canadian entrepreneurs are somewhat less aggressive in seeking out and exploiting economic opportunity in Canada than their US counterparts, the net effect would be to slow down the over-all growth rate until such time as the domestic capital market achieves characteristics comparable to those in the US and the UK and entrepreneurial attitudes in Canada change. It is one thing to argue that it is *possible* for a small, relatively affluent society to save enough to finance a level of investment adequate to sustain a full employment rate of growth. It is quite another to assume that there would be no difficulty in channelling the sources of funds to those needing them and to assume that the investment "needs" would be rigorously sought and exploited in an uncertain environment especially against a background hitherto characterized by a relatively high degree of caution.

Nor does it make much sense to refrain from borrowing or lending abroad when economic circumstances warrant. Furthermore, to prevent all foreign capital inflows would require a degree of restrictionism and inconvertibility of the Canadian dollar that is inconsistent with the traditional Canadian approach to free trade. If free trade in goods and services benefits Canada, as it demonstrably does, given all the exportable surpluses especially of agricultural produce and minerals, a policy of excessive restrictionism in foreign finance can only be viewed as an economic waste that at the same time would probably jeopardize the growth rate, even if domestic interest rates could be held down. Since a rise in domestic interest rates would doubtless ensue from restricting foreign capital inflows, the probability that the Canadian rate of economic growth would be lower is considerably enhanced.

This does not mean that foreign ownership of Canadian assets is an unmixed blessing. It raises all the issues of foreign control previously discussed in Chapter 4 and the growing problems of dividend and interest payments abroad. What the foregoing does suggest is that until the Canadian capital market becomes more fully developed and Canadian investment propensities become less cautious, the cost of attempts to choke off foreign financing will be a slower rate of economic development. Of course, economic growth depends on much more than those factors discussed in the present section and it is clear that many things might be done in other segments of the domestic economy to offset, at least partially, whatever adverse impact a reduction of foreign financing might have. None the less, since increased foreign capital inflows are both cause and consequence of growing Canadian economic prospects, it would seem undesirable from an economic point of view to jeopardize the latter by excessive concern with the former. However appealing the foreign domination issue is to politicians both in and out of office, the economic argument is at best equivocal. Furthermore attempts to legislate against foreign-controlled enterprises have serious effects upon domestic capital markets, as the Budget Speech of June 1963 amply illustrated. Since a fuller development of the Canadian capital market is one way to promote greater Canadian participation therein, detailed restrictions against foreign finance is a cumbersome and perhaps self-defeating way to bring about a result that may have political and nationalistic appeal but adverse economic consequences.

Appendix to Chapter 7

A NOTE ON THE CAPITAL–OUTPUT RATIO

The use of the capital-output ratio as a technique to deduce needed or warranted rates of growth of output, implies a close causal relationship between investment and output. As such it is highly mechanistic and neglects the institutional and other factors which intervene between an act of investment and the assumed rise in output. A plant may be built but for many reasons not used or used very inefficiently. The weather can have a large effect on output irrespective of the amount of investment, especially in agriculture. Furthermore, there is the problem of the length of the gestation period: That is, over what period will output eventually emerge? There are many items of investment that will not yield output until some time later. The dating of investment and output is a crucial matter in the present context. The magnitude of the realized capital-output ratio depends as well upon the sectoral allocation and phasing of investment, the kind of investments made, institutional factors which effect efficiency, the degree of excess capacity existing prior to the additional capacity, and all the other influences on output which may be deemed largely independent of investment (e.g., the weather, managerial and labour efficiency, and so on). This means, then, that the aggregate capital-output ratio needs to be interpreted with great care since its magnitude is in reality a product of a vast variety of circumstances. Output depends upon much more than capital. As Frankel puts it, "as a general statement of the resources required in production, it [the capital-output ratio] is positively wrong, as any one-factor production function must be."[1]

Nevertheless, the concept of the capital-output ratio has been at the centre of most discussions of economic growth since the Second World War and has been used by many distinguished economists. It should not therefore be lightly dismissed. The present appendix will examine briefly its use and limitations in analyses of the phenomenon of economic growth.

We may conveniently concentrate upon a simplified version of the Harrod-Domar approach.[2] An act of investment not only generates additional income ($=$ output) but also additional capacity which, if it is to be sustained according to the theory, requires an increase in demand. Thus if we designate the propensity to save by S^*, and the incremental capital-output ratio by k, it is clear that if all savings are invested in an *ex ante* sense, the capacity of the economy will rise by $(S/k)Y$ (where Y is income in any period). If this capacity is to be used aggregate demand must then rise by this amount

[1]M. Frankel, "The Production Function: Allocation and Growth," *American Economic Review*, Dec. 1962, p. 996.

[2]See R. F. Harrod, *Towards a Dynamic Economics* (London, 1952); E. D. Domar, "Capital Expansion Rate of Growth and Employment," *Econometrica*, April, 1946.

otherwise the system falls back or inflation occurs. In short, the increment in demand ($\triangle Y$) must just be equal to the increment in capacity if fluctuations are to be avoided. Thus:

(1) $$\triangle Y = (S^*/k)Y \text{ or } (\triangle Y/Y) = S^*/k.$$

This equation is to be viewed as an equilibrium condition in the sense that the "warranted rate of growth" must be consistent with the propensity to save and the capital-output ratio so that actual investment in any period is equal to planned investment.[3] If the actual rate of growth deviates from the ratio of the assumed psychological constant S^* to the assumed technological constant k, there will be either a cumulative decline in Y or inflation. As Bruton puts it, the ratio of S^*/k may be regarded as the rate of growth of income $\triangle Y/Y$ "*required* to use newly created capital" or as "the maximum *allowable* rate of growth possible without inflation."[4]

In this simple form, it is presumed that the actual investment in any fiscal period is determined by the increment in income over the preceding period multiplied (or "accelerated") by the capital-output ratio, k. Thus for equilibrium we required that[5]:

$$S^*Y_t = k(Y_t - Y_{t-1}).$$

In this form, which was Harrod's original conception, k is the accelerator coefficient and all investment is of the induced variety. However, much investment is autonomous and in Harrod's more complete version the warranted rate of growth is modified by the amount of such autonomous investment, A. When this factor is introduced the warranted rate of growth is less and may be designated as follows[6]:

$$\triangle Y/Y = (S - A)/k.$$

But this changes the entire picture for if A is part of investment, as it is by definition, then the aggregate capital-output ratio is no longer k: rather it is $(k \triangle Y + A)/\triangle Y$. Thus k in the Harrodian version is *only* a marginal capital-output ratio under the assumption that all investment is induced. It is clear that Harrod was interested mainly in k as an accelerator coefficient and not as a measure of the capital-output ratio, since he later inserts

[3]This equation, Harrod's "fundamental equation," is also an identity in the *ex post* sense and may be derived as follows. Given the identity of S and I *ex post* we have: $S = I$. Divide by Y to obtain $S/Y = I/Y = \triangle K/Y$, where $I = \triangle K$ (the increase in stock of capital). Taking $(S/Y = (\triangle K/Y)$ and multiplying the right side by $\triangle Y/\triangle Y$ we have $(S/Y) = (\triangle K/Y)$ $(\triangle Y/\triangle Y) = (\triangle Y)/(Y)$ $(\triangle K)/(\triangle Y)$. But $S/Y = S^*$ and $\triangle K/\triangle Y = k$, thus $\triangle Y/Y = S^*/k$. If, however, the original equation of $S = I$ is construed as an equilibrium condition, the "fundamental equation" should similarly be viewed.

[4]H. J. Bruton, "Growth Models and Underdeveloped Economies," *Journal of Political Economy*, Aug. 1955, p. 323.

[5]This is, of course, equivalent to the earlier equation since it can be rewritten as $S/k = (Y_t - Y_{t-1})/Y_t = \triangle Y/Y$.

[6]Harrod's original version split up what we have lumped together as A and included also exports less imports. For simplicity the above version is adequate. For a more recent discussion of the relationship between autonomous and induced investment see D. Hamberg and C. L. Schultze, "Autonomous *vs.* Induced Investment: The Interrelatedness of Parameters in Growth Models," *Economic Journal*, vol. LXXI, March, 1961, pp. 53–65.

induced investment into his fundamental equation thereby implying an altered capital-output ratio with the same accelerator coefficient. Indeed, the inclusion of A considerably modifies the instability principle, since it implies that with a larger amount of savings absorbed into investment unrelated to current growth, a smaller amount of savings is left to be "absorbed" by the accelerator principle.

If we abandon its accelerator implication and assume the reverse causation (i.e., that investment induces output increments or at least requires them in order to be sustained rather than the other way around) then the capital-output ratio may be used as formulated earlier and a warranted rate of growth equivalent to S^*/k is implied. But if much of the capital involved in k is autonomous, say government investment, then it need not be "depressed by the fact that demand does not grow *pari passu* with the growth of capacity in the public sector."[7] Indeed, much of private investment is made in anticipation of future demand changes. Thus it is evident that unless expectations are specified and, more importantly, the time span over which results are to be realized is made clear, there exists no such thing as a unique warranted rate of growth even should S^* and k prove to be rigidly fixed. Much depends upon the amount of investment deemed autonomous and the period of gestation. Of course, the very distinction between autonomous and induced investment is not subject to a high degree of quantitative precision and in fact is not always conceptually clear, which lends a rather mystical air to any concept of a "warranted" growth rate.[8]

Moreover, the warranted growth rate applies only to *capital* capacity. It is "warranted" in the sense that this is the actual rate of growth of income necessary to have the capital stock fully employed. A lower actual rate of growth implies "over-production" since, given the constants S^* and k, *ex post*

[7]Hamberg and Schultze, "Autonomous *vs.* Induced Investment," p. 55.

[8]Indeed Yeager argues that "the distinction between autonomous and induced investment has almost no operational meaning." (Leland B. Yeager, "Some Questions about Growth Economics," *American Economic Review*, March 1959, p. 59, n. 13.) The conceptual confusion is evident in many places. For example, Hamberg and Schultze ("Autonomous *vs.* Induced Investment," p. 54) construe induced investment as taking place in response to *either* actual or *expected* increases in demand. Making some investment responsive to expected demand changes over some unspecified time period supports Yeager's assertion. Furthermore, as Ackley points out, "the allegedly technological relationship which links an increased output to a greater requirement for capital goods does not . . . support a link between the *level of output* and the rate of investment . . . [although] the two are frequently confused, as for example by S. Weintraub, *Income and Employment Analysis* (Pitman, 1951), pp. 127–131. K. Kurihara, in K. Kurihara, ed., *An Introduction to Keynesian Dynamics* (Columbia University Press, 1956), pp. 88 ff., also calls the idea of this section the 'acceleration principle,' which seems unfortunate." (Gardner Ackley, *Macroeconomic Theory* (New York, 1961), p. 337 and n. 16.) Even with an unambiguous definition of the accelerator, its usefulness as an analytical tool has frequently been questioned: the usual caveats are outlined briefly in Ackley, *ibid.*, pp. 492–3 and A. W. Stonier and D. C. Hague, *A Textbook of Economic Theory* (London, 1953), pp. 225–32, and need not be repeated here. There is also considerable ambiguity in the use of the accelerator as a capital coefficient in the sense that it is not always clear whether it is a *behavioural* or *technological* relationship.

I would exceed *ex ante I*; hence the rate of investment and growth would decline assuming all *I* is induced. Conversely, if income grew by more than the warranted rate this would imply under-production since *ex post I* would be less than *ex ante I* and a further spurt in investment would occur until the system bubbled over into inflation after the limits to production imposed by available resources had been reached. In short, the warranted rate of growth pertains to full employment of capital.[9] But what of full employment of labour?

It is possible to develop a similar analysis with respect to labour. Assume the labour force is increasing by *l* per cent and output per worker by *w* per cent. If full employment of labour is to be maintained then aggregate demand must rise by $l + w + lw$. This is likewise both a required and maximum allowable growth rate. Thus to have full employment of *both* labour and capital income must grow at a rate equal to both $l + w + lw$ and (S/k). in other words

$$(S/k) = l + w + lw = (\triangle Y/Y)$$

is an equilibrium condition which yields a kind of "dual" warranted growth rate. If there are discrepancies between (S/k) and $l + w + lw$, then we encounter difficulties in either the degree of labour or capital utilization which presumably causes the system to "stumble" in some sense. But as Fellner has argued:

The condition here formulated is necessary but insufficient even in the crude version of the theory. Furthermore, even the crude version should recognize that credit policies may increase or decrease the rate of growth of the equilibrium output, given the stock-output ratio . . . The necessary refinements of the theory are connected mainly with the fact that the capital-output ratio and the rate of growth of output may adjust to the requirements of equilibrium. Even the possibility that the equilibrium value of the propensity to save might adjust should not be left out of account. . . . [The capital-output ratio] changes with the changing composition of output. . . . It also changes with the characteristics of innovations. . . .[10]

Furthermore, all the variables in the equation are subject to policy and hence not fixed, intractable constants. Some growth models, of course, allow for variations in S^*, *k*, and so on, but these are deemed to take place in a reasonably predictable way in response to an assumed set of institutional arrangements and individual reaction patterns. However none of the variables is rigidly fixed in the sense of being absolutely impervious to policy and hence are not predictably determinate. Even the *k* is not really a technological constant: it is a summation of the output in various industries in response to a particular investment allocation. The latter is peculiarly subject to governmental policy involving not only direct allotment of capital to particular industries but taxation, subsidy, and import policies designed to stimulate some industries more than others. Nor can the empirical evidence

[9]We need hardly remark that the phrase "full employment of capital" is a very elusive one. Indeed, the notion of "capital capacity" is exceedingly elastic and scarcely subject to precise estimation.

[10]William Fellner, "The Capital-Output Ratio in Dynamic Economies," in *Money, Trade and Economic Growth: Essays in Honor of John Henry Williams* (New York, 1954, pp. 116–17.

pertaining mainly to the US and the UK which indicates a high degree of secular constancy of the capital-output ratio, be construed as proof that this must also be the case in Canada or any other country. Indeed, the reasons adduced for the apparent constancy of the aggregate capital-output are far more revealing of the process of economic growth than the alleged constancy itself, even assuming the data to be reasonably accurate.

Thus the Harrod-Domar approach to economic growth involving the use of capital-output coefficients (often erroneously equated with the accelerator principle) has been severely criticized as not having much relevance on a wide variety of grounds.[11] Furthermore, the model is based upon the constancy of the various ratios whereas it is everywhere the aim of policy to alter these. It cannot help much in explaining economic growth to assume constancy in the very variables which will be changed in the growth process itself either autonomously or by deliberate planning. The entire approach therefore involves a degree of abstraction from the key determinants of growth which renders it little better than a mathematical exercise. Ackley points out, after analysing and criticizing the Harrod-Domar models, that he has said "practically nothing about the basic cultural determinants of growth, including the factors of motivation, values, economic organization, the skills of workers and managers, and the ingenuity of innovators and promotors, the willingness to invest resources in basic 'pure research' and in education, and a host of other factors."[12] In short, the Harrod-Domar approach abstracts from the most vital elements required to generate or initiate economic development.[13]

For all of these reasons, plus data limitations, we have not made extensive use of the capital-output ratio in Canada. Although in the last section of Chapter 7 dealing with "needed" amounts of investment we have employed certain estimates of the capital coefficient, it cannot be stressed too much that the results are subject to all of the foregoing strictures and must be construed only as the crudest sort of approximation and then only "if all other things remain equal."

[11]See for example, Ackley, *Macroeconomic Theory*, pp. 506 and 567, and especially Yeager, "Some Questions about Growth Economics," pp. 53–63.

[12]Ackley, *Macroeconomic Theory*, p. 567. This point is also stressed by Bert F. Hoselitz in *Sociological Aspects of Economic Growth* (Glencoe, Ill., 1960), esp. chap. 2.

[13]Another general approach uses a Cobb-Douglas production function of the form $Y = aK^\alpha L^\beta$ where K and L are the quantities of capital and labour respectively and a, α, β assumed constants where $(\alpha + \beta)$ may equal, exceed, or be less than 1. There are many difficulties with respect to this kind of approach such as changes in the *quality* of capital and labour, the magnitude of the constants, and so on. However, in this formulation, the capital-output ratio is not a determining variable. Rather it is a resultant of the various changes made in K and L as well as α and β. In short, while one can easily deduce average and marginal capital-output ratios from the production function, these are endogenous variables and are not used as determinants in the sense of the Harrod-Domar analysis. Since we are primarily interested in the capital-output ratio as a significant factor in determining the actual, warranted, or natural rate of growth, further discussion of growth models in terms of a Cobb-Douglas production function will not be undertaken here. Frankel, "The Production Function," has related the two approaches and achieved a more realistic synthesis.

8
MANAGEMENT, PRODUCTIVITY, AND RESEARCH

The fourth factor or agent of production is defined as the one that brings together land, labour, and capital in the proper place and in right proportions for productive activity. This is the agent that takes the initiative, makes the vital decisions regarding the activities of the enterprise, and to some extent bears a large part of the risks of failure in an uncertain environment. This obviously crucial function has been variously referred to as organization, entrepreneurship, management, and so on, although these terms are not necessarily used synonymously. While, however, the function may be easy enough to define, the activity itself is impossible to quantify. Entrepreneurial or managerial ability, that is, the degree of talent that the organizing factor has in performing this function (or rather these functions), cannot be measured in terms of man-hours, kilowatt hours, capital stock, or any other simple unit of measurement. Only the results relating to profits, productivity, and the like can be assessed and even these cannot legitimately be imputed solely to organizational talent, ability, or training.

Given these difficulties on the empirical side, in this chapter we will discuss chiefly technology and productivity which, although related to management, cannot be deemed to be causally linked in any clear-cut or unambiguous fashion. However, it is worthwhile at the outset to provide some estimates of the number of people who may be designated as "managers." No definitive measure of the quality of Canadian managerial talent is possible, but some impressionistic comments and comparisons with the similar US factor of production will be made. Of some interest is the legal form and size of organization within which decision-making takes place and we shall present some of the evidence on this score as well. It is clear that these measures are simply proxies and in no way represent any definitive characterization of that elusive agent, management. But the evidence to be presented below may help in a rough way to delineate broadly some aspects of management and its environment in Canada.

It is, however, to the *results* of entrepreneurship that we must look in assessing both its quality and quantity in Canada: thus the emphasis of this chapter will be on technology, including research and development, and productivity.

MANAGEMENT

MANAGERIAL SUPPLY

Some evidence of the number of employed people designated as "managerial" is presented in Table 8.1. Conceptually, this group includes persons whose duties primarily relate to the direction or management of organizations, either private or public, or of subdivisions of them. The individual's relationship to the organization could be that of employee or of proprietor.

Included in the group are directors, executives, managers and working proprietors of enterprises, managers and superintendents of establishments, departments, branches and agencies, and public administrators. Specifically, retail and wholesale dealers are included. Excluded from the group are professionals in private practice, self-employed craftsmen, tradesmen, farmers and other primary workers, and foremen and overseers.[1]

Using this definition there were some 581,000 persons in the managerial category as of 1962 and these accounted for 9.3 per cent of the employed labour force in that year. The general trend appears to be fairly steadily upward as far as the number of managers are concerned and somewhat less so in terms of proportion of the employed labour force. There are, however, some rather sharp declines in both the absolute numbers and the ratios. The former is particularly difficult to explain especially since people in this occupational classification normally are not released when downturns in the level of economic activity occur. It is doubtless the case that much of the sharp contraction in numbers particularly in 1948, 1954, 1955, 1958, and 1960 involves business failures of individual proprietors and possibly a redefinition of status as well with the same managerial function being performed in another

[1]Definition supplied by DBS.

TABLE 8.1

Trends in Managerial Supply*
1947-62

Year	Number of people (000)	Percentage of employed labour force
1947	449	8.9
1948	254	5.1
1949	375	7.5
1950	410	8.1
1951	422	8.2
1952	459	8.8
1953	496	9.4
1954	476	9.1
1955	443	8.3
1956	452	8.1
1957	509	8.8
1958	494	8.6
1959	534	9.2
1960	505	8.4
1961	539	8.8
1962	581	9.3

SOURCE: DBS, *The Labour Force: Industry and Occupation.*
*Newfoundland included in estimates from 1950 only.

occupational category. It could, of course, represent serious under-employment but the figures are highly suspect.

The general upward trend, however, seems to be reasonable and roughly correlates with the over-all growth of the economy in the post-war period. It is not possible to say whether Canada has enough managers since the qualitative aspect is so important and, in any event, the definition and measurement of this agent of production are far from adequate.

MANAGERIAL QUALITY

If the quantitative measure of the number of managers leaves much to be desired, any assessment of managerial quality is even more so and must be entirely impressionistic. Even if such objective indices of performance as profits, costs, or growth, existed for various firms or industries in a form rendering them comparable with other countries, this would still be an inadequate test since so many other factors necessarily condition the actual economic outcome of a particular firm. Yet the general impression exists that the quality of Canadian management is below that of the US, that Canadian managers, capable as they may be compared with some overseas companies, are a little less dynamic, flexible, and daring than their US counterparts. The Canadian attitude towards risk-taking in general appears to be less aggressive than that below the border[2] and, if the managerial class is correctly viewed as one of the more dynamic groups in any society, this would reflect upon Canadian management, at least so far as comparison with the US is concerned. A wide variety of impressionistic evidence seems to support this general view. As Fullerton and Hampson put it:

The composite picture which emerges . . . while by no means entirely con-clusive, suggests that there is some truth in the view that management of Canadian secondary industry as a whole is somewhat less progressive and forward-looking than that of its competitors in the United States, although this is clearly not true in many individual cases. In large part the relative weaknesses of Canadian management may be due to the greater shortages of trained personnel in this country, reflecting both our more recent indus-trialization and our more rapid growth.[3]

Or again,

We have met many executives in Canada and in the United States and we feel that American management is made up of a quantity of specialists which is often not the case in Canada again due to the size of certain industries. We feel that Canadian management has much to learn from contact with United States management. . . . On the other hand, our Canadian manage-ment often has problems with design, market analysis, sales, labour relations which all have to be handled by the same individual. Granted these problems are often less complex but they have to be considered just the same. Generally speaking, we would say that you (the United States) have a better quality of management but that this management is made up of many specialists in various lines of endeavour.[4]

Indeed some of the institutional aspects of the Canadian economy may reinforce whatever relative degree of inflexibility or inertia exists in the managerial class. The high degree of concentration of industry (examined below), which implies, though does not necessarily cause, a lower degree of competition domestically, may inculcate less of a com-petitive spirit. If the real monopoly profit is the "quiet life," this may affect the attitudes of Canadian managers. Again, the protective tariff for secondary manufacturing, the relatively easy and preferred access to

[2]For a brief discussion see I. Brecher and S. S. Reisman, *Canada–United States Economic Relations*, a report prepared for the RCCEP (Ottawa, 1957), pp. 121ff.
[3]D. H. Fullerton and H. A. Hampson, *Canadian Secondary Manufacturing Industry*, a study prepared for the RCCEP (Ottawa, 1957), p. 141.
[4]John H. Young, "Some Aspects of Canadian Economic Development," chap. v, unpublished PhD thesis, Cambridge University, 1955.

Commonwealth markets, the extent of non-resident control, the lack of vigorous enforcement of anti-combines laws,[5] these, and above all the small number of firms in any given Canadian industry, which makes informal collusion and anti-competitive practices easy to achieve, are doubtless more important determinants of Canadian managerial talent than any ethnic, racial, or nationalistic mystique.[6]

With economic development over time, however, it is possible that whatever skill differential exists between the general level of US and Canadian managerial talent may be narrowing. It has been suggested that

... the traditional lag of Canadian businessmen behind their American counterparts has been further reduced by the development of improved travel and communication facilities, the attendance of Canadians at American management schools, the opening of Canadian schools of business administration, and the wide dissemination of American management techniques and ideas through such media as business publications, journals and conferences.[7]

These, of course, are merely non-empirical observations and do nothing but convey what is a general impression, although there seems little reason to doubt the validity of the over-all characterization which is consistent with the somewhat different institutional structure in the US as indicated below.

The Economic Elite. If the foregoing assessment of managerial quality is necessarily tenuous, it is at least possible to provide some details of the characteristics of what has been referred to as the "economic élite." A study by John Porter[8] of 170 "dominant" corporations in Canada, indicated that of 1,304 directors, 907 were Canadian residents. This latter group is what he refers to as the economic élite. These are clearly not "managers" as construed in the previous section although some of them obviously fit this category. What the economic élite chiefly represents is the high-income group who control and to some extent manage a very significant share of Canadian business. Porter's study of the Canadian-born élite, including all chartered bank directors, revealed some features that may have relevance to the accessibility of élite status

5A recent study reports that a "review of the administration of the [Combines Investigation] Act between 1952 and 1960 indicates that the policy has been one of causing the minimum inconvenience to business that is compatible with avoiding the political stigma of being in favour of combines." G. Rosenbluth and H. G. Thorburn, "Canadian Anti-Combines Administration, 1952–1960," *CJEPS*, Nov. 1961 p. 501.

6Some features of the "economic élite" are described in the following section.

7Fullerton and Hampson *Canadian Secondary Manufacturing Industry*, p. 143.

8"Concentration of Economic Power and the Economic Elite in Canada," *CJEPS*, May 1956, pp. 199–220, and "The Economic Elite and the Social Structure in Canada," *ibid.*, Aug. 1957, pp. 376–94.

and thus indirectly may be related to managerial quality. He found that about two-thirds of those in his sample had received education beyond the high school level, either in a specialized profession but chiefly in university at a time when less than 4 per cent of the 18-to-21-year-olds in Canada attended college. Over one-third had also been enrolled in private secondary schools. Racially and linguistically, the élite is almost completely English-speaking of British origin despite the fact that this group constitutes less than half the general population. The only other ethnic group of more than negligible proportion was French, but this group constituted less than 7 per cent although French Canadians comprise about 30 per cent of the Canadian population.[9] As would be expected from this ethnic composition, the religious affiliation was overwhelmingly Protestant (86 per cent), with Catholics accounting for about 13 per cent of the élite and Jews barely one per cent. Furthermore, almost all the French Canadians in the sample were Roman Catholics. Since about 43 per cent of Canada's population is Catholic, this suggests that "the economic system does not provide Catholics with a very wide avenue of upward mobility."[10]

The general picture that emerges from Porter's study is that a substantial proportion of economic activity in Canada is "dominated" by a relatively small number of college-trained, English-speaking Protestants of British ancestry. While therefore Canada is a plural society in many respects, economic power is highly concentrated in the hands of a particular group which, it seems fair to say, shares a common value system and is otherwise closely interconnected and more homogeneous than the general population. Precisely how these characteristics of the economic élite relate to progress and efficiency is impossible to say without much further study. But the implications of Porter's evidence suggest that the possession of certain educational, ethnic, linguistic, and religious characteristics may be important conditions on the road to economic success. The importance of these factors, with the exception of education, will probably be reduced if more vigorous rates of growth are experienced in the future. Under more buoyant economic conditions, opportunities expand and there is less rigidity in the economic and social structure since a gain by one group is less likely to be at the expense of another. The reverse is true of a relatively static situation.

[9]Indeed it is reported that even in Montreal about 80 per cent of the value of corporate assets was controlled by English-speaking Canadians and that the great majority of places of work of French Canadians are English-owned (Phillippe Garigue, "Organisation sociale et valeur culturelles canadiennes-français," *CJEPS*, May 1962, p. 198.)

[10]"The Economic Élite and the Social Structure in Canada," p. 387.

It is impossible to document any close connection between the fore-going features of Canada's economic élite and the quality of Canadian management, although there are many possible lines of interrelationship. For example, one inference from Porter's evidence is that Canada has been drawing its managerial talent from a rather restricted segment of the Canadian population. Since there is no scientific reason for believing that this segment by virtue of cultural or natural capacity possesses any inherent superiority in terms of managerial or entrepreneurial capabili-ties, the implication is that the Canadian economy is failing to tap poten-tial resources for which an obvious need exists. Unlike natural resources, the failure to exploit the available supply of managerial potential from other than the group identified above cannot be attributed to deficiency of demand. Although comparable data are not available for the US, it seems that there is much less homogeneity within the American class of managers. The US has long been proud of its "melting pot" tradition which has apparently carried over into management as well, with the obvious exception of negroes. If true, this would reinforce the above impressions concerning the superior quality of US managerial resources in the sense that recruitment of US managers is less restricted than Canadian by religious affiliation and ethnic origin. Again, the position of the negro in the US is an exception, but this aspect of the colour problem is scarcely relevant to Canada. It is clear that much more study of this whole matter is required before reaching any more than highly tentative conclusions. We cannot therefore pursue the matter further in the present volume.

However, there is doubtless some more tangible connection between the managerial quality and the concentration of industry in Canada, even though the precise relationship is complex and tenuous. In the following section some of the evidence on firm size and concentration is presented.

FIRM SIZE AND CONCENTRATION

It is estimated that there are over half a million separate business firms in Canada (*c.* 1960)[11] which vary in size from less than $25,000 in assets and employing only 2 or 3 persons to giant corporations with assets exceeding $100 million and employing several thousand workers. A very large proportion of business assets in Canada is, not surprisingly, con-centrated in the largest firms. Rosenbluth has estimated that roughly

[11]This estimate virtually coincides with the number of "managers" previously shown. This should be taken to cast doubt mainly on the concept of "manager" used in the statistical tabulation rather than on the number of firms estimated above.

one hundred firms have assets in excess of $100 million each and that 57 of these are non-financial corporations (i.e., those whose main assets are physical means of production).[12] In 1956 these 57 non-financial giants owned about 38 per cent of the total value of real assets (land, buildings, equipment, and inventory) of all non-financial corporations and about 20 per cent of all real business assets including those of unincorporated firms.[13]

US data suggest that the 100 largest firms in manufacturing, mining, and distribution (i.e., non-financial enterprises) owned approximately 30 per cent of all industrial assets in 1958. Thus, the degree of asset concentration in the US is less than in Canada in the sense that 100 largest US firms control a smaller proportion of total corporate industrial assets in the US than the 57 largest Canadian firms in Canada.[14] Although there are many statistical pitfalls in such international comparisons, the two sets of data regarding asset concentration appear to be sufficiently comparable to warrant the conclusion of significantly greater concentration in Canada.[15]

Indeed, the figures for Canada even tend to understate the degree of concentration since they treat subsidiaries as separate entities. An attempt to take account of subsidiary-parent relationships suggests that in 1956, 44 privately owned non-financial firms "accounted for 44 per cent of the value of 'real' assets held by all privately owned non-financial corporations." Thus, concentration in terms of assets may be very much higher than in the United States.

If we examine concentration in terms of the proportion of output or employment in any industry accounted for by the largest four, six, or eight firms, similar conclusions emerge. The largest firms in Canada are

[12]G. Rosenbluth, "Concentration and Monopoly in the Canadian Economy" in M. Oliver, ed., *Social Purpose of Canada* (Toronto, 1961), p. 198.

[13]*Ibid.*, pp. 198–200. Four of the 57 firms are crown companies. Excluding these, the 53 remaining privately owned corporations owned about 29 per cent of all real, privately owned assets of non-financial corporations, one-quarter of the real assets of all corporations and roughly 14 per cent of the entire Canadian business economy.

[14]US data from N. R. Collins and L. E. Preston, "The Size Structure of Industrial Firms," *American Economic Review*, Dec. 1961, Table 1, p. 989.

[15]Rosenbluth's calculations are outlined carefully in the Appendix to "Concentration and Monopoly in the Canadian Economy," pp. 244–5 and, as far as the corporate sector is concerned, are comparable to those of Collins and Preston. One difficulty is the different coverage. The latter exclude utilities, services and so on while Rosenbluth's estimates include these. But, except for utilities, the degree of concentration of non-financial corporate assets is generally lower outside of the sectors included by Collins and Preston: hence, the different coverage is not apt to make the estimates sufficiently non-comparable to reverse the above conclusion.

heavily concentrated in manufacturing, transport, finance, mining, and utilities. These sectors together accounted for about half of GDP in 1961 or close to 60 per cent excluding government administration and defence. Earlier evidence for manufacturing suggests that the degree of concentration in terms of output or employment is much higher in Canada than in the US for virtually all industries for which comparable data are available.[16] The data are summarized in Table 8.2. It should be noted that the Canadian concentration ratio is defined in terms of employment while that of the US is construed in terms of value of output. Past evidence suggests that output is generally more highly concentrated than employment which means that concentration in Canada is understated in Table 8.2 relative to the United States. Again the data refer to earlier years, 1948 in Canada and 1947 in the US. However, while some increase in over-all concentration may have occurred, it is probably not large over a twelve-to-fifteen year period and, as far as the US and Canada are concerned, the change is doubtless in the same direction in so far as comparable economic forces are at work in the two nations. Thus, while more up-to-date evidence of a directly comparable nature to that of Table 8.2 is not available, the data of the table may be deemed roughly relevant to the present situation although for particular industries there may be important changes. The evidence indicates a higher degree of concentration in Canada in the 41 industries listed in Table 8.2. The conclusion that concentration in manufacturing is higher in Canada than the US is thus warranted and indeed reinforced due to the bias through using employment as the indicator in Canada and output in the US. Other evidence for Canada alone is shown in Table 8.3 for 1954 which generally bears out the above observations. A similar pattern would appear to prevail in the other concentrated segments of Canadian industry due to the much smaller markets in Canada combined with only slight differences in average firm size. Indeed there are roughly eight times as many firms in a US industry than in the same industry's counterpart in Canada, at least as far as a sample from the manufacturing sector is concerned.[17]

The reasons for this degree of concentration relate primarily to two main factors. As already mentioned the size of the Canadian market in particular product lines clearly restricts the number of "optimal" sized firms despite the pressures exerted by the "miniature replica effect" discussed in Chapter 4. But beyond the relationship between efficient firm

[16]G. Rosenbluth, *Concentration in Canadian Manufacturing Industries* (Princeton, 1957), chap. IV.
[17]*Ibid.*, pp. 80–5.

TABLE 8.2

Concentration in Canada and the United States:
Selected Manufacturing Industries.
1947-48

Industry	Concentration of employment in Canada, 1948		Concentration of output (value) in US, 1947	
	Number of largest firms	Percentage of employment accounted for by given number of largest firms	Number of largest firms	Percentage of output accounted for by given number of largest firms
Foods, Beverages, Tobacco				
Malt and malt products	9	100	8	69
Starch and glucose (corn prod.)	10	100	20	99.5
Distilleries	7	96	8	86
Macaroni, etc.	14	100	20	56
Breweries (malt liquors)	8	79	8	30
Wine	3	58	4	26
Soft drinks	5	40	8	14
Bread and other bakery products	8	35	8	26
Prepared stock and poultry feeds	9	34	8	27
Condensed milk	12	80	20	76
Biscuits and crackers	7	68	4	71.5
Tobacco processing (tobacco stemming and redrying)	4	71	4	88
Textiles, Leather, Fur				
Cordage, rope, twine	6	93	8	53
Leather belting	3	62	4	44
Narrow fabrics	3	54	4	17
Woollen fabrics	3	28	4	28
Woollen yarn	7	65	8	34
Corsets	3	37	4	16
Fur dressing and dyeing	5	59	8	42
Canvas products	4	25	4	10
Leather tanning	7	49	8	39
Fur goods	3	6	4	3
Cotton and jute bags (textile bags)	3	37	4	53
Wood and Paper				
Roofing paper	3	60	4	42
Excelsior	10	100	20	88
Boat building	20	44	20	52.5
Metals				
Pig Iron* (blast furnaces)	4	100	4	67
Primary aluminum	1	100	3	100
Ship building	4	42	4	42

*Canadian data based on capacity of equipment.

TABLE 8.2 (*continued*)

Industry	Concentration of employment in Canada 1948		Concentration of output (value) in US, 1947	
	Number of largest firms	Percentage of employment accounted for by given number of largest firms	Number of largest firms	Percentage of output accounted for by given number of largest firms
Nonmetallic minerals				
Gypsum products	5	100	8	94
Abrasive products	5	96	4; 8	49; 56
Petroleum refining	3	80	4	37
Asbestos products	3	64	4	57.5
Chemicals				
Matches	4	100	4	83
Printing ink	8	86	8	69
Paints and varnishes	6	49	8	36
Soap	3; 16	75; 94	4; 20	79; 93
Compressed gases	6	95	8	88
Hardwood distillation	2	100	4	72
Miscellaneous				
Umbrellas	3	84	4	22
Buttons	5	68	8	32

SOURCE: Gideon Rosenbluth, *Concentration in Canadian Manufacturing Industries* (Princeton, 1957), Table 25, pp. 77-9.

size and market size, which is a very difficult thing to pinpoint with much accuracy, there is the institutional fact that antitrust enforcement in Canada has been much weaker than in the US. This is especially true as regards mergers. Indeed, it is probably not too much to say that the Canadian approach to the so-called monopoly problem has been so weak as to have had an imperceptible effect upon market structure and little more influence upon market practices. The amendments in this regard during the Diefenbaker administration have further weakened Canada's anti-monopoly legislation and enforcement.[18]

There are, of course, great numbers of small firms in such sectors as trade, services, and agriculture (including forestry and fishing) as in the United States. But, in general, the evidence suggests that the degree of concentration of assets, output, and employment is higher in Canada

[18]For a brief review of Canadian antitrust laws see George W. Wilson, "How Effective Are our Antitrust Laws?" *Business Quarterly*, fall 1959, pp. 169–74. A more recent and extensive survey has been made by G. Rosenbluth and H. G. Thorburn, *Canadian Anti-Combines Administration* (Toronto, 1963).

TABLE 8.3

Concentration of Control in Some
Leading Canadian Manufacturing and
Primary Industries
1954

Industry	Percentage of net value added accounted for by six largest firms
Petroleum	
Crude production	68
Refining	93
Mining, smelting and refining	
Nickel-copper	100*
Lead-zinc	86
Copper-gold	88
Iron ore	100*
Aluminum†	100
Asbestos	94
Gypsum	97
Other manufacturing	
Pulp and paper	46
Chemicals	
Fertilizers	92
Acids, alkalies, and salts	63
Primary plastics	74
Medicinal and pharmaceutical	33
Paints and varnishes	54
Electrical apparatus and supplies	52
Primary iron and steel	84
Automobiles	97
Automobile parts	46
Rubber goods	77
Railway rolling stock	84
Primary textiles	
Synthetic fibres	100
Primary textiles (excl. synthetic fibres and knitted goods)	90
Agricultural implements	91

Source: Irving Brecher and S. S. Reisman, *Canada–United States Economic Relations*, a study prepared for the RCCEP (Ottawa, 1957), Table 31, p. 110.

*For the mining industries the "value added" is the gross value of shipments less cost of process supplies, ores and concentrates, containers, fuel and electricity. The industry figures include data for mines which were active but not actually producing, and the cost of fuel and electricity for these non-producers is deducted when arriving at the value added for the industry.   This practice sometimes gives a lower net value for the industry then for the six largest firms.   In some cases, of course, only six firms may be involved in the industry.

†One company only.

than the United States. To some extent the presumed monopolistic consequences of this situation in Canada are reduced by the fact that in several areas governmentally owned and operated firms are important forces. This is particularly noteworthy in transportation and communication, where the Canadian National Railways represents over half of the railway industry and is an important force in trucking as well. Air Canada is the largest airline in Canada while the Canadian Broadcasting Corporation is the largest radio and television broadcasting corporation. In addition to such dominance in these areas, the Polymer Corporation, which produces synthetic rubber products, Eldorado Mining and Refining Limited, which mines and refines uranium and produces nuclear fuels, and the Central Mortgage and Housing Corporation, which provides a large variety of services in the mortgage market as well as owning and managing rental housing units for war workers and veterans, are all government-owned enterprises of a business type which may be used as instruments of public policy and, in their respective areas, offset to some extent, the possible consequences of private concentrations of economic power. It should be stressed, however, that these government-owned enterprises have been established to operate much like private companies. Indeed, it is a point of some pride to the government to have these companies operate efficiently and show levels of profits as high as or even higher than in the private sector. It is not so much their existence *per se* that may offset the undesirable aspects of private concentrations as their *potential* in this regard should abuses of power become evident. For the most part, these crown companies are reluctant to deviate from business practices pursued by large private corporations. It is doubtless the case that, thus far at least, the real restraint in transportation comes less from the existence of the Canadian National Railways and Air Canada than from regulation by the Board of Transport Commissioners and the Air Transport Board.

Despite these important areas of government ownership and regulation, it seems to be a valid judgment that "problems due to 'bigness' . . . to extreme inequality of firm size, and . . . monopolistic control of markets by a small number of sellers are . . . of major importance in the Canadian economy."[19] Especially is this the case where the industries enjoy the benefits of tariff protection and have little to fear from anti-combines investigations—which seems to be the typical situation.

Some additional details concerning type of ownership for the manufacturing sector are presented in Table 8.4. It is noteworthy that only

[19]Rosenbluth, "Concentration and Monopoly in the Canadian Economy," p. 204.

TABLE 8.4

Manufacturing Establishments by Size and Type of Ownership
1958

Size of Assets and type of ownership	Number of establishments	Percentage of total*	Number of employees	Percentage of total	Selling value of factory shipments $000,000	Percentage of total
Under $25,000:						
Totals	12,521	34	25,518	1.98	124.3	.56
Individual ownership	8468	23.04	16,536	1.28	82.8	.37
Partnership	1654	4.50	4440	.34	17.9	.08
Incorporated	1152	3.13	3355	.26	15.4	.07
Co-operative	54	.15	104	.01	0.6	—
Not classifiable	1193	3.24	1083	.08	7.4	.04
$25,000-$99,999:						
Totals	9948	27.07	67,782	5.25	533.3	2.41
Individual ownership	4292	11.68	25,447	1.97	209.6	.95
Partnership	1551	4.22	10,789	.84	81.5	.37
Incorporated	3583	9.75	29.488	2.28	213.6	.96
Co-operative	265	.72	917	.07	16.3	.07
Not classifiable	257	.70	1141	.09	12.3	.06
$100,000-$499,999:						
Totals:	8833	24.04	184,460	14.29	2023.1	9.12
Individual ownership	990	2.70	12,657	.98	168.8	.76
Partnership	664	1.81	11,417	.88	127.6	.58
Incorporated	6614	18.00	155,282	12.03	1607.0	7.25
Co-operative	471	1.28	3477	.27	100.3	.45
Not classifiable	94	.26	1627	.13	19.4	.09
$500,000 or over:						
Totals	5439	14.8	1,012,842	78.4	19,482.5	87.9
Individual ownership	36	.10	2134	.17	31.4	.14
Partnership	54	.15	3217	.25	50.8	.23
Incorporated	4217	14.19	998,924	77.39	19,147.5	86.3
Co-operative	120	.33	6556	.51	215.8	.97
Not classifiable	12	.03	2011	.16	37.0	.17
Totals	36,741	100.00	1,290,602	100.00	22,163.2	100.00

SOURCE: *Canada Year Book 1961*, Table 16, pp. 656-7.
*Totals may not add to 100 per cent due to rounding.

15 per cent of the establishments have assets over half a million dollars but these account for over three-quarters of the total employment and close to 90 per cent of sales value of factory shipments. Virtually all establishments in the largest size class are incorporated while individual proprietorships predominate in the under $25,000 group. Of the total number of establishments about 45 per cent are incorporated, 38 per cent under individual ownership, 11 per cent partnerships, with co-operatives accounting for less than 3 per cent and the balance, about 4 per cent, not classifiable. But the incorporated establishments, though constituting less than half the total number of establishments, account for over 90 per cent of employment and almost 95 per cent of value of factory shipments. On the other hand individual proprietorships, although almost 40 per cent of the total, account for less than 5 per cent of employment and barely 2 per cent of value of factory shipments.

These patterns of heavy concentration within the corporate sector as far as manufacturing is concerned are not, of course, unusual. Similar evidence pertains in the US as well. But the relative importance of the corporation in other sectors is somewhat different, being in general higher in public utilities and transportation than in manufacturing but of negligible proportions in agriculture and less significant in the service, trade, construction, and mining sectors than in manufacturing.

SUMMARY

The foregoing mixture of impressionistic notions and empirical evidence reveals a highly diverse milieu within which management appears to function. It may, however, be useful to summarize some of the main findings briefly at this point. In general, it would appear that the typical Canadian manager, excluding the individual proprietor, is employed in a relatively large corporation with assets between $100,000 and $500,000. The firm is probably a subsidiary of a US enterprise, especially if it is in mining, refining, or secondary manufacturing. The Canadian manager is possibly less dynamic than his American counterpart and is typically a Protestant of British ancestry with a college degree. His firm also has a fairly high degree of market power particularly if it sells in the domestic market.

The significance of these impressions as far as the quality and effectiveness of management is concerned is difficult to determine. Nor can the attempt be made in the present volume. Furthermore, we must reiterate that the validity of these comments in specific instances is dubious. But as a rough general sketch it may not be unduly misleading.

However, as already noted, the real test of managerial ability from the national point of view lies in the area of efficiency. Regardless of the number of managers and their quality, the performance of the Canadian economy, in terms of productivity, is the objective test of achievement. Clearly, however, this means that our concept of management must broaden and include government management not only as it involves the operation of Crown companies but more importantly in conducting the affairs of government especially in the crucial areas of monetary, fiscal, and debt management policy. Appropriate management of the money supply and fiscal affairs, to say nothing of tariffs, labour policy, and anti-combines enforcement, can significantly affect the general climate within which private decision-making takes place. The efficiency of any major segment of the economy, and certainly of the economy as a whole, is largely a joint product of both public and private management in the sense that management has the major task of utilizing and combining present resources effectively. In this sense, trends in efficiency may be interpreted, albeit loosely, as one criterion of the efficiency of managerial talent in utilizing Canada's resources. The evidence on productivity trends is the subject of the next section.

PRODUCTIVITY

The concept of productivity is relatively straight-forward but, as is the case of management and capital, raises substantial problems of measurement. In general, productivity means output per unit of input and as such is the inverse of real cost per unit of output. However, there are always several inputs or factors of production required to produce any given quantity of output and obtaining an index of total real input or some common denominator of a unit of productive material is a hazardous statistical undertaking. The most frequent measure of productivity, therefore, utilizes that factor of production whose units are, or at least appear to be, somewhat more homogeneous than all others, namely labour. Man-hours or man-years expended to produce output are deemed to be appropriate indicators of productivity in general. Thus, the measure widely used is output per man-hour or per man-year.

The use of this as the main indicator of efficiency must not be taken to imply causation or to suggest that labour is the most important factor of production. Rather it is a pragmatic choice dictated by the availability of better data on labour time than for any other productive agent. Of course, man-hours or man-years of labour are not homogeneous, as Adam Smith long ago observed. But they appear to be more so than is the case for land, capital, and management, even if firm quantity estimates of the latter were available, and are used for this reason as well.

Defining productivity in this fashion does not, however, resolve all of the empirical problems. Output per man-hour or per man-year can refer to broad aggregates such as GNE per man-year employed or such narrow efficiency measures as output per man-hour for a particular firm or industry. There is also a choice between the use of current or deflated dollars in the numerator. It is scarcely surprising then that numerous estimates of productivity are available and that these frequently exhibit widely varying results.

The present section will examine first the trends in aggregative labour productivity and then productivity changes for several sectors in the Canadian economy. Since a major purpose here is to examine productivity trends to facilitate the projections of Part Three which pertain to the whole economy, estimates of output per man-hour or man-year at the industry level have not been presented. There are, in any event, greater statistical problems at the lower level of aggregation and the results do not appear sufficiently fruitful to warrant estimation for present purposes.

In the latter part of this section we will examine some of the trends in productivity of land and capital to supplement the discussion of labour productivity. For the most part, however, the main criterion of efficiency will be construed in terms of output per unit of labour input.

GLOBAL PRODUCTIVITY

Gross national product per man-year[20] in current dollars has been estimated as $409 in 1870 while by 1960 this productivity measure had risen almost 15 times to a level of $6,088. Not all of this can be considered as a real gain because of the substantially higher level of prices in 1960 (see Table 8.5). A very crude adjustment for the effects of changing prices suggests that "real" GNE per man-year increased from roughly $1,160 (in terms of 1949 dollars) in 1870 to over $4,300 in 1960, or not quite quadruple the aggregative productivity 91 years earlier. Compounded annually this yields a rate of increase of almost 1.5 per cent per year. However, there have been rather widely varying

[20]Man-years are assumed to be equal to number of persons employed during the year as shown in DBS employment statistics. Since this section was written, DBS has published productivity estimates for 1947–63 on the basis of both man-hours and persons employed. See DBS, *Indexes of Output Per Person Employed and Per Man-Hour in Canada Commercial Nonagricultural Industries, 1947–63* (Ottawa, April, 1965). These data are consistent with the evidence contained in the following pages.

TABLE 8.5

Gross National Expenditure per Man-Year
selected years 1870–1960

| Year | GNP per man-year | | Percentage change | Average annual percentage change |
	(current dollars)	(constant 1949 dollars)	(constant 1949 dollars)	
1870	409	1164		
1890	512	1489	27.9	1.26
1910	787	1942	30.4	1.25
1930	1553	2353	21.2	1.00
1940	1612	2608	10.8	1.07
1950	3603	3496	34.0	3.00
1960	6088	4333	23.9	2.17

SOURCE: Data for 1870, 1890 and 1910 from O. J. Firestone, *Canada's Economic Development, 1867–1953*, p. 223, Table 81. Data for these years in constant dollars of 1949 were converted from constant dollars of 1935–39 by the implicit GNE deflator. Other data from DBS, *National Accounts Income and Expenditure 1926–1956, 1961* and *1962*.

rates of increase as shown in Tables 8.5 and 8.6. In general, prior to 1940 rates of growth in productivity were between 1 and 1¼ per cent per year compounded annually, while since 1940 the rates have ranged between 2 and 3 per cent annually using decade comparisons. There is little doubt that productivity has been increasing at higher rates since the end of the Great Depression. Indeed the proportionate growth in the ten-year interval 1940–50 was higher than in the twenty-year intervals since 1870 shown in Table 8.5. Even using the decade of the 1950's the record is much better than the earlier periods indicated despite the slowdown from 1956–60.

But decade comparisons hide substantial year-to-year changes and may be seriously distorted by the choice of beginning and end years. Data showing GNE per man-year since 1926 in terms of both current values and dollars of 1949 are given in Table 8.6. The influence of the changing pattern of prices is obvious. That is, until the middle 1930's prices tended to be rather flexible downwards so that decreases in current dollar productivity exceeded those in real terms while increases were less, whereas after the mid-thirties the general upward drift in prices renders current value decreases in productivity less than the real and increases generally greater. Looking at the real changes (columns 4 and 5 of Table 8.6) the over-all pattern of productivity changes reflects the movements in GNE from year to year. Thus productivity decreased every year between 1929–32, 1945–47 and in 1954 and 1957, while

TABLE 8.6

Global Productivity
1926–62

Year	GNE per employed person, current dollars	Percentage change from year to year	GNE per employed person (1949 dollars)	Percentage change from year to year
1926	1451		2134	
1929	1594	.06	2355	−1.09
1933	1018	−7.71	1844	−5.87
1937	1278	6.95	2143	4.03
1938	1298	1.56	2182	1.82
1939	1368	5.39	2315	6.09
1940	1612	17.83	2608	12.65
1941	1950	20.96	2923	12.07
1942	2329	19.43	3341	14.30
1943	2469	6.01	3420	2.36
1944	2642	7.00	3551	3.83
1945	2661	0.72	3497	−1.52
1946	2529	−4.96	3255	−6.92
1947	2718	7.47	3189	−2.03
1948	3095	13.87	3220	.97
1949	3259	5.29	3259	1.21
1950	3603	10.55	3496	7.27
1951	4142	14.95	3629	3.80
1952	4627	11.70	3862	6.42
1953	4769	3.06	3964	2.64
1954	4788	.40	3886	−1.97
1955	5058	5.63	4087	5.17
1956	5476	8.26	4263	4.30
1957	5574	1.79	4213	−1.17
1958	5369	−3.67	4284	1.69
1959	5963	11.06	4311	.63
1960	6088	2.09	4333	.51
1961	6186	1.61	4376	.99
1962	6498	5.04	4522	3.33

SOURCE: Computed from Tables I.1 and I.3.

during expansion periods productivity has been positive and generally rising. During the Second World War enormous gains were recorded until 1942 and again during the boom following 1949. Productivity increases during the slowdown of the late 1950's were exceedingly small and generally less than 1 per cent per year through 1961.

These facts suggest a close positive relationship between the growth of total GNE and GNE per man-year, as many observers have pointed out.[21] In other words, year-to-year productivity changes depend largely on the direction of change in GNE since this total fluctuates more than employment. Thus, to ascertain any long-term trend in productivity requires comparisons over time intervals or more than one or two years.

The trend over the whole period 1926–62 suggests an annual average compound rate of productivity growth of about 2.2 per cent. The growth rate between 1950 and 1960 was likewise about 2.2 per cent. Taking the ten years 1952–62, however, suggests an average compound rate of only 1.6 per cent, reflecting the impact of sluggish growth from 1956 to 1961, while between 1949 and 1962 the figure is 2.4 per cent. These facts illustrate the varying results obtained through changes in the choice of end and beginning dates. However, generally speaking, the record indicates that real GNE per man-year increases over time within the range of 1.5–3.0 per cent, although few specific years fall within this range.

Another global productivity measure is gross domestic product (GDP) per man-year. Data showing GDP per man-year appear in Table 8.7 in index number form (1949 = 100) for 1935–61. The general pattern of this indicator is roughly comparable to the GNE measure although there are several significant differences even as to direction of change. From 1949 to 1961 GDP per man-year grew at an average annual rate of almost 2.5 per cent which is comparable to the average rate using GNE. Indeed, between 1949 and 1961 the percentage change using either measure was about 33 per cent. The annual growth rate between 1935 and 1961 is close to 2.8 per cent using GDP and 3.0 per cent using GNE. Over time, therefore, either global productivity measure yields roughly comparable results despite some important year-to-year discrepancies.

But these aggregative measures are themselves products of divergent trends in particular sectors and industries. For a somewhat fuller appreciation of the pattern of productivity, the following section provides estimates at a lower level of aggregation.

[21]See George W. Wilson, "The Relationship Between Output and Employment," *Review of Economics and Statistics*, Feb. 1960, and references cited therein.

TABLE 8.7

Global Productivity Indices
1935–61
(1949 = 100)

	GDP per man-year		GNE per man-year		GDP less agriculture per man-year	
Year	Index	Percentage change	Index	Percentage change	Index	Percentage change
1935	66.0		62.4		73.2	
1936	67.4	2.12	63.2	1.28	75.7	3.41
1937	69.1	2.52	65.8	4.03	76.8	1.45
1938	69.7	.87	67.0	1.82	76.2	−.78
1939	73.2	5.02	71.0	5.97	79.2	3.93
1940	82.9	13.25	80.0	12.65	89.4	12.80
1941	94.6	14.10	89.7	12.07	100.5	12.40
1942	107.5	13.60	102.6	14.30	106.8	6.27
1943	110.5	2.79	104.9	2.36	113.5	6.27
1944	115.1	4.16	109.0	3.91	117.6	3.61
1945	109.4	− 4.95	107.3	−1.52	114.2	− 2.89
1946	96.0	−12.24	99.9	−6.92	98.2	−14.01
1947	97.1	1.14	97.9	−2.03	97.9	−.31
1948	99.6	2.57	98.9	.97	99.6	1.73
1949	100.0	.40	100.0	1.21	100.0	.40
1950	106.7	6.70	106.9	6.90	105.1	5.10
1951	112.5	5.44	111.4	3.80	107.3	2.09
1952	118.7	5.51	118.5	6.42	109.4	1.96
1953	121.1	2.02	121.6	2.64	112.5	2.83
1954	119.6	−1.24	119.2	−1.97	114.8	2.04
1955	127.4	6.52	125.4	5.20	118.2	3.05
1956	132.6	4.08	130.8	4.30	121.3	2.54
1957	128.7	−2.94	129.3	−1.17	118.8	−2.06
1958	131.1	1.86	131.5	1.69	119.6	.67
1959	134.0	2.21	131.9	.30	122.0	2.01
1960	133.4	−.45	132.9	.76	120.7	−1.07
1961	133.7	.23	134.3	1.06	122.0	1.08

SOURCE: DBS, *Indexes of Real Domestic Product by Industry of Origin, 1935–1961* (Ottawa, 1963) and DBS, *National Accounts Income and Expenditure*, various issues.

SECTORAL PRODUCTIVITY

In Table 8.8 we have summarized in index form (1949 = 100) productivity estimates for the period 1935–61 for various sectors and industries.

Agricultural productivity is highly volatile, as would be expected given the unique dependence upon weather conditions which make output fluctuate largely independently of labour input. Thus, year-to-year changes in agricultural output per man-year run as high as 65 per cent

TABLE 8.8

Productivity Indices by Sector
1935–61
(1949=100)

Year	Agricultural output per man-year		Manufacturing output per man-year		Construction output per man-year		Transportation, storage and communication output per man-year		Wholesale and retail trade output per man-year	
	Index	Percentage change	Index	Percentage change	Index	Percentage change	Index	Percentage change	Index	Percentage change
1935	79.2		80.2		65.3		43.2		82.0	
1936	69.8	−11.86	83.0	3.49	88.0	34.70	46.8	8.33	84.5	3.04
1937	69.2	− .86	85.9	3.49	85.5	− 2.84	49.7	6.19	87.9	4.02
1938	87.3	26.10	81.5	− 5.12	73.5	−14.00	48.7	− 2.01	85.1	−3.18
1939	99.6	14.00	86.5	6.13	70.0	− 4.76	51.6	5.95	86.8	1.99
1940	103.0	3.41	92.8	7.28	104.2	48.80	63.4	22.80	91.7	5.64
1941	94.3	− 8.45	95.3	2.69	92.7	−11.03	77.8	22.70	95.5	4.14
1942	156.1	65.50	94.6	− .73	96.7	4.31	87.7	12.72	98.8	3.45
1943	99.2	−36.45	93.3	−1.37	94.5	− 2.27	98.0	11.70	101.8	3.03
1944	120.3	21.20	95.9	2.78	103.1	9.10	100.1	2.14	101.7	− .10
1945	89.8	−25.35	92.9	−3.12	102.0	− 1.07	98.7	− 1.40	101.6	− .10
1946	99.9	11.20	93.6	.75	98.4	− 3.53	90.5	− 8.30	107.2	5.51
1947	99.2	− .70	95.9	2.45	93.1	− 5.38	98.2	8.50	107.9	.65
1948	104.8	4.83	97.2	1.35	93.5	.43	99.8	1.62	99.7	−7.60
1949	100.0	− 3.85	100.0	2.88	100.0	6.95	100.0	.20	100.0	.30
1950	113.0	13.00	104.7	4.70	103.5	3.50	103.3	3.30	103.2	3.20
1951	139.3	23.27	106.4	1.62	99.9	− 3.48	113.1	9.49	100.7	−2.42
1952	180.8	29.79	107.8	1.32	100.1	.20	119.4	5.57	103.8	3.08
1953	172.1	− 4.81	111.9	3.86	110.2	10.18	120.9	1.26	107.3	3.37
1954	129.4	−24.81	114.5	2.32	117.4	6.53	117.9	− 2.48	105.1	−2.05
1955	175.0	35.23	122.7	7.16	121.6	3.58	133.6	13.31	111.2	5.80
1956	197.6	12.91	125.3	2.12	126.7	4.19	149.2	11.67	115.2	3.60
1957	171.0	−13.46	123.4	−1.52	128.7	1.58	149.5	.20	109.7	−4.77
1958	190.4	11.34	128.1	3.81	141.4	9.86	146.6	− 1.94	112.0	2.10
1959	195.9	2.89	134.8	5.23	131.0	− 7.35	160.6	9.54	115.6	3.21
1960	205.5	4.90	136.3	1.11	129.7	− .99	163.6	1.87	114.6	− .87
1961	186.2	− 9.39	140.5	3.08	138.4	6.71	172.1	5.20	114.8	.17

SOURCE: DBS, *Indexes of Real Domestic Product by Industry of Origin, 1935–1961* (Ottawa, 1963) and DBS, *National Accounts Income and Expenditure*, various issues.

and typically exceed 10 per cent. Furthermore, the frequency of negative changes is greater than that of any other sector, except construction,
and the magnitude of annual changes is far higher than elsewhere in the
economy. In general, however, despite the substantial volatility, agricultural productivity has increased from levels mostly below 100 (1949 =
100) prior to the Second World War to levels close to 200 in the late
1950's. The trend is sharply upward despite wide fluctuations about the
trend line.

In manufacturing, annual productivity increases since 1949 have
generally been within the 2 to 4 per cent range and exhibit less volatility
than the other sectors shown in Table 8.8. The growth in manufacturing
output per man-year since 1949 has been about 40 per cent, well below
agriculture and transportation, storage, and communication, but about
equal to construction and above trade.

The compound annual rates of productivity growth for each of the
sectors in Table 8.8 are shown in Table 8.9 for various periods. Agri-

TABLE 8.9

Sectoral Growth in Productivity: Annual Averages
selected periods 1935–60

Sector	1935–61	1949–61	1950–60
Agriculture	3.4	5.3	6.2
Manufacturing	2.2	2.9	2.7
Construction	2.9	2.8	2.3
Transportation, storage and communication	5.5	4.6	4.7
Wholesale and retail trade	1.3	1.2	1.0

SOURCE: Derived from Table 8.8.

culture again stands out as having the highest productivity increases for
each of the three periods distinguished, except for transportation, storage, and communication during the 1935–61 period. The lowest productivity growth rates are recorded in wholesale and retail trade, a sector
of the economy less susceptible to automation than almost any other
save government. Manufacturing and construction have recorded roughly
comparable gains in the 2 to 3 per cent range. The table indicates clearly
the varying rates of growth of labour efficiency among different sectors
of the economy which get "averaged out" when using global or aggregative measures. Even the evidence of Table 8.9 hides considerable diversity at the industry and firm level.

For making inter-country comparisons, however, data limitations
generally require more aggregative indicators and to answer the question

of Canada's relative productivity performance we shall use the global measures of labour productivity developed earlier.

On the whole, the Canadian economy has progressed reasonably well in terms of labour productivity compared with other countries, except during the decade of the 1950's. Rough estimates for the period 1913–59 suggest that GNE per man-year increased at a compound annual rate of 1.5 per cent which is above or equal to the recorded rates for Germany (1.4), France (1.5), the Netherlands (1.3), Denmark (1.2), and the United Kingdom (0.8), but below the rates for Japan (2.6), Italy (1.7), Norway (1.9), Sweden (1.7), and the United States (1.8).[22] However, between 1950 and 1959 Canada's productivity growth was only 2 per cent per year and below that of every country listed above except Denmark and the United Kingdom. Indeed, Norway, the Netherlands, France, Germany, Italy, and Japan recorded rates of growth well over 3 per cent per year, or between 50 and 300 per cent above the Canadian performance. Japan's estimated growth rate of GNE per man-year was a whopping 6.1 per cent per year between 1950 and 1959. There are, of course, serious problems of comparability using these estimates, but those for Canada included above are consistent with the estimates made in the present section and the wide differences during the later period are likewise consistent with what we know to be the case in Western Europe[23] and the previous discussion of the slowdown in Canada.[24] While, therefore, the figures may be less than completely accurate and not fully comparable, there is little doubt that Canadian economic progress has lagged badly in the latter half of the 1950's compared with most other countries in the Western world.

However, a slightly different comparison with the US and UK during the 1950's suggests that Canada's performance has been relatively good. In fact, Table 8.10 shows that over the whole decade gross output per man-year in Canada exceeded that of both the US and the UK although by only a slim margin. What this means, of course, is that the English-speaking countries of the Western World, and not only Canada, have experienced sluggish growth in productivity relative to Western Europe. The fact that Canada's performance is at least as good as that of the US and UK cannot be grounds for complacency.

But over the long pull, Canada's productivity performance compares favourably, if not spectacularly, with that of most Western countries and

[22]See *The Annual Report of the Council of Economic Advisers,* Jan. 1962 (Washington, 1962), p. 114.
[23]See J. F. Dewhurst, *Europe's Needs and Resources* (New York, 1961).
[24]See chap. 1.

TABLE 8.10

Productivity Change, Canada,
US, and UK
1950–60
(1950 = 100)

Year	Canada(a)	US(b)	UK(c)
1950	100	100	100
1951	105.4	105.6	97
1952	111.2	108.8	100
1953	113.5	111.9	103
1954	112.1	112.0	106
1955	119.4	117.2	109
1956	124.3	116.4	109
1957	120.6	118.1	111
1958	122.9	117.8	112
1959	125.6	122.7	118
1960	125.0	124.5	122

SOURCES: (a) Data from Table 8.7 referring to GDP per person employed.
(b) Data from *Annual Report of the Council of Economic Advisers*, January 1963 (Washington, DC, 1963). Data refer to real GNP per person employed.
(c) Data from G. D. N. Worswick and P. H. Ady, *The British Economy in the Nineteen-Fifties* (Oxford, 1962), p. 536. The data refer to GDP per person employed.

the evidence of the early 1960's suggests a resumption of the historical pattern. Nevertheless, the varying rates of growth over time periods of five to ten years indicates that positive productivity changes cannot be taken for granted. This in turn implies that both public and private management need to pay careful and constant attention to matters of efficiency.

One of the main determinants of productivity change is the effort expended to find improved processes and new ways of performing economic tasks more effectively. In the final section of this chapter we will examine research and development activity in Canada. Before turning to this important topic however some estimates of productivity of land and capital will be made and, wherever possible, comparisons with other countries will be attempted.

PRODUCTIVITY OF LAND

Output per unit of land is another useful indicator of productivity as far as agriculture is concerned. Data on yields per acre of major Canadian crops are shown in Table 8.11 from 1926–30 to 1955–59. It will be noted that productivity gains are much smaller than for labour productivity either in general or specifically for agriculture. For example, from the average for 1926–30 to the average for 1955–59, the largest gain in bushels per acre was recorded for oats and potatoes, about 20 and 60 per cent respectively, over the whole period, whereas agricultural output per man-year as a whole virtually doubled since the 1930's. For most of the crops, yields per acre have risen somewhat more slowly or in some cases have even declined (e.g., rye).

TABLE 8.11

Crop Yields for Major Canadian Crops:
selected periods 1926–59
(annual average bushels per acre)

	1926–30	1931–35	1936–40	1941–45	1946–50	1951–55	1955–59
Wheat	18.3	12.5	13.6	17.8	15.5	21.7	20.4
Oats	30.5	25.9	26.1	32.3	30.2	38.3	37.8
Barley	24.9	19.2	21.2	26.3	22.4	28.6	26.7
Rye	16.6	9.0	11.1	13.6	11.0	18.0	16.1
Flaxseed	8.4	4.3	5.6	7.4	8.1	9.9	8.8
Soybeans	—	—	—	18.8	20.8	23.0	25.2
Tame hay (tons)	1.62	1.53	1.63	1.67	1.52	1.83	
Potatoes (cwt.)	82.5	81.2	75.2	82.2	105.1	116.1	131.7
Peas	17.5	17.0	15.7	16.3	17.0	18.6	16.8
Beans	16.1	16.0	18.2	16.2	17.5	18.3	17.2
Field Roots (tons)	9.4	10.2	10.1	10.7	10.3	10.8	10.9

SOURCE: DBS, *Long-Time and Average Yields of Field Crops in Canada, by Provinces, 1908–1955* (Ottawa, 1957), and Table 5.2. for 1955–59 avearge.

As noted in Chapter 5, yields per unit of land in Canada have not been especially high since there is sufficient land to warrant extensive rather than intensive cultivation. Compared to the United States, the EFTA countries and EEC countries,[25] Canadian output per unit of land is the lowest of all three areas for wheat, rye, barley, and oats and for a total of these cereals plus corn. Estimates from the Food and Agricultural Organization have been put together in Table 8.12. In general, Canadian output per hectare,[26] the measure used in Table 8.12 for five major cereal crops, is not quite 1,400 kilograms,[27] compared with over

[25]EFTA is the European Free Trade Area. Frequently referred to as the "Outer Seven," it includes Austria, Denmark, Norway, Portugal, Sweden, Switzerland, and the United Kingdom. EEC is the European Economic Community, sometimes called the "Inner Six" and composed of Belgium, Luxemburg, France, Germany, Italy, and the Netherlands.

[26]One hectare = 2.471 acres.   [27]One kilogram = 2.2046 pounds.

TABLE 8.12

Land Used for, Production of, and Yields of Five Cereals, by Crop Area
annual average, 1948–52 and 1958–60

Crop and area	Land used (thousand ha.)		Production (thousand tons)		Yields per ha. (hundred kg.)	
	1948–52	1958–60	1948–52	1958–60	1948–52	1958–60
Total,						
five cerals	128,319	119,408	216,314	264,622	16.9	22.2
Canada	18,681	17,404	24,939	24,022	13.3	13.8
US	81,299	72,207	138,374	169,727	17.0	23.5
EEC	20,276	21,201	36,656	50,636	18.1	23.9
EFTA	8063	8596	16,345	20,237	20.3	23.5
Wheat	50,804	43,837	67,529	77,680	13.3	17.7
Canada	10,513	9060	13,472	11,566	12.8	12.8
US	27,756	21,458	31,066	35,864	11.2	16.7
EEC	10,234	10,868	18,467	24,662	18.0	22.7
EFTA	2301	2451	4524	5588	19.7	22.8
Rye	4292	3624	6929	7145	16.1	19.7
Canada	555	213	463	222	8.3	10.4
US	686	655	524	727	7.6	11.1
EEC	2235	2047	4426	5048	19.8	24.7
EFTA	816	709	1516	1148	18.6	16.2
Barley	10,658	15,428	18,231	30,913	17.4	20.0
Canada	2870	3399	4282	4916	14.9	14.5
US	4095	5919	5843	9509	14.3	16.1
EEC	1931	3321	3635	8588	18.8	25.9
EFTA	1762	2789	4471	7900	25.4	28.3
Oats	26,805	21,479	37,849	35,723	14.1	16.6
Canada	4623	4529	6338	6554	13.7	15.4
US	15,266	11,793	18,970	17,665	12.4	15.0
EEC	4281	3040	7326	6578	17.1	21.6
EFTA	2635	2117	5215	4926	19.8	23.3
Corn	35,760	(35,040)	85,776	(113,161)	24.0	32.3
Canada	120	203	384	764	32.0	37.6
US	33,496	32,382	81,971	105,962	24.5	32.7
EEC	1595	(1925)	2802	(5760)	17.6	(29.9)
EFTA	549	(530)	619	(675)	11.3	(12.7)

Source: John O. Coppock, *North Atlantic Policy: The Agricultural Gap* (New York, 1963), p. 143.

2,300 kilograms in the other three regions shown for 1958–60. There is some evidence of a relative deterioration as far as Canadian yields are concerned since a rather higher ratio of yields in Canada to those in the United States, EEC, and EFTA prevailed in 1948–52. This is true of all the crops listed in Table 8.12. These figures are consistent with the

TABLE 8.13

Crude Productivity of Land and Labour by Country
mid 1950's

Country	Production (wheat equivalent)	
	Kg. per ha. of agricultural land	Tons per man-year of labour input
Canada	750	61
US	1075	67
EEC	3040	15
BLEU	6130	38
France	2280	20
Germany	4200	19
Italy	2730	7
Netherlands	6800	33
EFTA	3170	22
Austria	3110	13
Denmark	5450	47
Norway	3460	16
Portugal	1170	4
Sweden	2830	30
Switzerland	4870	21
UK	3330	43

SOURCE: Coppock, *North Atlantic Policy*, p. 72.

previous findings that yields in Canada could be raised but that, until demand conditions warrant, the incentive to utilize land more intensively will simply not arise.

On the other hand, labour is far more scarce in Canada than land and the incentive to utilize manpower more effectively is obviously greater than in the case of land. A comparison with the countries in Western Europe regarding labour productivity in agriculture puts Canada and the United States on top with crop outputs of 61 and 67 tons per man-year respectively compared with an EEC average of only 15 and an EFTA average of 22 (see Table 8.13).[28]

In other words, output per unit of land is relatively lower in both the US and Canada than in Western Europe, while output per unit of

[28]The data of Tables 8.12 and 8.13 must be used with caution. They are at best crude estimates but appear sufficiently meaningful to warrant their use if only broad orders of magnitude are required.

labour input is much higher in North America. These divergent productivity levels reflect, albeit crudely, the far higher land-man ratio in
North America than in Western Europe. Thus, in North America it is
relatively more efficient to economize on manpower than on land: hence,
agriculture tends to be more extensive as far as land area is concerned.
The reverse is true in Western Europe.

CAPITAL PRODUCTIVITY

Trends in productivity of capital can readily be produced from the estimates of capital stock made in Chapter 7. Indeed, capital productivity
is simply the inverse of the capital-output ratio. Since the estimates of
the quantity of capital are so crude, we shall do no more here than
summarize the apparent trend. There is little assurance that this, in fact,
is a close representation of reality and all of the caveats given before
regarding the use of these estimates must be kept in mind.

The available evidence is presented in index form using 1949 as a
base in Figure 8.1. As expected the trend is downward rather sharply
which contrasts with the general increase in both land and especially
labour productivity over a comparable period of time. Thus, while on
the average it took $3 of capital to produce one dollar's worth of gross

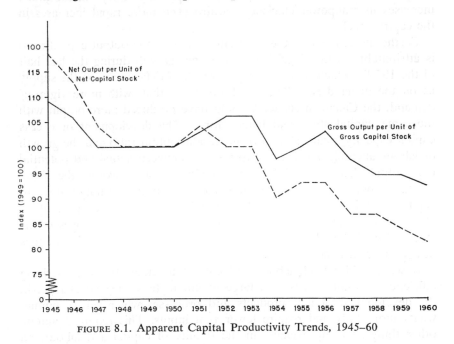

FIGURE 8.1. Apparent Capital Productivity Trends, 1945–60

output prior to the middle 1950's, recently this has risen to almost $4 of required capital: hence output per unit of capital input has declined by about 25 per cent over a fourteen-year period.

This must be interpreted with care. Not only are the estimates open to serious question but even if completely accurate, the decline in apparent capital efficiency does not necessarily mean a deterioration of the quality of Canada's growing capital stock. It simply means that with the present factor endowments, the substitution of capital for labour is economically efficient. As a result, the capital-labour ratio has risen steadily. Since productive activity is in fact a joint result of the co-operation of several factors of production, the interpretation of a rising trend of labour efficiency and decline in capital productivity is simply that, with an increase in the capital-labour ratio, much of the rise in labour productivity is due to the fact that each worker has relatively more capital to work with: hence, the rise in labour productivity is causally connected with the decline in capital productivity. In no sense can it legitimately be inferred that *less* capital investment relative to labour input is required simply because the apparent productivity of the former is declining. On the contrary, since labour productivity depends to such an extent on the quality and quantity of capital, continued increases in manpower efficiency require even more rapid increases in the capital stock.

Furthermore, much of the apparent decline in the output-capital ratio is attributable to the sluggishness of output growth during the last half of the 1950's, which is not so much a result of deficiencies on the supply as on the demand side. There is little doubt that, with more vigorous demand, the Canadian economy could have produced more output with the same capital stock and labour force. The development of excess capital capacity, manifest by a rising capital-output ratio and the growth of labour unemployment, attest to the gap between actual and potential real output that emerged following 1956. In other words, the rising capital-output ratio is less an indicator of sharply diminishing returns to capital than it is a symptom of economic slowdown since percentage changes in output are generally more rapid than similar changes in the stock of capital and, in the short run at least, reflect mainly changes in aggregate demand.

If we consider land, labour and capital together, the key to rising efficiency over-all resides to a large extent in technological change, in the development of new products and processes which satisfy human wants more fully and require fewer real inputs. This requires, among other things, an improvement in the quality of capital and labour, an up-grading of the skill level as well as new skills. An important determinant of these productivity-enhancing factors is the effort expended on research and development to which we now turn.

RESEARCH AND DEVELOPMENT

At the heart of technological advance and productivity increases is the search for new knowledge about the physical world which yields new ways of accomplishing old tasks and/or permits new tasks to be undertaken. The earliest mechanical improvements such as the all-important discovery of the wheel and the most recent efforts to place a man on the moon have this much in common, namely, that they represent scientific advance through some form of research. The "research" might originally have consisted simply in backyard, casual tinkering or merely in trying new arrangements of physical parts. But even so it had its foundation in the spirit of curiosity and inquiry. However casual early efforts may now appear, the same impulse underlies the very crudest of experimentation as well as the most highly organized and elaborate.

But what characterized the great bulk of research and development (R and D) prior to, say, 1940 was its *ad hoc*, generally unorganized nature especially as far as business was concerned. Even in government and the universities, however, the scale of research efforts, if more highly organized and more of a continuing activity than in business, was relatively small. Since 1940 and especially following the successful spliting of the atom, a veritable "industry of discovery" has grown up in all the highly developed countries of the world. If R and D was small-scale, sporadic, and unappreciated as a separate activity only two decades ago, today it is big business growing bigger, obviously here to stay and in danger of receiving accolades out of all proportion to possible results.

In this section we shall examine the growth of organized research in Canada and contrast this with the efforts of several other countries.

Organized research in Canada on a national basis began during the First World War with the establishment in 1916 of an advisory council by the government.[29] Its main functions were to plan and integrate research work, organize co-operative investigations, assist in financing

---

[29]Research activities along particular lines had been undertaken earlier by the government but these "represented a very minor part of the over-all responsibilities of the departments which conducted them." Royal Commission on Government Organization, *Report* 23: "Scientific Research and Development" (Ottawa, 1963), vol. 4, p. 194. (Hereafter cited as RCGO, *Report*, 23.)

post-graduate work, and make grants to university professors. No national laboratories were established until 1924 when the Research Council Act was revised. Since that time extensive facilities have been opened in and around Ottawa as well as the Prairie Research Laboratory in Saskatchewan, the Atlantic Regional Laboratory in Nova Scotia, a building research station at Norman Wells, NWT, and a small Pacific Regional Station in Vancouver, BC. The growth of activities of the National Research Council may be seen from Table 8.14. From a modest beginning in 1916–17 of barely $10,000 research expenditures

TABLE 8.14

National Research Council: Operating Expenditures
excluding expenditures for buildings, services rendered by other
departments, and non-research activity
selected years 1916-63
(dollars)

1916-17	10,155
1920	99,872
1925	121,011
1929-30	462,639
1935-36	629,338
1940	1,056,385
1950	8,157,506
1954-55	13,355,776
1959-60	26,055,700
1961	29,059,809
1962	33,857,417
1963	38,110,940

SOURCE: 1916-30 *Organization and Activities of the National Research Council Ottawa* (Ottawa Nov. 1931), pp. 111-12. 1933-40, from Annual Reports of the National Research Council of Canada for these years. 1950-63 prepared by the National Research Council's General Services Office.

rose steadily, though relatively slowly through the 1920's and 1930's. But in the postwar period outlays for research activity have increased sharply from $6.7 million in 1948–49 to over $38.1 million in 1962–63. In addition, atomic energy facilities have been erected at Chalk River, Ontario, and nuclear reactors, located not only at Chalk River but at Toronto, Hamilton, Rolphton, and Douglas Point, Ontario are now in operation.[30] Other federal government research activity is housed in Canadian universities or undertaken by various government departments such as Agriculture, Fisheries, Mines and Technical Surveys, and

[30]A joint Canada-India reactor has also been established in Bombay.

so on, using facilities throughout the country, or by industry under government contract.

A striking feature of Canadian governmental research is the extent to which it is conducted within government establishments. Over 80 per cent of all federal R and D was performed internally in 1961–62 compared with 78 per cent in 1952–53. The share of industry in total governmental research has declined sharply from 18 per cent to less than 10 per cent while universities and other (mainly provincial government) rose from 4 to almost 9 per cent.[31] Several provinces have established provincial research councils. These include the Nova Scotia Research Foundation established in 1946, the Saskatchewan Research Council (1947), and the Research Councils of Alberta (1921), BC, and Ontario (1928).

Industrial research of one kind or another is now viewed as an essential part of any business searching for ways to improve its products or seeking new products. However, the funds specifically allocated for a separate function defined as R and D have been rather meagre in the past. Large-scale R and D by business is mainly a post-war phenomenon as far as Canada is concerned. The paucity of business research in Canada has long been stressed and lamented. Indeed until 1905 it is reported that no firms "employed research for the improvement of their manufacturing processes or of their products."[32] As late as 1916, even after the stimulus of the First World War, a questionnaire by the Research Council of Canada indicated that only 37 firms out of the leading 2,400 in Canada had research laboratories and total outlays apart from salaries "did not exceed $135,000 in 1916."[33] A later survey for 1938 covering laboratories only reported that industrial laboratories had total wage and salary expenditures in that year of over $7 million and other current expenditures of almost $1.7 million with an employment of 2,410 people classified as professional.[34] There are problems of comparability with the earlier survey and in the 1938 survey the report stresses that "the data furnished by business concerns refer to service within their organizations that cannot be regarded as scientific laboratories in the strict sense of the word. . . . However, . . . the definition of the co-operating organizations was accepted."[35] Nevertheless, it would appear that the interest in research by 1938 was substantially greater

[31]RCGO, *Report*, 23, Table 3, p. 199.
[32]DBS, *Canada Year Book 1922–23*, p. 940.
[33]*Ibid.*
[34]DBS, *Survey of Scientific and Industrial Laboratories in Canada* (Ottawa, 1939), Tables 1 and 2.
[35]*Ibid.*, p. 3.

than in 1916, although still small. The experience during the Second World War led to a permanent enlargement of the amounts spent on research and development so that by 1959 a survey by DBS of 471 firms reporting R and D programs (of 2,800 companies surveyed) indicated R and D expenditures in Canada of almost $100 million and employment of 4,141 professionally trained personnel.[36] Although this represents a decline in all categories from a comparable 1957 survey[37] (due almost entirely to the cancellation of work on the "Arrow") and despite conceptual and empirical difficulties rendering comparison with earlier years hazardous, nevertheless the trend appears to be sharply upward. Yet industrial research still appears to be lagging well behind that of government and universities.[38]

It is difficult to quantify university research. In principle all aspects of university work are either creating or imparting knowledge and understanding. However, limiting research to the purely scientific and technological, it is clear that so long as departments of science or engineering have existed some research of the type involved in the present section has been undertaken.[39] In this sense it is perhaps fair to say that the universities of Canada were first in this field although the amounts involved were very small. For example, *total* expenditures by all colleges and universities in Canada were less than 0.4 per cent of GNE as late as 1958. As Dr. Steacie puts it,

. . . . In the very early days Canadians went abroad for almost all their higher education, and it is only in the last hundred and fifty years or so that university education existed at all in Canada. We first developed undergraduate education, but up to 40 years ago we were totally dependent on the United States, the United Kingdom, and Europe for all postgraduate education. Research in a Canadian university was a rare event in those days. After the first war there was a great development of graduate work in Canadian universities, but it was only after the second war that the Canadian universities really came into their own as centers of research and graduate education. This development is still going on, and still has a considerable distance to go. . . .[40]

---

[36]DBS, *Industrial Research-Development Expenditures in Canada, 1959* (Ottawa, 1961), p. 7.

[37]See DBS, *Industrial Research-Development Expenditures in Canada, 1957* (Ottawa, 1958).

[38]E. W. R. Steacie, "The Development of Industrial Research in Canada," Ottawa Board of Trade Annual Dinner Meeting, April 6, 1961, p. 4.

[39]The Honorary Advisory Council for Scientific and Industrial Research states that "Scientific research in Canada began in the 'eighties' with the institution in the universities of courses in experimental and practical science." *Canada Year Book 1922–23*, p. 939.

[40]"The Development of Industrial Research in Canada," pp. 2–3.

EXPENDITURES ON RESEARCH AND DEVELOPMENT
There are many conceptual and empirical problems in estimating the volume of spending devoted to a separate function or set of activities designated as research and development. Data collection on such activities are relatively recent in the few countries that have begun to be concerned with the magnitudes involved. Part of the apparent rise in R and D may indeed be a statistical illusion. Earlier figures on R and D may be grossly understated. As concern with R and D has grown and come to be more and more specialized in the industry of discovery, activities that were previously classified as current expenses have been included in R and D.[41] Furthermore there are difficult questions concerning what actually constitutes R and D if one is concerned with identifying activities directly related to raising productivity by new or improved processes and products. In general, it is the case in every country that the data on R and D are conceptually weak and empirically spotty. The series will improve over time as more systematic work goes into it, but as Kuznets puts it "if it is inventive activity that we wish to study, then we should not dim our view of it by using measures that are incomplete or so inclusive that inventive activity expenditures are only a small and probably variable fraction of the total."[42]

Since R and D estimates in Canada have only recently begun on a systematic basis, the evidence is especially shaky and no adequate historical time series exists.[43] Indeed, even in federal government research there is a "deplorable lack" of comprehensive data over the years.[44] It should not therefore be surprising to find widely varying estimates of total R and D expenditures for any given year.[45] For example, three

[41]Recently Yale Brozen has applied a correction factor for US data of plus 40% for 1921, 33% for each year 1921–1933, and 16% for 1938 to V. Bush's pre-1940 estimates and has added another 20% "for greater comparability with post-1940 data." ("Trends in Industrial Research and Development," *Journal of Business of the University of Chicago*, July 1960, p. 260.) See also E. F. Denison, *The Sources of Economic Growth in the United States*, Committee for Economic Development, Supplementary Paper no. 13 (New York, 1962), chap. 21.

[42]Simon Kuznets in NBER, *The Rate and Direction of Inventive Activity* (Princeton, 1962), p. 35. This whole volume should be consulted for an assessment of the nature of the problems of measurement, as well as the reference in the following footnote.

[43]For details of attempts to measure R and D in Canada in the past see George T. McColm, "Canadian Surveys of Research and Development," in *Methodology of Statistics of Research and Development*, National Science Foundation (Washington, DC, 1959), pp. 63–5.

[44]RCGO, *Report*, 23, pp. 196–7.

[45]Even in the US which has the most experience in attempting to measure research, discrepancies up to 300 per cent in estimates purporting to measure similar activities are not unknown. (See, for example, C. Kidd, *Science*, vol. 129,

estimates of total outlays for R and D were given as roughly $250 million, $310 million, and $380 million for 1959.[46] With such discrepancies for a recent year when serious efforts at measurement were made, the lack of a satisfactory time series is understandable. The data presented in the following tables should therefore be viewed as crude approximations at best. Table 8.15 provides some comparisons of Canadian R and D with the US and UK. The general pattern among these three countries receives support from other sources as well,[47] namely that Canadian R and D as a proportion of GNE is roughly between one quarter and one-half that of the US and UK. The data of Table 15 indicate more specifically that the ratio is one-third that of the UK and about 28 per cent of the US. On a per capita basis the ranking is similar although the discrepancies are wider.

TRENDS IN RESEARCH AND DEVELOPMENT

Rough comparisons of trends in R and D in Canada, the US and the UK on a real per capita basis are shown in Figure 8.2. The chart indicates only the broad general tendencies and is not to be presumed accurate for a particular year. But as a picture of long-run changes in this important activity it supports the evidence available and is consistent with informed opinion in this area. Broadly, the chart indicates a sharp rise in R and D per capita especially during the Second World War which, particularly in the US, continued to accelerate after 1947–48. Canada lags behind with per capita expenditures of about $20 in 1960 compared with about $26 in the UK and over $70 in the US.[48]

Somewhat more reliable estimates of federal government expenditures are available for the 1951–52 to 1961–62 period and are shown in Table 8.16. The sharp upward and continuous trend, broken only by the special circumstances in 1959 in connection with the "Arrow" contract, is noteworthy. The amount of government research performed by

---

p. 368; W. Shapley in *Methodology of Statistics of Research and Development*, p. 7, and S. Dedijer, "Measuring the Growth of Science," *Science*, vol. 138, pp. 781–7.)

[46]These figures were derived respectively from the following sources: RCGO, *Report*, 23, p. 198; C. J. Mackenzie, "The Significance of the Recent Scientific Explosion," an address to the Chemical Institute of Canada, Montreal, Feb. 15, 1961, Chart 1; and Dedijer, "Measuring the Growth of Science," Table 1, p. 783.

[47]Dedijer, "Measuring the Growth of Science," Table 1 and C. J. Mackenzie, "The New Scientific Technology," *Chemistry in Canada*, July 1963, p. 56.

[48]See also Dedijer, "Measuring the Growth of Science," where similar estimates have been made. However, Table 8.15 above which shows total 1959 R and D expenditures as $251 million in Canada would suggest a per capita figure of only $14.4 while the same table converting to per capita estimates has figures similar to those given above for the US & UK.

TABLE 8.15

Research and Development Expenditures
Canada, UK, and US
c. 1959

	Canada 1959			United Kingdom 1958-59			United States 1959		
	millions of dollars	% of GNP	dollars per head	millions of dollars	% of GNP	dollars per head	millions of dollars	% of GNP	dollars per head
Total expenditures*	251	0.72	14.4	1338	2.11	25.7	12,430	2.58	70.1
Financed by government	154	0.44	8.8	896	1.41	17.2	8030	1.67	45.3
Performed by government	126	0.36	7.2	445	0.70	8.5	1780	0.37	10.0
Financed by industry	78	0.23	4.5	403	0.63	7.8	4075	0.85	23.0
Performed by industry	97	0.28	5.5	784	1.23	15.1	9438	1.96	53.2

SOURCE: derived from the Royal Commission on Government Organization, *Report 23*: "Scientific Research and Development" (Ottawa, 1962), p. 198.
*Includes universities, etc.

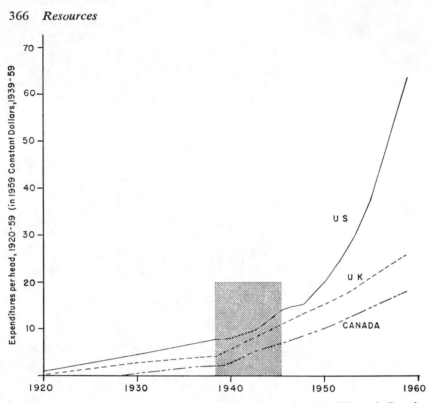

FIGURE 8.2. Research and Development Expenditures in US, UK, and Canada, 1920–59

SOURCE: C. J. Mackenzie, "The Significance of the Recent Scientific Explosion," an address to the Chemical Institute of Canada, Montreal, Feb. 1961, Chart 1.

industry rose substantially from 1951–52 to a peak in 1957–58 and then dropped sharply to lower levels in each year since. By 1961–62 the level was still only 40 per cent of the peak although the trend appeared to be rising. Nevertheless, in comparison with the US and UK, the extent to which Canadian industry shares in government expenditures, especially in the area of defence research, has been described as "astonishingly small."[49]

Thus, not only is Canadian R and D smaller on any basis than is the case with Canada's two leading customers and competitors, as far as international trade is concerned, but the share of it performed by industry is less. The implications of these facts have been variously interpreted as jeopardizing future productivity in Canada relative to other countries and as stimulating the departure of first-class scientists and

[49]RCGO, *Report*, 23, p. 207.

TABLE 8.16

Total Federal Government Expenditures by Sector Doing Research and Development
(millions of dollars)
1951–62

	1951-52	1952-53	1953-54	1954-55	1955-56	1956-57	1957-58	1958-59	1959-60	1960-61	1961-62
Current expenditures											
Federal government	63.7*	81.3	89.8	101.0	114.0	113.1	124.0	135.8	142.4	159.6	178.7
Industry†	3.2*	18.9	16.8	23.6	31.7	45.2	53.1	47.6	12.6	13.4	21.3
Educational organizations (universities)	3.7	4.4	4.5	5.2	5.6	7.0	7.5	10.1	13.5	15.7	17.7
Other (provincial research councils, etc.)	0.3	0.2	0.3	0.4	0.4	0.6	0.6	0.6	0.8	1.2	1.2
Federal government testing and evaluation of R & D not included elsewhere	—	—	—	—	2.0	2.1	1.0	1.5	0.9	1.0	2.9
Sub-Total	94.2*	104.8	111.4	130.1	153.6	168.0	186.2	195.7	170.3	191.0	221.7
Capital expenditures											
Federal buildings and works	13.3	20.2	15.4	15.3	18.5	26.4	26.4	28.1	31.8	33.8	36.2
Total	107.5*	125.0	126.8	145.4	172.1	194.4	212.6	223.8	202.1	224.8	257.9

*Figures for the Royal Canadian Air Force were not available for 1951-52. An estimated $23.3 million is included in the total but not allocated by sector.
†Atomic Energy of Canada Limited Research Contracts are included in Federal governments.
SOURCE: RCGO, Report, 23, p. 198.

engineers to other countries, both of which will damage Canada's international competitive position. However, a closer examination of the evidence suggests that the US and UK predominance is attributable to defence expenditures and that, if civilian-oriented R and D is considered, the proportion of GNE accounted for by all three countries is about the same (0.3 to 0.4 per cent).[50] Furthermore, defence research of the present variety does not "spill over" readily into civilian use.[51] Thus, the implications of the gross estimates of R and D in Canada seem to be somewhat less serious when examined as to type. Nevertheless, the need in Canada is clearly for an acceleration of R and D, for a closer co-ordination of governmental research, and undoubtedly for an altered policy as has frequently been recommended in recent years.[52] As Steacie has expressed it: "technically we owe everything to the United States and the United Kingdom, but technically we are still a colony. As far as research is concerned, industry is now largely where the universities were in 1930. . . . [this] situation is not permanently acceptable."[53]

PATENTS

Another frequently used set of data relating to "inventive" activity is the evidence regarding patents and patent applications. In a very general sense, patents may be construed as the successful completion of research effort at least as far as patentable inventions are concerned. The number of Canadian patents granted since 1873 is shown in Table 8.17. The gradual upward drift to 1932 is apparent followed by a decline then relative stability to about 1949 and a relatively sharp rise, especially after 1954, which evened off in 1959 at about 22,000. However, these statistics include all Canadian patents granted and do not reflect inventive activity within Canada since over 90 per cent of all Canadian patents are granted to non-residents. Indeed, patents granted to residents as a proportion of total patents granted has declined rather steadily since 1935 from slightly over 10 per cent to less than 5 per cent in each of the years 1957, 1958, and 1959. More recently this ratio has risen to about 5.6 per cent, but the persistent downward trend would suggest that a reversal seems unlikely. Detailed evidence is given in Table 8.18. As far as Canadian inventors are concerned, and in terms of patents

---

[50]Mackenzie, "The New Scientific Technology," p. 56. His Table 17 gives a breakdown between civilian and defence outlays by government.

[51]This point has been stressed by Robert A. Solo, "Gearing Military R and D to Economic Growth," *Harvard Business Review*, Nov.–Dec. 1962.

[52]See Mackenzie, "The New Scientific Technology"; RCGO, *Report*, 23; and Steacie, "Development of Industrial Research in Canada" to mention only a few.

[53]"Development of Industrial Research in Canada," p. 5.

TABLE 8.17

List of Canadian Patents Granted
calendar years 1872-1962

Year	Patents	Year	Patents	Year	Patents
1872	671	1902	4551	1932	10,426
1873	1016	1903	5793	1933	9300
1874	1218	1904	6005	1934	8842
1875	1266	1905	6111	1935	8007
1876	1337	1906	6027	1936	7935
1877	1277	1907	6727	1937	7906
1878	1172	1908	6376	1938	7676
1879	1137	1909	7112	1939	7351
1880	1252	1910	7192	1940	7631
1881	1510	1911	7408	1941	8318
1882	1846	1912	7485	1942	7792
1883	2178	1913	7809	1943	7781
1884	2456	1914	6968	1944	7284
1885	2233	1915	7032	1945	7433
1886	2610	1916	7327	1946	6755
1887	2596	1917	7099	1947	6965
1888	2257	1918	6752	1948	7815
1889	2725	1919	7577	1949	8400
1890	2428	1920	11,379	1950	8400
1891	2343	1921	7844	1951	9381
1892	3417	1922	12,609	1952	9522
1893	3548	1923	9174	1953	9609
1894	3800	1924	9144	1954	9743
1895	3152	1925	11,043	1955	11,487
1896	3526	1926	10,324	1956	14,919
1897	4062	1927	9521	1957	16,029
1898	3644	1928	9271	1958	17,252
1899	3420	1929	10,263	1959	21,610
1900	4187	1930	10,993	1960	21,630
1901	4545	1931	11,287	1961	22,050
				1962	21,135

SOURCE: *Annual Reports of the Commissioner of Patents*, various years.

granted to Canadian residents, there has been since 1935 a pattern roughly comparable to that of total patents granted, namely, a decline from 1935 to about the mid-1940's, a slow rise to about 1958, and a new higher plateau since 1960. But whereas total patents granted by the early 1960's were more than double those of the mid 1930's, the number of Canadian inventors was little over 50–60 per cent higher, which is reflected in the steady decline in the share of the latter already noted.

In Figure 8.3 we have summarized the trends in patents to Canadians. While Mackenzie's estimates of R and D suggest a steady increase since 1935 accelerating during the war and again after 1949, the number of

TABLE 8.18
List of Canadian Inventors in Patents Issued
1935-63

Fiscal year ending March 31	Number of Canadian inventors	Total patents granted	Percentage of Canadian inventors (approx.)
1935	885	8713	10.15
36	792	7791	10.17
37	703	8177	8.6
38	647	7720	8.4
39	620	7578	8.2
40	571	7234	7.9
41	608	7834	7.76
42	595	8346	7.14
43	500	7686	6.5
44	480	7803	6.15
45	486	7084	7
46	495	7412	6.7
47	520	6590	7.9
48	580	7175	8.1
49	570	7959	7.16
50	655	8513	7.7
51	627	8461	7.4
52	708	9516	7.5
53	742	9700	7.6
54	606	9414	6.3
55	570	10,282	5.5
56	652	11,862	5.5
57	761	15,513	4.9
58	772	16,261	4.8
59	899	18,293	4.9
60	1219	22,021	5.5
61	1258	22,014	5.7
62	1207	21,659	5.6
63	1194	21,225	5.6

SOURCE: *Annual Reports of the Commissioner of Patents*, various years.

patents granted to Canadian residents declined rather steadily through the wartime period and thereafter increased slowly with an apparent acceleration after 1958 and 1959. Too much should not be read into the divergent behaviour not only because Mackenzie's estimates are very impressionistic but also because there is no necessary connection between the two series, even though they may each be taken to represent aspects of what is loosely termed inventive activity. For example, it may well be the case that inventions are becoming progressively more complex and that in some sense the research needed for complex invention is rising. If so it is quite possible to have R and D expenditures rising while the number of patentable inventions is declining. Again, more of R and D

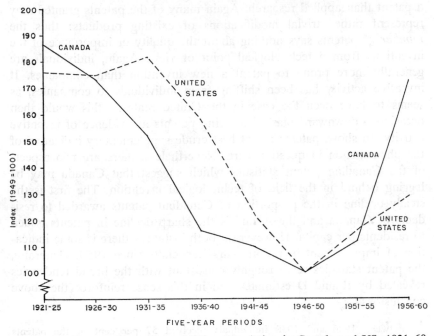

FIGURE 8.3. Patents Granted per Million Population in Canada and US, 1921–60
(annual averages for five-year periods)
SOURCES: DBS, *Canada Year Book 1945*, p. 128; above, Table 1.3; US Department of Commerce, *Statistical Abstract of the United States 1961*, pp. 5 and 540.

spending is being devoted to so-called basic research than in the past which is less likely to lead to a patentable invention. These and other rational possibilities could well explain the apparent trend discrepancies in the two series, to say nothing about the data limitations of the R and D estimates previously discussed.

A comparison with the United States in terms of patents granted per million of population indicates roughly comparable trends, namely a general decline from the early 1920's until 1946–50, with a steady increase thereafter. The sharper rise in Canada since 1946–50 must be interpreted with care since only about 5 or 6 per cent of Canadian patents are awarded to Canadian residents compared with over 90 per cent in the United States (see Figure 8.3).

There are, of course, many inadequacies in patent statistics when used as indicators of inventive activity. Not all increases in useful technological knowledge leading to innovations are patentable. In particular as already noted the fruits of basic research are less likely to lead to a patent than applied research. Again many of the patents granted may represent rather trivial modifications of existing products: thus the *number* of patents says nothing about the quality or importance of the inventions from a technological point of view. Again, individuals are generally more prone to patent a new invention than companies. If inventive activity has been shifting from individuals to companies, as seems to have been the case in the United States,[54] this would then occasion a downward bias when using patents as evidence of inventive activity. In short, patents are at best crude supplementary indicators of the phenomenon in question here. Nevertheless, there are two aspects of the Canadian patent statistics which suggest that Canada may be lagging behind in the field of technological invention. The first is the steady decline in the proportion of Canadian patents awarded to residents of Canada and the second is the sharp decline in patents issued to residents per capita. However, in both instances there is some indication of improvement in recent years, especially since 1959. Generally, the patent statistics seem roughly consistent with the broad tendencies revealed by R and D estimates and in this sense reinforce the above conclusions.

[54]Between 1926 and 1930 individuals received 57 per cent of the patents issued and companies 43 per cent while from 1951–19 ‾ the ratios were 39 and 59 per cent respectively with the Government accounting for 2 per cent. These data refer to the U.S. experience but are probably pertinent in Canada as well. See Denison, *The Sources of Economic Growth in the United States*, p. 238.

PART THREE

The Future

9

PROJECTIONS TO 1970 AND 1975

The foregoing outline of past economic trends in total output, productivity, resources, and so on permits us to attempt certain estimates of the future. We are especially concerned in this part to calculate future demand as well as needs and to match these against future resources to assess the ability of the Canadian economy to respond to the needs and demands of a growing population whose tastes, preferences, and incomes will all be expected to change over time. The concept of "needs" will be confined mainly to the consumer sector and will involve a calculation of the added output required to eliminate "poverty" in Canada. This is contrasted with demand as measured by expected total output (GNP) and its composition.

One of the main difficulties in making such estimates is the interrelationship among the various items. Even at the most aggregative level, as already pointed out in Chapter 2, it is not possible to estimate the future population without making certain assumptions about the rate of economic growth since demographic and economic factors bear some relationship to each other. Human beings are both users of output and providers of input (labour). While the rate and pattern of population growth condition the pace of economic progress and needs, the latter partly determines the former as well. However, the demographic factor is far more stable than the economic. Indeed, at any point in time, the number of those who will enter and leave the labour force age category in the next five to fiteen years is known. The number of those who will enter the labour force age group for the first time have already been born and the number who will reach 65 in the next decade or so are part of the objective facts of the present population age structure. Since death rates change very slowly, this means that, barring some major calamity, the net change in the number of people between 14 and 65 years of age is easily deducible. Only two factors may seriously affect the labour force estimate based upon the 14–65 age group. One is the participation rate which may vary substantially, especially as far as the female labour force is concerned. The other is migration, which may change not only in total amount from year to year but also in terms of age and sex composition. But aside from these factors, for which certain assumptions must of course be made, the stability and certainty of the age composition, including the number of people in the over-14 bracket, make the estimate of the labour force largely independent of economic conditions.

The same is roughly true of total population even though birth, marriage, and to a lesser extent death rates depend to some extent on the level of economic prosperity. However, changes in these are relatively slow and the precise relationship to economic conditions rather tenuous, as already pointed out.[1] For the next fifteen years it is reasonable to expect that these demographic factors will parallel closely the trends of the recent past. Thus, despite the interconnection as both cause and effect between demographic and economic factors, the former are usually deduced first and economic levels made the dependent variable.

Since total real output (GNP in constant prices) may be considered as the product of four variables (1) population, (2) labour force propensity (i.e., ratio of labour force to total production), (3) output per man-year, and (4) percentage of labour force employed, the procedure we shall follow in computing aggregate GNP (equal, of course to GNE) for 1970 and 1975 will be to provide independent estimates of each of these variables and then multiply them together. The estimates necessarily are based upon the past trends examined in Parts One and Two, although they will be modified where other information suggests that a change is to be expected. Following the estimate of GNE in 1970 and 1975 we shall proceed to a finer breakdown of its components.

CALCULATING THE GNE

POPULATION PROJECTION: 1970 AND 1975

Because of the lack of satisfactory data on other variables which influence population growth, the projected population of Canada until 1975 is largely based on the past trends in fertility and mortality rates

[1]See chap. 2, pp. 64–5.

and on the assumption of three levels of net immigration.[2] Immigration and emigration, the most volatile factors in population growth, will depend not only on the Canadian government's immigration policy, but also on relative economic conditions in Western Europe, the United States, and Canada. If economic expansion and higher standards of living result in Western Europe as a consequence of the recent economic integration there, one can expect that the flow of immigrants from Europe to Canada will diminish, particularly if unemployment in this country remains at relatively high levels. The world's growing need for natural resources could, on the other hand, ease the unemployment problem in Canada and this, coupled with a liberalization of the government's immigration policy, would tend to increase the flow of immigrants to Canada. It is unlikely, however, that immigration during the next decade will attain the levels registered in the immediate postwar years.

Table 9.1 provides the estimated population of Canada for two terminal years, 1970 and 1975, by specific age groups, for males and females, under three assumed levels of net immigration: 0, 25,000 and 50,000 persons per year. As the table indicates, the average annual rate of population growth during the years 1965–75 will be only about 2.0 per cent as compared with 2.7 per cent during the decade 1951–61.

From 1965 to 1975 the pre-school age group of 0–4 years old will remain at 12.3 per cent of the total population, the same level at which it stood in 1961. Elementary school age group, 5–14 years old, will constitute only 20.3 per cent as compared with 21.6 per cent in 1961. This decrease reflects the lower birth rates recorded in more recent years. However, an absolute increase in this age group will imply a continuing need for more school facilities.

The people 65 years and over will account for a slightly higher percentage of the total population in the years to come than in the past due to higher expectancy of life.

[2]The projected population of Canada in this study is based on "Population Projection, 1966–91" prepared by Dr. A. Stukel for the Royal Commission on Health Services. The estimates for terminal dates 1970, and 1975 have been obtained by interpolating back one year from the terminal years 1971 and 1976 used in the above-mentioned projection. Only three basic variables were used: mortality and fertility rates and net immigration. The latter was assumed at several levels because of sharp variations in the volume of immigration within a short period of time. In projecting mortality rates, the following factors were considered: the past rate of change; the main causes of death in each age group; and the mortality rates and their behaviour for each age group in other countries. The projections of fertility rates were based on the trends during the last decade. A slight increase for only one age group, 15–19, was allowed because of a trend towards earlier marriage.

TABLE 9.1
Projected Population 1970 and 1975
(thousands)

Age group	1970				1975				Average annual rate of growth	
	Male	Female	Total	%	Male	Female	Total	%	1965-70	1970-75
a. Net immigration—0 per annum										
0-4	1297.0	1238.0	2535.0	11.6	1490.0	1417.0	2907.0	12.2		
5-14	2312.0	2213.0	4525.0	21.0	2471.0	2362.0	4833.0	20.3		
15-64	6427.0	6341.0	12,768.0	59.3	7055.0	6990.0	14,045.0	59.2		
65 and over	804.0	928.0	1732.0	8.1	904.0	1076.0	1980.0	8.3		
Total	10,840.0	10,720.0	21,560.0	100.0	11,920.0	11,845.0	23,765.0	100.0	1.8%	2.0%
20-29	1626.0	1565.0	3191.0	14.8	1935.0	1865.0	3805.0	16.0		2.0%
b. Net immigration—25,000 per annum										
0-4	1324.0	1259.0	2583.0	11.8	1525.0	1452.0	2977.0	12.3		
5-14	2342.0	2238.0	4580.0	20.9	2515.0	2412.0	4927.0	20.3		
15-64	6525.0	6450.0	12,975.0	59.3	7215.0	7112.5	14,327.5	59.2		
65 and over	806.0	933.0	1739.0	8.0	910.0	1081.5	1991.5	8.2		
Total	10,997.0	10,880.0	21,877.0	100.0	12,165.0	12,058.0	24,223.0	100.0	2.0%	2.0%
20-29	1660.0	1599.0	3259.0	14.9	1980.0	1902.5	3882.5	16.0		2.0%
c. Net immigration—50,000 per annum										
0-4	1347.0	1276.0	2623.0	11.9	1556.0	1484.0	3040.0	12.3		
5-14	2364.0	2260.0	4624.0	20.9	2570.0	2450.0	5020.0	20.3		
15-64	6516.0	6510.0	13,125.0	59.3	7352.0	7265.0	14,617.0	59.3		
65 and over	809.0	936.0	1745.0	7.9	912.0	1088.0	2000.0	8.1		
Total	11,136.0	10,982.0	22,118.0	100.0	12,390.0	12,287.0	24,677.0	100.0	2.1%	2.2%
20-29	1681.0	1625.0	3306.0	15.0	2025.0	1941.0	3996.0	16.1		

The main family formation age group, 20–29 years old, will steadily increase its proportion from 13.0 per cent in 1965 to about 16.0 per cent in 1975. This increasing trend in the number of people of marriageable age is a consequence of the post-war baby boom. One may expect a growing demand for housing and durable consumer goods, which should help to sustain a higher level of aggregate demand.

The same trend is to be observed with respect to the portion of the population 15–64 years old, which is expected to increase to 59.3 per cent in 1975 as compared with 58.5 in 1961. There will be a growing number of new entrants into the labour force also due to the higher birth rates in the years following the Second World War. While the source of the potential labour force will increase and should accelerate the Canadian rate of economic growth, it will also be necessary to provide new job opportunities if severe unemployment is to be avoided.

These estimates indicate the number of people who must be provided for in 1970 and 1975. In aggregative terms a population of between 21.6 and 22.1 million in 1970 will "need" to spend about $23 billion (in dollars of 1949) on consumer goods and services merely to maintain the level of per capita personal consumption achieved in 1962. But the long-term trend in real per capita consumption has been rising and if past growth rates can be deemed manifestations of rising needs, by 1970 such expenditures should be about $27 billion (1949 dollars).

Even this higher estimate of needs is on the low side since it implies perpetuation of existing disparities in income distribution. A more realistic assessment of needs requires adding certain amounts to the consumption spending of those segments of the population whose income and hence consumption may at present be deemed substandard. A careful calculation of the disparity between actual and needed spending is not possible from existing data available in Canada. However, a crude calculation may be made by estimating the average consumption expenditures of those living on incomes defined as below the poverty level and the extent by which this falls below a reasonable minimum. If we define the poverty level of income as an amount which is less than half the average income at present enjoyed by Canadians, this implies that all families with incomes below $2,500 and all unattached individuals with incomes below $1,000 may be placed in the "poverty" classification.[3]

[3]Data from DBS, *Distribution of Non-Farm Incomes in Canada by Size, 1959* (Ottawa, 1962). It is assumed throughout that income and personal consumption expenditures are equal for incomes below the poverty level as defined in the text. The above mentioned level of poverty income is however probably understated. Various studies in the US define poverty incomes for families as those under $4,000 and for individuals under $2,000. See, for example, *Poverty and Depri-*

Using this definition of poverty and applying the non-farm income distribution to the whole of Canada[4] suggests that about 38 per cent of unattached individuals had incomes below $1,000 and 18 per cent of families had incomes below $2,500 in 1959. Thus, the total number of persons in the poverty income group may be estimated as roughly 3.5 million or about 20 per cent of the total population in 1959, which is consistent with recent findings in the United States. If we further assume that within the poverty income group the average income of unattached individuals was $600 and the weighted average for families was about $950,[5] it may be estimated that this group needed to spend $1.4 billion more (in 1959 dollars) in the aggregate to raise their levels of consumption above poverty. For 1959 this works out to a rise of consumption expenditures of $1.1 billion or roughly 6 per cent measured in dollars of 1949.

It must be emphasized that this calculation is exceedingly crude but it is surprisingly consistent with similar findings in the US[6] and may perhaps serve to highlight a problem that has been little noticed in Canada and, until recently, in the United States as well.[7] If nothing else the above attempt to measure the extent of poverty and deprivation in Canada may provide some impetus towards more carefully worked out estimates. There can, of course, be no presumption that those families and individuals with higher incomes necessarily have adequate food, clothing, shelter, medical care, recreation, and so on although it has not been possible to make an analysis of other income groups. Furthermore, we have assumed that *total* consumption needs to be increased rather than simply redistributing income. This appears to be a realistic assumption in so far as the post-war distribution of income has remained relatively stable.[8] This means that a net increase in total personal expendi-

---

vation in the United States, Conference on Economic Progress, Washington, DC, April, 1962, chap. III. The *Economic Report of the President* for 1964 (Washington, DC, 1964) uses a $3,000 per family and $1,000 to $1,500 per unattached individual as the poverty dividing line (see chap. 2). Other studies have somewhat more elaborate and different levels of income. However, even assuming the 20 to 30 per cent discrepancy between US and Canadian per capita GNP, the figures used in the text probably serve to understate the extent of poverty in Canada and are adopted here mainly to get a rough indication of the numbers involved on a conservative estimate.

[4]DBS, *Distribution of Non-Farm Incomes in Canada by Size, 1959*.

[5]Data derived from *ibid.*, Table 9, for families.

[6]Indeed, Dewhurst has estimated the shortfall of US aggregate consumption in 1950 as about 6 per cent. See J. F. Dewhurst and associates, *America's Needs and Resources: A New Survey* (New York, 1955), p. 107.

[7]See *Economic Report of the President* and the *Annual Report of the Council of Economic Advisers* (Washington, DC, 1964), chap. 2.

[8]See DBS, *Distribution of Non-Farm Incomes in Canada by Size, 1959*, p. 12; and chap. 1, p. 20 above.

ture on consumer goods and services by the poverty group is required which would imply a change in the distribution of income though not a redistribution. When we come to estimate consumption in 1970 and 1975 some attempt will be made to determine whether the projected demands will come up to needs as defined above. First, however, we must project aggregate demand (GNE) which rests on a calculation of the labour force in 1970 and 1975 to which we now turn.

THE LABOUR FORCE: 1970 AND 1975

Taking the high and low population projections of the previous section and using the range of labour force propensities that have typified recent non-war decades, namely 35–37 per cent, we can specify a high and low estimate for the labour force in 1970 and 1975. On this basis, the Canadian labour force in 1970 is expected to be between 7.5 and 8.2 million people and between 8.3 and 9.1 million in 1975.

Another way of estimating the labour force is to take the projections by sex for the over 14-year-old age group and apply estimates of the future participation rates by each sex respectively. At present male and female participation rates are 77.7 and 29.5 per cent respectively. The male rate is expected to decline slightly to about 76.5 per cent in 1970 and 76.0 in 1975 while the female rate should rise to about 34.5 in 1970 and 36.0 in 1975. Using these calculations, the labour force in 1970 should be between 8.0 and 8.2 million and in 1975 between 9.0 and 9.3.

Since the data on productivity to be examined in the following section run in terms of output per employed member of the civilian labour force, we must deduct estimates of the armed services in Canada for 1970 and 1975. Assuming these to be about 120,000,[9] this puts the civilian labour force between 7.4 and 8.1 million for 1970. Using similar techniques as above the civilian labour force in 1975 may be expected to lie between 8.2 and 9.2 million.

PROJECTION OF OUTPUT PER MAN-YEAR: 1970 AND 1975

As noted in Chapter 8, real GNP per man-year has historically risen at between 1.5 and 2.5 per cent compounded annually over long periods. However, in recent decades the growth of productivity has been rising and, with growing expenditures on research and development, automation, and other labour efficiency-enhancing activities, it seems more

[9]As of March 31, 1961, Canada's regular armed forces were as follows: Navy–20,655, Army–48,051 and Air Force–51,349, or a total of 120,055. The assumption of constancy of this figure is based upon two other assumptions: (1) that no major war will break out and (2) that no major relaxation of international tensions will occur.

reasonable to assume that the range will be between 2 and 3 per cent in future. In 1962, GNP per man-year employed was estimated as $6,498 in current (1962) dollars or $4,522 in dollars of 1949. Assuming no price changes, "real" GNP per man-year in 1970 and 1975 may be calculated by applying the low and high growth rates.[10] For 1970 this works out as between $5,299 and $5,719 per man-year in 1949 dollars or between $7,614 and $8,232 in 1962 dollars. For 1975 the estimates are $5,850–$6,642 in 1949 dollars and $8,406–$9,544 in 1962 dollars.

There are other techniques for making such estimates. As already noted, productivity trends differ among sectors of the economy. Taking a weighted average of the productivity gains (1950–60) of the sectors shown in Table 8.9 yields a productivity increase of roughly 2.6 per cent which is in the middle of the high and low figures used above.[11]

Other approaches to estimating the rate of productivity growth also yield figures within the range specified above. It does not seem unreasonable, therefore, to predict that GNP per man-year employed in 1970 will be between $5,300 and $5,700 (1949 dollars) or $7,600 and $8,200 (1962 dollars). In 1975, GNP per man-year employed may be estimated as between $5,900–$6,600 (1949 dollars) or $8,400–$9,500 (1962 dollars).

THE EXTENT OF UNEMPLOYMENT

Since 1951 the rate of unemployment in Canada has exhibited a rising trend as well as the usual cyclical behaviour. That is to say, although the rate of unemployment declines during the expansion phase of the business cycle, the post-war experience in Canada, at least until 1962, has been that unemployment does not fall to the previous low. The average unemployment for the years 1951–55 was 3.5 per cent of the labour force; between 1956–60 this increased to 5.7 per cent, and averaged 6.6 per cent in 1961 and 1962. However, since 1962 the unemployment rate has declined steadily so that it is possible the upward trend has been arrested. Certainly the rising trend could not be expected to continue to 1970 since this would imply rates of unemployment in excess of 10 per cent. Even present levels are considered too high and have already induced private and governmental actions to reduce unemployment. The causes of the growth of unemployment relate directly to

[10]That is, GNP per man-year in 1970 would lie between $4,522 (1.02)[8] and $4,522 (1.03)[8] using 1949 values while in 1975 the range would be $4,522 (1.02)[13] and $4,522 (1.03)[13].

[11]The other productivity estimates for 1935–61 or 1949–61 in Table 8.9 also yield weighted averages about halfway between the upper and lower limits specified in this section.

the slowdown in aggregate demand as well as to structural problems associated with the development of new processes and techniques requiring not only higher general skill levels but different skills as well. The failure of the skill composition of the labour force to match the rapidly changing needs combined with slow over-all growth are the particular forces underlying the growth of unemployment in recent years. It seems probable that the slow growth of aggregate demand of the late 1950's will not persist through the 1960's; it is doubtful, however, whether the difficulties on the supply side can be eliminated although some alleviation may be expected. In short, most of the causal factors should be less effective in the years ahead: hence, an unemployment rate of between 3 and 4 per cent may be anticipated.

It is possible that this may be somewhat optimistic in view of the failure to achieve anywhere near this level for a protracted period following 1956. Yet in the last three months of 1963, the seasonally adjusted rates of unemployment showed a steady decline and averaged 5.1 per cent of the civilian labour force. Estimates for March 1965 put the rate at 3.9 per cent. The trend has been sharply downward. Furthermore, the Canadian economy is clearly capable of achieving a more acceptable rate of unemployment and, indeed, has frequently done so in the past. Other countries, notably those in Northwestern Europe, have been able to sustain employment levels at 97 per cent, or higher, of the labour force over most of the 1950's and are characterized by labour scarcity rather than surplus.[12] In short, a rate of unemployment between 3 and 4 per cent is feasible for Canada and

---

[12]It is, of course, true that the definition and measurement of unemployment differ among countries so that direct comparisons of published data are not completely valid. Nevertheless a recent estimate of unemployment in several countries adjusted to conform with US definitions revealed the following.

| Country | Rates of unemployment adjusted to US definitions | | |
	1960	*1961*	*1962*
Canada	7.0	7.2	6.0
United States	5.6	6.7	5.6
France	1.9	1.7	1.8
Germany (Federal Republic)	1.0	0.5	n.a.
Great Britain	2.4	2.2	2.8
Sweden	n.a.	1.5	1.5

SOURCE: *Exploring the Dimensions of the Manpower Revolution*, vol. I of Selected Readings in Employment and Manpower compiled for the Subcommittee on Employment and Manpower (Washington, DC, 1964), p. 168. These estimates indicate that the very large discrepancies between North America and much of North Western Europe are not statistical illusions.

indeed should be a major goal of economic policy. We accept this range of unemployment here as the maximum that would be acceptable over a long period of time, and one within the realm of Canadian capabilities.

Using the 3 to 4 per cent figures, the employed civilian labour force in 1970 should lie between 7.1 and 7.9 million. Using the low and high estimates of GNP per employed civilian member of the labour force developed in the previous section yields a GNP estimate between $37.6 and $45.2 billion in 1949 dollars or $54.1–$65.0 billion in 1962 dollars. Since these are the extreme estimates it is likely that the actual figure would lie close to the mid-way point: hence, a "best guess" would be for a GNP in 1970 of $41 billion in 1949 dollars or almost $60 billion in 1962 dollars. By the same procedure the best guess for 1975 would be $53 billion in 1949 dollars and $76 billion in 1962 dollars (see Table 9.2).

Let us pause to examine the consistency of such estimates with past experience in Canada and with other recent forecasts.

These estimates imply a growth rate of about 4.7 per cent compounded annually from 1960 to 1970. From 1949 to 1962, the growth rate of GNP in dollars of 1949 was about 4.3 per cent whereas the over-all growth rate from 1926 through 1962 in the same terms

TABLE 9.2

GNP and Components, Actual 1960, and
Projections for 1970 and 1975
(billions of 1949 dollars)*

	1960		1970		1975	
	$	%	$	%	$	%
Personal expenditure on consumer goods and services	17.9	69.4	27.1	66.0	34.6	65.3
Government expenditure on goods and services	4.2	16.3	6.9	16.8	8.8	16.8
Business gross fixed capital formation and change in inventories	4.7	18.2	7.5	18.3	9.9	18.7
Exports less imports of goods and services	−0.9	−3.5	−0.5	−1.1	−0.4	−0.8
Gross national expenditure	25.8	100.0	41.0	100.0	53.0	100.0

*Figures may not add to totals due to rounding.

amounted to roughly 3.7 per cent. The estimates thus suggest an acceleration of the over-all rate of growth of real GNP both from its long-term average rate and recent experience. But one of the reasons for the long-term rate being only 3.7 per cent was the period of prolonged depression of the 1930's and economic slowdown of the late 1950's. The estimates in this section, in short, assume that no lengthy depression will typify the next ten to fifteen years and that the slowdown of the later 1950's will not recur, at least to the same extent. Much depends upon external demand conditions as well as domestic policy. In a more basic sense the higher growth rate implied in the above estimates assumes that world demand for traditional Canadian exports will not slacken and, in fact, is expected to rise and that domestic policy will be not only more vigorous but more expansionistic. There are good reasons for the former assumption in view of the growing scarcities, especially in the US, of many raw materials that Canada has in abundance. In particular, the rise in world literacy rates will require more paper and thus a constantly rising demand for newsprint and other pulp and paper products may be expected. Some difficulties may be encountered in agricultural products although the growing needs of China and other underdeveloped countries as well as the Soviet Union may offset this to some extent. Indeed, during the early 1960's wheat sales to the Sino-Soviet countries helped initiate the resurgence in Canada's growth rate. There are no signs that these countries will need less from Canada in the near future although trade relations with them are subject to a high degree of uncertainty. In general, there seem to be good reasons for expecting a relatively buoyant foreign demand for Canadian products—a buoyancy encouraged by the devaluation of 1962 —especially if Canada also makes more strenuous efforts in the realm of manufactured products.

Optimism with respect to domestic policy is less well founded. Nevertheless, if the export markets in fact turn out to be favourable, there will be less pressure on the Canadian balance of payments which, in the past, has served to curb the vigour with which expansionistic monetary and fiscal policies are pursued. Furthermore, it is generally believed that mistakes of policy made the economic slowdown of the late fifties worse than it otherwise would have been.[13] At least in the realm of monetary policy there was a rather single-minded purpose to check inflation which, combined with balance of payments problems, led to a more severe tightening of credit or less of an easing of credit than the output and employment situation appeared to warrant. If this is a valid appraisal,

[13]See Introduction.

it provides some good grounds for optimism. We can learn by past mistakes. Furthermore, there is a growing restiveness about the chronically high levels of unemployment that might well force both monetary and fiscal policy to concentrate less on preventing inflation and more on stimulating aggregate demand. If the trade balance turns out to be as anticipated,[14] this, combined with the other pressures, might well serve to alter the focus of policy in a direction more consistent with economic dynamism. In many respects this is more a matter of faith than of any compelling logic, but we think a case can be made for this view. In addition, the tax reduction in the US (February 1964) has had the effect most economists predicted and has served to stimulate US economic growth; it has thus provided a strong external demand for Canadian exports and supported a more rapid rate of growth throughout North America.

If external and internal conditions change in the manner described above, the somewhat higher growth rate estimated for the decade of the sixties and through the first half of the 1970's would seem to be feasible and not inconsistent with past trends. Indeed, the Economic Council of Canada suggests a potential growth rate of 5.5 per cent from 1963 to 1970 based on net immigration of 50,000 per year (compared with 25,000 used in the present set of estimates). Again, we have assumed an unemployment rate of 3.5 per cent while the Council assumes only 3 per cent.[15] In any event the Council's estimate of growth potential clearly suggests that our projection is not unduly optimistic.

Furthermore, with population growing by about 2 per cent per year, the estimated rise in real GNE per capita becomes 2.7 per cent compounded annually which is comparable with growth in per capita GNE between the late 1930's and 1962.

Other estimates of GNE in 1970 and 1975 are summarized in Table 9.3.

COMPOSITION OF THE GNE

A variety of techniques exist for estimating the composition of GNE. On the one hand one can simply project past trends on the various components as proportions of GNE. This does not involve any estimate of the size or even rate of growth of GNE which, in fact, may exert some influence on its proportionate composition. A second technique

[14]See within at pp. 000–000.
[15]Economic Council of Canada, *Economic Goals for Canada to 1970* (Ottawa, 1964), pp. 36–51.

TABLE 9.3

Aggregate Projections
1970 and 1975

Source	Population (millions) 1970	Population (millions) 1975	Labour force (millions) 1970	Labour force (millions) 1975	GNP (billions of 1949 dollars†) 1970	GNP (billions of 1949 dollars†) 1975
Caves and Holton	21.0	23.4*	7.2	8.0*	38.7	47.4*
Firestone	20.5*	22.4	7.9*	8.6	39.3*	47.6
RCCEP	21.6	24.0	7.9	8.9	40.5	50.1
Present study	21.8	24.2	7.8	8.7	41.0	53.0
Economic Council	21.7	—	8.1	—	43.1	—

*Computed from author's assumptions.
†All GNP estimates adjusted to 1949 dollars by the GNP deflator.
REFERENCES: Richard E. Caves and Richard H. Holton, *The Canadian Economy* (Cambridge, Mass., 1961).
O. J. Firestone, *"Growth and Future of the Canadian Market 1900 to 1975"* (Ottawa, July, 1956), mimeo.
RCCEP, *Final Report* (Ottawa, 1957).
Economic Council of Canada, *Economic Goals for Canada to 1970*, First Annual Review, Ottawa, Dec. 1964, Chaps. 3 and 4.

examines the relationship between the GNE components and their major determinants, some of which involve the size and rate of growth of GNE itself. We shall employ both methods using each as a check for consistency. The data will refer to constant dollars of 1949 which will later be converted to 1962 dollars.

PERSONAL CONSUMPTION EXPENDITURES

During high employment, non-war years, the ratio of personal expenditures on consumer goods and services to GNE has varied generally between 66 and 70 per cent, using constant dollars of 1949. The higher ratios have occurred when unemployment rates have been well above the 4 per cent mark. Consequently, since our previous GNE estimates imply unemployment at roughly the 3 to 4 per cent level, it is reasonable to suppose that in 1970 and 1975 the ratio would be at the lower end of the historical range for so-called "normal" years, namely 66–68 per cent. This would mean personal consumption expenditures of between $27.0–27.9 billion in 1970 and between $35.0 and $36.0 billion in 1975.

Alternatively, consumption can be estimated by using the so-called income elasticity of demand for broad categories of consumption expenditures. This is defined as the percentage change in consumption of a particular commodity or commodity grouping divided by the percentage change in personal disposable income. Since the latter is expected to change by about the same proportion as real GNP,[16] to estimate broad consumption categories we may simply multiply the income elasticity for each category by the percentage change in GNP from, say 1962, to 1970 and 1975 and use the derived percentage change to compute actual consumption in 1970 and 1975. Estimates of income elasticity have been made by Caves and Holton[17] and when used in the above fashion yield the estimates shown in Table 9.4. Total consumption expenditures estimated by this technique are $27.8 billion for 1970 and $35.9 billion for 1975 in 1949 dollars, both of which lie within the range previously deduced using the historical evidence on the proportion of personal consumption expenditures to GNP.

TABLE 9.4

Estimated Consumption
1970 and 1975

Category	1970	1975	1970	1975
	(billions of dollars of 1949)		(per cent of total)	
Food	6.953	8.989	25.0	25.0
Tobacco and alcoholic beverages	2.778	3.592	10.0	10.0
Clothing and personal furnishings	2.856	3.692	10.3	10.3
Shelter	3.344	4.323	12.0	12.0
Household operation	3.339	4.314	12.0	12.0
Transportation	4.276	5.528	15.4	15.4
Personal and medical care and death expenses	1.756	2.270	6.3	6.3
Miscellaneous	2.539	3.283	9.1	9.1
Total	27.841	35.901	100.0	100.0

SOURCES: See text.

Aggregate personal consumption expenditures of these amounts imply per capita consumption of $1,270 for 1970 and $1,480 for 1975 (in 1949 dollars) or a growth rate from 1950 of roughly 2.3 per cent per year, which is not much higher than the historical growth of real per capita consumption.

Thus, on a variety of grounds, the estimates of personal consumption made above seem reasonable and not significantly out of line with the past behaviour of the Canadian economy.

But with economic growth some relative decline in consumption may be expected. Thus the best guess-estimate of personal consumption

[16]See for example, D. W. Slater, *Consumption Expenditure in Canada*, a report prepared for the RCCEP (Ottawa, 1957), p. 69.
[17]R. E. Caves and R. H. Holton, *The Canadian Economy: Prospect and Retrospect* (Cambridge, Mass., 1959), p. 342.

expenditures is $27.1 billion for 1970 and $34.6 billion for 1975 (both in 1949 dollars).

It is difficult to assess whether this amount of consumption would close the gap between demand and needs as previously defined for the low income or poverty group as it existed in 1959. On the one hand it is generally believed that those in the poorest income categories tend to be outside of the regular market processes and hence do not share in economic progress to the same extent as the rest of the nation. This view is implicit in the familiar notions of "poverty its own cause" and "the rich get richer while the poor get poorer." The whole issue of a growing "underclass" more and more isolated from economic and social dynamism has recently been explored by Gunnar Myrdal.[18] We will not discuss this problem further here although it is clearly of great importance for Canada and seems not to have attracted much notice. However, at one extreme it implies that those in poverty at one point of time will remain at the same absolute income levels at some not too distant future time, or at least that their offspring will. This suggests that, if population increases in the "underclass" at the same rate as in the nation as a whole, the proportion of the population living in poverty, estimated earlier at 20 per cent in 1959, will remain the same. Other things being equal, this further suggests that consumption in 1970 and 1975 will have to be higher by roughly $1.4 and $1.5 billion (in 1949 dollars) respectively to eliminate the gap of underconsumption by the poor. The gap between consumption demand and needs would, under these assumptions, decline to 5 and 4.5 per cent in 1970 and 1975 respectively.[19]

On the other hand, if the lower income groups are not completely impervious to market forces or do not have their ranks augmented by growing unemployment, it is quite possible that in absolute terms, poverty, as defined above, may be reduced significantly perhaps requiring only a 2 to 4 per cent rise in consumption to close the deficiency gap. Much also depends upon policies undertaken to alleviate poverty. A reasonable guess might however be that in 1970 and 1975 approximately 3 to 4 per cent more needs to be spent on consumption assuming no significant reduction in the over-all equality of income distribution.

GROSS FIXED CAPITAL FORMATION

There are several methods of estimating capital requirements to achieve an output of $41 billion in 1970. As already noted, the gross capital-

---

[18]See his *Challenge to Affluence* (New York, 1963), Part I.

[19]It is possible that this is conservative if rates of population growth in the underclass exceed the national average or if technological unemployment increases their numbers.

output ratio has slowly been increasing in Canada and it would seem reasonable to project this at about 4 for 1970 and 1975. This would make the gross capital stock in 1970 amount to $164 billion which implies a growth rate of gross capital between 1960 and 1970 of 5.5 per cent compounded annually. This, in turn, means that gross fixed capital formation during 1970 will be $8.55 billion. Alternatively we may use the marginal gross capital-output ratio to deduce the increment in gross capital stock during 1970. Since we have previously estimated that GNE will rise by roughly 4.7 per cent, this implies that the increase in GNE during 1970 will be $1.84 billion. Assuming that the marginal gross capital output ratio lies between 4.3 and 4.8, we may estimate by this technique that gross capital formation in 1970 will be roughly $8.4 billion. A best guess is therefore $8.5 billion using both the average and marginal gross capital output ratios. This figure includes both public and private investment. Historically, public capital formation has constituted about 20 per cent of the total in 1949 dollars. Thus business gross fixed capital formation in 1970 may be projected at $6.8 billion and public investment at $1.7 billion. These estimates suggest that business gross fixed capital formation in 1970 will constitute around 16.6 per cent of GNE (all figures in dollars of 1949). For high employment years and years of fairly rapid economic growth, this ratio has varied between 15 and 19 per cent in the past. For the early part of the fifties the ratio reached as high as 20.5 per cent in 1956 prior to the slow-down. It seems clear, however, that these high proportions are non-sustainable over lengthy periods of time. Hence the figure of 16.6 per cent seems realistic.

To this must be added the investment in inventories. During years of fairly rapid over-all growth the proportion of inventory investment to GNE (in 1949 dollars) has ranged between 2 and 4 per cent. For the decade of the fifties as a whole the average ratio was about 2 per cent. Caves and Holton have estimated this component of GNP at 1.7 per cent.[20] A reasonably conservative estimate implying a level of inventory accumulation that would clearly be sustainable and not excessive would therefore be about $700 million. Thus total private investment may be estimated at $7.5 billion in 1970. By a similar technique total private investment for 1975 may be expected to amount to $9.9 billion (all figures in 1949 dollars).

GOVERNMENT EXPENDITURES ON GOODS AND SERVICES

This component of GNE is rather difficult to project since it involves mainly political decisions and is not uniquely related to economic fac-

[20]*Canadian Economy*, p. 346.

tors. Furthermore government spending in the present context refers to all levels of government, federal, provincial, and municipal, and at the federal level differs from the outlays as contained in the administrative budget which is widely publicized. Essentially the concept of "government expenditures on goods and services" as used in the national accounts seeks to measure only those outlays by government for currently produced goods and services excluding similar outlays by government business enterprises which are included in the private sector. Thus the totals of, for example, federal government receipts and expenditures in the national income sense differ from those in the regular administrative budget annually presented to Parliament. Between 1955 and 1962, for example, federal government budgetary expenditures as per the public accounts were regularly below federal government expenditures on goods and services as recorded in the national income estimates by amounts ranging from half a billion dollars to over one billion dollars.[21]

Fortunately for predictive purposes the ratio of government expenditures on goods and services as defined in the national accounting sense has, since 1951 when the new and higher defence spending plateau was reached, varied between 15 and 17 per cent. On a straight historical projection, therefore, since we are assuming no war and no mass unemployment, and given an upward bias in government spending, it seems reasonable to assume that this will be roughly 17 per cent of total GNE in 1970 and 1975. Alternatively, since we concluded in the previous section that public gross fixed capital formation would be $1.7 billion in 1970 and since the ratio of government capital formation to total government expenditures on goods and services in the national accounting sense typically constitutes around 25 per cent of the total, we may estimate total government expenditures in 1970 at $6.8 billion which is approximately 16.6 per cent of estimated GNE. Our best guess estimate for this component of GNE to total is $6.9 billion or 16.8 per cent of the projected GNE for 1970. A similar calculation suggests that government expenditures in 1975 would amount to $8.9 billion, also some 16.8 per cent of the level of GNE projected for 1975.

EXPORTS AND IMPORTS OF GOODS AND SERVICES

A proper appraisal of these two major components of GNP would involve a detailed analysis of the composition and geographical distribution of each component of exports and imports. However, neither time

[21]Details of the adjustments needed to convert budgetary to national accounts totals are given in DBS, *National Accounts Income and Expenditure, 1926–1956* (Ottawa, 1962), pp. 161–2.

nor resources has permitted such a comprehensive survey. Furthermore there exist several carefully made projections of each of these components. We will therefore use such projections as the basis for making our own, modifying them in the light of subsequent information and in conformity with the over-all estimates already made in previous sections of the present work.

The two most comprehensive appraisals of Canada's export prospects in recent years[22] suggest that exports of goods and services as a proportion of GNP will be 19 per cent in 1970[23] and 19.7[24] per cent in 1980 in dollars of 1949. If we examine the past historical trends, it would appear that the Caves and Holton proportion is too low for 1970. Furthermore, both estimates were made before devaluation of the Canadian dollar and prior to the slowdown. Hence both tend to understate exports and overstate imports. During the decade of the fifties the ratio varied between 22 and 24 per cent and in 1962 was 23.2 per cent. Assuming a slight general downward drift in the relative significance of exports, a ratio of 22.0 per cent may be expected in 1970 or a total value of export of goods and services of $9.0 billion in dollars of 1949. Assuming the ratio in 1975 to decline to 21.5 per cent, this implies a value of $11.2 billion. These estimates, although slightly on the high side of Slater's computations, lie within the range projected by the Royal Commission on Canada's Economic Prospects between 1955 and 1980 and will be accepted here as the best guesses for this important category of final demand.

On the import side, it is believed that with the growth rate of GNP implied in the aggregate projection made earlier, imports will exceed exports for the Canadian economy as they have typically done during periods of rapid growth. This would imply imports as a proportion of GNP slightly in excess of 22 per cent for 1970 and 21.5 per cent for 1975. Slater's study of imports estimates the import ratio as 23.5 in 1965 (using 1949 dollars) and 21.9 per cent in 1980.[25] Assuming a fairly steady decline in this ratio over time, estimates of 23.1 per cent for 1970 and 22.3 per cent for 1975 fit the pattern reasonably well.

---

[22]Caves and Holton, *Canadian Economy*, chap. 13; Slater, *Canada's Imports*, a study prepared for RCCEP (Ottawa, 1957); and R. V. Anderson, *The Future of Canada's Export Trade*, a study prepared for RCCEP (Ottawa, 1957).

[23]This is the Caves and Holton estimate adjusted from dollars of 1955 by the implicit national accounts price index for exports of goods and services after adding an estimate of $300 million for interest and dividend receipts in 1970.

[24]This is Slater's forecast adjusted to dollars of 1949. See *Canada's Imports*, p. 164.

[25]*Canada's Imports*, Table 33, p. 98.

These imply import levels of $9.5 billion for 1970 and $11.6 billion for 1975 in 1949 dollars.

Putting these estimates together suggests a balance of payments deficit on current account of $500 million for 1970 and $400 million for 1975 which are below the deficits prevailing during much of the 1950's and appear to be well within Canada's ability to handle especially with a significantly higher GNP. In other words, although the projections made here imply deficits on Canada's international transactions, these are not sufficiently large relative to anticipated GNP to constitute crisis conditions of the type which, along with the attempts to manipulate the free exchange rate, led to the emergency measures of 1962 and which would otherwise represent levels of GNP that were non-sustainable.

SUMMARY OF AGGREGATE DEMAND COMPONENTS

In dollars of 1949 the picture that emerges of Canada's major expenditure categories is shown in Table 9.2.

At this point we may pause to check the feasibility of attaining an output of $41 billion (in dollars of 1949) by 1970 and $53 billion by 1975. If the savings ratio implied in the foregoing is realized this works out at about 21.2 per cent for 1970 including that portion, about one-fifth, of government GNP purchases deemed to be investment[26]; the so-called "warranted" rate of growth is around 4.7 per cent assuming an incremental capital-output ratio between 4.3 and 4.8. Essentially this means that as far as capital is concerned, no serious obstacle appears if the Canadian economy in fact generates the savings in a fashion consistent with past experience and if Canadian business and government use these savings in an efficient manner. Furthermore, if the excess of imports over exports represents mainly capital equipment this would further expand capital capacity more substantially than if the deficit

---

[26]The savings ratio may be deduced as follows for 1970 from the above estimates which omit many detailed items and adjustments. If we assume that the national income governmental budgets are balanced then total taxes equal total expenditures or $6.9 billion. Business savings are composed of capital consumption allowances and retained income and account for about three quarters of business capital formation, or roughly $5.6 billion. Since personal saving is the difference between personal disposable income and personal consumption expenditures we must derive the former. Simply, personal disposable income is GNE less savings of business after taxes are deducted. Thus personal disposable income may be estimated as $41 — (5.6 + 6.9) = $28.5 billion and personal savings as $28.5 — 27.1 = $1.4 billion: hence total gross national savings is $7 billion which, of necessity, equals total investment (i.e. business capital formation, $7.5 billion plus exports minus imports, or —0.5). But adding government investment, estimated as 25 per cent of total government spending yields a savings and investment estimate of $8.7 billion or 21.2 per cent of GNE.

consisted entirely of consumer goods. There is clearly no bottleneck in terms of quantity of labour since we have deduced the output totals on the assumption of rates of unemployment over 3 per cent. Problems may be encountered in terms of labour and managerial quality although these would not appear to be sufficiently great to preclude the antici- pated growth of productivity of between 2 and 3 per cent per employed worker per year. This productivity growth is more likely to occur if realistic monetary and fiscal policies are pursued, if the calibre of Cana- dian management continues its apparent improvement,[27] and if the volume of research and development expenditures continues at the higher levels recently achieved. There will be greater difficulty in raising the general skill level of the whole labour force, but this should serve mainly to limit productivity gains to the 2–3 per cent range rather than to raise their levels in excess of 3 per cent which might otherwise prove possible.

There is obviously no bottleneck from the point of view of natural resources including energy and fuel sources. Indeed, as already shown in Chapter 5, the limitation on output of most of these items would be the failure of GNE to grow fast enough rather than the other way around.

In short, from the point of view of supply, there is no apparent shortage that would serve to prevent GNE from increasing to the levels estimated above.

We will not make estimates of the many subcomponents in the aggre- gates discussed above mainly because detailed projections will shortly be published by the Royal Commission on Health Services. Furthermore time and resources available for the present study do not permit a careful appraisal of all the factors essential for a finely disaggregated approach. To attempt such estimates here would be little more than an arithmetic exercise which the reader may readily undertake for himself. We may therefore conclude this part on the happy note that Canada clearly has the means of achieving ever higher standards of living for an increasing population.

[27]See chap. 8, p. 333.

EPILOGUE

As the centenary of her birth approaches, Canada as a nation is beset by division and doubt. To the historically-minded observer, it would seem that the problems of today could not possibly compare with those that confronted the new nation of 1867, and yet concern for the future viability of Canada is more deeply and widely felt throughout the nation today than at any time since Confederation. This concern is all the more rueful and melancholy because of the inability to define with concrete clarity the nature and sources of the nation's problems. It is not possible, as it was in 1867, to focus upon the United States as an inimical force posing a forthright military and political threat to which Canada could respond in a similarly forthright fashion. The United States is still today a threat in the minds of many Canadians, most particularly in the economic realms of trade and investment, but the indefinite and apparently indefinable nature of these fears, together with the mutual friendship and great goodwill that has grown between the two nations in the past hundred years, make it very difficult for Canada to respond clearly and constructively to the dangers she senses from this direction.

Similarly, in the spheres of domestic economic and political life, the problems, while much smaller in magnitude than they were a century ago, are more nagging and debilitating on account of their shapelessness and ambiguity. The economy is rich and modern and yet does not seem to be able to avoid or effectively combat unemployment and persistent regional disparities of income. The federal political system has proved equal to great challenges in the past, but today is under heavy attacks, some of which disclose the existence of a degree of rancour and embitterment that would seem impossible to ameliorate by measures short of the effective dissolution of Confederation.

These doubts and fears seem to be quite unjustified by the study of the Canadian economy and its future prospects which occupy the foregoing pages of this book. As our study and projections have indicated, the future of Canada, on economic grounds, is bright with promise. The nation has abundant natural resources, many of which are of a kind for which future world demand may confidently be expected to be very strong. She has relatively easier access to the world's single largest market, the United States, than any other country. With a level of income per head among the highest in the world, her ability to provide for a high level of capital formation is assured from domestic sources, and in addition, she enjoys almost unparalleled access to the great capital markets of the world. The Canadian people are well educated; the Canadian labour force is highly skilled, talented, and hard-working. Nor is Canada notably short of entrepreneurial and administrative talent, both public and private. The country is already supplied with an infrastructure of social fixed capital facilities that, despite some important gaps and limitations, is well developed and, compared with most countries, substantial in amount. The same may be said of the existing stock of private fixed capital facilities. The Canadian economy remains highly dependent on exports, but enjoys the stability of established markets with a high and growing degree of diversification, despite the predominant importance of staples. There are no critical resource scarcities or bottlenecks such as confront many of the underdeveloped countries of the world and make their economic progress difficult and problematical.

In brief, Canada should be able to look forward with confidence in her ability to progress. The prerequisites of economic growth and development are all abundantly provided and her history up to this point has shown that Canada is able to take advantage of her opportunities. Nevertheless, it needs to be emphasized, as we have already done in the preceding chapters, that past progress and the present availability of human and non-human resources are not by themselves sufficient to guarantee development, even of the most strictly material kind. The way in which resources are used, and for what purposes, are the critical factors for Canada of the 1960's. And since it is in the political and cultural life of a country that these decisive prime movers are to be found, the keys to Canada's future lie there. But it is precisely in the political and cultural spheres that serious problems exist which will severely test the viability of Canada as a united and independent national entity capable of development within herself and of contributing to the solution of international problems. Most of these questions have been examined or touched upon in other parts of this volume, especially in so far as their economic aspects are concerned. Our aim in this epilogue is simply to itemize those aspects of present-day Canada which, at this time of writing, loom largest as barriers to the realization of her national promise.

First in importance is the constitutional structure. Canada is a federal state with jurisdiction and responsibility divided between two levels of government, and these two levels are not merely administrative divisions but autonomous entities, both finding their legitimacy in the same document, the British North America Act of 1867. However, the BNA Act, by which Canada as a nation began history, stressed the need for a strong central government. It is in the nature of all but the worst forms of government that constitutional structures should change with time, and it is in the nature of a federal union that there should be changes in the distribution of powers and responsibilities between the different levels of government of which it is composed. However, during the past fifteen years or so the growth of governmental functions has been remarkably one-sided. The development of the services of the welfare state—health, pensions, social services, and social welfare—are all constitutionally provincial responsibilities; urban growth and redevelopment is a provincial responsibility; highways and roads are provincial responsibilities; education is a provincial responsibility. It is impossible to think of any federal function calling for large expenditures of public funds, that has grown comparably in recent years.

By itself this great growth of governmental functions would seem to call for either a shift of responsibilities from the provincial to the federal government, or a shift of taxing power in the opposite direction. What has developed in Canada is neither of these two direct solutions. The federal government has retained the financial power, but has, increasingly, used its fiscal resources in order to make expenditures and to implement policies in areas of provincial responsibility. This has led to a great prolification of federal policies—from the Trans-Canada Highway, to the subsidization of university students, to the National Pensions scheme.

Canada has, for a good many years now, been adopting *ad hoc* solutions for immediate problems, without attending to the larger constitutional issues that are involved. One should perhaps not be surprised that this policy of expediency is now threatening to break down. The worst manifestation of this is the rising demands for provincial autonomy amounting, in some parts of the country, to a demand for the effective dissolution of the federal union. This is not confined to Quebec, though elsewhere in Canada it lacks the racial elements that seem to have become essential features of Quebec's insistence upon a reconstruction of the Canadian constitution. It is noteworthy that the demands for provincial autonomy and financial independence have been accommodated and acquiesced in perhaps to a greater degree in Canada than in any other nation of the Western world, yet there is no lessening but instead a continuous swelling of provincial claims.

The growth of local and regional responsibilities is, of course, not unique to Canada, but of special significance is the extent to which, in Canada, these have already been allowed to weaken vital functions of the central government—a trend which threatens to continue. The United States, for example, has always had strong "states rights" sentiments, but they have never been allowed seriously to undermine, for example, federal control of monetary, fiscal, or tariff policies. The recent federal tax reduction in the United States was definitely not designed to allow the states to enter the vacated field, as was the case in Canada under recent federal-provincial taxation agreements. As we have previously noted, much of this trend in Canada must be ascribed to failures at the federal level to devise and implement effective economic policies within its own sphere of constitutional responsibility.

It may be argued that decentralization, the return to the smaller political units of certain details of policy and administration, is a desirable next step in the development of the modern welfare state. Myrdal, for example, has argued that

the purpose and accomplishment of planning in the Welfare State is, in fact, constantly to simplify, and largely to liquidate, old and new intervention: to substitute a few, mostly overall state policies for a growing mesh of detailed and direct ones and, in particular, to recondition the national community in such a way that for the most part it can be left to the cooperation and collective bargaining of the people themselves, in all sorts of communities and organizations beneath the formal state level, to settle the norms for their living together.[1]

But this implies a degree of development of national policy and administration that has not yet been achieved in most countries, and certainly not in Canada. The growth of autonomist and separatist tendencies is at least premature for Canada. It represents less the full development of a consensus regarding the legitimate sphere of federal government policy than a failure of such a consensus to arise amid doubts about the ability of the federal government to pursue wise and effective policies within its own sphere. One may readily grant that ultimately many details of policy should be returned to local and regional units of government.

[1]Gunnar Myrdal, *Beyond the Welfare State* (New Haven, 1960), p. 102.

Indeed, if it is a legitimate aim to try to encourage diversity, in government as in other spheres of social life, this is even more significant within a nation which values the individuality of the human spirit. But
Canada, at least, has not yet achieved that level of political maturity
where extensive reductions in federal authority and jurisdiction can be
viewed as symptomatic of social progress. Petty federal restraints and
interferences may well be done away with, but no wholesale renunciation
of jurisdiction by the federal government at the present time appears to
be consistent with the political or economic viability of Canada as a
nation.

The problems of "divided jurisdiction" that beset any federal state
are greatly exacerbated in Canada by the fact that the union is regarded
by many, and especially by those of the French language, as a union
of two races or two linguistic groups. The BNA Act has often been
referred to, in Quebec and elsewhere as constituting a "compact" between French and English Canadians. The fact that there is little historical or legal justification for such a view is of minor significance at a
time, such as the present, when strong sentiments of disaffection with
Confederation exist in French Canada. Whatever the nature of the
union between French and English in Canada may properly be thought
to be, it confounds the appreciation of constitutional problems because,
while it runs parallel to the constitutional organization in some ways, it
is tangential to it in others. French Canadians identify strongly with the
Province of Quebec and are inclined to think of Quebec City as their
capital. English Canadians have no comparable identification with a
province (except possibly in the case of Newfoundland) and Ottawa
takes on, for them, a role comparable to Quebec City. The curious result
of this is that Ottawa is not fully a *national* capital, but to a considerable degree is the capital of *English* Canada only—more so in the minds
of French Canadians than English Canadians perhaps, but that does not
make the result any the less peculiar. As a consequence, there are always
two, or perhaps three, games being played simultaneously on the board
of federal-provincial relations in Canada: Ottawa *versus* the provinces;
Ottawa *versus* Quebec; and Ottawa and the ten provinces, a free-for-all
with every player for himself.

The second of these three games is necessarily a delicate one. It is un-
avoidably played in a charged atmosphere, since it bears vitally on one
of the great non-rational emotions of modern political man—the emotion
of nationalism and ethnic identification. Nationalism in the modern
world is a sentiment akin to romantic love. Observed in others it is
risible, pathetic, and perhaps a little sad, but in oneself it burns with

the white heat of passionate dedication and unreason. Another nation's patriotic rituals engender in us the same contemptuous disdainful indulgence as the behaviour of others in love. But let us be the principals ourselves, and what holy dedication and Messianic zeal takes its place! Rational consideration of such matters is a difficult problem under the best of conditions—and Canada does not provide the best of conditions, for her national house contains more than one nationalistic sentiment, each displaying the typical patterns of dedication to its own and disdain for the other. One of the fundamental problems of Canadian nationhood is how to provide for different nationalistic sentiments and observances within a single national house without increasing irritation, acrimony, and ultimate divorce. It is a problem not yet solved in Canada. Perhaps it can never be fully solved, but today, for numerous reasons, it has come to the forefront as the leading threat to the continuation of Canada as a unified and independent nation.

The second of Canada's two major problems is also one that can never be "solved" in any final sense; it is the problem of how to live alongside the United States. Canadian problems of trade, international investment, defence, and international relations are important in themselves, but the proximity of the United States invests them with concern for the continuing survival of Canada as an independent nation. There can be no doubt that any small nation as closely aligned geographically and economically to a very large country as Canada is to the United States will inevitably face serious problems in maintaining her *de facto* political independence.[2] Yet this is not always the fault of the larger nation. The hypersensitivity to this problem in Canada is less the result of deliberate or even simply thoughtless American policy than of Canada's own lack of a sense of confidence in her ability to deal with these problems. The lack of confidence has been substantially deepened by the policies of recent years, many of which can only be described as blunders. The concern with the inflow of foreign capital and the balance of payments deficit which led, in 1961, to an effort to manipulate the Canadian exchange rate, culminated in an exchange crisis and the loss of the policy flexibility of a free exchange rate; the concern over foreign ownership of industry led to such poorly considered measures in the Budget of 1963 that most of them had to be withdrawn; the effort to use import tariff remissions as a form of export subsidy for the automobile industry has been widely criticized in Canada as contravening the spirit of the GATT and the defence of this policy by Ottawa

2There is some parallel here to the relationship between Finland and the Soviet Union, for example.

has been argumentative rather than rational; the response of the Canadian government to the US interest equalization tax in 1963 was to plead for special consideration which, in effect, gives the President of the United States a quite extraordinary degree of discretionary power over the Canadian balance of international payments—a consequence of its policy that the Canadian government did not appreciate at the time. These events have combined to produce a sense of inadequacy in Canada's ability to see the problems of its relations with the United States clearly, and to act wisely and effectively to meet them.

The assumption that Canada is culturally distinctive from the United States—an assumption which lies at the heart of Canadian nationhood, historically and today—is a large and nebulous subject, notoriously difficult to specify and delineate. The differences of tastes, preferences, attitudes, institutions, and so forth within the various regions of Canada seem to be larger than those between Canada and the contiguous areas of the United States. The latter differences hardly seem significant or important enough to justify paying an economic penalty of 20 to 30 per cent in terms of real GNP per capita, much of which might be reduced by some form of political or economic union of North America. If there is such a thing as a distinctive Canadian way of life it has yet to be crystallized sufficiently to be clearly identified, and to a casual observer the similarities with the United States are far more numerous and fundamental than the differences. Indeed, this may be one reason why whatever differences that do exist are continually overemphasized, and not infrequently have an anti-American basis. But excessive eulogy of perhaps insignificant differences only creates nagging doubts in the long run whether in fact they are important after all.

Canada, however, does have the opportunity of creating or developing a unique identity on the North American continent, and this, paradoxically, springs from that feature of her constitution that is today such a profound source of tension and concern—the mixture of two large linguistic and cultural groups, drawing their social and cultural inspiration from two different, though magnificently complementary, European sources. A real biculturalism, a real mixture of French and English in Canada would provide the kind of cultural climate that would set Canada, distinctively and constructively apart, and create a sense of accomplishment that would offset the seductive lure of closer attachment to the United States. This, and not the separatism of regional autonomy, would be the true fulfilment of the claims of Confederation. The long-standing failure to achieve a greater degree of bicultural harmony and intercourse contributes to the political disaffection between Ottawa and

Quebec which, in turn, is aggravated by the income disparities between French- and English-speaking Canadians.

The unfinished business of Canada in nationhood has wide ramifications, but all are interrelated. It is partly for this reason that successful resolution of the leading economic difficulties might well have high priority on Canada's agenda at the present time. But also we stress the economic aspects because we are confident that they are tractable. If a high rate of economic growth can be sustained, as would appear to be entirely feasible if wiser monetary, fiscal, and other economic policies are pursued than has been in the case over the past decade, this could provide the economic flexibility and opportunity necessary to tackle successfully many of the political, cultural, and other economic problems which will otherwise be aggravated by continuing economic stagnation or slow and halting growth. A good economic performance would also restore confidence in the federal government, the loss of which has induced much of the recent trend towards separatism and local autonomy. The improved economic performance since 1961 augurs well for Canada's future but only if it is not permitted to falter as it did in the latter half of the previous decade.

The appropriate general economic policies to take under given circumstances are no longer any mystery nor have they been since the mid 1930's. Under conditions of deficiency of aggregate demand (GNE) when unacceptably high rates of unemployment exist, the federal budget should run at a substantial deficit through some combination of deliberate tax rate reductions and rising public outlays. A deficit of a size that results from the unemployment itself rather than measures to combat it is clearly inadequate. At the same time, monetary policy should attempt to expand the money supply, increase the availability of credit, and reduce long-term interest rates. Reverse policies should prevail when strong inflationary pressures exist. To be sure, additional measures of a more direct sort are frequently required; but these should be instituted mainly to elaborate and refine the general orientation of policy outlined above rather than substitute for any failure to utilize the broad powerful instruments at the disposal of the government. Furthermore the public must come to accept the necessity of counter-cyclical finance and abandon the ancient dogma of an annually balanced budget or irrational fears of deficits in themselves. Nor should ministers of finance boast of budgetary surpluses or lament deficits when these constitute appropriate counter-forces to undesirable economic trends in the private sector. The task of the minister of finance is to be nation's economist, not its bookkeeper; the conventional wisdom of the business community will not serve him in the performance of this task. Post-war Canadian governments have frequently paid lip service to these general principles but their actions belie the intent.[3] In any event, outside of the academic profession there has been little attempt to convince the public of the importance of counter-cyclical, discretionary behaviour on the part of the monetary and fiscal authorities. As has been well said, "The Minister of Finance must be willing to explain, rather than apologize for, deficits and surpluses."[4] Nor must monetary policy again be permitted to fall into the hands of a person whose views of economic problems and relationships are so naive as to allow him to believe that inflation is the only serious danger the economy of the nation faces, and who therefore pursues a tight money policy even when rates of unemployment are high. Canada paid dearly for this blinkered fixation on price stability in the period after the downturn of the economy in 1957. Price stability of a reasonable degree could have been achieved with much less waste of human and physical resources. Nor should concern over the balance of payments be permitted to blind the authorities to the more serious problems of domestic unemployment. Indeed, high interest rates in Canada serve not only to keep unemployment excessively high but attract the foreign capital that some people view indiscriminately as a source of political servitude. Nor is it necessarily the case that rising aggregate demand is inconsistent with reasonably stable prices, especially when substantial excess capacity in both labour and capital exists. Indeed, rising demand may produce economies of scale and incentives to innovate which, even at full employment, will not cause such pressure on Canadian prices that exports are seriously threatened and imports stimulated. Canada's balance of payments has during the last decade served as a convenient excuse for ignoring sensible domestic policies. Yet in general there has been no irreconcilable conflict between appropriate monetary, fiscal, and balance of payments policies.

It is these serious mistakes of public policy whose consequences became so apparent during the mid-1950's that have caused the lack of confidence in Ottawa and lost the respect of most of Canada's economists. It will not be easy to restore confidence especially in the present political atmosphere. Furthermore, there are additional problems associated with residual poverty and structural unemployment whose resolution by the relatively simple expedient of counter-cyclical monetary and fiscal policy is scarcely to be expected. Canada, like other countries,

[3]For a brief discussion see *Report of the Royal Commission on Banking and Finance* (Ottawa, 1964), p. 507.
[4]*Ibid.*, p. 521.

needs to devise new remedies for new or persistent problems but unlike many other Western nations, Canada has not yet learned the lesson of the thirties. Thus, superimposed upon the new problems of the 1960's is the continuing failure to engage in straight-forward counter-cyclical actions which now need to be supplemented by carefully worked out new programs. The challenge of the sixties and beyond is thereby compounded; it requires, even though belated, implementation of what should have been long-established general economic policy as well as fresh approaches designed to attack problems not fully solvable by the more general measures.

It is, of course, possible that Canadian authorities have learned a bitter lesson from past mistakes and will follow a more responsible and consistent course of action in the future. If so, there is no reason why the Canadian economy cannot achieve the results we have projected in Part III. Indeed the projections were largely based upon this kind of optimism. And a dynamic economy can serve as a solvent for many of the divisive tendencies at present besetting the Canadian polity. Economic growth may create only the possibility of civilization, but its absence, especially in the Canadian case, can only lead to the further weakening of the political bonds forged a century ago.

EPILOGUE

A l'approche du centenaire de sa naissance, la nation canadienne est divisée et doute d'elle-même. Aux yeux de l'observateur qui s'intéresse à l'histoire, les problèmes de notre temps ne semblent pas comparables à ceux qu'affrontait la jeune nation de 1867 et, pourtant, on ressent aujourd'hui, quant à la viabilité du Canada, une inquiétude plus profonde et plus répandue qu'à tout autre moment depuis le début de la Confédération. Cette inquiétude est d'autant plus amère et sombre qu'on est incapable de définir clairement et concrètement la nature et les sources de ces difficultés. Il n'est pas possible, comme en 1867, de considérer les Etats-Unis comme une puissance hostile, constituant une menace militaire et politique immédiate, à laquelle le Canada pourrait répondre par une attitude semblable et aussi nette. Les Etats-Unis sont encore menaçants de nos jours, dans l'esprit de nombre de Canadiens, plus particulièrement dans les domaines économiques du commerce et des investissements ; toutefois la nature indéfinie et apparement indéfinissable de ces craintes, de même que, d'autre part, l'amitié réciproque et la grande bienveillance qui se sont développées entre les deux nations au cours des cent dernières années permettent difficilement au Canada de parer d'une façon claire et constructive aux périls qui le pressent de ce côté.

De même, dans la vie économique et politique du pays, les problèmes, qui sont beaucoup moins grands qu'il y a un siècle, sont d'autant plus agaçants et démoralisant qu'ils sont imprécis et ambigus. Nous avons une économie d'abondance et de caractère moderne, mais elle semble impuissante à éviter ou à combattre efficacement le chômage et à atténuer les différences de revenu qui persistent entre les régions. Le régime politique fédéral s'est montré à la hauteur de circonstances fort critiques dans le passé, mais il fait l'objet aujourd'hui de violentes attaques dont quelques-unes révèlent l'existence d'une certaine dose de rancœur et d'amertume qu'il semble impossible de faire disparaître sans aller jusqu'à la dissolution pure et simple de la Confédération.

Ces doutes et ces craintes paraissent injustifiés si l'on examine l'économie canadienne et ses perspectives d'avenir qui remplissent les pages précédentes du présent ouvrage. Comme notre étude et nos projections l'ont indiqué, l'avenir du Canada, en matière économique, est plein de promesses. La nation dispose d'abondantes ressources naturelles ; pour nombre d'entre ces dernières, elle peut s'attendre que la demande mondiale continuera d'être très forte. Il lui est relativement plus facile qu'à tout autre pays d'avoir accès au plus grand marché unitaire du monde, celui des Etats-Unis. La moyenne des revenus individuels est l'une des plus élevées qui soient, ce qui lui permet de trouver chez elle les moyens de former des capitaux considérables. De plus peu de pays sont aussi bien placés pour faire appel aux grands marchés financiers du monde. Les Canadiens sont instruits, la main-d'œuvre canadienne est hautement spécialisée, habile, et laborieuse. Le Canada ne souffre pas non plus du manque de chefs d'entreprise ou d'administrateurs dans les secteurs tant public que privé. Le pays est déjà doté d'une infrastructure étendue de biens sociaux à capital fixe qui, malgré certaines lacunes et insuffisances assez marquées, se compare favorablement, pour la valeur globale, avec celle dont disposent la plupart des autres pays. On peut en dire autant de la valeur réelle des biens privés à capital fixe. L'économie canadienne dépend étroitement de l'exportation, mais elle repose sur la stabilité de marchés établis qui présentent un degré élevé et croissant de diversification, malgré l'importance prépondérante des produits de base. Il n'existe ni pénurie ni goulot d'étranglement qui soient vraiment graves, comme il arrive dans beaucoup de pays sous-développés, ce qui rend leur progrès économique difficile et problématique.

En bref, le Canada devrait être en mesure d'envisager l'avenir, confiant dans ses moyens d'aller de l'avant. Les conditions préalables de croissance et de progrès économiques lui sont toutes abondamment acquises ; son histoire jusqu'à aujourd'hui a montré qu'il peut profiter des occasions qui lui étaient offertes. Néanmoins, il faut souligner, comme nous l'avons déjà fait dans les chapitres précédents, que les succès passés et la disponibilité actuelle des ressources humaines et matérielles ne suffisent pas en soi à assurer le progrès, même au niveau le plus terre-à-terre. La façon dont il utilise ses ressources et la fin à laquelle il les emploie constituent des éléments décisifs pour le Canada de 1960. Et puisque c'est dans la vie politique et culturelle qu'il faut chercher ces mobiles déterminants, c'est là que nous trouverons les clefs de l'avenir du pays. Toutefois c'est précisément dans les domaines politiques et culturels qu'il surgit des difficultés sérieuses qui mettent à rude épreuve la viabilité du Canada en tant qu'entité nationale unie et indépendante, capable de se développer à l'intérieur et de contribuer à la solution de problèmes internationaux. Nous avons abordé ou étudié la plupart de ces questions dans d'autres parties du présent ouvrage, surtout en ce qui a trait aux aspects d'ordre économique qu'elles présentent. Dans cet épilogue, nous visons simplement à détailler ces particularités qui, au moment où nous écrivons ces lignes, paraissent constituer les plus grands obstacles à la réalisation des espérances nationales du Canada.

Par ordre d'importance vient en tête la structure constitutionnelle. Le Canada est un Etat fédéral à juridictions et à responsabilités réparties entre deux niveaux de gouvernement ; ces deux niveaux ne sont pas de simples divisions administratives, mais ils marquent deux entités autonomes, trouvant leur raison d'être légitime dans le même document : la loi sur l'Amérique du Nord britannique de 1867.

Cependant cette loi en vertu de laquelle le Canada fit son entrée dans l'histoire à titre de nation soulignait la nécessité d'un gouvernement central puissant. Mais, il est de l'essence même de toutes les formes de gouvernement, hormis les plus mauvaises, que les structures constitutionnelles se modifient avec le temps, et il est de la nature d'une union fédérale que la répartition des pouvoirs et des responsabilités, aux différents échelons qui la constituent, ne reste pas immuable.

Toutefois, depuis une quinzaine d'années, l'importance des fonctions gouvernementales s'est accrue d'une façon singulièrement unilatérale. La mise en œuvre des services de la sécurité sociale — santé, pensions, avantages sociaux de tout ordre — d'après la constitution, est du ressort des provinces, comme, d'ailleurs, l'urbanisme, la voire, et l'enseignement. Il est impossible de citer une fonction fédérale déjà inscrite dans la constitution et exigeant une part importante des fonds publics, qui ait acquis une extension comparable au cours des récentes années.

En soi cette augmentation considérable de la centralisation semblerait comporter soit un déplacement des responsabilités des gouvernements provinciaux vers le gouvernement fédéral, soit la délégation des droits d'imposition dans le sens opposé. Aucune de ces deux solutions directes n'a été appliquée au Canada. Le gouvernement fédéral a conservé le pouvoir financier, mais il s'est servi de plus en plus de ses ressources fiscales pour effectuer des dépenses et pour mettre en œuvre des politiques qui ressortissaient au domaine des provinces. Cette tendance a suscité une prolifération de programmes fédéraux allant de la Route transcanadienne au versement de subventions aux étudiants et au projet de Caisse de retraite nationale.

Depuis nombre d'années déja le Canada applique des solutions d'espèce à des problèmes immédiats, sans penser aux sérieuses implications d'ordre constitutionnel qu'ils présentent. Il n'est peut-être pas surprenant que cette politique opportuniste menace en ce moment de faire faillite. La manifestation la plus grave de cet état de choses est la revendication croissante de l'autonomie provinciale qui, en certaines régions du pays, va en fait jusqu'à réclamer la dissolution de l'union fédérale. Ce phénomène n'est pas limité au Québec, bien que, dans les autres parties du pays, il ne comporte pas cet élément racial qui semble désormais former une caractéristique essentielle de l'insistance du Québec à exiger la refonte de la constitution canadienne. Il convient de noter que les requêtes en faveur de l'autonomie provinciale et de l'indépendance financière ont été acceptées et satisfaites à un degré peut-être plus grand au Canada que chez aucune autre nation du monde occidental ; et pourtant, loin de diminuer, les réclamations des provinces augmentent sans cesse.

L'accroissement des responsabilités locales et régionales n'est évidemment pas unique au Canada, mais ce qui importe particulièrement c'est de voir dans quelle mesure on a déjà laissé s'affaiblir chez nous des fonctions vitales du gouvernement central, tendance qui menace de continuer. Les Etats-Unis, par exemple, ont toujours nourri des sentiments très fermes à l'égard des « droits des Etats » , mais ils n'ont jamais permis que ceux-ci sapent sérieusement l'autorité fédérale en matière de monnaie, de fiscalité, et de politique tarifaire. La dernière diminution de l'impôt fédéral aux Etats-Unis ne visait définitivement pas à autoriser les Etats à envahir le domaine évacué, comme ce fut le cas au Canada en vertu des récents accords fiscaux conclus entre le fédéral et les provinces. Ainsi que nous l'avons noté précédemment, il nous faut, en grande partie, attribuer cette tendance à l'impuissance du fédéral à concevoir et à mettre en œuvre une politique économique efficace dans sa propre sphère de responsabilité constitutionnelle.

On peut faire valoir que la décentralisation, c'est-à-dire la remise entre les mains d'unités gouvernementales plus petites de certaines décisions accessoires de la politique et de l'administration, constitue la prochaine étape à laquelle doit maintenant arriver, dans son développement, l'Etat-providence moderne. Myrdal, par exemple, estime que

la fin et la réalisation de la planification dans l'Etat-providence sont, en réalité, de simplifier constamment et d'éliminer en grande partie des interventions anciennes et nouvelles ; de remplacer par quelques règlements administratifs, la plupart d'ordre général, la masse croissante de prescriptions détaillées et particulières ; et surtout de refaire la communauté nationale de telle façon qu'on puisse la confier en très grande partie à la coopération et aux conventions collectives des individus eux-mêmes groupés en toutes sortes de sociétés et d'organismes à un niveau inférieur à celui de l'Etat, en vue d'établir les normes de leur existence commune.[1]

Cependant une telle transformation suppose que la politique et l'administration nationales ont atteint un degré de développement encore inconnu dans la plupart des pays, et certainement dans le nôtre. La diffusion des tendances autonomistes et séparatistes est au moins prématurée au Canada. Elle ne veut pas vraiment dire que l'opinion s'est mise d'accord sur la place à donner au pouvoir fédéral ; elle traduit plutôt un manque de confiance dans l'aptitude du gouvernement fédéral à agir avec sagesse et efficacité dans son propre domaine, quel qu'il soit. On peut facilement admettre qu'ultérieurement nombre de questions de détail seraient remises aux gouvernements municipaux et provinciaux. Et même, si c'est un dessein louable d'encourager la diversité, au sein du gouvernement aussi bien qu'en d'autres domaines de la vie sociale, cela importe encore davantage quand il s'agit d'une nation qui tient à l'individualité de l'esprit humain. Pourtant le Canada n'a pas encore atteint ce degré de maturité politique qui permettrait de diminuer sensiblement l'autorité et la juridiction fédérales et d'y voir un signe de progrès social. Le gouvernement fédéral peut accepter de supprimer des contraintes et des ingérences peu sérieuses, mais, en ce moment, le fait pour lui de renoncer de tous côtés à ses pouvoirs ne paraît pas compatible avec les chances de survie politique ou économique de la nation canadienne.

Les problèmes de « partage de juridiction » qui assaillent tous les Etats fédéraux deviennent beaucoup plus irritants au Canada du fait que plusieurs citoyens, et particuliérement ceux de langue française, considèrent la Confédération comme l'union de deux races ou de deux groupes linguistiques. Au Québec et ailleurs, la loi sur l'Amérique du Nord britannique est souvent représentée comme un « pacte » conclu entre les Canadiens français et les Canadiens anglais. Il n'existe guère de justification historique ou juridique d'une telle attitude, mais cela offre bien peu d'importance à une époque comme la nôtre où de vigoureux sentiments de désaffection à l'égard de la Confédération se manifestent au Canada français. Quoi que l'on estime devoir penser de la nature de l'union conclude entre Français et Anglais au Canada, l'appréciation des problèmes constitutionnels ne s'en trouve pas facilitée, car si cette union reste dans les cadres de la constitution sur certains points, elle lui échappe

[1]Gunnar Myrdal, *Beyond the Welfare State* (New Haven, 1960), p. 102.

sur d'autres. Les Canadiens français s'identifient solidement à la province de Québec et ils sont enclins à considérer la ville de Québec comme leur capitale. Les Canadiens anglais n'ont aucun point comparable d'intégration à une province (sauf peut-être dans le cas de Terre-Neuve) et Ottawa, pour eux, joue un rôle semblable à celui de Québec. Il en résulte assez curieusement qu'Ottawa n'est pas tout à fait une capitale *nationale*, mais qu'elle est, dans une forte mesure, seulement la capitale du Canada anglais, plus particulièrement sans doute dans l'esprit des Canadiens français que des Canadiens anglais, mais cela ne rend pas le résultat moins étonnant. En conséquence, sur le tableau des relations fédérales-provinciales il se joue toujours deux parties et peut-être trois : Ottawa et les provinces ; Ottawa et Québec ; Ottawa et les dix provinces, joute de style libre où chaque joueur mène son propre jeu.

La deuxième partie est nécessairement délicate. Elle se joue toujours dans une atmosphère tendue puisqu'elle est essentiellement chargée de l'une des grandes émotions irrationnelles de l'homme politique moderne : le nationalisme et l'identification ethnique. Dans le monde de notre époque, le nationalisme est un sentiment comparable à l'amour romanesque. Vu chez les autres il fait sourire ; il est touchant et peut-être un peu triste ; mais, en soi-même, il brûle de la flamme pure de l'ardeur passionnée et de la déraison. Les rites patriotiques d'une autre nation provoquent en nous la même indulgence méprisante et dédaigneuse que dans le cas du comportement des amoureux que l'on observe. Mais si d'observateurs nous devenons acteurs, quelle sainte ardeur et quel zèle messianique s'emparent de nous ! L'examen rationnel de ces questions constitue un problème difficile même dans les meilleures conditions, ce qui n'est pas le cas au Canada présentement ; en effet, au foyer national vit plus d'un sentiment nationaliste, chacun manifestant les symptômes typiques du dévouement à sa propre cause et du dédain pour l'autre. L'une des difficultés fondamentales que rencontre la nation canadienne consiste à permettre l'existence de divers sentiments et rites nationalistes dans un seul foyer national sans accroître l'irritation et l'aigreur et aboutir au divorce final. C'est un problème qui reste à résoudre au Canada. On n'y arrivera peut-être jamais, mais ajourd'hui, pour bien des raisons, il surgit au premier plan comme la menace la plus imminente qui pèse sur la survie du Canada, en tant que nation unifiée et indépendante.

La seconde difficulté d'importance majeure à laquelle doit faire face le Canada en est une autre qui ne comporte aucune « solution » définitive; c'est la façon de vivre aux côtés des Etats-Unis. Les problèmes de commerce, de placements internationaux, de défense et de relations extérieures sont considérables en soi, mais la proximité des Etats-Unis y ajoute un élément d'inquiétude quant à la survie nationale d'un Canada indépendant. Il n'y a aucun doute que toute petite nation, aussi intimement liée des points de vue géographique et économique à un très vaste pays, comme le Canada l'est aux Etats-Unis, va inévitablement rencontrer de sérieux embarras pour maintenir effectivement son indépendance politique[2]. Et pourtant ce n'est pas toujours la faute du grand voisin. L'hyper-sensibilité qu'on montre au Canada à l'égard de ce problème est moins le résultat d'une ligne de conduite réfléchie ou même simplement non préméditée de la part des Etats-Unis que le manque de confiance du Canada dans son aptitude à sortir de cette impasse. Ce manque de confiance s'est singulièrement accusé ces dernières années par suite de l'adoption de décisions dont plusieurs pourraient être simplement qualifiées de bévues. L'inquiétude touchant la pénétration des capitaux étrangers et la balance déficitaire des comptes provoqua, en 1961, un effort en vue d'agir sur le taux du change canadien ; une crise monétaire s'ensuivit et il fallut renoncer aux avantages d'un libre cours du change ; l'inquiétude causée par l'accaparement de notre industrie par des étrangers entraîna des mesures tellement inconsidérées dans le budget de 1963 qu'on dut en retirer la plus grande partie ; la décision qu'on a prise d'accorder des remises tarifaires à l'importation, à titre de subside à l'exportation, dans le cas de l'industrie de l'automobile, a été beaucoup critiquée au Canada comme étant une disposition contraire à l'esprit du GATT ; les arguments qu'Ottawa a avancés pour défendre cette politique tenaient plutôt de la rhétorique que de la raison ; la réaction du gouvernement canadien devant la taxe de péréquation d'intérêts imposée par nos voisins en 1963 a été de demander un traitement spécial lequel, en fait, laisse au Président des Etats-Unis un degré assez extraordinaire de pouvoir discrétionnaire sur la balance canadienne des comptes internationaux, conséquence que le gouvernement canadien n'avait pas envisagée à l'époque. Ces maladresses mises ensemble ont laissé croire que le Canada n'était pas capable de dominer nettement les problèmes posés par ses relations avec les Etats-Unis et d'y trouver des solutions avisées et efficaces.

L'hypothèse voulant que le Canada soit un pays de culture distincte de celle des Etats-Unis — hypothèse qui fut et qui est toujours au fond même de l'existence de la nationalité canadienne — est un sujet vaste et nébuleux, notoirement difficile à préciser et à cerner. Les différences de goûts, de préférences, d'attitudes, d'institutions, etc., parmi les diver-

[2]Nous pouvons trouver ici un parallèle dans les relations qui existent entre la Finlande et la Russie par exemple.

ses régions du Canada, semblent être plus considérables que celles qui existent entre le Canada et les Etats-Unis. Ici les disparités ne paraissent guère assez importantes pour justifier le paiement d'une sanction économique de 20 à 30 pour cent évaluée en fonction du produit national brut par tête, qu'on pourrait réduire en grande partie grâce à une forme d'union politique ou économique de l'Amérique du Nord. S'il est vrai qu'il existe un mode de vie proprement canadien, il ne s'est pas encore suffisamment crystallisé pour qu'on puisse l'identifier nettement. Aux yeux d'un observateur non averti, les ressemblances que nous avons avec les Etats-Unis sont beaucoup plus nombreuses et importantes que les différences. C'est peut-être là, en fait, l'une des raisons pour lesquelles on insiste tant sur les différences qui existent et qu'on y met assez souvent un sentiment anti-américain. Mais à force d'insister sur des distinctions peut-être insignifiantes, on finit par être assailli de doutes et on se demande si après tout elles ont tellement d'importance.

Cependant le Canada a l'occasion de se créer une identité unique sur le continent nord-américain par suite même, et c'est assez paradoxal, de cette caractéristique de sa constitution qui est aujourd'hui une source si profonde de tension et d'inquiétude : le mélange de deux groupes linguistiques et culturels qui tirent leur inspiration sociale et intellectuelle de deux sources européennes différentes mais magnifiquement complémentaires. Un biculturalisme réel, une communauté véritable des Français et des Anglais au Canada fourniraient la sorte de climat qui, d'une façon distinctive et constructive, ferait de notre pays une entité à part et qui, en donnant le sentiment d'avoir fait œuvre utile, serait de nature à contrebalancer l'attrait séducteur d'un attachement plus étroit aux Etats-Unis. C'est par là, et non par l'action séparatiste de l'autonomie régionale, que nous parviendrons à remplir les fins de la Confédération. L'incapacité de longue date d'atteindre un plus haut degré d'harmonie et de relations biculturelles contribue à créer la désaffection politique qui existe entre Ottawa et Québec et qui est aggravée par les disparités de revenus entre les Canadiens de langue française et les Canadiens de langue anglaise.

La question non réglée de la nationalité canadienne comporte des ramifications étendues qui forment un tout. C'est en partie pour cette raison que la solution heureuse de nos principales difficultés économiques mérite d'être au premier rang des préoccupations du Canada en ce moment. Une autre raison d'insister sur les aspects économiques est que nous croyons qu'ils peuvent se plier à notre volonté. Si nous pouvons maintenir un taux de croissance élevé, comme cela semble entièrement réalisable, si en matière de monnaie et de fiscalité ainsi que dans d'autres secteurs de l'économie notre politique se révèle plus sage et plus avisée qu'au cours des dix dernières années, nous pourrions obtenir la souplesse et les avantages économiques nécessaires pour nous attaquer avec succès à nombre de problèmes politiques, culturels, et financiers qu'autrement un marasme persistant ou une croissance lente et hésitante pourraient aggraver. Un bon rendement économique pourrait aussi restaurer dans le gouvernement fédéral la confiance dont la perte a suscité en grande partie cette tendance récente vers le séparatisme et l'autonomie locale. La progression que l'on enregistre depuis 1961 sur le plan économique permet de bien augurer de l'avenir du Canada, à condition toutefois que, contrairement à ce qui s'est produit au cours des cinq années précédentes, rien ne vienne freiner ce nouveau « bond en avant » .

Depuis 1935 environ, on ne peut plus hésiter sur la politique-type à suivre dans des conditions économiques données. Lorsque, à l'échelle nationale la demande est déficitaire et la proportion des chômeurs anormalement élevée, le budget fédéral doit être assez largement déficitaire, ce déficit étant le fruit d'une politique délibérée, comportant essentiellement la réduction des impôts et l'augmentation des dépenses publiques. Par contre, tout déficit qui, au lieu d'être le fruit d'une politique concertée visant à combattre le chômage, n'est que la conséquence du sous-emploi, est au contraire malsain. Quant à la politique monétaire, elle doit, dans les mêmes circonstances, viser à accroître la masse monétaire, à développer les facilités de crédit, et à réduire le taux des prêts à long terme. En période d'inflation c'est la tactique inverse qu'il faut adopter. Certes, des mesures supplémentaires et plus directes sont souvent indispensables, mais elles doivent être prises surtout pour parfaire l'une ou l'autre des deux politiques définies ci-dessus, et non parce que le gouvernement n'a pas su utiliser les moyens puissants dont il dispose. Il faut en outre éduquer l'opinion publique, lui apprendre qu'une bonne politique permet de prévoir et de neutraliser l'alternance inflation-déflation, à ne plus considérer comme seul garant de finances saines un budget annuel équilibré et lui inculquer l'idée qu'un déficit n'est pas forcément un état de choses que l'on doit redouter. Le ministre des finances doit perdre l'habitude de ce féliciter des excédents budgétaires, et il ne doit pas non plus déplorer les déficits lorsque ceux-ci peuvent aider au redressement de l'économie. Un ministre des finances doit raisonner en économiste et non en boutiquier : la sagesse routinière en honneur dans le commerce n'est pas de mise lorsqu'il s'agit des finances de la nation. Les gouvernements canadiens qui se sont succédé depuis la fin de la dernière guerre, tout en affirmant leur adhésion à ces principes, ont souvent démenti par leur action leurs prises de position théoriques[3]. Quoi qu'il en soit, en dehors du cercle étroit des économistes professionnels, on n'a pour ainsi dire rien fait pour montrer à l'opinion que les autorités fiscales et monétaires doivent prévoir les mouvements cycliques et s'employer à en corriger les effets. Comme on l'a dit fort justement, « le ministre des Finances doit être prêt à expliquer les déficits et les excédents au lieu de s'en excuser ou de s'en vanter suivant le cas » [4]. Il faut éviter que la politique économique ne retombe entre les mains d'un homme assez naïf pour s'imaginer que l'inflation est le seul péril qui menace l'économie du pays, ce qui l'amène à s'opposer à toute libéralisation de la politique monétaire, même lorsque le nombre des chômeurs est extrêmement élevé. Le Canada a payé très cher ce souci de maintenir coûte que coûte la stabilité des prix, dans les années qui ont suivi la crise économique de 1957, alors qu'il y avait d'autres moyens, moins coûteux, sur le plan humain comme sur le plan matériel, de préserver cette stabilité, du moins dans les limites du raisonnable. Le désir d'assurer la balance des paiements ne doit pas aveugler au point de faire passer au second plan un problème autrement sérieux, qui est celui du chômage. En fait, la politique qui garantit aux investissements un taux d'intérêt élevé n'a pas pour seule conséquence de laisser sans emploi un nombre considérable de travailleurs : elle attire les capitaux étrangers, ce qui, aux yeux de certains, ne peut manquer d'entraîner une certaine sujétion politique. Par ailleurs il est faux qu'un accroissement de la demande soit nécessairement incompatible avec une certaine stabilité des prix, surtout lorsque ni la main-d'œuvre ni les capitaux ne font défaut. En fait, à un accroissement de la consommation peut très bien correspondre un essor et un renouveau économiques, qui, même si le chômage était résorbé, ne feraient pas monter les prix canadiens au point de menacer les exportations et de favoriser les produits étrangers. Au cours des dix dernières années la balance des paiements a trop souvent été invoquée pour éviter de repenser la politique économique du pays. Pourtant, en général, il n'y a jamais eu incompabilité entre la balance des paiements et de saines mesures fiscales et monétaires.

Ce sont toutes ces erreurs, que leurs effets n'ont que trop clairement dénoncées à partir de 1955, qui ont fait perdre à presque tous les économistes canadiens tout respect pour le gouvernement d'Ottawa et toute confiance en sa politique économique. Cette confiance, il ne sera pas aisé de la regagner, surtout dans le climat politique actuel. Et cela d'autant plus que certains problèmes annexes, liés à celui de la misère

[3]Voir à ce sujet *Report of the Royal Commission on Banking and Finance* (Ottawa, 1964), p. 507.
[4]Ibid., p. 521.

résiduelle et du chômage d'ordre structural, ne sauraient être résolus par une simple adaptation de la politique fiscale et monétaire au rythme cyclique. Comme d'autres nations, le Canada doit s'engager dans une voie nouvelle pour résoudre des problèmes nouveaux ou hérités du passé. Mais, contrairement à beaucoup d'autres pays de l'Ouest, le Canada n'a pas encore tiré de la crise des années 30 la leçon qui s'impose. Ainsi, aux problèmes propres à l'époque où nous vivons viennent s'ajouter ceux qui sont dûs au fait que, pendant des années, on ne s'est pas engagé résolument dans la voie des mesures anti-cycliques, mesures qui devront désormais être complétées par d'autres soigneusement élaborées pour résoudre les nouveaux problèmes. Au point difficile où nous sommes parvenus, c'est donc une double série de réformes qui s'impose : il faut, d'une part, et avec tout le retard que cela comporte, s'engager dans la voie de celles qui auraient dû depuis longtemps appliquées et, d'autre part, en prévoir d'autres pour résoudre les problèmes nés depuis 1960, qui ne sauraient être entièrement résolus par les mesures prévues plus haut.

Il est certes possible que les autorités canadiennes aient à présent compris la leçon qu'il faut tirer des erreurs du passé, et qu'elles suivent dorénavant une politique plus sage et plus cohérente. Si tel est le cas, il n'y a aucune raison pour que l'économie canadienne ne réponde pas aux prévisions que nous avons faites dans la troisième partie. C'est d'ailleurs en se fondant sur cet espoir que ces prévisions ont été faites. N'oublions pas que la prospérité économique permettrait de résoudre bien des litiges qui empoisonnent actuellement la vie politique canadienne. Le développement économique rend possible une civilisation, il ne la crée pas. Mais s'il fait défaut, la situation politique s'en ressent et, dans le cas du Canada, cela veut dire l'affaiblissement des liens politiques forgés il y a un siècle.

Un Commentaire

par Albert Breton

UN COMMENTAIRE

Ce n'est certes par hasard qu'un volume, dont le but est d'évaluer les besoins et les ressources du Canada, consacre son introduction et sa conclusion aux aspects politiques de ce pays. Il n'y a pas là de quoi se surprendre, les situations et composantes politiques ayant toujours eu au Canada la priorité sur les perspectives économiques. Heureux sommes-nous que cet état de choses n'ait pas eu des effets aussi graves que certains auraient pu anticiper ! Nous le devons pour une part à la grande richesse du Canada et, pour une seconde part, au fait que les coûts économiques des priorités politiques—qui ont, notons-le ici, très probablement appauvri les Canadiens—n'ont jamais dépassé en pratique un certain minimum.

Quoiqu'il en soit le chapitre d'introduction du présent volume nous rappelle les origines de la Confédération canadienne, les problèmes qu'elle est venue résoudre, l'évolution qu'elle a subie, et les problèmes auxquels elle fait face aujourd'hui. On note en particulier que la Confédération fut établie pour apporter une solution aux conflits entre Canadiens d'expression française et d'expression anglaise et pour arrêter l'expansionisme américain. On ajoute à cela que le Canada semble faire face encore aujourd'hui à des manifestations différentes de ces deux mêmes problèmes de base. Face à l'attraction et à la pression des Etats-Unis, le gouvernement canadien a adopté au tout début de la Confédération trois types de politiques majeures : la construction d'un chemin de fer transcontinental, une politique d'immigration, et une politique tarifaire. Tel que le soulignent les auteurs du chapitre, seule la première de ces trois politiques a eu du succès, la seconde ayant eu des effets ambigus et la troisième ayant produit presque des effets contraires à ceux qu'on espérait en 1879. En effet, l'établissement de tarifs par le Canada a stimulé les Américains à venir investir derrière le mur protectioniste et, en conséquence, le spectre étasunien est réapparu pour alimenter à nouveau un vieux fonds nationaliste canadien « anti-yankee » dont l'origine remonte à l'époque coloniale elle-même. Soulignons ici que le nationalisme canadien a eu comme effet indirect de déplacer l'attention des Canadiens des vrais problèmes auxquels notre pays devait et doit encore faire face, tout en donnant naissance à un ensemble de politiques économiques pour le moins bizarres.

En ce qui concerne le second problème du Canada, à savoir, les relations entre Canadiens d'expression française et d'expression anglaise, les auteurs du chapitre d'introduction considèrent qu'elles rappellent toujours celles de l'époque de la Confédération : il se pourrait même qu'elles se soient détériorées. C'est tout au moins l'impression que laisse la lecture des quelques pages consacrées à cette question. En effet, on y craint une menace sérieuse pour la Confédération du fait de certaines conduites actuelles dans la province de Québec.

A ce sujet, notre impression est un sentiment d'exagération chez les auteurs à propos des tensions et conflits entre Canadiens français et Canadiens anglais. Il est symptomatique à notre avis que leurs opinions s'appuient non pas sur les politiques ou sur les déclarations officielles du gouvernement du Québec, si ambiguës et de foi douteuse qu'elles aient parues à certains moments mais plutôt sur les activités et les menaces de quelques groupes marginaux dans la société québécoise. Quant à nous, nous restons persuadé que la chose vraiment étonnante au Canada n'est pas que les relations entre les Canadiens français et les Canadiens anglais soient difficiles, mais plutôt qu'elles soient si faciles. S'il est vrai que les différences religieuses, ethniques, ou culturelles peuvent provoquer des conduites irrationnelles, que l'on songe à l'histoire de l'humanité pour constater que les Canadiens ont eu jusqu'à ce jour des comportements fort civilisés. Toutefois, pour ne pas être vaincu en bons sentiments, nous ajouterons qu'il y a encore place pour des améliorations dans les relations inter-ethniques au Canada.

Dans les pages qui suivent, notre propos sera double. D'une part, nous analyserons les matériaux contenus dans les diverses parties de ce panorama économique du Canada, matériaux choisis pour nous fournir une image de l'évolution de l'économie canadienne depuis les années trente et du cadre dans lequel cette évolution a pris place. D'autre part, simultanément à cette analyse critique, nous esquisserons les grandes lignes qui se dégagent de chacun des chapitres de la présente étude.

PREMIERE PARTIE : TENDANCES ECONOMIQUES D'HIER

Le premier chapitre intitulé « Perspectives d'accroissement » mentionne que, depuis la fin des années trente jusqu'au début des années soixante, les dépenses nationales brutes per capita dans l'économie canadienne, ont subi en dollars réels (de 1949) une augmentation au taux de 2.8 pour cent composé annuellement. Précisons immédiatement qu'il est certain que le choix d'une autre période pour calculer ce taux en aurait produit un, substantiellement différent et, nous semble-t-il, un peu plus bas. Par contre, ce dernier taux aurait eu l'avantage d'être plus conforme à la capacité réelle de l'économie canadienne en longue période, tout en demeurant à un niveau respectable. Il reste vrai par ailleurs que l'augmentation imposante des dépenses nationales brutes, implicite même lorsque le taux de croissance est inférieur à 2.8 pour cent, a été accompagnée par des changements importants dans la répartition de ces dépenses. A cet égard, il est à remarquer que parmi les quatre groupes consommateurs, exportateurs, gouvernements, et investisseurs qui se partagent les dépenses nationales brutes, les deux premiers ont vu leur part respective diminuer de 8 pour cent, alors que celle des gouvernements augmentait de 9 pour cent et celle des investisseurs de 7 pour cent.

Les transformations que nous venons de souligner ont été, tel que le notent les auteurs du chapitre que nous étudions actuellement, accompagnées de changements dans la quantité et la composition des biens et des services à la disposition des Canadiens, de modifications dans la distribution du revenu, dans la structure industrielle, dans la composition de la main-d'œuvre, et dans la structure occupationnelle elle-même. Dans ce dernier cas, on doit remarquer qu'il s'est agi d'une évolution vers l'établissement d'une structure occupationnelle du type propre aux économies industrielles modernes.

En ce qui concerne le remaniement de la distribution des revenus, il est à mentionner que les gages et salaires se répartissent plus également entre les individus et les familles en 1951 qu'en 1931. Cependant, les inégalités dans le revenu sont demeurées constantes entre 1951 et 1957. Signalons en dernier lieu, avec les auteurs du présent volume, qu'une comparaison entre la distribution des revenus de 1931 et celle de 1951 doit se faire avec précaution, étant données les conditions particulières existant en 1931. Toutefois selon nous, l'égalisation des revenus est assez importante entre ces deux années pour que la dépression de 1931 ne puisse l'expliquer complètement.

A propos du changement dans la structure industrielle, le seul fait important à rapporter est la diminution de 15 pour cent à 5 pour cent du secteur agricole dans le produit national brut entre 1927–29 et 1959–61. Quant aux secteurs de la construction, des produits manufacturés, de l'administration publique et de la défense, leur part respective du produit national est demeurée constante au cours de cette même période. Il nous paraît valable de noter ici que l'utilisation de catégories plus fines pour évaluer les changements dans la structure industrielle n'aurait vraisemblablement pas permis d'observer la constance des parts que nous avons rapportées.

Au sujet des transformations dans la composition de la main-d'œuvre, les auteurs du chapitre que nous analysons indiquent qu'elles ont reflété assez fidèlement les changements dans la structure industrielle. On signale en plus une augmentation importante du nombre de professionnels et d'ouvriers qualifiés et une augmentation moins importante que celle-ci du nombre d'ouvriers semi-qualifiés et non-qualifiés.

Dans un autre domaine, celui des tendances de longue durée observées dans les indices de prix, les auteurs du présent volume définissent dans son ensemble comme période d'inflation, celle qui se situe entre la fin des années trente et le début des années soixante. On y souligne aussi que les indices de prix ont augmenté à un taux beaucoup moins élevé à la fin de cette période qu'à son début.

L'analyse que nous venons de rappeler suggère cependant que les recherches soient davantage poussées. Ainsi, on pourrait se demander si les indices de prix sont une mesure exacte du niveau des prix. En effet, il est utile de retenir que presque tous, sinon tous, les facteurs qui ne sont pas considérés explicitement pour l'établissement des indices, tels par exemple les changements dans le revenu des gens formant l'échantillon sur lequel le calcul des indices est basé ou encore les changements dans la qualité des produits qui entrent dans la pondération des indices, introduisent un biais vers le haut de ces indices. En conséquence, il est possible au cours de certaines périodes, que les indices marquent une hausse des prix alors que le niveau de ces derniers diminue. Dans la conjoncture actuelle, ces considérations importent. Il n'est pas impossible que depuis 1957–58, le niveau des prix au Canada soit en fait tombé même si les indices continuent à pointer vers une hausse.

Il nous semble aussi qu'il serait avantageux que soit faite une analyse des transformations qui ont pu survenir dans le degré de flexibilité des prix et dans celui des salaires. C'est qu'une fraction importante des ajustements qui doivent se produire dans l'économie se fait par l'intermédiaire des marchés. Or, ceux-ci remplissent ce rôle en jouant sur les prix. Aussi est-il nécessaire que soit déterminée la plus ou moins grande flexibilité des prix pour qu'une connaissance plus exacte de l'évolution et des adaptations de leur niveau soit établie.

Les diverses tendances que nous avons résumées au cours des paragraphes qui précèdent sont importantes et d'un grand intérêt. Elles sont un préalable à l'examen de la capacité d'une économie à répondre aux problèmes qui lui sont posés, en l'occurence ici : les besoins que cette économie doit satisfaire étant données les ressources dont elle dispose. Une étude de certaines autres tendances reste maintenant à entreprendre. Nous pensons en particulier qu'on pourrait faire l'analyse des faits qui se rattachent aux tendances observables dans le degré de protection tarifaire et non-tarifaire de la période considérée. On pourrait encore discuter des tendances qui concernent les subsides directs et indirects (principalement ceux qui prennent la forme d'une réduction d'impôt) accordés soit aux individus, soit aux familles, soit aux entreprises et aux organisations par les divers gouvernements.

Voilà autant d'aspects fondamentaux sur lesquels nous aimerions revenir plus tard. Pour l'instant, signalons que plusieurs secteurs et plusieurs marchés de l'économie canadienne sont effectivement en déséquilibre. Plus précisément, notons que dans un certain nombre de cas les déséquilibres tendent à disparaître et que dans d'autres ils semblent s'établir en permanence. Une telle situation est coûteuse en regard du bien-être de la population. Or, il est possible que cette situation soit liée aux divers facteurs mentionnés ici. Aussi serait-il bon qu'on en fasse l'investigation.

En ce qui concerne les tendances de la masse monétaire au Canada durant la période étudiée, on pourrait ajouter ici un développement plus élaboré. S'il est difficile par des exercices économétriques de tracer le cheminement exact de l'influence de la monnaie sur l'activité « réelle », c'est-à-dire sur l'activité économique mesurée en regard d'un numéraire, il ne faut toutefois pas oublier que ces expériences économétriques ne sont qu'approximatives de l'économie « réelle », qu'effectivement cette dernière ne peut pas remplacer, même en principe, les économies monétaires dans lesquelles nous vivons. En conséquence donc, il aurait fallu qu'on accorde un rôle à la monnaie, tout au moins en ce sens qu'une masse monétaire déficiente aura de mauvais effets sur l'activité économique.

Dans une section importante du premier chapitre que nous analysons, on examine en durée et en mutations les effets d'un mécanisme primordial du changement qui s'opère dans l'économie canadienne au cours de la période sous observation. Simplifié, ce mécanisme se définit comme suit : le plus important déterminant de l'investissement qui prend place au Canada est le niveau d'exportation. En d'autres mots, une augmentation des exportations provoque une augmentation des investissements qui entraîne à son tour dans la période subséquente une élévation du revenu. Par contre, une réduction des exportations a un effet contraire. C'est là une hypothèse du fonctionnement de l'économie canadienne basée sur le fait qu'une large proportion des exportations canadiennes est composée de matières premières exploitées principalement dans le but de la vente à l'étranger plutôt qu'à la consommation et à la production domestique.

Il nous semble que le mécanisme auquel nous venons de référer corresponde à un phénomène réel de l'économie canadienne, phénomène que certains aimeraient fouiller de manière plus détaillée. En second lieu, on pourrait se demander si les « tests » statistiques employés par les auteurs du chapitre, comme par d'autres avant eux, sont absolument valables pour démontrer l'existence d'un pareil mécanisme. Notre raison principale à ce propos est qu'une augmentation des exportations produirait directement « à travers » un simple multiplicateur keynésien, une augmentation du revenu national, et, dans une période subséquente, celle-ci entraînerait une augmentation des investissements. Il s'agit là d'un mécanisme qui ressemble à celui des auteurs, mais pourtant fort différent. C'est pourquoi, nous semble-t-il, l'emploi de tests plus « sophistiqués » permettrait de réellement accepter ou rejeter l'existence du mécanisme présenté dans ce volume. Quoiqu'il en soit, il nous est apparu utile qu'on ait discuté cette question. C'est en effet ainsi que le passé peut être compris et utilisé autant que par la présentation détaillée de séries statistiques.

Le chapitre suivant, « Schémas de la population » , analyse les transformations démographiques qui se sont produites au Canada au vingtième siècle. Ici aussi l'accroissement est impressionnant même s'il est irrégulier.

On fait mention qu'au cours de la période qui va de 1901 à aujourd'hui, la population canadienne s'est augmentée à un taux moyen de 2.04 pour cent par année. C'est là un accroissement remarquable qui s'explique par trois facteurs : 1° le niveau élevé du taux brut des naissances en dépit de variations importantes allant de 21 à 28 par mille enregistrée au cours de la période ; 2° la réduction considérable du taux brut des mortalités, réduction qui favorisa davantage les femmes que les hommes; 3° l'immigration nette, c'est-à-dire la différence entre l'immigration et l'émigration brutes.

A propos de la réduction du taux de mortalité, les Canadiens ont vu leurs espérances de vie s'augmenter de manière considérable. Ainsi le Canada peut se comparer sur ce point avec tous les autres pays développés dans le monde. Cependant, le taux de mortalité infantile demeure à un niveau plus élevé que dans d'autres pays industrialisés.

Au sujet de l'immigration nette, on constate que les statistiques varient suivant les divers moments de la période observée. En fait, les taux de migration nette sont tantôt positifs, tantôt négatifs, si bien que depuis la Confédération l'immigration nette totale a été pratiquement nulle. Toutefois, au cours des vingt-cinq dernières années, elle a contribué d'une façon positive et importante à l'accroissement de la population du Canada.

A mesure que la population canadienne augmentait, elle se transformait dans sa composition. Signalons en particulier dans la pyramide de répartition de la population selon son âge, un accroissement considérable des jeunes et des « personnes plus agées » , fait qui a provoqué une hausse du nombre relatif de gens qui dépendent, au point de vue du revenu réel, de la main-d'œuvre active. On peut encore remarquer des transformations dans la distribution des personnes selon leur origine ethnique. Par rapport à la population totale, la proportion des personnes d'origine française est demeurée virtuellement constante, celle de gens d'origine anglaise a diminué, tandis que la proportion des personnes des autres origines augmente.

En dernier lieu, on observe le déplacement frappant de la population canadienne vers les villes et le développement nécessaire de ces dernières pour parer à cette marée humaine.

La lecture du chapitre dont nous venons de rappeler les grandes lignes amène sans doute à se demander quelles sont exactement les mécanismes économiques auxquels on a fait allusion. Ces mécanismes, dit-on, sous-tendraient les changements démographiques, mais comment peut-on en être assuré ? Sont-ils vraiment ceux qu'il importe de proposer pour expliquer les phénomènes observés ? En effet, certains s'inquièteront de savoir si les hypothèses suggérées, si plausibles qu'elles soient, permettant d'établir une relation entre les taux de natalité et ceux de nuptialité d'une part, et l'activité économique d'autre part, ne sont pas précisées de manière qu'il soit possible de les utiliser pour expliquer soit des relations positives, soit des relations négatives. Par ailleurs, une description précise des mécanismes à l'œuvre aiderait à évaluer la signification des mouvements démographiques, par rapport, par exemple, au critère du bien-être, ou par rapport à celui d'efficacité, ou à tout autre qu'on pourrait choisir.

Le chapitre intitulé « Les Différences régionales », qui fera maintenant l'objet de nos réflexions, porte sur les différences entre les diverses régions du Canada et sur certaines tendances économiques de longue durée qu'on a pu y observer.

Dans ce chapitre, on concentre l'attention sur la distribution interrégionale du revenu et sur certaines composantes de ce revenu ; on considère aussi la répartition du revenu à l'intérieur de chaque région. On constate en particulier au sujet de cette dernière une relation commune aux régions comme à l'ensemble du pays à savoir : le revenu est distribué plus également par classe de revenu quand le niveau moyen de ce dernier est plus élevé. En d'autres mots, à peu d'exceptions près au Canada, plus la région est pauvre, plus le revenu se distribue de façon inégale.

D'autre part, on rapporte au sujet de la répartition interrégionale du revenu, qu'il semble y avoir stabilité dans la fraction du revenu disponible provenant du produit national brut attribuée à chaque région. Toutefois cette stabilité dissimule des changements importants dans certains autres aspects de l'activité économique. Telles sont par exemple, la diminution de la proportion des investissements totaux accordés aux provinces atlantiques, ou encore la diminution de la fraction de la population totale du Canada vivant dans ces mêmes provinces et dans les Prairies. Si ces dernières variations n'ont pas influencé la grande stabilité de la répartition du revenu par régions, cela est dû pour une large part aux compensations par paiements de transfert payés par le gouvernement fédéral lesquels maintiennent le revenu disponible à un niveau plus élevé qu'il ne le serait s'il était déterminé par les seules forces économiques.

Dans le même chapitre, on note aussi que les industries lourdes se concentrent surtout en Ontario et à un moindre degré dans la province de Québec. On trouve enfin l'industrie légère dans toutes les provinces canadiennes mais principalement ailleurs qu'en Ontario et dans la province de Québec.

En première remarque, nous aimerions observer que ce qui frappe davantage dans l'étude qui nous occupe est le déséquilibre profond de la situation économique des diverses régions du Canada lesquelles, on le sait, forment un marché commun. Bien qu'on nous ait fourni assez peu de matériel pour porter un jugement éclairé, il nous semble que ce déséquilibre soit maintenu plutôt que corrigé par les politiques qui ont été imaginées pour améliorer la situation. A cet égard, et relativement au chapitre du présent travail qui nous intéresse maintenant, nous aimerions suggérer qu'on projette une étude en profondeur qui porterait sur le jeu des divers mécanismes d'ajustement et sur les obstacles qui les empêchent d'agir dans l'économie canadienne.

Dans le chapitre que nous commentons, il est intéressant de noter que l'étude adopte une position du Rapport de la Commission royale sur les perspectives économiques du Canada. On mentionne en effet que le niveau de vie des provinces atlantiques serait encore plus bas qu'il ne l'est, n'eut été certaines politiques du Gouvernement fédéral. En courte période, cela est indéniable. En longue période, il est cependant légitime de se demander si, justement, le bas niveau de vie des provinces atlantiques ne résulte pas largement des politiques du gouvernement fédéral. En effet, ne doit-on pas blâmer des politiques gouvernementales qui ont comme conséquence d'enrayer, au lieu de les accélérer, des mécanismes économiques qui par eux-mêmes peuvent fonctionner ? Une meilleure information sur la direction dans laquelle les mécanismes économiques décrits opèrent devrait être obtenue afin de soutenir nos avancés. Il serait dès lors possible d'apporter une réponse à la question de savoir si la situation s'améliore ou se détériore davantage.

Le dernier chapitre de la première partie de l'étude que nous traitons, intitulé « L'Influence extérieure » porte son attention à la place du Canada dans le monde, à l'influence de l'étranger sur certains domaines de notre activité économique. On y rapporte avec clarté les données sur l'évolution de nos importations et de nos exportations de biens comme de services (les invisibles). On montre jusqu'à quel point le Canada dépend de son commerce extérieur et jusqu'à quel point cette dépendance signifie, dépendance de son commerce avec les Etats-Unis. Ces remarques sont accompagnées d'une discussion au sujet des changements survenus dans la composition des importations et des exportations, par catégories générales de produits. On découvre ici que le Canada dépend beaucoup moins de ses exportations de blé et de ses sous-produits qu'il y a quelques années. Par contre notre pays est aujourd'hui beaucoup plus assujetti par ces exportations de bois, de pâte de papier, de minéraux, et de métaux qu'il ne l'était autrefois. Quant à nos produits manufacturés, ils occupent à peu près la même proportion de nos exportations. Notons enfin qu'au point de vue de nos importations, la part des produits manufacturés s'est augmentée, même si on observe que dans plusieurs catégories de biens importés, la fraction des produits finis diminue.

Comme ailleurs dans l'étude, on discute dans le présent chapitre de la viabilité de la Confédération canadienne. On affirme que le déplacement de la direction des exportations du Canada, auparavant surtout acheminées vers le Royaume-Uni et l'Europe de l'Ouest et maintenant dirigées vers les Etats-Unis, a réduit la portion relative du commerce est-ouest à l'intérieur du Canada, et augmenté la part de notre commerce nord-sud. Il en est résulté une propension plus grande au régionalisme économique déjà présent dans chaque région du pays. Il est important d'observer à l'égard de cette situation très plausible et très intéressante qu'elle doit être liée à un fait déjà mentionné, à savoir que si les gouvernements canadiens ont dû historiquement payé des subsides, voté des tarifs et des taxes pour maintenir la Confédération, ils devront en toute probabilité maintenant augmenter les subsides et les tarifs pour compenser la perte du commerce est-ouest ainsi que les effets bénéfiques de ce dernier sur l'ensemble du commerce du Canada. Ajoutons ici que jusqu'à présent personne n'a établi la vigueur des phénomènes que nous avons mentionnés ; seule la direction des forces postulées semble bien être dans le sens indiqué.

Au sujet de la balance des paiements du Canada, on note que bien qu'elle soit soumise à des variations importantes ; les déficits et les surplus n'ont jamais perduré au cours de l'histoire du pays pour une très longue période de temps. Voilà un fait important qui resitue les débats échevelés des dernières années sur cette question, dans leur contexte propre. Par ailleurs, on indique que les déficits ont été accompagnés de mouvements de capitaux. On signale, à propos de ces derniers, qu'historiquement ce sont eux qui ont précédé les déficits et non le contraire.

Pour ce qui regarde les mouvements de capitaux importants dans la balance des paiements du Canada, on rapporte qu'ils ont provoqué une augmentation absolue considérable de la dette nette extérieure du Canada. Cependant par rapport au produit national brut, cette dette a diminué de façon marquée. Le rapport que nous analysons note d'autre part le fait intéressant suivant : la propension moyenne du Canadien moyen à investir aux Etats-Unis est passablement plus élevée que celle de l'Américain moyen à investir au Canada. Enfin, on observe que l'augmentation de la dette nette extérieure du Canada a été accompagnée d'une transformation notable de la composition de cette dette, à savoir : la fraction des investissements directs a considérablement grandi au détriment des investissements de portefeuille.

Après avoir établi les tendances à la hausse de la propriété et du contrôle étranger de certains actifs canadiens, les responsables du chapitre discutent les implications de ce contrôle sur le taux de croissance de l'économie canadienne et sur la structure de cette dernière principalement en regard des exportations du Canada. On conclut à ce sujet de manière fort détaillée, que l'influence du contrôle économique ne peut pas se séparer d'une discussion des tarifs canadiens et étrangers et cela malgré le fait que la technologie importée avec le capital ne soit pas toujours ajustée au prix des facteurs de production existant au Canada.

Le chapitre que nous venons d'analyser propose une image qui, selon nous, est assez exacte des influences économiques étrangères qui jouent sur l'économie canadienne. Le point de vue qui y est présenté nous semble en effet très juste, et les vérités qui y sont contenues auront avantage à être diffusées.

DEUXIEME PARTIE : LES RESSOURCES

Dans un chapitre intitulé « Les Ressources actuelles et futures » on décrit les ressources à la disposition des Canadiens pour satisfaire leurs besoins et ceux des autres pays désireux d'acheter ces biens. Les auteurs portent en fait leur attention sur l'évolution de la quantité et de la qualité de nos richesses classifiées ici d'après la distinction classique à savoir : le sol et les ressources naturelles, le travail, le capital, et l'organisation.

En première remarque nous aimerions rappeler que, même si on reconnaît l'importance des ressources naturelles dans l'économie du pays, il importe de retenir que celles-ci déterminent davantage l'orientation générale et la composition de la production totale que le taux de croissance de cette économie. A ce propos, n'est-il pas en effet exact que le commerce est un substitut à l'existence de ressources naturelles et qu'il permet un développement aussi grand s'il est bien manié ?

Tel qu'on le souligne brièvement, le Canada est du point de vue de ses dimensions physiques un grand pays dans lequel on observe de grandes variations géologiques et climatologiques. Intéressantes en elles-mêmes, ces considérations expliquent aussi selon nous une part considérable de la distribution géographique de la population et de la production. Il nous semble que quelqu'un pourrait bien s'arrêter sur ce dernier aspect et discuter pour le moins jusqu'à quel point les forces physiques sont transformables ou jusqu'à quel point elles ne le sont pas. Ne s'agit-il pas en effet d'une donnée relativement permanente qui conditionne bien des activités et contre laquelle les politiques officielles des gouvernements du pays se sont souvent élevées ?

Parmi les diverses richesses à la disposition des Canadiens, le sol en est une fondamentale. On nous indique qu'il est la base de notre agriculture et de nos forêts. On nous rappelle enfin qu'il fournit l'espace nécessaire au logement des personnes, à la construction des industries, au développement des transports. Enfin, il convient fort bien aux loisirs de plein air et à certaines autres activités qu'il est inutile de nommer ici.

Au sujet du sol utilisé pour fins agricoles, le rapport étudié soumet que par rapport au début du siècle, de plus vastes parties de notre terre arable sont aujourd'hui exploitées. Le taux de développement est cependant beaucoup plus bas depuis quelques années. Comparativement à sa production, notre agriculture utilise une très grande partie du sol ; dans le monde entier, elle est une des plus vastes mises en exploitation du sol, sinon la plus extensive. De plus, c'est une agriculture qui emploie peu d'irrigation et peu d'engrais. Elle est ainsi capable d'une élévation notable de sa production. Enfin, elle est, dans la conjoncture économique d'un marché domestique limité et de protection des produits étrangers, assez peu susceptible de développer ses grandes possibilités.

Pour ce qui regarde les forêts canadiennes, le pays fait face à des réserves si considérables que le potentiel exploitable excède de beaucoup les exploitations actuelles. On nous rapporte en effet que la quantité de bois que les gouvernements du pays autorisent à couper est en deça de ce qui devrait être autorisé et plus encore, ce qui est abattu est en deça de ce qui est autorisé. Ainsi, le Canada pourrait mettre en valeur ses forêts beaucoup plus vigoureusement qu'il ne le fait.

Quand on considère l'ensemble des autres usages de notre sol — résidences, industries, transports — le rapport fait état que moins de 1 pour cent du territoire canadien sert à ces fins. Ainsi, ici encore nos ressources abondent.

Notre richesse en eau, nous disent les auteurs du présent chapitre, sert à la consommation domestique, à l'élimination des déchets, à la production d'énergie. Elle est encore un réservoir de poissons et de plus elle appartient au monde des loisirs, usage qu'on ne considère pas. On ne consomme jamais plus de 10 pour cent de nos réserves d'eau dans toutes les régions du pays. En moyenne pour tout le Canada, l'utilisation de l'eau est égale à 4.1 pour cent de l'offre annuelle. Mieux encore dans les provinces d'Alberta et de Colombie Britannique, la consommation est inférieure à 2 pour cent des réserves. En somme, notre abondance est ici encore remarquable.

Bien que la situation manque de clarté pour les poissons d'eau douce de l'intérieur du pays, nos richesses en pêcherie apparaissent aussi comme dépassant nos besoins. Le homard excepté, sous des conditions économiques qui le permettent ou l'exigent, il nous serait possible de retirer de l'Atlantique et du Pacifique une plus grande quantité de poissons de mer. Enfin, une sous-exploitation ou une sur-exploitation pouvant affecter le développement optimum de nos réserves de poissons, toute évaluation de ces réserves, soit actuelles, soit futures, devra tenir compte des conditions biologiques de reproduction et de croissance des poissons.

Au sujet de nos stocks de minéraux connus, on note dans l'étude qu'il est difficile d'en donner un estimé exact puisque seule une fraction des terres à explorer, l'a été. En conséquence, les dépôts et les réserves connues sont en général inférieurs aux réserves totales. Ce fait importe pour interpréter des données, car l'exploration est en fonction de la demande, c'est-à-dire de la profitabilité estimée des ressources. Pour ce qui est des réserves actuelles d'un certain nombre de minéraux, il appert que, dans un certain nombre de cas, elles suffiront pour quelques années seulement et que dans d'autres elles serviront encore longtemps.

Le chapitre que nous étudions, se termine par une évaluation de l'énergie à la disposition du Canada. On conclut à ce sujet, comme pour nos autres richesses que nos possibilités sont énormes et capables de satisfaire à nos besoins pour de longues années à venir.

En somme, si on tient compte de ce que nous avons résumé au cours des derniers paragraphes, nous pouvons maintenant nous demander si pour telle ou telle richesse naturelle, il y aurait lieu d'en mousser l'exploitation ou encore, si nos ressources sont développées à un rythme optimun dans les cas où la demande mondiale est assez élevée pour en rendre l'exploitation profitable. Une réponse à ces questions importe si l'on considère que l'investissement de capital social, dans le but de produire une meilleure exploitation de certaines de nos ressources, pourrait avoir pour effet d'augmenter le revenu des Canadiens. Ne s'agit-il pas ici de mesures que l'on doit prendre avant que de bons substituts soient trouvés pour nos ressources développpables ?

Dans un chapitre intitulé « La Population active canadienne », on note que la main-d'œuvre ou que les gens au travail constituent les 35 pour cent de la population totale du pays ; on remarque de plus qu'entre 1901 et 1961, le monde au travail s'est accru de 260 pour cent alors que la population totale s'élevait de 240 pour cent. Le taux de croissance de la main-d'œuvre du pays a été en outre affecté par quatre facteurs principaux. Ce sont : *a*) l'augmentation du nombre d'années obligatoires de scolarité ; *b*) un âge de retraite plus jeune qu'auparavant pour plusieurs personnes ; *c*) un plus grande nombre de femmes au travail qu'autrefois ; *d*) des immigrants en âge de travailler plus nombreux. En dernier lieu, les responsables du présent chapitre font observer que durant la période 1901–61 la main-d'œuvre masculine a triplé et la féminine s'est multipliée par sept, de telle sorte que la femme canadienne représente aujourd'hui 28 pour cent du monde au travail par rapport à 13 pour cent au début du siècle.

Au cours de la période 1921–61, l'étude souligne un taux stable de participation de la main-d'œuvre, soit 53 pour cent. En fait, ce qui s'est produit, se présente comme suit : le taux de participation des hommes a diminué et celui des femmes augmenté, ce qui a contribué à maintenir la stabilité du taux global de participation.

On examine par la suite la distribution industrielle et occupationnelle de la population canadienne au travail. Au sujet de la répartition industrielle des travailleurs, on a découvert que les possibilités d'emploi dans l'industrie productrice de biens ne se sont augmentées que de 26 pour cent, ce qui implique une chute de 58 pour cent à 45 pour cent de la portion que ce type d'industrie prenait de l'ensemble des travailleurs. On observe d'autre part que les industries produisant des services ont vu doubler leurs possibilités d'emploi entre 1931 et 1961. Au sujet de la distribution occupationnelle de la main-d'œuvre, on rapporte pour la période 1931–61, une augmentation de 155 pour cent chez les collets blancs, de 67 pour cent chez les travailleurs manuels, de 90 pour cent chez le personnel des services, et une baisse de 35 pour cent chez les travailleurs de l'industrie primaire.

Dans une section qui suit, on met en relation immigration et émigration d'une part, et, d'autre part population au travail. On y fait aussi l'analyse de certaines caractéristiques du chômage d'après la guerre de 1939–45. On explique principalement ce dernier par les changements structurels survenus au cours de la période. Cette hypothèse, certains pourraient se le demander, se vérifie-t-elle si sont considérés les tests de type empirique utilisés pour la soutenir ? Ces derniers, en effet, constituent-ils un argument pour ou contre l'explication de type « structura-liste » employée ici ? D'autre part, pourrait-on rattacher l'argumentation de cette section à certaines autres parties de cette étude, particulièrement celles qui se rapportent à la critique des politiques fiscales et monétaires depuis la fin de la guerre ?

Cependant, certaines autres questions viennent à l'esprit. En effet, dans une optique où l'on croit que les changements dans la qualité de la main-d'œuvre importent beaucoup pour comprendre la contribution des travailleurs à la production d'un pays, qu'en est-il de l'évolution de la qualité de notre population au travail ? Par exemple, n'y aurait-il pas lieu de connaître la plus ou moins grande amélioration de l'éducation de nos travailleurs mesurée en regard de leur nombre d'années d'étude ? De même, la connaissance de la santé des gens au travail mesurée en regard de leur nombre de jours d'absence au travail pour cause de maladie, ne nous apprendrait-elle pas beaucoup ? Enfin bien que ceci présenterait sans doute des difficultés de mesure, ne serait-il pas instructif et utile de savoir quels changements se sont produits dans la mobilité des travailleurs ?

Dans un chapitre intitulé « Le Capital » on s'arrête à l'étude de nos réserves en capital et aux flux des investissements dans notre économie. Après les préliminaires d'usage rattachés aux difficultés de tout ordre que présente le concept de capital (difficultés qui existent aussi bien pour les ressources naturelles, la main-d'œuvre, etc., mais que les économistes tiennent à attribuer au concept de capital seul), les responsables du chapitre décrivent en utilisant avec habileté le peu de statistiques à leur disposition, l'évolution des réserves de capital physique canadien. Entre autres, entre 1945 et 1960, on observe que le stock brut a presque doublé et que le stock net a doublé. On note aussi qu'en 1945, les 80 pour cent du stock de capital sont constitués par des structures de tous genres (bâtiments, maison, chemin, etc.) et les 20 pour cent qui restent par la machinerie et l'équipement. Par contre en 1955, le capital de structure n'atteint plus que 75 pour cent du capital total et celui de machinerie atteint 25 pour cent. Ainsi ce dernier qui en 1945 formait 25 pour cent du capital industriel canadien, en forme en 1955 50 pour cent, soit une augmentation du double.

Si pour fins de comparaison statistique on oppose les relations, capital par rapport à la production du Canada et des Etats-Unis, on constate une différence marquée, cette fraction étant de 2.9 aux Etats-Unis et 3.9 au Canada. C'est une différence de plus de 25 pour cent, si on la mesure en regard du rapport canadien. De plus, il semble que le rapport du capital à l'output ait tendance à croître dans le temps. Enfin, on mentionne que le coefficient marginal du capital à la production varie considérablement dans le temps, mais entre les niveaux 4.3 et 4.8.

Du point de vue du flux d'investissements, on nous souligne une grande « volatilité », c'est-à-dire un taux élevé des changements dans les dépenses pour investissements. Cependant, de 1946 à 1961, la portion des investissements publics et privés attribuée à la construction domiciliaire a été relativement stable, soit à environ 20 pour cent du total. On remarque aussi au cours de la même période une stabilité autour de 60 à 65 pour cent du total, de la part des investissements pris par la construction non-résidentielle, la machinerie, et l'équipement. Enfin, l'investissement public (construction non-domiciliaire) est passé de 14–15 pour cent entre 1947 et 1951 à 18–19 pour cent à la fin des années cinquante et au début des années soixante.

Le flux d'investissement doit être financé. Il l'a été dans notre pays par l'épargne personnelle, l'épargne commerciale et gouvernementale, et par celle du monde extérieur. En 1959–61, 90 pour cent des épargnes brutes provenait du secteur commercial, principalement sous la forme de fonds de dépréciation. En 1947, cette source ne fournissait que 70 pour cent de l'épargne brute totale. Au sujet des investissements domestiques, on nous rapporte que 82 pour cent d'entre eux sont financés par l'épargne domestique. Toutefois, la part financée par l'épargne des résidents canadiens pourrait être aussi basse que 73 pour cent des investissements domestiques. Cependant, si les investissements gouvernementaux sont inclus, tels qu'ils le doivent d'ailleurs, ce dernier pourcentage s'apprécie quelque peu. On nous apprend en dernier lieu, que depuis 1930 jusqu'à 1960, la part de l'épargne dans les dépenses totales brutes s'est abaissée de 18 pour cent à 16 pour cent.

Dans une dernière section du chapitre qui traite du capital, on examine la possibilité pour le Canada de financer complètement tous ses investissements à partir de l'épargne privée sans pour cela réduire le taux de croissance du pays. Selon nous, on conclut correctement que cela pourrait être possible à la condition que l'on brise toutes les règles du jeu (par exemple, lever un embargo) et s'ouvrir en conséquence à des représailles.

Dans un appendice technique au présent chapitre, on démontre aisément que les modèles de croissance du genre de ceux d'Harrod et de Domar ne sont que de peu d'utilité. En effet, il n'est pas facile de les rendre opérationnels d'une part, et d'autre, de leur joindre les autres aspects de la croissance économique. Peut-être y aurait-il lieu ici de considérer des modèles plus « sophistiqués » de croissance économique ?

Il est difficile de commenter de manière satisfaisante le contenu du chapitre que nous avons revu au cours des paragraphes précédents. Il faut en effet se rappeler les difficultés réelles en statistiques auxquelles les auteurs du chapitre ont dû faire face pour décrire notre stock de capital et son évolution. On aurait dû peut-être attacher une plus grande importance à la description de l'évolution des marchés financiers au Canada. Notre pays n'est-il pas en effet l'un des rares pays à haut niveau de vie qui ait eu un marché de capital de pays sous-développé ? Ce dernier fait qui peut s'expliquer sans doute de bien des façons pourrait peut-être aussi servir à interpréter certaines perspectives de la structure de l'économie canadienne.

Dans un chapitre intitulé « L'entrepreneur, la technologie, et la productivité » on considère avec les économistes en général un quatrième facteur de production, à savoir, les entrepreneurs ou encore les structures d'organisation qui servent à combiner et à fondre les trois facteurs habituels de production : les ressources, la main-d'œuvre, et le capital.

En particulier, on précise malgré que les renseignements connus ne soient pas absolument fiables, qu'environ 9.3 pour cent de la main-d'œuvre fait partie de la classe des administrateurs (managers). On ajoute à ce premier fait qu'on observe peu l'augmentation de cette proportion.

Mais ce n'est pas tant le nombre d'administrateurs qui importe comme leur qualité. Aussi, sans qu'on prétende que la qualité des administrateurs canadiens soit excellente ou nulle, on nous cite des témoignages à l'effet que les entrepreneurs canadiens sont moins dynamiques que les entre-preneurs américains. Tout en demeurant sceptique vis-à-vis ces propos, on accepte le moindre dynamisme de nos entrepreneurs puis on le relie à la grande concentration de notre économie, aux tarifs, à l'absence d'application rigoureuse de la loi contre les pratiques restrictives, et au manque de contrôle domestique. On le rattache aussi à l'entraînement moins élevé, aux qualifications moins nombreuses, et à la compétence inférieure des entrepreneurs canadiens. Il importe d'insister ici avec les responsables du chapitre que l'évidence dans les faits pouvant supporter les divers propos et relations qu'ils ont avancés est extrêmement ténue.

On remarque par ailleurs que l'élite économique du Canada est très peu nombreuse, qu'elle contrôle une portion considérable de notre économie. On la décrit comme ayant des traits aux contours bien définis que ce soit la langue, l'origine ethnique ou l'éducation. Tout cela évoque l'image d'une société favorisant peu la concurrence et dans laquelle l'accès à certains postes est contré par des barrières sociales. Relative-ment à ce phénomène, nous aimerions souligner que les investissements américains ont de façon évidente pour nous, un effet marqué sur la diffusion du pouvoir des élites et sur le développement du nationalisme canadien en réponse à cette diffusion.

Cette concentration du pouvoir économique entre les mains d'une élite relativement peu nombreuse s'accompagne d'une concentration importante des actifs dans un petit nombre d'entreprises. Ainsi, en 1956 au Canada, 57 grosses corporations possédaient 38 pour cent de la valeur de tous les actifs réels, alors qu'aux Etats-Unis en 1958, 100 corporations géantes possédaient 30 pour cent de la valeur des actifs réels. C'est là une centralisation beaucoup plus forte ici qu'aux Etats-Unis, phénomène qu'on retrouve d'ailleurs dans le degré de concentration dans l'emploi et dans la production.

Dans une section subséquente, on fait tour à tour l'analyse de la productivité de la main-d'œuvre, du sol, et du capital. A cette fin, on impute à chacun de ces facteurs pris séparément toutes les variations de la production. Par cet artifice, on découvre que la productivité du travail s'est accrue au taux de 1.5 pour cent composé annuellement de 1870 à 1960 et à un taux de 2.2 pour cent par année entre 1926 et 1962. D'autre part, on note que la productivité du sol est faible et qu'elle n'augmente que lentement. Finalement, on observe que celle du capital a diminué.

A notre avis, les conclusions qu'on tire de ces observations doivent être interprétées avec soin. En effet, puisqu'on ne mesure pas la productivité marginale et puisque toute la production est imputée à chacun des facteurs séparément, il n'est pas facile de conclure au sujet des forces économiques en jeu. C'est la difficulté que présente comme méthode d'analyse la moyenne arithmétique relativement à l'analyse par régressions. En outre, on doit remarquer que les productivités moyennes obtenues au moyen des méthodes qui furent utilisées se réconcilient difficilement avec les offres des divers facteurs au cours des mêmes périodes. Il reste cependant que les tendances décrites ont un intérêt en elles-mêmes.

Dans une dernière section du chapitre, on examine brièvement l'évolution de la recherche scientifique au Canada. Bien que les renseignements exacts soient rares et peu fiables, les responsables de cette partie du présent ouvrage signalent qu'au cours des dernières décennies, les sommes d'argent attribuées à la recherche et à son développement ont augmenté. On ajoute à ce fait, qu'on a aussi observé concomitamment une diminution des nombres de brevets industriels accordés à des résidents canadiens. Ce sont là deux tendances réconciliables mais bien inutiles, étant acquis le peu de qualité des données elles-mêmes.

TROISIEME PARTIE : LE FUTUR

Dans un court chapitre de la troisième partie du livre qui nous intéresse, on projette sur 1970 et 1975 certains aspects de l'économie canadienne. Tel qu'il est habituel de le faire pour ce genre de travaux, on assume que la production peut se relier à la main-d'œuvre et à la production en hommes-années. Pour ce qui est de la population totale du Canada, on estime qu'elle atteindra 21.8 millions en 1970 et 24.2 millions en 1975. Au sujet de la participation au travail de cette population future, on prévoit qu'elle atteindra 7.8 millions en 1970 et 8.7 millions en 1975. Afin d'établir ou de proposer un estimé de la production totale, on assume tout d'abord que de 3 à 4 pour cent des travailleurs seront en chômage durant les années sur lesquelles portent les prévisions ; en second lieu, on assume que le taux d'augmentation de la production par homme-année sera de 2.6 pour cent annuellement. On obtient à partir de là pour la période 1960–70, un taux de croissance de la production totale de 4.7 pour cent par année, ce qui équivalent à un produit national brut de 41 milliards en 1970 et de 53 en 1975.

Au sujet des diverses sources de demande pour la production prévue, les auteurs du chapitre examinent celles des investisseurs et des gouvernements. Enfin, ils traitent de la demande et de l'offre provenant de l'extérieur. En utilisant deux méthodes différentes, on estime à propos de la consommation domestique, qu'elle variera entre 66 et 68 pour cent du produit national brut. C'est un pourcentage auquel cette consommation s'est historiquement tenue. Par l'emploi du rapport moyen et du rapport marginal capital sur production on en vient ensuite à préciser un taux brut d'investissement total pour la période 1960–70, de 5.5 pour cent par année, à condition que soit maintenu entre 4.3 et 4.8 le rapport marginal capital sur production.

A propos de dépenses gouvernementales on prévoit qu'elles se maintiendront au pourcentage atteint au cours des dernières années, à savoir environ 17 pour cent du produit national brut. Par ailleurs on prévoit que les exportations atteindront 22 pour cent du produit national brut et que nos importations se situeront à 23.1 pour cent du même produit. La balance des paiements du Canada sera en conséquence déficitaire d'un demi-milliard, somme inférieure à celle des dernières années écoulées.

Les diverses prévisions ou évaluations faites dans le chapitre qui nous intéresse sont toutes consistantes entre elles et sont toutes fondamentalement des projections mécaniques qui utilisent les comptes nationaux comme cadre de références. A ce dernier propos, qu'on nous permette de remarquer que les économistes utilisent de plus en plus un système d'équations dans lequel les mécanismes économiques sont introduits de façon explicite. Ces méthodes plus complexes n'ont sans doute pas été employées parce que peu appropriées à un volume comme celui-ci.

Dans son ensemble le présent volume que nous avons commenté brièvement fait un vaste panorama de l'économie canadienne. Il ne tend pas à proposer une vision nouvelle de la situation. Il est orienté vers le public canadien qu'il pourra renseigner sur les faits importants du système économique dans lequel il vit.

LIST OF TABLES

LIST OF FIGURES

INDEX